CIMA

PRACTICE & REVISION KIT

STRATEGIC

PAPER E3

ENTERPRISE STRATEGY

This Kit is for exams in 2013.

In it we:

- Discuss the **best strategies** for revising and taking your E3 exam
- Show you how to be well prepared for the **2013 exams**
- Give you **lots of great guidance** on tackling questions
- Demonstrate how you can **build your own exams**
- Provide you with **three** mock exams

FOR EXAMS IN 2013

BPP LEARNING MEDIA

First edition 2010
Fourth edition January 2013

ISBN 9781 4453 6616 6
(Previous ISBN 9781 4453 8089 6)
e-ISBN 9781 4453 9279 0

British Library Cataloguing-in-Publication Data
A catalogue record for this book is available from the British Library

Published by

BPP Learning Media Ltd
BPP House, Aldine Place
142-144 Uxbridge Road
London W12 8AA

www.bpp.com/learningmedia

Printed in the United Kingdom by Ricoh

Ricoh House
Ullswater Crescent, Coulsdon
CR5 2HR

Your learning materials, published by BPP Learning Media Ltd, are printed on paper obtained from traceable sustainable sources.

We are grateful to the Chartered Institute of Management Accountants for permission to reproduce past examination questions. The suggested solutions in the exam answer bank have been prepared by BPP Learning Media Ltd.

BPP
LEARNING MEDIA

Contents

Question index

The headings in this checklist/index indicate the main topics of questions, but questions often cover several different topics.

Questions set under the old syllabus's *Management Accounting – Business Strategy (MABS) exam* are included because their style and content are similar to those that appear in the Paper E3 exam.

BPP
LEARNING MEDIA

Planning your question practice

Our guidance from page xix shows you how to organise your question practice, either by attempting questions from each syllabus area or by **building your own exams** – tackling questions as a series of practice exams.

Topic index

Listed below are the key Paper E3 syllabus topics and the numbers of the questions in this Kit covering those topics.

If you need to concentrate your practice and revision on certain topics or if you want to attempt all available questions that refer to a particular subject you will find this index useful.

Note: Case Study questions tend to cover a wide range of topics. However, parts of these questions have been listed when they deal with a specific topic.

Syllabus topic	Question numbers
Ansoff's matrix	21, 26, 46
Balanced scorecard	57, 58, 59, 60, 61, 63
Benchmarking	16, 17
Business process re-engineering (BPR)	47, 48
Change agents	7, 37, 42, 45
Change and communication	38
Change and context	36
Change and culture	37, 50
Change management styles	40
Control systems	49, 51, 54, 57, 64(d), 72(c)
Corporate appraisal (SWOT)	1
Corporate social responsibility (CSR)	5, 10, 11, 12, 18, 43, 65(a), 67(b)
Critical success factors (CSFs)	51, 62, 73(d)
Customer profitability analysis	54
Data mining, data warehousing	28, Mock Exam 2 (Qn 3)
Disposals and divestment	20
E-business and e-commerce	29, 30
Environmental analysis	13, 14(a), 31
Ethics and social responsibility	12
Ethical issues	7, 8, 9, 71, 72(d), 73(c), Mock Exam 2 (Qn 2)
Force field analysis	40(a)
Five forces analysis (Porter)	2, 31
Franchises	64
Generic strategies	29, 31, 65(b), 70, Mock Exam 2 (Qn 1)
Implementing change	32(b), 38, 39(c), 40, 42, 46, 50
Information systems	29(b), 49, 67(c)
Industry lifecycle	19
IS strategy	31, 32, 33, Mock Exam 1 (Qn 2)
IT strategy	32, 33, 34
Joint ventures	22, Mock Exam 1 (Qn 1)
Knowledge management	52(b), Mock Exam 2 (Qn 3)
Key Performance Indicators (KPIs)	62
Leading change	37
Management styles	50
Market entry strategies	23, 45
Methods of growth	21, 45
Mission statements	6, 7,19, 69(a)
Nature of change	Mock Exam 1 (Qn 1)
Objectives	42, 65(a), 66(b)
Organisational culture	37, 50
Outsourcing	34, 35(b)

Syllabus topic	Question numbers
Performance management / control	49, 52, 53, 54, 72(c)
Performance measurement	54, 55, 56
Portfolio analysis, product portfolio	18, 69(c)
Process innovation	47
Product life cycle	18
Relationship marketing	28
Resistance to change	37, 38, 40, 41, 44, 46, 59, 61, 66(d), 68(b)
Scenario planning	14(b), 71(b)
Stage models of change	41, 43(c), 65(c)
Stakeholders / Stakeholder management	4, 5, 6, 7, 11, 27, 39(a), 69(a), Mock Exam 1 (Qn 4)
Strategic alliances	39(b)
Strategic information	56
Strategic objectives	3
Strategic management accounting	71
Strategic options	12, 20, 24, 25, 26, 27, 66(a), 67(a), 68(a), 69, Mock Exam 2 (Qn 1)
Strategic planning	3, 16, 70(b), 71(a), 72(a), 73(a), Mock Exam 1 (Qn 2),
Sustainability	64(c)
Triggers for change	41
Types of change	36, 38(a), 44
Value chain	15, 30, Mock Exam 2 (Qn 4)

Using your BPP Learning Media Practice and Revision Kit

Tackling revision and the exam

You can significantly improve your chances of passing by tackling revision and the exam in the right ways. Our advice is based on feedback from CIMA. We focus on Paper E3; we discuss revising the syllabus, what to do (and what not to do) in the exam, how to approach different types of question and ways of obtaining easy marks.

Selecting questions

We provide signposts to help you plan your revision.

- A full **question index**
- A **topic index**, listing all the questions that cover key topics, so that you can locate the questions that provide practice on these topics, and see the different ways in which they might be examined
- **BPP's question plan**, highlighting the most important questions
- **Build your own exams**, showing you how you can practise questions in a series of exams

Making the most of question practice

We realise that you need more than questions and model answers to get the most from your question practice.

- Our **Top tips** provide essential advice on tackling questions and presenting answers
- We show you how you can pick up easy marks in questions, as picking up all readily available marks can make the difference between passing and failing
- We include **marking guides** to show you what the examiner rewards
- We summarise **Examiner's comments** to show you how students coped with the questions
- We refer to the **BPP 2012 Study Text** (for 2013 exams) for detailed coverage of the topics covered in each question

Attempting mock exams

There are three mock exams that provide practice at coping with the pressures of the exam day. We strongly recommend that you attempt them under exam conditions, because they reflect the question styles and syllabus coverage of the exam. To help you get the most out of doing these exams, we provide guidance on how you should have approached the whole exam.

Our other products

BPP Learning Media also offers these products for practising and revising the E3 exam:

Passcards	Summarising what you should know in visual, easy to remember, form
Success CDs	Covering the vital elements of the E3 syllabus in less than 90 minutes and also containing exam hints to help you fine tune your strategy
i-Pass	Providing computer-based testing in a variety of formats, ideal for self-assessment
Interactive Passcards	Allowing you to learn actively with a clear visual format summarising what you must know
Case Study Kit	The compulsory question in each Strategic level exam is based on a common pre-seen case study, issued in April and October each year. The BPP Case Study Kit provides analysis of this pre-seen Case Study and special practice questions based on the themes in the Case Study.

You can purchase these products by visiting www.bpp.com/learningmedia

Revising E3

The E3 exam

This will be a time-pressured exam that combines a relatively small amount of calculations with more wide-ranging discussions of aspects of business strategy. It is very important that you have a good understanding of the process of designing and implementing strategy as a whole, that you can appreciate the strategic issues being identified in a question.

Topics to revise

You need to be comfortable with **all areas of the syllabus** as questions, particularly the compulsory Section A Question, are likely to span a number of syllabus areas. **Question spotting will** absolutely **not work** on this paper. It is better to go into the exam knowing a reasonable amount about most of the syllabus rather than concentrating on a few topics.

Interaction with the competitive environment

- Strategies are developed in a context, so it is important to understand how an organisation's external environment and its stakeholders affect strategy development.
- Make sure you also understand the different approaches organisations can take to strategic planning: in particular, appreciating the differences between the rational planning model and more emergent strategies.
- Information systems (IS) and information technology (IT) can have a significant impact on an organisation and its competitive position.

Evaluating strategic position and strategic choices

- Alongside external factors and context, the internal resources and capabilities of an organisation also shape its strategic options
- You need to be prepared to identifying different strategic options, making use of key models such as Ansoff's matrix or Porter's generic strategies
- You may need to evaluate the appropriateness of different strategic options for an organisation
- You need to have a good general understanding of the process of strategy formulation

Change management

- Implementing a strategy is likely to involve tools and techniques associated with change management, and you may need to evaluate the tools, techniques and strategies an organisation is using to manage a change process
- You may also need to recommend how change can be managed successfully to support an organisation's strategy, and how resistance to change can be overcome

Implementation of strategic plans and performance evaluation

- Performance measurement is very important for an organisation to be able to evaluate the performance implications of a given strategy, and whether it is delivering the benefits an organisation hoped it would.
- Performance measures can be both financial and non-financial
- An organisation may need to improve its knowledge management strategies or its information systems to provide the information it needs to monitor performance effectively.

Question practice

Question practice under timed conditions is essential, so that you get used to the pressures of answering exam questions in **limited time**. In your practice, you need to get used not only to applying your knowledge to the specific context given by the scenario, but also to allocating your time between the different requirements in each question. It's particularly important to do questions from both sections of the paper in full to see how the numerical and written elements balance in longer questions.

Question practice is also important so that you get used to **applying your knowledge** to the problems given in question scenarios. You need to make sure your answers are directly relevant to the scenario, rather than describing theories and models more generally. Practising questions is an invaluable way of acquiring this skill.

Passing the E3 exam

Avoiding weaknesses

You will enhance your chances significantly if you ensure you avoid these mistakes:

- Little or no time spent studying the preseen material ahead of the exam
- Failure to read the question and the question requirements
- Failure to pick up key points from the scenario, eg size of organisation, history and culture of organisation, objectives and goals of organisation
- Failure to apply knowledge to the specific circumstances of the scenario
- Failure to make realistic recommendations or practical suggestions
- Time management – spending excessive time on strong areas or too long on areas you struggle with
- Poor English, poor structure and poor presentation

To help you avoid these weaknesses, it is important you get into good habits early on. Five such good habits are:

- **Plan your answer carefully**, making sure you identify ALL the requirements of the question
- **Identify the key verbs** (evaluate, discuss etc) used in the question, and make sure your answer fulfils the requirements of the verbs. (A list of the verbs CIMA use in their exams is included at page xviii.)
- Make sure the points you make are **relevant to the question**; for example, do they help explain what a company should do, why it should do it, or how it could do it? Examiners' comments from exams under the old syllabus reveal a frustration at candidates' apparent inability to answer the question set. To score well in this exam, you have to produce an answer which is relevant to the question actually set.
- Only use **theory** if you are **specifically asked** to; do not waste time writing all you know about a theory when you have not been asked to do so.
- Mostly importantly of all, **tailor your answer specifically to the question** and the organisation described in the scenario. Make sure you are giving **practical advice** which is appropriate for that organisation, not just general business advice. One way to help with this is to regularly refer to the name of the organisation in the scenario, or its key personnel, in your answer.

Using the preseen material

Although you should do some research on the preseen material for the Section A case study in advance of the exam, the focus for your answer should come from the **unseen** material.

If the research you have done based on the preseen material is not relevant when you see the unseen material, don't worry.

The main mark-scoring points will come from the **unseen** material. As a result, the main focus of your attention when planning and writing your answer should be on the unseen material. Only include material from the preseen – or from your research on it – if it is **specifically relevant** to the unseen material and the question requirements set.

Using the reading time

We recommend that you spend the first part of the reading time choosing which of the Section B questions you will do, on the basis of your knowledge of syllabus areas tested and whether you can fulfil **all** the question requirements. We suggest that you should note on the paper any ideas that come to you about these questions.

However, don't spend the reading time going through and analysing the Section B question requirements in detail; leave that until the three hours writing time. Instead you should be looking to spend as much of the reading time as possible looking at the **Section A scenario**, and in particular identifying the significance of the additional information you have been given in the **unseen material**.

Whilst you're reading the paper, remember to keep thinking about strategic issues for every scenario that you read.

Choosing which questions to answer first

Spending most of your reading time on the Section A scenario will mean that you can get underway with planning and writing your answer to the Section A question as soon as the three hours start. It will give you more actual writing time during the one and a half hours you should allocate to it, and it's writing time that you'll need.

During the second half of the exam, you can put Section A aside and concentrate on the two Section B questions you've chosen.

However, our recommendations are not inflexible. If you really think the Section A question looks a lot harder than the Section B questions you've chosen, then do those first, but **DON'T run over time on them.** You must leave yourself an hour and a half to tackle the Section A question. When you come back to it, having had initial thoughts during the reading time, you should be able to generate more ideas and find the question is not as bad as it looks.

Numerical analysis and computation

Although the majority of the marks available in E3 will be for discussion and analysis, the exam is likely to offer some marks for the analysis of numerical data, and for performing calculations. It is unlikely that the calculations themselves will be particularly complex, but it will be very important that you understand the significance of the numerical data and use it to **support the strategic arguments** in your answer.

Knowledge and application

You will need to bring two different professional attributes to this exam to score well.

The first, simpler one, is **technical knowledge**. You need to be familiar with the key models and theories used at all stages of the strategic process. However, the emphasis here is on 'key': you will not be expected to discuss obscure academic ideas in detail.

The second attribute is the ability to **apply these basic ideas**. As a general principle, there are likely to be only a few marks available for knowledge itself. The emphasis in strategic level exams is on using knowledge to analyse and resolve practical problems. When analysing a problem, you need to decide which **models** and **ideas** offer help in solving it, explain how they do so, and then make **practical suggestions** for future action.

This second requirement (application) is far more difficult to master than the first (knowledge). You cannot acquire the ability to apply ideas simply by reading or even by learning things by heart. Most people find that they must practise the skills of problem analysis and application by tackling example questions.

Remember that any strategies you recommend must be suitable and feasible for the organisation, and must be acceptable to shareholders, managers and other key stakeholders.

Depth of explanation

Remember that depth of discussion is also important. Discussing a point will often involve writing a paragraph containing 2-3 sentences not simply giving a list of ideas. Each paragraph should:

- Make a point
- Explain the point in sufficient detail as required by the action verb
- Relate the point to the scenario and demonstrate why it is important to the organisation in the scenario.

As a general guideline, a well-explained point can be worth up to 2 marks.

However, simply **identifying** a relevant point is only likely to score ½ mark or 1 mark. To score all the marks available you will have to **discuss, explain** or **evaluate** the point as required by the action verb in the question requirement.

Remember that the marking schemes for discussion questions will be fairly general, and you will gain credit for all relevant points. Good discussion focused on the question scenario, with evaluation of advantages and disadvantages supported by relevant examples, will score well.

Gaining the easy marks

Not surprisingly, given that this is a strategic level paper, we cannot say for certain where the easy marks will be. It is likely there will be a small number of marks available for purely technical knowledge, so you should aim to get these. (This reinforces the importance of making sure you have revised the whole syllabus, rather than only covering selected topics). There may also be some relatively easy marks for doing some numerical calculations and providing sensible analysis based on those calculations.

However, in the main, you are likely to gain the majority of the relatively easier marks, (or to avoid losing easy marks) through following certain basic techniques:

- Setting out answers clearly and professionally, and writing short, punchy paragraphs
- Clearly labelling the points you make in discussions so that the marker can identify them all rather than getting lost in the detail
- Providing answers in the form requested, (eg producing a report if a report is asked for); using the correct level of details for the question verb used; and making recommendations if required

The exam paper

Format of the paper

		Number of marks
Section A:	1 compulsory question, totalling 50 marks, with a number of subsections, all relating to a pre-seen case study and further new unseen case material	50
Section B:	2 out of 3 questions, 25 marks each. These do not relate to the pre-seen case study.	50
		100

Time allowed: 3 hours, plus 20 minutes reading time

All three syllabus subjects at strategic level (E3, P3 and F3) must be studied concurrently. The *pre-seen* case study material for the Section A question is the same for the three strategic level subjects.

CIMA guidance

CIMA has indicated that credit will be given for focusing on the right principles and making practical evaluations and recommendations in a variety of different business scenarios, including manufacturing, retailing and service organisations, and including both the public and private sectors of the economy.

A likely weakness of answers is excessive focus on details. Plausible alternative answers could be given to many strategic questions, so model answers should not be regarded as all-inclusive.

Preseen

CIMA has indicated that they do not want students spending excessive amounts of time doing research based on the preseen material. The exam questions will be specific, and so there will be few marks earned from general background research.

Marks will be earned by answering the specific questions set, which will draw heavily on material provided in the unseen case study.

Numerical content

The paper is likely to have about 10% numerical content, but questions may also require candidates to analyse and interpret numerical data rather than simply performing calculations.

Breadth of question coverage

Questions in *both* sections of the paper may cover more than one syllabus area. This feature, coupled with the very limited amount of choice you have in which questions to answer in this exam, suggests it will be very unwise to try to question spot for E3.

Knowledge from other syllabuses

Candidates should also use their knowledge from other Strategic level papers. One aim of this paper is to prepare candidates for the TOPCIMA T4 – Part B case study.

Past papers

Nov 2012

This exam is Mock exam 3 in this Kit.

Section A

1 Benefits of emergent strategy; analysis of product profitability, ways to improve product profitability; impact of customer relationship marketing on customer retention; benefits of, and barriers to, e-business

Section B

2 Internal and external triggers for change; evaluation of forces driving and resisting change (Force field analysis); type of change; overcoming resistance to change

3 Analysis of strategic opportunities, using Ansoff's matrix; evaluation of opportunities, on the basis of suitability, acceptability and feasibility; recommendation of strategic option

4 Benefits and drawbacks of different organisational structures; benefits and drawbacks of centralised decision-making process; recommendation of appropriate organisational structure

Sept 2012

This exam is Mock exam 2 in this Kit.

Section A

1 Strategic evaluation of a proposal to close a business unit of a company; implications of the proposed closure for the company; selection of generic competitive strategies for business units to pursue

Section B

2 Potential conflicts with CIMA's Code of Ethics; resolving ethical conflicts; issues to include in an ethical code

3 Benefits of knowledge management; introducing a knowledge management strategy; data mining

4 Value chain and competitive advantage; project/change management.

May 2012

Section A

1 Factors influencing the attractiveness of a franchise; sustainability; changes to planning and management control systems.

Section B

2 Environmental analysis; Corporate Social Responsibility issues in abandoning a mission statement; stakeholder management using Mendelow's matrix

3 Types of change; evaluating proposals for new information systems; overcoming resistance to change

4 Balanced Scorecard and strategy implementation; recommending measures for a balanced scorecard.

March 2012

Section A

1 Factors which could affect the success of a new business model; advising whether the new model fits with strategic and financial objectives, and CSR principles. Porter's generic strategies and developing a sustainable competitive advantage; Lewin's stage model and facilitating changes in working environment.

Section B

2 Implications of an 'ethical business policy' for shareholders; managing relationships with different stakeholder groups.

3 'SMART' objectives; managing organisational change; role of change agents in implementing change.

4 Information required for planning and decision-making; potential improvements to existing information available; benefits of benchmarking.

Nov 2011

Section A

1 Calculating impact of three strategies on income, and then advising whether strategies should be implemented; strategic and financial objectives; BCG matrix; overcoming resistance to change

Section B

2 Evaluation of industry profitability using Porter's Five Forces; Porter's Diamond

3 Changes necessary to improve performance; ethical codes

4 Evaluating performance management systems, and recommending improvements; performance measures

Sept 2011

Section A

1 Strategic evaluation of three potential strategies; Corporate Social responsibility; Information systems

Section B

2 Evaluation of control system; Balanced Scorecard, and practical issues with implementing Scorecard

3 Ansoff's matrix; evaluation of a possible acquisition; issues in managing change

4 Stakeholder management; mission statement; change agents; ethics.

May 2011

Section A

1 Strategic decision about a relocation; Overcoming resistance to change; strategic improvements to achieve goals

Section B

2 PEST & Five forces analysis; Porter's generic strategies; information systems strategies

3 Control systems & critical success factors; changes required to improve control systems

4 Stakeholder analysis; CSR and responsible business practice.

March 2011

Section A

1 Stakeholder management; mission statements; evaluating a proposed acquisition in relation to financial performance and CSR; BCG matrix and strategies for strategic business units

Section B

2 CSR policies; Models of change in relation to implementing a CSR policy

3 Financial control; knowledge management strategies

4 Benefits and content of IT & IS strategies; implementation of them

November 2010

Section A

1 Porter's generic strategies; strategic objectives and strategy formation; project evaluation

Section B

2 Control systems and performance measures; customer profitability analysis

3 Comparison of market entry strategies (organic growth vs acquisition); change agents and managing change

4 Information systems strategy; information technology strategy and information management strategy

September 2010

Section A

1 Approaches to strategic planning; strategic management accounting; scenario planning; ethical dilemmas

Section B

2 Control measures and strategic performance; role of information systems in implementing strategic plans

3 Stakeholder analysis and conflicting stakeholder objectives; mission statements

4 Balanced Scorecard and performance measures; using Balanced Scorecard to achieve changes in strategy and culture

May 2010

Section A

1 Approaches to strategy; organisational structure; control issues with overseas agents; forecasting; ethical dilemmas

Section B

2 Porter's Value chain; analysis of strengths and weaknesses; implementing e-commerce solutions

3 Strategic implementation; Critical Success Factors; Key Performance Indicators

4 Ansoff's matrix; Managing changes in organisational structure

Specimen paper

Section A

1 Approaches to strategic planning; evaluating alternative operational strategies; ethical dilemmas; critical success factors; information systems

Section B

2 Stakeholder mapping and stakeholder analysis, evaluating strategic options

3 Balanced Scorecard and performance measures; using Balanced Scorecard to achieve changes in strategy and culture

4 Porter's generic strategies; use of information systems to support business strategy

What the examiner means

The table below has been prepared by CIMA to help you interpret exam questions.

Learning objective	Verbs used	Definition	Examples in the Kit
1 Knowledge			
What you are expected to know	• List	• Make a list of	
	• State	• Express, fully or clearly, the details of/facts of	
	• Define	• Give the exact meaning of	
2 Comprehension			
What you are expected to understand	• Describe	• Communicate the key features of	**14 (b)**
	• Distinguish	• Highlight the differences between	**28 (a)**
	• Explain	• Make clear or intelligible/state the meaning or purpose of	**15 (a)**
	• Identify	• Recognise, establish or select after consideration	**19 (a)**
	• Illustrate	• Use an example to describe or explain something	
3 Application			
How you are expected to apply your knowledge	• Apply	• Put to practical use	
	• Calculate/compute	• Ascertain or reckon mathematically	**66 (a)**
	• Demonstrate	• Prove the certainty or exhibit by practical means	
	• Prepare	• Make or get ready for use	
	• Reconcile	• Make or prove consistent/ compatible	
	• Solve	• Find an answer to	
	• Tabulate	• Arrange in a table	
4 Analysis			
How you are expected to analyse the detail of what you have learned	• Analyse	• Examine in detail the structure of	**30 (a)**
	• Categorise	• Place into a defined class or division	**6 (a)**
	• Compare and contrast	• Show the similarities and/or differences between	**73 (a)**
	• Construct	• Build up or complete	**27 (b)**
	• Discuss	• Examine in detail by argument	**5 (b)**
	• Interpret	• Translate into intelligible or familiar terms	
	• Prioritise	• Place in order of priority or sequence for action	
	• Produce	• Create or bring into existence	**1 (a)**
5 Evaluation			
How you are expected to use your learning to evaluate, make decisions or recommendations	• Advise	• Counsel, inform or notify	**7 (c), (d)**
	• Evaluate	• Appraise or assess the value of	**2 (a)**
	• Recommend	• Propose a course of action	**8 (a), (b)**

Planning your question practice

We have already stressed that question practice should be right at the centre of your revision. Whilst you will spend some time looking at your notes and the Paper E3 Passcards, you should spend the majority of your revision time practising questions.

We recommend two ways in which you can practise questions.

- Use **BPP Learning Media's question plan** to work systematically through the syllabus and attempt key and other questions on a section-by-section basis
- **Build your own exams** – attempt the questions as a series of practice exams

These ways are suggestions and simply following them is no guarantee of success. You or your college may prefer an alternative but equally valid approach.

BPP's question plan

The plan below requires you to devote a **minimum of 40 hours** to revision of Paper E3. Any time you can spend over and above this should only increase your chances of success.

Review your notes and the chapter summaries in the Paper E3 **Passcards** for each section of the syllabus.

Answer the key questions for that section. These questions have boxes round the question number in the table below and you should answer them in full. Even if you are short of time you must attempt these questions if you want to pass the exam. You should complete your answers without referring to our solutions.

Attempt the other questions in that section. For some questions we have suggested that you prepare **answer plans or do the calculations** rather than full solutions. Planning an answer means that you should spend about 20% of the time allowance for the questions brainstorming the question and drawing up a list of points to be included in the answer.

Attempt Mock exams 1, 2 and 3 under strict exam conditions.

Syllabus section	2012 Passcard chapters	Questions in this Kit	Comments	Done ☑
Strategic models (b/f management level E2)		2	Answer in full. This question (from the November '11 exam) looks at Porter's five forces model and his Diamond model. Both are key strategic models, but this question highlights how, in E3, you will be expected to apply models to a scenario rather than just explaining them.	☐
Strategic development & strategic options	1-9	3	Prepare an answer plan. To score well in this question you would need to make sure your answer is tailored directly to the company given in the scenario. General discussions around objectives (part a) and strategic planning (part c) will score poorly.	☐
		5	Answer in full. This question (from the May '12 exam) combines the topics of CSR and stakeholder management. Notice, in particular, how part (b) requires you to discuss CSR specifically in the context of a company's decision to abandon its mission statement.	☐
		6	Prepare an answer plan. This is a question on stakeholder analysis, from the September '10 exam. Part (a) refers specifically to Mendelow's matrix, and you need to apply the matrix in part (b) to advise how to deal with stakeholder conflict. Part (c) looks at mission statements and social responsibility, which are quite popular exam topics.	☐
		7	Prepare an answer plan. This question (from the September '11 exam) combines a number of topics: stakeholders; mission statements; change; and ethics.	☐
		8	Answer part (b) in full. Ethics form an important part of the E3 syllabus. However, ethical issues are not limited to whether individuals comply with CIMA's Code of Ethics, as this question illustrates.	☐
		9	Answer in full. This question combines ethical issues with stakeholder management. Part (b) in particular illustrates how difficult it can be for organisations to manage relationships with all their stakeholders if those stakeholders have conflicting goals.	☐
		11	Prepare an answer plan. Although part (a) mentions Mendelow's matrix, the key issue here is evaluating how much power and interest the different stakeholder groups have. If you're struggling with part (c), try to think about real life. How have supermarkets tried to demonstrate they are socially responsible?	☐
		12	Prepare an answer plan. This question addresses the topical issue of corporate social responsibility. However, remember E3 is a business strategy exam, so you need to balance sustainability and CSR issues with an organisation's objective to deliver value for its owners.	☐
		14	Prepare an answer plan for part (b) only. Scenario planning is an important strategic technique you need to be familiar with. This is quite a factual question, so it will demonstrate whether or not you know the stages involved in scenario planning.	☐

Syllabus section	2012 Passcard chapters	Questions in this Kit	Comments	Done ☑
		16	Answer in full. In effect, parts (a) & (b) of this question from March '12 are exploring the differences between traditional management accounting and strategic management accounting. But make sure your answers relate specifically to the scenario. The same applies for part (c) about benchmarking.	☐
		19	Prepare an answer plan. Do you understand how the industry life cycle influences business' strategies and objectives?	☐
		20	Answer in full. The action verb in parts (b) and (c) is 'evaluate', so you need to provide a balanced argument as to whether the assertions made are valid or not. Part (c) is also important because it looks at the strategic options for disposals (as opposed to the Ansoff matrix and options for growth which students often seem more familiar with).	☐
		21	Answer in full. Part (a) of this question from September '11 should be a relatively straight forward application of Ansoff's matrix. But, make sure you apply your answer to the scenario, and don't just describe the matrix.	☐
		22	Answer in full. This question tests your knowledge of joint ventures, and the risks of expanding through a joint venture. However, make sure you understand the requirement for part (b) very carefully: you are asked to discuss the benefits for country C rather then the joint venture companies.	☐
		25	Answer in full. This question is based around the 'suitability, acceptability, feasibility' framework used for evaluating strategic options. As always, make sure you think about the specific context of the scenario and who the key stakeholders are.	☐
		27	Answer in full. This question (from the Pilot paper) is a good example of a question which is essentially practical rather than theoretical. Analyse the stakeholders who could influence an organisation; evaluate the strategic options that organisation is considering, and then recommend which option the organisation should pursue.	☐
		29	Prepare an answer plan. This question (also from the Pilot paper) combines an assessment of competitive strategy (using Porter's generic strategies) with an assessment of how an organisation can use Information Systems to help it deliver its strategy.	☐
		30	Answer in full. This question from the May 2010 exam, looks at another of Porter's theories – the value chain, and again combines it with an IT perspective: how e-commerce can change the value chain in an organisation.	☐
		31	Answer in full. This question from the May 2011 paper has a similar format to Question 29 since it looks at how the generic strategies could help an organisation determine its strategy, and then how Information Systems could support that strategy.	☐

Syllabus section	2012 Passcard chapters	Questions in this Kit	Comments	Done ☑
		32	Answer in full. This question from the March 2011 looks at a range of issues to do with IS/IT – areas of the syllabus that the examiner has reported candidates frequently answer poorly.	☐
		33	Prepare an answer plan; to get more practice on questions about IS/IT.	☐
Change management	11 – 12	38	Prepare an answer plan. This question looks at a number of different aspects of change management: types of change (part (a)), communicating change (part (b)), and resistance to change (part (c)).	☐
		39	Answer in full. This question combines a number of strategic ideas: stakeholders, strategic alliances and change implementation. Make sure your answers to all the parts relate specifically to the scenario and don't become a generic discussion.	☐
		40	Prepare an answer plan. The focus of this question is on resistance to change, and overcoming resistance to change.	☐
		42	Answer in full. Part (a) of this question from the March '12 exam looks at objectives and the importance of making them 'SMART', whereas Parts (b) and (c) look at issues around implementing change.	☐
		43	Prepare an answer plan. Parts (a) and (b) of this question (from the March 2011 exam) deal with CSR policies, and then part (c) looks at how these policies could be implemented. Lewin's stage model of change is specifically referenced in the question.	☐
		44	Answer in full. Notice the way part (a) links into part (b). In part (a) you are asked to explain where it would be appropriate to use different types of change. This should help identify which type of change is more appropriate for the circumstances in the scenario (part (b)). Part (c) is another question which looks at ways of overcoming resistance to change.	☐
		45	Answer this question, from November 2010, in full. This is another question which looks at aspects of change in the context of wider strategic issues. In this case, the strategic context is acquisitions, and the 'change' element concerns the role of change agents.	☐
		46	Answer in full. Part (b) of this question (from the May 2010 exam) looks at potential difficulties in changing an organisational structure and how the process could be managed. Part (a) of the question provides useful revision of Ansoff's matrix; so the two parts together illustrate the way a single question can examine different aspects of the syllabus.	☐
Implementing strategic plans	10, 13, 14	49	Prepare an answer plan. This question (from September 2010) looks at the role of controls in improving performance and implementing strategies.	☐

Syllabus section	2012 Passcard chapters	Questions in this Kit	Comments	Done ☑
		51	Answer in full. This question about control systems and critical success factors was answered very poorly when it was examined (in May 2011). In particular, candidates appeared to struggle with part (c).	☐
		52	Prepare an answer plan. This question (from the March 2011 exam) covers two different topics – ratio analysis, and knowledge management, and is a useful reminder of the way questions can combine topics from different areas of the syllabus.	☐
		53	Answer in full. Your 'evaluation' of the current system – in part (a) – should identify weaknesses in the system which you can them recommend improvements for, in part (b).	☐
		54	Answer this question from the November 2010 exam in full.	☐
		56	Prepare an answer plan. This question addresses the difficulties of performance measurement in international divisions following an acquisition; so you need to be aware of the limitations of measurement techniques (ROI; RI) as well as their uses for a company.	☐
		57	Answer this question (from September '11) in full. Again, think about the linkages between the parts of the question. If the company is wondering how it could apply the balanced scorecard, might this suggest that one of the weaknesses in the current system is that it doesn't address a wide enough range of perspectives?	☐
		58	Prepare an answer plan. This question (from May '12) should be a relatively straight-forward application of the balanced scorecard.	☐
		59	Prepare an answer plan. Part (a) of this question deal with change management issues, and then part (b) looks at how the balanced scorecard could be used to manage strategic performance.	☐
		62	Answer in full; from the May 2010 exam. This is another question on the balanced scorecard. Make sure the measures you recommend in part (b)(ii) are specifically relevant to the scenario rather than being generic measures.	☐
		63	Prepare an answer plan for parts (a) and (b), but answer part (c) in full. This question is from the Pilot Paper, and part (c) is particularly important – because it highlights that you need to think about how the balanced scorecard can help deliver strategy and change in an organisation.	☐
Pre-seen and unseen case studies		64	Answer in full. This is the compulsory Section A question from the May 2012 exam.	☐
		65	Answer in full. This is the compulsory Section A question from the March 2012 exam.	☐

Syllabus section	2012 Passcard chapters	Questions in this Kit	Comments	Done ☑
		66	Answer in full. This is the compulsory Section A question from the November 2011 exam. Note that the pre-seen material is the same for Questions 65 & 66, highlighting how the Examiner can use the pre-seen material as the basis for a range of different requirements, based largely on the additional material provided by the unseen scenario.	☐
		67	Answer in full. This is the compulsory Section A question from the September 2011 exam.	☐
		68	Answer in full. This is the compulsory Section A question from the May 2011 exam.	☐
		69	Answer in full. This is the compulsory Section A question from the March 2011 exam.	☐
		70	Answer in full. This is the compulsory Section A question from the November 2010 exam.	☐

Build your own exams

Having revised your notes and the BPP Passcards, you can attempt the questions in the Kit as a series of practice exams, making them up yourself or using the combinations from past exams that we have listed below.

	Specimen paper	May 2010	September 2011	November 2010	March 2011	May 2011	September 2011	November 2011	March 2012	May 2012
Section A										
1	73	72	71	70	69	68	67	66	65	64
Section B										
2	27	30	6	33	32	11	7	2	9	5
3	29	46	49	45	43	31	21	8	16	44
4	63	62	59	54	52	51	57	53	42	58

Whichever practice exams you use, you must also attempt **Mock exams 1, 2 and 3** at the end of your revision.

BPP
LEARNING MEDIA

QUESTIONS

STRATEGIC MODELS

Questions 1 & 2 cover key strategic models which are assumed knowledge brought forward from E2.

1 Qualispecs 45 mins

Qualispecs has a reputation for quality, traditional products. It has a group of optician shops, both rented and owned, from which it sells its spectacles. Recently, it has suffered intense competition and eroding customer loyalty, but a new chief executive has joined from one of its major rivals *Fastglass*.

Fastglass is capturing *Qualispecs*' market through partnership with a high-street shopping group. These shops install mini-labs in which prescriptions for spectacles are dispensed within an hour. Some competitors have successfully experimented with designer frames and sunglasses. Others have reduced costs through new computer-aided production methods.

Qualispecs has continued to operate as it always has, letting the product 'speak for itself' and failing to utilise advances in technology. Although production costs remain high, *Qualispecs* is financially secure and has large cash reserves. Fortunately, the country's most popular sports star recently received a prestigious international award wearing a pair of *Qualispecs*' spectacles.

The new Chief Executive has established as a priority the need for improved financial performance. Following a review she discovers that:

(i) targets are set centrally and shops report monthly. Site profitability varies enormously, and fixed costs are high in shopping malls

(ii) shops exercise no control over job roles, working conditions, and pay rates

(iii) individual staff pay is increased annually according to a pre-determined pay scale

Everyone also receives a small one-off payment based on group financial performance.

Market analysts predict a slowdown in the national economy but feel that consumer spending will continue to increase, particularly among 18-30 year olds.

Required

(a) **Produce** a corporate appraisal of Qualispecs, taking account of internal and external factors, and **discuss** the key strategic challenges facing the company. **(16 marks)**

(b) Corporate appraisal offers a 'snapshot' of the present. In order to focus on the future, there is a need to develop realistic policies and programmes. **Recommend**, with reasons, strategies from your appraisal that would enable Qualispecs to build on its past success. **(9 marks)**

(Total = 25 marks)

2 BBB international bank (11/11) 45 mins

BBB is an international bank with retail banking operations in many countries. BBB's retail banking is geared primarily towards individual customers and is provided through branches as well as the Internet. BBB offers a wide variety of retail banking products including savings and cheque accounts, debit and credit cards, insurances, mortgages and personal loans. BBB has a strong international brand image and a long record of success, particularly in Western countries.

BBB has offered retail banking services in country R for the last three years (since 20X8). BBB decided to invest in R because, at the time, R had a rapidly growing economy, and in 20X8 BBB considered there were good retail banking opportunities as only 50% of the population of R had a bank account. BBB initially invested $200 million entering R and establishing its own branch network there. It also purchased a local bank in R for $150 million just after the start of the global financial crisis in 20X7.

R liberalised its economy twenty years ago which means it now allows the free flow of capital into and out of the country. The banking sector contains some state-owned institutions that compete strongly for retail banking business. The largest state-owned bank, SB, has half of R's retail banking business and has a strong position of dominance. This has been strengthened recently due to a reorganisation in its senior management and the launch of some successful new retail banking products. These new products have proved to be very popular with customers and are very profitable.

One banking analyst has recently commented that "R's government has chosen to energise the banking sector through SB. It is less keen on foreign competition. The potential rewards for retail banking in R are great. There is plenty of growth left in this market and the margins are excellent. However, R's population is very conservative, they don't like change." Within R, mortgage and consumer lending has grown at 20% per year compound from 20X7 to the present day. BBB's economic intelligence unit has forecast that this growth will continue for the foreseeable future because this reflects the policy of R's government.

There are a number of foreign banks which have been established in R for over 15 years and these are all profitable. They have 35% of R's retail banking market. Since the beginning of the current year, BBB has identified two foreign banks which entered R at the same time as BBB, but which have withdrawn from R. One of the foreign banks has stated its reason for withdrawal as being 'Our operations in R have reduced group profitability.'

Required

(a) **Evaluate**, using Porter's Five Forces model, BBB's future potential for a profitable retail banking business within country R. **(14 marks)**

(b) **Advise** BBB, using your analysis from part (a) of your answer, whether it should continue its retail banking business in country R. **(5 marks)**

(c) **Advise** BBB how it could use Porter's Diamond in its preliminary analysis when considering future investment in new foreign countries. **(6 marks)**

(Total = 25 marks)

STRATEGY DEVELOPMENT AND STRATEGIC OPTIONS

Questions 3-35 cover strategy development and strategic options, the subjects of Parts A and B of the BPP Study Text for Paper E3.

3 CTC Strategic objectives (*MABS*, 11/06) 45 mins

CTC, a telecommunications company, has recently been privatised by the government of C after legislation was passed which removed the state monopoly and opened up the communications market to competition from both national and overseas companies – a process known as deregulation.

Prior to the deregulation, CTC was the sole, protected, supplier of telecommunications and was required to provide 'the best telecommunications service the nation can afford'. At that time the government dictated the performance levels required for CTC, and the level of resources it would be able to bring to bear to meet its objectives.

The shares were floated on the C Stock Exchange with 80% being made available to the population of C and up to 20% being made available to foreign nationals. The government of C retained a 'golden share' to prevent the acquisition of CTC by any foreign company. However, the privatisation meant that many of the traditional ways in which the industry had operated would need to change under the new regulations. Apart from the money received from the flotation, the government privatised CTC in recognition of both the changing global environment for telecommunications companies, and the overseas expansion opportunities that might exist for a privatised company. The government recognises that foreign companies will enter the home market but feels that this increased competition is likely to make CTC more effective in the global market.

You have recently been appointed as the management accountant for CTC and have a background in the commercial sector. The Board of Directors is unchanged from CTC's pre-flotation days.

Required

(a) **Explain** to the Board of Directors why the objectives of CTC will need to change as a result of the privatisation of CTC and the deregulation of the market. **(10 marks)**

(b) **Produce** two examples of suitable strategic objectives for CTC, following its privatisation and the deregulation of the market, and explain why each would be an appropriate long term objective. **(4 marks)**

(c) **Advise** the Board of Directors on the stages of an appropriate strategic planning process for CTC in the light of the privatisation and deregulation. **(11 marks)**

(Total = 25 marks)

4 Scientific equipment supplier (*MABS*, 11/09) 45 mins

E is a multinational company operating in a number of different countries around the world. The company imports and supplies a full range of scientific equipment to both private and public education systems in the countries in which it operates. In one of these countries, Y, there has recently been an election and a change of government.

As the global economic situation has worsened and there is currently no economic growth, tax revenues for most countries have shrunk. Therefore, governments are under pressure from their electorates to be seen to be effective in their relationships with business.

The government of country Y has announced that it wishes Y to benefit more from the business conducted by E and other multinationals operating within the country. The government of Y has given E 12 months to employ at least 50% of its staff from the local population. Additionally, E is required, in the same period, to find a local partner and to sell to it 25% of the business at a price to be determined by the government of Y. The government of Y has said that further sale of company assets to local business will be required in the future, at a time which has not yet been determined.

Many of the staff of E, based in Y, are already from the indigenous population and do not agree with the government's policy. They feel this will damage the performance of E and is likely, eventually, to put their jobs at risk. The Managing Director of E is concerned that the government's policy will damage the economy of Y.

However, the unions in Y, which are very supportive of the new government, are in favour of the proposals but have said they would prefer the initial local ownership to be set at a larger percentage.

E's business in Y is profitable. In response to the government's proposals, the Board of Directors of E is considering the following three suggestions:

1. Sell the whole division operating in Y and leave the country.
2. Remain in Y and comply with the wishes of the government.
3. Stay in Y and seek legal advice about resisting the government's proposals.

Required

(a) **Produce** a stakeholder analysis for E in country Y. **(16 marks)**

(b) **Evaluate** the three suggestions that the Board of Directors is considering in response to the proposals of the government of Y. **(6 marks)**

(c) Based on your evaluation in part *(b)* **recommend**, with justification, the most appropriate course of action for E. **(3 marks)**

(Total = 25 marks)

5 RGG pesticide manufacturer (5/12) 45 mins

RGG plc (hereafter RGG) was incorporated in 1902 and operated as a pesticide manufacturer owned by a Western European Government. In 1992 RGG was privatised and its Articles of Association restricted its operations to countries within Europe.

This restriction is reflected in RGG's mission statement which states 'In accordance with our tradition, RGG will only sell pesticides to customers in European countries'. In 1992 this stance was very popular with investors and many people bought shares in RGG because of it.

For the last seven years, (since 20X5), RGG has experienced declining profits, a depressed share price and its finance director believes it is vulnerable to a take-over. In the latest financial year (to 31 March 20Y2) it had revenues of £50 million, made a loss of £1 million and employed a total of 1,505 full-time and part-time staff.

RGG's managing director, S, who is a CIMA member, has received a suggestion from a member of staff of RGG that its mission statement is out-dated and restricts business expansion. S would like to abandon the mission statement and sell pesticides wherever it is profitable to do so. S believes that RGG could get a substantial amount of business from markets outside Europe which would mean better job security for RGG employees.

When S proposed, at a recent Board meeting, that RGG abandon its mission statement, a non-executive director objected because 'this is not what our shareholders want. They have bought their shares in RGG because of our mission statement and like the idea of restricted sales. It would be wrong for the Board to go against their wishes'.

S asserted 'We have over 5,000 shareholders, most of whom own no more than 250 shares. Nobody knows what our shareholders want or why they invest in us, but I doubt they want to artificially restrict our sales. Our mission statement reflects 1992 not now, and so it should be abandoned.'

Required

(a) **Explain** TWO methods that S could use to form an understanding of RGG's external environment. **(4 marks)**

(b) **Discuss** if it is consistent with Corporate Social Responsibility for RGG to abandon its mission statement.

Your answer should address the following aspects of this proposal:

RGG's Economic, Legal and Ethical responsibilities. **(16 marks)**

(c) **Recommend**, using Mendelow's model, strategies that RGG could adopt to manage its relationships with different types of stakeholder, with regard to the suggestion that it should abandon its mission statement.

Note: In your answer to part (c) you are not required to draw Mendelow's diagram. **(5 marks)**

(Total = 25 marks)

6 WRL gold mining company (*MABS*, 9/10) 45 mins

WRL is a multi-national gold mining company. Its mission statement explains that 'WRL exists to make the maximum possible profit for its shareholders whilst causing the least damage to the environment. WRL will, at all times, be a good corporate citizen'.

Three years ago, in 20X7, WRL was granted a licence to mine for gold by the national government of Stravia, a small country whose economy is mainly based on agriculture. The national government of Stravia was very keen to develop its economy and saw gold mining as an important aspect of this. The area where WRL was granted the licence is very remote and has no towns or cities nearby. There are small villages near the site of the gold mine. One of the conditions of the licence is that WRL would employ local people wherever possible, which it has done. WRL is entitled under the terms of the licence to dispose of the waste from the gold mining wherever is convenient for it.

The terms of the licence granted a payment by WRL to the national government of Stravia, payable in US dollars, which in 20X9 totalled $50 million. This is a significant amount of foreign exchange for Stravia's economy. Similar levels of payment by WRL to the national government are likely to continue annually for the foreseeable future. The mine has operated profitably since it began.

WRL's mine is in an area controlled by the Eastern state government. The Eastern state government was not involved in the negotiations to bring WRL to Stravia and is not entitled to any payment from WRL. However, Stravia's national government granted the Eastern state government $1 million in 20X9 from the payments which it received from WRL.

The Eastern state government discovered that WRL's proposed mining techniques use a great deal of water which becomes polluted. The cheapest way for WRL to dispose of this polluted water is to dispose of it in a lake near the mine and it intends to do this.

The Eastern state government feared that if the polluted water was disposed of in the lake this would kill all the aquatic life in the lake and have a long-lasting adverse effect on the lake and the surrounding area. Therefore, the Eastern state government took legal action against WRL in the Eastern state courts to prevent the disposal of the polluted water in the lake.

During the court action, WRL argued that if it was not allowed to dispose of the polluted water in the lake its mining operations in Stravia would become uneconomic and the mine would have to close. A small number of WRL's shareholders argued that it was better to close the mine than to pollute the lake.

The state courts granted the Eastern state government's request to prevent WRL disposing of the polluted water in the lake. However, upon appeal to the National Supreme Court, WRL has been granted permission to pump the polluted water into the lake as its licence imposes no restrictions.

Required

(a) (i) **Categorise**, according to Mendelow's matrix, any **three** of the stakeholder groups of WRL with respect to the decision about the disposal of the polluted water. You should explain what the power and interests of the three stakeholder groups you have categorised are likely to be.

Note: You are not required to draw the Mendelow matrix. **(9 marks)**

(ii) **Advise** the Board of WRL of the actions it should take to resolve the problem of its stakeholders' competing objectives. **(7 marks)**

(b) **Discuss** the extent to which WRL's mission statement is consistent with its plan to put the polluted water in the lake. **(9 marks)**

(Total = 25 marks)

7 LAS corporate headquarters (9/11) 45 mins

LAS is a public company that has its corporate headquarters in Asia. It is listed on the London Stock Exchange. Its latest annual report was criticised in a leading international financial newspaper because of its 'exclusive focus on the interests of shareholders which ignored any other interested parties'.

LAS was established in 1851 and its purpose, at that time, was stated to be 'to trade in Empire commodities'. Since then, the nature of LAS's business has changed radically and it is now a property company with investments in many countries. In the year ended 30 June 20X1, LAS managed properties valued at £800 million. LAS does not have a mission statement.

LAS's Financial Director, CR, is a CIMA member. He has suggested that the corporate headquarters be moved from Asia to London for the following reasons:

- London is a major international financial centre whereas its current host country is not. It would be easier for LAS to arrange finance from a London base and some of its transactions costs would be cheaper.
- LAS's business takes place in 28 different countries. None of these countries has more than 5% of LAS's business and there is no particular reason to site LAS in one of them.

The Board has agreed to this proposal and is considering using a change agent to help it in this process. LAS has decided that when the corporate headquarters is moved to London by the end of 20X1, it would mean that 80 employees in Asia would lose their jobs. Their prospects for finding a replacement job are not good.

Required

(a) (i) **Identify** which 'other parties', besides shareholders, are likely to be interested in LAS's annual report. **(2 marks)**

(ii) **Discuss** how LAS could use Mendelow's matrix to classify these interested parties and rank their needs. **(4 marks)**

(b) **Discuss** the purpose of, and advantages LAS could derive from, a mission statement. **(4 marks)**

(c) **Advise** LAS of the benefits of using a change agent to help in the move of its corporate headquarters to London. **(7 marks)**

(d) **Advise** the Finance Director if his suggestion to move the corporate headquarters is a breach of CIMA's Code of Ethics. **(8 marks)**

(Total = 25 marks)

8 NNN Transport company (11/11) 45 mins

NNN plc, a transport company, has recently experienced a number of problems and trading conditions have become difficult in its business. NNN plc has invested very little recently in replacement vehicles, buildings and driver recruitment and training. As a result, its operational performance has declined and its unit costs per mile have risen to uncompetitive levels. Its latest financial report, for the year ended 31 March 20X1, was subject to a qualified audit opinion because the external auditors had serious concerns about NNN plc's ability to continue in business. The auditors had identified a number of causes for concern, namely:

Revenue: some customers paid by cash but this was not always recorded and the auditors felt that the declared revenue did not fully represent the actual revenue.

Cash: there were substantial discrepancies. The auditors identified a possible shortfall of £1,000,000 but they were unsure whether this was due to criminal activity or inadequate cash accounting.

Criminal activities: NNN plc employs 210 people. Following a police investigation in 20X0, two directors, one manager and six drivers were prosecuted for people smuggling whilst using NNN plc's equipment. All nine employees were found guilty and sent to prison. During the trial of these employees the judge commented: 'There appears to have been a culture of criminality within NNN'. On 1 February 20X1 NNN plc was fined £2,000,000 because of the actions of these employees.

The auditors noted that seven of the nine employees who started their employment with NNN plc two years ago had not been subject to background checks or required to produce references. Two of these seven employees had criminal records. NNN plc does not have an internal audit department or an internal security department.

Financial results: although NNN plc had forecast a profit of £5,000,000 for year ending 31 March 20X1, the outturn was a loss of £5,000,000.

In September 20X1, NNN plc's bankers appointed a receiver and on 1 October 20X1 NNN plc was sold to a venture capitalist, WGG. WGG plans to sell NNN plc for a profit by the end of 20X3, but in order to do this NNN plc will have to satisfy the following conditions. It must :

- Have an unqualified audit report
- Be making a profit
- Not be engaged in any criminal activities
- Have introduced an ethical code

Required

(a) **Recommend** the changes required to be made so that NNN plc satisfies the first three conditions set by WGG. Your answer should make recommendations under the following headings:

Accountancy related changes

Performance related changes

Organisational related changes **(16 marks)**

(b) **Recommend**, with reasons, THREE principles that should be contained within an ethical code for NNN plc. **(9 marks)**

(Total = 25 marks)

9 JJJ electrical manufacturer (3/12) 45 mins

JJJ manufactures electrical products. It is based in country Q which has a liberal developed economy. In the last four years, JJJ has suffered from decreasing profits due to increased competition from imported products which have reduced its market share. JJJ has always stressed that it has an 'ethical business' policy which is based on the following aspects:

- All of JJJ's products are sourced and made exclusively within Q.
- JJJ sells all its output within Q.
- JJJ pays high regard to its employees' working conditions and strictly adheres to all legislative requirements.
- JJJ has stated its commitment to the principles of fair trade although it does not currently trade with any developing economies.

Market research indicates that JJJ's customers and shareholders value its ethical business policy.

JJJ's chief buyer has identified several suppliers in country K, which is a developing economy. Suppliers from K could supply components to JJJ at a price which would undercut its existing domestic suppliers within Q by 40%. If JJJ bought from the suppliers in K, it would enable it to significantly reduce its product costs and compete on price against the imported products which have been reducing its market share.

JJJ's chief buyer believes the reasons for the low prices of the suppliers based in K are:

1. K's labour costs are 60% lower than those in Q. K's labour laws allow children from 10 years of age upwards to work in factories whereas in Q, no one under the age of 16 can work in a factory. K has a national minimum wage for adults which is only 10% of the national minimum wage for adults in Q. K has no national minimum wage for people under the age of 18.
2. Q has extensive health and safety legislation which, it is estimated by JJJ's Management Accountant, adds approximately 18% to its products' costs. K has little health and safety legislation.

Required

(a) **Advise** JJJ whether the four aspects of its 'ethical business policy' could cause concerns for its shareholders.

Assume that the components are not sourced from suppliers in K when answering this question.

(9 marks)

(b) Assume that JJJ has decided to source components from suppliers in K.

Advise whether, and how, JJJ could continue with its ethical business policy in its relationship with the following interest groups:

(i) its suppliers in K **(4 marks)**

(ii) its suppliers in Q **(4 marks)**

(iii) its customers in Q **(4 marks)**

(iv) its shareholders **(4 marks)**

(Total = 25 marks)

10 Genetically modified plants (*MABS*, 5/09) 45 mins

Genetically modified (GM) plants are produced by adding a gene from another species. This is so that the plants are more resistant to weed killer or pests, and are able to grow with less water or in other difficult conditions. GM crops are substantially more profitable for farmers than normal crops because they produce far larger yields per acre. GM crops are seen by many as the great hope for ending starvation around the world.

There are concerns, however, especially in Europe, about the possible long-term negative impact of genetically modifying crops. There is further opposition based on fears that conventional crops growing in fields some distance away from a GM crop can be damaged by the GM crop's DNA.

B is a privately owned biotechnology company based in Europe. B has developed a process which makes seeds pest resistant **without** genetically modifying those seeds. Up to now, the company has only operated at the laboratory scale and has no production facilities capable of producing commercial quantities of the seeds.

Due to the nature of the biotechnology industry, B has been very secretive about the research work it is conducting. However, the news of the recent invention has caused a lot of excitement in the scientific community. Within this community this non-GM technology, developed by B, is seen to have the potential to contribute significantly to both the economy and the well being of populations in poorer countries.

Recently, however, B has faced increasing protests from environmental lobby groups and elements of the local community near its laboratories. These groups want B to stop developing and testing these non-GM seeds. These stakeholder groups claim, incorrectly, that the seeds are genetically modified.

The government of the country in which B is based is currently conducting an enquiry into the safety of GM crops. The enquiry is not likely to reach a conclusion for another 18 months. The expected conclusion is a ban on the research and development of GM crops. Some other countries have already banned research and development into GM crops, whilst other countries have approved such research.

Although B does not genetically modify seeds, the Board believes that the company will suffer from the adverse publicity that will result from a ban on research and development into GM crops.

The Board of B is considering the following options:

1. The company could work to convince the stakeholders that it is not genetically modifying seeds and that it is in the best interests of everyone that it is allowed to carry on with its research.
2. The company could move to a country where there is a more tolerant attitude to research and development in the area of biotechnology.

Required

(a) **Discuss** the corporate responsibility that B has towards the government, the environmental lobby groups and the local community as stakeholders. **(8 marks)**

(b) **Recommend** how B can improve relationships with the government, the lobby groups and the local community. **(9 marks)**

(c) **Discuss** the corporate social responsibility (CSR) issues relating to B's option to relocate, using the four dimensions of CSR; legal, ethical, economic and philanthropic. **(8 marks)**

(Total = 25 marks)

11 HWS shop chain (5/11) 45 mins

HWS is a chain of shops which sells groceries. HWS was established in 1844 by a group of ethically motivated investors. Its mission was stated as '.. to sell the best quality groceries at the cheapest prices'. Because of their religious beliefs the original investors restricted HWS from selling any alcohol or tobacco products. This restriction represented what was considered responsible business practice at that time. However, this restriction was an informal one and did not appear in the mission statement or the memorandum and articles of association of HWS.

HWS became a 'Public Limited Company' (Plc) and was floated on the London Stock Exchange four years ago, in 20X7. Its current market value is £450 million. Its most recent reported profit was £40 million. Its current shareholders are:

	% of share capital	Number of investors	Motive for investing
HWS charitable trust	10	1	Uses funds to benefit health of the population
HWS employees	10	5,080	Part of remuneration
HWS directors	2	6	Part of remuneration
Pension funds	15	2	Long-term security for pensioners
Investment trusts	15	4	Medium/long-term investors
RCB : private equity fund	25	1	Seeks short-term profits
UK clearing bank	20	1	HWS is a client
Private investors	3	15,000	Many and varied

Last year, HWS decided to become the '24/7/365 grocer'. This means that all its shops are always open, that is, 24 hours a day, every day of the year. Since then, HWS has found that many of its customers wanted to buy alcohol and tobacco products, particularly those customers using its shops between 2 am and 6 am. The Board of HWS has decided to implement a new retailing strategy and sell alcohol and tobacco products, beginning next month. HWS believes that this will give a substantial boost to its profits. HWS's Managing Director has announced in a statement to the Stock Exchange that '...this widening of our product portfolio should increase profits by at least £10 million a year by the end of next year'. This announcement has attracted criticism from the HWS charitable trust which stated: '...this is against the whole ethos of HWS'.

Required

(a) **Evaluate**, using Mendelow's matrix, the levels of power and interest of HWS's shareholders in the decision to sell alcohol and tobacco. You should justify your evaluations. **(14 marks)**

(b) **Advise** HWS's Board of TWO other stakeholders who would be interested in the decision to sell alcohol and tobacco. You should state the reason for the interest of these stakeholders. **(4 marks)**

(c) **Advise** HWS's Board how it could respond to the increasing demands in society for responsible business practice. **(7 marks)**

(Total = 25 marks)

12 Timber company (*MABS*, 11/07) 45 mins

D is an international logging company, which cuts down timber and supplies sawmills where the timber is seasoned and then cut to appropriate sizes for use in a range of industries. D will work with any timber, ranging from softwoods used in construction or paper manufacture to exotic hardwoods used in expensive furniture. Its usual approach is to secure the rights from a landowner, or in some cases a national government, to cut timber. This can often involve the payment of large initial cash deposits to these suppliers, money which D usually borrows. A logging team then cuts down the trees as quickly as possible and hauls the timber to a convenient river where it is floated to a sawmill. Moving on rapidly to the next site, the loggers usually leave considerable surface damage behind them.

Since an increasing proportion of the company's work has been in the tropical rainforest, it has recently come under pressure from environmental groups that have protested that it is not socially responsible to act in this way. Whilst the softwood forests can be regenerated in a couple of decades by replanting, hardwoods in tropical forests take far longer to mature.

The Chief Executive of the company has argued that he is not concerned about these protests since, as far as he is concerned, the company always acts ethically, as it has the agreement of the national government in any country in which the company operates.

A recent development in the timber industry has been the harvesting of timber from the bottom of reservoirs which have been created by flooding valleys. Although the capital equipment required for this approach is significantly more expensive than that used in conventional logging, the operating costs are lower. Waterlogged trees in reservoirs have balloons attached, are cut, float to the surface and are towed to a sawmill. The underwater process is quieter and less disruptive to wildlife and the environment.

It has been estimated that there are over half a billion trees, or 20 years' supply, submerged in reservoirs across the world, but it can take considerable research and expense to find them.

As long as the timber has remained submerged deeply enough, it is of the same quality as timber harvested from the land. There is currently only one company conducting underwater logging, although a number of other companies are also considering this development.

Some of the board of directors feel that D should pursue this underwater approach and abandon land based logging. The Chief Executive and one other director feel that the underwater approach carries too high a risk.

Required

(a) (i) Briefly **explain** the differences between business ethics and corporate social responsibility (CSR). **(5 marks)**

(ii) **Discuss** the CSR issues relating to D's business and how the company might improve its CSR position. **(8 marks)**

(b) With reference to D, **evaluate** the two approaches to logging and recommend which you think is more appropriate for D. **(12 marks)**

(Total = 25 marks)

13 Water charity (*MABS*, 5/08) 45 mins

Based in a European country, BBB is a charity which raises funds to provide portable equipment to remove the poison arsenic from drinking water in villages, in less developed countries. Run by a Board of Trustees, the organisation operates on 'laissez-faire' management principles. There are few full-time paid employees and BBB is heavily dependent upon the work of volunteers. Although these volunteers are dedicated, many have said that they do not feel the organisation knows where it is going and have said that they are not confident about the future of BBB.

Funding comes from appeals to the general population, which are made through newspaper advertisements. BBB does not use the Internet to promote or raise donations and, generally, does not use available technology to any extent in its organisation. Additionally, BBB receives corporate donations, most of which come from old school friends of the trustees. There is no government funding.

Recently BBB has had difficulty in attracting donations and is at risk of not being able to carry on its work. The charity industry has become more competitive and many other organisations within it have become more aggressive in their marketing and promotion.

None of the Board of Trustees has a commercial background. The Chairman of Trustees has recently been to a number of conferences where the value of foresight and the need to conduct a frequent and thorough 'environmental analysis' have been discussed.

The Chairman has accepted that there is a serious gap in the knowledge that the trustees have about the environment in which BBB operates. Recognising that BBB needs a more proactive approach to the environment in which it operates, your help as a management accountant has been sought.

Required

(a) **Discuss** how conducting a frequent and thorough environmental analysis would help the Board of Trustees of BBB. **(14 marks)**

(b) **Explain** the concept of foresight and two techniques for the development of foresight. **(5 marks)**

(c) **Discuss** the difficulties that BBB might, as an organisation, experience in developing a process of environmental analysis. **(6 marks)**

(Total = 25 marks)

14 Scenario planning (*MABS*, 5/07) 45 mins

B is a media company, publishing lifestyle magazines for the consumer market. These lifestyle magazines contain articles and advertisements about fashion, health and beauty products, homes, furniture, and hobbies and are bought by people aspiring to a high standard of living.

Increasingly, consumers are turning to other media for the information and entertainment traditionally provided by this type of magazine.

Traditionally, 60% of B's revenue has been derived from selling advertising, the balance being provided by the cover price of each magazine. Over the last four years both the revenue and profits have declined as there has been a steady reduction in the sale of both advertising space and the number of magazines sold.

The industry is very dependent upon the level of discretionary disposable income. If this income is at a low level, fewer luxury goods are advertised. However, people still buy the magazines to read about these goods.

The company has tried to expand abroad but has failed, expensively, to achieve this. Similarly, attempts to enter other segments of the home market, particularly teenage magazines, have failed. Both of these failures have come as a surprise to the Board of Directors who thought that they understood the respective markets well enough to make the appropriate decisions.

New technology, in the form of digital media, has also affected the magazines industry. These changes have been felt in both production methods, such as broadband distribution of proof copies, and the choice of media, such as the Internet, available to consumers. To a large extent, the speed of these developments was a surprise to the directors of B.

Required

As management accountant, you have been seconded to work with the organisation's forecasting and planning function, to improve its long-range planning.

(a) **Evaluate** the benefits to B of implementing a process of systematic environmental analysis. **(12 marks)**

(b) **Describe** the essential stages that should be included in a scenario planning process that could be introduced by B. **(13 marks)**

(Total = 25 marks)

15 Service company value chain (*MABS* 11/08) 45 mins

C is a manufacturer of test equipment for electronic circuits. In the past, C was a dominant player in the international market. However, over the past three years, the company has found that its profits have declined as it has lost market share to other companies in the market.

C's business model consists of the following stages:

1 C's highly skilled engineers first visit client sites and, after discussions with the client's engineers, identify and design the appropriate testing equipment to meet the client's requirements. C's engineers are still recognised as the best in the industry, and customers agree that they produce the most effective solutions to the increasingly complex problems presented by C's clients. This stage of the process is seen as a very collaborative process between the engineers employed by C and the engineers employed by its clients.

2 In the laboratories at C, the equipment design goes through a fairly complicated process. Prototypes are developed, based on the discussions in stage 1. These prototypes are then tested. Once a final design is agreed, the plans are passed to the manufacturing department for production.

3 The manufacturing department of C then produces the appropriate equipment to the desired specification and installs it at the client's site.

4 After the equipment has been installed, C conducts maintenance on an annual basis.

It is standard practice within the industry for clients to pay a total price for design, manufacture and initial installation of the equipment and an annual maintenance charge after that. Total prices are quoted before design work commences. It is unusual for companies in the industry to maintain other manufacturers' equipment.

Although clients recognise the high quality of the solutions provided, they are increasingly complaining that the overall prices are too high. Clients have said that although other suppliers do not solve their problems as well as C, they do charge less. As a result, C has reduced its prices to compete with other companies. There is a suspicion that the manufacturing and installation stages of the business are not contributing sufficiently to the business because the costs may be too high.

Some of the Board of Directors of C have recognised that this situation cannot continue and have recommended that a value chain analysis be conducted, to identify the way forward for C. The Board feels that it is important that it identifies which activities in the current business model actually add value and whether all of them should be continued. One of the directors has suggested that C should actually be a solutions provider and not a manufacturer.

Although most directors are in agreement with the proposed value chain analysis, the managing director has argued that value chain analysis is a bad idea. He says that he has heard a number of criticisms of the value chain model.

You are the management accountant for C. The finance director has asked you to do the following:

Required

(a) **Explain** the benefits that C might gain from conducting a value chain analysis. **(12 marks)**

(b) **Explain** the criticisms of Porter's value chain model that could be relevant to C. **(8 marks)**

(c) **Describe** an alternative form of value chain analysis which could be more appropriate for C. **(5 marks)**

(Total = 25 marks)

16 BBB advertising agency (3/12) 45 mins

BBB is an advertising agency, specialising in work for the hotel industry. BBB has no formal mission statement or strategy. However, BBB's management board agrees that it should grow and make profits as it always has done.

BBB's market niche is small and competition is intense. BBB is unaware of the total size of its market niche but believes that it is increasing. Within its market, BBB estimates it is the second or third largest company. BBB thinks it wins most of its work because of the high quality of its output, but thinks sometimes price is the determinant for securing a new client.

BBB, which employs 15 staff, has always found it difficult to attract sufficient staff. BBB sometimes has to turn down work due to a lack of staff. It passes such work onto other advertising agencies. When this happens BBB earns commission. However, due to the seasonal nature of the hotel industry, there are times when BBB has surplus capacity. The management board believes BBB could increase its profit if it increased the number of its staff in order to accept some of the work that it currently turns down.

BBB's accountant provides management accounting information to the management board to support planning and decision-making. This consists of budgetary control and standard costing information. The accountant produces budgetary control monthly reports which are very detailed and show every expenditure over £25. The annual budget is flexed each month to reflect that month's level of activity. The accountant produces very detailed monthly variance reports relating to labour, variable overheads and fixed overheads. The accountant produces a monthly profit figure.

Work undertaken for clients is priced by adding a standard uplift to total cost. A blanket overhead recovery rate is used in arriving at total cost. On occasions, some of BBB's clients have complained that they have been charged too much. However, on other occasions BBB believes that it may have undercharged its client.

The management board has stated that it 'urgently needs additional information to support its planning and decision-making'. A member of the management board attended a recent seminar which discussed benchmarking and is investigating whether this technique could assist BBB.

Required

(a) **Advise** BBB's management board what additional information it needs to support its planning and decision-making. **(10 marks)**

(b) **Recommend**, with reasons, THREE improvements to the planning and decision-making information provided to BBB's management board. **(9 marks)**

(c) **Advise** the management board how BBB could benefit from the use of benchmarking. **(6 marks)**

(Total = 25 marks)

17 Benchmarking in a charity (*MABS*, 5/05) 45 mins

E5E is a charity concerned with heart disease. Its mission statement is to:

- Fund world class research into the biology and the causes of heart disease
- Develop effective treatments and improve the quality of life for patients
- Reduce the number of people suffering from heart disease
- Provide authoritative information on heart disease

E5E obtains funding from voluntary donations from both private individuals and companies, together with government grants. Much of the work it does, in all departments, could not be achieved without the large number of voluntary workers who give their time to the organisation and who make up approximately 80% of the workforce.

E5E does not employ any scientific researchers directly, but funds research by making grants to individual medical experts employed within universities and hospitals. In addition to providing policy advice to governmental departments, the charity's advisors give health educational talks to employers and other groups.

The Board recognises the need to become more professional in the management of the organisation. It feels that this can be best achieved by conducting a benchmarking exercise. However, it recognises that the introduction of this process may make some members of the organisation, particularly the volunteers, unhappy.

Required

As Financial Controller:

(a) **Discuss** the advantages and disadvantages of benchmarking for E5E. **(8 marks)**

(b) **Advise** on the stages in conducting a benchmarking exercise in the context of E5E. **(13 marks)**

(c) **Advise** on how those implementing the exercise should deal with the concerns of the staff, particularly the volunteers. **(4 marks)**

(Total = 25 marks)

18 Product portfolio (*MABS*, 5/06) 45 mins

3C is a medium-sized pharmaceutical company. It is based in Asia, but distributes and sells its products worldwide.

In common with other pharmaceutical companies, 3C has a large number of products in its portfolio, though most of these are still being developed. The success rate of new drugs is very low, as most fail to complete clinical trials or are believed to be uneconomic to launch. However, the rewards to be gained from a successful new drug are so great that it is only necessary to have a few successful drugs on the market to be very profitable.

At present 3C has 240 drugs at various stages of development; being tested or undergoing clinical trials prior to a decision being made whether to launch the drug. 3C has only three products that are actually 'on the market':

- Epsilon is a drug used in the treatment of heart disease. It has been available for eight months and has achieved significant success. Sales of this drug are not expected to increase from their current level.
- Alpha is a painkiller. It was launched more than ten years ago, and has become one of the leading drugs in its class. In a few months the patent on this drug will expire, and other manufacturers will be allowed to produce generic copies of it. Alpha is expected to survive a further twelve months after it loses its patent, and will then be withdrawn.
- Beta is used in the hospital treatment of serious infections. It is a very specialised drug, and cannot be obtained from a doctor or pharmacist for use outside the hospital environment. It was launched only three months ago, and has yet to generate a significant sales volume.

The directors of 3C meet every month to review the product portfolio and to discuss possible investment opportunities. At their next meeting, they are to be asked to consider three investments. Due to a limited investment budget, the three investments are mutually exclusive (that is, they will only be able to invest in ONE of the options). The options are as follows:

- The directors can invest in a new version of Alpha, Alpha2, which offers improved performance. This will allow 3C to apply for a new patent for Alpha2, and maintain the level of sales achieved by Alpha for an additional five years. Alpha2 has successfully completed all its clinical trials, and can be launched immediately.
- The directors can invest in a major marketing campaign, to promote the use of Beta to specialist hospital staff. While this investment should lead to a significant growth in the sales of Beta, 3C is aware that one of its competitors is actively promoting a rival product with similar performance to that of Beta.
- The directors can invest in the final stage of clinical trials for Gamma. This is a 'breakthrough' drug, as it has no near rivals on the market. Gamma is used in the treatment of HIV, and offers significantly better success rates than any treatment currently available. The team of 3C specialists managing the development of Gamma is confident it can successfully complete clinical trials within six months. The team also believes that Gamma should be sold at the lowest price possible, to maximise the benefits of Gamma to society. However, the marketing department of 3C believes that it would be possible to earn very large profits from Gamma, due to its success rate and breakthrough status.

Required

(a) **Briefly explain** how the product life cycle model can be used to analyse the current product portfolio of 3C (that is, BEFORE the planned investment). **(8 marks)**

(b) **Evaluate** the potential impact of each of the three investment options (Alpha2, Beta and Gamma) on the product portfolio of 3C, referring to your answer to part (a) above. **(9 marks)**

(c) **Discuss** the social responsibility implications of each of the three investment options, for the directors of 3C. **(8 marks)**

(Total = 25 marks)

19 Printing company (*MABS*, 5/09) 45 mins

D is a printing company that was founded by three people 20 years ago. At that time, the company used a new technology which had been developed by one of the founders. Another founder member was a finance professional. The third person is Mr Z, who has a strong, dynamic, personality. Mr Z has been the driving force behind the development and growth of the business to its present size of 350 employees. With a charismatic leadership style, Mr Z was very proud of the fact that he knew all employees by their first names and considered everyone to be part of one big team. Everyone understood exactly what the company stood for and how things should be done.

As the company has grown, Mr Z feels he is not in touch with newer members of staff and that they do not understand his, and the company's, values.

In addition, the technology used by D is no longer considered innovative and there are a number of other competitors operating in exactly the same way. D is still market leader within the industry, but only by a few percentage points. Mr Z feels that the industry has reached the maturity stage of its lifecycle.

An acquaintance of Mr Z, a management consultant, has suggested that the company should have a published mission statement and a clear set of strategic objectives.

Required

(a) **Identify** the characteristics of the maturity stage of the industry lifecycle. **(5 marks)**

(b) **Discuss** the issues that the management of D would need to consider when creating an appropriate mission statement. **(15 marks)**

(c) **Discuss** the characteristics of strategic objectives that would be appropriate for D at this stage of the industry lifecycle. **(5 marks)**

(Total = 25 marks)

20 Conglomerate value (*MABS*, 5/08) 45 mins

CCC is an established company in public ownership comprising the following divisions; construction and building, engineering and machinery, real estate. Although the company has traded profitably, its earnings have been subject to wide variations and some of the shareholders are concerned about the Board's policy of 'conglomerate diversification'.

In the last year the company had the following earning figures:

	Earnings $m
Division	
Construction and building	50
Engineering and machinery	20
Real estate	30
Group	100

Note. It should be assumed that the above divisional earnings are stated after tax.

Industry	*Current average market sector P/E*
Construction and building	8
Engineering and machinery	13
Real estate	23

CCC is currently valued on the stock market at $1,000 million, and proposed/current dividends are approximately half analysts' expectations.

Construction and building

This activity represents the original business before CCC started to make acquisitions. The divisional management has described the business as 'mature, stable, and offering the prospect of modest but sustained growth'.

Engineering and machinery

This activity represents the first acquisitions made by CCC whereby a number of small companies were bought and consolidated into one division. The divisional management has described the business as 'mature but offering the prospect of profit growth of 10% per annum'. Additionally the division has a broad customer base servicing a number of government agencies – minimising the risk of cash flow problems.

Real estate

This division represents the most recent acquisition made by CCC and has provided profit growth of over 20% per annum in the three years since it was formed. The divisional management, which is recognised as the most dynamic management team within CCC, feels that this rate of growth can be continued or surpassed.

HQ Organisation

Each division has its own headquarters office in a different town and the group headquarters, which has the responsibility for raising capital and operating a group treasury function is also separately located. The group headquarters is located in the capital, is quite luxurious and has a staff of 50 including the main board directors. Group headquarters, and the staff, is funded by a management charge on the divisions.

Investors

An informal group of institutional shareholders, which holds approximately 20% of CCC's equity has requested a review of the Board's strategy and a rationalisation of the company's portfolio. These shareholders feel that the Board of Directors has destroyed value and that the company should take the opportunity to dispose of the real estate division, reduce costs by closing the group headquarters and relocate the board and treasury functions to one of the divisional headquarters. This, they have said, would allow the company to pay a large, one off, dividend to reward shareholders for their tolerance of poor past performance.

The Board of Directors feels that the suggestions are unreasonable and that its strategy has served the best interests of all shareholders.

Required

(a) **Explain** the term 'conglomerate diversification'. **(3 marks)**

(b) (i) **Evaluate** the comments made by the institutional investors that the Board 'has destroyed value'. **(3 marks)**

(ii) **Evaluate** the suggestions made by the institutional investors that

' the company should take the opportunity to dispose of the real estate division, reduce costs by closing the group headquarters and relocate the board and treasury functions to one of the divisional headquarters'. **(7 marks)**

(c) **Identify** and **evaluate** alternative methods available to the Board for the disposal of the real estate division, should it decide to do so, and recommend the method of disposal most appropriate to CCC. **(12 marks)**

(Total = 25 marks)

21 TKC group (9/11) 45 mins

TKC is a publicly listed UK company consisting of three divisions: leisure, engineering and financial services. The three divisions have similar sized revenues and employ, in total, 900 people. The only division which is currently profitable is engineering, which has not been affected by the severe downturn in consumer spending which started three years ago (in 20X8) and is still continuing. The UK government has forecast that consumer spending will not recover to its 20X7 levels for at least another four years. This reduced level of consumer spending has impacted very detrimentally on TKC's leisure and financial services divisions.

TKC's corporate strategy has been to 'buy any business where TKC's exceptional management skills give an opportunity to earn exceptional profits'. However, this strategy has recently been called into question, as since the start of the recession in 20X8, TKC's cash reserves have been exhausted. It no longer makes a profit and its share price has declined by 80% from its historic high in 20X7. TKC's Board is finding it difficult to manage its business because of the very different nature of the three divisions' activities, which means that they are subject to different external environmental influences.

Recently, the Board of TKC has been considering the future direction of its business. It has an opportunity to acquire a large engineering company, BAB, which is in financial difficulties. BAB currently employs 500 people. If TKC made this acquisition it would become the largest engineering business, in terms of revenue, in the UK. It would also have a substantial export business which it does not currently have.

The Board of TKC has been reviewing its current organisational structure and has decided to divest itself of the leisure and financial services divisions. The purpose of this corporate reorganisation is to achieve a more concentrated business focus and a return to profitability.

Required

(a) **Advise** the Board of TKC of the future strategic directions available to it as indicated by Ansoff's product-market scope matrix. For each of the cells in the matrix give an example of a strategy TKC could use to carry out each of the future strategic directions. **(8 marks)**

(b) **Discuss** the potential benefits and disadvantages of the possible acquisition of BAB. **(7 marks)**

(c) **Recommend** what things TKC should plan:

(i) for the corporate reorganisation; **(5 marks)**

(ii) for the proposed acquisition of BAB if this proceeds. **(5 marks)**

(Total = 25 marks)

22 Telecommunications joint venture (*MABS*, 5/09) 45 mins

The telecommunications market in C, a developing country, has recently been deregulated and opened to foreign competition. The national telecommunication company was split into four separate companies, each of which has approximately 25% of the local market. The national telecommunication company was using old equipment and was in need of considerable capital investment. Each new company is individually quoted on the local stock market and the shares are held by both institutional shareholders and members of the general public.

The government of C made the decision to open the telecommunications market up to private investment to ensure that the country benefitted from the recent improvements in communications technology. There was some strong resistance to the privatisation from other stakeholders in C and the government is under political pressure to ensure that the country benefits from any foreign involvement.

Y is a successful and well established international telecommunications company. It has grown by acquiring companies in established markets. The company wishes to expand into C and is considering how to achieve this. If successful, this will be the first time that Y has entered a market at such an early stage of market deregulation.

The managing director of Y has stated that she would prefer to acquire one of the existing companies in C because this is the approach Y has always used.

However, other members of the Board of Directors have suggested that the best way forward may be to form a joint venture with one of the existing companies in the market. If Y were to adopt this strategy, this would be the first strategic alliance into which the company had entered.

The managing director of Y is concerned about the risks involved in joint ventures and has said that she is concerned about the reported lack of success of joint ventures.

Required

(a) **Explain** the characteristics of a joint venture. **(5 marks)**

(b) **Discuss** the benefits to country C of a joint venture between Y and one of the telecommunication companies in C. **(10 marks)**

(c) **Evaluate** the risks that Y should consider before entering into a joint venture with one of the telecommunications companies in C. **(10 marks)**

(Total = 25 marks)

23 Electronic tracking equipment (*MABS*, 11/09) 45 mins

D is a manufacturer of specialised electronic tracking equipment used by police forces. The equipment allows the tagging, and tracing, of valuable equipment and also of prisoners. The company, which was started only five years ago, has a virtual monopoly in its own country. However, there are limited opportunities for growth in that country. As in most countries, the police forces in D's country are funded by the government. The Board of Directors, which owns the company, wish to see the same level of growth in revenue and profits continue.

The equipment, which has been available for five years, is protected by a number of patents and involves some sophisticated technology both in terms of the manufacturing process and the components which each device contains. Since the equipment is physically robust, there is only a limited replacement market.

The external cases for the tracking equipment are bought in from an outside supplier but most of the other components are manufactured by D in its own factories.

The Board of Directors of D has decided that to pursue a growth strategy it will need to develop an export market and wants, within five years, to develop a presence in all major markets in the world. The Managing Director has said that he expects the company to grow rapidly into a multinational company, operating in a number of countries.

The Board has identified a number of countries as possible areas in which D might operate. The Board of Directors of D recognises that the political, economic, cultural and legislative environments differ from those which exist in its own country and that this might create problems for performance and control of operations abroad.

Required

(a) **Evaluate** FOUR market entry strategies that D could use to develop a market in one of its identified countries. **(16 marks)**

(b) **Recommend**, with justification, the most appropriate strategy for market entry for D. **(3 marks)**

(c) **Discuss** the performance and control issues that D may face if it starts operations in other countries. **(6 marks)**

(Total = 25 marks)

24 Plastics manufacturer (*MABS*, 11/07) 45 mins

F is a leading manufacturer of plastics. Its major products are beer crates and small containers for food sold in supermarkets. Together these two product ranges constitute 90% of F's business, the remainder coming from selling more technologically sophisticated products.

The company is faced with a number of difficulties and may have to issue a profits warning in the coming year. Although the profit levels have been uneven for the past five years, this is the first time that F will have to report significantly reduced profits.

F has been adversely affected by the aggressive marketing of foreign companies importing beer crates into the market, such that F's market share has fallen from 80% to 60% in the past three years. Consolidation in the brewery industry has meant that profit margins for crate manufacturers have been squeezed.

The company is heavily dependent upon the home market, which accounts for 75% of its total sales. Exports have been mainly of food containers for supermarkets in neighbouring countries.

F has invested heavily in research and development (R&D) and, although there is one exciting proposition in electro–plastics, most expenditure has been on projects selected by R&D managers who have little commercial awareness. There is the possibility that some new products may be developed from the electro-plastics research.

F is highly centralised, with many decisions taken by the 20 members of the board of directors. The workforce is highly unionised, with a number of different unions represented. Each factory has several negotiating committees set up to agree pay and conditions. Negotiations are often time consuming and confrontational. This has resulted in very precise job definitions, which are strictly adhered to. This has further resulted in considerable inflexibility, together with a complicated system of labour grades.

The directors have had little communication with stock market analysts and investors, who have little knowledge of the company other than what is shown in the published accounts. An informal group of institutional shareholders has asked for a strategic review and has suggested that F should withdraw from the beer crate market.

Required

(a) (i) **Discuss** the main difficulties faced by F. **(5 marks)**

(ii) **Identify** and **evaluate** alternative strategies that F could adopt to address its difficulties and recommend those that are most appropriate. **(12 marks)**

(b) **Explain** why the failure to keep the shareholders more informed is a significant weakness for F. **(8 marks)**

(Total = 25 marks)

25 Biotechnology company (*MABS*, 5/08) 45 mins

DDD is a biotechnology company which develops drugs. It was founded seven years ago by three scientists when they left the university medical school, where they had been senior researchers. The Company employs 10 other scientists who joined from different universities. All of these employees are receiving relatively low salaries but participate in a share option scheme. This means that when DDD is successfully floated on the stock exchange they will receive shares in the company.

DDD currently has a number of new, innovative drugs in development, but the earliest any of these drugs might come to market is two years from now. It is expected that there would be one successful drug launched in most years after that for at least six years. However, successful drug launches are never guaranteed, due to the speculative nature of biotechnology and the long period of clinical trials through which any new drug must pass. DDD has to invest a significant amount of resources into the development of each potential drug, whether they are successfully launched or not. Currently, it has 12 drugs in development, a number of which may not be successfully launched. Due to the speculative nature of the industry, companies such as DDD are unable to obtain bank loans on commercial terms.

DDD is funded by an exclusive arrangement with a venture capital company. However, there is only sufficient cash in place to maintain the present level of activity for a further nine months. The venture capital company owns 15% of the equity of the company. The rest is owned by the three founders. It has always been the intention of the venture capital company and the founders that, once the company has a sufficient number of drugs in production and on the market, the company would be floated on the stock exchange. This is expected to happen in five years' time.

Recently there have been a number of approaches to DDD which might solve its cash flow problems. The three founders have identified the following options:

1. The venture capital company has suggested that it will guarantee the cash flow until the first drug is successfully launched in commercial quantities. However, it would expect its equity holding to rise to 60% once this offer is accepted.
2. A large pharmaceutical company has offered to buy DDD outright and retain the services of the three founders (in research roles) and a few of the staff.
3. Another biotechnology company has offered to enter into a merger with DDD. This company has also been established for seven years and has one drug which will be launched in six months. However, of the four other potential drugs it has in development, none are likely to be commercially viable for 5 years. This company would expect the three founders to stay with the newly merged company but feels a rationalisation of the combined staff would be needed.

As the financial advisor to the three founders you have been asked to comment on the approaches that have been made.

Required

(a) **Describe** the 'Suitability, Feasibility and Acceptability (SFA) framework as used for evaluating strategic options. **(6 marks)**

(b) Using the SFA framework, **evaluate** the strategic options identified by the founders. **(12 marks)**

(c) **Identify** and **evaluate** one other strategic option that the founders might pursue. **(5 marks)**

(d) **Recommend** the most appropriate strategic option based on your analysis above. **(2 marks)**

(Total = 25 marks)

26 Educational publisher (*MABS*, 11/09) 45 mins

B is an established publisher of training manuals and other training material for members of professional bodies and for personal development. The products are sold all over the world by major bookshops and online book vendors. Although the company has a website, it does not sell directly to colleges or private individuals.

Currently, all stages of the production and distribution processes are conducted within mainland Europe. All stages of these processes are conducted in-house by B.

Over the past five years, sales of B's training manuals have declined and the company is expecting to make little, if any, profit in the coming year.

B's manuals are of the traditional style, that is, an extensive amount of printed material bound in a single volume. An initial market study has shown that B's training manuals do not appeal to readers, because they are under heavy time pressure and are unable to devote sufficient time to reading these manuals. The manuals, because of their bulk, are also considered to be difficult to work with.

There are three other direct competitors in the market, which is highly competitive. In this market the products are difficult to differentiate and profit margins are low. Although B has no firm evidence, the directors believe that all three of their competitors are more profitable than B. However, the directors are not aware that any of the competitors are operating in a different way to B, and their training manuals are virtually identical to those offered by B.

The directors of B believe that there are product development and market development opportunities that could be pursued. They also believe that the cost structure of the products could be improved. However, they are prepared to consider any reasonable alternative strategy that will improve the competitive position of the company.

Required

(a) **Explain** how more detailed knowledge about B's competitors would help the directors of B. **(7 marks)**

(b) (i) **Evaluate** THREE strategies that would enable B to be more competitive. **(12 marks)**

(ii) **Recommend**, with justification, the most appropriate strategy for B to implement in the short term. **(3 marks)**

(iii) **Recommend**, with justification, the most appropriate strategy for B to implement in the long term. **(3 marks)**

(Total = 25 marks)

27 Agriland (Pilot paper) 45 mins

ZZM is a multinational company which buys agricultural products for use in its manufacturing process. ZZM has committed to observe all guidelines and codes of conduct for multinationals. This policy was prompted by ZZM's desire to be a good corporate citizen.

ZZM has been trading profitably for ten years with farmers' co-operatives in Agriland, an agricultural country. ZZM's business is an important part of Agriland's economy. ZZM has made efforts to improve both the production techniques of the farmers and the living conditions of farm workers and their families. ZZM has built a number of schools and also a district hospital in Agriland.

The farmers' co-operatives have freedom to trade with anyone but have chosen to deal exclusively with ZZM. ZZM has enjoyed harmonious relationships within Agriland but this now seems threatened by a number of factors.

The Government of Agriland has been under the control of the same political party for the previous 15 years. Recently there have been allegations of corruption made against the Government and its popularity has decreased: some analysts think it might lose the next general election. The main opposition party is very nationalistic and opposed to free trade. It has stated that if it is elected it will nationalise all foreign owned businesses without compensation.

The farm workers' union in Agriland has asked for an immediate 10% pay rise as farm workers' pay has not increased for two years although prices have increased by 20%. The farm workers have never been militant but this is changing. In some areas of Agriland, farm workers have gone on strike.

At a recent meeting between the President of Agriland and ZZM, the President said there was a common interest in preventing the main opposition party from winning the next general election. The President suggested a number of strategies which could be followed:

1. ZZM could give a substantial donation to the President's party for its election funds.
2. ZZM could agree to an extra tax on its Agriland operations. This could be used to increase the national minimum wage for farm workers.
3. ZZM could open an agricultural processes factory within Agriland to assist economic development.

The President stated his strategies were not mutually exclusive. He added that if ZZM was not able to help him, then he would seriously consider nationalising ZZM's operations without any compensation

Required

(a) **Advise** how stakeholder mapping could assist ZZM in deciding the options to pursue with respect to Agriland. **(4 marks)**

Note: You are **not** required to draw Mendelow's matrix.

(b) **Construct** a stakeholder analysis for ZZM's business in Agriland. **(9 marks)**

(c) **Evaluate** the options suggested by the President and **one** other option which you identified. **(8 marks)**

(d) **Recommend** the option which you consider ZZM should follow. Explain the reason(s) for your recommendation. **(4 marks)**

(Total = 25 marks)

28 Relationship marketing (*MABS*, 11/08) 45 mins

B is a public company that operates 100 supermarkets in a European country. There are a number of other supermarkets operating in the country and the market is fiercely competitive. All of the supermarkets find it difficult to generate any customer loyalty and have found that customers are very price sensitive.

Like all other supermarkets in the country, B suffers a higher staff turnover than other retail outlets and this is recognised as one of the reasons for relatively low customer satisfaction and retention.

The marketing director has suggested that the company would benefit from introducing a credit card that its customers could use in its supermarkets and in other retail outlets within the country. At present, although all supermarkets in the country accept credit cards for payment for goods, no other supermarket offers its own credit card.

The marketing director claims that, in addition to the appeal to the customers, the credit card would allow B to gather large quantities of data about its customers. He feels this would offer advantages in terms of data mining, data warehousing and relationship marketing.

You are the management accountant for B. The finance director has said that she is unfamiliar with these techniques and has asked you to provide some explanations and advice in the context of B's business.

Required

(a) **Distinguish** between data mining and data warehousing. **(6 marks)**

(b) **Describe** relationship marketing in the context of B's business applying the "six markets" model. **(12 marks)**

(c) **Recommend**, with reasons, three strategies that B can use to develop relationship marketing and improve customer loyalty. **(7 marks)**

(Total = 25 marks)

29 GHK Restaurants (Pilot paper) 45 mins

GHK is a restaurant chain consisting of eight restaurants in an attractive part of a European country which is popular with tourists. GHK has been owned by the same family for the previous 15 years and has always traded at a profit. However, a number of factors have meant that GHK is now in danger of making a trading loss. There has been a substantial drop in the number of tourists visiting the region whilst, at the same time, the prices of many of the foodstuffs and drinks used in its restaurants has increased. Added to this, the local economy has shrunk with several large employers reducing the size of their workforce.

The owners of GHK commissioned a restaurant consultant to give them an independent view of their business. The consultant observed that the eight restaurants were all very different in appearance. They also served menus that were very different, for example, one restaurant which was located on a barge in a coastal town specialised in fish dishes, whereas another restaurant 20 miles away had a good reputation as a steak house. The prices varied greatly amongst the restaurants; one restaurant in a historic country house offered 'fine dining' and was extremely expensive; yet another located near a busy railway station served mainly fast food and claimed that its prices were 'the cheapest in town'. Three of GHK's restaurants offered a 'middle of the road' dining experience with conventional menus and average prices. Some of the restaurants had licences which enabled them to serve alcohol with their meals but three restaurants did not have such licences. One restaurant had a good trade in children's birthday parties whereas the restaurant in the historic country house did not admit diners under the age of 18.

The consultant recommended that GHK should examine these differences but did not suggest how. The owners responded that the chain had grown organically over a number of years and that the location, style and pricing decisions made in each restaurant had all been made at different times and depended on trends current at that time.

Required

(a) **Advise** the owners of GHK how the application of Porter's Three Generic Strategies Model could assist them in maintaining or improving the profitability of their restaurants. **(10 marks)**

Note: You are not required to suggest individual generic strategies for each of GHK's restaurants.

(b) **Advise** how GHK could employ a range of organisational information systems to support whichever generic strategy it chooses to adopt. **(15 marks)**

(Total = 25 marks)

30 JGS Antiques (5/10) 45 mins

JGS is a long-established retailer which specialises in the sale of antiques*. JGS is owned by a married couple who both work in the business. They have no employees. Their premises consist of a large modern shop and there is an apartment above this in which the owners live. Over the last five years the local area has become very fashionable and the shop is now surrounded by smart restaurants, cafes and up-market fashion outlets. This area has also become a very popular place to live which has meant that property values have increased substantially. The owners believe that if they disposed of their premises they would make a substantial capital gain. The owners have noticed that the fixed costs of their property, including insurance, local tax, security and maintenance have risen very sharply during the last five years.

Since establishing the business the owners have developed their expertise. They now have a national reputation in the antiques trade and many repeat customers. They traded profitably each year from 1980 until two years ago, but in the last year have made an operating loss for the first time. The owners are often consulted by other antique traders and collectors by letter and telephone and they have developed a considerable income stream by charging for their advice. However, they have found that their location is becoming increasingly problematic. Although the popularity of their area of town has increased and led to many more people living and visiting the area, unfortunately for the owners most of these people are not interested in antiques. They are young people who like the area but do not have the disposable income to spend on antiques.

A further problem is that the shop is not situated in a large city and it is very inconvenient for many antique traders and collectors to visit. The owners believe the location has recently restricted the success of their business. The owners know that a very popular development in the antiques trade has been the establishment of 'Antiques Fairs' where antiques are bought and sold. Some of these have established international reputations and have many thousands of visitors. However, because of JGS's location and the need to keep their shop open, the owners do not attend these. The owners recently set up a website which has basic information about their business on it such as their address, telephone number and the opening times of their shop. The website has received a large number of hits but it does not seem to have increased sales.

[* Antique = 'a decorative object that is valuable because of its age'. *(Oxford Concise Dictionary)*]

Required

(a) **Analyse** the strengths and weaknesses of JGS using the value chain model.

Note: You are not required to draw a value chain diagram in any part of your answer to this question. **(8 marks)**

(b) The owners propose to convert their website to facilitate e-commerce in order to increase turnover and profit.

Advise the owners of JGS what they will have to do immediately, and also on a continuing basis, to carry out this e-commerce solution. **(8 marks)**

(c) **Evaluate** how the introduction of e-commerce could affect JGS's value chain. **(9 marks)**

(Total = 25 marks)

31 Futurist hotel (5/11) 45 mins

CB is a recently qualified CIMA accountant. He has just started a job as a Marketing Accountant for a newly built hotel, the Futurist. Currently, the Futurist has no marketing staff.

The hotel, which has not yet opened for business, intends to generate profit from its rooms and its restaurants. However, other hotels in the local area get much business by providing a 'wedding package'. A wedding package usually includes the provision of a venue for the wedding ceremony, a meal for the wedding guests, entertainment after the wedding and overnight accommodation for the bride and groom.

These competitor hotels market their weddings in a number of different ways. One hotel, the 'De Luxe', situated in a castle in a beautiful, rural setting, charges a minimum price of £50,000 for its wedding package which includes a meal for 100 guests and rooms for a bridal party of 10 guests for one night. The De Luxe has won many international awards for its food and for the high standard of its facilities and bedrooms.

In contrast, another competitor hotel, the 'Royal Albert' offers its wedding package for 100 guests for a total cost of £1,000, with no overnight accommodation provided in the basic price. The Royal Albert is a budget hotel situated next to a busy transport inter-change in the nearby town.

There are another five hotels which the Futurist regards as competitors: these other hotels charge between £35 and £50 for each guest attending a wedding at their hotel.

CB has been asked to join a team consisting of the hotel's General Manager and the Restaurants Manager to formulate a strategy for the Futurist to offer a wedding package.

Required

(a) (i) **Identify** TWO models that the team could use to analyse the external environment. Briefly **explain** the models. **(4 marks)**

(ii) **Explain** how these models could assist the team in formulating a wedding package strategy for the Futurist hotel. **(6 marks)**

(b) (i) **Explain** how an understanding of Porter's three generic competitive strategies could help the team design a successful wedding package strategy for the Futurist hotel **(9 marks)**

(ii) **Advise** the team how information systems strategies could support the three generic competitive strategies. **(6 marks)**

(Total = 25 marks)

32 LM recruitment agency (3/11) 45 mins

LM is a recruitment agency which has experienced very rapid organic growth since it was established four years ago. Currently, it has an annual revenue of £15 million and employs 90 staff, the majority of whom are recruitment consultants. LM is organised into three divisions: Executive Recruiting, Medical Consulting and Financial Services. Each of the divisions has a managing partner who is a member of the Board of LM. The three divisions operate in very different niche markets and each managing partner has a great deal of autonomy in the way he manages his own division. This autonomy is reflected in the information technology and systems (hereafter IT) used by each of the three divisions. As LM has grown rapidly and organically, so has its information requirements.

LM is managed by an Executive Board which consists of a Chairperson, a Finance Director and the three divisional managing partners. All the partners have an equity stake in the business. Last year (20X0), LM appointed a new Finance Director with considerable experience of IT. The Finance Director decided to review LM's increasing reliance on IT. LM's spending on IT in 20X0 was £1 million, the same as its forecast profit for the current year.

Following the review of LM's use of IT, the Finance Director identified the following aspects of LM's IT provision:

- LM does not have a central IT department: IT is the responsibility of each managing partner within his own division and each managing partner has different levels of expertise and interest in IT.
- No member of LM's Board has a designated responsibility for IT.
- There is no recognition within LM of the potential strategic significance of IT for its business. LM does not have an IT strategy.
- Within LM and its divisions, there are very different standards for IT. This means that hardware, such as PCs and laptops are not standard and there are different replacement policies. LM does not use a common suite of software so there are often difficulties in transferring information within LM.
- LM has a corporate website which was designed by an external consultant three years ago. The front page of the corporate website displays LM's identity. However, if users navigate to the divisions' pages, these have a variety of styles and degrees of maintenance. For example, the Executive Recruiting pages are always up to date; however, the Financial Services pages are currently 'Under Construction'. No-one within LM has the responsibility for maintaining the corporate website.

Required

(a) **Advise** the Board:

(i) Why LM should have a common overall strategy for its Information Technology and Information Systems. **(8 marks)**

(ii) What the strategy should include. **(7 marks)**

(b) **Recommend** how LM should implement the strategy which you have suggested in (a) (ii). **(10 marks)**

(Total = 25 marks)

33 Y Gardening services (11/10) 45 mins

Y is the proprietor of a small business which provides gardening services. It has been established for three years. Y does not employ anyone in her business as she prefers to keep her business simple and to minimise the amount of administration. Y operates her business as a 'lifestyle business': A lifestyle business has been defined as: 'A small commercial enterprise operated more for the owner's enjoyment and satisfaction than for the profit it earns'. Her business is not a high-growth business. It exists to provide her with an income sufficient to give her the lifestyle she desires.

Y has invested in her business so that she has all the machinery to enable her to provide a wide range of gardening services. She has established a list of ten key customers which together yield her sufficient income. She frequently gets requests from potential new customers because of her excellent reputation for creativity and reliability. However, she will only take on a new client if an old client leaves; this rarely happens.

Y has invested very little in information technology. She has a mobile phone which has all her customers' numbers entered in the memory. She also maintains a large diary each year which records the work she has done and which is the basis for her invoicing. Y writes her invoices by hand and thinks that all her customers pay her regularly, although she never checks if there are any amounts outstanding. Once a year she lends her diary to her accountant who deals with her tax affairs. Y has kept all the yearly diaries from the start of her business. Y does not own a computer.

Y was married six months ago and her husband is a full-time student so all of the family income comes from Y's gardening business. Y has recently learnt that she is having a baby and she is concerned that her income will be insufficient to support her family. Y is aware that a contract for the maintenance of a large luxury hotel's grounds will be up for tender in the near future. The hotel contract will run for the next two years, with the possibility of a rolling annual extension, dependent upon Y meeting the high levels of quality and service expected by the hotel. The hotel has a reputation for excellence and will be a very demanding client. However, the hotel pays premium prices to its suppliers which it monitors very closely for adherence to contract specifications.

If she secures the contract, Y's income would increase and become adequate for her new needs. However, in order to carry out the contract and continue to service the ten existing customers, Y would need to employ at least three gardeners and an administrative assistant to deal with the hotel's requirements.

Required

Assuming Y secures the hotel contract:

(a) **Discuss** whether she will be able to maintain her lifestyle business strategy. **(4 marks)**

(b) Advise Y of the purposes and benefits of using in her business:

(i) an information systems strategy

(ii) an information technology strategy

(iii) an information management strategy. **(12 marks)**

(c) **Recommend** what actions Y will have to take to implement each of the three strategies referred to in (b). **(9 marks)**

(Total = 25 marks)

34 IT outsourcing (*MABS*, 5/05) 45 mins

The insurance industry is characterised by large organisations producing, packaging and cross-selling a number of different 'products' to their client base. Typical products include life insurance, health insurance, house insurance and house contents insurance. Therefore, cost efficiency, repeat business and database manipulation are of significant importance.

BXA is a medium sized insurance company that has grown over the past fifty years by a number of relatively small mergers and acquisitions. Its business is focused on life, automobile and private property insurance. Over the last few years the insurance industry has undergone significant change with increasing consolidation and the squeezing of margins.

The Board of BXA recognises that it is quite old fashioned in its approach to business, particularly in its attitude to information technology. Much of the computing is done on personal computers, many of which are not networked, using a variety of 'user written' programs. There are a number of different computer systems in the organisation that have been inherited from the companies that have been acquired in the past. However, these computer systems have not been fully consolidated. It is recognised that this lack of compatibility is causing efficiency problems.

BXA has recently been approached by CXA, an insurance company of a similar size, with a view to a merger. Although BXA has never combined with an organisation of this size before, the Board recognises that this merger could present an opportunity to develop into a company of significant size but that this may also present further problems of system incompatibility.

BXA has decided to proceed with the merger, but the Board recognises that this might only make the situation worse with regards to information management strategy of the resulting combined company.

The Finance Director has asked you, as project accountant, to investigate the potential of outsourcing the information technology function as part of the post-merger consolidation process.

Required

(a) **Discuss** the advantages and disadvantages of outsourcing the IT function for the merged organisation at each of the strategic, managerial and tactical levels of the organisation. **(15 marks)**

(b) Briefly **describe** the characteristics of the supplier that BXA will be looking for in the selection of the contractor to take on the outsourcing. **(5 marks)**

(c) **Identify** the factors which should be included in the service level agreement with which the contractor will be expected to comply in achieving the levels of performance that BXA will require. **(5 marks)**

(Total = 25 marks)

35 Supplying and outsourcing (*MABS*, 5/07) 45 mins

C is a major pharmaceutical manufacturing company producing and supplying a variety of prescription drugs in its home market. C currently uses its own fleet of vehicles to deliver to the wholesalers. There are six competitors who supply drugs which can be used to treat the same diseases as those produced by C.

Up until three years ago, the supply chain for the industry consisted of the manufacturers, and a group of ten wholesalers which covered the whole country and which supplied approximately 4,000 independent pharmacies. These independent pharmacies are all small companies which source their drugs from the wholesalers.

Traditionally, patients would see a doctor who would write a prescription for the correct dose of the required drug which the patients had to take to the pharmacy to get their supply. This was the only way they could obtain their medication. Because of a government subsidy, regardless of the medication prescribed, all prescriptions are charged at a fixed rate.

Three years ago, the legislation changed and for the first time supermarkets were allowed to employ a qualified pharmacist and to supply prescription drugs. Because of their size and buying power, the supermarkets are now refusing to deal with the wholesalers and are insisting on being supplied directly by the pharmaceutical manufacturers.

These changes have not been well received by the independent pharmacies. There has been a significant volume of comment in the press about pressure groups which see this as another encroachment by 'big business' on the small independent traders. Some government ministers have also expressed concern about the increasing market power of the supermarkets.

C is considering changing its distribution network so that it no longer supplies the wholesalers but will sell directly to all the independent pharmacies and will share the wholesalers' margin with them.

Although the transport manager has said that he believes the arrangements can be dealt with in-house, some of the Board of Directors feel that it might be better to outsource all the transport function.

The Board of Directors recognises that there would need to be significant changes in the way the company operates were either, or both, proposals to be implemented. These changes would also have a significant effect on the stakeholders of the business.

Required

(a) **Discuss** the advantages and disadvantages, to C, of the proposal to supply directly to the independent pharmacies. **(10 marks)**

(b) **Discuss** the advantages and disadvantages, to C, of the proposal to outsource the transport function should the proposal to directly supply independent pharmacies be adopted. **(8 marks)**

(c) **Advise** the project team how C might best communicate the decision, to directly supply independent pharmacies, to each of its principal stakeholders. **(7 marks)**

(Total = 25 marks)

CHANGE MANAGEMENT

Questions 36-46 cover change management, the subject of Part C of the BPP Study Text for Paper E3.

36 Contact Services 45 mins

An increasing number of people in Vizland, a European country, are wearing contact lens rather than traditional spectacles (glasses).

In Vizland, customers who need contact lenses visit an optician (eye doctor) who assesses the type and strength of lens they need, and then writes a prescription to enable the customer to buy the relevant lenses.

Customers then have to take their prescriptions to a pharmacy (chemist) to get the lenses made up. This can sometimes take a long time and customers have to call back to collect the lenses a few hours later. This annoys customers who prefer a 'while-you-wait service', and so the larger pharmacies are encouraging their regular customers to order their prescriptions online so that the lenses can be prepared in advance of the customer collecting them. Recently, a number of pharmacies have also been encouraging the opticians to send the prescriptions directly to them electronically so that the lenses can be prepared in advance ready for the customer to collect.

Contact Services is a privately owned software company which has developed a specialised software package for the pharmacies to deal with the prescriptions from the opticians and from customers ordering online. Contact Services' current corporate objective is to be a 'skilled professional company providing high quality, dedicated software services to the pharmacy industry.'

In recent years, Contact Services has been reasonably successful in selling its software, and has experienced a gradual growth in turnover and operating profit. However, it is not the only company which offers software solutions for the pharmacy industry, and it currently only holds a market share of around 25%.

Contact Services has three directors, each of whom has a significant amount of shares in the business.

The chief executive is an entrepreneur whose natural tendency is to identify opportunities and take any risks necessary to exploit them. He joined Contact Services just over a year ago, and feels the time is right to expand the company to a size and profitability that makes it an attractive acquisition target, thereby providing him with an exit route to cash in some or all of his investment in Contact Services.

The sales and marketing director also feels that Contact Services needs to expand into new markets to increase its growth. However, the software development director does not share this enthusiasm for expansion.

The chief executive feels that Contact Services can grow by developing a generic software package which can be used more widely by the retail industry. He thinks that by removing the specific references to contact lenses and pharmacies, the software package could be adapted for use in other retail sectors. The existing pharmaceutical package would be retained but it would be marketed as a specialist version of the generic package.

The software development director resists this proposed change of strategy very strongly. His team of developers are already under constant pressure to meet the demands of the existing pharmacy customers. The pharmacies regularly request updates to the software to allow them to implement technical innovations that improve customer service.

The software development director would like additional resources to be devoted to developing a more standardised software package for their current customers. He is annoyed at the way Contact Services' salesmen regularly commit the company to producing customised software solutions for individual customers and promising delivery dates that the software delivery team struggle to meet.

The rush in development work is leading to users reporting an increasing number of faults in the software. As a result, Contact Services' reputation is suffering, and several large pharmacies who are key customers have recently expressed dissatisfaction with the quality of their software package.

Required

(a) **Analyse** the type of change the chief executive is proposing for Contact Services. **(10 marks)**

(b) **Discuss** the internal factors at Contact Services that may influence the success or failure of the chief executive's proposal to develop a generic software package. **(15 marks)**

(Total = 25 marks)

37 Heritage Trust 45 mins

The Heritage Trust is a charity which was founded in 1830 with the aim of acquiring buildings of national interest and preserving them for the public to visit, along with the art collections and antiques within them. The Trust now owns over 200 houses nationwide, many of which also have large gardens.

Historically, about 30% of the Trust's income has come from government grants, reflecting the importance the Government attaches to preserving the nation's heritage. About 50% of the Trust's total income comes from membership fees. (Members pay an annual subscription which then allows them free entry to any of the Trust's properties.) The remaining 20% comes from a combination of admission charges (which non-members pay to visit the properties) and sales in the gift shops and restaurants which many properties have.

The income is used for the continued preservation of the properties and their art collections, as well as paying for the administrative costs of the Trust, including staff costs. Each property has a salaried manager, who lives on site, although a number of volunteers also help with the upkeep of the properties.

The Trust is governed by a Board of Trustees, who are well-known and respected figures in the field of heritage and the arts. The Trust's strategy is developed by the Director General (DG) in conjunction with the Trustees.

The Board of Trustees and the DG have always believed that there are a number of 'flagship' properties which people want to preserve and support. These properties encourage people to become members of the Trust and to renew their memberships each year, regardless of whether they actually visit the properties.

In the annual budget, a share of the central membership income is allocated to each individual property. The amount each property receives depends on whether or not it is a 'flagship' property, and how important the collections within the property are believed to be.

Being the manager of a 'flagship' property is considered an important position and enjoys many privileges, including spacious private accommodation within the property itself, and a dedicated personal assistant.

Recently, the government has announced plans to halve its grants to the Trust, meaning the Trust will have to significantly increase its income from commercial activities to make up the shortfall in funding. The DG resigned in protest at the government's actions. However, the Trustees recognised the scale of the problem facing the Trust, and appointed a new DG from the private sector to develop a new business strategy. The new DG was previously the CEO of a major retail chain.

The DG has produced a strategic planning document, which includes a number of controversial proposals:

- In future, the central budget will be allocated to properties according to visitor popularity. This is designed to stimulate properties to come up with interesting and innovative ideas to increase visitor numbers.
- Removing the property managers' personal assistants, and giving them IT training where necessary so that they can do their own administration
- Recruiting five regional business development managers to increase commercial income by selling a wider range of souvenirs from the gift shops, and hosting open air concerts and theatre productions in the grounds of the properties
- Recruit an e-commerce business manager to develop an online store

The 'flagship' property managers have reacted furiously to the DG's suggestions. The idea of linking budgets to visitor numbers has been greeted with dismay, and the DG has been accused of devaluing the historical significance of the properties in a search for popularity.

A number of these managers have written to individual members of the Board of Trustees with their concerns about the DG's proposals, while others have contacted local television companies and the local press and have given interviews which are critical of the DG's proposals.

All the managers across the Trust have also been particularly critical of the lack of consultation about the proposed changes. They argue running the Trust is very different to running a retail chain and the new DG hasn't taken time to understand the culture and values of the Trust before publishing her plans.

The new DG has been shocked at the strength of opposition to her plans and has asked you to help her deal with it.

Required

(a) **Explain** the role of a change agent in leading change. **(5 marks)**

(b) **Discuss** FIVE underlying organisational cultural issues that have led to the resistance to the Director General's proposals. **(15 marks)**

(c) **Recommend** the steps that could be taken to overcome the resistance to the proposals. **(5 marks)**

(Total = 25 marks)

38 Goldcorn 45 mins

Goldcorn is a multinational company that manufactures automobiles which it sells in the low- to medium-price sectors of the market. It is listed on an international stock market.

Goldcorn manufactures three different types of product: small cars, large cars, and trucks.

The company currently has four manufacturing sites: one in western Europe, one in eastern Europe, one in Asia, and one in North America. Each of the factories currently manufactures all three products and, in general, sells them in the region of the world in which that factory is located.

While sales are internationally diversified, market research has shown that different geographical regions require different designs and features. As a result, each factory has developed each of the products separately with different features and capabilities which are appropriate to the market in its own geographical region.

Each of the factories operates as a separate profit centre. However, profitability has declined in all four of the factories in recent years meaning that profitability for the company as a whole has also fallen steeply.

The central board has attempted to improve matters by reviewing costs, and applying a series of cost reduction programmes. It has also carried out some internal benchmarking exercises on costs and efficiencies.

The benchmarking exercises have shown that some of the factories can produce some vehicles at a lower cost than others, but the results are not consistent. For example, the Asian factory produces small cars more cheaply than any of the other factories, but it is the highest cost producer of large cars.

What is more, when there is a major change in exchange rates, the whole cost comparison exercise changes.

The CEO is concerned that although Goldcorn has repeatedly engaged in cost reduction programmes by selective redundancies, reducing capacity, changing reporting structures and outsourcing the production of various components, there has been no permanent cost reduction of any significance.

There has recently been an unexpected major new entrant into the industry from South East Asia, which has low costs and sells its vehicles at low prices. The CEO believes that if Goldcorn is going to be able to compete with this new entrant it will have to reduce costs much more significantly than it has been able to do in the past.

In response, the finance director has suggested that Goldcorn considers globalising production.

The key features of his proposal are that:

- Each of the three products would be made in only one basic design, and all of the world production of each product would be made at a single factory. Consequently only three factories would be needed, so one would be closed.
- Each factory would be a cost centre rather than a profit centre. Responsibility for sales and marketing would be centralised functionally worldwide.

Given the perceived significance of the threat of the new entrant, the finance director argues that these changes should be pushed through urgently, with the aim of completing the change programme within six months.

He believes that that larger scale specialist production would significantly reduce production costs. However, he has suggested that the situation should be reviewed in two years' time given the uncertainties involved in such a major change.

Required

(a) Critically **analyse** the type of change programme envisaged in the finance director's current proposal compared to those carried out in the previous cost reduction exercises. **(10 marks)**

(b) **Discuss** the reasons why Goldcorn should communicate the nature of the changes to the key stakeholders affected by the finance director's change programme. **(8 marks)**

(c) **Analyse** the possible barriers to change that may arise and cause resistance to the implementation of the finance director's proposal. **(7 marks)**

(Total = 25 marks)

39 ChemiCo 45 mins

Chemico is a chemical engineering company, based in an eastern European country. It is the largest and most important employer in the region, which is a relatively poor area with only one small town in reasonable commuting distance.

Chemico's main shareholders are international financial institutions, who have also provided finances in the form of loans.

At the moment, the company is performing well. Annual sales and profits have been increasing, the share price is strong, and the company has a number of large orders on its order book. It also has a favourable reputation among customers, which include some major household names.

However, Chemico's directors realise that the company's profitability is likely to diminish in the longer term, because new engineering technologies are being developed which will reduce (although not eliminate) the demand for their products.

The directors have been considering the option to diversify by developing a new product, using the same basic engineering and chemical processes as the existing products. However, this new product can present higher risks of toxic incident, and environmental campaigners have written to the local authorities highlighting the inherent risks involved in developing the new product.

Chemico's directors are also aware that one of its competitors is also developing a similar new product. Initial scientific research has concluded that Chemico's new product is generally more effective than its rival's in the process it was designed for. However, the rival product doesn't pose any toxic risk.

Chemico's director's are currently considering the possibility of entering a strategic alliance with the competitor for the joint development of the new product.

Chemico is also considering a move into manufacturing specialist plastics. The plastics manufacturing business is one of the major users of Chemico's current products. However, Chemico would need to develop completely new manufacturing processes for it to be able to be able to make the plastics in house.

The directors feel the investment required could be justified because there is strong growth in western Europe for the plastics, and the margins earned would be much higher than on their current products. However, initial investigations have also shown that Chemico could enter the market by buying a small local plastics company from the current owner who wishes to retire.

Required

(a) Assume Chemico decides to pursue the first proposal and develop the new chemical product itself. **Discuss** the main stakeholders' likely reactions to that proposal, and the degree to which they are likely to resist the proposal. **(9 marks)**

(b) **Evaluate** the issues which Chemico's directors should consider with respect to entering a strategic alliance with the competitor for the joint development of the new product. **(7 marks)**

(c) **Discuss** the change implementation issues which are likely to arise if Chemico decides to acquire the plastics company. **(9 marks)**

(Total = 25 marks)

40 ProfTech 45 mins

ProfTech is a privately-owned training college which specialises in providing courses in business subjects such as accounting, marketing and law.

It is currently the largest training college in its country, but its market position is increasingly coming under threat from Youtrain Co which has developed an electronic learning (e-learning) facility which is proving very popular with students. Students value the flexibility it gives them as to when they choose to learn.

ProfTech's directors are keen for ProfTech to develop its own e-learning product, and have approved the budget for the investment in the electronic hardware and software required to support such a product. However, the e-learning programme also requires considerable investment in tutor time to convert the existing taught materials into electronically accessible modules.

The directors have said that within two years they want all students to have the option of having either face-to-face or online tuition for every course that ProfTech offers. Some of the tutors who are in favour of e-learning have already developed their online courses, and are offering them for students, but a number of tutors have yet to do so.

The majority of ProfTech's tutors argue that the best way for students to learn is through face-to-face contact with tutors, and they remain unconvinced of the benefits of e-learning. Very few of the tutors have taken advantage of the in-house courses which have been arranged for them to show them how the e-learning software works, and how to prepare e-learning materials. Consequently, many of the tutors don't understand how the software works, yet they still automatically blame the IT department if any problems arise with the e-learning material they are preparing.

Not surprisingly, the impact of e-learning at ProfTech is very varied. Some courses make extensive use of online learning and technology, while others are still taught largely by traditional classroom methods. A number of students have commented critically on this variation.

ProfTech's directors are worried about imposing e-learning on their staff in the face of known resistance. However, they are equally concerned that the impression ProfTech is giving to current and prospective students, in an increasingly competitive and international marketplace, is far from impressive.

The current partial and unsystematic use of e-learning is becoming a significant competitive disadvantage.

Required

(a) Briefly **discuss** how ProfTech's directors could use force field analysis in connection with the e-learning facility. **(6 marks)**

(b) **Discuss** the reasons why the tutors are opposing e-learning. **(6 marks)**

(c) **Advise** the directors of the approaches they could take to ensure that the change to e-learning is successfully implemented. **(13 marks)**

(Total = 25 marks)

41 Callcom 45 mins

Callcom is a major telecommunications provider, and is listed on the stock exchange in the European country where it is based.

Until the mid-1980s, Callcom was a state-owned company, which held a monopoly over telecommunication services in its country. However, in 1984 the government deregulated the market and began granting licences to new rival suppliers. In 1986, Callcom was privatised.

Since the privatisation, competition has developed strongly in the telecommunications industry, while the industry itself has grown significantly. It now contains a range of landline telephone (fixed voice) providers, mobile service providers, internet service and cable TV providers.

Callcom has attempted to diversify and offer mobile phone and broadband services in additional to its traditional landline services. However, it has been unable to achieve a profitable market share in the mobile phone market and recently sold this part of its business to a larger mobile phone operator.

Callcom has been more successful in attracting broadband customers and has secured a large number of broadband subscribers. However, the growth in broadband services across the market as a whole has led to a decline in fixed voice market revenues.

A number of broadband providers have also developed the voice over internet protocol (VOIP) technology which allows broadband customers to hold telephone conversations for no additional call costs. Although Callcom has developed its own VOIP technology, VOIP presents a major challenge to Callcom, which has traditionally relied on fixed voice services as its largest and most stable revenue stream.

VOIP technology also raises important staffing implications. It is not yet clear exactly what the new VOIP networks will mean for staffing levels and skill requirements at Callcom, although it is likely that telecommunications providers will need less telephone exchanges and network buildings, and lower levels of network staff.

A high proportion of Callcom's engineers belong to the telecommunications union, and when Callcom announced some job cuts last year, the trade union members voted for industrial action to support their colleagues. The industrial action lasted for several weeks and had a significant effect on both Callcom's financial performance and its reputation in the industry.

Another legacy of Callcom's history as a state-owned monopoly is that it still has a relatively bureaucratic culture and structure, and so is slower to respond to market opportunities than some of its younger rivals.

There are several potential 'new wave' growth opportunities, using VOIP technology and wireless communication. However, to take advantage of these Callcom's engineers will need training additional training in how to install wireless access points in public venues. The engineers have argued they should receive a large pay increase to compensate them for using the new skills required for this job, and have threatened further strike action if a pay award is not forthcoming.

Required

(a) **Analyse** the external and internal triggers for change in Callcom's strategy and operations. **(7 marks)**

(b) **Evaluate** how successful Callcom has been at managing change prior to the wireless access point project, and explain how a stage model of change could help Callcom manage the wireless access point project. **(13 marks)**

(c) **Discuss** the reasons why Callcom's engineers might resist the change programmes. **(5 marks)**

(Total = 25 marks)

42 MMM University departments (3/12) 45 mins

MMM is a university whose mission is 'to be the best'. It has a wide range of educational activities and is organised into six departments:

1. Arts
2. Medicine
3. Law
4. Engineering
5. Natural Sciences
6. Theology

Each of the six departments above is controlled by a senior manager, known as a Head who has operational responsibility for their department's activities throughout the university.

On the advice of management consultants, it has now been decided to reorganise the University and establish the following three new departments which will replace the current six departments listed above:

1. Student experience: this includes teaching, welfare, progression, pass rates and quality for both undergraduates and postgraduates.
2. Research: this includes academic research and commercial research.
3. All profit-making activities other than commercial research.

Each of the new departments will be managed by one of the existing Heads. MMM wants to introduce a control system for its Heads and departments that will measure their performance against strategic and operational targets using quantitative and qualitative criteria. MMM's executive board has the following objectives for the new control system:

- To develop the Heads' motivation
- To encourage the Heads to accept responsibility for achieving strategic and operational targets
- To encourage activities that generate income from external activities

MMM's executive board believes that the departmental reorganisation and the introduction of the new control measures will require cultural change within the university.

Required

Advise MMM's executive board:

(a) how it could use the 'SMART' model to achieve the new control system's objectives. **(10 marks)**

(b) of the activities it must undertake to manage the process of:

(i) changing the university's culture **(5 marks)**

(ii) introducing the new departmental structure **(5 marks)**

You must NOT use Lewin's three-step model of change as the basis of your answer to requirement (b).

(c) **Discuss** the role that a change agent could play in the change process in MMM. **(5 marks)**

(Total = 25 marks)

43 XYZ Chemical Co (3/11) 45 mins

XYZ is a privately owned company which manufactures industrial chemicals. The manufacturing process produces large quantities of waste and is very noisy and smelly.

XYZ sources some of its raw materials from economically underdeveloped countries.

XYZ has an ethnically diverse workforce.

XYZ has always tried to stay within its country's laws.

However, recently there have been a number of accidents which XYZ's safety manager thinks were due to operator error.

XYZ would like to be listed on a stock exchange as this would provide access to capital which would assist XYZ's plans for expansion. XYZ does not have a policy for Corporate Social Responsibility (CSR). However, XYZ's auditors have advised XYZ that a CSR policy would be required if the company is to be listed.

Required

(a) **Advise** XYZ of the benefits of a CSR policy. **(10 marks)**

(b) **Recommend** the contents of a suitable CSR policy for XYZ dealing with its manufacturing process, procurement policy, labour force and compliance with the law. **(6 marks)**

(c) **Advise** XYZ how it could use Lewin's model of staged change to implement a CSR policy. **(9 marks)**

(Total = 25 marks)

44 WAL biscuit manufacturer (5/12) 45 mins

WAL is a manufacturer of biscuits which it sells to retailers. Its current year's revenue of £120 million represents approximately 3% of the UK market. WAL has a centralised marketing information system based on a software package bought seven years ago, in 20X5. This package is financial accounts orientated: the only management information provided to support the marketing staff consists of reports showing revenue, profit, inventory value, receivables and payables balances. WAL's marketing staff and the Marketing Director, M, have complained that they are not provided with information such as customers' profitability, market share and market growth which would support their strategic decision-making. They consider the inadequacies of the current marketing information system to be so serious that they would like a Big Bang* change which would mean moving straightaway to a new marketing information system that would give them the information they need. They feel WAL is being left behind by its competitors and is losing customers.

The Company Secretary, R, manages WAL's IS/IT staff. R was responsible for buying the existing marketing information software in 20X5 and he would also be responsible for the procurement of its replacement. R has identified three possible solutions to meeting the marketing staff's needs: the first two are evolutionary, the third would be a 'Big Bang'.

Solution 1

Modification: the existing marketing information system would be redesigned by WAL's in-house IS/IT staff to meet the needs of the marketing staff. Although WAL's IS/IT staff have limited experience of the type of work which would be required, they are confident the redesign could be done within a year. The IS/IT staff are unsure of the cost.

Solution 2

Development: WAL's in-house IS/IT staff would develop new bespoke software to meet the marketing staff's needs. The IS/IT staff have stated that '*because WAL's needs are unique, costs can only be roughly estimated. However, this solution is likely to be considerably more expensive than the 'Modification' solution. The final cost would be dependent upon the length of the project. It should take a minimum of six months to develop new software but it might take as long as two years. We have little experience of software development but are very enthusiastic about trying*'.

Solution 3

Purchase: WAL could purchase the biscuit industry standard marketing information system software: this would be an expensive purchase but the product is well proven. Some of WAL's marketing staff have experience of using this software in other companies, are very appreciative of its benefits and believe it would help them considerably in their jobs. The software supplier claims that '90% of the biscuit industry uses our product and if you buy it we guarantee to have it working inside WAL within three months of you buying it'.

R believes that he represents the majority of opinion within the IS/IT staff who very much prefer that change should be evolutionary. They would be very resistant to change if it was carried out in any other way. R also pointed out that WAL has experience of 'Big Bang' organisational change in the recent past which failed because WAL's culture didn't change to reflect this.

R stated, 'It looks straightforward to go out and buy a software package but it's a lot more complicated than people think and it's my department that would have to do all the work.

* 'Big Bang': any sudden forceful beginning or radical change

Required

(a) **Explain** the circumstances in which it would be appropriate to use:

(i) Evolutionary change
(ii) 'Big Bang' change

(4 marks)

(b) (i) **Evaluate** each of the three solutions proposed by R. **(9 marks)**

(ii) **Recommend**, with reasons, which of the three solution identified by R should be adopted. **(3 marks)**

(c) **Advise** how WAL could overcome the resistance to change which would arise if Solution 3, the *purchase* solution, were to be adopted.

(9 marks)

(Total = 25 marks)

45 JKL's growth (11/10) 45 mins

JKL is a small European company based in the south of the UK which employs 35 people. It has an annual revenue of €9 million. One aspect of its recently formulated strategy is an aspiration to expand into a neighbouring country, France, by means of organic growth.

The reason that JKL's strategy for expansion is based on organic growth is due to JKL's past experience. Two years ago, the directors of JKL negotiated the purchase of a UK business, LMN, located in the west of the UK. At the time of this acquisition, LMN was regarded by JKL as having complementary capabilities and competences. However, within a short time after the acquisition, JKL judged it to have been a failure and LMN was sold back to its original owner at a loss for JKL.

JKL employed consultants to analyse the reasons for the failure of the acquisition. The consultants concluded that the failure had happened because:

1. JKL and LMN had very different accounting and control systems and these had not been satisfactorily combined;
2. JKL and LMN had very different corporate cultures and this had posed many difficulties which were not resolved;
3. JKL had used an autocratic management style to manage the acquisition and this had been resented by the employees of both companies.

The consultants recommended that JKL should consider the use of change agents to assist in any future acquisitions.

JKL has learnt that a French competitor company, XYZ, may shortly be up for sale at a price which would be very attractive to JKL. XYZ has a very good reputation in its domestic market for all aspects of its operations and its acquisition would offer JKL the opportunity to widen its skill set. None of JKL's staff speaks fluent French or is able to correspond in French. A small number of XYZ's staff speak English fluently but none of its staff are able to correspond in English.

Required

(a) **Discuss**, in the context of JKL, the respective advantages and disadvantages of pursuing a strategy of expansion by:

(i) Organic growth
(ii) Acquisition

(8 marks)

(b) **Recommend** what actions JKL should take to prevent the difficulties that occurred in the failure of the acquisition of LMN from happening if it acquires XYZ. **(9 marks)**

(c) **Recommend** how a change agent could assist in the successful acquisition of XYZ.

(8 marks)

(Total = 25 marks)

46 XZY Asia (5/10) 45 mins

XZY, a publicly quoted company has expanded rapidly since its formation five years ago, in 20X5. Its rapid growth rate, based on a broad range of well-regarded products manufactured and sold exclusively within Asia, has led to high profits and an ever increasing share price. However, in the last year, XZY has found its growth rate difficult to sustain. XZY's core strategy has been described by its CEO as 'selling what we know to who we know'. However, this view has been criticised by a number of financial analysts and journalists who have warned that if XZY's growth rate is not maintained its share price will fall and the value of the company will reduce. XZY has a functional organisational structure and currently employs around 800 employees. The number of employees has grown by 20% since 20X8.

The Human Resource Director of XZY has suggested that she carries out a review of XZY with the purpose of saving a significant amount of money by reorganising the company and reducing employee numbers. In this way, she considers she would be making a contribution towards maintaining XZY's profit growth rate. The CEO is interested in this idea but he is aware that changing organisational structure can be difficult. The CEO knows from his previous experience that such reorganisations do not always achieve their intended results.

Required

(a) **Evaluate**, using Ansoff's product market scope matrix, the alternative strategies XZY could follow to maintain its growth rate in profits and share price. **(12 marks)**

Note: Ansoff's model is also described as the growth vector matrix. You are not required to draw this model.

(b) **Advise** the CEO of the difficulties which may be encountered in changing the organisational structure of XZY and reducing employee numbers. **(5 marks)**

(c) **Recommend** how the CEO could manage the process of changing the organisational structure.

(8 marks)

(Total = 25 marks)

IMPLEMENTATION OF STRATEGIC PLANS

Questions 47-63 cover implementation and control, the subject of Part D of the BPP Study Text for Paper E3.

47 Operating theatre (*MABS*, 5/06) 45 mins

4D is a large teaching hospital. While it offers a full range of hospital services to its local community, it also has a large staff of professors and lecturers who teach and train all kinds of medical student. 4D has a very good reputation for clinical excellence.

One of the areas in which 4D is very highly regarded is the training of surgeons. Three of the nine operating theatres in the hospital can be observed from a gallery, though only a limited number of students can watch any operation due to space constraints. This allows the students to watch an experienced surgeon carry out a procedure and then ask questions of their lecturer or the surgeon. Later in their training, students can use the same facilities to carry out operations while being observed by experienced staff and fellow students.

The IT department of 4D has just developed a new Information System for use in operating theatres. This system (OTIS – the Operating Theatre Information System) uses web technology to allow students anywhere in the world to videoconference with a lecturer during an operation. The students can observe the operation and the surgical team, and discuss the procedure with the surgeon and their lecturer. The system also works 'in reverse' so a surgeon at 4D can watch a student perform an operation elsewhere in the world, and provide guidance and support. The OTIS system is currently being tested, prior to introduction.

Required

(a) (i) **Distinguish** between Business Process Re-engineering (BPR) and Process Innovation (PI), and explain the role of information technology in each of these techniques. **(6 marks)**

(ii) **Discuss** whether, in your opinion, the Operating Theatre Information System (OTIS) implementation is an example of BPR or PI. **(4 marks)**

(b) **Evaluate** THREE benefits to 4D and TWO benefits to society, of the Operating Theatre Information System (OTIS) **(15 marks)**

(Total = 25 marks)

48 Insurance Company (*MABS*, 11/09) 45 mins

C is one of several insurance companies which offer insurance policies covering general risks relating to individuals and families. Cost efficiency is a major factor in the success of the companies in this industry. Competition is fierce.

Over the past three years C has seen the volume of business increase but profits have remained static due to declining margins.

Although some of the processes within C are computerised, most of the processes which involve communication with customers are still paper-based. Responses from telephone enquiries involve paper-based communications both with the enquirers and internally within C. Additionally, sales staff visit potential customers in their homes to try to sell them insurance policies for their homes and their possessions. These transactions are again paper-based. This process is often slow and has led to complaints both from customers and from the company's sales staff.

C has also been receiving a regular, and increasing, number of complaints from current and potential customers about errors in the paperwork that they receive.

The Board of Directors of C has announced that there is a need for a business process re-engineering exercise to be conducted with the intention of modernising the business. The intention is to streamline the business model as much as possible and to increase the profitability of the company. C intends to computerise almost all of the work done within the company.

A number of staff have expressed concern about business process re-engineering and its implications for those who work at C.

Required

(a) Briefly **explain** the principles of business process re-engineering (BPR). **(7 marks)**

(b) **Explain** the stages involved in implementing a BPR exercise that might be undertaken by C. **(8 marks)**

(c) **Discuss** the improvements that the Board of Directors of C might expect from the application of BPR to C's business model. **(10 marks)**

(Total = 25 marks)

49 MNI University (9/10) 45 mins

MNI is a university in a European country. It employs 350 academic staff and 420 other staff. It has 8,000 full-time students. Following a visit from government appointed auditors it was criticised for the following reasons:

- The university operated at a deficit; its expenditure exceeded its income.
- Student drop-out and failure rates were greatly in excess of the national average.
- It could not accurately produce a head-count of the number of students enrolled.
- Internal control of cash receipts was defective and in several areas there were discrepancies.
- The level of student complaints was very high and increasing.
- It had a large number of debtors, mainly ex-students, and was not doing anything to collect outstanding amounts.
- It had an abnormally high level of staff turnover.
- The quality of education provided by MNI had been given the lowest possible rating 'Poor'.

Following this visit, MNI replaced its Vice-Chancellor*. The majority of MNI's funding comes from central government which has instructed the new Vice-Chancellor to prepare a new Strategic Plan for the next five years. The new Strategic Plan will be required to address the criticisms identified in the audits.

[*:The Vice-Chancellor is the University's Chief Executive Officer]

Required

(a) **Categorise**, under the headings Operational, Management and Strategic, the recent criticisms made about MNI. **Advise** the Vice-Chancellor how control measures could assist in the successful implementation of the new strategic plan. **(7 marks)**

(b) **Recommend**, with reasons, what controls the university could use to assist in the improvement of any three of the areas criticised in the recent audit. **(9 marks)**

(c) **Advise** the Vice-Chancellor how information systems could support the successful implementation of the new strategic plan. **(9 marks)**

(Total = 25 marks)

50 Management styles (*MABS*, 11/07) 45 mins

B is a multinational company with more than 20 divisions operating in various light engineering industries supplying automobile and aircraft manufacturing companies. Each division is managed by a chief executive officer (CEO) reporting directly to the board of directors of B.

B has recently acquired C, a smaller company with only 5 divisions which also operate in light engineering and supply similar customers to B's existing businesses. Each division is managed by a CEO reporting to the board of directors of C.

In the previous acquisitions that B has made, the acquired companies have been allowed to continue operating independently. This is despite the fact that there are overlapping or competing divisions in the combined enterprise. There is no certainty that this approach will continue.

Using Goold and Campbell's classification, B operates a system of 'strategic planning', and C operates a system of 'strategic control'.

B has announced that the board of directors of C will retire and each of the former divisions of C will report directly to the board of B.

The board of directors of B recognises that this will represent a considerable change in culture, working practices and expected behaviour for the CEOs of the divisions of C. It is concerned that there may be problems in ensuring the commitment of those CEOs to both B and its 'strategic planning' style.

As part of the acquisition team you are responsible for the transition to the new structure.

Required

(a) **Discuss** the differences between 'strategic planning' and 'strategic control'. **(4 marks)**

(b) **Discuss** the impact that the change in planning culture is likely to have on the CEOs of the former divisions of C. **(11 marks)**

(c) **Explain** how the changes to the reporting arrangements could be implemented to ensure the commitment of those CEOs to B. **(10 marks)**

(Total = 25 marks)

51 JIK kitchen manufacturer (5/11) 45 mins

JIK is a manufacturer, retailer and installer of domestic kitchens. It started business in 1980 and its market segment has been low to medium income earners. Until recently, its business model had been based on selling high volumes of a standard kitchen, brand name 'Value', with a very limited degree of customer choice, at low profit margins. JIK's current control system is focused exclusively on the efficiency of its manufacturing process and it reports weekly on the following variances: Materials price, Materials usage and Manufacturing labour efficiency.

JIK uses standard costing for its manufacturing operations. Currently, JIK employs 40 teams, each of which is required to install one of its 'Value' kitchens per week for 50 weeks a year. The average revenue per 'Value' kitchen installed is £5,000. JIK would like to maintain this side of its business at the current level. The 'Value' installation teams are paid a basic wage which is supplemented by a bonus for every kitchen they install over the yearly target of 50. The teams make their own arrangements for each installation and some teams work seven days a week, and up to 12 hours a day, to increase their earnings. JIK usually receives one minor complaint each time a 'Value' kitchen is installed and a major complaint for 10% of the 'Value' kitchen installations.

Two years ago JIK had launched a new kitchen, brand name 'Lux-Style'. This kitchen is aimed at high net-worth customers and it offers a very large degree of choice for the customer and the use of the highest standards of materials, appliances and installation. JIK would like to grow this side of its business. A 'Lux-Style' kitchen retails for a minimum of £50,000 to a maximum of £250,000. The retail price includes installation. Last year, the average revenue for each Lux-Style kitchen installed was £100,000. Currently, JIK has 2 teams of Lux-Style kitchen installers and they can install up to 10 kitchens a year per team. These teams are paid salaries without a bonus element. JIK has never received a complaint about a Lux-Style kitchen installation.

JIK's business is generated from repeat orders, recommendations, and local press advertising. It employs two sales executives who earn an annual salary of £35,000 each. It offers a twelve month money back guarantee and this has to be honoured for 1% of its installations.

JIK has always been profitable but was surprised to see that in its results for the last year it only made 0.1% net profit on its turnover.

Required

(a) **Evaluate** the appropriateness of JIK's current control system. **(7 marks)**

(b) **Recommend** TWO Critical Success Factors (CSFs) which could assist JIK achieve future success. You much justify your recommendations. **(6 marks)**

(c) **Advise** JIK of the changes it will need to make:

(i) To its current control system following the introduction of the CSFs recommended in part (b) of your answer. **(4 marks)**

(ii) To its standard costing system, reporting frequency and information requirement to achieve improved control. **(8 marks)**

(Total = 25 marks)

52 NGV government department (3/11) 45 mins

NGV is a government department which researches biotechnology which has been defined as:

'Any technological application that uses biological systems, living organisms, or derivatives thereof, to make or modify products or processes for specific use'. [Source: United Nations.]

NGV was formed in 1980 and since then it has been operated as a cost centre. Each year the Director of NGV agrees a budget with the government minister to whom he is responsible. If there is a deficit or a surplus at the end of the year this is not carried forward to the next year. NGV normally has a deficit at the end of the year. NGV receives no income other than its budget which, for the current year (20X1), is £20 million. Within NGV there are 180 cost centres which spend the annual budget. NGV does not have a management accounting function but the Director knows approximately, on a monthly basis, the total spending which has taken place within NGV. There is no formal system in place for forecasting spending. The Director thinks that NGV will probably spend between £20 and £25 million in 20X1. NGV has no record of its capital equipment as this is purchased, on its behalf, by a central government ministry and, therefore, appears on that central government ministry's balance sheet.

Often the work done by NGV results in an innovation which can be developed commercially. When this happens, other government departments are responsible for patenting the innovation and its subsequent commercial exploitation. NGV does not pay any of the costs associated with patenting and commercial exploitation but neither does it receive any revenues generated from the patents or their commercial usage. Some of the past innovations developed by NGV have been extremely successful commercially and have generated significant revenues for other government departments and commercial organisations.

NGV currently employs 320 staff: 25% of these are regarded as being amongst the world leaders in their research expertise. In the past, when NGV staff have produced an innovation with commercial potential they have frequently left NGV a short time later and moved to a much better paid position in the private sector. Sometimes staff leave in the middle of a research project which cannot then be completed because of the loss of their expertise. The Director is worried about what he calls a 'brain-drain' and he is concerned that there is no system for capturing tacit knowledge i.e. the 'know-how of the individual member of staff. However, many of NGV's staff are long-serving employees who have not yet produced any significant research 'break-throughs'.

The Director of NGV has been told by the government minister to whom he reports that NGV is going to have to 'Join the real world, produce an adequate return on investment (ROI) and produce a strategy showing how this will be achieved'. From the next financial year NGV will not be allowed to run at a deficit but will be allowed to carry forward and use any surplus.

Required

(a) **Discuss** the extent to which the Director of NGV could use financial ratio analysis to exercise financial control and assist NGV in producing an adequate return on investment (ROI). **(12 marks)**

(b) **Recommend** how NGV should implement a knowledge management strategy. **(13 marks)**

(Total = 25 marks)

53 ZZZ manufacturing company (11/11) 45 mins

ZZZ is a manufacturing company employing 1,200 people which makes components for the automotive industry. ZZZ has had 'preferred supplier' status with a major car manufacturer, MMM, for the last three months. This means ZZZ is guaranteed a minimum amount of business with MMM each week. The preferred supplier status is reviewed annually. MMM insists on a year-on-year reduction of 4% in the prices charged by ZZZ. ZZZ's current level of guaranteed business with MMM is £2 million per week which constitutes 95% of ZZZ's revenue.

MMM operates a just-in-time production and purchasing system and it has a policy of not inspecting the components supplied to it by ZZZ. However, if there are two reports of any of ZZZ's components failing, either during production or later in a vehicle driven by one of MMM's customers, ZZZ would lose its preferred supplier status. ZZZ has a number of competitors which would like to replace it as MMM's preferred supplier.

ZZZ's Managing Director, H, has the following objectives, which have been imposed upon him by ZZZ's Board of Directors:

- Maintain ZZZ's preferred supplier status with MMM;
- Keep ZZZ's expenditure within the limits set each year in the budget which is approved by its Board of Directors;
- Develop the management skills of ZZZ's 32 operational managers

H is held responsible for the successful achievement of the objectives and he may lose his job if any are not met. H believes that the best way to achieve his objectives is by the use of a performance management system (PMS) which he has designed. H's PMS is based exclusively on budgetary control. This PMS uses quarterly reports prepared by ZZZ's budget accountant. These reports compare budgeted and actual expenditure for each of ZZZ's 2,000 cost centres.

The quarterly reports are reviewed by H and later discussed with ZZZ's operational managers. The operational managers are shown the aggregate amount of under or overspending in the cost centres but are not allowed to know the detail underlying this. This is because H believes that the details of ZZZ's finances should only be known to members of the Board of Directors.

All ZZZ's investment in new capital equipment, amounting to £20 million in the previous financial year, was spent in two of the manufacturing cost centres. ZZZ's investment proposals are originated and prepared by H and submitted for approval to ZZZ's Board of Directors. The operational managers are not involved with the preparation of investment proposals. To date, no investment proposal submitted by H has been refused by the board.

Required

(a) **Evaluate** the effectiveness of ZZZ's performance management system in assisting H achieve his objectives. **(11 marks)**

(b) **Recommend**, with reasons, FOUR improvements ZZZ could make to its current performance management system. **(8 marks)**

Note: In your answer to part (b), you must NOT include the balanced scorecard as one of your recommendations.

(c) **Recommend**, with reasons, TWO performance measures that would show ZZZ's operational managers the progress they are making towards maintaining ZZZ's preferred supplier status with MMM. **(6 marks)**

(Total = 25 marks)

54 DLC telephone services (11/10) 45 mins

DLC is a company which provides private telephone network services. It sells its services exclusively to business customers and, since its foundation three years ago (in 20X7), DLC has been very successful. DLC has been able to charge a premium price for its services and in financial years 20X8 and 20X9 achieved a Return on Capital Employed (ROCE) of 50% and 48% respectively. DLC's success has been built on excellence in two key success factors: Technological Innovation and Customer Service. DLC currently employs 80 people and this year will have annual revenue of $24 million.

Technological innovation

DLC has been able to continually innovate its services based on the 'leading edge' skills of its founder and chief executive, X, who previously worked in a research institute. DLC's technological innovation also requires substantial, continued capital investment and DLC spent $6 million on this in 20X9. X owns 100% of DLC's share capital. X has been able to attract several of her former colleagues to join DLC and they have contributed to the culture of research excellence and technological innovation.

Customer service

DLC's business has been the design, installation and maintenance of private telephone networks for large organisations. A recent contract completed by DLC was for a large media organisation to provide a network to support 7,000 current users, with provision for this number to be extended to 10,000 within three years. This type of business is very rewarding for DLC as it is not price sensitive. However, meeting the service requirements of the client is vitally important.

DLC's control system

DLC's only financial control system is a traditional one of budgetary control. Budgets are prepared using the actual levels of expenditure for the previous budget year together with an additional amount designed to reflect forecast levels of inflation. Monthly management accounts are prepared in which actual expenditure is compared to budgeted expenditure. DLC also computes monthly its overall Return On Capital Employed (ROCE) which X considers to be the best control measure available for her to use.

DLC has no system which explicitly sets targets and reports upon Technological Innovation and Customer Service. X considers DLC's performance in these two areas is best represented by the company's ROCE. DLC's sales achievement against budget is reported upon in total: there is no attempt made at sectional analysis. When X started DLC, she knew every detail about every customer and contract and their levels of profitability. However, as DLC has expanded she can no longer do this, which she feels is a weakness.

DLC's strategic aims

DLC has no formal written statement of strategy. However, X has expressed the following strategic aims: she wants the company to continue expanding within the same market/business segment, and to provide a rewarding lifestyle for herself and secure well-paid jobs for DLC's employees.

Required

(a) **Discuss** the usefulness and limitations of DLC's control system. **(12 marks)**

(b) **Advise** X how non-financial performance measures could assist in the evaluation of DLC's two key success factors. **(6 marks)**

(c) **Evaluate** how Customer Profitability Analysis could assist in the achievement of X's strategic aims for DLC. **(7 marks)**

(Total = 25 marks)

55 Performance measurement (*MABS*, 5/07) 45 mins

D is a management consultancy partnership providing complex computer modelling services to utility companies. Three partners started the business ten years ago but rapid growth in the past four years has seen it increase to fifteen partners. Each partner has a team working exclusively for, and reporting directly to that partner. Competition between the teams is fierce and, sometimes, heated. The loyalty of each team to its respective partner is very strong.

Members of each team are rewarded with an annual team bonus based on the amount of new business they bring in each year. However, recently it has been discovered that teams have been competing with each other for the same potential new client.

Partners recruit all consultants as trainees, usually after they have obtained a doctorate in pure mathematics or economics. After a six months probationary period they are either confirmed in post or asked to leave. The rewards for those that stay are high with at least 60% of income derived from the team bonus. Typically a basic salary of $40,000 would be boosted to $100,000 if the team has worked aggressively and found new clients.

The service that the partnership provides is highly specialised and at the forefront of available technology. Each team will write computer simulations to address its clients' problems. These models are not made available outside the company and, on some occasions, have not even been shared with other teams in the consultancy.

At a recent partners' meeting, it was agreed that the inter-team rivalry was not working in the partnership's best interest, since teams were competing in such a way as to damage the firm's reputation, profitability and its prospects for growth. Recognising that the current performance measurement system encouraged this behaviour, the partners agreed that an appropriate performance measurement system should be introduced which was less one-dimensional. The partners believed this would encourage better practice in terms of knowledge sharing and a coordinated approach to their existing clients and potential clients. They have recognised that the introduction of a multi-dimensional performance measurement system will involve a significant training programme for their teams to redirect their current focus away from only finding new business.

Required

As a first stage in this process, you have been appointed as management accountant and practice manager.

(a) **Advise** the partners of the functions that an effective performance measurement system will perform for D.

Note. You are not required to describe, in detail, any particular system. **(10 marks)**

(b) **Recommend** the process that should be used in developing the performance measurement system to be used within D. **(15 marks)**

(Total = 25 marks)

56 International acquisition (*MABS*, 5/08) 45 mins

EEE is a divisionalised company, based in F, where it is quoted on the stock exchange. EEE manufactures and sells small electrical equipment products. As a country, F is more highly developed than the neighbouring countries. EEE has enjoyed a strong home market and has exported to the neighbouring countries.

EEE has had a reputation for producing high quality products. Recently, it has come under increasing competitive pressure from new, privately held, companies based in the neighbouring countries.

It appears that competitors based in these neighbouring countries have been selling lower quality products than EEE and have been undercutting it quite significantly in terms of price. Sales in both EEE's home and export markets have been badly affected by the actions of these competitors in the neighbouring countries.

EEE has looked at a number of possible solutions to this situation and has decided to acquire a manufacturing company in one of the neighbouring countries and move all of its production there, completely closing the manufacturing division in F. This would mean that EEE would purchase one of the companies that has recently become a competitor. EEE would maintain its present divisionalised structure within its home country F and treat the acquired company as a new division.

The Board of Directors recognises the need to carefully select a suitable acquisition target company. The Board also recognises that careful consideration will need to be given to the most suitable approach to performance management once the acquisition has been made. The Board is considering an approach based on either Return On Investment (ROI) or Residual Income (RI).

Required

(a) **Advise** the Board on what information would be required to assess the suitability of an acquisition target. **(15 marks)**

(b) (i) **Discuss** the difficulties that EEE may experience with the performance measurement of its division, post acquisition. **(6 marks)**

(ii) **Discuss** the disadvantages that EEE may experience if it chooses to use ROI as its primary performance measure. **(4 marks)**

(Total = 25 marks)

57 SAH yachts (9/11) 45 mins

SAH is a family owned company employing 32 people, which builds and sells medium sized yachts which normally retail at £100,000. SAH operates in a very competitive market. SAH's yachts are usually bought by amateur sailors with high disposable incomes who value quality, reliability and performance. In the current year it plans to sell 25 yachts. SAH's Managing Director, N, has a vision for the company to be 'regarded as the best yacht builder for the private owner'.

SAH has always emphasised the high quality of its yachts and knows that its customers are very knowledgeable. Each yacht is built to a specific order and there is usually a period of at least one year between an order being placed and the yacht being delivered to the customer. SAH's construction process is very traditional: most of its designs are at least 20 years old and much of the construction work on its yachts is done by hand. SAH regards its workforce as 'craftspeople' who have learned their skills through their work experience. SAH employs school-leavers and provides apprenticeships lasting seven years. However, most of its competitors employ university graduates who have studied yacht design and construction.

SAH designs all its yachts manually which is very time consuming, although most of its competitors now use CAD/CAM* suites for their designs. SAH does not have any staff with CAD/CAM experience. SAH uses natural materials: for example, cotton for the sails. However, recently some natural materials have become difficult to obtain and the prices of these have risen by as much as 40% in the last two years. Many of SAH's competitors have replaced natural materials with synthetic ones as these are easier to obtain, cheaper and give enhanced performance.

In 1985, SAH employed a consultant who designed a standard costing system for use in its manufacturing operations. This system is still in use at SAH today. N relies on the standard costing system which is his only control system for the company. N knows that the manufacturing cost of a yacht amounts to 60% of its total cost and believes that if he is in control of 60%, he is in control of the majority of cost. However, N has experienced some difficulty in his role as the control system only reports financial results. N would like a system that gives him integrated control over all aspects of the business and has been considering the use of a Balanced Scorecard.

SAH's business comes from repeat orders and recommendations. However, it has experienced criticism in the last year because it failed to meet the promised delivery time for 30% of its orders and has lost business because the potential customers said that SAH's yachts looked 'old-fashioned' and were 'too slow'.

Cash flow is particularly important for SAH, because of the long lead times for each yacht, and has been under pressure recently. SAH has had to increase its overdraft facility by £50,000 to £150,000 and this is nearly fully used. Every year since its inception SAH has reported a profit but for the last financial year its Return on Capital Employed was 3%, which N has stated is unacceptable.

**CAD/CAM: Computer-Aided Design, Computer-Aided Manufacturing*

Required

(a) **Evaluate** the strengths and weaknesses of SAH's current control system. **(9 marks)**

(b) **Advise** N:

(i) how the Balanced Scorecard could be applied and used within SAH. You should also suggest and justify ONE measure for each of the balanced scorecard's perspectives. **(10 marks)**

(ii) of THREE potential problems he might encounter if he introduces the Balanced Scorecard. **(6 marks)**

(Total = 25 marks)

58 CCC car insurance (5/12) 45 mins

T is the Chief Executive Officer of a motor car insurance company, CCC. T, together with the Board of Directors, developed a mission statement last year (20X1) following a detailed analysis of the company's operations and market place. The mission statement states that 'CCC wants to continually grow through its commitment to quality and delivering value to its customers'. CCC has developed a complementary vision statement which aspires to:

- Provide superior returns to our shareholders
- Continually improve our business processes
- Delight our customers
- Learn from our mistakes and work smarter in the future

CCC's overriding objective, also developed last year, is to double the size of its revenue by the end of 20X5.

T has identified the following areas of concern:

- Poor customer service has led to CCC losing 15% of its customers in 20X1/20X2. The customer sales manager had sponsored an initiative to reward customers with a discount if they renewed their motor insurance. However, most of the sales executives were not familiar with the details of this scheme and did not mention it to customers considering renewing their insurance. The discount scheme had not affected the rate of loss of customers.
- The average age of CCC's personal computers (PCs) was five years. There have been many complaints from CCC's staff that their PC's are not adequate for their current demands. The last time an initiative had been undertaken to bring PCs up to date was three years ago.
- CCC's internal auditors had conducted performance reviews in three departments during 20X1. They found a common pattern in all three departments: many of the staff had only minimal educational qualifications which were inadequate for the jobs they were doing. This resulted in an unacceptable level of errors being made. No initiatives had been undertaken to address this problem.
- Investors have been critical of the low dividend yield on their CCC shares.

T is worried because, despite the time and effort put into the development of the mission and vision statements and the overriding objective, CCC is not making sufficient progress towards achieving its revenue target. Its revenue growth rate in 20X1 was 10%.

CCC's shortfall against its revenue target was discussed at a recent Board meeting. The Corporate Affairs Director stated that "the Board is 100% behind our strategy and vision but it's just not happening. I have experience in my previous company of working with an integrated model, the Balanced Scorecard. Could the Balanced Scorecard help CCC?"

Required

(a) **Advise** T how a Balanced Scorecard could assist in delivering CCC's vision and strategy. **(5 marks)**

(b) Assume that CCC has adopted a Balanced Scorecard approach to help it achieve its vision.

Recommend FOUR perspectives, and for each perspective show:

- An objective
- A measure
- A target
- An initiative

(16 marks)

(c) **Discuss** briefly TWO drawbacks of the Balanced Scorecard. **(4 marks)**

(Total = 25 marks)

59 JALL independent retailer (9/10) 45 mins

JALL is an independent retailer of office products selling 2,000 different items such as paper, stationery, printer cartridges, diaries and planners. JALL has been established for over 50 years and has successfully served the needs of its customers in the small town where it operates its three shops. The nearest competitor for JALL is ten miles away. JALL employs 50 staff and had revenue of €7,000,000 in the last financial year.

JALL has been owned by the same family since it began and many of its staff have worked in the shops all their lives. Staff turnover has always been very low and staff morale very good. JALL's managers know all their staff and major customers personally. JALL's managers are prepared to listen to suggestions and complaints and they like to 'keep a finger on the pulse' of the business. Staff appraisals are conducted informally once a year when the profit-sharing bonus is announced. JALL has paid its staff a bonus every year since it was established. JALL's customers benefit from competitive prices and a very high standard of service. JALL's suppliers are very pleased to work with JALL because its procurement procedures are very efficient and it always pays its accounts within the credit period.

Recently there have been a number of changes at JALL. Customers have noticed signs in the shop window stating 'Clearance sale: all items must go!' Suppliers have noticed that they are not always being paid on time. Within the shops, a manager is not always present and the staff have been told that JALL is to be sold to LNR, a large national chain of stationery retailers. When the staff enquired about the safety of their jobs they were told by their manager that there will be a meeting, at a future date, when they would be told whether or not they would be made redundant. However, the existing managers will keep their present jobs under the new ownership.

The effects of these changes are:

- Staff are very worried about their future with JALL and morale is at an all time low.
- Suppliers are thinking about changing their credit terms with JALL and are concerned about their future trading relationship.
- Customers are unsure about the future of JALL and some have switched their business to other retailers.
- JALL's revenue has fallen considerably and there is little inventory on display within the shops.

Required

(a) **Advise** the management of JALL:

(i) Why it might encounter resistance to the change in ownership. **(6 marks)**

(ii) How it could overcome this resistance to change. **(7 marks)**

(b) **Advise** the management of LNR:

(i) How it could use the Balanced Scorecard to manage its strategic performance. **(6 marks)**

(ii) How it could construct targets for JALL's staff within an incentive scheme and use these targets to support the Balanced Scorecard. **(6 marks)**

(Total = 25 marks)

60 Computer company (*MABS*, 11/08) 45 mins

DD is a research company operating in the computer hardware industry. It has been established for three years. The company employs 30 scientists and engineers working in three research teams. One of those teams has invented an innovative processor which is significantly faster than any processor that is currently available commercially. It is likely that the new processor will be usable in computers used for industrial and, possibly, gaming purposes. The other teams are working in similar areas, developing processors.

The company is privately funded by an entrepreneur (Mr X), who made $350 million from the sale of his previous computer business.

Although all of the researchers have done new and innovative work, which has led to a number of published academic papers, no patents have been filed since the company started. Therefore, none of DD's innovative products has ever become commercially available.

Mr X has, to date, allowed his research staff to conduct research which is focused on creativity rather than commercial viability. He does not want to lose any of the current research staff but now wants to encourage them to be more commercially aware.

Mr X has decided that the company must now capitalise upon the innovative computer processor that one of the DD teams has invented. He intends that some of the focus should shift to the development of commercially available products rather than purely research activities.

Mr X recognises that this will be a significant change in strategy and culture for the company and that the change will require significant planning and management. Mr X intends to hire marketing staff and five additional engineers to bring the processor, and any other potential products, to market as soon as possible.

Currently there is no performance measurement system in place within the company. Mr X believes that the Balanced Scorecard might be the best performance measurement system for DD.

Required

(a) **Explain** the components of the Balanced Scorecard model. **(4 marks)**

(b) **Recommend**, with reasons, two measures that DD should use in **each** of the components of the Balanced Scorecard model. **(16 marks)**

(c) **Discuss** how the Balanced Scorecard should be introduced and used, in order to help DD achieve the proposed change in strategy and culture. **(5 marks)**

(Total = 25 marks)

61 Global environmental charity (*MABS*, 5/09) 45 mins

E is a global environmental charity. E is internationally recognised for its work in the area of sustainable development and the protection of endangered species and habitats.

Some supporters of E have criticised the organisation for its lack of clear direction in an increasingly competitive environment. Donations to charities have been declining, year on year, for the past five years.

The structure of E is unusual in that there is an autonomous division in each country in which the charity operates. There are 45 autonomous divisions, each headed by a CEO. It is the responsibility of each divisional CEO to report to the Supervisory Board of 10 trustees, which is based in a European country. Four times a year, the 45 CEOs meet for two days to discuss performance and their plans for the future. The meetings usually finish with no clear decisions about a unified direction for the charity to take. The divisions act independently for the next three months. This has led to a number of crises, both financial and non-financial, in the past five years.

As a result, the Supervisory Board has recognised that the charity cannot continue with the existing lack of direction, control and accountability. The Supervisory Board has decided to introduce a performance measurement and control system which will help it to implement a clear strategic direction for the charity. The Supervisory Board recognises that this will be a significant change for the CEOs and managers, and the Board expects considerable resistance.

A consultant has suggested E should introduce a balanced scorecard system of performance measurement and control.

Required

(a) **Discuss** the advantages and disadvantages for E of introducing a balanced scorecard system of performance measurement. **(12 marks)**

(b) **Discuss four** reasons why the CEOs of E might resist the proposed changes. **(8 marks)**

(c) **Recommend** the steps that could be taken to overcome the resistance to change. **(5 marks)**

(Total = 25 marks)

62 RCH (5/10) 45 mins

In a widely published model, Johnson, Scholes and Whittington characterise the strategic management process as consisting of three inter-related elements:

- Strategic analysis
- Strategic choice
- Strategic implementation

Required

(a) Explain why strategic implementation is included in the Johnson, Scholes and Whittington model.

Note: You are not required to draw the model. **(5 marks)**

RCH, an international hotel group with a very strong brand image has recently taken over TDM, an educational institution based in Western Europe. RCH has a very good reputation for improving the profitability of its business units and prides itself on its customer focus. The CEO of RCH was recently quoted as saying 'Our success is built on happy customers: we give them what they want'. RCH continually conducts market and customer research and uses the results of these researches to inform both its operational and longer term strategies.

TDM is well-established and has always traded profitably. It offers a variety of courses including degrees both at Bachelor and Masters levels and courses aimed at professional qualifications. TDM has always concentrated on the quality of its courses and learning materials. TDM has never seen the need for market and customer research as it has always achieved its sales targets. Its students consistently achieve passes on a par with the national average. TDM has always had the largest market share in its sector even though new entrants continually enter the market. TDM has a good reputation and has not felt the need to invest significantly in marketing activities. In recent years, TDM has experienced an increasing rate of employee turnover.

RCH has developed a sophisticated set of Critical Success Factors which is integrated into its real-time information system. RCH's rationale for the take-over of TDM was the belief that it could export its customer focus and control system, based on Critical Success Factors, to TDM. RCH believed that this would transform TDM's performance and increase the wealth of RCH's shareholders.

Required

(b) (i) **Identify four** Critical Success Factors which would be appropriate to use for TDM. **(4 marks)**

(ii) **Recommend**, with reasons, **two** Key Performance Indicators to support **each** of the **four** Critical Success Factors you have identified. **(16 marks)**

(Total = 25 marks)

63 RTF (Pilot paper) 45 mins

RTF is an architectural practice owned by 3 partners and employing 20 other staff. Its vision has been stated as: 'Your future designed by RTF: Today!' Its business is focused on designing housing schemes for local governments and also individual houses for wealthy clients. The emphasis in the housing schemes has been to produce high-quality homes to standard designs and ensuring that the schemes were completed on time and within budget. RTF has established a library of designs which it has successfully used and which can be reused. The relationships which RTF has established with local government employees have been important for the successful completion of its contracts. RTF has a corporate contacts database where every local government employee it has dealt with is recorded. This has proved invaluable to RTF.

RTF's other main income stream comes from the design of individual, 'one-off', houses for wealthy clients. The partners have always enjoyed this work as it gives them the opportunity to express their professional talents. However, the recently appointed Management Accountant has concerns about this business as she believes the partners spend a disproportionate amount of their time on this work. One fundamental control system within a professional practice is the system for recording time which forms the basis for costing work. Unlike most of its industry which uses proprietary software, RTF relies upon a manual system for recording time spent on each project and the results are often inaccurate.

The partners have always believed that a staff development policy is important for success. They have invested in improving the educational and technical background of their staff. RTF has a strong relationship with its local university. One result of this relationship is a computerised design package, '2020Design', which RTF and the university jointly developed and own. The package speeds up the design process and offers the possibility of significant cost savings. If this package is applied within RTF it could result in either a greater throughput of work from the existing staff, staff reductions or some combination of both of these.

RTF has carried out market research regarding the potential demand for 2020Design. This research indicates that 2020Design will be a viable commercial product. In what will be a significant strategic and cultural change for RTF it intends to market 2020Design and has employed a Marketing Manager. The Marketing Manager intends to licence agents to sell 2020Design in RTF's home country and abroad.

RTF does not have any systematic way of relating its operations to its vision or of measuring performance. However, one of the partners has heard of the Balanced Scorecard and has suggested that this might be an appropriate model for RTF to use.

Required

(a) **Explain** the four different perspectives of the Balanced Scorecard model. **(4 marks)**

(b) For each of the four perspectives, **discuss** and **recommend** two appropriate measures which would assist RTF. **(8 marks)**

(c) **Recommend** how RTF could introduce and use the Balanced Scorecard to help it achieve the required changes in strategy and culture. **(13 marks)**

(Total = 25 marks)

SECTION A CASE STUDIES

Case study questions 64 – 73 combine pre-seen and unseen material in the same way that they will be combined for the E3 exam.

64 B Supermarkets (5/12) 90 mins

Pre-seen case study

You should assume the date 'now' is May 2012.

Introduction

B Supermarkets (B) was founded as a grocery retailer in a European country in 1963. Its sales consist mainly of food and household items including clothing. B now owns or franchises over 15,000 stores world-wide in 36 countries. The company has stores in Europe (in both eurozone and non-eurozone countries), Asia and North America. B's head office is located in a eurozone country. B has become one of the world's largest chains of stores.

B's Board thinks that there are opportunities to take advantage of the rapid economic growth of some Asian countries and the associated increases in demand for food and consumer goods.

Structure

The B Group is structured into a holding company, B, and three subsidiary companies which are located in each of the regions of the world in which it operates (Europe, Asia and North America). The subsidiary companies, referred to as "Regions" within B, are respectively B-Europe, B-Asia and B-North America.

Store operations, sales mix and staffing

B operates four types of store: supermarkets, hypermarkets, discount stores and convenience stores. For the purpose of this case study, the definition of each of these types of store is as follows:

A *supermarket* is a self-service store which sells a wide variety of food and household goods such as washing and cleaning materials, cooking utensils and other items which are easily carried by customers out of the store.

A *hypermarket* is a superstore or very large store which sells the same type of products as a supermarket but in addition it sells a wide range of other items such as consumer durable white goods, for example refrigerators, freezers, washing machines and furniture. Hypermarkets are often located on out-of-town sites.

A *discount store* is a retail store that sells a variety of goods such as electrical appliances and electronic equipment. Discount stores in general usually sell branded products and pursue a high-volume, low priced strategy and aim their marketing at customers who seek goods at prices which are usually less than can be found in a hypermarket.

A *convenience store* is a small shop or store in an urban area that sells goods which are purchased regularly by customers. These would typically include groceries, toiletries, alcoholic beverages, soft drinks and confectionery. They are convenient for shoppers as they are located in or near residential areas and are often open for long hours. Customers are willing to pay premium prices for the convenience of having the store close by.

B sells food products and clothing in its supermarkets and hypermarkets at a higher price than many of its competitors because the Board thinks that its customers are prepared to pay higher prices for better quality food products. B also sells good quality consumer durable products in its supermarkets and hypermarkets but it is forced to sell these at competitive prices as there is strong competition for the sale of such goods. B's discount stores sell good quality electrical products usually at lower prices than those charged in its supermarkets and hypermarkets, B only sells electronic equipment in its discount stores. Customers have a greater range from which to choose in the discount stores as compared with supermarkets and hypermarkets because the discount stores specialise in the goods which they sell. B's convenience stores do not have the availability of space to carry a wide range of products and they charge a higher price for the same brand and type of goods which it sells in its supermarkets.

Although B owns most of its stores, it has granted franchises for the operation of some stores which carry its name.

Nearly 0.5 million full-time equivalent staff are employed world-wide in the Group. B tries when possible to recruit local staff to fill job vacancies within its stores.

Value statement and mission

In recognition of the strong competitive and dynamic markets in which it operates, B's Board has established an overall value statement as follows: "We aim to satisfy our customers wherever we trade. We intend to employ different generic competitive strategies depending on the market segment in which our stores trade."

The Board has also produced the following mission statement:

"B practises sustainable investment within a healthy ethical and thoughtful culture and strives to achieve customer satisfaction by giving a courteous and efficient service, selling high quality goods at a reasonable price, sourcing goods from local suppliers where possible and causing the least damage possible to the natural environment. By this, we aim to satisfy the expectations of our shareholders by achieving consistent growth in our share price and also to enhance our reputation for being an environmentally responsible company."

Strategic objectives

The following objectives have been derived from the mission statement:

1 Build shareholder value through consistent growth in the company's share price.

2 Increase customer satisfaction ratings to 95% as measured by customer feedback surveys.

3 Increase commitment to local suppliers by working towards achieving 40% of our supplies from sources which are local to where B stores trade.

4 Reduce carbon emissions calculated by internationally agreed measures by at least 1% per year until B becomes totally carbon neutral.

5 Maximise returns to shareholders by employing different generic competitive strategies depending on the market segment in which B stores trade.

Financial objectives

The Board has set the following financial objectives:

1 Achieve consistent growth in earnings per share of 7% each year.

2 Maintain a dividend pay-out ratio of 50% each year.

3 Gearing levels as measured by long-term debt divided by long-term debt plus equity should not exceed 40% based on book value.

Governance

The main board comprises the Non-executive Chairman, the Chief Executive and nine Executive directors. These cover the functions of finance, human resources, corporate affairs (including legal and public relations), marketing, planning and procurement. There is also one executive director for each of the three regions, being the Regional Managing Directors of B-Europe, B-Asia and B-North America. There are also nine non-executive main board members in addition to the Chairman.

The main Board of Directors has separate committees responsible for audit, remuneration, appointments, corporate governance and risk assessment and control. The Risk Assessment and Control Committee's tasks were formerly included within the Audit Committee's role. It was agreed by the Board in 2009 that these tasks should be separated out in order not to overload the Audit Committee which has responsibilities to review the probity of the company. B's expansion has been very rapid in some countries. The expansion has been so rapid that B has not been able to carry out any internal audit activities in some of these countries to date. The regional boards do not have a committee structure.

Each of the Regional Managing Directors chairs his or her own Regional Board. All of the Regional Boards have their own directors for finance, human resources, corporate affairs, marketing, planning and procurement but their structure is different for the directors who have responsibility for the stores. In B-Asia, one regional director is responsible for the hypermarkets and supermarkets and another is responsible for discount stores and convenience stores. In B-North America, one regional director is responsible for the hypermarkets and supermarkets and another is responsible for discount stores (B does not have any convenience stores in North America). In B-Europe there is one regional director responsible for supermarkets and hypermarkets, one for discount stores and one for convenience stores. In all regions the regional directors have line accountability to their respective regional managing director and professional accountability to the relevant main board director. There are no non-executive directors on the regional boards. Appendix 1 shows the main board and regional board structures.

Treasury

Each of B's three regions has a regional treasury department managed by a regional treasurer who has direct accountability to the respective Regional Director of Finance and professional accountability to the Group Treasurer. The Group Treasurer manages the central corporate treasury department which is located in B's head office. The Group Treasurer, who is not a main board member, reports to the Director of Finance on the main board.

Shareholding, year-end share prices and dividends paid for the last five years

B is listed on a major European stock exchange within the eurozone and it wholly owns its subsidiaries. There are five major shareholders of B, including employees taken as a group, which between them hold 25% of the 1,350 million total shares in issue. The major shareholders comprise two long term investment trusts which each owns 4%, a hedge fund owns 5%, employees own 5% and the founding family trust owns 7% of the shares. The remaining 75% of shares are owned by the general public.

The year-end share prices and the dividends paid for the last five years were as follows:

	2007	*2008*	*2009*	*2010*	*2011*
	€	€	€	€	€
Share price at 31 December	47.38	25.45	28.68	29.44	31.37
Net Dividend per share	1.54	1.54	1.54	1.62	1.65

Planning and management control

B has a very structured planning process. Each regional board produces a five year strategic plan for its region relating to specific objectives set for it by the main board and submits this to the main board for approval. The main board then produces a consolidated strategic plan for the whole company. This is reviewed on a three yearly cycle and results in a revised and updated group five year plan being produced every three years.

B's management control system, which operates throughout its regions and at head office, is well known in the industry to be bureaucratic and authoritarian. Strict financial authority levels for development purposes are imposed from the main Board. There is tension between the main Board and the regional boards. The regional board members feel that they are not able to manage effectively despite being located much closer to their own regional markets than the members of the main Board. The main Board members, on the other hand, think that they need to exercise tight control because they are remote from the markets. This often stifles planning initiatives within each region. This tension is also felt lower down the organisation as the regional board members exercise strict financial and management control over operational managers in their regions in order to ensure that the main Board directives are carried out.

Competitive overview

B operates in highly competitive markets for all the products it sells. The characteristics of each of the markets in which it operates are different. For example, there are different planning restrictions applying within each region. In some countries, B is required to operate each of its stores in a partnership arrangement with local enterprises, whereas no such restriction exists within other countries in which it trades. B needs to be aware of different customer tastes and preferences which differ from country to country. The following table provides a break-down of B's stores in each region.

	B Europe	*B Asia*	*B North America*
Supermarkets and hypermarkets	3,456	619	512
Discount stores	5,168	380	780
Convenience stores	4,586	35	

B is one of the largest retailing companies in the world and faces different levels of competition in each region. B's overall market share in terms of retail sales for all supermarkets, hypermarkets, discount stores and convenience stores in each of its regions is as follows:

	Market share
Europe	20%
Asia	1%
North America	1.5%

The following table shows the sales revenue and net operating profit earned by B in each of its regions for the year ended 31 December 2011:

	B Europe *€ million*	*B Asia* *€ million*	*B North America* *€ million*
Revenue	89,899	10,105	9,708
Net Operating Profit	4,795	743	673

B is constantly seeking other areas of the world into which it can expand, especially within Asia where it perceives many countries have an increasing population and strengthening economies.

Corporate Social Responsibility (CSR)

B is meeting its CSR obligations by establishing environmental targets for carbon emissions (greenhouse gas emissions), careful monitoring of its supply chain, undertaking sustainable investments and investing in its human capital.

Environmental targets for carbon emissions:

B's main board is keen to demonstrate the company's concern for the environment by pursuing continuous improvement in the reduction of its carbon emissions and by developing ways of increasing sustainability in its trading practices. A number of environmental indicators have been established to provide transparency in B's overall performance in respect of sustainability. These published measures were verified by B's statutory auditor and are calculated on a like-for-like basis for the stores in operation over the period measured.

In the year ended 31 December 2011, B reduced its consumption of kilowatt hours (kWh) per square metre of sales area as compared with the year ended 31 December 2008 by 9%. The target reduction for that period was 5%. In the same period it reduced the number of free disposable plastic bags provided to customers per square metre of sales area, by 51% against a target of 60%. Its overall greenhouse gas emissions (measured by kilogrammes of carbon dioxide per square metre of sales area) reduced by 1% in 2011 which was exactly on target.

B provides funding for the development of local amenity projects in all of the countries where B stores operate. (An amenity project is one which provides benefit to the local population, such as providing a park, community gardens or a swimming pool.)

Distribution and sourcing:

Distribution from suppliers across such a wide geographical area is an issue for B. While supplies are sourced from the country in which a store is located as much as possible, there is nevertheless still a requirement for transportation across long distances either by road or air. Approximately 20% of the physical quantity of goods sold across the group as a whole is sourced locally, that is within the country in which the goods are sold. These tend to be perishable items such as fruit and vegetables. The remaining 80% of goods are sourced from large international manufacturers and distributors. These tend to be large items such as electrical or electronic equipment which are bought under contracts which are set up by the regional procurement departments. B, due to its size and scope of operations, is able to place orders for goods made to its own specification and packaged as under its own brand label. Some contracts are agreed between manufacturers and the Group Procurement Director for the supply of goods to the whole of the B group world-wide.

B's inventory is rarely transported by rail except within Europe. This has resulted in lower average reductions in carbon emissions per square metre of sales area by stores operated by B-Asia and B-North America than for those stores operated by B-Europe. This is because the carbon emission statistics take into account the transportation of goods into B's stores.

Sustainable investments:

B aspires to become carbon neutral over the long term. The Board aims to reduce its carbon emissions by investing in state of the art technology in its new store developments and by carrying out modifications to existing stores.

Human Resources:

B prides itself on the training it provides to its staff. The training of store staff is carried out in store by specialist teams which operate in each country where B trades. In this way, B believes that training is consistent across all of its stores. In some countries, the training is considered to be at a sufficiently high level to be recognised by national training bodies. The average number of training hours per employee in the year ended 31 December 2011 was 17 compared with 13 hours in the year ended 31 December 2010. In 2011, B employed 45% more staff with declared disabilities compared with 2010.

Information systems and inventory management

In order to operate efficiently, B's Board has recognised that it must have up-to-date information systems including electronic point of sale (EPOS) systems. An EPOS system uses computers or specialised terminals that can be combined with other hardware such as bar-code readers to accurately capture the sale and adjust the inventory levels within the store. EPOS systems installation is on-going. B has installed EPOS systems in its stores in some countries but not in all its stores world-wide.

B's information systems are not perfect as stock-outs do occur from time-to-time, especially in the European stores. This can be damaging to sales revenue when stock-outs occur during peak sales periods such as the days leading up to a public holiday. In Asia and North America in particular, B's information technology systems sometimes provide misleading information. This has led to doubts in the minds of some head office staff about just how robust are B's inventory control systems.

As is normal in chain store groups, there is a certain degree of loss through theft by staff and customers. Another way that loss is suffered is through goods which have gone past their "sell-by" date and mainly relates to perishable food items which are wasted as they cannot be sold to the public. In most countries, such food items which cannot be sold to the public may be sold to local farmers for animal feed.

Regulatory issues

B's subsidiaries in Asia and North America have sometimes experienced governmental regulatory difficulties in some countries which have hindered the installation of improved information systems. To overcome some of these regulatory restrictions, B-Asia and B-North America have, on occasions, resorted to paying inducements to government officials in order for the regulations to be relaxed.

APPENDIX 1

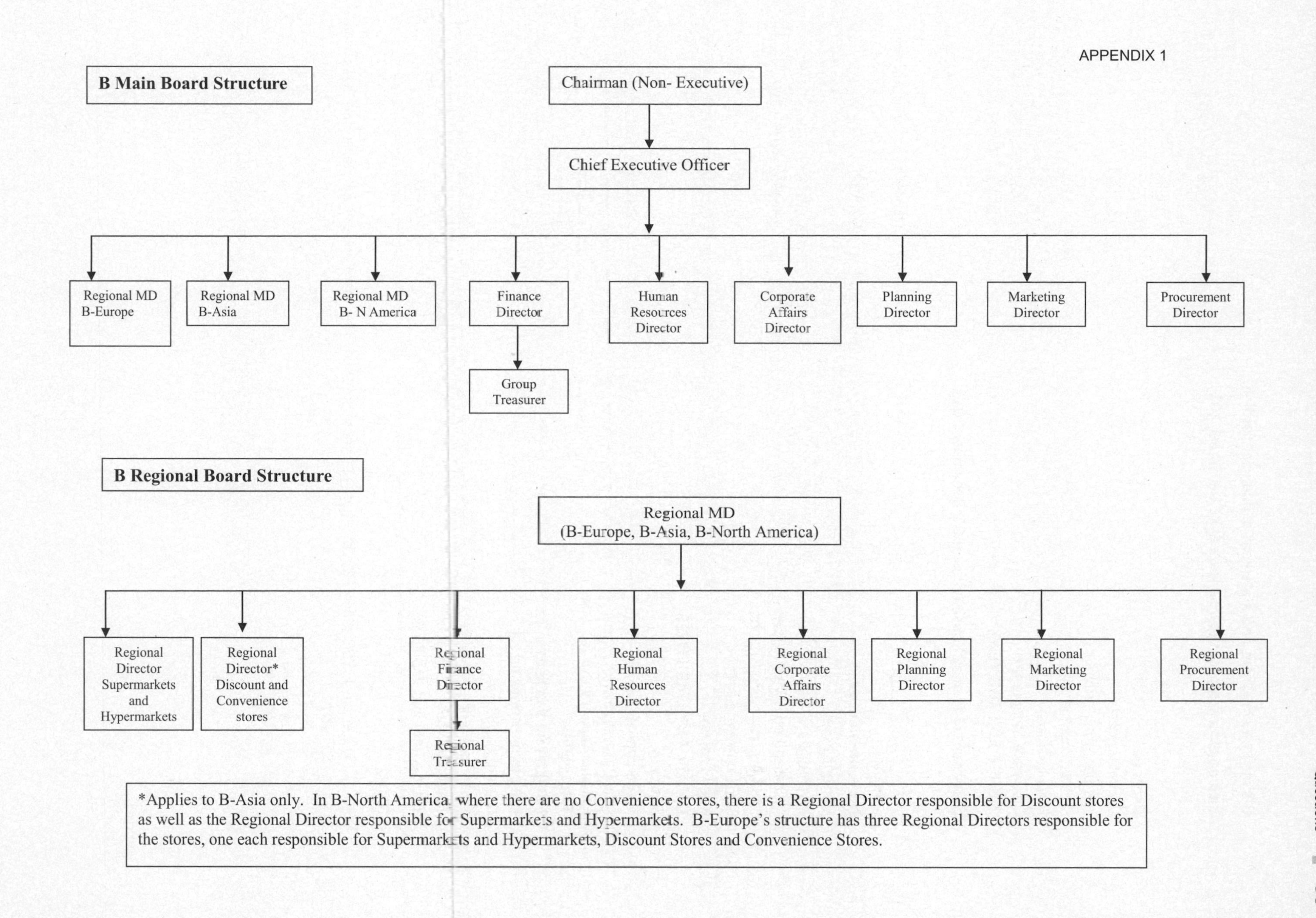
B Main Board Structure
Chairman (Non- Executive)
Chief Executive Officer
Regional MD B-Europe
Regional MD B-Asia
Regional MD B- N America
Finance Director
Group Treasurer
Human Resources Director
Corporate Affairs Director
Planning Director
Marketing Director
Procurement Director
B Regional Board Structure
Regional MD (B-Europe, B-Asia, B-North America)
Regional Director Supermarkets and Hypermarkets
Regional Director* Discount and Convenience stores
Regional Finance Director
Regional Treasurer
Regional Human Resources Director
Regional Corporate Affairs Director
Regional Planning Director
Regional Marketing Director
Regional Procurement Director
*Applies to B-Asia only. In B-North America where there are no Convenience stores, there is a Regional Director responsible for Discount stores as well as the Regional Director responsible for Supermarkets and Hypermarkets. B-Europe's structure has three Regional Directors responsible for the stores, one each responsible for Supermarkets and Hypermarkets, Discount Stores and Convenience Stores.

B's income statement and statement of financial position.

Income statement for the year ended 31 December 2011

	Notes	€ million
Revenue		109,712
Operating costs		(103,501)
Net operating profit		6,211
Interest income		165
Finance costs		(852)
Corporate income tax		(1,933)
PROFIT FOR THE YEAR		3,591

Statement of financial position as at 31 December 2011

		€ million
ASSETS		
Non-current assets		57,502
Current assets		
Inventories		7,670
Trade and other receivables		1,521
Cash and cash equivalents		3,847
Total current assets		13,038
Total assets		70,540
EQUITY AND LIABILITIES		
Equity		
Share capital	1	2,025
Share premium		3,040
Retained earnings		18,954
Total equity		24,019
Non-current liabilities		
Long term borrowings		15,744
Current liabilities		
Trade and other payables		30,777
Total liabilities		46,521
Total equity and liabilities		70,540

Notes:

1 There are 1,350 million €1.50 shares currently in issue. The share price at 31 December 2011 was €31.37.

Unseen Case Material

Franchising discount stores within Country P

B Supermarkets (B) is evaluating the possibility of expanding its business into Country P which is in Europe. Country P has an underdeveloped economy. However, it was described by a leading international bank as a 'Global Growth Generator': that is, one of the countries with 'the most promising growth prospects for 2010-2050'.

B does not currently conduct any business within Country P. B would like to test the market there. B's Marketing Director has suggested that one possible way of doing this would be to introduce discount stores within Country P by granting franchise agreements to local entrepreneurs (the franchisees) within Country P. This would also have the advantage for B of limiting its capital investment in Country P, as the entrepreneurs would be responsible for providing the premises so B will not incur any capital costs for buildings relating to any franchise. The equipment will be supplied by B.

B has had success when it has granted franchises in many countries. This experience has enabled B to establish the following fee structure which it would apply to franchises in Country P.

Country P fee structure: charged by B per franchise

'One-off' fees: charged at the start of the franchise	**€**
Franchise fee	60,000
Training fee	20,400
Equipment fee	150,000

Annual fees (payable at the end of each financial year)	
Royal fee	15% of revenue
Service fee	5% of revenue
Marketing contribution fee	5% of revenue

To justify the launch of discount store franchises in Country P, B's Marketing Director has set a minimum required income of €3 million per year for B, to be earned from the annual fees charged to the franchises (that is, from the royalty fee, the service fee and the marketing contribution fee).

B's Marketing Director estimates that the cost of capital for entrepreneurs in Country P is 12%.

In addition to the one-off fees and the annual fees, B has estimated the following average monthly operating costs and revenues for each discount store franchise:

Per month	**€**
Revenue	100,000
Fixed costs	2,000
Variable operating costs	65% of reveue

The variable operating costs are additional to the annual fees which are payable to B.

Sustainability

In its mission statement (see 2nd page of pre-seen material) B claims to 'Practise sustainable investment'. B also aspires to '...enhance our reputation for being an environmentally responsible company'. B is also keen to demonstrate its concern for the environment by pursuing continuous improvement in the reduction of its greenhouse gas emissions and by developing ways of increasing sustainability in its trading practices. B has developed a number of environmental indicators to provide transparency in its overall performance in respect of its sustainability (see 4th page of pre-seen material).

If B does undertake expansion into Country P, 90% of its products will have to be imported into Country P: half by road, half by air. The distribution of the imported products within Country P will be done by road transport. If the discount stores are opened they will be in new purpose built premises which will be designed to be energy efficient. B's Marketing Director believes that it will be possible to operate the discount stores in Country P as 'carbon-neutral' businesses. B will expect the discount store franchises in Country P to comply with all aspects of its corporate social responsibility policy (see 4th page of pre-seen). Each discount store will be able to operate without giving its customers free disposable plastic bags.

Planning and management control

B has a very structured planning process (see 3rd page of pre-seen material). Its management control system is 'bureaucratic and authoritarian'. B's Planning Director is aware of the internal tensions within the company regarding the planning and management control systems.

If the discount store franchises proceed within Country P, B's Planning Director sees it as an opportunity to introduce a substantial degree of reform to the planning and management control systems currently operating within B. Country P would function as a test site for planning and management control system reform for B. If this experience proves to be successful then the Planning Director would suggest to B's main Board that reform should be extended throughout the company. The Planning Director has suggested to B's Board that if the reform of the planning and management control systems is introduced then B Europe's Regional Director for Discount Stores:

- Could use a reformed planning and management control system in Country P.
- Would be responsible for achieving a profit target for discount stores in Country P which would be agreed with B's Chief Executive Officer.
- Would be able to employ whatever planning and management control systems he preferred in Country P. He would be required to submit a monthly return to the Finance Department at B's Head Office.
- Could use whatever Information System he wanted in Country P. However, this would have to be compatible with B's management control system for data entry and reporting purposes. The design and operation of the reporting systems used within Country P would be the exclusive responsibility of the Regional Director for Discount Stores.
- Would have the authority to decide which products are sold in Country P's discount stores and source them from anywhere.
- Would have sole responsibility for making all decisions about the entrepreneurs in Country P; such as appointment, renewal and cessation.

The Corporate Affairs Director has reacted strongly against the Planning Director's proposals for reform of the planning and management control system. He said 'In my opinion this is not how we do things. Our procedures have served us well in the past. Tinkering with our culture in this way is a waste of money and could be dangerous.'

Required

(a) **Calculate** the number of discount store franchises that need to be granted in Country P to earn the minimum required income of €3 million per year. **(4 marks)**

(b) (i) **Advise** the minimum period for which a franchise should be granted in Country P to make it financially worthwhile for an individual franchisee.

You should ignore the capital cost to the franchisee of providing the premises. **(4 marks)**

(ii) **Advise** which additional factors are likely to influence entrepreneurs about the desirability of investing in a discount store franchise in Country P.

You answer should include factors under the following headings:

- Marketing/Branding
- Risk
- Franchise implementation and operation **(17 marks)**

(c) **Evaluate** how Country P's discount store business could assist B Supermarkets in achieving 'sustainable investment' and increased sustainability in its trading practices. **(10 marks)**

(d) **Advise** B's Chief Executive of the advantages AND disadvantages for B which might arise if the reforms to the planning and management control system within Country P, that have been suggested by the Planning Director, were introduced throughout B Supermarkets. **(15 marks)**

(Total = 50 marks)

Pre-seen material for Questions 65 & 66 – M plc

Note: This pre-seen applies to both Question 65 (from the March 2012 exam) and Question 66 (from the November 2011 exam).

You should assume the date 'now' is November 2011.

Pre-seen Case Study

Introduction

M plc is a long established publisher of newspapers and provider of web media. It is based in London and has had a full listing on the London Stock Exchange since 1983. The company has three operating divisions which are managed from the United Kingdom (UK). These are the Newspapers Division, the Web Division and the Advertising Division.

Newspapers Division

The Newspapers Division publishes three daily newspapers and one Sunday newspaper in the UK. The Division has three offices and two printing sites. Between them the three offices edit the three daily newspapers and the Sunday newspaper. The Newspaper Division has two subsidiary publishing companies, FR and N. FR is based in France within the Eurozone and N in an Eastern European country which is outside the Eurozone. Printing for all the Division's publications, except those produced by FR and N, is undertaken at the two printing sites. FR and N have their own printing sites.

Web Division

The Web Division maintains and develops 200 websites which it owns. Some of these websites are much more popular in terms of the number of "hits" they receive than others. Web material is an increasing part of M plc's business. In the last ten years, the Web Division has developed an online version of all the newspapers produced by the Newspapers Division.

Advertising Division

The sale of advertising space is undertaken for the whole of M plc by the Advertising Division. Therefore, advertisements which appear in the print media and on the web pages produced by the Newspapers Division (including that produced by FR and N) and the Web Division respectively are all handled by the Advertising Division.

Group Headquarters

In addition to the three operating divisions, M plc also has a head office, based in the UK, which is the group's corporate headquarters where the Board of Directors is located. The main role of M plc's headquarters is to develop and administer its policies and procedures as well as to deal with its group corporate affairs.

Mission statement

M plc established a simple mission statement in 2005. This drove the initiative to acquire FR in 2008 and remains a driving force for the company. M plc's mission is "to be the best news media organisation in Europe, providing quality reporting and information on European and world-wide events".

Strategic objectives

Four main strategic objectives were established in 2005 by M plc's Board of Directors. These are to:

1. Meet the needs of readers for reliable and well informed news.
2. Expand the geographical spread of M plc's output to reach as many potential newspaper and website readers as possible.
3. Publish some newspapers which help meet the needs of native English speakers who live in countries which do not have English as their first language.
4. Increase advertising income so that the group moves towards offering as many news titles as possible free of charge to the public.

Financial objectives

In meeting these strategic objectives, M plc has developed the following financial objectives:

(i) To ensure that revenue and operating profit grow by an average of 4% per year.

(ii) To achieve steady growth in dividend per share.

(iii) To maintain gearing below 40%, where gearing is calculated as debt/(debt plus equity) based on the market value of equity and the book value of debt.

Forecast revenue and operating profit

M plc's forecast revenue and net operating profit for the year ending 31 March 2012 are £280 million and £73 million respectively.

Extracts from M plc's forecast income statement for the year ending 31 March 2012 and forecast statement of financial position as at 31 March 2012 are shown in the appendix.

Comparative divisional performance and headquarters financial information

The following information is provided showing the revenue generated, the operating profit achieved and the capital employed for each division and the operating costs incurred and capital employed in M plc's headquarters. This information covers the last two years and also gives a forecast for the year ending 31 March 2012. All M plc's revenue is earned by the three divisions.

Newspapers Division	*Year ended 31.3.2010 £million*	*Year ended 31.3.2011 £million*	*Forecast for year ending 31.3.2012 £million*
Revenue external	91	94	94
Revenue internal transfers	90	91	96
Net operating profit	45	46	48
Non-current assets	420	490	548
Net current assets	4	8	(10)

Web Division	*Year ended 31.3.2010 £million*	*Year ended 31.3.2011 £million*	*Forecast for year ending 31.3.2012 £million*
Revenue internal transfers	55	60	66
Net operating profit	10	13	16
Non-current assets	37	40	43
Net current assets	1	1	(2)

Advertising Division	*Year ended 31.3.2010 £million*	*Year ended 31.3.2011 £million*	*Forecast for year ending 31.3.2012 £million*
Revenue external	162	180	186
Internal transfers	(145)	(151)	(162)
Net operating profit	10	18	19
Non-current assets	3	6	7
Net current assets	1	1	(2)

Headquarters	*Year ended 31.3.2010 £million*	*Year ended 31.3.2011 £million*	*Forecast for year ending 31.3.2012 £million*
Operating costs	8	9	10
Non-current assets	37	39	43
Net current assets	1	1	(1)

Notes:

1 The Advertising Division remits advertising revenue to both the Newspapers and Web Divisions after deducting its own commission.

2 The Web Division's entire revenue is generated from advertising.

3 The revenues and operating profits shown for the Newspapers Division include those earned by FR and N. The converted revenue and operating profit from N are forecast to be £20 million and £4 million respectively for the year ending 31 March 2012. FR is forecast to make a small operating profit in the year ending 31 March 2012. The Board of M plc is disappointed with the profit FR has achieved.

Additional information on each of M plc's divisions

Newspapers Division

FR is wholly owned and was acquired in 2008. Its financial statements are translated into British pounds and consolidated into M plc's group accounts and included within the Newspaper Division's results for internal reporting purposes.

Shortly after it was acquired by M plc, FR launched a pan-European weekly newspaper. This newspaper, which is written in English, is produced in France and then distributed throughout Europe. M plc's board thought that this newspaper would become very popular because it provides a snapshot of the week's news, focused particularly on European issues but viewed from a British perspective. Sales have, however, been disappointing.

N, which publishes local newspapers in its home Eastern European country, is also treated as part of the Newspapers Division. M plc acquired 80% of its equity in 2010. At that time, M plc's board thought that Eastern Europe was a growing market for newspapers. The subsidiary has proved to be profitable mainly because local production costs are lower than those in the UK relative to the selling prices.

The Newspapers Division's journalists incur a high level of expenses in order to carry out their duties. The overall level of expenses claimed by the journalists has been ignored by M plc in previous years because it has been viewed as a necessary cost of running the business. However, these expenses have risen significantly in recent years and have attracted the attention of M plc's internal audit department.

There has been significant capital investment in the Newspapers Division since 2009/10. The printing press facilities at each of the two printing sites have been modernised. These modernisations have improved the quality of output and have enabled improved levels of efficiency to be achieved in order to meet the increasing workloads demanded in the last two years. Surveys carried out before and after the modernisation have indicated higher levels of customer satisfaction with the improved quality of printing.

The increased mechanisation and efficiency has reduced costs and led to a reduction in the number of employees required to operate the printing presses. This has led to some dis-satisfaction among the divisional staff. Staff in the other divisions have been unaffected by the discontent in the Newspapers Division. Staff turnover has been relatively static across the three divisions, with the exception of the department which operates the printing presses in the Newspapers Division where some redundancies have occurred due to fewer staff being required since the modernisation.

Web Division

The web versions of the newspapers are shorter versions of the printed ones. There is currently no charge for access to the web versions of the newspapers. Revenues are generated from sales by the Advertising Division of advertising space on the web pages. Some of the websites permit unsolicited comments from the public to be posted on them and they have proved to be very popular. The Web Division is undertaking a review of all its costs, particularly those relating to energy, employees and website development.

The Web Division's management accounting is not sophisticated: for example, although it reports monthly on the Division's revenue and profitability, it cannot disaggregate costs so as to produce monthly results for each of the 200 websites. The Division is at a similar disadvantage as regards strategic management accounting as it lacks information about the websites' market share and growth rates. This has not mattered in the past as M plc was content that the Web Division has always been profitable. However, one of M plc's directors, the Business Development Director (see below under The Board of Directors and group shareholding) thinks that the Web Division could increase its profitability considerably and wants to undertake a review of its 200 websites.

Advertising Division

The Advertising Division remits advertising revenue to both the Newspapers and Web Divisions after deducting its own commission. In addition, the Advertising Division offers an advertising service to corporate clients. Such services include television and radio advertising and poster campaigns on bill boards. Advertisements are also placed in newspapers and magazines which are not produced by M plc, if the client so wishes. An increasing element of the work undertaken by the Advertising Division is in providing pop-up advertisements on websites.

Planning process

Each division carries out its own planning process. The Newspapers Division operates a rational model and prepares annual plans which it presents to M plc's board for approval. The Web Division takes advantage of opportunities as they arise and is operating in a growth market, unlike the other two divisions. Its planning approach might best be described as one of logical incrementalism. Increased capital expenditure in 2010/11 helped the Advertising Division to achieve an 11% increase in revenue in that year. The Divisional Managers of both the Web Division and the Advertising Division are keen to develop their businesses and are considering growth options including converting their businesses into outsource service providers to M plc.

The Board of Directors and group shareholding

M plc's Board of Directors comprises six executive directors and six non-executive directors, one of whom is the Non-executive Chairman. The executive directors are the Chief Executive, and the Directors of Strategy, Corporate Affairs, Finance, Human Resources and Business Development. The Business Development Director did not work for M plc in 2005 and so had no part in drafting the strategic objectives. She thinks that objective number four has become out- dated as it does not reflect current day practice. The Business Development Director has a great deal of experience working with subscription-based websites and this was one of the main reasons M plc recruited her in March 2011. Her previous experience also incorporated the management of product portfolios including product development and portfolio rationalisation.

There are divisional managing directors for each of the three divisions who are not board members but report directly to the Chief Executive.

One of M plc's non-executive directors was appointed at the insistence of the bank which holds 10% of M plc's shares. Another was appointed by a private charity which owns a further 10% of the shares in M plc. The charity represents the interests of print workers and provides long-term care to retired print workers and their dependents. Two other non-executive directors were appointed by a financial institution which owns 20% of the shares in M plc. The remaining 60% of shares are held by private investors. The board members between them hold 5% of the shares in issue. None of the other private investors holds more than 70,000 of the total 140 million shares in issue.

It has become clear that there is some tension between the board members. Four of the non-executive directors, those appointed by the bank, the charity and the financial institution, have had disagreements with the other board members. They are dissatisfied with the rate of growth and profitability of the company and wish to see more positive action to secure M plc's financial objectives.

Some board members feel that the newspapers market is declining because fewer people can make time to read printed publications. Some of the non-executive directors think that many people are more likely to watch a television news channel than read a newspaper.

Editorial policy

M plc's board applies a policy of editorial freedom provided that the published material is within the law and is accurate. The editors of each of the publications printed in the UK and France and of the websites have complete autonomy over what is published. They are also responsible for adhering to regulatory constraints and voluntary industry codes of practice relating to articles and photographs which might be considered offensive by some readers.

There is less scrutiny of the accuracy of the reporting in N's home country than in other countries. The Eastern European country in which N is situated has become politically unstable in the last two years. Much of this unrest is fuelled by the public distaste for the perceived blatant corruption and bribery which is endemic within the country's Government and business community. It is well known that journalists have accepted bribes to present only the Government's version of events, rather than a balanced view. There is also widespread plagiarism of published material by the country's newspapers and copyright laws are simply ignored.

Corporate Social Responsibility

A policy is in place throughout M plc in order to eliminate bribery and corruption among staff especially those who have front line responsibility for obtaining business. This policy was established 15 years ago. All new employees are made aware of the policy and other staff policies and procedures during their induction. The Director of Human Resources has confidence in the procedures applied by his staff at induction and is proud that no action has ever been brought against an employee of M plc for breach of the bribery and corruption policy.

M plc is trying to reduce its carbon footprint and is in the process of developing policies to limit its energy consumption, reduce the mileage travelled by its staff and source environmentally friendly supplies of paper for its printing presses. The Newspapers Division purchases the paper it uses for printing newspapers from a supplier in a Scandinavian country. This paper is purchased because it provides a satisfactory level of quality at a relatively cheap price. The Scandinavian country from which the paper is sourced is not the same country in which N is situated.

Strategic Development

The Board of Directors is now reviewing M plc's competitive position. The Board of Directors is under pressure from the non-executive directors appointed by the bank, the charity and the financial institution (which between them own 40% of the shares in M plc), to devise a strategic plan before June 2012 which is aimed at achieving M plc's stated financial objectives.

[Pre-seen material continues on the next page]

APPENDIX 1

Extracts from M plc's forecast group income statement and forecast statement of financial position

Forecast income statement for the group for the year ending 31 March 2012

	Notes	*£ million (GBP million)*
Revenue		280
Operating costs		(207)
Net operating profit		73
Interest income		1
Finance costs		(11)
Corporate income tax	1	(19)
FORECAST PROFIT FOR THE YEAR		44

Forecast statement of the group financial position as at 31 March 2012

	Notes	*£ million (GBP million)*
ASSETS		
Non-current assets		641
Current assets		
Inventories		2
Trade and other receivables		27
Cash and cash equivalents		2
Total current assets		31
Total assets		672
EQUITY AND LIABILITIES		
Equity		
Share capital	2	140
Share premium		35
Retained earnings		185
Non-controlling interest		16
Total equity		376
Non-current liabilities		
Long term borrowings	3	250
Current liabilities		
Trade and other payables		46
Total liabilities		296
Total equity and liabilities		672

Notes:

1 The corporate income tax rate can be assumed to be 30%.

2 There are 140 million £1 shares currently in issue.

3 The long-term borrowings include £83 million of loan capital which is due for repayment on 1 April 2013 and the remainder is due for repayment on 1 April 2019.

65 M plc (3/12) 90 mins

Unseen Case Material

M plc publishes three well known daily newspapers and of these the 'Daily Informer' is the longest established. The Daily Informer has positioned itself as 'the family newspaper with the broad focus.' It has sections on news, sport, politics, the arts, environment, fashion, technology, medicine, children's interests and world events. However, critics within the newspaper industry have stated that the Daily Informer has no clear identity and does not target any particular segment of the newspaper reading market. Its circulation has decreased by 38% during the last ten years. The Daily Informer made a loss in each of the last two years.

The Daily Informer is published six days a week: it is not published on Sundays. The daily sales of each edition of the newspaper amount to 150,000 copies and its selling price is £0.50 per copy. Each issue of the Daily Informer has 3 pages of advertising sold at £7,500 a page.

The Daily Informer employs 330 people made up of:

- 200 journalists and editorial staff: average salary £42,000
- 130 other staff: average salary £37,000

The Daily Informer:
Forecast income statement for year ended 31 March 2013

	£000s
Revenue	
Circulation	23,400
Advertising	7,020
Total revenue	**30,420**
Costs	
Journalists and editorial staff	8,400
Other staff	4,810
Production costs:	
Fixed	3,180
Variable	5,180
Advertising costs	1,000
Distribution costs	4,680
IT	4,000
Third party pictures/photos	3,000
Total Costs	**34,250**
Loss	**(3,830)**

One of the Daily Informer's competitors, the 'Opinion', recently changed from being a paid for newspaper to being free to its readers. This has resulted in a large increase in the newspaper's circulation and a reduction in journalists and editorial jobs and other staff. The general economic situation is bad for employment and many of the Opinion's former staff are unemployed.

It is noticeable that the Opinion has changed its character: it contains much more advertising, no in-depth reporting and the main content focuses on reporting the activities of footballers and other celebrities.

The Chief Executive of M plc, W, wants to investigate the possibility of the Daily Informer also becoming a free newspaper (hereafter referred to as 'FREE') and has asked S, the divisional managing director of the Newspaper Division, to examine the consequences of such a change. S has instructed the editor of the Daily Informer, E, to prepare a business forecast for FREE.

S has stated that the following criteria should be followed:

- FREE must target the same market segment as its competitor 'Opinion'
- Advertising space should be sold at £7,000 per page
- FREE's first financial objective should be to break-even within the next year

If the Daily Informer becomes 'FREE', it will, together with the 'Opinion' newspaper, form a new market segment of free newspapers. These will be the only such national UK newspapers.

E has stated that as FREE would no longer have a broad focus it would be possible to produce it with a smaller number of journalists and editorial staff. It is unlikely that FREE would continue to appeal to the Daily Informer's current readership. However, FREE would have a much greater popular appeal and achieve a higher circulation than the Daily Informer. E also believes that FREE would be able to sell substantially more advertising space, which was the experience of the Opinion when it changed its status.

The Daily Informer is currently distributed by its own staff using an in-house transport fleet. Most of the outlets which sell the Daily Informer are small retailers (that is, local newsagents and small shops). This means that currently the transport fleet has to make deliveries to 750 separate locations.

FREE would be available at 200 key points: for example, transport interchanges, such as train and bus stations and outside bars, restaurants, cinemas and sports centres. Each of these key points would distribute many more newspapers than the small retailers who are currently used for distribution. FREE would outsource the distribution to a transport specialist and this together with the reduced number of distribution points would lead to a substantial reduction in distribution costs for FREE as compared to the Daily Informer.

This new method of distribution would have an impact on the former distribution channel. The small retailers would no longer be able to sell the Daily Informer and this would lead to redundancies for some of the people in low paid jobs employed by the retailers. E knows from his previous experience working on another free newspaper that the readers are likely to only read FREE for a brief period of time, up to 30 minutes, and then they will throw away the paper. This could lead to a significant littering problem.

Forecast 'FREE' circulation		**1,000,000 copies per day**
All Savings/Increases below based on forecast income statement for the Daily Informer for year ended 31 March 2013 and apply for the whole of the year to 31 March 2013		*Comment*
Saving: Reduction of journalists and editorial staff jobs	125 jobs reduction	Less requirement for journalists due to change in character of newspaper
Saving: Other staff	£2,600,000	Savings in other staff due to changes in production arrangements
Increase: Production costs	50%	Some costs rise but others fall due to economies of scale and use of recycled newsprint. The variable cost of one copy of FREE is £0.03. Fixed costs do not alter.
Increase: Advertising costs	£500,000	Increase due to change in character of newspaper
Saving: Distribution costs	45%	Savings because of altered subscription
Saving: IT	50%	Savings due to change in character of newspaper
Saving: Third party pictures/photos	25%	Savings due to change in character of newspaper

Competitive environment

The Daily Informer currently competes against ten other daily newspapers which cover various segments of the newspaper reading market. All of these newspapers contain between 7 and 10 pages of advertisements per issue. Some newspapers specialise in TV and sports coverage, others are directed towards women and one specialises in reporting financial markets and company news. Changes in reading habits and the growth of alternative news media have meant that the number of people in the UK who are prepared to pay for a newspaper is decreasing.

As the newspaper industry is a mature one, its technology is well-developed and production methods are similar across the industry. Since the Newspaper Division modernised its printing press facilities in 2009/10 (see 3rd page of pre-seen material) most of its competitors have followed suit.

Some journalists, often referred to as 'stars', are very important in UK newspapers and can command large salaries because they attract readers. These journalists often move between different newspapers.

When M plc is considering a major change to one of its businesses, it carries out a preliminary management accounting exercise. In the case of FREE, the exercise consists of calculating the number of pages of advertising it will be required to sell in order to cover all its costs and the implications of such a change. The result of this exercise, both qualitative and quantitative, will be used to inform any subsequent decision about whether or not to launch FREE.

Required

(a) (i) **Calculate** the number of pages of advertising required to be sold in the year ending 31 March 2013 in order for FREE to break-even.

Base your calculation on 312 published days. **(8 marks)**

(ii) **Discuss** the factors which could affect FREE's ability to achieve the sales of the number of pages of advertising you have calculated in (i). **(6 marks)**

(iii) **Advise** S, the divisional managing director of the Newspaper Division, of the extent to which the publication of a free newspaper fits M plc's strategic and financial objectives (see 2nd and 3rd pages of pre-seen). **(7 marks)**

(iv) **Advise** S, the divisional managing director of the Newspaper Division, whether the effects of the proposed change to FREE are consistent with Corporate Social Responsibility principles relating to employment, the environment, and FREE readership. **(8 marks)**

(b) **Evaluate,** using Porter's generic competitive strategy model, the likelihood of the proposed change to FREE giving the Newspaper Division a sustainable competitive advantage.

(12 marks)

(c) **Advise** E how he could use Lewin's three-step model of change to assist the staff to make the transition to the new working environment of FREE.

(9 marks)

(Total = 50 marks)

66 M plc – Web division (11/11) 90 mins

Important note: Before attempting this question, make sure you have read the pre-seen material 'M plc' which can be found before Question 65.

Web Division

M plc maintains 200 websites and access to these is currently free of charge. M plc's most important website supports the 'Daily News' newspaper which is published seven days a week in the UK. This website has been operating for five years and normally receives 100,000 visits (hits) a day. The business model is that all M plc's websites generate income from advertising.

Current advertising revenue

The Daily News website currently carries five pages of advertising each day for which it charges advertisers £6,000 per page. M plc's Business Development Director, X, has identified a decline in advertising revenue from the Daily News website. X knows that the advertisers are attracted by the number of visits the website receives. However, the visitors come from a wide background with different social characteristics and economic resources. The advertisers would prefer to deal with a more tightly focused readership. This has led advertisers to reduce their spending to the current level of five pages per day, seven days a week.

X has commissioned market research which indicates that advertisers would:

(i) increase the number of daily pages of advertising they buy if the Daily News website was subscription-only;

(ii) not pay the current price per page if the number of subscribers was fewer than 60,000;

(iii) expect to pay a decreasing amount per page as the number of subscribers decreased.

Move to subscription base

X believes it would be beneficial if the Daily News website ceased to be free and became available only by subscription. This would generate an additional revenue stream for the Web Division. She has discussed this idea with the Web Division's Managing Director, Y, who has asked her to provide detailed advice about the consequences of such a change.

Forecast subscription revenue

X will offer subscribers a choice. They could either pay a daily subscription giving access for one 24 hour period or they could pay a weekly subscription giving access for seven days. X has estimated the number of subscribers for three possible pricing strategies. Each strategy has a daily price and a weekly price. The strategies are totally independent. Details of the strategies are shown in the table below.

Strategy	*Daily subscriptions Price per day*	*Daily subscriptions Forecast number of subscribers each day*	*Weekly subscriptions Price per week*	*Weekly subscriptions Forecast number of subscribers each week*
1	£0.25	4,000	£0.50	17,000
2	£0.50	3,500	£0.75	15,000
3	£0.75	1,500	£1.50	6,000

Forecast advertising revenue

The pricing strategies for the subscriptions in the table above would give rise to the total subscriptions shown in the table below. In addition, the table below shows the expected advertising revenue for each page sold and the expected number of pages sold for each subscription strategy.

Strategy	*Total number of subscribers each week*	*Forecast advertising revenue per page sold* £	*Forecast number of pages sold per day*
1	45,000	4,000	7
2	39,000	3,750	9
3	16,500	2,500	10

Performance management.

Although M plc has aggregate financial information for the Web Division it does not compute individual website's profit or loss. X believes that some of the 200 websites are profitable, should be invested in and could be candidates for changing to a subscription-only basis. X also believes that some of the 200 websites are unprofitable and should be closed down. She knows that the different websites consume different amounts of resources and activities. Under the current accounting arrangements the demands made on the division's activities by individual websites are not recognised.

X recognises that the task of reviewing the portfolio of 200 websites will be a complex one. Her previous experience indicates that better decisions are made when additional characteristics of products, besides their financial profile, for example, their relative market performance, are considered. However, X does not have detailed market information about the 200 websites. She is aware that the major search engines, such as Google, Yahoo and Bing can supply data relating to different market sectors and showing aspects such as market share and growth rates about individual websites. This data, which must be paid for, can be supplied for current and historic usage.

Strategic headcount reduction programme

M plc's Board of Directors is reviewing the company's competitive position (see pre-seen material). Four of the non-executive directors are dissatisfied with the profitability of the company (see 4th page of pre-seen). As a response to this criticism, the three divisional managing directors have been instructed by M plc's Chief Executive to find ways of enhancing efficiency and reducing costs.

The Web Division's Human Relations Manager, Z, has been directed by Y to recommend how this instruction could be carried out. Z has suggested the Web Division carries out a strategic headcount reduction programme. The Web Division currently employs 380 people in 10 different departments. Not all departments employ the same number of people: the largest department, Web Development, employs 62 people; the smallest department, Web Security, employs 11 people. Z has recommended a reduction of 100 staff across the division which would cut the Web Division's costs by £2.5 million, thus, enhancing M plc's competitive position.

Z has suggested that the best way of implementing the headcount reduction programme is that each of the 10 departments should declare 10 redundancies. Z has suggested that each departmental manager should choose who will lose their job. The departmental managers will be responsible for notifying those members of their staff who will be losing their jobs. Z insists that preference for redundancy should be given to employees over the age of 50 who are earning high salaries. Z believes that the participation of the departmental managers in the programme will have a positive motivational effect upon them, and this could lead to savings in later years which would exceed the estimated £2.5 million saving each year arising from the strategic headcount reduction programme.

Required

(a) (i) **Calculate** the impact of each of the THREE possible pricing strategies suggested by X on the Web Division's *weekly* income.

(10 marks)

(ii) **Advise** X of the other factors that should be considered before deciding to change the Daily News website to a subscription-only basis.

(10 marks)

(b) **Advise** the Business Development Director, X:

(i) Of the extent to which the proposed change to a subscription-only basis for the Daily News website represents a conflict with M plc's strategic and financial objectives;

(7 marks)

(ii) What arguments she should use to persuade the board of M plc to agree to the proposed change.

(3 marks)

(c) **Advise** X how she could use a portfolio analysis model, such as the Boston Consulting Group matrix, to review the portfolio of 200 websites to help her decide which to continue and which to discontinue.

(7 marks)

(d) (i) **Recommend**, with reasons, THREE improvements to the strategic headcount reduction programme that has been proposed by the Human Relations Manager, Z.

(6 marks)

(ii) **Advise** Z of approaches he could use to deal with any resistance to the changes resulting from the strategic headcount reduction programme from staff remaining in the Web Division.

(7 marks)

(Total = 50 marks)

Pre-seen material for Questions 67 & 68 – F plc

Note: This pre-seen applies to both Question 67 (from the September 2011 exam) and Question 68 (from the May 2011 exam).

You should assume the date 'now' is May 2011.

Pre-seen Case Study

Introduction

F plc is a food manufacturer based in the United Kingdom. It generates its revenue from three divisions named the Meals, Snacks and Desserts divisions. Each division specialises in the production of different types of food and operates from its own factory located on three different sites in England. F plc's head office is located in a remote part of England and is about equidistant from each of the company's three divisions.

Currently, F plc has a total employment establishment of about 10,000 full-time equivalent employees, about 97% of whom are employed in its three divisions. It is constantly running with about 700 full-time vacancies, mostly in the Desserts Division. This vacancy factor in the Desserts Division impedes its productivity.

The company was founded over 150 years ago by an entrepreneurial farmer who saw the opportunity to expand his farming business by vertically integrating into food production. Instead of selling his crops on the open market, he established a mill and produced flour. From this, it was a natural progression to diversify into producing other crops which were then processed into different ingredients for food products.

The company grew steadily and it became clear at the beginning of the 20th Century that increased production facilities were needed. It was at this point that the company built its first factory which at the time was a state of the art manufacturing facility. As demand continued to grow during the 20th Century, the company required additional manufacturing facilities and made a public offering of shares in 1960 to finance this expansion. The public offer was successful and F Limited was established. The original family's holding in the company fell to 25% at this point. Although a second factory was opened with the capital that had been raised, F Limited continued to manage the company on a centralised basis.

The next phase of development came in the late 1980's when F Limited became F plc. After this, F plc had a successful rights issue which raised sufficient capital to enable a third factory to be built. It was at this point that the divisionalised and de-centralised structure was established. Prior to this, the company managed its factories directly from its head office. The family shareholding fell to 20% at this point, with one family member holding 10% of the shares and family trusts holding the other 10%.

The environment in which F plc trades is dynamic, particularly with regard to the growth of legislation relating to food hygiene and production methods. F plc now exports many of its products as well as obtaining ingredients from foreign producers, which means that F plc must observe legislative requirements and food standard protocols in different countries.

Mission statement

F plc's mission statement, which was set in the year 2000, is as follows:

"F plc is committed to continually seek ways to increase its return to investors by expanding its share of both its domestic and overseas markets. It will achieve this by sourcing high quality ingredients, using efficient processes and maintaining the highest standards of hygiene in its production methods and paying fair prices for the goods and services it uses."

Strategic aims

The strategic aims are set in order to enable F plc to meet the obligations contained in its mission statement. F plc aims to:

(i) increase profitability of each of its divisions through increased market share in both domestic and overseas markets
(ii) source high quality ingredients to enhance product attractiveness
(iii) ensure that its factories adhere to the highest standards of food hygiene which guarantee the quality of its products
(iv) strive to be at the forefront in food manufacturing techniques by being innovative and increasing efficiency of production with least waste.

Corporate Social Responsibility

F plc takes Corporate Social Responsibility (CSR) seriously. The post of Environmental Effects Manager was created two years ago and a qualified environmental scientist was appointed to it. The Environmental Effects Manager reports directly to the Director of Operations. The role of the Environmental Effects Manager is to develop initiatives to reduce environmental impacts, capture data on the environmental effects of divisional and head office operations and report to the Board of Directors on the progress towards the achievement of F plc's CSR targets. An extract from F plc's internal CSR report for 2010 is shown in Appendix 1. F plc does not publish its CSR report externally.

Last year, F plc received criticism in the national press in England and in other countries for exploiting some of its suppliers in Africa by paying low prices for ingredients. This resulted in an extensive public relations campaign by F plc to counter these accusations. It established a programme to channel funds to support farmers in Africa via payments made through African government agencies. The programme, which is managed through F plc's head office, received initial financing from F plc itself and is now widening its remit to draw funding from other sources including public funding from the European Union.

The Board of Directors

The Board of Directors comprises five executive and five non-executive members all of whom are British. No member of the Board is from an ethnic minority.

The Chairman is a senior non-executive director and a retired Chief Executive of a major quoted retail clothing company based in England. He received a knighthood two years ago for services to industry.

The Chief Executive is 52 years old and was Director of Operations at F plc before taking up his current post three years ago.

The Finance Director is 49 years old and a qualified CIMA accountant. He has experience in a variety of manufacturing and retail organisations.

The Director of Operations is 65 years old and is a member of the original family which founded the business. He has been employed by F plc for all of his working life. He took up his current post three years ago following the promotion of the previous post holder to the role of Chief Executive.

The Marketing Director is 43 years old and has held various positions in sales and marketing for different organisations before being appointed to the Board. He came to the attention of the Chief Executive when he was instrumental in a successful initiative to market a new shopping complex in the city in which F plc's head office is based. At the time, the Marketing Director was the Chief Marketing Officer for the local government authority in the area.

The Director of Human Resources, the only female member of the Board, is 38 years old and holds a recognised HR professional qualification. Last year she was presented with a national award which recognised her achievements in the development of human resource management practices.

In addition there are four other non-executive directors on the Board. Two of them previously worked in senior positions alongside the Chairman when he was Chief Executive of the retail clothing company. One of them was the clothing company's finance director, but is now retired and the other was its marketing director but is now the sales and marketing director for a pharmaceutical company. One of the other non-executive directors is a practising lawyer and the other is a sports personality of national renown and a personal friend of the Chairman.

The Divisional General Managers, responsible for each of the three divisions, are not members of F plc's board. The Divisions are organised along traditional functional lines. Each division is managed by a Divisional Board which is headed by a Divisional General Manager. Each Divisional Board comprises the posts of Divisional Operations Manager, Divisional Accountant, Divisional Marketing Manager and Divisional Human Resources Manager. Each division undertakes its own marketing and human resource management. The divisional accountants are responsible for the management accounting functions within their divisions. Each member of the divisional boards is directly accountable to the Divisional General Manager but have professional accountability to the relevant functional F plc executive board members.

Financial position and borrowing facilities

Extracts from F plc's financial statements for the year ended 31 December 2010 are shown in Appendix 2.

F plc's long term borrowings are made up of a £160 million bank loan for capital expenditure and a £74 million revolving credit facility (RCF).

The bank loan is secured on F plc's assets and is repayable on 1 January 2018.

The RCF allows F plc to borrow, make repayments and then re-borrow over the term of the agreement. This provides F plc with flexibility because it can continue to obtain loans as long as it remains at or below £80 million, being the total amount agreed for this facility. The RCF expires on 31 December 2013.

Planning process

The planning process employed by F plc is one which can be described as adhering to classical rational principles. This has been the method of planning used for many years and culminates in the production of a five year forecast. The annual budget cycle feeds in to the strategic plan which is then updated on an annual basis. All F plc's revenue is derived through the operations of the three divisions. The only income generated by F plc's head office is from investments. The five year forecast for sales revenue and net operating profit for each division and F plc in total, after deduction of head office operating costs, is shown in Appendix 3. This shows that F plc is seeking to increase its sales revenue and net operating profit over the five year plan period.

Competition within the industry

F plc is one of the largest food production companies in England. It had an overall share of about 6% of its home market in 2010. Its nearest competitors held 5% and 7% market share respectively in 2010. The products in the industry have varying product life cycles. Competition is intense and there is a high failure rate for new products. Usually, new products require significant marketing support particularly if a new brand is being established.

Organisational culture within each division

Different cultures have emerged within each division.

Meals Division:

In the Meals Division, each function operates with little direct interference from the Divisional Board members. The approach is to allow each function to operate with as little control as possible being exercised by the Divisional Board.

Snacks Division:

In the Snacks Division, the emphasis of the Divisional Board is on product research and development and marketing. The Snacks Divisional Board expects its divisional marketing staff to undertake market research into customer tastes and preferences and then for products which satisfy these to be developed by its divisional research staff.

Desserts Division:

In the Desserts Division, the finance function is the dominant force. The finance functions in the other two divisions exert less influence over operations than is the case in the Desserts Division. It is not unusual for the Divisional Accountant in the Desserts Division to have confrontational meetings with managers of other functions. Such confrontation is particularly evident in the monthly meetings between the Divisional Accountant and the Divisional Marketing staff. It is clear that within the Desserts Division, the Divisional General Manager, a food technologist by profession, and the Divisional Accountant, formerly an auditor with a local government authority, maintain strict control over the operation of the division.

Further details relating to the three divisions are as follows:

Meals Division

The Meals division is located in the South of England. It specialises in manufacturing frozen meals, which are designed to be easy for consumers to quickly heat up and serve. The meals are sold to supermarkets and other retail outlets. Some are manufactured under F plc's own brand and others are manufactured under supermarkets' own labels. The division is also increasing its sales to welfare organisations which support elderly and infirm people. These organisations purchase simple frozen meals in bulk which they then heat up to provide a hot meal each day to those people in their care. In 2010, the Meals Division earned 14% of its revenue from outside the United Kingdom.

One of the Meals Division's most profitable products is a steak pie that is flavoured with special gravy that was developed by one of F plc's founding family members in the early part of the 20th Century. F plc's competitors cannot copy this gravy because the ingredients have to be combined in a very precise manner and then cooked in a particular way. The recipe for this gravy is known only to F plc's Director of Operations and the manager of the pie factory.

Two of the Meals Division's products are currently subject to investigation by the Food Standards Authority of a European country. Please see Appendix 1 under the heading "Food labelling" for more information on this.

Snacks Division

The Snacks Division, located in the East of England, mainly manufactures confectionery such as packet savouries and chocolate bars. Its main customers are supermarkets and retail shops. It has a growing market in continental Europe and in 2010 the division earned 19% of its revenue from non-United Kingdom sales. Many of its products are F plc's own brands, although, similarly with the Meals Division, it supplies products to supermarkets under their own label.

The Snacks Division successfully launched a new premium brand of chocolate bars in the UK in 2010.

Desserts Division

The Desserts Division is located in the North of England where road, rail and air links are not well developed. This has resulted in high transportation costs for goods into and out of the factory. Originally, this location was chosen because the lease terms for the factory were very competitive but in recent times the local taxes placed on the factory have become expensive. There is some limited room for expansion on the site the factory occupies but the local government authority has repeatedly rejected the expansion plans when the Division has sought the necessary planning permission to put its plans into action. This has caused the Divisional Board to consider whether it should move its entire operation to another part of England where its expansion plans may be more easily accomplished.

The Division has experienced technical and managerial staff shortages. The workforce of the Division has an establishment of 4,700 full-time equivalent employees. Despite there being a ready supply of manual labour for production work, the Desserts division runs with an average of 385 full-time vacancies at any one time.

The Division's products range from cold desserts, particularly ice cream, which can be eaten directly from the packaging, to those which require some preparation by the final purchaser before the product can be consumed. The Divisional Marketing Department has been investigating the possibility of negotiating 'Freezer deals' by which the Desserts Division would supply ice cream freezers to independent retailers which sell the Division's ice cream products. An independent retailer is a shop or outlet that is not part of a larger chain. This is in order to investigate the possibility of increasing the Division's share of the ice cream market sold by independent retailers.

The Division's sales increase in the periods which lead up to national and international festive periods such as Christmas and Chinese New Year. The Division is constantly researching new markets in an effort to increase its foreign earnings. Revenue from outside the United Kingdom in 2010 represented 23% of the Division's total revenue.

Inventory control and IT systems

There have been a number of problems across all three divisions in respect of inventory control. Poor inventory control has led to high levels of wastage and obsolete inventory being carried. This has been particularly problematic in respect of perishable ingredients. In the case of the Desserts Division, the Divisional Accountant has estimated that 5% of the Division's potential revenue has been lost as a result of not being able to satisfy customer orders on time, due to poor inventory control.

F plc operates a standard information management system across all the Divisions and at Head Office. The Information Technology in use has been unreliable due to technical malfunctions since the information management system was installed in 2001. Monthly management accounts, provided by each division to head office are often late, sometimes not being made available for up to three weeks into the subsequent month.

Internal audit

Until now, F plc's Internal Audit function, which is based at Head Office, has tended to concentrate its efforts on reviewing activities in the Meals and Snacks divisions as they each produce lower revenues and net operating profits in absolute terms compared with the Desserts division. The Internal Audit function's approach of applying a "light touch" to the Desserts Division is also in recognition of the influence exerted by the Divisional Finance function over the Division's operational activities.

Strategic development

The Board of Directors is now midway through its strategic planning cycle and is considering how the company should move forward. There is a proposal to build and operate a factory in West Africa to reduce air kilometres being flown in supplying the Meals Division with fresh vegetables. It is intended that the African factory will freeze the vegetables and then transport them to the Meals Division's factory in England by refrigerated ship.

[Pre-seen material continues on the next page]

APPENDIX 1

Extracts from F plc's internal Corporate Social Responsibility report for the year ended 31 December 2010.

This report was produced by the Environmental Effects Manager and presented to the Board of F plc in January 2011.

Fair trading

In accordance with its mission statement, F plc is committed to paying a fair price for the ingredients it uses in its products, particularly to farmers in the less developed economies of the world.

Waste reduction and recycling

F plc set a target for the financial year 2010 that waste of ingredients should be cut by 2%, measured by weight, from the 2009 levels. The actual ingredient waste was 2.5% lower in 2010 than in 2009 as measured by weight.

A target was also set for F plc to recycle 90% of its used packaging in the year 2010. It was recorded that 85% of total used packaging in 2010 was actually recycled.

Food labelling

Legal requirements demand accuracy in food labelling, in respect of ingredients, product description and cooking instructions in many countries. F plc employs a Compliance Manager to ensure that relevant labelling laws in each country, with which the company trades, are adhered to. A target is set for F plc to justify 100% of its claims in food labelling. Two products manufactured in the Meals Division are currently undergoing investigations by the Food Standards Authority of a European country following allegations that the labelling is inaccurate.

Transportation

Following adverse press coverage relating to the high number of kilometres travelled when importing and exporting goods from and to overseas countries, F plc introduced a target that its use of air travel should be reduced by 10% in 2010 compared with the amount used in 2009. F plc fell short of its target by only reducing air kilometres travelled by 3% in 2010 compared with 2009. Road kilometres travelled increased by 5% in 2010 compared with 2009.

Efficiency of energy usage in production

In an effort to reduce carbon emissions from the three divisions and head office, a target was set that by 2015, F plc will become carbon neutral in terms of its usage of energy. Energy usage in 2010 was at the same level as in 2009. It has been proposed that energy efficient lighting should replace the current energy inefficient lighting at all three factories and at head office in 2011 and smart meters should be installed in all of F plc's premises to keep the waste of electricity to a minimum.

APPENDIX 2

Extracts from F plc's income statement and statement of financial position

Income statement for the year ended 31 December 2010

	£ million (GBP million)
Revenue	986
Operating costs	(938)
Net operating profit	48
Interest income	1
Finance costs	(16)
Corporate income tax	(10)
PROFIT FOR THE YEAR	23

Statement of financial position as at 31 December 2010

	Notes	*s£ million (GBP million)*
ASSETS		
Non-current assets		465
Current assets		
Inventories		90
Trade and other receivables		112
Cash and cash equivalents		20
Total current assets		222
Total assets		687
EQUITY AND LIABILITIES		
Equity		
Share capital	1	140
Share premium		40
Retained earnings		61
Total equity		241
Non-current liabilities		
Long term borrowings	2	234
Current liabilities		
Trade and other payables		212
Total liabilities		446
Total equity and liabilities		687

Notes:

1. There are 560 million ordinary shares of £0.25 each in issue.
2. The long term borrowings comprise £160 million loan for capital expenditure which is repayable on 1 January 2018 and a £74 million revolving credit facility which expires on 31 December 2013.

APPENDIX 3

Five year forecast of sales revenue and net operating profit for each division and F plc in total and operating costs for head office:

	2010 (Actual)	*2011*	*2012*	*2013*	*2014*	*2015*
Meals Division						
Sales revenue	266	287	310	335	362	391
Net operating profit	31	34	40	47	54	63
Snacks Division						
Sales revenue	176	194	213	234	258	283
Net operating profit	44	48	53	58	64	71
Desserts Division						
Sales revenue	544	571	600	630	661	694
Net operating profit	72	80	90	101	112	125
Head office						
Operating costs	(99)	(107)	(112)	(118)	(124)	(130)
F plc total						
Sales revenue	986	1,052	1,123	1,199	1,281	1,368
Net operating profit	48	55	71	88	106	129

67 F plc (9/11) 90 mins

Unseen Case Material

Freezer deals

The Desserts Division has been reviewing its Marketing strategy. One of F plc's strategic aims (see 1st page of pre-seen material) is to 'increase profitability of each of its divisions through increased market share in both domestic and overseas markets'. The Divisional General Manager is willing to authorise a 'once and for all' additional expenditure of £2 million to achieve an increase in market share. However, he is very insistent that any spending must have a payback period of 1 year and increase market share.

The Divisional Accountant does not support the General Manager in these views. The Divisional Accountant believes that the most appropriate time frame for evaluating the success of the £2 million investment would be three years.

Following several months of research, the Desserts Division Marketing staff has targeted, within the UK, the market segment of ice cream sold by independent retailers as a means to increase the profitability and market share of the division. An independent retailer is 'a shop or outlet that is not part of a larger chain'. The Desserts Division currently has a 7% share of this market. Independent research has estimated that the total size of this market segment is £50 million in sales each month.

The Desserts Division Marketing staff has been investigating 'Freezer deals' which mean that the Desserts Division would supply ice cream freezers to independent retailers. The Freezer deals offer the independent retailers differing levels of marketing support and either a free, or discounted, freezer. In return, the independent retailers would be required to give a variable commitment to stock the Desserts Division's products. The Freezer deals under consideration are named 'Exclusive', 'Half-Way House' and 'Free and Easy'. The Desserts Division intends to offer only one of the Freezer deals to all UK independent retailers.

Freezer deals: key points

Exclusive

- Under this deal the independent retailer will be obliged to sell the Desserts Division's products exclusively for a period of three years.
- The Exclusive deal will be supported by the Desserts Division which will supply point-of-sale marketing materials. This support will cost the Desserts Division £16 per month per retailer.
- Freezer supplied free of charge: the retailer would be limited to one freezer under this deal. The Desserts Division is responsible for the maintenance of the freezer but any costs are expected to be minimal during the freezer's working life.

Half-Way House

- At least 50% of the independent retailers' ice cream products must be Desserts Division products.
- The Half-Way House deal will be supported by the Desserts Division which will supply point-of-sale marketing materials. This support will cost the Desserts Division £10 per month per retailer.
- Freezer supplied at discounted price: the retailer would be limited to one freezer under this deal.

Free and easy

- No obligation to stock Desserts Division products.
- The Free and Easy deal will offer no marketing support from the Desserts Division.
- Freezer supplied at a discounted price: the retailer would be limited to one freezer under this deal.

Based on his own expert knowledge and the results of specially commissioned market research, the Desserts Division Marketing Manager has produced the following information.

Freezer deal	Cost of purchase of each freezer to Desserts Division	Freezer supplied to retailer for	Estimated take-up	Estimated average additional sales made by Desserts Division to each retailer per month	Desserts Division's estimated contribution margin on additional sales
Exclusive	£500	Free	5,000 retailers	£800	5.5%
Half-Way House	£500	£200	2,700 retailers	£500	7.5%
Free and Easy	£500	£200	135 retailers	£200	10%

Additional information

(i) The freezers which will be supplied are all new and come from a reputable manufacturer. They have been designed to operate in the independent retailers' environment and have a predicted working life of three years.

(ii) As the Desserts Division has spare capacity, the implementation of any of the Freezer deals would not cause any incremental spending on Fixed Costs.

(iii) Each participating independent retailer will advertise the Desserts Division's products in its shop.

(iv) The Freezer deals enable the Desserts Division to conduct market research directly with consumers.

Corporate Social Responsibility

The day-to-day responsibility for F plc's Corporate Social Responsibility (CSR) is carried out by the Environmental Effects Manager (EEM) (see 2nd page of pre-seen material). The EEM has an annual budget of £100,000 which pays her salary and the costs of her office: she has no staff. She reports directly to the Director of Operations (DoO) and part of her role is to report to F plc's Board on the progress 'towards the achievement of F plc's CSR targets'.

However, because the DoO is so busy, the EEM has few opportunities to speak to him. The EEM never meets F plc's Board although her CSR report (see Appendix 1 of Pre-seen material) is submitted to it. The EEM does not receive any formal feedback from the Board about her report. As the post of EEM was established only two years ago not all managers within F plc have yet met her. There is some resistance to the role of the EEM within F plc as some managers believe CSR is better carried out locally whilst others see CSR as a distraction from their jobs.

The EEM has to respond to an increasing amount of environmental legislation, advice and guidelines coming from national governments and international organisations such as the European Union and the United Nations. Given the complexity of F plc with three divisions, a head office and 10,000 employees, it is clear that, at times, the EEM has more work than she can cope with.

At her last meeting with the DoO, over three months ago, she complained that her role is not taken seriously by some senior managers, and that her current activities do not help F plc achieve its CSR targets.

Required

(a) **Recommend**, with reasons, which of the three 'Freezer deals' the Desserts Division Board should offer to the independent retailers.

Note: There are 12 marks available for calculations in requirement (a). Ignore the time value of money. **(25 marks)**

(b) **Advise** the Board of F plc, giving your reasons:

(i) whether it should have a strategic aim dealing with Corporate Social Responsibility. **(6 marks)**

(ii) whether F plc should include its internal Corporate Social Responsibility report in its annual report. **(6 marks)**

(iii) how the Environmental Effects Manager could contribute more towards F plc meeting its Corporate Social Responsibility targets. **(7 marks)**

(c) **Advise** the Board of F plc how it could use Information Systems to implement, monitor and report upon its Corporate Social Responsibility policy. **(6 marks)**

(Total = 50 marks)

68 F plc - desserts division (5/11) 90 mins

Important note: Before attempting this question, make sure you have read the pre-seen material 'F plc' which can be found before Question 67.

Moving the Desserts Division

The Board of the Desserts Division has decided to investigate the possibility of relocating the Division to the West of England. The Board of F plc will approve the relocation providing the following conditions are satisfied:

1. The relocation produces a positive Net Present Value (NPV). F plc has instructed the Desserts Division to use a hurdle rate of 15% and to base its evaluation on a 10 year time horizon. All the cash flows associated with this project should be regarded as occurring at the end of the year in which they occur.
2. The relocation has a payback period of 3 years or fewer.
3. There are no adverse effects on F plc's public image.
4. The relocation makes a positive contribution to F plc's Corporate Social Responsibility targets.
5. The relocation is consistent with F plc's mission statement.
6. The move contributes towards achieving F plc's strategic aims.

A commercial property agent has identified a possible suitable site in the West of England. The site is on a newly developed industrial estate and consists of a modern factory, offices and distribution facilities. The costs of relocation, payable in Year 0, will be £1,820,000.

Starting from Year 1 of the factory's operations the local taxes in the West of England would be £75,000 cheaper each year than in the North of England. The local government authority in the West of England is keen to attract new investment and has indicated it would look favourably upon any future plans for expansion. The local government authority will give, in Year 0, an incentive payment to the Desserts Division of £1,000 for each job created in the factory and distribution areas and £2,000 for each job created in the offices. There is a good supply of labour of all types available in the area. As this new site is much closer to the Desserts Division's suppliers and customers there would be, from Year 1, savings in transport costs of £300,000. There will also be a reduction in 'Road Kilometres Travelled' equivalent to 15% of F plc's total Road Kilometres Travelled based on 2010 results.

F plc's Director of Human Resources has forecast that the Desserts Division will employ, in total, 5,600 people at the new site in the West of England. The mix of Desserts Division's workforce at the new site would consist of 10% in the offices and 90% in the factory and distribution areas. It should be easy to secure all the labour needed. However, F plc's Director of Human Resources is worried that the relocation, if it goes ahead, would generate large-scale redundancies amongst the Desserts Division's employees in the North of England, even though they will be offered the opportunity of relocating to the new site. She has estimated that as many as 98% of the current workforce (See pages 5 and 6 of pre-seen) would become redundant and this would cost the Desserts Division £1,000 for each employee in redundancy pay in Year 0.

There will also be an increased annual cost, starting in Year 1, of £200,000 because labour is more expensive in the West of England.

The Chief Executive of F plc and the Desserts Division

The problems with divisional culture (see 3rd page of the pre-seen material) and with inventory and IT (see 4th page of the pre-seen) have come to the attention of the Chief Executive of F plc. The Chief Executive has told the Desserts Division Board that the current situation is unacceptable and that the following goals must be achieved:

Goals

1. **The confrontational meetings between the Divisional Accountant and the Marketing staff must change their character and a constructive working relationship must be established between the Divisional Accountant and the Divisional Marketing staff.**

   The Divisional Marketing staff members have complained to the Divisional Accountant that they don't always agree with or understand his figures and that they feel that the Divisional Accountant is spying on them.

   As the finance function is 'the dominant force' in the Desserts Division, the Board has delegated responsibility for the achievement of this goal to the Divisional Accountant. The Divisional Accountant has recognised that he is, in part, the cause of this problem. The Divisional General Manager has told the Divisional Accountant that a successful resolution of Goal 1 is very important for both of their future careers within F plc.

2. **The Desserts Division must reduce its levels of wastage of ingredients to 2% of materials usage: these levels are currently 3.8% which cost £7.5 million in 2010.**

   A large proportion of the wastage is caused by poor storage of food raw materials. Some raw materials, for example, chocolate, have been subject to theft by warehouse staff. Other raw materials are wasted because they go bad and become unfit for human consumption.

3. **The Desserts Division must carry out a physical inventory-count at the end of each month. There must not be a difference greater than 1% between the theoretical and actual inventory-counts at any time. Currently, the difference is usually 5%.**

   The inventory-counts are performed by any staff who want to earn overtime. Consequently, there is no regular group of people carrying out this work. The warehouse staff who issue ingredients are not required to participate in the inventory-counts although sometimes they do take part. The results of the inventory-counts have been unreliable and supplementary counting of high value/large quantity ingredients has been necessary.

4. **All customers' orders must be met on time and the Division must achieve 100% of its potential revenue. Poor inventory control will no longer be tolerated.**

   Poor inventory control means that some inventory balances are misleading. Some items are shown in inventory when there are none. There are other items which are not shown in inventory even though they are present. This has led to customers' orders being delivered late, usually by one or two days. This has led to some customers closing their accounts.

5. **The Desserts Division's monthly management accounts must be with Head Office within three working days after month-end.**

   The management accounts are often delayed because necessary information is missing or incomplete. The system for ordering and the receipt of goods into the factory is a paper- based one and has often been the cause of discrepancies between theoretical and actual inventory balances. This system is incompatible because its information is not in a form which can be directly entered into F plc's standard information management system.

The Chief Executive has told the Desserts Division's General Manager that any expenditure required for the implementation of any proposed changes required to achieve the five goals must be self-financing.

Required

(a) **Advise** F plc's Board as to whether or not it should approve the Desserts Division's proposed relocation to the West of England.

Your answer should include an evaluation of the six conditions of approval set by F plc's Board, including the results of your Net Present Value calculation for condition 1.

There are 10 marks available for calculations. **(20 marks)**

(b) **Advise** the Divisional Accountant how he could deal with any resistance to change he might encounter when attempting to achieve the Chief Executive's first goal. **(15 marks)**

(c) **Recommend** improvements which would enable the Board of the Desserts Division to achieve goals 2 to 5 as set by the Chief Executive of F plc. **(15 marks)**

(Total = 50 marks)

Pre-seen material for Questions 69 & 70 – DEF Airport

Note: This pre-seen applies to both Question 69 (from the March 2011 exam) and Question 70 (from the November 2010 exam).

You should assume the date 'now' is November 2010.

Pre-seen Case Study – DEF Airport

Overview

DEF Airport is situated in country D within Europe but which is outside the Eurozone. The local currency is D$. It is located near to the town of DEF. It began life in the 1930s as a flying club and was extended in 1947, providing scheduled services within central Europe. A group of four local state governments, which are all in easy reach of the airport (hereafter referred to as the LSGs), took over the running of the airport in 1961. The four LSGs are named North (NLSG), South (SLSG), East (ELSG) and West (WLSG). These names place their geographical location in relation to the airport. In the early 1970s flights from the airport to European holiday destinations commenced with charter flights operated by holiday companies. In 1986, the first transatlantic flight was established and the airport terminal building was extended in 1987.

By 1989 the airport was handling 500,000 passengers per year which is forecast to increase to 3.5 million for both incoming and outgoing passengers in the current financial year to 30 June 2011. The airport mainly serves holidaymakers flying to destinations within Europe and only 5% of the passengers who use the airport are business travellers.

DEF Airport was converted into a company in 1990 and the four LSGs became the shareholders, each with an equal share. The company is not listed on a stock exchange. The airport has undertaken extensive development since 2000, with improvements to its single terminal building. The improvements have mainly been to improve the airport's catering facilities and to increase the number of check-in desks. There has also been investment in the aircraft maintenance facilities offered to the airlines operating out of the airport.

Governance

The Board of Directors has four Executive directors: the Chief Executive, the Director of Facilities Management, the Finance Director and the Commercial Director. In addition there is a Company Secretary and a Non-Executive Chairman. In accordance with DEF Airport's Articles of Association, the Non-Executive Chairman is drawn from one of the four LSGs. The Non-Executive Chairman is the sole representative of all four LSGs. The Chairmanship changes every two years with each of the four LSGs taking turns to nominate the Chair.

The four LSGs have indicated that they may wish to sell their shareholdings in the airport in the near future. If any LSG wishes to sell its shares in the airport it must first offer them to the other three LSGs. Any shares that are not purchased by the other LSGs may then be sold on the open market. A local investment bank (IVB) has written to the Chairman expressing an interest in investing in the airport in return for a shareholding together with a seat on the Board.

Mission statement

The Board of Directors drew up a mission statement in 2008. It states "At DEF Airport we aim to outperform all other regional airports in Europe by ensuring that we offer our customers a range of services that are of the highest quality, provided by the best people and conform to the highest ethical standards. We aim to be a good corporate citizen in everything we do."

DEF Airport development plan

The Board of Directors produced a development plan in 2009. The Board of Directors consulted with businesses in the area and followed central government airport planning guidelines. It was assumed that the views of other local stakeholders would be represented by the four LSGs which would feed comments to the Board through the Chairman.

The plan relates to the development of DEF Airport and its forecast passenger growth for the next two decades. The Board proposed that future development of the airport will be phased and gradual in order to avoid unexpected consequences for the local communities and industry.

Strategic objectives

The following strategic objectives have been established in the development plan:

1. Create a planning framework which enables DEF Airport to meet the demands of the forecast passenger numbers;
2. Reduce to a minimum the visual and audible impacts of the operation of the airport on the local environment;
3. Ensure that the airport is financially secure;
4. Improve land based access to the airport;
5. Minimise the pollution effects of the operation of the airport.
6. Maintain / increase employment opportunities for people living close to the airport.

By the year ending 30 June 2015, DEF Airport is expected to support about 3,000 local jobs and have a throughput of 5 million passengers per year, an increase of 1.5 million from the 3.5 million passengers forecast for the current financial year ending 30 June 2011. In order to accommodate the forecast increased number of passengers and attain the development objectives, it will be necessary for the airport to extend its operational area to the east of the land it currently occupies.

Financial objectives

Extracts from DEF Airport's forecast income statement for the year ending 30 June 2011 and forecast statement of financial position as at that date are presented in the Appendix. The four LSGs have made it clear to the Board of Directors that the airport must at least achieve financial self-sufficiency. The financial objectives of the airport are to ensure that:

1. The airport does not run at a loss;
2. All creditors are paid on time;
3. Gearing levels must not exceed 20% (where gearing is defined as debt to debt plus equity) and any long-term borrowings are financed from sources approved by the four LSGs.

Corporate Social Responsibility

A key feature of DEF Airport's development plan is to develop "Sustainable Aviation" initiatives in order to reduce the effects of flying on the environment. One effect on the environment is that the airport is subject to specific planning restrictions affecting flights between the hours of 11 p.m. (2300 hours) and 7 a.m. (0700 hours) to reduce aircraft noise. Flights are permitted between these times, but must be specially authorised. Typically, flights between these times would be as a result of an emergency landing request.

A leading international consultancy, QEG, which specialises in auditing the corporate social responsibility (CSR) issues of commercial enterprises, has offered to provide a CSR audit to DEF Airport free of charge. QEG is based in the USA and hopes to expand by offering its services to European enterprises.

DEF Airport's competitors

TUV Airport is located about 100 kilometres away from DEF Airport and serves a highly populated industrial city. The Board of Directors of DEF Airport considers TUV Airport to be its main competitor. There are another three competing airports within 80 kilometres of DEF Airport. TUV Airport purchased one of these three competitor airports and subsequently reduced services from it in order to reduce the competitive threat to itself.

Airlines

Airlines are keen to negotiate the most cost effective deal they can with airports. DEF Airport applies a set of standard charges to airlines but is aware that some of its competitor airports have offered inducements to airlines in order to attract DEF's business.

Airlines across the world are facing rising fuel and staff costs as well as strong competition from within the industry. There has been an overall increase in customer demand for air travel in recent years and low-priced airlines have emerged and are threatening the well-established, traditional airlines. Consequently, the traditional airlines have begun to cut the number of destinations to which they fly.

There are several low-priced airlines that serve DEF Airport's competitors, but only one, S, also operates out of DEF Airport. S is exploring ways in which it might increase its flights to and from DEF Airport.

DEF's Board of Directors has been approached by a North American airline that wishes to operate services from DEF Airport. This airline specialises in flights for business and first class passengers. However, this airline insists that it would pay DEF Airport in US$. This is contrary to the airport's policy of accepting payment only in D$, which is the local currency.

Analysis of revenue by business segment

The forecast split of total revenue of D$23.4 million by business segment for the current financial year ending 30 June 2011 is:

	%
Aviation income	48
Retail concessions at the airport	20
Car Parking	15
Other income	17

(Other income includes income from property rentals, and other fees and charges.)

DEF Airport offers discounts for prompt payment.

Aviation income

In addition to the standard charges, which are set out below, there is a range of surcharges which are levied on airlines for such items as "noisy aircraft" (charged when aircraft exceed the Government limits for acceptable noise levels), recovery of costs and expenses arising from cleaning or making safe any spillages from aircraft and extraordinary policing of flights (for example, arrests made as a result of anti-social behaviour on aircraft).

Standard charges made by DEF Airport to the airlines:

Charges per aircraft

Landing charges – large aircraft:	D$300
Landing charges – medium aircraft:	D$170

Parking charges for the first two hours are included in the landing charge. Thereafter, a charge of D$200 per hour is imposed for each large aircraft and D$250 per hour for each medium aircraft. The parking charge is lower for large aircraft because they take at least two hours to clean and refuel, so they almost always have to pay for an hour's parking, and also because there is less demand for the parking areas used for large aircraft. Medium aircraft tend to take off again within one hour of landing. Approximately 10% of medium sized aircraft landings result in the airline incurring parking charges for one hour. This is normally either because their scheduled departure time requires them to park or because of delays imposed by air traffic restrictions, technical malfunctions or problems with passengers.

Charges per passenger
Passenger Load:

Flights to European destinations:	D$1.60 per departing passenger
Flights outside Europe:	D$4.00 per departing passenger
Passenger security	D$1.20 per passenger arriving or departing

Retail concessions

DEF Airport provides the facilities for a range of shops, bureau de change (dealing in foreign exchange currency transactions for passengers), bars and cafes for the budget conscious passenger.

DEF Airport has a monopoly in the provision of retail concessions and therefore faces no competition.

Car parking

Car parking is an important source of DEF Airport's revenue. The airport has extended its own car parking facilities for customers over recent years. Car parks occupy a large area of what was green belt land (that is land which was not previously built on) around its perimeter. The land was acquired by the airport specifically for the purpose of car parking. A free passenger bus service is provided to take passengers to and from the car parks into the airport terminal building.

Competitors have established alternative car parking facilities off-site and provide bus services to and from the airport's terminal. The parking charges made by the competitors are lower than those levied by the airport. Competitor car park operators offer additional services to passengers, such as car maintenance and valeting, which are undertaken while the car is left in their care.

DEF Airport does not have a hotel on its premises. There is a hotel within walking distance of the airport which offers special rates for passengers to stay the night before their flight and then to park their cars at the hotel for the duration of their trip.

Other income

This heading contains a mixture of revenue streams. The Commercial Director reported that some have good growth prospects. Property rental income is likely to decline though as there has been much building development around the airport perimeter.

DEF Airport security

Passengers and their baggage are required to go through rigorous security checks. There is a fast track service provided which can be accessed by all passengers at an extra charge. This is intended to speed up the security process. However, on some occasions this leads to passengers on the normal route becoming frustrated because they are required to wait in lengthy queues to pass through the security checks. Airport security staff are required by law to search all departing passengers and their baggage for suspicious or dangerous items. On the very rare occasions that they discover anything they report their concerns to the police. There are always several police officers on patrol at the airport at any given time and so the police can respond to any report very quickly.

In addition to passenger and baggage screening, DEF Airport security staff are responsible for the security of parked aircraft and airport property. They do this primarily by monitoring all arriving and departing vehicles and their drivers and by monitoring the many closed circuit television cameras that cover the airport.

The airport has had a good record with regard to the prevention of theft from passenger baggage. This is frequently a serious matter at other airports, but DEF Airport has received very few complaints that baggage has been tampered with. DEF Airport's Head of Security regards the security of baggage as very low risk because of this low level of complaints.

The Head of Security at DEF Airport was appointed to his current role in 1990, when the airport was very much smaller than it is today. He was a police sergeant before he joined the airport staff. Immediately before his appointment he was responsible for the front desk of DEF town's main police station, a job that involved managing the day-to-day activities of the other police officers on duty. He was happy to accept the post of Head of Security because the police service was starting to make far greater use of computers. He had always relied on a comprehensive paper-based system for documenting and filing reports.

The Head of Security is directly responsible for all security matters at DEF Airport. In practice, he has to delegate most of the actual supervision of staff to shift managers and team leaders because he cannot be expected to be on duty for 24 hours per day or to manage the security arrangements in great detail while administering the security department. The overall responsibilities of the Head of Security have not been reviewed since his appointment.

Strategic options

The Board of Directors is now actively considering its strategic options which could be implemented in the future in order to meet the strategic objectives which were set out in the airport's development plan.

APPENDIX 1

Extracts of DEF Airport's forecast income statement for the year ending 30 June 2011 and statement of financial position as at 30 June 2011

Forecast income statement for the year ending 30 June 2011

	Note	*D$000*
Revenue		23,400
Operating costs	1	(25,450)
Net operating loss		(2,050)
Interest income		70
Finance costs		(1,590)
Corporate income tax expense		(130)
LOSS FOR THE YEAR		(3,700)

Forecast statement of financial position as at 30 June 2011

		D$000
ASSETS		
Non-current assets		150,000
Current assets		
Inventories		400
Trade and other receivables		9,250
Cash and cash equivalents		3,030
Total current assets		12,680
Total assets		162,680
EQUITY AND LIABILITIES		
Equity		
Share capital	2	17,700
Share premium		530
Revaluation reserve		89,100
Retained earnings		23,200
Total equity		130,530
Non-current liabilities		
Long term borrowings	3	22,700
Current liabilities		
Trade and other payables		9,450
Total liabilities		32,150
Total equity and liabilities		162,680

Notes:

1. Operating costs include depreciation of D$5.0 million.
2. There are 17.7 million ordinary shares of D$1 each in issue.
3. The long-term borrowings comprise a D$6.3 million loan for capital expenditure which is repayable on 1 July 2015 and D$16.4 million owed to the 4 LSGs. This has no fixed repayment schedule and is not expected to be repaid in the next year.

69 DEF & WLS (3/11) 90 mins

Unseen Case Material

IVB

IVB, a local investment bank (see Governance section of the pre-seen material), has a track record of investing in businesses that are under-performing in terms of profit. In the past, when IVB has achieved control of such a business, it has engaged in severe cost-cutting to boost the profitability of the business. This prepares the business for a rapid sale to a third party at a substantial profit for IVB. IVB describes itself as 'the business turnaround expert'. IVB has carried out this process four times since 2007. The results for IVB have been profitable for its shareholders but it has been heavily criticised by the financial media because its actions have led to large-scale job losses in the businesses it has 'turned around'.

Cargo handling

The Board of DEF has initiated an internal project to introduce cargo handling services at DEF which would become operational in 2014. However, the Board has learnt that an American aviation cargo handling company, WLS, is now up for sale by its owners. WLS was founded in 1965 and operates from numerous airports in America, Europe and Africa. WLS arranges for the dispatch and receipt of a large variety of consignments which are sent by air. WLS believes one of the main reasons for its success has been the use it has made of information systems. It believes these information systems to be the most advanced in its industry.

As a cargo handling company, WLS offers a wide range of services to its customers including:

- Collection and delivery of items from the customer's premises to the airport
- Specialist packing: WLS claims it can 'handle anything from a full grown elephant to a grand piano'
- Storage: short-term, long-term and refrigerated storage
- Customs clearances and all administration for any consignment
- Baggage handling services

Extracts from WLS's recent financial statements are shown below:

For the year ended 31 December	**2007**	**2008**	**2009**	**2010**
	D$000	**D$000**	**D$000**	**D$000**
Revenue	2,874	3,313	3,978	4,972
Profit after interest, finance costs and tax	632	795	1,074	1,492
Net cash inflow	50	82	111	224
Balances as at 31 December	**2007**	**2008**	**2009**	**2010**
	D$000	**D$000**	**D$000**	**D$000**
Receivables	144	165	199	234
Debt: nominal value	200	200	200	200
Equity	308	1,103	2,177	3,669

WLS is not a quoted company. The Board of DEF has been advised by the agent carrying out the sale of WLS that it could be purchased for D$4,000,000 cash. The agent explained that WLS's owners wanted to retire and were looking for a quick sale.

WLS and Corporate Social Responsibility

DEF's current Chairman is a politician who takes a keen interest in environmental and Corporate Social Responsibility issues. The Chairman has discovered an audit report prepared by QEG (see CSR section of the pre-seen case) which reviewed WLS's operations in 2010. Within the audit report QEG criticised WLS because:

- It has a very high carbon footprint*
- In some countries, it has unfair and discriminatory employment practices
- Its customer service standards were widely perceived to be 'poor' and a US consumer organisation had accused WLS of having a 'couldn't care less attitude'

(* A **carbon footprint** is 'the total set of greenhouse gases emissions caused by an organisation, event or product'. Source: UK Carbon Trust.)

QEG awarded its lowest possible rating, one star out of a possible five, to WLS and concluded that 'it is not a good corporate citizen'.

The Commercial Director of DEF would like to review the Airport's current and potential revenue streams and he has asked the Management Accountant for help with this. Together they have compiled the table below:

Business segment	**Forecast revenue D$000 year ending 30.6.2011**	**Anticipated cash flow**	**Market prospects**
Aviation income	11,232	Strongly positive	Mature market, intense competition, some future growth possible
Retail concessions at the airport	4,680	Positive	Strong regional market share, high growth rate of recent past has slowed down greatly since 2009. Future growth prospects uncertain because of national retail slowdown
Car parking	3,510	Marginally positive	Market share and growth rate prospects are restricted by increasing competition
Other income: property rentals and other fees and charges	3,978	Marginally positive. Was negative in 2009	The different parts of this revenue stream makes it difficult to understand its market position but thought by the Commercial Director to be declining both in growth and share
TOTAL	**23,400**		

Business segment	**Revenue D$000 year ended 31.12.2010**	**Cash flow**	**Market prospects**
WLS	4,972	Positive	The market for cargo handling services is expanding greatly. DEF has no market share at present because it does not offer these services

Required

(a) (i) **Explain** alternative approaches that can be used by Boards of Directors, in general, to manage conflicting objectives between their stakeholders. **(5 marks)**

If IVB becomes a shareholder in DEF and is granted a seat on the Board:

(ii) **Discuss** why DEF's mission statement might change. **(5 marks)**

(b) The Board of DEF is considering acquiring WLS.

Advise DEF's Board if the proposed acquisition of WLS is an appropriate strategic option.

Your answer should include:

(i) an evaluation of WLS's financial performance **(20 marks)**

Note: There are 7 marks in this section for your calculations and a further 13 marks are for your commentary on your calculations.

(ii) The information highlighted in the audit report prepared by QEG. **(10 marks)**

(c) **Recommend** to the Board of DEF, using an appropriate model (for example, the Boston Consulting Group Portfolio Matrix), future strategies for each of DEF's current and potential business segments.

(10 marks)

(Total = 50 marks)

70 DEF Airport (11/10) 90 mins

Important note: Before attempting this question, make sure you have read the pre-seen material 'DEF Airport' which can be found before Question 71.

Unseen Case Material – DEF Airport

DEF Airport's competitiveness

The Board is concerned about the competitiveness of the airport and there is disagreement within the Board about the best means of competing. One Board member, who has spent most of his working life at DEF Airport, believes that the airport has a local monopoly in its immediate location and that this locational advantage is all that is needed for a successful competitive strategy.

However, other Board members who have recent working experience at other profit-making airports, within and outside Europe, think that DEF's competitive advantage has been reduced by the low-priced airlines that operate from other airports. Within Europe the low-priced airlines have been very successful and passengers are willing to travel further to an airport for cheaper flights, making DEF's location less significant. The low-priced airlines emphasise low fares, cost-containment and operating efficiencies such as online check-in facilities and no ticketing.

The Commercial Director has recently been researching the topic of competitiveness to assist his Board colleagues. He has noted that there are two very distinct types of customer serviced by, and, producing revenue for, DEF Airport. The first type of customer is the 'clients' of the airport: namely the airlines, and these create 'Aviation Income' and contribute to 'Other Income'. The other type of customer is the airline passenger who will use the Retail and Car Parking facilities at DEF Airport because they are passengers on airlines which are using DEF Airport. Both types of customer will have its own particular needs and wants and DEF Airport may have to meet these in different ways if it is to achieve sustainable competitive advantage.

The Commercial Director has also informed his colleagues of the findings of a recent survey of European air passengers. The survey of business and first class travellers revealed that business and first class passengers valued 'Distinctiveness' and this was a big factor in their choice of airport.

'Distinctiveness' was defined in the survey by such factors as having:

- the leading airlines operating from the airport not the low-priced airlines
- luxury passenger lounges
- high class restaurants
- large duty free shops with an extensive range of the most exclusive brands

One passenger in the survey summarised 'Distinctiveness' as 'Offering something which nobody else offers'.

Future strategic development

DEF Airport's process of strategic development is set within the context of its mission statement published in 2008 which states "At DEF Airport we aim to outperform all other regional airports in Europe by ensuring that we offer our customers a range of services that are of the highest quality, are provided by the best people and conform to the highest ethical standards. We aim to be a good corporate citizen in everything we do."

Following on from the mission statement, the Board of Directors produced a development plan in 2009. The Board of Directors consulted with businesses in the area and took account of central government airport planning guidelines. It was assumed that the views of other local stakeholders would be represented by the four LSGs which would feed comments to the Board through the Chairman.

The plan relates to the development of DEF Airport and its forecast passenger growth for the next two decades. It is proposed that future development of the airport will be phased and gradual in order to avoid unexpected consequences for the local communities and industry. A key feature of DEF Airport's development plan is to develop "Sustainable Aviation" initiatives in order to reduce the effects of flying on the environment.

Strategic development

DEF's strategic objectives are set out in the pre-seen material.

Future ownership

The four LSGs have indicated that they may wish to sell their shareholdings in the airport in the near future. If any LSG wishes to sell its shares in the airport it must first offer its shares to the other three LSGs. Any shares that are not purchased by the other LSGs may be sold on the open market. A local investment bank (IVB) has written to the Chairman expressing an interest in investing in the airport in return for a shareholding together with a seat on the Board.

IVB has a track record of investing in businesses that are under-performing in terms of profit. In the past when IVB has achieved control of such a business it has engaged in severe cost-cutting to boost the profitability of the business. This prepares the business for a rapid sale to a third party at a substantial profit for IVB. IVB describes itself as 'the business turnaround experts'. IVB has carried out this process four times since 2007. The results for IVB have been very successful in terms of profit for its shareholders but it has been heavily criticised because its actions have led to large-scale job losses in the businesses it has 'turned around'. The Chief Executive of DEF Airport has expressed strong concern to the Chairman about the approach from IVB as he believes that such investment could have very serious consequences for the airport.

Cargo Handling Services

The Director of Facilities Management has been researching the possibility of offering cargo handling services at DEF Airport as a way of increasing profits. The introduction of such services would enable DEF Airport to more fully utilise existing plant and buildings and would not require capital investment. However, DEF Airport would have to increase its expenditure on fixed costs and would also have to employ additional direct labour. The Director of Facilities Management estimates that the earliest the cargo handling services would become operational would be in 2014 as DEF Airport would have to obtain government permissions and secure contracts with shipping agents and transportation companies.

The Director of Facilities Management has discussed this project with the Finance Director who said she welcomed any project which would improve DEF Airport's finances. However, she added 'because the project is some time away and is based on a number of estimates, it is unlikely to get the Board of Directors' approval unless it offers at least D$200,000 a year in profit from 2014.

The Director of Facilities Management has assembled the following estimates about the introduction of cargo handling services:

1. If the cargo handling services had been in operation in the year to 30 June 2010 this would have generated a revenue of D$1.5 million which would have increased by 10% per year until the first year of actual operations in the year to 30 June 2014.
2. If cargo handling services are introduced into DEF Airport there will be fixed costs of D$400,000 each year from the date of their introduction.

If DEF introduces cargo handling services in 2014, arising from the cargo handling revenue, there will be:

- a 10% probability of a 40% contribution margin
- a 20% probability of a 30% contribution margin
- a 70% probability of a 25% contribution margin

Required

(a) **Advise** the Board how DEF Airport could achieve sustainable competitive advantage as defined by Professor M Porter.

Your advice should include discussion under the following headings:

(i) Overall cost leadership; **(7 marks)**

(ii) Differentiation; and **(7 marks)**

(iii) Either: Cost focus **or** Differentiation focus. **(7 marks)**

Note: You are **not** required to draw Porter's generic competitive strategy model

(b) If IVB becomes one of the shareholders in DEF Airport, **advise** the Board:

(i) why its approach to strategy formation and its mission might be challenged by IVB; **(6 marks)**

(ii) which of the **six** strategic objectives in the development plan might be opposed by IVB; give reasons for your choices; **(6 marks)**

(iii) how the future operations of the Airport might be affected. **(7 marks)**

(c) **Recommend**, with reasons, whether the cargo handling services project should be undertaken. Your recommendations should be based solely on the outcome for 2014.

Note: 6 marks are available for calculations **(10 marks)**

(Total = 50 marks)

Pre-seen material for Questions 71 & 72 - Aybe

Note: This pre-seen applies to both Question 71 (from the September 2010 exam) and Question 72 (from the May 2010 exam).

You should assume the date 'now' is May 2010.

Pre-seen Case Study - Aybe

<u>Background</u>

Aybe, located in Country C, was formed by the merger of two companies in 2001. It is a listed company which manufactures, markets and distributes a large range of components throughout Europe and the United States of America. Aybe employs approximately 700 people at its three factories in Eastern Europe and supplies products to over 0·5 million customers in 20 countries. Aybe holds stocks of about 100,000 different electronic components.

Aybe is regarded within its industry as being a well-established business. Company Ay had operated successfully for nearly 17 years before its merger with Company Be. Company Ay can therefore trace its history back for 25 years which is a long time in the fast moving electronic component business.

The company is organised into three divisions, the Domestic Electronic Components division (DEC), the Industrial Electronic Components division (IEC) and the Specialist Components division (SC). The Domestic and

Industrial Electronic Components divisions supply standard electronic components for domestic and industrial use whereas the Specialist Components division supplies components which are often unique and made to specific customer requirements. Each of the three divisions has its own factory in Country C.

Composition of the Board of Directors

The Board of Directors has three executive directors, the Company Secretary and five non-executive directors. The Chairman is one of the five independent non-executive directors. The executive directors are the Chief Executive, Finance Director and Director of Operations. There is also an Audit Committee, a Remuneration Committee and a Nominations Committee. All three committees are made up entirely of the non-executive directors.

Organisational structure

Aybe is organised along traditional functional/unitary lines. The Board considers continuity to be a very important value. The present structure was established by Company Ay in 1990 and continued after the merger with Company Be. Many of Aybe's competitors have carried out structural reorganisations since then. In 2008, Aybe commissioned a review of its organisational structure from a human resource consultancy. The consultants suggested alternative structures which they thought Aybe could employ to its advantage. However, Aybe's Board felt that continuity was more important and no change to the organisational structure took place.

Product and service delivery

Customers are increasingly seeking assistance from their component suppliers with the design of their products and the associated manufacturing and assembly processes. Aybe's Board views this as a growth area. The Board has recognised that Aybe needs to develop web-based services and tools which can be accessed by customers. The traditional method of listing the company's range of components in a catalogue is becoming less effective because customers are increasingly seeking specially designed custom made components as the electronics industry becomes more sophisticated.

Financial data

Aybe's historical financial record, denominated in C's currency of C$, over the last five years is shown below.

	Year ended 31 December:				
	2009	2008	2007	2006	2005
	C$m	C$m	C$m	C$m	C$m
Revenue	620	600	475	433	360
Operating profit	41	39	35	20	13
Profit for the year	23	21	16	9	5
Earnings per share (C$)	0·128	0·117	0·089	0·050	0·028
Dividend per share (C$)	0·064	0·058	0	0	0

Extracts from the 2009 financial statements are given at Appendix A. There are currently 180 million ordinary shares in issue with a nominal value of C$0·10 each. The share price at 31 December 2009 was C$0·64. No dividend was paid in the three years 2005 to 2007 due to losses sustained in the first few years after the merger in 2001.

Aybe's bank has imposed an overdraft limit of C$10 million and two covenants: (i) that its interest cover must not fall below 5 and (ii) its ratio of non-current liabilities to equity must not increase beyond 0·75:1. Aybe's Finance Director is comfortable with this overdraft limit and the two covenants.

The ordinary shareholding of Aybe is broken down as follows:

	Percentage of ordinary shares held at 31 December 2009
Institutional investors	55
Executive Directors and Company Secretary	10
Employees	5
Individual investors	30

The Executive Directors, Company Secretary and other senior managers are entitled to take part in an Executive Share Option Scheme offered by Aybe.

Performance Review

Aybe's three divisions have been profitable throughout the last five years. The revenue and operating profit of the three divisions of Aybe for 2009 were as follows:

	DEC Division	*IEC Division*	*SC Division*
	C$m	*C$m*	*C$m*
Revenue	212	284	124
Operating profit	14	16	11

Financial objectives of Aybe

The Board has generally taken a cautious approach to providing strategic direction for the company. Most board members feel that this has been appropriate because the company was unprofitable for the three year period after the merger and needed to be turned around. Also, most board members think a cautious approach has been justified given the constrained economic circumstances which have affected Aybe's markets since 2008. While shareholders have been disappointed with Aybe's performance over the last five years, they have remained loyal and supported the Board in its attempts to move the company into profit. The institutional shareholders however are now looking for increased growth and profitability.

The Board has set the following financial objectives which it considers reflect the caution for which Aybe is well known:

(i) Dividend payout to remain at 50% of profit for the year;

(ii) No further equity shares to be issued over the next five years in order to avoid diluting earnings per share.

Capital budget overspends

Aybe has an internal audit department. The Chief Internal Auditor, who leads this department, reports directly to the Finance Director. Investigation by the Internal Audit department has revealed that managers with responsibility for capital expenditure have often paid little attention to expenditure authorisation levels approved by the Board. They have justified overspending on the grounds that the original budgets were inadequate and in order not to jeopardise the capital projects, the overspends were necessary.

An example of this was the building of an extension to the main factory at the DEC division that was completed in 2009 at a final cost of nearly C$3 million which was almost 50% over budget. The capital budget for the extension was set at the outset and the capital investment appraisal showed a positive net present value. It subsequently became apparent that the site clearance costs and on-going construction expenditure were under-estimated. These estimates were provided by a qualified quantity surveyor who was a contractor to Aybe. The estimates supplied by the quantity surveyor were accurately included in Aybe's capital investment appraisal system which was performed on a spreadsheet. However, no regular checks were carried out to compare the phased budgeted expenditure with actual costs incurred. It came as a surprise to the Board when the Finance Director finally produced the capital expenditure project report which showed the cost of the extension was nearly 50% overspent.

Strategic development

Aybe applies a traditional rational model in carrying out its strategic planning process. This encompasses an annual exercise to review the previous plan, creation of a revenue and capital budget for the next five years and instruction to managers within Aybe to maintain their expenditure within the budget limits approved by the Board.

Debates have taken place within the Board regarding the strategic direction in which Aybe should move. Most board members are generally satisfied that Aybe has been turned around over the last five years and were pleased that the company increased its profit in 2009 even though the global economy slowed down. Aybe benefited from a number of long-term contractual arrangements with customers throughout 2009 which were agreed in previous years. However, many of these are not being renewed due to the current economic climate.

The Board stated in its annual report, published in March 2010, that the overall strategic aim of the company is to:

"Achieve growth and increase shareholder returns by continuing to produce and distribute high quality electronic components and develop our international presence through expansion into new overseas markets."

Aybe's Chief Executive said in the annual report that the strategic aim is clear and straightforward. He said "Aybe will strive to maintain its share of the electronic development, operational, maintenance and repair markets in which it is engaged. This is despite the global economic difficulties which Aybe, along with its competitors, has faced since 2008. Aybe will continue to apply the highest ethical standards in its business activities."

In order to facilitate the achievement of the strategic aim, Aybe's Board has established the following strategic goals:

1. Enhance the provision of products and services which are demanded by customers;
2. Invest in engineering and web-based support for customers;
3. Maintain the search for environmentally friendly products;
4. Pursue options for expansion into new overseas markets.

The Board has also stated that Aybe is a responsible corporate organisation and recognises the social and environmental effects of its operational activities.

Concern over the rate of growth

Aybe's recently appointed Director of Operations and one of its Non-Executive Directors have privately expressed their concern to the Chief Executive at what they perceive to be the very slow growth of the company. While they accept that shareholder expectations should not be raised too high, they feel that the Board is not providing sufficient impetus to move the company forward. They fear that the results for 2010 will be worse than for 2009. They think that Aybe should be much more ambitious and fear that the institutional shareholders in particular, will not remain patient if Aybe does not create stronger earnings growth than has previously been achieved.

Development approaches

The Board has discussed different ways of expanding overseas in order to meet the overall strategic aim. It has, in the past, been reluctant to move from the current approach of exporting components. However the Director of Operations has now begun preparing a plan for the IEC division to open up a trading company in Asia. The DEC division is also establishing a subsidiary in Africa.

[Pre-seen material continues on the next page]

APPENDIX A

Extracts of Aybe's Income Statement and Statement of Financial Position

Income statement for the year ended 31 December 2009

	2009
	C$ million
Revenue	620
Operating costs	(579)
Finance costs	(4)
Profit before tax	37
Income tax expense	(14)
PROFIT FOR THE YEAR	23

Statement of financial position as at 31 December 2009

	2009
	C $million
ASSETS	
Non-current assets	111
Current assets	
Inventories	40
Trade and other receivables	81
Cash and cash equivalents	3
Total current assets	124
Total assets	235
EQUITY AND LIABILITIES	
Equity	
Share capital	18
Share premium	9
Other reserves	8
Retained earnings	75
Total equity	110
Non-current liabilities	
Bank loan (8% interest, repayable 2015)	40
Current liabilities	
Trade and other payables	73
Current tax payable	8
Bank overdraft	4
Total current liabilities	85
Total liabilities	125
Total equity and liabilities	235

71 Aybe Asia (9/10) 90 mins

Unseen Case Material

Aybe's expansion into Asia

Prior to 2010, the IEC division of Aybe had carried out a limited amount of business in Asia. Following Aybe's decision to pursue business opportunities in Asia, it moved very quickly in 2010 and established a separate trading company with a local partner in Asia to sell the products of the IEC division. The ownership of the company is shared; 50% by Aybe and 50% with a local entrepreneur. Aybe has chosen this structure because of legal requirements. A further legal requirement is that in the case of the company failing, dissolving or ceasing to trade, Aybe will be required to reimburse the local entrepreneur the amount of his original investment. Currently, this liability is estimated to be C$ 500,000.

Initially, this expansion was very successful with good levels of demand being experienced for IEC's products. Recently, however, a number of environmental factors have rapidly changed. These include a forecast of declining demand for IEC's products in Asia due to adverse world economic factors and a move towards protectionism in some Asian countries. IEC has also been unfortunate in that its direct labour costs in Asia have increased by more than the planned level. Economic intelligence suggests that this inflation will continue increasing year on year until the end of 2015.

Options for change

Aybe has always applied a rational planning model in carrying out its strategic planning process. However, Aybe has decided to comprehensively review its overall strategic aim to 'Achieve growth and increase shareholder returns by continuing to produce and distribute high quality electronic components and develop our international presence, through expansion into new overseas markets'. The Director of Operations has been the champion of IEC's expansion into Asia and has been asked by the Board of Directors of Aybe to advise whether Aybe should continue to develop IEC's business in Asia or whether it should close its separate trading company business and concentrate on its domestic market.

Director of Operations

The status of the Director of Operations and his career within Aybe are linked to the expansion of the company's business into Asia. One of the reasons for his appointment to Aybe is his Asian experience. He would like to become the Chief Executive of Aybe. At the time of the decision to expand into Asia the Director of Operations was involved in a professional dispute with Aybe's Management Accountant who shortly afterwards left the company. After a short period when Aybe had no Management Accountant it was realised that this was a serious weakness and a replacement appointment was made.

Director of Operations' advice

The Director of Operations has provided the table below relating to IEC's three product groups which constitute 95% of its Asian business. The remaining 5% of IEC's Asian business operates at break-even.

IEC division: forecast Asian business 2011

Product group	**A**	**B**	**C**
	C$	C$	C$
Average selling price per unit	350	6,200	85
Average variable cost per unit	200	2,500	60
Sales volume in units per year	2,800	100	58,000

The Director of Operations is under a lot of pressure not to disappoint the Board of Aybe and has made a quick estimate of the profit which he considers will be about C$2 million in 2011. The Director of Operations invited the Management Accountant to a meeting to discuss the Board's request for advice regarding future business prospects in Asia. He suggested that to save time the Management Accountant should present the Director of Operations' estimate to the Board meeting which was shortly to discuss whether or not to continue with IEC's Asian operation.

The Director of Operations explained that the business environment in Asia is very dynamic which makes it difficult to predict too far ahead. In his previous company, the Director of Operations had used scenario planning when faced with similar uncertain environments. The Director of Operations acknowledged that there had been a number of changes in the business environment affecting IEC. He had made some forward projections based on his experience of Asia and his knowledge of Asian markets. He stated that although the Asian expansion had not worked out exactly as planned, it still held very good potential for IEC, and he was very committed to it. He also said that he realised that the Management Accountant was new to the company.

However, the Board was pressing for early advice from the Director of Operations. The Director of Operations referred to his table, (given above) and stated that it supported his estimate that IEC's Asian business would be able to achieve, at a minimum, C$2,000,000 profit per year. On this basis IEC's Asian business would make a worthwhile contribution to Aybe's performance and should definitely be supported and continued.

The Management Accountant replied that he had consulted widely within Aybe about the prospects for IEC's business in Asia and the consensus was that the prospects were not good. It was expected that revenue would decline after 2010 and operating costs would increase. The Management Accountant has also established that there are specific fixed costs of C$1 million per year associated with IEC's Asian business. The Management Accountant stated that before presenting anything to the Board he wanted to independently calculate profitability based on the Director of Operations' table and any other relevant information. The Director of Operations said that this was unnecessary and would only waste time. He also said that accuracy should be balanced against speed in order to allow Aybe to take advantage of business opportunities in Asia.

The Management Accountant replied that he had to be given time to do his job and it was his duty to form an independent opinion and to present it to the Board.

The Director of Operations said that the duty of a Management Accountant was to help management not obstruct it. The Director of Operations said he knew far better than the Management Accountant and the rest of Aybe about business in Asia and that the Management Accountant should do as he is told when instructed by a Director of the Board. The Director of Operations also added that if the Management Accountant wanted to keep working in Aybe he should give the Director of Operations his support and not argue about technicalities. He added 'The last time I had a fall-out with a Management Accountant she was asked to leave Aybe: I hope you won't fall into the same trap'.

Required

(a)

(i) **Discuss**, in the context of its Asian business, whether it is appropriate for Aybe to continue to use the traditional rational model for its strategic planning. **(6 marks)**

(ii) **Recommend**, with reasons, **two** alternative approaches to strategy that could be appropriate for Aybe to use. **(6 marks)**

(iii) **Advise** Aybe of the factors it should consider before withdrawing from the trading company which it has established with its partner in Asia. **(6 marks)**

(b) **Advise** the Board of Aybe:

(i) How strategic management accounting could contribute to the success of its current and future strategies. **(6 marks)**

(ii) How scenario planning could be used to help make the decision about whether or not to withdraw from the trading company in Asia. **(6 marks)**

(c) **Evaluate** the Director of Operations' claim that IEC's Asian business will achieve, at a minimum, C$2,000,000 profit in 2011. **(10 marks)**

Note: There are 6 marks for calculation in requirement (c)

Situations such as the one encountered by Aybe's Management Accountant are described by CIMA's Code of Ethics as ***Threats*** (CIMA Code of Ethics 100.10). The Code suggests a range of ***Safeguards*** that may eliminate or reduce ***Threats*** to an acceptable level.

(d) **Explain** the nature of the ***Threat*** faced by the Management Accountant. **Recommend**, with reasons, **two** internal and **two** external ***Safeguards*** which could eliminate or reduce the ***Threat***. **(10 marks)**

(Total = 50 marks)

72 Aybe (5/10) 90 mins

Important note: Before attempting this question, make sure you have read the pre-seen material 'Aybe' which can be found before Question 71.

Unseen case material - Aybe

The business environment in Asia

Aybe has taken advice from a number of expert sources about market prospects in Asia. The research concluded Asian markets have excellent potential for growth and profitability, because of increasing industrialisation, for one of Aybe's divisions, IEC. The markets are fast-moving and highly adaptive. Some countries in Asia are highly entrepreneurial whilst in others there is much involvement of the State in business. In some countries there is a mixed economy. In general, Asia encourages free markets but this is also allied to a requirement in some countries for local involvement in any business enterprise. Most Asian countries make extensive use of sophisticated information systems and information technology. A considerable amount of outsourcing from Western countries has taken place to Asia's benefit. Although this had originally been in areas of manufacturing, outsourcing has now developed extensively and many service and administrative functions have also been outsourced to Asia. All of these influences have led to a variety of organisational structures in Asian business.

Director of Operations

Aybe is organised along traditional functional lines and one of the most important departments is 'Operations'. The director with responsibility for this department is the Director of Operations. The Director of Operations had recently joined Aybe and one of the reasons for his appointment was his experience in managing the electronics division of a multinational company in China. He is very energetic and ambitious and had been supported in his appointment at Aybe by the Non-Executive Director (NED) who chairs the Nominations Committee. This NED considers that the Director of Operations has the potential to become the Chief Executive Officer (CEO) of Aybe within the next five years.

Expansion of electronic components business into Asia

Prior to 2010, the IEC division of Aybe had carried out a limited amount of business in Asia. The results of this business are shown in the column 'Actual 2009'.

Aybe's Management Accountant has prepared a forecast for the period 31 December 2010 to 2014 which shows the incremental effects of expansion into Asia of products from the IEC division. Aybe has been fortunate in that the Asian government in the country where it intends to trade has granted a tax 'holiday' for eight years to new overseas businesses. This means that Aybe's operations will not be liable to tax. Country C has a double taxation treaty with the Asian country. This forecast is shown below:

	Actual 2009 C$m	Forecast 2010 C$m	Forecast 2011 C$m	Forecast 2012 C$m	Forecast 2013 C$m	Forecast 2014 C$m
Incremental revenue	5.00	5.15	5.30	5.46	5.63	5.80
Incremental costs	1.00	1.03	1.06	1.09	1.13	1.16
Incremental profit for the year	4.00	4.12	4.24	4.37	4.50	4.64
	C$	C$	C$	C$	C$	C$
Incremental earnings per share	0.022	0.023	0.024	0.024	0.025	0.026
Incremental dividend per share	0.011	0.011	0.012	0.012	0.013	0.013

In preparing this forecast the Management Accountant has used a well established procedure within Aybe which included detailed consultation with Board members and operational managers. Additionally, external market research had been commissioned to assist with such matters as potential demand and customer preferences. Discussion, consultation and consensus have always been considered important aspects of strategic decision-making within Aybe and the Management Accountant has been praised by the Finance Director for following this procedure in her preparation of the five year forecast.

The Director of Operations and Management Accountant

A Board meeting has been scheduled to discuss the continued expansion into Asia. Prior to this, the Director of Operations had asked for a meeting with the Management Accountant to discuss her forecast. At the meeting the Director of Operations was extremely critical about the profit projections within the forecast and he enquired how these had been constructed. The Management Accountant explained that there had been a wide process of consultation both inside and outside of Aybe and that she had followed the normal company procedure for preparing the forecast.

The Director of Operations said that the normal procedures within Aybe were 50 years out of date. He said that business is dynamic and that planning just slowed everything down. He stated that the best way of making strategy was to react to events and to seize opportunities and that consultation and consensus resulted in stagnation. As regards the Management Accountant's profit projections, he felt these were totally unrealistic. The Director of Operations said that he has extensive experience of the electronics markets in Asia, and this, together with his instincts, has led him to a completely different view of the potential for Aybe if the expansion took place.

The Director of Operations then stated the following assumptions for the incremental effects of the Asian expansion:

(a) Take the actual results given above for year ended 31 December 2009 as the base year for the forecast.
(b) Revenue will increase by 25% compound per year from the base year to the end of the forecast period.
(c) Incremental operating costs will be 20% of revenue each year during the forecast period.

The Director of Operations instructed the Management Accountant to prepare a new five year forecast, for presentation at the Board meeting, using the above assumptions. The Director of Operations instructed the Management Accountant to destroy her original forecast. The Management Accountant stated that this was not the way things are normally done at Aybe and that the Director of Operation's projections for revenue were unrealistically optimistic. The Director of Operations replied that it was not the role of a management accountant to question a director's professional expertise but rather a good management accountant should help him by carrying out his requests. The Director of Operations was not willing to discuss the matter further with the Management Accountant and pointed out that he had the unqualified support of a NED. The Director of Operations insisted the management accountant do the following:

- Produce a revised five year forecast incorporating the Director of Operations' assumptions;
- Present the revised forecast at the forthcoming Board meeting;
- Destroy the Management Accountant's original forecast.

Required

(a) (i) **Discuss** the relevance of the style of strategy currently in use at Aybe to the development of the Asian markets. **(5 marks)**

(ii) **Advise** the Board of **two** alternative approaches to strategy which you consider Aybe could use in the development of the Asian markets. Explain why you consider your choices may be appropriate. **(6 marks)**

(b) **Evaluate** the suitability of Aybe's current organisational structure in respect of the proposed expansion into Asian markets. **(9 marks)**

(c) (i) **Explain two** control problems Aybe might encounter if it chooses to conduct its business in Asia using agents. **(4 marks)**

(ii) **Advise** Aybe of appropriate control measures it could use to deal with the problems you have explained in (c)(i). **(6 marks)**

(d) (i) **Construct** an incremental profit forecast for the Asian expansion for the period 2010 – 2014 using the assumptions proposed by the Director of Operations and the actual results for year ended 31 December 2009. **(4 marks)**

(ii) **Discuss** the consequences for the shareholders of the revised incremental profit forecast constructed in d(i). **(6 marks)**

(iii) **Evaluate** how the views of the Director of Operations about the Management Accountant's profit forecast and the role of management accountants represent an ethical dilemma for the Management Accountant of Aybe. **(10 marks)**

(Total = 50 marks)

73 Power Utilities (Pilot paper) 90 mins

Strategic level pre-seen case material

Background

Power Utilities (PU) is located in a democratic Asian country. Just over 12 months ago, the former nationalised Electricity Generating Corporation (EGC) was privatised and became PU. EGC was established as a nationalised industry many years ago. Its home government at that time had determined that the provision of the utility services of electricity generation production should be managed by boards that were accountable directly to Government. In theory, nationalised industries should be run efficiently, on behalf of the public, without the need to provide any form of risk related return to the funding providers. In other words, EGC, along with other nationalised industries was a non-profit making organisation. This, the Government claimed at the time, would enable prices charged to the final consumer to be kept low.

Privatisation of EGC

The Prime Minister first announced three years ago that the Government intended to pursue the privatisation of the nationalised industries within the country. The first priority was to be the privatisation of the power generating utilities and EGC was selected as the first nationalised industry to be privatised. The main purpose of this strategy was to encourage public subscription for share capital. In addition, the Government's intention was that PU should take a full and active part in commercial activities such as raising capital and earning higher revenue by increasing its share of the power generation and supply market by achieving growth either organically or through making acquisitions. This, of course, also meant that PU was exposed to commercial pressures itself, including satisfying the requirements of shareholders and becoming a potential target for take-over. The major shareholder, with a 51% share, would be the Government. However, the Minister of Energy has recently stated that the Government intends to reduce its shareholding in PU over time after the privatisation takes place.

Industry structure

PU operates 12 coal-fired power stations across the country and transmits electricity through an integrated national grid system which it manages and controls. It is organised into three regions, Northern, Eastern and Western. Each region generates electricity which is sold to 10 private sector electricity distribution companies which are PU's customers.

The three PU regions transmit the electricity they generate into the national grid system. A shortage of electricity generation in one region can be made up by taking from the national grid. This is particularly important when there is a national emergency, such as exceptional weather conditions.

The nationalised utility industries, including the former EGC, were set up in a monopolistic position. As such, no other providers of these particular services were permitted to enter the market within the country. Therefore, when EGC was privatised and became PU it remained the sole generator of electricity in the country. The electricity generating facilities, in the form of the 12 coal-fired power stations, were all built over 15 years ago and some date back to before EGC came into being.

The 10 private sector distribution companies are the suppliers of electricity to final users including households and industry within the country, and are not under the management or control of PU. They are completely independent companies owned by shareholders.

The 10 private sector distribution companies serve a variety of users of electricity. Some, such as AB, mainly serve domestic users whereas others, such as DP, only supply electricity to a few industrial clients. In fact, DP has a limited portfolio of industrial customers and 3 major clients, an industrial conglomerate, a local administrative authority and a supermarket chain. DP finds these clients costly to service.

Structure of PU

The structure of PU is that it has a Board of Directors headed by an independent Chairman and a separate Managing Director. The Chairman of PU was nominated by the Government at the time the announcement that EGC was to be privatised was made. His background is that he is a former Chairman of an industrial conglomerate within the country. There was no previous Chairman of EGC which was managed by a Management Board, headed by the Managing Director. The former EGC Managing Director retired on privatisation and a new Managing Director was appointed.

The structure of PU comprises a hierarchy of many levels of management authority. In addition to the Chairman and Managing Director, the Board consists of the Directors of each of the Northern, Eastern and Western regions, a Technical Director, the Company Secretary and the Finance Director. All of these except the Chairman are the Executive Directors of PU. The Government also appointed seven Non Executive Directors to PU's Board. With the exception of the Company Secretary and Finance Director, all the Executive Directors are qualified electrical engineers. The Chairman and Managing Director of PU have worked hard to overcome some of the inertia which was an attitude that some staff had developed within the former EGC. PU is now operating efficiently as a private sector company. There have been many staff changes at a middle management level within the organisation.

Within the structure of PU's headquarters, there are five support functions; engineering, finance (which includes PU's Internal Audit department), corporate treasury, human resource management (HRM) and administration, each with its own chief officers, apart from HRM. Two Senior HRM Officers and Chief Administrative Officer report to the Company Secretary. The Chief Accountant and Corporate Treasurer each report to the Finance Director. These functions, except Internal Audit, are replicated in each region, each with its own regional officers and support staff. Internal Audit is an organisation wide function and is based at PU headquarters.

Regional Directors of EGC

The Regional Directors all studied in the field of electrical engineering at the country's leading university and have worked together for a long time. Although they did not all attend the university at the same time, they have a strong belief in the quality of their education. After graduation from university, each of the Regional Directors started work at EGC in a junior capacity and then subsequently gained professional electrical engineering qualifications. They believe that the experience of working up through the ranks of EGC has enabled them to have a clear understanding of EGC's culture and the technical aspects of the industry as a whole. Each of the Regional Managers has recognised the changed environment that PU now operates within, compared with the former EGC, and they are now working hard to help PU achieve success as a private sector electricity generator. The Regional Directors are well regarded by both the Chairman and Managing Director, both in terms of their technical skill and managerial competence.

Governance of EGC

Previously, the Managing Director of the Management Board of EGC reported to senior civil servants in the Ministry of Energy. There were no shareholders and ownership of the Corporation rested entirely with the Government. That has now changed. The Government holds 51% of the shares in PU and the Board of Directors is responsible to the shareholders but, inevitably, the Chairman has close links directly with the Minister of Energy, who represents the major shareholder.

The Board meetings are held regularly, normally weekly, and are properly conducted with full minutes being taken. In addition, there is a Remuneration Committee, an Audit Committee and an Appointments Committee, all in accordance with best practice. The model which has been used is the Combined Code on Corporate Governance which applies to companies which have full listing status on the London Stock Exchange. Although PU is not listed on the London Stock Exchange, the principles of the Combined Code were considered by the Government to be appropriate to be applied with regard to the corporate governance of the company.

Currently, PU does not have an effective Executive Information System and this has recently been raised at a Board meeting by one of the non-executive directors because he believes this inhibits the function of the Board and consequently is disadvantageous to the governance of PU.

Remuneration of Executive Directors

In order to provide a financial incentive, the Remuneration Committee of PU has agreed that the Executive Directors be entitled to performance related pay, based on a bonus scheme, in addition to their fixed salary and health benefits.

Capital market

PU exists in a country which has a well developed capital market relating both to equity and loan stock funding. There are well established international institutions which are able to provide funds and corporate entities are free to issue their own loan stock in accordance with internationally recognised principles. PU is listed on the country's main stock exchange.

Strategic opportunity

The Board of PU is considering the possibility of vertical integration into electricity supply and has begun preliminary discussion with DP's Chairman with a view to making an offer for DP. PU's Board is attracted by DP's strong reputation for customer service but is aware, through press comment, that DP has received an increase in complaints regarding its service to customers over the last year. When the former EGC was a nationalised business, breakdowns were categorised by the Government as "urgent", when there was a danger to life, and "non-urgent" which was all others. Both the former EGC and DP had a very high success rate in meeting the government's requirements that a service engineer should attend the urgent break-down within 60 minutes. DP's record over this last year in attending urgent breakdowns has deteriorated seriously and if PU takes DP over, this situation would need to improve.

Energy consumption within the country and Government drive for increased efficiency and concern for the environment

Energy consumption has doubled in the country over the last 10 years. As PU continues to use coal-fired power stations, it now consumes most of the coal mined within the country.

The Minister of Energy has indicated to the Chairman of PU that the Government wishes to encourage more efficient methods of energy production. This includes the need to reduce production costs. The Government has limited resources for capital investment in energy production and wishes to be sure that future energy production facilities are more efficient and effective than at present.

The Minister of Energy has also expressed the Government's wish to see a reduction in harmful emissions from the country's power stations. (The term harmful emissions in this context, refers to pollution coming out of electricity generating power stations which damage the environment.)

One of PU's non-executive directors is aware that another Asian country is a market leader in coal gasification which is a fuel technology that could be used to replace coal for power generation. In the coal gasification process, coal is mixed with oxygen and water vapour under pressure, normally underground, and then pumped to the surface where the gas can be used in power stations. The process significantly reduces carbon dioxide emissions although it is not widely used at present and not on any significant commercial scale.

Another alternative to coal fired power stations being actively considered by PU's Board is the construction of a dam to generate hydro-electric power. The Board is mindful of the likely adverse response of the public living and working in the area where the dam would be built.

In response to the Government's wishes, PU has established environmental objectives relating to improved efficiency in energy production and reducing harmful emissions such as greenhouse gases. PU has also established an ethical code. Included within the code are sections relating to recycling and reduction in harmful emissions as well as to terms and conditions of employment.

Introduction of commercial accounting practices at EGC

The first financial statements have been produced for PU for 20X8. Extracts from the Statement of Financial Position from this are shown in Appendix A. Within these financial statements, some of EGC's loans were "notionally" converted by the Government into ordinary shares. Interest is payable on the Government loans as shown in the statement of financial position. Reserves is a sum which was vested in EGC when it was first nationalised. This represents the initial capital stock valued on a historical cost basis from the former electricity generating organisations which became consolidated into EGC when it was first nationalised.

Being previously a nationalised industry and effectively this being the first "commercially based" financial statements, there are no retained earnings brought forward into 20X8.

APPENDIX A

EXTRACTS FROM THE PRO FORMA FINANCIAL STATEMENTS OF THE ELECTRICITY GENERATING CORPORATION

Statement of financial position as at 31 December 20X8

	P$ million
ASSETS	
Non-current assets	15,837
Current assets	
Inventories	1,529
Receivables	2,679
Cash and Cash equivalents	133
	4,341
Total assets	20,178
EQUITY AND LIABILITIES	
Equity	
Share capital	5,525
Reserves	1,231
Total equity	6,756
Non-current liabilities	
Government loans	9,560
Current liabilities	
Payables	3,862
Total liabilities	13,422
Total equity and liabilities	20,178

[The unseen material begins on the next page]

Unseen Case Material (Exam day material for Paper E3 only)

Background

EGC was privatised just over a year ago and is now Power Utilities (PU). The new Board of Directors of PU is accountable to the shareholders, the major one being the Government which holds 51% of the shares.

In an early move by PU, it has taken over two of the private electricity distribution companies. One of these, DP, located in the Eastern Division of PU, serves a limited portfolio of industrial customers and three major clients. The takeover was not disputed with DP's Board recommending to its shareholders acceptance of the bid. PU now holds 90% of DP's shares.

The Board of Directors of PU has established a Management Board at DP which is independently chaired by a nominee from PU's Board. The previous Executive Directors on DP's board have all retained their posts and their remuneration includes a performance bonus based on DP's overall profitability. The previous Chairman of DP has retired.

Customer service

During the time when EGC was nationalised, customer break-downs had been categorised by the Government as Urgent (when there was a danger to life) and Non-urgent (all other breakdowns).

There was a requirement for Urgent break-downs that a service engineer should be with the customer within 60 minutes or less. Before privatisation the electricity distribution industry had a very high success rate in meeting this requirement with 99.9% of customers being attended within 60 minutes and nobody ever waited longer than 90 minutes for attention.

Non-urgent break-downs were attended to in turn but there was no maximum time requirement for an engineer to attend. There were always a significant number of Non-urgent break-downs to attend to and customers might wait as long as six months for attention.

During the last year there have been an increasing number of complaints to DP from its customers regarding the slow attendance of service engineers following a reduction in their numbers. It was often now the case that customers with Urgent break-downs had to wait for up to a day for attention and the situation for customers with Non-urgent break-downs also had got worse.

Options for change

The Technical Director (TD) of DP has been investigating the deteriorating standards of customer service. He believes that there are two possible ways forward which he proposed to put to the Board of Directors of DP.

The first would be to invest a considerable amount of resources to improve the existing in-house customer service carried out by DP's service engineers. The other response would be to outsource customer service. The financial data relating to both these options is given below:

Financial implications

In-house

If the customer service is kept in-house, DP will have to spend money recruiting additional engineers and training and equipping all the engineers to a very high standard. In order to meet the service targets of 100% attendance within 60 minutes for Urgent break-downs (which it is estimated will amount to 6,000 each year) and also that up to 2,000 Non-urgent break-downs are resolved each year, DP will employ 75 engineers. The cost of establishing this new service network together with infrastructure, recruitment, training and equipment set up costs in the first year only will amount to P$50,000,000. In addition, there would be an annual running cost of P$8,000,000.

Outsource

DP has had a quote from a reputable service company, RSC. RSC would employ 38 service engineers and would charge DP P$250 for each Urgent break-down which it attended and P$150 for each Non-urgent break-down which it attended. It has enough capacity to attend all the break-downs which DP estimates will occur each year. However, it cannot commit to attending 100% of Urgent break-downs within 60 minutes: RSC estimates it will only be able to attend 99% of Urgent break-downs within 60 minutes. The remainder will take between 2 and 4 hours before RSC can get its engineers to the customer.

As a condition of RSC accepting the contract it will require a 'one off' payment of P$30,000,000 when the contract is signed.

Other information

Industry history shows that there is a probability of fatality or serious injury when the response to an Urgent break-down is delayed. In the case of DP, it is estimated that every urgent break-down not attended by a service engineer within 60 minutes carries a 0.1% chance of a fatality or serious injury.

Investments such as the one proposed by the TD are regarded by DP as having an opportunity cost of capital of 10%.

The TD and the Management Accountant (MA)

In their discussions about the outsourcing of the customer service the MA had asked the TD if it was possible to quantify the financial cost of fatality or serious injury caused by the non-attendance of an engineer within 60 minutes to an Urgent break-down. The TD said it was not worth doing this as the chance was so small and he did not want to distract the Board in its decision making with irrelevant data. The MA agreed that the probability of a fatality or serious injury was low but nevertheless as DP aspired to being a good corporate citizen and in the interests of transparency this information should go before the Board.

The TD stated that these forecasts were his, he took responsibility for them and he would not be placing the information about fatality and serious injury before the Board. The TD stated that he would answer any question put to him by the Board but that the MA should concentrate on his own job and let the TD get on with his.

Required

(a) (i) **Compare and contrast** the rational planning model with the Incrementalist approach to strategic planning. **(6 marks)**

(ii) **Advise** the Board of Directors of DP of another approach to forming strategy which would be most suitable for its organisation's changed circumstances as a privatised company. **(4 marks)**

(b) (i) **Analyse** the two alternative methods of servicing DP's customers.

Note: All 10 marks are for calculation in this requirement. **(10 marks)**

(ii) **Discuss** the consequences of the two methods of servicing DP's customers. **(5 marks)**

(c) **Evaluate** the extent to which the views of the Technical Director regarding the disclosure of information about non-attendance at Urgent break-downs within 60 minutes represent an ethical dilemma for the Management Accountant. **(10 marks)**

(d) In the light of the changed circumstances of DP, and your findings and evaluation above:

(i) **Recommend**, with reasons, four Critical Success Factors (CSFs) which would be appropriate for DP as a company. **(8 marks)**

(ii) **Discuss** the main attributes for an effective Information System by which DP would be able to manage the Urgent and Non-urgent breakdowns. **(7 marks)**

(Total = 50 marks)

ANSWERS

1 Qualispecs

Text reference. SWOT analysis is assumed knowledge for E3, because it is covered in the E2 syllabus.

Alternative answers. This question is a good illustration of the fact that there is usually no single right answer for a strategic level answer. In particular, the requirement to 'Produce a corporate appraisal' provides scope for a variety of different approaches. The first answer tries to show a wide range of strengths, weaknesses, opportunities and threats for its corporate appraisal. However, we have also presented a second answer (in a text box) which shows less factors but describes each in more detail. This approach – of focusing on the key points and explaining them clearly – is a good way of scoring well under the time pressures you will face in strategic level papers.

Part (a)

Top tips. To score well in this requirement you need to note that requirement involves two distinct parts, separated by the word 'and'.

The first part requires you to 'produce a corporate appraisal' and the post-exam guidance makes it clear that the Examiner was expecting a SWOT analysis approach rather than one based on environmental scanning and internal appraisal. How were you to know this? Firstly, there is not really enough data available for you to be able to carry out a thorough external and internal review. Secondly, the material given is in a significantly summarised form, which is ideal for the SWOT analysis approach.

The second part of the requirement asks you to 'discuss the key strategic challenges'. In effect, this means breaking down the SWOT into a small number of key risks or threats.

Also, make sure you look at both parts (a) and (b) of the question before answering it so that you do not repeat yourself. It is important that you decide how the parts are different. Part (a) asks you to describe the present situation of Qualispecs. Part (b) asks you what to do to improve that situation.

Qualispecs corporate appraisal

Strengths

- New CEO with good track record in the industry, intimate knowledge of a major competitor and willingness to take vigorous steps
- Reputation for quality products helps maintain margins and goodwill
- Celebrity exposure which can help increase awareness and sales
- Strong financial position including large cash reserves permits long term investment in strategic developments.

Weaknesses

- Failure to utilise new technology that could cut costs and improve service
- High production costs that put them at a price disadvantage
- Failure to use reward system for motivation to build customer focus
- Over-centralisation prevents local initiative

Opportunities

- Formal celebrity endorsement
- Fashion 'eye-wear', including designer frames and sunglasses could improve margins and customer retention
- Availability of new production technology to cut costs and improve service throughout
- Aging population means increased need for spectacles as sight can deteriorate with age
- Increased spending among 18-30 year old customers especially on fashion products

Threats

- Effects of economic slowdown on discretionary spending such as fashion goods
- Decline in customer loyalty/increasing competition from innovative rivals using new technology
- New technologies such as laser treatment that dispense with need for spectacles
- On-line providers able to make up and provide spectacles and contact lenses to customer prescriptions

Key strategic challenges

Qualispecs is in danger of being left behind by its competitors. The erosion of its customer base shows that it can no longer allow its product to 'speak for itself'. Unless it takes vigorous steps, its rivals will draw further ahead and its decline will accelerate.

1 **To embrace new technologies**. If Qualspecs doesn't reduce its costs and prices whilst also improving its speed of service it will become increasingly uncompetitive.
2 **To become more dynamic and customer centred.** Its unimaginative **reward policy** reduces the productivity of its staff and managers and their willingness to provide good ideas that could enhance the company's success.
3 **To reach out to new customers**. Its established reputation gives Qualispecs a reliable income. To increase this it needs to find new customers such as higher-spending younger customers.

Part (b)

Top tips. This part of the question requires you to recommend specific strategies. The Examiner's suggested solution was based on converting threats to opportunities and weaknesses to strengths; matching strengths with opportunities and remedying weaknesses. It would probably also be possible to base an answer on Porter's generic strategies. The Ansoff matrix could also provide some useful ideas for new products and markets.

Qualispecs is fortunate in that its finances are sound and it has large cash reserves. It would be appropriate to use some of that financial strength to make investments that will improve the company's competitive position. *Qualispecs* should seek improvements in three main areas of its operations.

- Innovation
- Performance management
- Distribution

Innovation

Two areas are ripe for innovation: **products** and **production methods**. In both areas, *Qualispecs* has to catch up with its competitors. The economic downturn means that growth will be most easily achieved in the 18-30 year old market. Fashion-consciousness is important here, so the design and variety of prescription spectacles and sunglasses must be improved. At the same time, suitable promotion must be undertaken, perhaps making use of sports star endorsement.

Production methods must be examined for opportunities to reduce cost and improve efficiency. The one hour laboratory approach should be considered, as discussed below.

In addition to these two matters, it would be appropriate for *Qualispecs* to begin to foster a **culture of innovation**. Given its existing stagnation, there are almost certainly several other aspects of its operation that would benefit from new ideas. Such cultural change is linked to our next area of consideration.

Performance management

We mentioned performance management in our earlier discussion of key strategic challenges. The principle could also be applied in the form of **management bonuses** based on the overall performance individual shops and regions and individual pay increases and bonuses related to sales and profit performance. Such a change would require greater autonomy for managers at shop level in particular if it were to have significant effect, so there would have to be some delegation of control over such matters as working conditions, job roles and pay rates.

Distribution

Qualispecs must do something about the wide variation in its shops' performance. A careful examination of costs and revenues is needed. There is also a need to look at the shops estate from a marketing point of view. The estate may be in need of renovation or even complete redesign. The company should aim to make its shops pleasant and interesting places to visit. *Fastglass* has entered into partnership with a high-street shopping group. This may be an innovation that *Qualispecs* could imitate as part of its attention to product development. A **fashion retailer** would be a good choice of partner for a new group of in-store shops concentrating on the new designer styles, for example. A partnership approach to costs and revenues may be possible and appropriate.

Qualispecs must also examine the *Fastglass* mini-lab approach with an open mind. This method may be worth adopting, assuming the technology is not protected, but caution should be employed: a full examination of costs and market prospects should be carried out and implications fully explored.

Alternative approach to answer for Question 1: (see note at start of answer)

Part (a)

Strengths – (Internal)

Reputation

The company has an excellent reputation for quality products. This will enable the company to launch new products with confidence that existing customers will have faith in their products and services, thus increasing market penetration.

Financial strength

The company is on a sound financial footing, including large cash reserves. This is advantageous as it will allow Qualispecs (Q) to make investments in new technologies such as those used by Fastglass, (F) without the need to secure external finance.

Weaknesses – (Internal)

Technology

The technologies employed by Q appear dated, as the company has 'failed to utilise advances'. This has resulted in a lack of competitive edge against companies such as F resulting in lost customer loyalty as well as a higher cost base.

Poor internal control

The company produces internal information that shows variable profitability and lack of control over job roles. The failure to act upon this information means that the company has continued to trade from shops that are not very profitable and hence drag down the company's results. The lack of control over job roles may lead to confusion amongst staff creating inefficiency and lower levels of customer service.

Opportunities – (External)

New technologies

The technologies that Q has not utilised may be employed using Q's cash reserves. This will allow the company to compete more effectively against F and stem the tide of lost customer loyalty. Additionally, the new technologies should lower the currently high production costs.

Youth market

Although there is a predicted slowdown in the economy we are told customer spending will rise in the 18-30 year olds market segment. Q could target its product development and marketing approaches to this segment to gain market share in a demographic that is known to contain high spending and image conscious consumers. This could be aided by the endorsement of the popular sports star.

Threats – (External)

Competition

Q faces increased competition from companies such as F employing superior technologies. The intense competition that Q faces will cause problems such as a falling customer base, which will result in lower repeat custom and falling economies of scale. The Q brand may also suffer in comparison to successful industry rivals.

Market slowdown

The national economy is predicted to slow down which could affect Q's sales. Even though consumer spending is predicted to be strong this will primarily benefit the stronger competitors with differentiated products and services. As Q is currently uncompetitive it stands to miss out on any increase in spending whilst seeing the economy shrink as a whole.

Key strategic challenges

Uncompetitive technologies

In order to become competitive Q needs to invest in newer technologies. Its current technologies make its production methods slow and expensive.

<u>Outdated marketing</u>

Letting 'the product speak for itself' is an outdated marketing concept. A failure to research, understand and supply customer needs allied to promotional activities undermines Q attempts to be more competitive.

<u>Disjointed structures</u>

The lack of cohesion over pay and job roles is undermining Q's ability to provide a consistent service offering. Failure to do so will confuse staff which my impact upon customers and harm the brand.

Part (b)

<u>Invest in new technologies</u>

One hour technology capability will solve a number of the issues discussed above. It will enable the strengths of Q, beings it brand and cash, to be matched to the opportunity of new technologies. Additionally, the weaknesses of uncompetitive technologies resulting in slow and expensive production costs, will be reduced or eliminated. This measure will also allow Q to compete on an equal footing with F, and if it invests in even more recent innovations perhaps out-compete F in the growing youth market too.

<u>Marketing Campaign</u>

Q could attempt to arrange celebrity endorsements with sports, music or film stars in order to enhance their brand. The famous sports star endorsement appears to have been a fortunate accident, the benefits of an official endorsement could be huge in terms of brand exposure, customer loyalty and maybe premium pricing.

Particular emphasis could be placed on the growing 18-30 year olds market segment. There will be a cost in terms of payments to the celebrities and marketing campaign. Marketing, however is an area that is currently both a weakness of Q that can be eliminated and an opportunity that can be exploited.

<u>Focus on profitable locations</u>

Q appears to operate some stores that are profitable whilst others are not, which drags down overall group profitability. Q should conduct a review of each site's historic and potential future profitability and focus its resources where it is most likely to make maximise returns for shareholders.

For example those sites with very high rental should have their leases reviewed to see if they can be broken or notice served to either look for alternative premises in the town or the store closed. In this way Q will be maximising its returns in respect of a key constraint (floor space).

2 BBB International bank

Text reference: Porter's Five Forces model and his Diamond model are both covered in the E2 syllabus and so are assumed knowledge for E3. However, there is a brief recap of the main points of both models in the Introduction chapter at the start of the E3 Study Text.

Marking scheme

			Marks
(a)	Evaluation of each of the Five Forces – up to 3 marks each	Up to 15	
	Comment that Five Forces model looks at profitability of industry so does not imply the banking industry in R will be equally profitable for all banks	Up to 2	
		<u>Total up to</u>	14
(b)	Benefits of remaining in R	Up to 2	
	Disadvantages of remaining in R	Up to 2	
	Advice about whether R should remain in R or not	Up to 4	
		<u>Total up to</u>	5

(c)	Outline of the diamond model and general discussion of how it can be used – 1 mark per point	Up to 3	
	Discussion of how BBB could use the diamond model in its future decisions	Up to 4	
		Total up to	6
		Total	25

Top tips:

Part (a): It is important to remember that Porter's Five Forces model looks at the profitability of an **industry** rather than a single firm. However, just because an industry is profitable doesn't mean that all of the companies in it will be equally profitable. This appears to be the case with the banking industry in R.

In part (a) you should work through the Five Forces in turn and evaluate their strength in relation to the banking industry in R. This will then give you an indication of the likely profitability of the banking industry as a whole.

However, remember the requirement asked you specifically to evaluate BBB's future potential to make a profit, not the potential for the industry as a whole to make a profit.

Planning this question is vital, to ensure you avoid repeating points between parts (a) and (b).

Part (b): A number of the features that will influence BBB's decision relate to the Five Forces (eg competitive rivalry). The question requirement highlights this by asking you to 'use your analysis from part (a).

However, in part (b) you need to focus specifically on BBB's ability to sustain a profit in country R. In this respect, it is important to consider whether BBB has any resources or competences which will allow it to establish a sustainable competitive advantage in R. If it doesn't, then it is unlikely to be able to sustain a profit there, and so should leave the market.

Remember that the question requirements asked you to 'Advise....' so you need to give clear advice to BBB at the end of your answer as to whether it should continue in country R or not.

Examiner's comment. Part (a) was not well answered. Although many candidates were able to describe the Five Forces correctly, and could apply them to the scenario in general terms, candidates then failed to consider the effect that the Forces would have on BBB's profitability. However, the question required candidates to evaluate the effect of the Forces specifically on BBB's profitability, not, for example, to discuss them in the context of the banking industry as a whole.

(a)

Threat of new entrants

The threat of new entrants is limited by **barriers to entry**.

Capital investment - The main barrier to entry to the banking market in R is the **capital investment** required to enter that market. In total, BBB spent $350 million to enter the market ($200 million to establish its own branch network, and $150 million to acquire a local bank).

Dominance of SB - In addition, **SB's dominant position** in the market (being a state-owned organisation, accounting for half of R's retail banking business) might act as a potential disincentive to potential new entrants thinking about investing in R.

Recent withdrawals - The fact that two foreign banks have recently withdrawn from R may also discourage potential new entrants from investing there. The banks' claims that their operations in R served to reduce group profitability suggest that R may not be a very profitable market to invest in.

Competitive rivalry

Strong competition – The state-owned institutions provide tough competition for retail banking business in R. Within this context, SH has established a position of dominance, accounting for half of this business. In addition, a number of well-established foreign banks account for a further 35% of R's retail banking market.

Although the well-established foreign banks are all profitable, it appears the more recent entrants have been less successful. Two of the banks which entered R at the same time as BBB have withdrawn due to the poor levels of profitability their operations in R have generated. Therefore, although there appear to be high margins in the banking industry in R, it appears that banks need to have reached a certain size (a critical mass) before they can begin to earn those margins.

Market growth – Nonetheless, the banking analyst's report indicates there is plenty of growth left in the banking market in R, and the margins are excellent. This suggests the competitive rivalry may not be as intense as it might otherwise be, but the dominant position of the established banks still suggests there is a **high level of rivalry** in the banking market in R.

Bargaining power of consumers

The banking market in R is geared primarily towards personal banking, but individually, customers will only have a low degree of bargaining power.

Choice of bank accounts - However, the degree of choice customers in relation to which bank to use increases their bargaining power. For example, people in R could choose to bank with: SB; one of the other state-owned institutions; BBB, or one of the other foreign owned-banks.

It is likely to be relatively easy for customers to switch from one bank to another, which again could increase customers' bargaining power.

Conservatism - R's population doesn't like change, which means they will are naturally more likely to use one of the established banks than a relatively new foreign entrant such as BBB. In effect, this could reduce the bargaining power of customers on the existing banks. By contrast, though, it could increase their bargaining power over new entrants such as BBB. BBB is likely to have to offer the customers significantly better deals than existing domestic banks in the short term to attract new customers.

Threat of substitute products

Although there are a number of different banks which consumers could use, these reflect the level of competitive rivalry in the industry, rather than the threat of substitute products.

Similarly, although there is scope for consumers to switch to internet banking services rather than using the branch network, this again represents a switch within the industry rather than a substitute product.

In this respect, there don't appear to be any substitutes for banking products as a whole, so the threat here is low.

Bargaining power of suppliers

Liberalised market – R has a liberalised economy which allows the free movement of capital in and out of the country. This suggests that BBB (and the other banks in the industry) should easily be able to supply their capital requirements in R under normal market conditions, although the global financial crisis could have an impact on these market conditions overall.

The scenario does not indicate any other key suppliers who could influence BBB's operations in R, so we cannot make any judgement about their strength of their bargaining power.

Potential for future profits

Overall, it appears there is a relatively high level of competitive rivalry in the industry and customers also have a moderate level of bargaining power. However, the threat of new entrants and the threat of substitute products appears to be reasonably weak.

Looking at these forces together suggests that the market should be a profitable one, and this corroborates the analyst's view.

However, the market is not necessarily equally profitable for all the banks in it. Consequently, the potential profitability for BBB's banking business within R is likely to be lower than that of SB's.

(b)

Market profitability and growth – The analysis in part (a) suggests that the retail banking market in R should remain a profitable one. There is plenty of growth left in the market, not least because a high proportion of the population do not currently have bank accounts (This figure was 50% three years ago in 20X8). As more of the population open bank accounts, the size of the banking market in the country will necessarily increase.

Competitive rivalry – However, although the market overall is profitable and growing, there is still likely to be a high degree of competitive rivalry in it.

SB presents the strongest competitive threat to BBB. SB already accounts for half of the retail banking business in R, and its position has been strengthened by its recent re-organisation, and the launch of some successful (and profitable) new products.

Consumer preference – Consumers' attitudes to change should also be a concern to BBB. The customers' dislike of change means they are likely to continue using SB and established banks rather than switching to BBB. Even though BBB has a strong brand image and a long record of success, this may not be sufficient to convince customers to switch to BBB.

Profit levels - The fact that BBB is already successful in a number of other countries means that it should only continue in R if it can sustain an acceptable level of profit there. It appears that the two foreign banks who entered the market at the same time were not able to do this, and so they left.

BBB does not appear to have any sources of sustainable competitive advantage which will enable it to be more successful than these banks, or to reduce SB's dominance in the market.

Advice: Therefore BBB should be advised not to continue its retail banking business in country R.

Top tips:

Part (c): Porter's diamond assesses the factors which increase a country's national competitiveness for a given industry.

So, a useful approach to this question would be to work through each aspect of the diamond in turn, and consider how they could influence BBB's decision to invest in a country.

Note, the perspective you need to take here is whether a country is likely to make a good investment for BBB, rather than simply whether it has a competitive banking industry. It is possible that if the determinants of national competitiveness are already too well developed, a country may not be a good place for a new entrant to invest in. In particular, if the existing demand conditions are very high, will BBB have any aspects of competitive advantage over the existing firms already there?

(c)

Potential competitiveness: Porter's diamond suggests that there four key determinants which make some countries inherently more competitive than others as locations for different industries. When it is considering future investment in new foreign countries, BBB should try to invest in countries which have a favourable environment for retail banking, and so will maximise the chances of its investment being successful.

Firm strategy, structure and rivalry – Considering these factors will help BBB assess the level of competition it is likely to face in the country. The situation in R illustrates how the structure and rivalry of the banking industry (dominated by the state-owned bank, SB) have a major impact on the competition any potential new entrants will face there.

Factor conditions – A business needs to assess that the inputs it needs to do business successfully are available in a country before it moves there. As a service business, a key factor in BBB's success will be the quality of the staff it employs. Therefore, it needs to be sure that any countries it considering entering have a suitable potential workforce for it to recruit from.

Demand conditions – This analysis will help indicate how demanding customers' requirements are, for example in terms of quality and product innovation. BBB would then have to consider how well its products will meet the customers' requirements.

Although Porter suggested that a tough domestic market will encourage competitiveness among the existing firms in that market (and thereby increase the national competitive advantage for an industry), if customer requirements are too demanding this may make entering the market an unattractive strategic option for BBB.

Related and supporting industries – In order for BBB to operate successfully in a country, the infrastructure in the country must be suitable to support its operations.

Government – In addition to the four main determinant listed above, Porter also highlighted the importance of government policy in shaping a country's national competitiveness. The influence of government could be particularly important factor for BBB to consider. For example, in R, the government doesn't appear keen on foreign competition in the banking sector, which may make R a less attractive place for foreign banks to invest.

However, if BBB does use the Diamond to help assess possible new countries to invest in, it should do so with a degree of caution. For example, some critics argue that ultimately it is companies, not countries, which determine competitive advantage, and a company's success is determined by its strategies and management, rather than being located in a specific country.

3 CTC Strategic objectives

Text reference. Strategic objectives, which are relevant to parts (a) and (b), are dealt with in Chapter 2 of your BPP Study Text. Stakeholders are also discussed in Chapter 2.

Top tips. Neither the scenario nor any of the requirements make use of the word 'stakeholder', but it should spring to your mind as soon as you begin thinking about this question. CTC has some very important new stakeholder groups to consider and their interests will be the main formative influence on what the company sets out to do. Stakeholders will be a major consideration for both part (a) and part (b).

Part (a)

Top tips. When answering this question you need to think of the contrasting aims and objectives of private sector organisations with those in the public sector. Simply saying what the new objectives should be will not be enough to pass this question. Instead you need to think in terms of **change,** and consider what the company's objectives were before privatisation, and how these will change after the company is privatised.

Don't overlook the demands of corporate governance; this is about both what is to be done and also how it should be done.

The solution below adopts a stakeholder approach. An alternative approach would be to make a series of points related to the primacy of profit in a commercial firm compared to a state monopoly, the need to hold market share at home, the need to gain sales revenues by expanding product range and providing services abroad and the need to protect its share price by good corporate governance and adequate communication with investors.

Examiner's comments. Most candidates mentioned the pre-privatisation objectives of economy, efficiency and effectiveness and identified the new role of shareholders and their importance in setting objectives. However, many candidates failed to recognise the importance of overseas expansion as an objective.

As a state monopoly, CTC's role was expressed in terms of its **service to the nation as a whole**. Its focus was on the public sector aspirations off **efficiency, effectiveness and economy**, but it was **not subject to market discipline** and its finances were controlled by government. The lack of market input and the highly technical nature of its operations make it likely that its main operational concern was **engineering competence**, rather than customer interests. However, the government, as principal stakeholder, imposed requirements around performance and service levels to be achieved.

Shareholders as new stakeholders

CTC now has a new and important class of **stakeholder** in the form of its **shareholders**. They will have firm ideas about their requirements in the form of growth, earnings and dividends.

Importance of customers

The company faces a de-regulated market where competition will intensify. It will need to pay great attention to the views and needs of its **customers**; they are a stakeholder group that is likely to wield far more influence than previously, since they will be able to choose new suppliers when new providers of telecommunications services enter the market following its deregulation.

Impact on objectives

These influences will affect objectives at all levels in the organisation and will require a significant realignment of attitudes. In particular, there will be **pressure to reduce costs; to develop new and attractive products**; and to **improve customer service**, particularly in the matter of installing new equipment and dealing with faults.

The **respective requirements of shareholders and customers** also highlight a potential conflict which will need to be addressed by the directors when setting the company's objectives.

Shareholders will want to **maximise profitability** which may be achieved by raising prices. But customers will seek the lowest price they can get.

Although the **government** is no longer the main external stakeholder, it will still be interested in CTC's performance. The company will continue to make a large contribution to the economy of C as a major employer and taxpayer; it also has the potential to develop as a major centre of technological excellence.

While government will step back from direct involvement in the running of CTC, it is likely that it will retain an interest in its overall success, and possibly a closer involvement in such matters as the promotion of technological development and overseas expansion, which if successful could increase CTC's **tax liability** to the government.

Corporate governance

A final influence on the strategic objectives of the privatised company will arise in the field of **corporate governance**. As a quoted company, CTC will be subject to the normal regulations and codes of practice laid down by its quoting stock exchange. It may also be subject to special **government regulation** designed to prevent it from using its size and current dominant position to discourage competitors. These influences are also likely to have a marked effect on the directors attitudes and practices.

Overall, the objectives of CTC will need to change to **focus on profitability and shareholder reward**, as well as customer satisfaction which becomes increasingly important in a deregulated market. Alongside this, the directors will need to ensure the business' controls and governance are adequate to comply with its new regulatory requirements.

Part (b)

Top tips. You must think carefully here. First, note that you are being asked for objectives *not* a mission statement: the objectives you select must be strategic (long term, not short term), but they can be very specifically aimed at particular aspects of strategy. Approaching the problem from the stakeholder angle would be a good way to proceed here, but make sure you explain *why* the objective is appropriate to CTC.

The second important point is that the objectives you provide must be SMART.

However, note (b) is only worth four marks so do not spend too long on this requirement.

Objective 1

To achieve an average of 5% annual growth in share valuation for the next five years or until competitors achieve a total of 25% market share.

This objective is relevant to the concerns of shareholders. It is specific, measurable and time-bounded. It is also realistic, in that it acknowledges that the company's existing privileged position is likely to be damaged by the entry of competitors into its markets.

Objective 2

To create, within twelve months, an affordable and humane restructuring plan that will reduce staff costs by 20% and to implement the plan over the following three years without provoking a major labour dispute.

This objective addresses the continuing strategic need for cost efficiency to allow CTC to compete effectively in a deregulated market. It recognises the need to balance that need against the interests of the existing employees and the practical difficulties of implementing a headcount reduction.

Part (c)

Text reference. An overview of strategic planning models is given in Chapter 1 of your BPP Study Text.

Top tips. As you will be aware, there is a range of views about how strategy is and should be made. You will not have time to consider them in detail here!

There are 11 marks available for this requirement, which is too few for a wide discussion and too many for a simple answer based on one of the partial theories such as incrementalism or emergence.

The key to resolving this dilemma is to use the **rational model** to **guide your answer**, with passing reference to the other approaches as you go. The Examiner gives you a clue that the rational model is relevant by referring to the 'strategic planning **process**' (BPP emphasis).

However, by asking you to '*advise*' the Board, the Examiner is asking that your answer be appropriate for CTC, so you must apply your knowledge to the scenario rather than simply recounting the rational model.

Easy marks. The rational model is fairly all-embracing, but even if you cannot remember all of the detail and terminology, you ought to be able to get some of it down on paper, and then apply it to CTC.

Examiner's comments. In general, this question was well answered. However, some candidates still attempted to describe the text book stages of the rational model, without applying them to CTC in the light of the privatisation.

As a very large, newly privatised company, CTC needs to use a cautious and thorough approach to developing its strategy; if it does not, it runs a severe risk of being taken by surprise by the new and rapidly developing conditions under which it will have to operate. The classic **rational planning model** should therefore form the basis of its strategic processes.

This model will guide it through a series of logical stages. However, it is important to understand that although the rational model is linear in appearance, it is most effectively used if **feedback** between the various stages is created. Many of the processes involved can be run simultaneously, or even in reverse order if it becomes appropriate to reconsider earlier conclusions and decisions.

Company mission

CTC should give careful attention to what it is trying to achieve as a company. It should attempt to define its overall mission, and the strategic objectives that support that mission. Stakeholder interest and influence should be considered as part of this process, and any potential conflicts should be identified and resolved.

Environmental analysis

The company must ensure that it understands the ways in which it is affected by, and affects, the **environment in which it operates**. This will be a major task, since its comfortable state monopoly position has been disrupted; new competitors are very likely to enter its markets and, as a result, its customers are likely to discover that they have acquired significant bargaining power. CTC should analyse its wider environment using a 'PEST' analysis, and should consider the immediate industrial or task environment using Porter's Five Forces model as a guide. Environmental analysis is one of the stages of the rational model that is never complete; the company should undertake a policy of **continuing environmental scanning** for threats and opportunities.

Position audit

At the same time as it is seeking to understand its environment, CTC also needs to appraise its own internal **strengths** and **weaknesses**, and to understand its **core competencies** and **competitive position**. Its competitive advantage depends primarily on the possession of assets or competences that competitors cannot easily obtain or imitate; for instance, its network of telephone lines; intellectual property in the form of patents and proprietary designs; and the experience and knowledge of its staff.

The company should include in this phase an analysis of just how it creates value, using the **value chain** model.

Corporate appraisal

Environmental scanning and position audit permit the preparation of a SWOT analysis summarising the most important strengths, weaknesses, opportunities and threats pertaining to the company. This should then help CTC identify its strategic options.

Strategic options

CTC should consider its options in the context of *Porter*'s analysis of generic strategies: **cost leadership** and **differentiation**. (The narrow **focus** strategy is inappropriate to such a large business).

Advantages also accrue to a company that achieves **lock-in**; this is the condition of owning the industry standard as proprietary technology. This is likely to be very relevant to CTC with its recent monopoly and large installed technology base.

Given the opportunities for growth in the global telecommunications industry, which lay behind the government decision to privatise CTC, CTC may also consider its strategies for **product** and **market development** as described in the Ansoff matrix.

Evaluation of strategic options

Having generated a range of possible strategies, CTC should assess them for **suitability**, in terms of its overall strategic mission and posture; **acceptability** to stakeholders; and **feasibility** in terms of the resources required. The selected strategy should also be **sustainable** in the longer term, and contribute to the company's longer term competitive advantage.

Strategy selection

It will also be necessary to consider CTC's **structure and means of growth**. CTC might choose to expand **organically** or by **takeover**. The latter option might be a sensible way to expand internationally, for example. Other options include **alliances** and **joint ventures**. There may also be subsidiary part of the current organisation that are actually distractions and could usefully be divested.

Strategy implementation

Once a strategy has been selected, it must be implemented, and the implementation must be controlled. **Implementation** will require the development of functional and departmental strategies and plans. CTC's development from its current status as a recently privatised monopoly is likely to create significant complexity in its human resources management function, for example. Control will require the identification of **critical success factors** and the design of suitable strategic **performance measures** linked to them.

Review and revision

As noted earlier, strategy development is not a linear process and it does end with strategic control. A very important role for feedback lies in the potential stimulation of reconsideration of the earlier stages of the model as outlined above, particularly as the reality of the market begins to be felt.

Also CTC should be aware that strategy may not actually develop in the ordered, linear way the rational model suggests. By contrast, CTC is more likely to experience an **emergent** process, with modifications being made to its strategy development in response to changing environmental factors or other constraints.

4 Scientific equipment supplier

Text reference: Stakeholders are covered in Chapter 2 of the BPP Study text.

Part (a)

Top tips. This is a relatively straightforward requirement. However, make sure you note that the analysis is for E in country Y only, not for E in general.

Also, remember that you are asked to produce a stakeholder analysis for a particular scenario, not to draw Mendelow's matrix, or to spend time discussing it in general terms. There are no marks available for doing this.

The marks in the question are for analysing the stakeholders identified in the scenario according to their power and interest. So a sensible approach would be to use the four quadrants of Mendelow's matrix as headings (eg (i) high power; high interest; (ii) low power; high interest, etc) and then analyse which groups of stakeholders fit into each heading.

High power; High interest

Government of Y – The government has the power to influence E's operations: requiring E to change the mix of staff it employs, and to sell a percentage of its business to a local partner.

At an overall level, the government has a high interest in E because it will want to try to maximise the tax revenue it can derive from E. In this respect the government will have to perform a bit of a juggling act though – it cannot suppress E's business too far, because the tax revenue it receives from E is very valuable to it, especially in the context of declining tax revenues.

More specifically, the government also has a high degree of interest in E because it is one of E's major customers. (The government is responsible for funding the purchase of equipment for public education systems).

Unions – The Unions have relatively high power because of their alignment with the new government, in particular their views on increasing the local ownership of firms.

The Unions' views on local ownership suggest they are hostile to foreign firms operating in Y. As E is a foreign multinational, the unions will have a high interest in E's operations in Y.

Low power; High interest

Employees of E – The current employees will have a high interest because the government policy could put their jobs at risk.

To this end, the staff do not agree with the government's policy, but it appears they cannot do anything to influence it, meaning they have low power.

Management of E – Although E's management team have a high interest in the company's performance, they also appear to have little or no power in being able to influence government policy. The MD's concern that the government's policy will damage Y's economy seems to have been ignored by the government.

E's management team in Y also have a specific interest in deciding how to respond to the government's policy.

Other multinational companies in Y – The other multinationals operating in Y will be affected by the government's policy in a similar way that E is. Like E, the other multinationals do not appear to have any power to influence government policy, but they have a high degree of interest in the outcome of that policy.

Specifically, the other multinationals may be interested to see how E responds to the government's policy announcements.

However, it is possible that the multinationals may all join together to lobby the government collectively to reconsider its policies about foreign multinationals in the country. While individual companies only have low power, it is possible that if all the multinationals in Y acted as one they may be able to exert greater power over the government.

Private customers – E's customers in the private education system have an interest in ensuring that they can still obtain the scientific equipment they need. In particular, they will be interested in how their relationship with E will change in the light of the government's policies, not least whether E will continue to operate in Y. However, the customers will have little or no power to influence that decision.

Local businesses in Y – The government's policy requires E to find a local partner and sell 25% of its business in Y to that local partner.

While this does not give the local business any significant power as such, it could present the local partner with a significant opportunity if E decides to stay in Y and work with it. Therefore local businesses are likely to have a high degree of interest in E's decisions.

Low power; low interest

E's shareholders – As a multinational company, E operates in a number of other countries as well as Y. While E's shareholders will be interested in the company's performance as a whole, they are likely to be less interested in the issues affecting business individual countries. The level of interest in Y will be determined by the significance of the turnover and profit generated in Y in relation to the group's results as a whole.

However, in the same way that E's management and the other multinational companies operating in Y appear to have little power to influence government policy, so too E's shareholders are likely only to have relatively low power.

Part (b)

Top tips: There are only 6 marks available here for evaluating the three suggestions, whereas there were up to 16 marks available for part (a) of this question. So, make sure you allocate your time appropriately between the different parts of the question. Nonetheless, there are a number of various issues you could consider here, so try to think of practical issues: for example, how will the circumstances of any sale affect the price E can attain for the business? Note that you are asked to evaluate the suggestions so this means considering both potential advantages and disadvantages. You may well decide that none of the proposals is actually favourable to E, but as you are evaluating the different suggestions try to think which one you think will be least disadvantageous, because this should then be the one you recommend in part (c).

Sell the whole division

Selling price - We do not know how significant the market in Y is to E's business as a whole, but obviously this could have a significant bearing on any decision about selling the whole division operating there.

Aside from this point, if E decides to sell the division now, it is likely that the sale price will be relatively low, reducing the attractiveness of a sale as a strategic option for E.

The worsening global economic situation and the lack of economic growth are likely to have reduced business confidence among potential buyers. This confidence will be further reduced if, as the MD suggests, the government's policy in Y further damages the economy there.

Against this economic backdrop, it is unlikely E would be able to find a buyer who would be prepared to pay the full price for the business.

Resource constraints – Any potential buyer will also need to evaluate their ability to operate the division as a standalone entity. As a multinational company, E has the necessary supply chain and infrastructure to be able to import the equipment it needs to supply different countries. A buyer which operated solely in Y may not have the capacity to do so, making the purchase of E's operating division in Y unattractive to them.

Remain and comply with the government's wishes

There are two elements to the government's proposal: (i) that at least 50% of the workforce must be from the local population, and (ii) that E must sell a proportion of its business to a local partner.

Workforce composition - Many of E's staff are already from the indigenous population, so this element of the proposal should not cause E many problems.

Local partner - However, the enforced sale of 25% of the business to a local partner may be more problematic, particularly as the government can set the sale price. Given the government's hostility to foreign companies, they are likely to set a low price for the sale.

However, E may be prepared to comply with the suggestion if it can find a suitable partner to work with. If E could persuade a consortium of its customers from the private education sector to become its local partner, this could be an acceptable option. The arrangement would satisfy the government's requirement for a local partner, but it would also strengthen E's relationship with the private education suppliers, thereby making it their preferred supplier.

Seek legal advice about resisting the government's proposals

If E challenges the government's proposals, there is a danger that the government, supported by the unions, will retaliate by imposing even harsher sanctions on E.

We do not know what the public perception of multi-national companies is in Y, but it is possible that the public may support the government's stance, so again E may not benefit by resisting the government's proposals.

Moreover, E needs to remember that the government (as the budget holder for the public education system) is one of its major customers.

Therefore if E challenges the government, the government may retaliate by buying its scientific equipment from a different supplier. This will again damage E's profitability, and adversely affect the sales value of the company – either as a whole or for a 25% share. Consequently, resisting the government's proposal is unlikely to be a suitable strategy.

Part (c)

Top tips: Make sure your answer here is consistent with your evaluation in part (b). However, don't simply repeat the evaluation. The verb here is 'recommend' so you must make it clear which one of the three options E should take, and then justify why this is the case.

The evaluation in (b) suggests that complying with the government's wishes is the most appropriate course of action, and so this is the recommended one.

The requirement of having at least 50% of the staff from the local workforce is unlikely to have much impact on E's operations.

Although the requirement to sell 25% of the business will reduce E's profit levels, this is still likely to be preferable to selling the whole division (Option 1) or risking more punitive measures and losing the government as a customer (Option 3).

Moreover, if E can find a local partner which is supportive, it may help generate additional business in Y. In this respect, the idea of partnership with a consortium of the private education establishments is a relatively desirable option.

In this case, if the government – in time - requires a full (100%) transfer of E's assets to a local company, the consortium might take over all of the local business, but continue to import equipment from E. This would mean that even though it no longer owns any asset in the country, E could still make a profit from Y.

5 RGG pesticide manufacturer

Text reference: Corporate social responsibility and stakeholders are covered in Chapter 2 of the BPP Study text.

Marking scheme

			Marks
(a)	SWOT: identify threats and opportunities	Up to 2	
	PEST: identify sources of risk, drivers for change, and opportunities and threats	Up to 2	
		Total up to	4
(b)	Economic responsibilities – up to 2 marks for each relevant point discussed		
	Relevant points include (but are not limited to): maximising shareholder wealth; duty to reverse decline; opportunities for growth.	Up to 6	
	Legal responsibilities – up to 2 marks for each relevant point discussed		
	Relevant points include (but are not limited to): duty to act in best interests of shareholders; accountability to shareholders, but not obliged to consult shareholders; need to change Articles of Associationders; duty to reverse decline	Up to 10	
	Ethical responsibilities – up to 2 marks for each relevant point discussed		
	Relevant points include (but are not limited to): S's personal behaviour complying with CIMA's Code of Ethics; complying with majority wishes of the Board; possibility of irresponsible use of pesticides by customers.	Up to 6	
		Total up to	16
(c)	Definition of stakeholders, or identification of importance of power and interest	1	
	For recommending how to manage relationships with different groups of stakeholders – up to 1 mark for each 'quadrant' in Mendelow's matrix	Up to 4	
		Total up to	5
		Total	25

(a)

Top tips.

Part a. This is a relatively straightforward requirement. The two models the examiner used in his answer were SWOT analysis and PEST analysis – both of which are key strategic models. However, Porter's five forces model would also have been a valid model to use here.

Note that you are only asked about RGG's external environment, so the 'strengths' and 'weaknesses' aspects of SWOT analysis are not relevant here; only 'opportunities' and 'threats'. Equally, don't simply describe the models in generic terms, but make sure you explain how S could *use them* to form an understanding of RGG's external environment.

Two models which S could use to form an understanding of RGG's external environment are **SWOT analysis** and **PEST (or PESTEL) analysis**).

SWOT analysis – A corporate appraisal (SWOT) analyses an organisation's strengths and weaknesses, and the opportunities and threats which are present in its external environment. In order to gain an understanding of RGG's external environment, S needs to focus on these **opportunities** and **threats**.

For example, carrying out a SWOT analysis should highlight that the prospect of **being taken over is a threat** for S, while the prospect of **expanding into countries outside Europe** represents a potential **opportunity** for it.

PEST analysis can also help S to identify the external factors which constitute opportunities or threats to RGG. In this way, PEST analysis can also help identify factors in the external environment which could become triggers for change for RGG.

The PEST acronym stands for:

Political factors – for example, any government regulations on the chemicals which could be used in fertilisers

Economic factors – for example, the rate of economic growth or recession. The reference to economic factors could also reinforce the importance of looking at potential sales of RGG's pesticides in countries outside Europe.

Social factors – for example, social attitudes towards the use of pesticides in farming, compared to organic farming.

Technological factors – for example, new inventions and new product development; for example, environmentally-friendly fertilisers.

Sometimes, these four factors are also supplemented by **E**nvironmental and **L**egal factors, such that PEST becomes PESTEL.

Porter's Five Forces looks at the competitive forces which determine the level of profits that can be sustained by an industry; in RGG's case the pesticide manufacturing industry.

The five competitive forces are:

(i) The threat of new entrants to the industry
(ii) The bargaining power of customers
(iii) The bargaining power of suppliers
(iv) The threat of substitute products
(v) The competitive rivalry between the existing firms in the industry.

By understanding the strength of these forces, S will be able get an understanding of the level of profits which the pesticide manufacturing industry is likely to be able to maintain. Porter's model suggests that the stronger the competitive forces it faces are, the lower the level of profits which an industry will be able to sustain.

(b)

Top tips.

Part (b). To score well in this question it is essential that you link your answer directly back to the scenario. You have not been asked to discuss corporate social responsibility in general terms, but specifically whether the decision to abandon RGG's mission statement is consistent with the basic principles of CSR. As a result, the focus of your answer needs to be on the decision.

Equally, make sure you remember the question is about the CSR implications of RGG abandoning its mission statement, not the CSR implications of producing pesticides. Nonetheless, it appears that one of the aims of the mission statement was to stop pesticides failing into irresponsible hands (where they could be used to harm the ecological environment, or made into weapons.) This highlights the link between the refusal to export and CSR.

As the requirement specifically highlights the three aspects of CSR (economic, legal and ethical responsibilities) you should use these as headings for your answer, and give all three aspects relatively equal weighting in your answer.

Examiner's comments. Part (b) was not well answered. Although most candidates discussed RGG's economic responsibility to its shareholders reasonably well, their discussions of legal and ethical implications of abandoning the mission statement were much weaker. Most candidates incorrectly focused on the general ethical and legal implications of selling pesticides in general, rather than on the specific legal and ethical issues relating to RGG abandoning its mission statement.

Corporate Social Responsibility – Corporate Social Responsibility (CSR) represents an organisation's obligation to maximise positive stakeholder benefits whilst minimising the negative effects of its actions.

By identifying the importance of economic, legal and ethical issues, CSR highlights the range of stakeholders who have an interest in an organisation. Equally, RGG needs to consider these three different aspects when deciding if the decision to abandon its mission statement is consistent with CSR.

Economic responsibilities

Maximising shareholder wealth – RGG's primary economic responsibility is to maximise the wealth it generates for its shareholders; and it appears that this is a key consideration in S's proposal.

Current economic position – In recent years, RGG has experienced a decline in its profits, and it made a loss of £1 million in the last financial year. RGG's share price has also fallen as a result. Given RGG's responsibility to maximise the wealth it generates for its shareholders, it should therefore seriously consider any proposals which would allow it to boost its profits and thereby reverse the current decline.

Business expansion – S's proposal appears designed to help RGG boost its profits. By restricting its business to countries within Europe, RGG is unable to benefit from any growth which could be achieved by expanding into markets outside Europe.

If S's belief that RGG could generate a substantial amount of business from markets outside Europe is correct, then RGG's economic performance, and the wealth it generates for its shareholders, should also improve substantially as a result of such an expansion. Therefore, from an economic perspective, the proposal to abandon the mission statement is socially responsible.

Legal responsibilities

Although the notion of social responsibility implies more than simply 'acting lawfully', a socially responsible company needs to ensure it complies with its legal responsibilities and does not act illegally.

Duty to shareholders – The Board of Directors at RGG have a legal duty to act in the best interests of the owners of the company: the shareholders.

However, there appears to be some disagreement among the Directors about what the shareholders want, or what would serve their best interests. S clearly believes that abandoning the mission statement would be in the shareholders' best interests because it would enable RGG to expand and thereby hopefully increases its profits.

By contrast, one of the non-executives argues that the shareholders value the fact that RGG only sells its pesticides to European countries.

Legal obligations – In theory, RGG could ask its shareholders to vote on whether they want to retain the mission statement or not. However, the Board is not legally obliged to consult with the shareholders on such a decision. Equally, RGG is not legally obliged to have a mission statement, so it would not be acting illegally by abandoning the statement.

Accountability and authority – The Board of directors has been appointed by the shareholders to manage RGG on their behalf. Consequently, while the Board remains accountable to the shareholders it also has the authority to make decisions about the management of the company. Therefore, provided that any decision about the mission statement is properly discussed by the Board, and agreed by it, then the decision is consistent with corporate social responsibility, particularly given the potential economic benefits it could bring.

Ultimately, however, if the shareholders do not believe that the Board is acting in their best interests then they can vote not to re-elect the Board, and they even have the right to replace it.

Articles of Association – In effect, RGG's mission statement is reinforcing its Articles of Association which also restrict its operations to countries within Europe. Therefore, while the Board would be acting legally if it abandoned the mission statement *per se*, any decision to start trading outside Europe would not be legal unless the Articles were amended first to permit such an expansion.

Ethical responsibilities

Ethical principles – It is important that the Directors comply with ethical principles in relation to the proposal. For example, the principle of **objectivity** dictates that S should make the proposal because it is in the best interests of the company, rather than because it serves some personal interest or bias of his own.

However, it does not appear that a proposal designed to increase sales and therefore boost profits will conflict with any fundamental ethical principles, and so from this perspective it is ethical.

Safeguarding jobs – Equally, the proposal seems ethical because the subsequent expansion it could enable should help improve job security for RGG's staff. The finance director believes RGG in its current format is vulnerable to a take-over, which would leave at least some of the 1,505 staff at risk of redundancy.

However, if RGG is able to expand outside Europe and its performance improves, this should provide greater job security for its employees.

Lack of consultation – However, there is potentially an ethical issue in abandoning the mission statement without consulting RGG's shareholders, even though there isn't a legal responsibility to do so.

We have already noted that RGG's Board has a duty to act in the best interests of the shareholders. However, if the majority of the shareholders do still like the idea of restricted sales, as the non-executive director has suggested, then abandoning the mission statement and the attendant restriction would not reflect the shareholder wishes.

It seems that nobody knows that the shareholders want. Therefore, abandoning the mission statement without first establishing what they *do* want, would not be socially responsible behaviour.

Reasons for restriction – In this respect, it may also not be socially responsible for RGG to abandon the statement without first understanding why the restrictions were introduced in the first place. For example, there could be concerns that the pesticides might be misused in some countries, or even that they could be used in making chemical weapons. If RGG's name becomes associated with that misuse, such an association could be very damaging for the company's brand and reputation.

Equally, however, if there is a danger that RGG's pesticides will be misused in some countries outside Europe, then to the extent that abandoning the mission statement means that the pesticides could now be sold to those countries, the proposal to abandon the statement would not be socially responsible.

(c)

Top tips.

Part (c). Like part (a), this should have been a relatively straightforward requirement. However, note that the requirement asked you to 'recommend the *strategies RGG could adopt* to manage its relationships with different types of stakeholders' rather than simply to describe Mendelow's matrix and the different types of stakeholder groups it identifies. For example, instead of simply identifying stakeholders with high interest and high power as key players, you need to recommend ways that RGG can ensure that any proposals it makes are acceptable to these stakeholders.

Power and interest – Mendelow's matrix suggests that RGG should assess the relative levels of power and interest that different stakeholder groups hold in relation to the proposal to abandon the mission statement, and this should then help RGG identify which stakeholder groups are the most important for it to manage.

High power; high interest

Key players – RGG needs to ensure that its key stakeholder groups **support the suggestion**, or at least that the suggestion is **acceptable to them**. Because they hold a high level of power and are likely to use it, this group of stakeholders could thwart the proposal if they opposed it. Therefore, it will be important for RGG to **take the views of any key stakeholder groups into account** before deciding whether or not to proceed with the proposal.

High power; low interest

Keep satisfied – RGG will need to **treat these stakeholders with caution**, because while their low interest means they are currently like to be passive, their high power means they are **capable of becoming key players** if they become concerned about the proposal. One way of keeping these stakeholders satisfied would be to explain what the benefits of the proposal will be well in advance of any decision being made about whether to abandon the mission statement or not.

Low power; high interest

Keep informed – Although stakeholders in this category have a high level of interest in the suggestion, their low level of power means they will have little ability to influence the decision as to whether or not to abandon the mission statement. Consequently, Mendelow's model suggests it should be sufficient for RGG to keep these stakeholders informed about the decisions it makes in order to satisfy their interest in the suggestion.

However, if RGG decides it wants to implement the suggestion, it should also try to persuade these stakeholders about the merits of the proposal, to avoid the risk that any who oppose it will try to activate stakeholders who currently have high power but low interest and encourage them to oppose the suggestion.

Low power; low interest

Minimal effort – Because stakeholders in this group have a low level of interest, and would only have a limited ability to influence the decision even if they took an interest it, RGG should spend very little effort managing its relationships with them. This should then leave it with more time to manage its relationships with the stakeholders who are more strategically important.

6 WRL gold mining company

Text reference. Stakeholders and stakeholder management are discussed in Chapter 2 of your BPP Study Text.

Marking scheme

			Marks
(a) (i)	Each stakeholder correctly identified and categorised, with their power and interest explained. (Only three stakeholder groups should have been included.)	Up to 3	
		Total up to	9
(ii)	Each appropriate action recommended	Up to 2	
		Total up to	7
(b)	For each valid point about why the mission statement is consistent with the plan	Up to 2	
	For each valid point about why the mission statement is inconsistent with the plan	Up to 2	
	Conclusion	2	
		Total up to	9
		Total	25

Part (a)

Top tips: This should have been a relatively straightforward question, in which you identified and categorised the stakeholder groups mentioned in the scenario and then categorised their levels of power and interest.

Note that you are only required to categorise **three** stakeholder groups. However, there are seven stakeholder groups identified in, or inferred by, the case study: (i) the Board of WEL; (ii) local people; (iii) employees working in the mine; (iv) shareholders in general; (v) the minority shareholders who oppose the decision; (vi) the Eastern state government; and (vii) the Stravia national government.

For tutorial purposes, all seven have been categorised here, and their interest and power explained. However, **you should only have included three in your answer**.

Note also that the question asks about stakeholders' power and interests specifically in relation to the decision about the disposal of the water, not about WRL's operations in general. Make sure your answers relate specifically to the decision. And, make sure you only consider stakeholders identified in the scenario; do not introduce additional stakeholder groups of your own.

Examiner's comments: This question was generally well answered. Nevertheless, some candidates still provided only a general discussion of the stakeholder groups instead of focusing their levels of power and interest. And the main weakness of this answer was that some candidates introduced stakeholders that were not identified in the scenario, and for which they earned no marks.

(i)

High interest; High power

1. **Board of WRL:** If WRL is not allowed to dispose its water in the lake, its mining operations in Stravia would become uneconomic and the mine would have to close.

   The Board's **interest** is therefore high, because the decision is crucial to WRL's continued operation in Stravia.

   As the Board makes the decision about where to dispose of the water (and is given free rein in this decision by the licence) its **power** is also high.

2. **Stravian national government:** The licence fee which WRL pays the government ($50 m in 20X9) represents a significant amount of income for the government.

   Given the government's desire to develop its economy, and the role it sees for gold mining in this development, the national government has a high **interest** in the outcome of the decision.

   Power: The government granted WRL its licence to mine for gold, which shows the government has a degree of power over WRL's operations. The government's licencing power means it is also likely to have the power to revoke the licence if it is unhappy with the way WRL is operating (for example, if the government feels the environmental cost of disposing the polluted water in the lake outweighs the economic benefits of WRL's operations in Stravia.

3. High interest; Low power

   Employees working in the mine: WRL's mine is in a very remote area, so if it were to close there are likely to be very few alternative job opportunities for the local people currently working for WRL. Therefore they have a high **interest** in the continued operation of WRL's mine.

   However, the local employees are only likely to have low **power** over the decision because it is unlikely that they have senior or high-profit jobs within WRL. Equally, it is unlikely they will have any significant influence over the governments (either the Eastern state government or the national government).

Alternative stakeholder groups you could have included:

High interest; Low power

Local people: The local people are likely to be interested for two reasons: first, the mine offers jobs for local people; but second, disposing the polluted water in the lake will have a long-lasing adverse effect on the lake and the surrounding area. This second factor could be a particular concern if the people use the lake as a source of drinking water or for catching fish for food.

These two reasons together mean that the local people could have a **conflict of interests** about the decision, although their level of interest in it is likely to be high. Nonetheless, they are likely to only have low **power** over the decision because they are unlikely to be able to exert any influence over the government or WRL.

Eastern state government: The state government's **interest** is such that it took legal action against WRL to try to prevent the polluted water being disposed of in the lake.

However, the local government's decision has been over-ruled by the National Supreme Court, suggesting that ultimately the local government only has relatively low **power**.

Minority shareholders: A small number of shareholders feel sufficiently concerned about the impact of the polluted water on the lake that they would rather close the mine than pollute the lake. In this respect, they have a high **interest** in the decision.

However, the fact that their number is only a small minority of shareholders means they will have little **power** to affect any decisions.

<u>Low interest; High power</u>

There are no stakeholder groups in this category

<u>Low interest; Low power</u>

<u>WRL's shareholders</u>: WRL is a multi-national company which exists to make the maximum profit for its shareholders. Although the shareholder's level of interest will be influenced by the contribution the Stravian mine makes to WRL's profits overall, it is likely that Stravia is just one among many countries in which WRL operates, and so the shareholders' **interest** in decisions affecting any one specific mine are likely to be low.

The shareholders could exert significant power if they all joined together and voted to force WRL to stop polluting the lake. However, this seems very unlikely as the shareholders are likely to be more interested in the profits from the mine. Consequently, if they are not willing to act collectively to vote against the pollution, their **power** to influence the decision can be categorised as low.

(ii)

Tutorial note: In (a) (i) we have organised stakeholders in relation to the four quadrants in Mendelow's matrix.

The requirement for (a) (ii) asks for advice about WRL's Board should deal with stakeholders, so Mendelow's matrix is again a good framework here because it provides suggestions for how to deal with stakeholders with different power and interests.

However, note three points:

- There is no indication in the requirement that you should only look at the three stakeholder groups you categorised in (a) (i); instead, you should look at how the Board should aim to deal with conflicting interests across all stakeholder groups
- You are advising the Board of WRL (not the government)
- You should try to make your advice specific to the scenario, and not let it become generic advice based on Mendelow's matrix (eg: don't just say: 'Make the strategy acceptable to them'. This will **not** be sufficient to earn a good proportion of the 7 marks available here).

Examiner's comments: This question was not well answered, because many candidates focussed (incorrectly) on how WRL could overcome the pollution problem, rather than how it could deal with conflicting stakeholder objectives. Candidates must make sure they read the question requirements carefully to avoid mistakes such as this.

<u>High interest; high power</u>

(Stravian national government)

Because the national government has both high interest in the decision and high power over it, it is a key player. Therefore, WRL needs to make sure its **actions and strategy are acceptable** to the government.

However, as the government views gold mining as an important way of developing the economy, and it has given WRL the licence to dispose of waste water wherever is convenient, it seems likely that a strategy based on economic benefits rather than environmental costs will be acceptable to the government. Therefore, there doesn't appear any reason that WRL will need to change its plans to make them acceptable to the government.

<u>High interest; low power</u>

(Local employees working in the mines; Local people; Eastern state government; Minority shareholders)

Although these groups have a high interest in the decision, they only have relatively low power to influence it. Therefore, the Board should make sure these groups are **kept informed** about its plans, but it does not need to be concerned with making sure its plans are acceptable to them. Their lack of power makes it difficult for these groups to disrupt WRL's plans.

<u>Low interest; low power</u>

(*Shareholders in general*)

As this group only has a low interest in the decision, as well as low power over it, the Board should only spend minimal effort considering the shareholders' position in respect of the decision.

Mission statement – As well as categorising the stakeholders according to their power and interest, the Board should also try to relate the stakeholders' objectives to its own mission statement, and ensure that it acts in the way that best follows its mission statement.

In this respect, WRL's primary objective is to make the maximum possible profit for its shareholders. Although WRL has also expressed an aim to minimise the damage it causes to the environment, this is likely to be a secondary objective behind the need to be profitable. The Board's dealings with the different stakeholder groups should reflect this prioritisation.

Part (b)

Top tips: This is another question which requires a high level of application rather than simply a demonstration of knowledge. You were not asked to discuss the role of mission statements in developing a strategic plan, or to discuss the merits of having a mission statement. Instead you should have identified, and discussed, those areas of the plan to pollute the lake which were consistent with the mission statement identified in the scenario, and those areas of it which were not consistent.

Examiner's comments: Most candidates correctly realised that putting the polluted water in the lake was not consistent with parts of the mission statement. However, far fewer candidates went on to discuss that, if WRL did not pollute the lake, this would conflict with the intention to maximise profit.

WRL's mission statement highlights both the economic and environmental aspects of mining, and the potential conflict between profit and pollution which it is facing in relation to its operations in Stravia.

Areas of consistency with the plan:

"Make the maximum possible profit for its shareholders" – The mine has **operated profitably** since it began. However, if WRL were not able to dispose of the polluted water in the lake, it would become uneconomic and would **have to close**. So to the extent that the plan enables WRL to continue with a profitable operation, it is consistent with the mission statement.

"WRL will... be a good corporate citizen" – In line with the condition in its mining licence, WRL **employs local people** wherever possible and so brings jobs and incomes to the local economy.

WRL has generated a significant amount of foreign exchange for Stravia's economy, and mining is playing an important part in developing the economy. So, in this respect, WRL has been acting as a good corporate citizen - but WRL would no longer be able to make its positive contribution to Stravia's economy if it had to close the mine because it had become uneconomic.

Moreover, WRL is **acting lawfully** in accordance with its licence, which is why the National Supreme Court upheld its right to dispose of the polluted water in the lake. Again, by acting lawfully, WRL is being a good corporate citizen.

Areas of inconsistency with the plan

"Causing the least damage to the environment" – The decision to dispose the polluted water in the lake has been taken because this is the **cheapest option** not the one which causes the least environmental damage.

"WRL will, at all times, be a good corporate citizen" – Disposing of the polluted water in the lake will kill all the aquatic life in the lake, and have a long-lasting adverse effect on the lake and the surrounding area. In this respect, the decision does not portray WRL as a good corporate citizen.

It could also be argued that acting against the wishes of the local state government and proceeding with the plan is also not the behaviour of a good corporate citizen.

Stakeholder wishes – The mission statement focuses on achieving profit for shareholders and suggests shareholders' interests are solely economic. However, there are a minority of shareholders who would rather close the mine than pollute the lake. So, if WRL proceeds with the plan it will be acting against the interests of these shareholders.

Extent of consistency

WRL's decision to dispose of the polluted water in the lake is consistent with the economic aspects of the mission statement (to maximise profit) but it is not consistent with some aspects of being a good corporate citizen or with minimising damage to the environment.

However, part of the problem here is that there appears to be a degree of incompatibility in the mission statement. WRL seems faced with a choice of *either* maximising profits *or* causing the least damage to the environment. It cannot do both, although the mission statement seems to suggest it should try to.

7 LAS corporate headquarters

Text references: A brief recap of stakeholder analysis is given in the introductory chapter at the start of the Study Text. Mission statements and stakeholder management are covered in Chapter 2 of the Study Text. The role of change agents is covered in Chapter 12. Business ethics is covered in Chapter 2, while directors' responsibilities are covered in Chapter 1.

Top tips:

Be careful not to spend too long on part (a) (i): it is only worth 2 marks. The reference to 'interest' in 'other *interested* parties' should have given you the hint that this question wanted you to identify 'other stakeholders.' However, given the mark limit, you should have simply identified – in general terms – what stakeholders are, and then identified some stakeholders for LAS. You shouldn't have spent time discussing any specific stakeholder groups in any detail here.

Similarly, part (a) (ii) is only worth 4 marks, so don't spend too long discuss Mendelow's matrix in general terms. The key point here is how LAS can use the ideas of power and interest to classify different stakeholder groups and rank their needs (based on their relative levels of power and interest). Importantly though, note that the requirement refers to LAS classifying different stakeholder groups, so you should refer specifically to LAS's stakeholders, rather than only providing a generic discussion Mendelow's matrix.

In part (b), did you note that there are effectively two parts to the requirement: (i) Discuss the purpose of a mission statement? (ii) Discuss the advantages to LAS of having a mission statement? The first part is a more general discussion, but the second part should be linked specifically to LAS (for example, responding to the fact that the nature of LAS's business has changed radically since it was established 'to trade in Empire commodities').

For part (c), although the requirement refers to LAS's move to London, there is relatively little detail in the question which you can use as a framework for your answer. Consequently, one approach would be to think what the role of a change agent is (in general terms) and think how elements of that role could be useful in relocating LAS's headquarters. To score well, you need to focus your answer clearly on the benefits to LAS of using a change agent. Answers which focus on the activities a change agent undertakes, or the skills a change agent requires, in general terms will score few marks.

Part (d): The idea of stakeholders (from part (a)) could have given you some hints about the potential issue in part (d). On the one hand, the directors have a duty to the company's shareholders, but they also have to treat other stakeholders (eg employees) fairly. However, just because a decision may have adverse consequences for one group of stakeholders, does that make it unethical? Has it breached any of the fundamental principles of CIMA's Code of Ethics?

Notice that the verb requirement here is 'advise' so you need to give some clear advice at the end of your answer as to whether or not you think the suggestion is a breach of CIMA's Code.

Once again, though, you should not spend time simply describing the Code, or listing elements from it in detail. A maximum of two (out of 8) marks in this question were available for describing the principles of the Code in general terms.

The key to scoring well in this question was applying the Code to the scenario in order to provide the advice required.

(a) (i)

Stakeholders – The other parties with an interest in LAS's annual report will be its other stakeholders (in addition to its shareholders.)

Stakeholders are groups or individuals who have an interest in an organisation's strategy. Shareholders are one stakeholder group, but other stakeholder groups are likely to include: customers, employees and management, suppliers, local communities, interest and pressure groups.

(ii)

Analysis of interest and power – Mendelow's matrix encourages an organisation to look at the level of interest different stakeholder groups have in its strategy and the amount of power they could have to influence it.

LAS could use the matrix to classify the different stakeholder groups in terms of their interest and power, and this classification could then be used to rank their needs:

Key players – Key players will be those who have a **high degree of interest** in LAS's strategy, and **high power** to influence it. Stakeholders in this group will be most important ones to LAS, and any strategy it adopts must at least be acceptable to them.

High power; low interest – These are the second most important group. While they have a low interest at the moment, they are capable of becoming key players if their interest in the organisation increases.

Low power; high interest – Although these groups of stakeholders (often including employees) have important views, they have little ability to influence strategy and so their needs can be treated as lower priority.

Low power; low interest – Stakeholders with low power and low interest are the least important group of stakeholders so LAS should give **minimal effort** towards meeting their needs.

(b)

Purpose – A mission statement conveys an organisation's fundamental objectives. Although there isn't a standard format that mission statements have to follow, they can highlight the **purpose** of an organisation; what its **values** are; what the **commercial logic** and nature of its business is; and the policies and **standards of behaviour** that underpin the way it does business.

Advantages

Analyse purpose and values – LAS's stated purpose when it was founded was 'to trade in Empire commodities.' However, this is no longer relevant, since LAS in now an international property company.

In order to prepare a mission statement, LAS would need to analyse what it believes the key purpose and values of the company currently are, and this analysis could be helpful for LAS's strategic planning (for example, it may suggest new strategic options.)

Communication to external stakeholders – The mission statement will help communicate LAS's identity and purpose to the different countries and markets in which it does business. Understanding its values and beliefs could help potential customers decide whether to choose LAS to manage their property business in preference to competitors.

Motivation for staff – If the mission statement is published throughout the company so that all the staff are aware of it, this could help motivate the staff by making them feel their work is significant and is contributing to the corporate values.

(c)

Relocating LAS's headquarters from Asia to London could be a significant change for LAS. However, for it to be effective and benefit LAS, it needs to be effectively implemented.

Facilitating change – A change agent is an individual (or group) who helps to bring about strategic change in an organisation. If LAS uses a change agent to help in the move, this means that there is someone focused specifically on the successful implementation of the move. In effect, the change agent can act as an intermediary between the **change sponsor** (most likely, the Board) and the staff responsible for actually implementing the move (the **change implementers**).

Experience – Although the change agent could be appointed from LAS, it seems more likely that LAS will appoint an external consultant to act as their change agent. This should mean that they have **experience from facilitating similar changes** in the past, which LAS's management team may not otherwise have. Moreover, the agent will take responsibility for **facilitating the change** thereby leaving LAS's management team to remain focused on other business and strategic issues.

However, it is important the **Board doesn't devolve too much responsibility for the move to the change agent**. The change agent may have little direct authority over the change implementers (particularly LAS's managers) and so the move's effectiveness could depend on how well the Board and the agent work together, along with the people actually implementing it.

Change agent's role –The change agent's exact role will depend on the brief they are given by LAS. However, elements of it may include:

- Defining any problems associated aspects of the move
- Examining what causes these problems and considering how the factors causing the problems can be overcome
- Suggesting possible solutions for the problems
- Selecting a solution from those suggested, and implementing it
- Gaining support from all involved in the move to help overcome problems and implement solutions

In more general terms, a change agent could be very helpful in providing advice and information for LAS throughout the moving process.

Dealing with emergent issues – Although LAS's senior management and the change agent are likely to have planned out the move in advance, it is important to recognise that (because change processes are dynamic) there may need to be adaptations to the original plans when the move is actually implemented. The change agent can play a key role in managing this balance between planned change and uncontrolled, emergent change.

(d)

Code of Ethics – CIMA's Code of Ethics highlights five fundamental principles dealing with **integrity; objectivity; professional competence and due care; confidentiality; and professional behaviour**. The Finance Director's suggestion will only constitute a breach of CIMA's Code if it contravenes one of these principles.

Although the decision to move the headquarters was made by the Board of LAS as a whole, the Finance Director must take some responsibility for it: partly because he made the original decision, and partly because, as a member of the Board, he shares in the collective responsibility of the Board.

Redundancies – The relocation of LAS's headquarters to London will mean that 80 employees in Asia lose their jobs, and they are unlikely to be able find replacement jobs. Consequently, the decision to relocate is likely to have an adverse impact on these 80 employees. However, the fact that people are being made redundant does not necessarily make the decision to move LAS's headquarters unethical. Sometimes difficult decisions have to be made in the best interests of an organisation.

Fiduciary responsibility – The Directors are obliged to act in a way which is most likely to promote the success of the company for the benefit of its shareholders. In this case, it appears that there are genuine business reasons to relocated to London: for example, finance can be arranged more cheaply, and some of LAS's transactions costs would be lower.

Given this, it seems that the Finance Director is simply carrying out his fiduciary duty to the shareholders by suggesting the relocation to London.

Objective decision - There is no indication that the director has been forced to suggest London as an alternative site for the headquarters, nor that he has any self-interest in doing so. Given that LAS's business is spread relatively thinly across 28 different countries, there is no apparent reason why a location in any of those countries would necessarily be more suitable for the headquarters than London.

Therefore, the decision to move to London appears to be made for objective business reasons: driven by lower financing costs.

Advice

Consequently, although the suggestion will have adverse consequences for the 80 employees who will lose their jobs, the suggestion does not appear to constitute a breach of CIMA's Code of Ethics.

Nonetheless, the Directors need to ensure that when the relocation does occur, the employees who are losing their jobs are treated fairly and in accordance with legal requirements; for example, in relation to the notice periods they are granted and the level of redundancy pay they receive.

8 NNN Transport company

Text reference: Ethical principles and CIMA's ethical code are discussed in Chapter 2 of the BPP Study Text for E3.

Top tips.

In Part (a) you were asked to recommend the changes required for NNN plc to meet three conditions: have an unqualified audit report; make a profit; and not be engaged in any criminal activities.

The scenario clearly identifies a number of problems in NNN's current practices. So a useful approach to this question would be to assess how the current problems would prevent NNN from meeting the conditions, and therefore what needs to be done in order that NNN *can* meet the conditions.

However, remember, that E3 is a business strategy paper, not an accounting or auditing paper. Therefore, although the first set of recommendations you are for must focus on accountancy related changes, you should not spend time discussing, in detail, specific accounting controls NNN could introduce into its cash and revenue accounting procedures.

It is equally important that you consider performance related changes and organisational related changes, because these are likely to have a significant impact on NNN's ability to make a profit, and to improve the processes and culture within the organisation. For example, the scenario identifies that NNN plc does not have an internal audit department or an internal security department, so two of the organisational changes it could make could be to introduce these departments.

(a)

WGG plans to sell NNN in two years' time, and so any changes will need to be implemented quickly. The scale of the changes required, in conjunction with the speed of the changes required, suggests that a turnaround strategy is necessary.

Accountancy related changes

Issues highlighted by auditors – As well as their overall concern about NNN's ability to continue in business, the auditors were specifically concerned about the controls over NNN's accounting for revenue and cash, and the inaccuracies in its forecasting.

As NNN needs to have an unqualified audit report at the end of 20X3, it would be advised to address the auditor's areas of concern as a matter of priority. NNN's finance director should also discuss the specific issues of concern with the auditors and confirm the improvements they will expect to see before they are prepared to issue an unqualified audit report.

Given the urgent and time-bound nature of the changes, NNN's management team may need to recruit some external consultants to help them improve the company's systems and controls. If the audit firm has a consultancy division, NNN might be able to use some of these consultants to achieve this.

Accounting system and procedures – There appear to be major concerns around the completeness of NNN's recorded revenues and its cash figures. Given the likely importance of both of these figures in the accounts, NNN will have to review it accounting systems and procedures to ensure that revenue and cash are both accurately accounted for.

It is not clear if NNN's systems are adequate but they are not being properly operated by staff, or whether the systems and controls themselves are flawed. For example, NNN needs to establish why the discrepancies in cash are arising, in order that it can make the necessary improvements to cash control. If the systems themselves are inadequate, NNN needs to introduce more robust systems and controls in order to prevent a cash shortfall from recurring. For example, NNN needs to review the physical security over cash handling to try to ensure that no cash if being stolen.

Forecasting and budgets – NNN's profit forecasts were very inaccurate, and a number of stakeholders (such as investors and suppliers) are likely to have serious concerns that a forecast £5 million profit for 20X1 actually became a £5 million loss. The inaccuracy of the forecasts also reflects poorly on management's control of the business.

It is not clear how reliable NNN's forecasts have been in the past, but NNN needs to understand the reasons for the shortfall in profit in 20X1. £2 million can be explained by the fine imposed on the company, but this still leaves £8 million unexplained.

In particular, NNN needs to establish whether its forecasting process is flawed (and its forecasts were unrealistically optimistic) ; whether the forecasts were reasonable and the shortfall was due to problems with actual performance; or whether the shortfall was due to a combination of issues in both forecasting and actual performance.

If it emerges that the problems were due to unreliable forecasts, then NNN will need to review its methodologies and assumptions. It the shortfall is due to problems in actual performance, the causes of these will need to be identified and addressed as part of the performance related changes.

Performance related changes

Operational efficiency – By the time NNN is sold in two years' time, it needs to be making a profit.

Even after adjusting for the £2 million fine it suffered, it still made a loss of £3 million in 20X1.

It seems likely that this loss has come as a direct result of operational inefficiencies arising from NNN's lack of investment. Therefore NNN will need to improve its operational efficiency if it is going to become profitable again.

Investment – Given that the lack of investment in vehicles, buildings and human resources appears to be the main cause of NNN's declining operational performance and competitiveness, it seems to be crucial that NNN addressed this lack of investment.

It would seem sensible that NNN prepares a capital budget, and then ensures individual investment proposals undergo an appropriate investment appraisal – for example, a net present value calculation – before they are authorised.

Performance targets – It is also important that NNN monitors how the competitiveness of key operational indicators improves once any operational improvements have been made. In this respect, NNN needs to regularly monitor key performance indicators (such as unit costs per mile) , and it possible it should also benchmark its performance against key competitors.

Organisational related changes

Recruitment processes – The trial judge and the auditors both seem to have concerns about the prospect of criminality within NNN, and failures in the recruitment process appear to have contributed to this; for example, through the failure to carry out background checks on employees or to take up employees' references.

Therefore, NNN needs to examine its recruitment processes (or, if the processes are appropriate, to check they are being properly applied) to ensure that the staff it employs are suitable, and to minimise the risk of any future criminal activities being carried out by any of them.

Recruitment consultants – NNN should consider using recruitment consultants to help source staff. The recruitment consultants should carry out background checks on potential candidates before they are recommended to NNN.

Internal security department – The auditors identified substantial discrepancies in NNN's cash figures, and a shortfall of up to £1 million. This suggests that NNN holds significant amounts of cash, and therefore it needs to safeguard this cash.

NNN could establish an internal security department to monitor cash handling activities and investigate any discrepancies. NNN should also consider using physical security methods to help reduce cash losses: for example, installing safes and closed circuit television in areas where cash is handled, or carrying out random searches on employees who handle cash to check they haven't stolen any.

Internal audit department – NNN does not currently have an internal audit department. However, it is likely that an internal audit department would already have highlighted the problems around revenue, cash and recruitment processes raised by the external auditors, and given NNN the chance to start addressing them.

Therefore, NNN should establish an internal audit department to check that the company's processes and procedures are fit for purpose, and that they are being implemented properly.

In addition to the specific activities carried out by the internal audit and security departments, NNN's senior managers should also consider ways of making the overall culture at NNN into a more honest and ethical one. The introduction of an ethical code (as requested by WGG) should help in this respect.

(b)

Top tips

Part (b): The requirement specifically asked you to recommend THREE principles that should be contained within an ethical code.

It seems sensible to draw on CIMA's Code of Ethics as a framework for your answer here as far as possible. However, you also need to apply your answer to NNN plc, rather than just discussing principles from the Code in general terms. Equally, remember that the principles in the Code are designed for use by professional accountants, rather than a transport company as a whole. Not all of the principles from CIMA's Code will be relevant here (eg Professional Competence and Due Care.) So you need to be selective about which principles you select here to ensure they are specifically relevant to the scenario and the question.

Equally, you need to remember than CIMA's Code of Ethics is not the only source of ethical principles. For example, you could also have considered more general ethical principles such as honesty and fairness.

We have included some additional principles in the text boxes below our answer to indicate that there are more than three possible valid principles you could have recommended here. Provided you recommended a relevant principle, and gave reasons to support your recommendation, you would earn marks for it.

Integrity – The principle of integrity suggests that NNN plc needs to be straightforward and honest in all its professional and business relationships. Integrity also implies fair dealing and truthfulness.

One of the issues associated with integrity is that NNN plc should ensure that its forecasts are reliable. Investors look at the forecasts as estimates of how well the business is performing, but it would seem that these forecasts have been somewhat misleading for the last year, and have significantly over-stated performance expectations.

Confidentiality – It is important that NNN plc's staff and management do not disclose any confidential information about the business, its business relationships or its performance unless they have a right or duty to disclose that information.

For example, personal details about NNN's staff should be kept confidential. However, if a member of staff suspects that a colleague is engaging in people smuggling or another criminal activity, they should report their concerns to an appropriate person.

Legality – Although 'behaving ethically' means more than simply acting legally, it is nevertheless important that NNN and its staff comply with the law in all their activities. In effect, if acting legally is a pre-requisite for acting ethically, and NNN doesn't act legally it certainly won't be acting ethically.

The substantial fine NNN has recently received highlights the cost of acting illegally, notwithstanding the damage to NNN's reputation which would have resulted from the trial.

Equal opportunities – Again, this is as much a legal requirement as an ethical principle, but NNN should treat all people equally; for example, by not unfairly discriminating against potential employees on the grounds of age or gender.

Objectivity – The staff and management at NNN plc should not allow bias, conflicts of interest or the undue influence of others to compromise their professional or business judgement.

Sustainability - Although NNN is under pressure to turn around its performance within two years, it should try to implement strategies that will contribute to the business' long-term success, rather than focusing solely on short-term profitability.

Environmental impact – This looks at one specific dimension of sustainability. NNN should try to ensure that it minimises any detrimental impact that its operations have on the natural world, for example, by reducing carbon emissions from its vehicles.

9 JJJ electrical manufacturer

Text reference. Business ethics are discussed in Chapter 2 of your BPP Study Text. Stakeholder management is also consider in Chapter 2.

(a)

Top tips.

The question requirement specifically refers to the 'four aspects' of JJJ's ethical business policy, so you need to refer to all four aspects in your answer. A sensible way to do this will be to use each of the aspects as a heading in your answer, and then work through them in turn.

Also note the requirement deals specifically with whether the aspects of the policy will cause concerns for the *shareholders*... not a more general discussion about the benefits of limitations of the policy.

The reference to shareholders should have alerted you that, in effect, this question is exploring the potential conflict between JJJ's ethical policies and its ability to generate wealth for its shareholders (by generating dividends and increases in share price.) To what extent will the ethical policies hinder JJJ's ability to generate wealth for its shareholders?

All of JJJ's products are sourced and made exclusively within Q

Cheaper suppliers – JJJ's chief buyer has identified several suppliers in country K who could supply components at a price which is 40% lower than that JJJ pays to its current, domestic suppliers.

If JJJ continues to source all the components for its products domestically, its **costs will be higher** than if it sourced them from the suppliers in K. In turn, if this means that JJJ's profits are lower than they would be if it used components imported from K. It could also mean that JJJ might lose sales, if customers choose to buy cheaper imported rival products instead of JJJ's. Therefore, this aspect of the ethical business policy could concerns for JJJ's shareholders, because it conflicts with the aim of maximising shareholder wealth.

Customer preference – However, market research has also shown that JJJ's customers value its ethical business policy. This means that JJJ's customers may be prepared to pay more for its products, on account of its ethical business policy. Although it is unlikely that the extra amount that customers are prepared to pay will cover the 40% difference in cost, JJJ should consider its customers' attitudes before making any change to the policy. For example, if there is a danger that customers will stop buying JJJ's products if it discontinues its ethical business policy, then such a change will also concern the shareholders because it will again conflict with the aim of maximising shareholder wealth.

JJJ sells all its output within Q

Restricting growth – Although JJJ's share of the market has been reduced in the face of competition from imported products, this aspect of the ethical business policy prevents JJJ from trying to replace any losses of revenue by expanding into foreign markets. In this respect, if the policy prevents growth – or even JJJ's ability to maintain its existing revenues – then it could cause concern because, again, it conflicts the aim of maximising shareholder wealth.

Conversely, the policy could **reduce risk**, by avoiding exposure to the risk of trade.

Exporting and Fair Trade – If JJJ were to start exporting to developing economies, a Fair Trade policy might imply that it should sell its exports to those economies at more favourable terms than those which it would offer to developed countries.

In this respect, the combination of exporting to developing economies and a Fair Trade policy could again conflict with the idea of shareholder wealth maximization.

Employees' working conditions and adherence to legislative requirements

Adherence to legislative requirements – The element of the policy which states that JJJ adheres to all legislative requirements should not cause any concerns for the shareholders.

JJJ, like all other companies operating within Q, has to comply with all relevant laws, and therefore JJJ's competitiveness shouldn't suffer as a result of complying with the law. Equally importantly, if JJJ doesn't adhere to legislative requirements it could be fined, or may even be preventing from operating – both of which outcomes would be detrimental to the aim of maximising shareholders' wealth.

Nonetheless, adhering to the law could still leave JJJ exposed to international competitors who practice 'social dumping,' by selling products from countries which do not have equivalent labour protection laws.

High regard to employees' working conditions – It is not clear how far the 'high regard' which JJJ gives to employees' working conditions extends beyond its legal requirements, and what the cost implications of providing these favourable working conditions are.

If JJJ's policy simply means that it takes care to ensure that its working conditions comply with all legislative requirements, then this should not cause concern for its shareholders.

However, if JJJ's working conditions exceed legal requirements – for example, by providing very generous wages and benefits – then this could be a concern for the shareholders. The shareholders might feel that JJJ is incurring unnecessary costs (by providing favourable working conditions above the legal requirements) which could be seen as conflicting with shareholder wealth maximisation.

Commitment to the principles of fair trade

Paying a fair price for components – 'Fair trade' principles would oblige JJJ to pay a fair price for any inputs or components it sources from a developing economy. However, because all of JJJ's inputs currently come from within Q, they will not be affected by a 'fair trade' policy.

Therefore, this aspect of the policy should not currently cause any concerns for JJJ's shareholders.

Overall impact of the policy

Customer values – The shareholders' concerns with the policy are likely to arise if they feel it is making JJJ's products more expensive than competitors' products, thereby leading to reduced margins.

Basis of differentiation - However, this may not necessarily be the case. As the market research has indicated, JJJ's customers value its ethical business policy. This could mean that some customers buy JJJ's products because they share the values of the ethical business policy. In this respect, the policy may provide JJJ with a means of differentiating itself from other manufacturers. As such, the shareholders should consider the extent to which the policy might actually increase their wealth rather than reducing it.

(b)

Top tips.

The question requirement indicates that you need to consider two separate issues here:

(i) Whether JJJ could continue its ethical business policy in relation to each stakeholder

(ii) The actions it needs to take to continue its ethical business policy with each stakeholder.

It should be clear from the scenario that sourcing components from K represents a conflict with the current ethical business policy. However, to score well in this question you need to consider the differential impact that this conflict could have on JJJ's relationship with different stakeholder groups. And crucially (as the second point, above, suggests), you need to consider how JJJ could manage its future relationships with the different stakeholder groups. For example, how will the way JJJ managers its relationships with suppliers in K differ from the way it manages its relationships with suppliers in Q?

Examiner's comment. Many candidates recognised that sourcing components from suppliers in K was a conflict with the current ethical business policy, but few answers went further than simply recognising that a conflict existed. Few considered the nature of the conflict in relation to each of the interest groups, and there was little or no discussion of how JJJ could manage its future relationships with each of the different groups.

(i) Suppliers in K

Commitment to fair trade – JJJ's commitment to fair trade principles will become more important once it starts dealing with suppliers in developing economies. This will dictate that JJJ pays suppliers a 'fair' price for the components it receives, although this price may still be significantly lower than the price it currently pays to suppliers within Q.

Employees' working conditions and legislative requirements – The key issues in relation to this aspect of JJJ's policy are likely to arise from the differences in legislative requirements and accepted working conditions in K compared to Q.

Although K's labour laws allow children to work from the age of 10, JJJ's customers in Q may not feel that employing children of that age represents an ethical business policy, particularly as there is no minimum wage in K for people under the age of 18. Therefore, JJJ's reputation could be damaged as a result of its association with the suppliers in K, even though the suppliers are adhering to all the legislative requirements in their own country.

Consequently, if JJJ wants to continue with its ethical business policy it may need to impose some additional requirements on its suppliers in K:

Child labour – JJJ could insist that the suppliers it uses in K do not employ anyone under the age of 16 in their factories, thereby matching the employment legislation Q.

However, such an action could be challenged as imperialist, by preventing suppliers in K from employing people they are legally entitled to employ. An alternative approach might be to accept that the suppliers will employ children from the age of 10, but to insist that some minimum standards are in place; for example, that a minimum wage is applied for the child labour as well as workers over the age of 18.

Health and safety – As with legislation for child labour, K has very little health and safety legislation compared to Q, so JJJ could insist that the suppliers in K follow the same health and safety standards which are used in Q.

However, this could again undermine the cost advantages of using suppliers in K, because complying with Q's health and safety legislation adds approximately 18% to the cost of JJJ's products. Therefore, as with child labour, JJJ may be better advised to accept that K's health and safety standards are not as strict as Q's, but it could still insist that its suppliers follow certain key health and safety procedures even if they are not required by law.

(ii) Suppliers in Q

Products are sourced and made exclusively in Q – The decision to source components from suppliers in K directly contradicts the first aspect of JJJ's ethical business policy: that all of its products are sourced and made *exclusively* within Q.

JJJ's existing suppliers in Q will be very likely to highlight this point, because the decision to source components from suppliers in K will mean some, if not all, of JJJ's existing suppliers will lose income they currently receive from JJJ.

Although JJJ could argue that it still adheres to all legislative requirements, and the terms it has offered its new suppliers endorse its commitment to fair trade principles, it would seem impossible for JJJ to convince its suppliers in Q that it can continue with its existing ethical policy, where the decision use suppliers in K contradicts the first aspect of the policy so explicitly.

However, JJJ also needs to consider whether the fact that its products are sourced exclusively within Q actually adds any value to an ethical policy. Whilst its existing suppliers in Q will be disadvantaged as a result of the change, suppliers in K will benefit from it. Therefore, JJJ could argue that the choice of where to source its components is essentially an economic one, and it is no more, or less, ethical to source components in Q than K. In this case, JJJ could consider removing the first aspect from its policy.

Alternatively, JJJ could discuss its decision with its existing suppliers in Q, thereby allowing them the opportunity to establish operations in K themselves, or to source products from there themselves. These options might allow the existing suppliers to maintain the contracts they have with JJJ.

(iii) Customers in Q

Market research has indicated that JJJ's customers value its ethical business policy, although it is not clear whether they value all aspects of the policy equally highly or whether some aspects of it are more important to them than others.

Differentiation – If JJJ uses its current policy as a basis of differentiation from competitors, then the changes mean it will not be able to continue with the policy in its current format. In particular, if JJJ is trying to differentiate its products from cheaper imported products on the basis that its products are made exclusively within Q, it could not continue to do this once it sources components from suppliers in K.

Equally, JJJ will have an obligation to inform its customers that its products are no longer source and made entirely in Q.

Price – However, although JJJ's customers may feel that the change compromises some of the detailed aspects of the policy, JJJ should also highlight the benefits which the change could have for them. If JJJ can source components more cheaply, in turn it can offer more competitive prices to its customers.

Fair Trade – Equally, if JJJ's customers value the 'Fair Trade' element of JJJ's policy, the fact that it is now trading with suppliers in a developing country could be seen as a benefit. By sourcing components from K, JJJ will be helping to provide income and sustain jobs in that country.

Furthermore, if JJJ insists that its suppliers provide working conditions which exceed the minimum legal requirements in K, it could argue it is still demonstrating high regard for its employees.

Sustainability – However, JJJ also needs to think about the future of its own employees in Q. The fact that it has been suffering from decreasing profits and a declining market share suggests that, if JJJ does not look for alternative sources of components, it could be forced out of business – causing unemployment in Q, and meaning that the customers will no longer be able to buy their electrical products from it at all.

(iv) Shareholders

Although JJJ's shareholders value its ethical business policy, it is not clear how far this policy influenced any shareholders' decisions to buy – or hold – shares in the company.

Equally, however, it would difficult to continue with its ethical policy in its current format when a major business decision (to change suppliers) directly contradicts with one aspect of the policy.

Honesty - In this case, JJJ should be honest with its shareholders, and explain to them that it has decided to source components from suppliers in K, and accordingly it will have to make a change to its ethical business policy.

Shareholder value – While some shareholders may not be happy about the change, JJJ needs to highlight the reasons why it was necessary. The shareholders should already be aware of JJJ's decreasing profits and declining market share, so JJJ should explain that the decision to source components from suppliers in K was taken to try to reverse these trends.

In this respect, JJJ can explain that it was seeking to act in the best interests of its shareholders, with a view to maximising shareholder wealth. However, in order to do this, JJJ has had to revise its ethical business policy.

JJJ should point out that it has not abandoned its ethical business policy – and is still committed to safeguarding the working conditions of employees and to the principles of fair trade. However, it has had to sacrifice its commitment to source products exclusively within Q to try to safeguard the future of the company.

10 Genetically modified plants

Text reference. Corporate social responsibility and stakeholders are discussed in Chapter 2 of your BPP Study Text.

Top tips. In parts (a) and (b), three key stakeholder groups are identified in the question requirements: the government, environmental lobby groups, and the local community.

In both parts of the question, a sensible approach would be to look at each of the separate groups in turn. So, for part (a) you should have looked at B's corporate responsibility towards: (i) the government, (ii) the environmental lobby groups, and (iii) the local community.

Similarly, for part (b) you should have divided your answer into three parts and looked at how B could improve relationships with: (i) the government, (ii) the lobby groups, and (iii) the local community.

One of the key issues here seems to be communication. Although B's work does not involve the genetic modification of the seeds the lobby groups and the local community, incorrectly, believe they do. If B can make the groups understand what it does more accurately, that could well improve relationships with the groups.

Note, however, that you were not required to undertake a detailed stakeholder analysis, and so you should not have wasted time doing so.

Part (a)

Responsibility to the government

Legal obligations – B has a duty to comply with all the legislation which is currently in force in its country. This will include employment laws and health and safety laws, for example governing the working conditions in which B's staff work.

However, B does not have any direct responsibility to the government in respect of the seeds it produces. Not only are B's seeds not genetically modified (GM), but also the national government has not actually passed any legislation banning the research and development of GM crops.

Financial obligations – B has a responsibility to pay corporate taxes on its profits and account for the relevant payroll taxes on its staff.

Innovation and leadership – Although the primary responsibility in developing the non-GM technology is to the international community and to poorer farmers as a whole, rather than the government, B might be seen to have a secondary responsibility to the government as an industry leader. If B can develop the new technology and develop it so that the seeds can be produced on a commercial scale, this could be a source of new jobs and additional revenue for the government. Moreover, it will establish B's country as the leader in this field, generating prestige and a favourable international reputation.

Responsibility to environmental lobby groups

Explain seeds are not genetically modified – The lobby groups' opposition to B's work comes from the fact that they believe B's seeds are genetically modified. However, as this is incorrect, B should explain to the lobby groups that it is not genetically modifying the seeds.

Although B does not have to explain any details of its work which could be commercially sensitive, it should nevertheless explain the nature of its work sufficiently to illustrate that it is not genetically modifying the seeds in the way the lobby groups believe. Although B cannot stop the lobbyists opposing its work, it does have a responsibility to ensure that the lobbyists are aware that it is not actually genetically modifying seeds.

Highlight the potential benefits of its work – There is a danger that by trying to stop B developing the seeds, the lobby groups will be preventing the development of a product which could be beneficial to society as a whole.

To this end, B should highlight the potential benefits of its seeds, and, in particular, how they could be a major benefit to populations in the developing countries of the world.

Responsibility to the local community

Explain the nature of its work – In the same way that B needs to explain to the lobby groups that it is not genetically modifying seeds, so it also needs to explain this to the local community to try to reduce their opposition to its work. Again, B needs to explain that opposing its work could prevent B from developing a product which could be very beneficial to society as a whole.

Responsibility as an employer – B is also likely to have a responsibility to the local community as an employer of local people. As an employer, B contributes jobs and income to the local community, and it should consider the potential impact on the local community if its moves to a new country.

Good corporate citizen – More generally, B has a responsibility to the local community to be a good corporate citizen. For example, as a research and development company with highly skilled staff, B could support some educational initiatives in local schools and colleges.

Part (b)

One of the main problems B seems to be facing is that key stakeholder groups do not really understand the nature of its work. Therefore, **educating them** about its processes will be crucial for B to improve relationships with them.

The government

Explain benefits – B should explain to the relevant government minister the potential benefits that the research could bring to the country. It is vital that B explains that its process does not involve genetic modification, and therefore offers a possible **commercial alternative to GM crops**.

If B carries on with its research, and subsequently produces its seeds in commercial quantities, this could have significant economic benefits for the country. B could generate significant **export earnings**, and as production grows, the local economy would also benefit through the **creation of jobs and supporting services**.

Explain the science – The government is likely to employ scientists of its own, particularly as it is currently conducting an enquiry into the safety of GM crops. B's scientists should try to develop good relationships with the government scientists to explain that B's technology is safe, and that its processes do not involve genetically modifying the seeds.

Co-operate with government enquiry – It is also important that B is seen to be co-operating with the current government enquiry into GM crops. This might make the government and other key stakeholders view B more favourably, and it will give B the opportunity to show its processes do not involve genetic modification of crop seeds.

Nonetheless, B should not disclose information which is commercially sensitive, because this could allow competitors to obtain details of its work, and develop similar processes of their own.

<u>Environmental lobby groups</u>

Explain processes do not involve genetic modification – The lobby groups remain convinced that B's work *does* involve genetically modifying crops, and B has to persuade them this is not the case. It is likely that the lobby groups, like the government, have scientists working for them, so B could look to **explain the principles of their work to the scientists** to get them to appreciate that B's processes do not involve genetic modification.

Explain wider benefits – As well as explaining its processes, B should be looking to explain the wider benefits of its work. If it can develop pest-resistant seeds, this will allow farmers (particularly in developing countries) to grow better crops and hopefully also improve their standard of living. This could also bring wider environmental benefits: if the farmers can improve the yield of their current land, this might reduce deforestation rates and erosion, because there will be less pressure to bring extra land under cultivation.

<u>The local community</u>

Press and media stories – Many people in the local community will not understand the detail of what B does, but will only be aware of B's work through the stories reported in the press and the media. It is therefore important that B increases its communications with the media, so that they can present B's side of the story as well as is opponents' views. To this end, B could hold regular press releases, and possibly could even invite some journalists to see some of its processes, to highlight that they do not involve genetically modifying any crops. Again though, B has to strike a balance between giving people more information and preserving commercial sensitive details.

Local government – The local government could be another important stakeholder in the local community, so B should also look to improve communications with it. If the local government (and in particular any local government scientists) accept that B's work is safe and doesn't involve any genetic modification, then the local community may also be more likely to accept it.

Support community projects – B might also be able to improve its relationship with the local community by getting more involved with local people. For example, it could sponsor some local events, or provide some financial support to community projects.

Part (c)

> The question for part (c) also gives you a clue about how to structure your answer, by listing the four dimensions of CSR. A sensible approach would have been to look at each of these four dimensions in turn. There are 8 marks available, and 4 dimensions, so you should look to score 2 marks for each aspect.
>
> However, your answer should have related the four CSR aspects specifically to B's decision to re-locate. General discussions about aspects of CSR would not have scored well.

<u>Legal</u>

B has no legal obligation to be based in one country as opposed to another. Therefore, if it chooses to move to another country it is free to do so.

Clearly, B will still need to comply with the laws and regulations of the country it moves to, but it is unlikely these will be more rigorous than those it currently has to follow.

One issue which B will need to be aware of, however, is that if there are any **international standards** governing genetic engineering processes and practices, then it will need to ensure it complies with these whichever country it is based in.

Ethical

The main ethical issue in this scenario appears to be that the lobby groups feel that B's work is unethical because it allegedly involves the **genetic modification** of seeds. B's own directors know that their work does not involve genetic modification, and so the ethical objections are not justified on scientific grounds. However, it is likely that the lobby groups will continue to object to B's work, wherever it is located.

B's motive for moving to a new country is that it the new country is more supportive of biotechnology research and development. So there may be a perception in this country that the **greater good** of being able to produce seeds which help to feed people better outweighs the concerns that some groups have about genetic modification. In which case, if relocating helps B develop the product and then produce it commercially, the move should be supported.

Economic

Demand for genetically modified food is growing worldwide, and this looks to provide B with good opportunities for economic growth. B has an economic objective to **generate a profit for its owners** and so if moving to a new country helps it to **grow and achieve more profit**, then that is a valid reason for moving.

Moreover, if B grows and becomes a successful business, its success will also benefit its new host country. The government will benefit from **tax revenues**, and the local economy could benefit through B's **investment** in it, and through the demand for supporting goods and services.

Ultimately, if B becomes very successful, it could prompt other similar companies to move to the country, and could lead to the development of a biotechnology cluster there. This again would be economically beneficial to B's new host country.

Philanthropic

Although the new country has a more tolerant attitude to research and development than B's current country, some locals may still be unhappy about the potential impact of a new business on their amenities and their way of life. However, B should be keen to work with the local community so that the community supports it rather than resents it.

One of the ways B can gain the local community's support is by improving people's quality of life, and **giving something back to society**. For example, B could support some local education projects: either by helping to fund new schools or colleges, or by running some education programmes for local farmers.

11 HWS shop chain

Text reference: Stakeholder analysis is covered in Chapter 2 of the BPP Study text.

Top Tips:

Part (a): Although the requirement refers to *shareholders*, the reference to Mendelow's matrix, and to levels of power and interest, should have indicated very clearly that this question was about *stakeholder* analysis, although the stakeholders you had to analyse were the different groups of shareholders identified in the scenario. However, it is important that you realise that the relative power of different shareholder groups is not determined solely by the size of their shareholding. The group which is probably the most powerful (the Directors) actually has the lowest shareholding. Also, remember you need to analyse power and interest specifically in relation to the decision to sell alcohol and tobacco, not in relation to HWS's strategy or performance more generally.

For part (b), note that you were only asked to advise the Board of TWO other stakeholder groups who would be interested in the decision to sell alcohol and tobacco.

Nonetheless, there are a number of possible groups you could choose from here. In addition to the two we have suggested in our answer, you could have suggested HWS's competitors; politicians or healthcare workers/doctors (interested in the potential impact on the health of HWS's customers and the cost of treating alcohol/tobacco related illnesses) or potential investors (interested in the impact of the 25% increase in profits). Provided you identified a relevant group, and supported your advice with a logical argument, you would have scored the marks available here.

Although the context of part (c) is Corporate Social Responsibility (CSR) and Ethics, you should not have discussed these concepts in general terms. Equally, although the decision to sell alcohol and tobacco could have social implications, you should not have focussed solely on the decision to sell these two products. Instead, your answer to part (c) should have looked at (socially) responsible business practices more widely; and how HWS can demonstrate that it acts in a socially responsible manner.

(a)

High power; high interest

HWS directors – Although the directors collectively have the lowest holding of the eight groups of shareholders (2%), they have the highest power over the decision, because it is they who have decided to implement the new retailing strategy. Similarly, it is the directors who have the power to modify the new retailing strategy – either, for example, if it does not prove to be as profitable as had been hoped, or else in response to pressure from other stakeholder groups.

Equally, the fact that they have taken the decision to implement the new strategy identifies the directors as having a high level of interest in the strategy, and the Managing Director's statement to the Stock Exchange reinforces this.

RCB: private equity fund – RCB has the highest individual shareholding in HWS, with 25% of the share capital. Although it still only hold's a minority of HWS's total equity, the size of RCB's holding puts it in a relatively powerful position.

Moreover, RCB's focus on the short-term profitability of its investments will also increase its interest in the decision, given the Managing Director's statement that the strategy should increase HWS's annual profits by at least 25% [£10m/£40m] by the end of the next year.

Additional point:

It is not clear from the scenario whether RCB's holding has changed in recent years, or how it has changed if it has. However, if its holding is increasing this could soon increase RCB's power further.

Stock Exchange regulations mean that any shareholder (or group of shareholders acting together 'in concert') which holds 30% or more of the equity in a company has to make an offer to acquire that company.

In this case, if RCB's holding increases the 5 percentage points from 25% to 30% this would then mean RCB has to make an offer to acquire HWS.

The scenario does not indicate whether or not RCB wants to reach this position, but if it does make a successful offer for HWS in due course – and subsequently acquires the company – then its power over HWS's strategic decisions will increase further.

UK Clearing Bank – The Bank's power comes partly from the fact that it is the second-largest shareholder (holding 20% of HWS's share capital) but also from the fact that HWS is one of its clients. As with RCB, the Bank's holding is still only a minority holding, although it is a sizeable minority, but in conjunction with having HWS as a client this will give the Bank a high level of power over HWS's decisions.

Similarly, the Bank will be interested in the commercial success of the new strategy, because of the potential impact this could have on HWS's gearing and future cash flows (and its potential ability to pay back any capital or interest owing to the bank).

High power; low interest

Pension funds; investment trusts – Together, the pension funds and investment trusts hold 30% of HWS's share capital, and so collectively they could have a high degree of power. Individually, however, each of the funds or trusts would hold less power.

Collectively, the funds' and trusts' shareholdings are worth £135m at current market value [30% × £450m] which may suggest the investors have a high degree of interest in HWS's on-going success. However, there is no indication what proportion of their respective portfolios these HWS shares constitute, and it is likely that the proportion could actually be quite small. This will reduce the investors' interest in the decision.

Moreover, as institutional investors, it is likely that they are more interested in HWS's overall financial performance rather than the individual decisions the company takes. And, although the decision to increase the product portfolio may be significant for HWS, in effect it is only bringing HWS's product portfolio more in line with other newsagents and grocers stores.

Low power; high interest

HWS Charitable trust – Unlike the Directors, the HWS Trust is not directly responsible for any of the decisions taken by the company. Moreover, the Trust's shareholding (10%) is not large enough to give it any significant power over the company's decisions.

However, the Trust has a very high level of interest in the decision, as indicated by the strongly worded statement it issued. Given its role in working to improve the health of the population, the Trust will be particularly critical of HWS's decision to sell alcohol and tobacco, given the potentially adverse impacts both can have on people's health.

HWS employees – Again, in contrast to the Directors, the employees have little power to shape any of the HWS's decisions. However, because the security of their jobs is likely to depend on the company's ongoing success they will have a high level of interest in how the decision affect's future profits. Moreover, because on average the employees hold shares worth about £9,000 each [(10% × £450m)/5,080] they will have a high level of interest in how the stock market reacts to the announcement, and how the announcement affects HWS's share price.

Low power; low interest

Private investors – 15,000 investors collectively only hold 3% of HWS's share capital, which means that individually each investor only holds a very small percentage of the share capital. Consequently, these investors (either individually or collectively) have very low power to influence any decisions HWS may make.

Moreover, given that, on average, each investor's holding is worth about £900 [(3% × £450m)/15,000] it is unlikely that many of these private investors will take a keen interest in HWS's business decisions.

(b) **Customers –** The reason why HWS has decided to sell alcohol and tobacco is in response to customer demand, particularly from customers using its shops between 2am and 6am. In this respect, these customers probably have the highest level of **interest of** any stakeholder group in the new strategy.

However, other customers may also be interested in the decision, but may not be in favour of it. For example, they may feel that alcohol and tobacco are damaging to health and so the number of outlets selling them should be restricted not increased.

Local communities – The main demand for alcohol and tobacco products appears to be from customers using the shops between 2am and 6am. Local residents living near HWS shops may be concerned that the decision to sell alcohol and tobacco will lead to an increase in noise and litter, because the residents may (rightly or wrongly) feel that people shopping for alcohol and tobacco late at night could be drunk and rowdy.

(c) **Mission statement** – Although HWS was established by a group of ethically motivated investors, its current mission statement doesn't actually make any reference to ethical behaviour or responsible business practice. In this respect, HWS could demonstrate its commitment to responsible business practice by modifying its mission statement to something like: '... to sell the best quality groceries at competitive prices whilst still acting in a socially responsible way.'

Importantly, acting in a socially responsible way may not always be compatible with the sentiment of HWS's current mission statement: to sell 'at the cheapest prices.' For example, one way HWS could adopt socially responsible business practices is through buying **'Fair Trade' products** for its stores. These guarantee that the producers (who are often based in developing countries) receive a fair price for their products (eg coffee). However, as a result, 'Fair Trade' products are often sold at a slightly higher price than other similar products.

Corporate values – As well as including a reference to social responsibility in its mission statement, HWS's sense of social responsibility also need to be communicated to the employees, so that they appreciate what the company stands for and how they are expected to behave. For example, the staff could receive training about responsible sales practices, and how this affects their routine activities. More strategically, HWS could also ensure that CSR issues are considered in any strategic decisions it makes. For example, the social impact of any new projects could be included acknowledging in capital investment decisions rather than simply looking at the short term financial aspects.

Reporting on performance – HWS could report on its responsible business practice, either in its annual report or in a separate document. For example, if HWS becomes involved in **local community schemes**, or makes **donations to charity** these could be highlighted in the report. HWS could designate one of its directors to be responsible for this report, thereby demonstrating a commitment from senior management to CSR.

Another important issue which HWS could report on is **sustainability**. One consequence of society's increasing demands for responsible business practice is that companies are looking to embrace sustainable business practices as a core part of their business strategies. It is not clear from the scenario how far HWS is doing this, but one way it could respond to society's demands is by promoting sustainability throughout its business; for example, through reducing carbon emissions, and through responsible supply chain management. Again, the ideas of Fair Trade would also be relevant here.

12 Timber company

Text reference. Chapter 2 of the BPP Study Text discusses corporate social responsibility, and also summarises the differences between business ethics and corporate social responsibility.

Marking scheme

				Marks
(a)	(i)	Explanation of business ethics (BE)	2	
		Explanation of Corporate Social Responsibility (CSR)	2	
		Explanation of the difference between BE and CSR (CSR is a much broader concept that BE)	1	
			Total up to	5
	(ii)	For each valid issue discussed regarding D's CSR position	1 mark each	
		For each valid suggestion about how D could improve its CSR position	2 marks each	8
			Total up to	
(b)		For each relevant point relating to the new approach, well evaluated	2 marks each	
		For each relevant point relating to the current approach, well evaluated	2 marks each	
		Clear recommendation on which option should be taken, justified by evaluation of the two approaches	Up to 2	
			Total up to	12
			Total	25

Part (a)

Top tips. Whilst, in general, strategic level question requires you to use the information provided in the scenario to inform your answer, (a) (i) is knowledge-based requirement. The key to doing well here is to present a clear definition of, first, business ethics and then corporate social responsibility, before highlighting the differences between two.

However, the way to approach (a) (ii) is to draw information from the scenario to shape your answer. You should have related the corporate social responsibility (CSR) issues specifically to the scenario given. A general discussion of how companies can deal with CSR would not have scored well.

Easy marks. The scenario should generate a number of issues for you to talk about; and for the majority of the question, the examiner wanted you to relate your answers specifically to the scenario. However, if you knew the subject material well, (a) (i) would have offered 5 easy marks.

> **Examiner's comments.** This question was reasonably well answered, and candidates demonstrated a sound understanding of CSR.

(i) Business ethics and corporate social responsibility

The notion of corporate social responsibility (CSR) has become used interchangeably with the term ethics.

However, the two are not the same.

Business ethics can be defined as behaviour which supports justice, integrity, honesty and goodness, and is guided by ethical theory.

Corporate social responsibility (CSR) is a broader concept. It includes a commitment for businesses to act ethically, but also to act in a way what provides benefits to society. This benefit to society can be related partly to economic development, but CSR also extends to look at the ways companies deliver environment improvements, community projects, or any other measures to improve quality of life.

In this context, we can see that business ethics only forms one part of corporate social responsibility. A company also has **economic** and **legal duties**, in addition to its **ethical duties**. However, the major value of corporate social responsibility is that it encourages companies to take account of **social costs and benefits** when they are fulfilling their economic duties.

(ii) CSR issues facing D's business

Environmental damage. The loggers usually leave considerable surface damage behind them once they have finished felling the trees. Because they are working as quickly as they can to move onto the next money-making job, they are relegating environmental concerns below purely financial ones.

Sustainability of forests. One of the major issues surrounding D's business is the sustainability of the timber it is harvesting – particularly the hardwood timbers. Again, the logging process is concerned more with obtaining timber to sell rather than considering the longer term environmental impact of the actions.

Acting in the best interests of society. Although D claims it always acts ethically because it has the agreement of the national government in any country in which it operates, this assumes that the government and D are the only two stakeholders with an interest in the projects. Moreover D's claim assumes that national governments always act in the best interests of society.

However, in practice, neither of these cases are always true. Also the methods used by D to get the government's agreement to logging should be appropriate. If D offered inappropriate inducements to government ministers in a country then it will have acted unethically by corrupting ministers.

Ways to improve CSR position

When considering these issues D should remember that it is a commercial organisation, and it has a **responsibility to its owners** (shareholders) as well as the environmental stakeholders. So, D's management needs to balance the aims of continuing profitability with those of environmental sustainability.

Review logging practices. At the operational level, D should review the ways the trees are felled to ensure that **ecological damage is minimized**.

Restore habitat. As far as possible, once the lumberjacks have finished logging, D should aim to restore a habitat to the condition it was in before logging started.

This should include **replanting areas** which have been deforested with appropriate trees to improve the sustainability of the forest.

D should also seek to minimise any impact its work has on **indigenous populations** living in areas where it works. If villages have to be relocated as a result of the logging works, D should support those whose livelihoods have been destroyed.

Work with environmental groups. At a more strategic level, D should work with the environmental groups that have criticised them, and consult with them about ways in which it can **reduce its negative environmental impact.**

One of the ways it may be able to do this is to **restrict its logging to sustainable forests only**.

Ensure safety and working conditions of employees. Logging is a dangerous industry to work in. D should ensure safe working practices, even if these are beyond the minimum legal standards in each country. It may be possible for D to exploit workers in some countries by giving low pay and inadequate facilities. D may fulfil its CSR obligations better by improving standards for its workers.

Giving something back. Simply taking the natural resources of a country may not be a good example of CSR. D could consider building schools to provide education to the children of lumberjacks in an effort to assist development of the country. Medical care may also be valuable.

Part (b)

> **Top tip.** This question again requires you to relate your answer specifically to the question, and the issues facing D. You were asked to *evaluate* the two approaches to logging, and so your answer should include a balanced argument 'for' and 'against' each approach. However, remember that this is a *business strategy* paper, so your answer should include business issues as well as environmental ones.
>
> Note you were also asked to *recommend* which strategy you think is more appropriate to D so you must present a conclusion based on the relative merits of the approaches evaluated to get full marks.
>
> The Examiner commented that the main weakness in student answers was the failure to make a recommendation about which of the two approaches is most appropriate for D.

Logging on dry land

Continuity of working practices. One of the advantages of continuing to work on dry land is that it means D will not have to change any of its working practices, and will not have to retrain any of its staff.

D's current working practices appear profitable, and it has no problems obtaining finance from the bank, therefore if it continues with its existing practices it should be able to continue generating profits for its owners.

However, in order to continue with its existing practices, D needs a continuing source of trees to fell.

Diminishing timber resources. Perhaps the most critical problem it will face in the medium to long term will be a reduction in the supply of trees to fell. This will be particularly true for hardwood resources. Hardwood trees take a long time to grow, and so even if they are replanted now the forests will take decades to regenerate.

Price increases. As a consequence of this shortage of supply, D may find the price it has to pay landowners or national governments for the rights to cut timber will increase. While D may pass on some of these higher costs to consumers, it is likely that a shortage in timber supplies will adversely affect D's profitability.

Current logging practices – with timber being logged faster than trees are replanted, and with little concern being given to environmental impact – are increasingly unsustainable. If D were to adopt this approach, it would face **increasing pressure from environmental groups** to adopt a more socially responsible approach to logging. And this social responsibility needs to take account of the rights of local populations as well as the timber resources.

Moreover, **other corporate stakeholders** – such as banks – are now taking corporate social responsibility increasingly seriously. Therefore if D is not seen to be acting in a socially responsible manner it may find it harder to raise loans.

Underwater business

Less environmental damage. One of the main overall benefits of the underwater business is that it has less negative environmental impact than logging on dry ground.

Also, estimates suggest that there is a **plentiful supply of timber** (20 years' supply) submerged in reservoirs.

As land based timber resources become scarcer, the underwater business will become increasingly attractive. If D moves into this area now and becomes an expert underwater harvester it may be able to develop a **competitive advantage** as the market leader.

Favourable CSR reputation. D will also get a good reputation if it follows this more socially responsible approach. There may also be **financial benefits** if end-users switch to using timber from the reservoirs because it is an environmentally friendly resource. In addition, D may be able to secure cheaper funding from its banks as a socially responsible company.

Serving environmentally conscious consumers. As the recycled paper and other industries demonstrate, many consumers are prepared to seek out and pay a premium price for products which have not caused environmental damage during their production. Providing timber harvested underwater to manufacturers and merchants will enable a premium price to be charged and a competitive advantage gained.

D is also likely to get some (international) **public relations exposure** from taking this new approach to socially responsible timber harvesting.

However, there are some significant issues to consider with the underwater business.

Initial costs. The new venture will require significant initial capital investment to acquire the equipment needed to harvest the timber underwater. This equipment is significantly more expensive than the equipment needed for logging on dry land.

The underwater business will also **need staff with different skills**. D will either need to retrain its existing staff, or possibly hire new staff (making its existing staff redundant if its discontinues its existing business on dry land).

Risk. There may be **operational difficulties with actually finding the timber**. Although estimates suggest that, globally, there are over half a billion submerged trees, D will need to locate them precisely in order to be able to harvest them efficiently. It may be able to do this with remote sensing equipment, but again, it is unlikely to have these skills or expertise currently, and these skills will take time to acquire.

Recommendation

Although there will be practical issues involved in changing the business' approach, the underwater business provides an attractive alternative to D's current land based operations. It will provide D will a source of sustainable supplies, and will allow it to demonstrate its corporate social responsibility.

13 Water charity

Study Reference. Environmental analysis (PEST analysis) and Porter's 'Five forces' model are assumed knowledge for E3 because they are covered in the E2 syllabus.

Foresight is covered in Chapter 3 of the BPP Study Text for E3.

Marking scheme

			Marks
(a)	Identification of benefits of environmental analysis to BBB, up to 2 marks each	Up to 4	
	Each valid example of how knowledge of the 'Five forces' will help BBB, clearly related to BBB, up to 2 marks each	Up to 8	
	Each valid example of how knowledge of PEST factors will help BBB, clearly related to BBB, up to 2 marks each	Up to 8	
		Total up to	14
(b)	Definition of foresight	1	
	For each well explained foresight technique (up to maximum of two techniques), up to 3 marks each	Up to 4	
		Total up to	5
(c)	Each difficulty well discussed and relevant to BBB, up to 2 marks each	Up to 6	
			6
		Total	25

Part (a)

Top tips. The question requirement doesn't specify which models to refer to in conjunction with environmental analysis, but the examiner's own answer uses Porter's Five forces and PEST analysis.

The question does not ask you to discuss environmental analysis itself, or PEST or Five forces as models. Instead it asks you to discuss how environmental analysis would help the Trustees. So the way to approach this question is to use the models to generate ideas, but then apply those ideas specifically to BBB's circumstances. It is the application which will earn you the marks in this question.

PEST is the most obvious model to use when considering environmental analysis. However, the scenario doesn't provide a great deal of information about the general environmental, so you should have realised that there wasn't sufficient scope to score 14 marks on PEST analysis alone.

Moreover, the reference in the scenario to the increasing competitiveness of the industry should have alerted you that Porter's Five forces model is also relevant here. One of the key issues the charity is facing is how to attract donations in an increasingly competitive industry. How could the ideas behind the Five forces model be useful to the Trustees here?

Easy marks. PEST and Five forces analysis are both core models so you should be able to use them in conjunction with the information from the scenario to identify some benefits to BBB from conducting environmental analysis.

Examiner's comments. There are still some candidates who fail to apply their knowledge as required in the question. This question did not require candidates to write all they know about PEST or the five forces. Instead they should have identified the benefits of environmental analysis to BBB – but many candidates failed to do this.

A common error students made was to prepare a PEST or Five Forces analysis without considering how they could help BBB address its opportunities or threats.

If the trustees of BBB conducted a thorough environmental analysis, this would allow them a better understanding of the **environmental factors** (political/legal, economic, social/cultural, technological) and **competitive forces** affecting their organisation. Understanding these factors and forces would help BBB shape its own strategy to help it survive and develop, not least by improving the information it has available to assist it in its decision-making.

Environmental factors

Political factors – BBB receives **no government funding**. This may be because it has not applied for any funding, or because government policy is not to make grants to charities. By reviewing government policy – either at national or EU level – BBB make be able to identify opportunities which will allow it to qualify for government funding. BBB should also review policies and legislation to see if there are any **tax breaks** available to it which it is not yet taking advantage of.

Economic factors – Because BBB relies entirely on voluntary donations (either from individuals or corporations), consumer confidence and economic growth are likely to affect the level of donations it receives. In an economic downturn, people and corporations are likely to look at ways of reducing their **discretionary spending**, and reducing charitable donations may be one way of achieving this. Therefore, BBB may be able to improve the accuracy of its **revenue forecasting** by taking account of general economic trends.

Also, by looking at economic trends and industry sectors' financial performance more closely, BBB may be able to target its appeals for donations more effectively. For example, if some **industry sectors are performing well**, then BBB would be better advised to approach companies in that for donations rather than companies in sectors which are performing poorly.

Social/cultural factors – It is likely that different social groups will have different **attitudes towards charitable donations,** and in particular to charitable donations towards overseas causes. If BBB was able to identify which groups in society give most generously, it may then be able to target its advertising campaigns more effectively. For example, particular towns and cities may have large ethnic populations with **family ties to the areas which BBB is seeking to help**; in which case, placing advertisements in the local press in those towns may be an effective way of increasing donations.

Technological factors – At the moment, BBB does not use the internet at all in its advertising campaigns. However, **online advertising** could be a cost-effective way of reaching potential donors, not least because online advertising has a **global reach** which BBB's current newspaper advertising is unlikely to have.

BBB could also investigate whether it could get some banner adverts or click-throughs on the websites of some of its existing corporate donors, linking in to the way the companies fulfil their corporate social responsibilities.

It is also important for BBB to be aware of any **technological advances** which could **improve the equipment** they provide to decontaminate the water, or which could provide **alternative ways of removing the arsenic** from the water.

Competitive forces

Although Porter's five forces model is usually applied by commercial organisations, it is still relevant to BBB especially since the charity industry is becoming increasingly competitive. By considering it, the trustees would be aware of the following factors which could impact their charity:

Competitive rivalry – BBB should consider what other charities are providing similar water aid to less developed countries. In particular, it should look at the **ways they are raising funds**, given the difficulty BBB has had in attracting donations. Part of the reason for this could be that people are **giving to other charities instead of BBB**, responding to the **advertising campaigns** of those other charities in preference to BBB's. BBB may be able to get some insights from competitors' campaigns to make its own adverts more effective.

New entrants – The increase in competition may reflect the **emergence of new charities**, and BBB needs to be aware of new charities with similar aims and goals to it starting up. If BBB knows about any new charities starting up it can **time some of its campaigns and promotions to coincide with the launch** of the new charity – thereby retaining its own donors rather than seeing them give money to the new charity instead.

Donors – Donors are the equivalent of buyers in Porter's model, because they are the people who provide BBB's revenue. Because **donations are discretionary**, the buyers have quite a **significant influence over BBB's performance**: if they choose to reduce their donations, BBB is relatively powerless to stop them doing so.

Substitutes – In theory, any **alternative ways which donors may choose to spend their money** could be seen as substitute products and services to BBB. This means that the threat of substitute products and services affecting BBB's revenue is quite significant.

One significant threat to BBB is that donors will switch to make donations to other charities or good causes; for example, a donor may invest in medical research rather than supporting BBB.

It will be particularly important to BBB that it retains its large corporate donors, and recognising the threat of substitutes should alert BBB to the importance of making sure these donors keep giving to it rather than other good causes. As part of this, BBB could consider producing a periodic report for its donors which shows how their money is helping the villages, thereby illustrating the value and importance of its work.

Part (b)

Top tips. The Examiner wrote an article on foresight and foresight techniques in '*Financial Management*' magazine the month before the exam in which this question was set. This serves as an important reminder that you should read any articles in CIMA magazines which are relevant to E3 as part of your preparation for the exam.

The question itself is a test of knowledge and does not need to be related to BBB. If you had read the Examiner's article, it should have offered you some easy marks.

Foresight can be described as the art and science of **anticipating the future,** by looking at how present actions could shape the future. Unlike forecasting, foresight does not attempt to predict the future, but rather to **identify a range of possible outcomes based on an understanding and analysis of current trends**. This could allow organizations to be better prepared for the future because they have anticipated possible changes which could affect them.
An organisation can use a number of techniques to improve its foresight. These include:

Tutorial note. Note the question only asks for two techniques which could be used to develop foresight. Therefore you should only have included **two** in your answer. However, we have included a wider range of techniques in the text box below for learning purposes. Any two of these would have earned you the marks available here.

Scenario planning – In scenario planning, organisations look at the factors, trends and uncertainties that could shape their industry, and then develop a range of plausible scenarios based on the key areas of uncertainty. These scenarios illustrate a range of possible futures for the organisation, so that it can consider the implications of those futures on its business, and can develop possible strategies to deal with the uncertainties it may face.

Delphi technique – A number of experts are asked to independently and anonymously give their opinions and insights on a particular trend and how it may develop. These initial results are summarised and the summary is returned to the experts. They are then asked to reconsider their original answers and respond again in the light of the responses from the group. This process is repeated until a consensus is reached.

Morphological analysis – The attributes of a product or strategy are listed as column headings in a table, and then as many variations of each attribute as possible are list in each column. In effect, a matrix of components is created. One entry from each column is then chosen to create a new mixture of components. This new mixture could represent a new product or strategy. The range of possible new mixtures illustrates the range of possible new products or strategies.

Visioning – An organisation's management develop an image of a possible or desirable future state. This image may initially be quite vague, but it is then developed into a more definite goal, accompanied by a strategic plan for how to achieve that goal. For visioning to be useful for an organisation, the image or goal articulated has to be a realistic and achievable alternative to the current state, and one which is preferable to the current state.

Opportunity mapping – An opportunity map is a qualitative and experience-based analysis aimed at identifying gaps in the current user experience of an organisation's product portfolio. By comparing the desired qualities of a product or strategy against the current qualities, an organisation may be prompted to change its priorities and strategies in order to deliver those desired qualities.

Trend extrapolation – This is a projection technique based on the assumption that certain social, economic or technological trends or patterns identified in the past will manifest themselves again in the future. The logic is that it is possible to forecast future trends by observing how certain patterns have changed in the past and projecting or extrapolating those changes into the future. The impact of those changes on the organisation should be considered, along with possible ways the organisation can respond to them.

Part (c)

Top tips. One of the keys to answering this question is to note that none of BBB's Trustees have a commercial background and so they are unlikely to have any experience of developing a process of environmental analysis. This lack of experience is likely to cause them problems as they try to carry out an environmental analysis for the first time.

The organisation's culture and structure are also important: for example, how will the laissez-faire management style or the fact that BBB is primarily staffed by volunteers affect the introduction of an environmental analysis process?

As always, make sure your answer draws directly on the material in the scenario. This question isn't about the problems of carrying out environmental analysis in general, but is about the specific difficulties BBB will face in doing so.

BBB currently operates on laissez-faire management principles and there is no focus on where the organisation is going. In order to implement a process of environmental analysis, BBB may have to make changes in a number of aspects.

Data management and technology. Environmental analysis often involves gathering and analysing significant amounts of information. BBB does not currently make use of available technology to any extent in its organisation. The apparent aversion to technology could inhibit BBB's attempts to develop an environmental analysis process.

Staff resources. BBB is staffed primarily by **volunteers**, and has very few full-time paid employees. Moreover, it is likely that the volunteers are **field-based**, concentrating on either raising funds for BBB's working or managing aid projects. However, environmental analysis will best be carried out **by office-based analysts** with access to the IT resources required for data analysis. It is debatable whether BBB currently has anyone suitable for this work.

Leadership and management. For the benefits of environmental analysis to be maximised, there will need to be a clear focus and direction to the analysis; for example, the key environmental factors to focus on will need to be defined. However, the current management approach appears to be one which does not give clear **focus or direction**. Therefore, developing a process of environmental analysis may require a change in the **organisational culture** (at least, among the senior management), and the introduction of more formal **structures and processes**.

However, it is debatable whether the current senior managers have the necessary **management skills** to implement such a significant **change management** programme.

Lack of experience. Because none of the Trustees has a commercial background it is unlikely that any of them has any experience of developing a process of environmental analysis. This, again, could lead to problems in defining both the aims and goals of the process, and also the practicalities of how it is introduced.

14 Scenario planning

Text reference. Environmental analysis, including PEST analysis, is assumed knowledge from E2. Scenario planning is discussed in chapter 3 of the BPP Study Text for E3.

Marking scheme

			Marks
(a)	For each benefit of implementing a process of environmental analysis	1	
	For applying the benefit to the case material		
	For evaluating each benefit given	1	
		1	
	Note: Students can only be awarded a maximum of 5 marks if no *evaluation* of benefits is provided		
		Total up to	12
(b)	For each stage described, up to 1 mark each but limited to ½ mark each if only presented as a bullet point	1	
	An additional 1 mark for each stage if it is clearly linked to the question scenario	1	
		Total up to	13
		Total	25

Part (a)

Top tips. It is important to distinguish what the two parts of this question are examining. (a) is a general assessment of the benefits of environmental analysis; (b) is much more narrowly defined and relates to a specific management tool – scenario planning process.

The key to doing well in (a) is to stick to what the question asks. It asks for an *evaluation* of the benefits of a system of environmental analysis. It does not ask for an explanation of what it is, and so it does not require you to carry out a PEST analysis. However, an evaluation should include discuss the limitations of the benefits as well their positive sides.

When this exam was sat, some students interpreted (a) to mean evaluate the benefits to B of implementing a process of systematic environmental analysis of the publishing industry as a whole. Others interpreted the question as asking for an evaluation of the benefits of implementing a process of systematic, rather than ad hoc, environmental analysis. Although these were both minority interpretations, the Examiner accepted them as valid.

However, the model answer below is based on the majority interpretation of the question – with the systematic environmental analysis relating to B itself, and the comparison being between implementing the systematic environmental analysis and not having any environmental analysis at all.

> **Examiner's comments.** In (a), many candidates chose to provide a detailed 'PEST' or 'Five forces' analysis rather than answering the question set; such an approach earned very few marks, because it was largely irrelevant.

Understanding the company's strategic environment

B has recently tried to diversify into new market segments and to expand its business overseas, but both of these ventures have failed despite the Board thinking they understood their target markets well.

This suggests that the Board's awareness of the environment in which the business is operating is not as good as it thought it was. Moreover, it suggests that the business failures could have been avoided with a better understanding of the business environment.

Similarly, the directors have been surprised by the speed with which new technology has been adopted by the magazine industry. This again suggests that the Board's awareness of the external technological environment is not as good as it needs to be for B to compete successfully in the industry. For example they could be overtaken in the advertising market by media owners able to offer a combined print and internet advertising capability.

Internal versus external focus

The fact that the technological changes in the industry have come as a surprise to the directors indicates that they have been focusing too narrowly on their own business rather than also being aware of their strategic environment. Business strategy is concerned with maintaining and improving the fit of the organisation with its environment. Lacking knowledge of its environment means that B's management are in no situation to develop successful strategies.

Therefore B would benefit from gathering information on the general environment in which it is operating to help redress the balance between the internal and external focus of the business.

Benefits from systematic environmental analysis

Identifying Opportunities – B would be aware of new opportunities so that it could capitalise on them rather than seeing their competitors take advantage of them. This is crucial to the long-term success of the business, because if B does not successfully identify new opportunities its business will not be able to grow.

The converse is also true. If B does not undertake environmental analysis, there will be a threat that its publications or their formats will become obsolete and ultimately that it will go out of business.

Understanding the market – B's recent attempts to expand overseas and to diversify into new domestic markets (teenage magazines) have both failed, at significant cost to the business. If the company had had a better understanding of these markets it may not have chosen to try to enter them. Similarly, if it had a better understanding of the range of potential new markets it may have chosen alternative segments to target.

Understanding the customers – We have seen that consumers are increasingly turning to new media away from traditional publishing media. If B was aware of its customers changing needs it could respond to them, and thereby hope to reverse the decline its sales and profitability.

Similarly, if there were particular niches in the market where there was unsatisfied demand, B may be able to move to fill them.

Market analysis – By looking at the market as a whole, B would be able to analyse trends in the industry and benchmark its performance against its competitors.

Technological advances – B needs to be aware of the technological developments in its industry so that it can adapt to them. This will allow it to take advantage of new production possibilities, and will also mean that the directors are not surprised by the speed of developments in the industry.

Strategic Intelligence

When they are all taken together, these benefits will provide B with a level of strategic intelligence to inform strategic decisions which it currently does not have. On the one hand, strategic intelligence will give the directors greater knowledge about B's business environment and enable them to anticipate change, which in turn will hopefully allow it to reverse the trend of declining sales and revenues which it has suffered over the last four years.

On the other hand, and equally importantly, once it has improved strategic information B will hopefully be able to avoid the costly failures it has suffered due to failed expansions into new markets.

Limitations of systematic environmental analysis

Although environmental analysis will allow B the possibility of improved strategic information, the company should also beware some of the problems attached to it.

The speed of technological change, particularly in digital media, means that there is a danger B's analysis will quickly become out of date. Consequently there is a risk that business decisions could be made based on invalid assumptions. Therefore rather than introducing a formal process of environmental analysis, B may be better served by a more informal process of information gathering about its competitors' activities and its markets.

A more informal process will also be cheaper to implement, particularly if B was thinking about using external consultants to prepare the formal analysis for them.

Part (b)

Top tip. A number of different methods have been proposed for how to produce scenario plans so there is no single 'right' answer. The solution shown here uses a 10 point plan (after Schoemaker) and this is the method discussed in the BPP Study Test.

However, provided you have described the stages of any similar plans (for example, Mercer), following a logical structure, you would get credit for this. You could also have considered contingency planning scenarios as well as scenarios about long-term futures insofar as they follow the same approach. However, if you merely presented the process headings without *describing* them you would not score enough marks to pass this requirement.

Again, the verb is very important – you are asked to describe the stages, not simply to list them.

Note also that the question only asks for the stages of a process that 'could be introduced by B' it does not ask for any specific references to B's industry. Although we have used references to B to help illustrate the stages we have described in our answer, the marking grid for this question did not allow any marks for specific references to the industry. You should not have spent time trying to think of specific references where you were not required to do so by the question.

Scenario planning process

Scenario planning does not try to predict the future. Rather it attempts to describe a range of plausible scenarios, and the action plans required if they do occur.

B's management should create a team to develop the scenarios, including a range of staff from across the company.

There are a number of methods of producing scenario plans (for example those proposed by Mercer, or Shoemaker) but the following are the key stages B should consider in building scenarios.

1. **Define the scope of the scenario**. This will include an assessment of the time frame involved, and the range of products and/or markets it wants to include in the scenario. Scenario planning could be used for a specific product, or extended to look at magazine publishing as a whole, so it will be very important to define the scope of the scenarios which the company wishes to look at. However, the key issue is to decide what insights are likely to be the most valuable to the company, and to set the scope so that it focuses attention in those areas.

2. **Identify the major stakeholders** that drive change or affect the industry (within the scope of the scenario identified in stage 1). Stakeholders should be both internal and external, including B's competitors.

3. **Identify the basic trends** affecting the industry and the business environment. For B, one of the key trends to consider will be technological change and the impact electronic media and the internet are having on magazine publishing. Again though, the trends should be relevant to the scope identified in stage 1.

4. **Identify the key areas of uncertainty** and their drivers. Uncertainties in scenario planning should be viewed as future possibilities, and should be based upon the political/legal, economic, social/cultural and technological (PEST) factors identified in the environmental analysis which B has been advised to undertake. In addition, the uncertainties should also consider B's own organisational competencies and capabilities.

5. **Construct initial scenarios** based on the key areas of uncertainty. The scenarios should be created by shaping the key uncertainties into coherent themes. For example, for B one scenario might be that a

slowdown in economic growth reduces the uptake of digital media distribution channels due to companies rationing capital investment. An equally valid scenario might be the reverse, with continued economic prosperity fuelling an increasing propensity for lifestyle features to be distributed through digital media including interactive television.

Each scenario will have different implications for B, and this is a critical aspect of scenario planning – the outcomes of the scenarios can then be used to assist business planning and forecasting.

6 **Check for consistency and plausibility**. For the scenario planning process to be useful, the scenarios presented must be able to happen, in the timescale identified in the scope of the scenario.

7 **Develop learning scenarios**. At this stage, the initial frameworks identified in stage 5 should be expanded into full descriptions of the scenario as if it were actually occurring.

B's senior management should become involved in the process at this stage, and should start considering the implications of each scenario in terms of the potential impacts they could have on their business.

8 **Identify research needs**. As a result of the work done in stage 7, B should be able to see which aspects of potential scenarios present risks and threats to its business. However, in order for it to be able to assess whether the risks are materialising, it must have some key indicators by which to measure them. For example, monitoring the percentage of households which have internet connectivity would give B an indicator of the extent to which paper-based publishing can be superseded by digital media.

9 **Develop quantitative models**. This stage builds on stage 7, to put together business models to forecast the effects of different scenarios on B's activities and future profitability/cash flow.

10 **Use scenarios to formulate competitive strategy**. The value of the strategic planning process is that it assists a company's decision-making in times of uncertainty. The process should have exposed the key areas of uncertainty which B faces, and in this final stage of the process management should develop strategic courses of action which they can apply to each of the scenarios.

15 Service company value chain

Study Reference. Porter's value chain and Stabell & Fjelstad's alternative are both discussed in Chapter 4 of the Study Text.

Top tips. The Examiner who set this question had written an article in the CIMA '*Financial Management*' magazine shortly before the relevant exam and in it he explained that Porter's value chain is more appropriate to traditional manufacturing activities rather than to service or consultancy activities. This idea is central to this question.

The whole point here is that the detail of C's activities does not fit with the traditional value chain model. Although there is a manufacturing element to C's work, the main focus is on designing the equipment rather than making it. In this respect, C's activities are better viewed as a 'value shop'.

Consequently in (a) you should have looked at how C can use value chain analysis to consider, in general terms, how its various activities add value to the business and contribute to its competitive advantage, rather than trying to analyse C's activities in terms of how they fit together in terms of Porter's value chain.

You should not have wasted time drawing and/or describing Porter's value chain, nor trying to map C's activities onto it. The question did not ask you to, and therefore there were no marks available for doing so.

Requirement (b) again picks up on the issue that Porter's value chain is more suitable for manufacturing activities than service activities. Another issue is that, in Porter's model, the value creation process is entirely internal to an organisation. But this is not the case with C, because the design process involves a lot of consultation between C's engineers and their clients' engineers.

Requirement (c) is best answered by using Stabell & Fjelstad's alternative representation of the value chain for professional services firms (which is the model the Examiner featured in his article). The stages of C's business model fit very neatly into this model.

However, if you weren't aware of this model, you would have struggled to score well in this part of the question. So, as a general point, when preparing for your exams, always make sure you read any Study Notes articles in 'Financial Management which are relevant for your exams.

Easy marks. If you had read the Examiner's article, and therefore were aware of weaknesses of Porter's value chain model in a service context, and of Stabell & Fjelstad's alternative model, parts (b) and (c) should have offered some easy marks.

Examiner's comments. Although this was a popular question it was poorly answered by many candidates, who failed to apply their answers to the questions set. The question asked about the benefits and limitations of value analysis to C, not about the benefits and limitations of value chain analysis in general. Very few marks were earned for simply described the value chain model.

For part (c), most candidates had clearly read the article in 'Financial Management' magazine and displayed good knowledge of the alternative model. This part of the question was well answered by most candidates.

Marking scheme

			Marks
(a)	For each benefit explained specifically in relation to C	Up to 2	
		Total up to	12
(b)	For each criticism explained and related to C	Up to 2	
		Total up to	8
(c)	Recognition of value chain as alternative model	1	
	For each of the alternative primary activities described	Up to 2	
		Total up to	5
		Total	25

Part (a)

Identify sources of value – The value chain illustrates the way business activities **link together** to **add value** from the **end-user's perspective.** As customers are increasingly complaining that prices are too high, C could use the ideas of the value chain to identify whether there are some activities which are not adding value from the customer's perspective and should therefore either be discontinued or done more cheaply.

Alongside identifying sources of value, the value chain also illustrates **how costs are caused** in a business. One of the key benefits of the value chain is in forcing an organisation to look at the **relationship between the value being added and the costs being incurred** in its business activities.

See the business as a whole – The value chain could also be useful for C in that it will encourage it to look at the business as a whole, rather than considering individual functions or process stages in isolation. To this end, the idea of **linkages** in the value chain is very important.

Identify potential sources of competitive advantage – One of the main purposes of the value chain is to help firms secure competitive advantage; for example, either by combining activities in new and better ways, or by managing linkages to increase efficiency and therefore reduce cost.

In this respect, the value chain can used to complement Porter's **generic strategies.** At the moment, it appears that C is following a **differentiation strategy** because it solves clients' problems better than its competitors do. However, it appears that **clients' lower cost solutions** are becoming increasingly more attractive to clients.

Therefore, the value chain can help **support C's management in deciding their strategy** going forward – in particular, whether they want to maintain a differentiation strategy in the light of clients' comments about costs.

Identify process improvements – A firm can secure competitive advantage by inventing new or better ways to do activities. By forcing a firm to look at all its activities, value chain analysis may highlight processes which could be **re-designed** or **outsourced**. For example, it is possible that C could **outsource the manufacturing part** of its business and concentrate on design activities.

Benchmark against competitors – C's clients have remarked that their competitors might not solve their problems as well as C, but they charge less. C could use the value chain as a model for analysing their competitors' activities, to see what activities they are doing differently, and where they are making cost savings.

Implement performance measurement – At the moment, there is a suspicion that the manufacturing and installation activities are not contributing as much to profits as they could, due to their costs being too high. However, there **do not appear to be any performance measures** to confirm this.

C could use the value chain as the basis for analysing the **value added by each stage of the process**, and for introducing **key performance measures based on the costs and value added** at each stage of the process. Once such measures are introduced, the directors will have much more reliable information about the contribution each stage makes to the business profitability overall.

Part (b)

It is not designed for use with service businesses – The most notable criticism of the value chain model is that it cannot easily be applied to service organisations. One of C's key capabilities is the expertise of its engineers, and they use their expertise to design solutions in response to the complex problems presented by their clients. Although **solution design is a critical business process for C** it does not fit with neatly with the primary activities described in the value chain. They are more suitable to processes in manufacturing organisations which deal with tangible inputs and outputs.

Role of technology development – Technology development is a secondary activity in Porter's value chain, however most of C's work is technology development. Therefore, technology development is actually the main **primary activity** for C.

The idea of the value system is difficult to apply to network organisations – The focus of the value chain is on how value is created within the **internal structure** of an organisation's value network, but it is much harder to apply to the wider context of value networks. This is important for C, because the solution design stage is a **collaborative process between C's engineers and the client's engineers**; and therefore does not fit with the idea of an entirely internal process.

This idea of a collaborative network would become even more important if **C outsourced its manufacturing** stage.

Detailed costing required – To make best use of the value chain idea requires a degree of **activity based costing** to establish the costs of the value activities. Given that C has to rely on suspicions about how much each stage of its business model contributes to profit, it is unlikely that C currently uses any activity based costing. Therefore it would be time-consuming and expensive to introduce, particularly if new systems have to be introduced to capture the costing data required.

Viewed as unnecessary and overly complicated – In addition, the engineers at C may not see the value of analysing their business in the depth that is required for a full value chain analysis. It is unlikely the engineers will appreciate the benefit of investing time and energy in the value chain analysis, because it will not help them with their design work, at which they are already skilled experts. If they feel that management are introducing seemingly unnecessary **bureaucracy and administration** the engineers' motivation for producing good quality designs may suffer as a result.

The cost of the analysis may exceed the benefits – The time and effort involved in setting up the value chain analysis (particularly if new cost capture systems are required) will be considerable. However, there is no guarantee that the value chain model will lead to increased profitability. Although detailed analysis could identify the stages of C's business which clients value most, and areas where C's costs could be reduced, this in itself will not necessarily reduce the loss of market share which C has suffered at the hand of its competitors.

Part (c)

The **design element of C's business is becoming increasingly important** at the expense of the manufacturing aspect. Consequently, C could be more usefully analysed as a professional services consultancy firm, rather than a manufacturing firm.

Therefore, while the support activities in the original value chain model remain appropriate, it would be more appropriate to change the primary activities to reflect Stabell & Fjeldstad's alternative representation of a **value chain for professional services firms**.

Problem acquisition and diagnosis – This activity relies on a combination of marketing effort and professional excellence. In C's case, the professional excellence of the engineers is required for solving the client's complex problems, and marketing effort is required to promote C's reputation for solving problems with the best solutions, thereby acquiring new clients for the engineers to work with.

Finding solutions – Again, this activity requires the professional expertise of C's staff. Unlike the 'Operations' activity in the original value chain model, this activity does not involve any physical transformation; rather it will involve C's engineers working with client staff to design possible solutions to their problems. (This represents stage 1 of C's business model.)

Choice between solutions – This activity also involves close consultation with the client. At this stage, C's engineers, in conjunction with their clients' engineers, will test the possible solutions before deciding on their preferred solution. (This represents stage 2 of C's business model).

Solution implementation – The preferred solution is then manufactured according to the design specification agreed with the client. (This is stage 3 of C's current business model).

Control and feedback – Once the solution has been built, it will need to be tested to check it works as intended before being installed. The ongoing annual maintenance also acts as a control, and should identify any repair work or modifications which are required to the equipment.

16 BBB advertising agency

Text reference. Benchmarking is considered in Chapter 4 of your BPP Study Text. The concept of strategic management accounting is discussed in Chapter 1.

Marking scheme

			Marks
(a)	For each aspect of additional information BBB needed – 1 mark each		
	(Possible aspects of additional information include: market/customer information; competitor information; costing/pricing information)		
	For discussing each aspect of the additional information – up to 2 marks each		
		Total up to	10
(b)	For each improvement recommended – 1 mark	Up to 3	
	For reasons justifying how the improvements will benefit BBB's planning and decision-making – Up to 2 marks per improvement	Up to 6	
		Total up to	9
(c)	For definition of benchmarking: including comparative nature of benchmarking (1 mark), and types of benchmarking (1 mark)	Up to 2	
	For each benefit of benchmarking advised – up to 2 marks each	Up to 6	
		Total up to	6
		Total	25

Top tips.

Part (a). Note that the requirement asks about the additional *information* which BBB needs to supports its planning and decision-making, not the activities it could undertake to obtain that information. For example, environmental analysis or competitor analysis are activities which BBB could undertake. The information which BBB needs is the size of the market and/or BBB's market share.

A sensible way to approach this question would be to analyse the weaknesses in the information which is currently available to BBB for planning and decision-making, which should then help you identify the additional information it needs in order to address those weaknesses.

Part (b). Here again, note the requirement asks you to recommend improvements to the *information* provided, rather than BBB's planning or decision-making process.

It is also important to plan your answers to part (a) and (b) carefully, so that the improvements you recommend in part (b) link to the additional information you have advised about in part (a). However, you need to ensure that your answer to part (b) doesn't merely repeat your answer to part (a).

For example, if your answer to part (a) identified that BBB needed more external information, then one of the improvements you could have recommended in part (b) is that the information provided to the Board includes a PEST analysis or analysis of Porter's Five Forces.

Part (a)

The current management accounting information provides a very detailed analysis of BBB's internal financial performance, but BBB does not appear to have any information about non-financial aspects of its performance, or any external information.

External information – It would be useful if the Board had additional information about BBB's market niche and its competitors, for example, about the size of the market, and BBB's share of that market.

Market size – BBB is currently unaware of the size of its market niche, and whether or not that niche is growing. Information about the size of the market and the rate at which it is growing (or declining) will be very useful for BBB because it can help identify how much scope there is for it to grow as well.

Market share – The fact that BBB has to 'estimate' that it is the second or third largest company in its niche indicates that it doesn't accurately know the size of its competitors or its market share. However, this information would be useful not only for monitoring BBB's current performance, but also for evaluating possible future growth plans or strategies.

Basis of competition – BBB is not sure whether it is the high **quality** of its output or its **prices** which are most important in securing new clients. This lack of information about what its customer value makes it harder for BBB to determine what its most effective competitive strategy should be: if customers value the high quality of its output, a differentiation strategy would be appropriate; if customers are attracted by low prices, this suggests a cost leadership strategy could be more appropriate.

Competitor pricing – It seems that BBB does not compare its prices against the prices which its competitors are charging for similar jobs. Consequently, BBB's clients sometimes complain they have been charged too much, while on other occasions BBB feels it has charged too low a price. However, both of these examples suggest that BBB would benefit from being aware of its competitors' prices so that it can ensure that it sets its own prices at a competitive level in relation to its competitors.

Industry forecasts – BBB could also look at industry forecasts for the travel and tourism sectors as a whole. The levels of demand which the sector is expecting, and therefore how well hotels might expect to be performing, could affect how much they are prepared to pay for advertising, or are able to pay.

Costing methods – BBB's approach to pricing work for clients accentuates the internal focus of BBB's planning and decision-making, but it also helps to explain why there are concerns that BBB is charging too high or too low a price for items.

By adopting an inflexible approach to costing and pricing, BBB may be setting uncompetitive prices in relation to competitors' prices, or in relation to what its customers want. This again highlights the importance of BBB having additional information about customers and competitors. For example, before setting a price for a client,

BBB should try to find out what price the customer has paid for similar pieces of work previously, or what price competitors have charged other customers for similar pieces of work.

Historical focus – An additional problem the Board faces is that the accountant's monthly figures appear to only show actual performance against budget.

Forecast - However, it would be useful if they also showed a **forecast**. This could allow the Board to highlight any shortfalls between the forecast position and their desired future position. In this way, if the forecast highlights any expected profit gaps, it could alert the Board that they need to plan for ways to reduce the gap.

Forecasting could also help with **human resources planning**. For example, forecasting could alert BBB to potentially busy periods when it would be beneficial for BBB to hire additional, freelance designers to satisfy the levels of demand it is facing.

(b)

Strategic management accounting

Currently, the information provided by the management accountant seems to reflect 'traditional' management accounting – concentrating on internal, financial performance.

However, the information provided to BBB's board could be more useful for planning and decision-making purposes if it reflected the ideas of strategic management accounting, which includes external and non-financial information, as well as financial information.

The current management accounting information appears very detailed (for example, showing all expenditure over £25), but it is debatable how useful this level of information is for BBB's management board. Equally, it appears that the nature of BBB's current detailed variance analysis might be more appropriate for a manufacturing company than for an advertising agency.

Summary information - Therefore, it is recommended that only a summary of the management accounting information and variance analysis is included in the management information, rather than the current detailed information.

External environment - In place of the current detailed information, the Board should receive information about the external environment – for example, summaries of the competitive forces (Five Forces) which are affecting the industry, and environmental analysis (PEST) highlighting the opportunities and threats which BBB is facing.

However, it is unlikely to be appropriate to include this external information each month. Instead it would be more useful to only include updated information when there are any significant changes to highlight.

Competitive position – competitors and customers

BBB is currently unaware of the total size of its market niche, or its market share within that market. Therefore it could be useful to find out information on these areas and include it in BBB's management information periodically.

Customer preferences - Perhaps more importantly, however, BBB is also unsure whether it wins business because of the high quality of its work or the prices it charges. This makes it difficult for BBB to determine whether its generic strategy should be based on differentiation (and quality) or cost leadership (and lower prices).

Competitor analysis - Equally it will be difficult for BBB to determine its generic strategy without understanding its competitors' strategies and their competences. For example, if BBB wants to pursue a differentiation strategy it will need to be confident that the quality of its work is superior to that of its competitors.

In this respect, it would be useful for BBB to analyse its strengths and weaknesses in relation to what customers want, and what its competitors provide. A summary of this analysis could be provided to the Board in the context of a SWOT analysis (which would also highlight key external issues as opportunities and threats).

Non-financial information

Currently, the information provided to the board looks solely at BBB's financial performance. However, issues such as the **quality** of BBB's advertising, and **customer satisfaction** with its work could also affect its future performance.

Issues around quality and innovation could be particularly important if BBB decides to pursue a differentiation strategy. In this respect, it would be useful if the information provided to the Board includes **key performance**

indicators, to enable the Board to monitor BBB's performance in areas of the business which are crucial to its competitive success.

Non-financial performance indicators – Therefore, in addition to the financial performance information which is currently provided it would also be useful if the management pack also included non-financial performance indicators; for example, by including key performance indicators monitoring customer satisfaction scores.

In this respect, BBB could possible consider introducing a multi-dimensional performance measurement system, such as the Balanced Scorecard. This would highlight the importance of considering a range of perspectives, not just financial ones, in the context of planning and decision-making.

(c)

Top tips.

When thinking about your answers to parts (a) and (b), you should hopefully have identified that BBB does not have any information about its competitors and their performance; which in turn means it cannot assess how well it is performing in relation to its competitors.

Therefore one of the benefits of benchmarking is that it could provide BBB with more information about its competitors, and their performance compared to BBB's.

To score well in this question it is important that you think about the benefits of benchmarking specifically for BBB; rather than simply advising the board about the generic benefits of benchmarking. Equally, note that you are only asked to advise the Board about the benefits of benchmarking; so you should not spend any time discussing its potential limitations.

However, you should have been able to score a couple of easy marks at the start of your answer by explaining what benchmarking is.

Examiner's comment. Most candidates were able to define benchmarking, and most also made an attempt to highlight a range of benefits of benchmarking. However, many answers talked about the benefits of benchmarking in generic terms, rather than considering the benefits which could be obtained specifically by BBB.

Benchmarking – Benchmarking is the establishment, through data gathering, of targets and comparators, which can be used to identify relative levels of performance and underperformance. It is then hoped that performance will improve as a result of identifying best practices.

Benchmarking could involve comparing the performance of one function within an organisation against other functions within that organisation, or it could involve comparing an organisation's performance against external organisations. These could either be direct competitors (competitive benchmarking), or organisations which are acknowledged to exhibit best practices, regardless of their industry (functional benchmarking).

Benefits to BBB

Comparative information – A key feature of benchmarking is that it involves a **comparison** of performance, and this kind of comparative information is something which BBB currently appears to be lacking when judging its performance.

Competitive benchmarking – Although there are a range of different types of benchmarking BBB could undertake, it seems that the most likely one for it to use is competitive benchmarking.

If BBB undertakes a competitive benchmarking exercise, this will mean that it has to increase its awareness of its **competitors' behaviour and strategies** – something which has currently been lacking, due to the internal focus of the current management information.

For example, BBB is currently unsure what impact price plays in its securing new clients. However, benchmarking its prices against its customers would indicate whether BBB's prices tend to be more expensive – or cheaper – than its competitors. In turn this could help BBB identify what role price plays in a customer's decision about which agency to choose.

Equally, such information could help BBB plan its future strategy; if BBB's prices are more expensive than its competitors, this suggests that a differentiation strategy would be more appropriate than a cost leadership or low price strategy.

Performance improvement - Equally, however, if BBB identifies that its competitors are able to control costs more efficiently that it can, or are achieving higher levels of client satisfaction, this should provide BBB with a stimulus to improve its performance in these areas.

In addition, if BBB can identify what its competitors are doing differently to it (to facilitate their superior performance) this should provide BBB with useful information about how it could improve its own processes, or change its own strategy, to improve its performance.

Avoid complacency – One of the dangers of BBB's current internal focus, is that the Board has no way of gauging how well BBB is performing in relation to its competitors. Therefore, the Board may think BBB is performing well, when actually its competitors are performing better than it. By comparing BBB's performance to its competitors', benchmarking would help remove the danger of such complacency.

17 Benchmarking in a charity

Text reference. Benchmarking is dealt with in Chapter 4 of your BPP Study Text.

Marking scheme

			Marks
(a)	Up to 1 mark for each advantage of benchmarking discussed	Up to 4	
	Up to 1 mark for each disadvantage of benchmarking discussed	Up to 4	
		Total	8
(b)	- Senior management commitment	1	
	- Decide and understand process; develop appropriate measures	Up to 2	
	- Monitor process measurement system	Up to 2	
	- Identify appropriate organisations to benchmark against	Up to 2	
	- Analyse data; discuss results with management and staff	Up to 2	
	- Implement improvement programmes	Up to 2	
	- Monitor and control; strive for continuous improvement	Up to 2	
	Where up to 2 marks are available for each point, 1 mark is to be given for mentioning the point, the second mark is for adding detail around it and embedding it in the case.		
		Total	13
(c)	1 mark for each valid point made		
	(These may include: obvious commitment from senior management; clear explanation of purpose of exercise; focus on process not individuals; involvement of staff in mapping process, or involvement in development of KPIs; making use of staff's knowledge and expertise)	Up to 4	4
		Total	25

Part (a)

Top tips. The key to answering this question well is to appreciate that while it is asking about the advantages and disadvantages of benchmarking, it is doing so in the specific context of E5E. Therefore you mustn't just write about the advantages and disadvantages of benchmarking in general, but you must apply these to the specific context of the charity.

Remember also you are asked to discuss them , so you need to consider the advantages and disadvantages in some detail, not simply list them.

Easy marks. There are very few really easy marks here. If you knew very little about benchmarking, you might be tempted to waffle on about variants of the general theme of improved efficiency (our first point below). This would not get you many marks at all, unfortunately. On the other hand, if you are familiar with the appropriate section of your BPP Study Text, a pass mark should be quite easily attainable.

Examiner's comments. The usual frustrations: lack of application of theory to the scenario and a lack of depth – basic lists, with little explanation, do not constitute a 'discussion'.

Advantages of benchmarking

Benchmarking allows an organisation to learn from best practice; this may be found in other, similar, organisations, in very different organisations that have some point of similarity, or within the organisation itself. One category of benefits will revolve around **improvements in economy, efficiency and effectiveness** and for a charity such as D4D will typically include some of those listed below.

- **Reduced costs** of operation,
- **Improved service** levels for all groups of stakeholders
- **Simplification of processes**
- **Improved quality**

There are further benefits.

Both full time staff and volunteers may have their **assumptions challenged.** This may be disturbing, especially in the charity sector, but can reinvigorate operations by removing complacence and improving understanding of what is worthwhile and what is not.

Charities compete with one another for funds; benchmarking allows **effective monitoring of fund raising (and spending) strategies**.

Connected with the two effects mentioned above, is the provision of **evidence to stakeholders** that the charity is fulfilling its purpose efficiently.

Disadvantages of benchmarking

There is an **increased flow of information** that must be monitored, summarised and assessed. These processes are not cost-free and they can lead to management overload. In a charity, the work involved in benchmarking can be discouraging for volunteer staff.

Overload can also occur when a successful benchmarking exercise produces a large volume of requests to participate from organisations that have themselves little to offer in potential improvements.

Benchmarking usually involves the exchange of information with other organisations. There is a threat to **confidentiality,** both commercial and personal.

Poor results from a benchmarking exercise can be disproportionately **discouraging and demotivating**, particularly to managers.

The benchmarking process itself can **distract managers' attention** from their primary responsibilities. Even when this does not happen, managers may put too much emphasis on improving the efficiency with which they do the things they have always done and fail to ask if new ways of doing things would be better overall.

Part (b)

Top tips. Although the question asks you to 'advise on the stages...', the key to this question is identifying the stages of which are involved in a benchmarking exercise. However, do not simply list the stages of a benchmarking exercise: the question requirement makes it very clear you have to relate them to the specific context of E5E.

Easy marks. Some things are obvious: partner organisations must be found; appropriate measurements must be taken and compared; improvements must be made if available. You could almost score a pass mark by discussing such ideas and relating them to the scenario.

Stage 1 – Obtain management support

The first stage is to **ensure senior management commitment** to the benchmarking process. This will only be genuinely available when the senior managers have a full appreciation of what is involved: senior people are quite capable of changing their minds when it becomes apparent that they did not anticipate the actual levels of cost or inconvenience, for example. The Board of E5E has actually proposed that a benchmarking exercise take place, but they will be as likely as any other senior management team to change their minds.

Stage 2 – Set objectives

The areas to be benchmarked should be determined and objectives should be set. Note that here, the objectives will not be in the form of aspirations for improvement to specific processes and practices, but more in the nature of stating the extent and depth of the enquiry. In E5E, for example, under fundraising, it might be decided to look carefully specifically at the security of cash collections.

Stage 3 – Identify key performance measures

Key performance measures must be established. This will require an understanding of the systems involved, which, in turn, will require discussion with key stakeholders and observation of the way work is carried out. A simple example of how this stage would be carried out within E5E might be to examine the processes for assessing applications for research grants.

Stage 4 – Choose organisations to benchmark against

Internal benchmarking may be possible where, for example, there are local fund-raising branches or shops. Where internal departments have little in common, comparisons must be made against equivalent parts of other organisations. The aim will be to find an organisation that does similar things but which is not in competition with E5E. For example, another charity that undertakes educational work, but is not involved in medical research would provide a suitable benchmark for E5E's educational work. This is a kind of **functional benchmarking**.

Stage 5 – Measure performance

Measure own and others' performance. Negotiation should take place to establish just who does the measurement: ideally, a joint team should do it, but there may be issues of **confidentiality** or **convenience** that mean each organisation does its own measuring.

Stage 6 – Compare performance

Raw data must be carefully analysed if appropriate conclusions are to be drawn. It will be appropriate to discuss initial findings with the **stakeholders** concerned: they are likely both to have useful comment to offer and to be anxious about the possibility of adverse reflection upon them. This may be particularly applicable to the volunteer staff within E5E, who may be sensitive about their amateur status.
From the performance measures identified, E5E's management should identify where improvements are needed.

Stage 7 – Improvement programmes

Design and implement improvement programmes. It may be possible to import complete systems; alternatively, it may be appropriate to move towards a synthesis that combines various elements of best practice. Sometimes, improvements require extensive **reorganisation** and **restructuring**. In any event, there is likely to be a requirement for **training**. Improvements in administrative systems often call for investment in new equipment, particularly in IT systems.

Stage 8 – Monitor improvements

The continuing effectiveness of improvements must be monitored. At the same time, it must be understood that **improvements are not once and for all** and that further adjustments may be beneficial.

Part (c)

Top tips. The wording of the question gives you the clue that you need to be sympathetic to the concerns of the staff in your answer to this question. An autocratic approach clearly would not score many marks: instead you need to take a concerned, humane stance and think about the setting. Application to the scenario is vital here, because the concerns will be specific to the volunteer status of many of the workforce and to the nature of a benchmarking process.

Also, think about the change management issues involved here. If you remember nothing else about change management, you should be aware of the need to tell people what is going on: rumour and speculation will become a serious problem if there is a deficit of communication.

Communication with staff and volunteers

Any type of investigation with an eye to change will cause apprehension and possibly alarm. People like to feel comfortable; they are comfortable with what they know and uncomfortable with the prospect of unspecified change. The first priority, therefore, must be to give the **fullest possible information about the purpose and**

nature of the benchmarking programme. This is best done face to face by senior managers in a series of small meetings, but where this is impractical, as may be the case with volunteers running branches and shops, the information should be disseminated down the usual communication channels of the hierarchy.

Part of the message should be that **senior managers support the programme** and that they see it as important.

The communication effort should continue throughout the life of the programme, reporting on progress and improvements made.

Encouraging staff involvement

The second main route to dealing with the concerns of staff lies in the way the programme is carried out. It must be emphasised that there is no element of personal assessment: procedures and methods are being examined, not individual performance. The staff should be encouraged to contribute as much as they can to the benchmarking process. They will be able to give important information on how systems *actually* work, to help in the development of key performance measures and to assist with the evaluation of proposed new methods. Many volunteers will have **wide experience of management** and **methods in other organisations** and, as a consequence, will have much to contribute.

18 Product portfolio

Text reference. The product life cycle and product portfolios are discussed in chapter 4 of your BPP Study Text. Social responsibility is discussed in Chapter 2.

Marking scheme

			Marks
(a)	Diagram of product life cycle, if given	1	
	Explanation of how the product life cycle model can be used to analyse a product portfolio	Up to 4	
	Classification of 3 C's current products in the portfolio, with explanation for classification, up to 1 mark each	Up to 3	
		Total up to	8
(b)	Evaluation of each option on the product portfolio, up to 3 marks for each option	Up to 9	9
(c)	Up to four social responsibility issues and implications discussed, each worth up to 2 marks	Up to 8	8
		Total	25

Part (a)

Top tips. Although the question specifies the model you are expected to refer to, you must remember that there are very few marks available for simply explaining the model.

However, in this case drawing the diagram for the product life cycle would be a good place to start. If you show the positions of 3C's products on a sketch of the standard life cycle curve, you can then think what those positions tell you about 3C's portfolio.

Note that this question was about the product life cycle, not the BCG matrix (see the Examiner's comment below).

Easy marks. The life cycle model is simple and if you can get the names of the phases roughly right you should collect some easy marks. A good diagram will show both sales and profit.

Examiner's comment. The words 'product portfolio' do not always imply that the BCG matrix should be used primarily for consideration of the *balance* of the portfolio. In the case of the life cycle model, balance means that the portfolio shows a succession of products at different stages in their individual life cycles.

The product life cycle (plc) is a simple model of the way that the sales of a product and the profits earned by it vary from its launch to its exit from the market. The model is crude in that a product's progress through the phases can be heavily influenced by marketing activity and, in any case, many products do not follow the standard pattern. Nevertheless, the concept is a useful tool for basic **portfolio analysis**.

The PLC for 3C's current product portfolio can be depicted as follows.

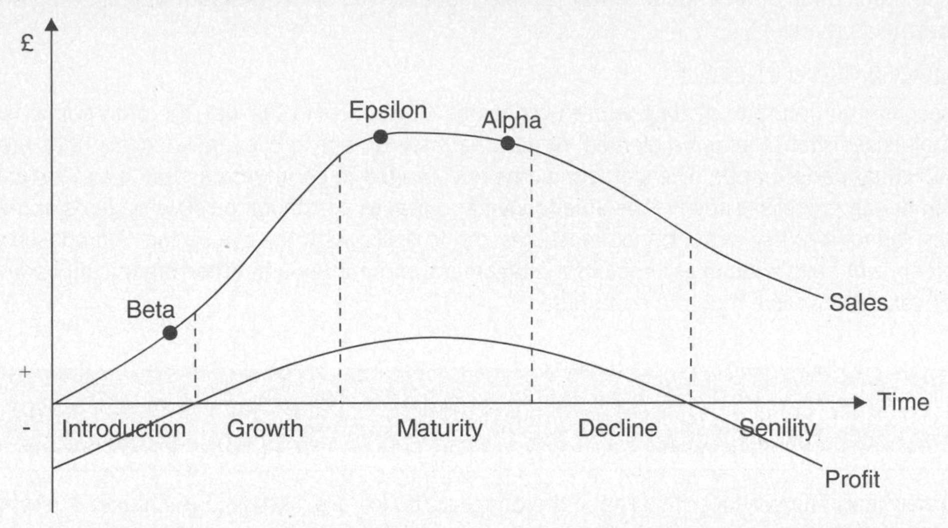

(i) **Beta** has been positioned in the introduction phase, because it has been only recently launched, and has not yet generated significant sales volume. However, Beta is likely to have a fairly accelerated Introduction stage, as it is a specialised product, for which there is already demand within the hospital market.

(ii) **Epsilon** has been positioned at the peak of the cycle. Although it has not been available for long, it has already 'achieved significant success' (and its introduction/growth curve may therefore have been steeper than shown in our 'standard curve' model). Sales are not expected to increase (hence its position at the peak).

(iii) **Alpha** has been positioned just at the point of decline. It has been available much longer than the other products, so its maturity stage may have been longer than our 'standard curve' model suggests. Decline will soon follow, because of the expiry of the patent and the entry of low-cost generic competitors: the decline/senility stage will last 12 months.

It would be usual with any portfolio analysis technique to look for **balance**: in plc terms this means that the portfolio should include products at several stages in their life cycles, so that as one declines, another is emerging to take its place.

3C's current portfolio seems adequate in this respect, in that while Alpha is expected to enter a rapid decline phase, Epsilon is generating high sales in its maturity phase as an acceptable 'cash cow', and Beta has been launched and has potential for growth.

However, the fact that Beta is unlikely to generate sales volume to replace Alpha (because it targets a specialist market niche) is likely to be of concern: hence the need to secure succession by launching Alpha2. There are also 240 drugs at various stages of development, so it should be possible to continue the succession into the future.

Part (b)

Top tips. In this part of your answer you have to look into the future and consider the probable effect of each option on 3C's portfolio as a whole. It is not enough say what will happen in plc terms to the three drugs concerned. You must also say what effect each option is likely to have on the future *balance* of the portfolio. **Risk** will be an important factor to consider.

3C has three investment options. Each must be considered in terms of the risks and benefits it offers, both in itself and within the context of the product portfolio. It is also important to consider the implications of *not* choosing each option.

Alpha2

Investment in Alpha2 may be seen as extending the maturity phase of Alpha by five years – or as introducing a new product (with accelerated introduction and growth due to existing brand loyalty), giving 3C two well-performing products in that category rather than just one. The overall effect on the portfolio will be to **ensure product succession** and produce moderate improvements in both sales and profitability.

This is a **low risk strategy** since clinical trials of Alpha2 are complete and the drug could go straight into production. Moreover, Alpha2 will be able to **build on existing brand loyalty** *and* **present barriers to entry** to the generic competitors to Alpha (who will be a step behind again). The disadvantage of this option is that the launch of generic copies could limit Alpha2's sales and profitability, unless the improved performance of Alpha can be successfully marketed.

If Alpha2 is not chosen, 3C will rely on Epsilon for most of its sales and profits in the near to mid term.

Beta

Beta is clearly felt to have good potential for growth, being in the early stage of its life, but it is unlikely to replace Alpha in the product portfolio as the latter declines, as it is a much more **specialised niche product**. Even if the rival product is as successful as Beta, it will not be of a generic type; prices and profitability should remain high, though total sales of Beta will be hit by competition from the rival.

The current investment option is based on direct marketing/promotional competition: with 'active promotion' by the rival, there is no guarantee of added market share – but there should be significant growth in sales in the short term.

Gamma

Seen in isolation, Gamma is the **high risk, high reward option**. It has yet to complete its clinical trials and there is no guarantee that these will be successful. On the other hand, a breakthrough treatment for HIV could be confidently expected to generate an extremely large volume of sales and high profit (with no near rivals on the market). Even if the low profit, high social benefit route is chosen, the rewards could be high.

Seen from the portfolio management point of view, Gamma would be a good succession option compared with Beta: it is likely to have an accelerated introduction and growth stage (due to existing market demand and no competition), and is ultimately likely to have a higher revenue peak at maturity.

There is some logic, therefore, in suggesting that either Alpha2 or Gamma should be the chosen option, with choice largely depending on 3C's appetite for risk.

Part (c)

Top tips. Although it is possible to discuss social responsibility issues in a lot of detail, it is unlikely you will have the time to do so in your exam. In the same way, the questions are unlikely to be on particularly complex areas of CSR or ethics. That is certainly the case with this question, which is about a very basic topic: for whose benefit do business organisations exist?

You are not expected to produce a definitive answer to this question: the requirement uses the verb 'discuss', which is quite unusual. Although in some questions, you are expected to make a reasoned recommendation, that is not the case here. Here all you need to do is consider the various relevant points.

Remember that you have to consider all *three* investment options though: do not concentrate solely on the dramatic potential of Gamma.

General social responsibility (CSR) implications

3C is required to operate within the confines of the **laws** of the countries in which it does business and, as an innovative pharmaceutical company, it is subject to extensive **regulation and ethical scrutiny** relating to its drug development and manufacturing activities.

There are certain key **stakeholders** in pharmaceutical development, including those who need/use the drugs. There is a general ethical obligation to alleviate suffering where possible, and uphold the public interest. However, as a commercial organisation, 3C exists primarily to make profit for its owners.

CSR implications of Alpha2

The implications of Alpha2 fundamentally rest on the issue of **fair competition** and **offering consumers value for money** for an essential product. Generic copies of drugs are often equally effective and able to be provided at lower cost (particularly in developing countries for whom the cost of importing patent brands is prohibitive): it is socially responsible to encourage basic pain-killers to be widely available. The case for Alpha2 rests on whether it bears out the claims of improved performance (which will be made by 3C's marketers) in such a way as to justify consumers paying a higher price.

CSR implications of Beta

The key implication of investment in a marketing campaign for Beta is likely to be the ethics of that campaign in its approach to medical practitioners and hospital buyers, in this specialist market (generally based on personal selling). Medical practitioners and procurement professionals have their own codes of ethics which prohibit them from altering their decisions or recommendations as a result of inducements (corporate hospitality, gifts and so on) – but this may be the 'temptation' for 3C in aggressive competition with its rival.

CSR implications of Gamma

There is already an ethics-related conflict between the aims of the development specialists (to offer a life-saving drug at the lowest possible price, to maximise the benefit to society) and those of the marketing department (to maximise profits by charging a high price for a monopoly product).

The worldwide HIV/AIDS epidemic has attracted enormous public interest both in support of individual sufferers (creating pressure to alleviate suffering where possible) and as a social justice issue (since the poorest countries are the worst affected). Many interest and pressure groups are lobbying for drugs to be made available (or patents shared) on a preferential or non-commercial basis.

3C has **responsibilities to its owners to reap optimal profits** from the drug's strong competitive advantage, in what is a high-risk, high-cost industry. However, it also has an **ethical responsibility** to make the drug as widely available as possible. Nor is this only a pricing issue: arguably, 3C would be socially responsible to invest in manufacturing Gamma – and irresponsible *not* to invest in its development, given that the drug has the potential to be successful.

There is no easy solution to the profitability dilemma, but it may be possible to compromise via differential pricing: eg making the drug available on favourable terms to medical charities in poorer countries. The problem here would be that such a dual pricing policy would inevitably attract both complaint from individuals who had to pay the full price, and arbitrage, with the attendant risk that profits would be undermined.

There is also a secondary social responsibility issue of raising the market's hopes of the new treatment *before* clinical trials have confirmed its success and safety, and rendered it legally and commercially viable.

19 Printing company

Text reference. Industry lifecycles are discussed in Chapter 4 of your BPP Study Text. Mission statements are discussed in Chapter 1.

Top tips. The verb for **Part (a)** is to 'Identify' the characteristics. 'Identify' is only a level 2 verb, so you do not need to give a detailed discussion or evaluation of the characteristics.

Also, the question requirement does not ask you to link your answer to the scenario, so you do not have to do so. And remember, there are only 5 marks available for part (a), so don't spend too long on it even if you think it is the easiest part of the question! For example, you shouldn't have wasted time drawing a detailed diagram of the whole industry lifecycle.

Unlike Part (a), your answer for **Part (b)** does have to relate directly to the scenario and company D. So don't just discuss mission statements in general terms, but discuss specifically what issues D would face in trying to create one.

A useful way of generating possible ideas for your answer might be to think of the advantages and disadvantages of mission statements. But remember, the question isn't asking for advantages and disadvantages as such. So you must present your answer as the issues D's management needs to consider, rather than as a series of advantages or disadvantages. For example, one of the perceived problems with mission statements is that they can be too general to have any real impact on employee's behaviour. So, the relevant issues which D's management needs to consider is how to make the mission statement specific enough and relevant enough to day-to-day activities to influence employee's behaviour.

Part (c) also requires you to apply your knowledge to the scenario. However, you could have used the idea of 'SMART' objectives as a useful framework for discussing the relevant characteristics. SMART identifies five characteristics and there are five marks available, so a brief discussion of each – in the context of D – should have allowed you to score well on this part of the question.

Part (a)

Products – In the mature phase of the industry lifecycle, there will be a high degree of **standardisation** among the products offered by different competitors. Product quality will also be high, as producers look to offer **superior quality** products to their rivals.

Competitors – There will be strong competition in the industry, but the fierceness of the competition may force some of the weaker players to leave the industry.

Buyers – There will be a mass market, so buyers will be widespread. Brand switching will be common: because the product is standardised, buyers will only incur relatively low switching costs in switching brands.

Profits – Profits will be eroding under the pressure of competition in the industry, and due to consumers' bargaining power. Margins will also be reduced by increased advertising and marketing costs.

Strategy – The competitive pressures in the industry will lead to firms seeking ways to reduce costs to try to preserve their margins.

Part (b)

Impact on employees' behaviour – One of the main reasons for D to have a mission statement is to make its employees aware of its organisational culture. So the mission statement will need to illustrate D's basic values and beliefs, to let the employees recognise the behaviours which are expected of them.

D's culture and values are currently strongly **shaped by Mr Z's behaviour and ideas**. For example, the desire to know everyone's first names suggests an open culture and a friendly environment. But D will need to ensure the values it encourages are **appropriate to the competitive environment**.

Impact of industry lifecycle – As the printing industry enters the mature stage of its lifecycle, D may be find itself facing increasing competitive pressure and the need to reduce costs. The mission statement will need to ensure that it promotes behaviour which is consistent with this. It may be that D's management feel that maintaining the friendly working environment will help maintain staff motivation and therefore may help keep costs low.

However, the mission statement will need to make staff appreciate the need to **work efficiently in a competitive environment**, rather than simply being friendly with one another.

Practical and realistic aims – D needs to ensure that its mission statement sets realistic and attainable aims, but also that it can actually deliver practical benefits. As the industry moves into its mature phase, D will need to work harder to retain its customers. So the mission statement should also try to identify how D will give value to its customers.

To do so in a meaningful way, it needs to identify aims which staff will be able to apply, otherwise they will simply ignore the mission statement as a management gimmick.

No experience of mission statements – D, and its staff, have never had a mission statement before. Creating one for the first time could be an issue in itself, for both management and staff. It will take time and effort for management to develop the statement, so they need to feel the organisation will benefit from having it.

Equally, the staff will need to accept it and feel it is relevant to them. If they basically ignore it, its value will be significantly reduced.

Specific aims – If the staff can't relate the statement to the work they do, it will not have any effect. So the statement needs to be **specific** enough that staff can see how it applies to their everyday work. For example it should indicate how staff should treat each other, and how staff should treat customers, suppliers and other external stakeholders. One of the main criticism of mission statements is that they can be too general to have any impact what people do, so D needs to avoid this problem.

Deliver competitive advantage – One of the key elements of a mission statement is a summary of a company's distinctive capabilities and competences.

Although D has historically grown by exploiting the technology one of its founders developed, that technology is no longer new or unique. Because the industry lifecycle is in its mature stage, it is likely that many of D's competitors have now all developed similar technology to it.

Therefore, the mission statement shouldn't emphasise the current technology too much, and it could be more useful to highlight that **finding new technologies** and **developing new innovations** will be the source of new growth in the future.

Flexible to changing environment – If D does look to introduce new ideas, then the mission statement needs to be flexible enough to accommodate them. If the mission statement essentially forces D to replicate what it is currently doing, rather than to look forward and develop, then it could be counter-productive in the long run.

Appropriate to competitive strategy – D has used the new technology its founders developed to establish itself as the market leader. As such, D may initially have been pursuing a differentiation strategy. However, as the industry enters the mature stage of its life cycle, it may be more important to highlight the **cost effectiveness** of D's printing solutions, rather than their **distinctive** product features.

In this case, D's mission statement will need to make clear this change of emphasis.

Market position – D is still marginally the market leader in the industry, and so the mission statement might include a statement that it intends to maintain that market leading position. That might be a bold statement to include, however, given that its technology is no longer innovative and so its competitors can look to capture market share.

Nonetheless, the mission statement should still include an indication for D's customers and other external stakeholders of where it sees its position in the industry in the longer term.

Part (c)

D's objectives need to reflect the fact that the industry is moving into the mature stage of its lifecycle.

Specific objectives – D's objectives need to be specific so that management clearly know the key issues for them to focus on. For example, given the strong competition and declining margins in a mature market, D could set objectives about the market share and level of profitability it wants to achieve.

Measurable – D's objectives need to be measurable so that the management can measure the company's actual performance indicators and see how well they compare to the objectives. For example, D could quantity the percentage market share it wants to achieve.

Achievable – There is no point setting objectives which are not achievable, because they will be ignored. For example, in a mature market it would unrealistic for D to set a target of growing sales by 10% per year.

Relevant – Objectives need to be relevant to a company's mission. In this context, the relevance of D's objectives will depend on the mission statement it writes. For example, if the mission emphasises the continued importance of innovation for D, an objective which looks to reduce research and development expenditure would not be appropriate.

Time-related – Objectives need to have clear timetables for achieving the measures specified, so wherever possible D should prescribe completion dates for the objectives it sets.

20 Conglomerate value

Text Reference. Conglomerate (unrelated) diversification, and methods of disposal and divestment are both covered as strategic options in chapter 6 of the Study Text.

Marking scheme

				Marks
(a)	Clear definition of conglomerate diversification		1	
	Additional marks for clarifying what the definition means		2	
				3
(b)	(i)	Calculation of market capitalisation for each division	1 ½	
		Numerical demonstration that group does not add value	1	
		Interpretation of figures from institutional shareholders' perspective	1	
		Concluding remark about adding/destroying value	1	
			Total up to	3

(ii)	Evaluation of suggestion to dispose of real estate division	Up to 4	
	Evaluation of suggestion to reduce costs	Up to 3	
		Total up to	7
(c)	Each disposal method accurately described and related to the scenario, up to 3 marks for each method, of which 1 for identification, and 2 for evaluation	Up to 10	
	Clear recommendation, justified according to evaluation	2	
		Total up to	12
		Total	25

Part (a)

Top tips. Requirement (a) is a pure test of knowledge. However, it is only worth 3 marks, so you should only write a brief explanation and then move on to parts (b) and (c).

Conglomerate – or unrelated – diversification is a strategy in which a **business moves beyond its present industry** into products or markets which are unrelated to its present industry.

The resulting conglomerate is a collection of businesses which **do not have any real operational relationships** to each other, and do not a common identity through being part of the same group. The only connection between them is a common parent.

Because the businesses are in different industries, conglomerate diversification does not generate any operating synergies from combining the different businesses. However, the parent can **spread its risk,** or change the balance of its **product portfolio** by entering new markets or new products.

Equally, the parent may use conglomerate diversification as means of **exploiting under-utilised resources** – for example, it may buy an underperforming business, and then turn it around by introducing better management.

Part (b)

Top tips. You need to recognise that both parts of requirement (b) ask you to '*evaluate*' assertions made by the institutional investors. Your evaluations should identify the aspects of the assertions which you think are valid and also those which you think are not valid. A simple market capitalisation calculation would identify that the Group's valuation is significantly less than it should be.

Also, note that in (b) (ii) there are two different suggestions to consider: (i) a sale of one of the divisions; and (ii) a rationalisation of the head office functions / facilities. A sensible approach would be to evaluate the two suggestions separately because there are very different issues at stake in each of them. Closing the Group headquarters is essentially a cost rationalisation exercise, but closing a division will affect revenue generation. With respect to the proposed sale of the real estate division: what will be the effect on the Group's profitability and its growth prospects? Would one of the other divisions be a better candidate for disposal?

Examiner's comments. This question was reasonably well answered, but many candidates did not properly evaluate the institutional investors' comments by discussing whether they were valid or correct.

Many candidates simply undertook the market capitalisation calculation without then discussing what it means.

(i) The institutional investors claim that the Board 'has destroyed value' implies that CCC group's overall valuation of $1,000 million is less than it should be given the potential value of each of the divisions.

	Earnings	*Market sector average P/E*	*Market capitalisation*
	$m		$m
Construction and building	50	8	400
Engineering and machinery	20	13	260
Real estate	30	23	690
Total	100		1,350
Group valuation			1,000

The calculations suggest that if the divisions were operating separately, and were quoted separately on the stock market, their **market capitalisation would be $1,350 million**. Therefore, at face value, it seems that the Group has 'destroyed' $350 million of value.

However, because it is based on the sector average P/E ratios, this calculation assumes that the performance of **each of the divisions is in line with their sector average**. It is possible that some of the divisions are themselves under-performing, which may explain some of the shortfall.

Nonetheless the scale of the shortfall does suggest that the Board is destroying value, and so the institutional investors call for strategic review is justified.

(ii) While a review of the Group's strategy is necessary, such a review should consider all of the operating divisions as well as the Group and head office functions, rather than being limited in scope to the areas the institutional investors suggest.

<u>Disposal of real estate division</u>

The real estate division currently contributes 30% of the Group's earnings, and is the **fastest growing** of the divisions (over 20% per year in the last three years). The divisional management team expects this rate of growth to be sustained.

The real estate market sector also has the **highest P/E ratio**, suggesting the sector affords good growth prospects, and supporting the divisional management team's optimistic forecasts.

In terms of CCC's overall portfolio, the real estate division appears to offer **better growth prospects** than either the construction or engineering divisions, although the engineering division is likely to have relatively secure earnings by virtue of its contracts with government departments. Nonetheless, disposing of the Real Estate department does not appear to be a good strategic move.

The **Engineering and machinery division** looks a more suitable candidate for disposal, despite its government contracts. It makes the **lowest contribution to group earnings**, and has a lower growth rate than the Real estate division.

Although the **Construction and building division** has the lowest growth rate, it **generates 50% of the Group's earnings** and CCC would be unlikely to want to dispose of a division which contributes such a large proportion of earnings.

Moreover, we should also consider the **institutional investor's potential motives** in recommending the sale of the Real Estate division. They are looking for a **large one-off dividend**, which suggests a short term strategy. In this respect, it is likely that CCC could sell the Real Estate division for a much **higher price** than the Engineering division, thereby generating more cash to pay a dividend. However, that is unlikely to be in the Group's longer term strategic interests.

<u>Relocating Group headquarters</u>

The Group headquarters are 'quite luxurious' and located in the capital which suggests that they are quite expensive. Therefore it is likely that **cost savings** could be made, by relocating to one of the divisional headquarters. There may be reasons why the offices need to be located in the capital (for example, being close to the stock market) in which case the Board need to explain this to the investors.

Equally, there may not be space in any of the divisional headquarters to relocate all the Group staff (50) there; in which case, the Group could still look at finding **new offices where overhead costs will be lower**. This could also be a good opportunity to review whether the Group really needs 50 staff or whether the team can be streamlined.

In the context of the suggestions that the Group is 'destroying value' it should be looking to **demonstrate value for money in its spending**. Controlling costs and making cost savings will be one way of doing this. Moreover, by reducing Group costs, the management charges levied on the divisions could also be reduced.

Part (c)

Top tips. Requirement (c) like (b) (ii) is also, in effect, a multi-part requirement: you need to identify alternative methods; evaluate them; and then finally recommending the most appropriate one.

The approach we have used in the answer below is to look at each alternative method in turn, before making a recommendation in the light of our comments on each method. As in part (b), because the action verb asks you to 'evaluate' you need to assess both the advantages and the limitations of each potential method the Board could use for the disposal.

For parts (b) and (c) you may find it useful to consider whether the 'institutional investors' (who only hold 20% of the equity) are representative of all the shareholders. Do the institutional investors' wishes for a large one-off dividend represent the interests of the other 80% of shareholders? For example, might some of the other investors prefer longer-term growth over a short-term dividend?

Marks available. The marking guide for this question allows up to 3 marks for each disposal method accurately described and related to the scenario, up to a total of 10 marks, suggesting you are expected to suggest 3 or 4 different methods. A further 2 marks are available for recommending the most appropriate method.

The answer below includes five alternative methods which the Board could consider. Given the mark allocation, you would not have needed all five to pass this question, but all five are valid options, and so are included for tutorial purposes.

Nonetheless, whichever methods you do include, it is important that you make a recommendation as to which is the most appropriate to CCC.

Easy marks. You should be able to identify a range of possible disposal methods. By then assessing how well they address the issues arising from the shareholders comments in the scenario, you should be able to how appropriate the possible methods are in this context.

If the Board does decide to sell the real estate division there are a range of alternative methods it could use for the disposal:

Sale as a going concern to another business

This would represent, in effect, the reverse of the transaction by which CCC acquired the real estate division. The division would be **sold to another company**, in exchange for either **cash or shares** in the acquiring company. All the responsibilities and costs of running the division would pass to the acquiring company, as would all future profits.

If the sale were made for cash, it could provide CCC with an **inflow of cash** to meet the shareholders demands for a large, **one-off dividend payment**.

However, it would mean that **CCC loses 30 percent of its earnings**, and any future earnings growth which the real estate division would have generated. This could mean that the Group's subsequent **ability to pay dividends in future years is reduced**. Moreover, stripping out the division with the highest P/E ration would cause CCC's share price to fall; in turn reducing the value of the remaining Group, and possibly again laying the Board open to a charge of 'destroying value.'

Finally, the sale of a division would mean that the Group **overhead costs** have to be apportioned over only two divisions rather than three, again reducing the Group profitability unless significant overhead savings were made.

Demerger

A demerger would mean that instead of simply being a division of CCC Group, the real estate operation becomes a **separate company in its own right**. The existing shareholders of CCC Group are likely to **receive shares in the new company** in proportion to their existing holding in CCC.

The logic behind a demerger is usually that the existing formation is creating **negative synergies**, and therefore the new company will generate greater earnings operating independently rather than being part of the Group. Given the suggestion that CCC is currently 'destroying value' this could well be the case.

However, from CCC's perspective a demerger is less attractive. As with a cash sale, CCC Group would lose 30 per cent of its earnings. But unlike the cash sale, the **demerger would not generate a cash inflow** into the business.

Therefore this option **would not provide for a one-off dividend to the shareholders**, because it is a non-cash option. If shareholders want a one-off cash boost they will have to generate it themselves by selling their shares in the newly demerged company.

However, one advantage of this approach from the shareholders perspective is that they have **shares in both companies**. If they remain dissatisfied with the performance of CCC Group, they could elect to sell their shares in it, and just retain their shares in the new real estate company.

Liquidation of assets

The real estate **division could be closed**, its staff made redundant (or redeployed elsewhere in the Group) and its **assets sold off** at market price.

However, given that the real estate is a profitable and growing business this is unlikely to be a desirable option; not least because a sale of assets is **likely to command lower prices than the sale of the business as a going concern**.

A liquidation of assets would be a cash sale, and so would provide a cash inflow to underwrite a one-off dividend payment. However, given that both options would lead to CCC losing 30 per cent of its group earnings, it is likely that it would **prefer the option which generates more cash** in return.

Moreover, there is a likely to be **negative publicity** surrounding the closure of the division, and any associated redundancies, which may have a further negative impact on the Group's performance.

Management buy-out

In a management buy-out, the **management of the real estate division would buy the division** from CCC, with the intention of driving forward its growth and increasing its profitability.

However, an important issue here is the **price which the managers would agree to pay** for the division. On the one hand, it is likely they will have to obtain **funding from venture capitalists** to support their own capital in the purchase, so they will want to keep the purchase price as low as possible to minimize their debt and future interest charges.

On the other hand, the divisional **managers are likely to know more about the business** and its prospects than the Group managers, and also any external purchasers.

These two factors together are likely to mean that the price a management buy-out team offer for the sale is **likely to be lower than the price which could be earned from an open market sale** of the business as a going concern.

Again, the Group needs to remember that after the buy-out the real estate will be a separate entity so Group **earnings will be reduced by 30 per cent**. Therefore it should not accept a sale price which is too low, particularly if it intends to make a one-off dividend payment to the institutional investors.

However, a management buy-out may be considered the most attractive option from a **public relations perspective**. The Group could present the sale of a successful division to its management positively – emphasising the way they are being given the opportunity to control the division's strategy and its future.

Management buy-in

This approach, in effect, combines aspects of a management buy-out and a sale of the business as a going concern. Like a management buy-out, a **group of people collectively buy the division**. However, unlike a management buy-out, the **purchasers come from outside the company**. So after a management buy-in the real estate division would become a privately owned real estate company.

From CCC's perspective, the management buy-in is another option which could **generate a cash inflow**, and so would provide the funds to satisfy the investors demands for a one-off dividend. Depending on the extent of the purchasers' knowledge of the business, CCC may be able to earn a higher selling price from a management buy in than from a management buy-out.

However, a management buy-in does not afford the same positive aspects in terms of public relations.

Recommendation

CCC could either look at the disposal as a means of **maximising value** from the Group, or **raising cash** to pay a one-off dividend. A de-merger is probably the option which would maximise value, but it will not generate cash. However, a management buy-out will generate cash proceeds, and, by allowing the divisional management full control of the real estate division should allow its capabilities to be exploited fully. Although the new entity will be outside the group, the public relations aspect of a sale to management will be more positive than an open market sale.

Therefore, CCC would be advised to sell the real estate division through a management buy-out.

21 TKC group

Text reference: Ansoff's matrix is discussed in Chapter 5 of the BPP Study Text for E3.

Part (a)

Top tips.

The scenario highlights that TKC is considering two major strategic issues: acquiring an engineering company, and divesting two of its divisions.

Although 'acquisition' and 'divestment' are not specifically included in the matrix, you should use them to help suggest strategies which TKC could use for each of the four strategic directions indicated by Ansoff's matrix.

For example, the acquisition would help TKC to increase its market share in the engineering market in the UK (market penetration), and it could give TKC access to new products (product development?) or new markets (market development?) which could help it achieve growth further.

By contrast, 'divestment' could be seen as having almost the opposite effect as diversification, so this may suggest TKC is unlikely to be interested in diversification. Nonetheless, the question still asks you for an example of a possible strategy for each quadrant in the matrix, so you still need to give an example of a possible diversification strategy. Given the circumstances, related diversification is more likely to be appropriate rather than unrelated diversification.

The fact that TKC intends to dispose of its leisure and financial services divisions is also important for the example strategies you suggest. You should not have attempted to apply Ansoff's matrix to the leisure and financial services division (because they will no longer be part of TKC once they have been divested).

Examiner's comments: It was disappointing to see how many candidates failed to apply Ansoff's matrix to the scenario information in part (a). A common mistake was that candidates attempted to apply the model to the leisure and financial services divisions of TKC. However, they had been specifically told in the scenario that these two divisions were to be divested. Therefore, applying the model to these divisions was irrelevant and would have earned no marks.

Similarly, providing a generic description of each quadrant of the model would also have earned very few marks. Answers must be applied to (the relevant divisions of) TKC.

Ansoff's product-market matrix looks at the mix of products and markets a firm can use to try to achieve growth, and identifies four options:

Market penetration – increasing sales within **current markets** (increasing the firm's market share in those markets) using **existing products**

Market development – selling **existing products** to **new markets**

Product development – selling **new products** but to **existing markets**

Diversification – introducing **new products** and selling them to **new markets.**

TKC is currently considering two proposals – the acquisition of BAB, and the disposal of the leisure and financial services divisions – and it could look at these proposals to see how they could help it carry out the future strategic directions indicated in Ansoff's matrix.

Market penetration – TKC and BAB both operate in the engineering market in the UK. Therefore, acquiring BAB could be seen as a market penetration, because it would allow TKC to increase it's market share to the point that it becomes the largest engineering business in the UK.

Market development – TKC does not currently have any export business, but BAB does. Therefore, the acquisition could provide TKC with the opportunity to sell its existing products into the export markets in which BAB already operates.

Product development – We do not know how similar the engineering products or services which BAB sells are to TKC's, however it seems likely that will be at least some similarity. Consequently, the acquisition could lead to some synergistic benefits in respect of product development; for example, TKC and BAB's engineers working together to develop new products. These new products could then be offered to both TKC and BAB's customers.

Diversification – The decision to divest itself of the leisure and financial services divisions demonstrates TKC's desire to achieve a more concentrated business focus. This may suggest that the Board are not currently interested in diversification, particularly unrelated diversification. However, it possible they could be interested in **related diversification**, for example, acquiring a supplier who produces some of the parts used in the engineering business.

Part (b)

Top tips.

The scenario should give you a number of ideas to help you answer this requirement. Some of these are fairly straightforward : the combined organisation will be the largest engineering business in the UK; BAB has an export business; TKC is in financial difficulties. However, some need a bit more analysis; for example, TKC has exhausted its cash reserves, and its share price has fallen – how will it fund the acquisition?

To score well in part (b) you should try to present a well-balanced discussion (of advantages and disadvantages), applied directly to the acquisition of BAB. A general discussion of the advantages and disadvantages of acquisitions (compared to organic growth) were not required here, and would not have earned any marks.

Benefits

Market leader – After the acquisition, TKC would have the largest engineering business, by revenue, in the UK. This size should also allow it to benefit from greater economies of scale than it currently enjoys.

Export markets – TKC does not currently have any export business, but the acquisition will give it a substantial export business. This could be particularly important given the prolonged recession in the UK and the risk that it could adversely affect TKC's engineering business in the future. Having export markets, which are at different stages in their business cycles to UK markets, should help provide TKC with alternative sources of growth even if the UK engineering market enters a downturn.

Application of management skills – TKC's corporate strategy is based on applying its 'exceptional management skills' to help it make significant profits from companies it has acquired. The fact that BAB is currently in financial difficulties could make an ideal target for TKC to acquire and turn around, using its exceptional management skills, and the fact TKC already has experience of managing an engineering business.

Disadvantages

Financial difficulties – Although the fact that BAB is in financial difficulties may allow TKC to acquire it for a relatively cheap price, acquiring a business in financial difficulties could still be a risk, particularly as TKC's 'exceptional management skills' have recently been called into question, and its cash reserves have been exhausted.

Impact on resources – Depending on how BAB performs post-acquisition, it may prove to be a further drain on TKC's resources. Moreover, because TKC's cash reserves have already been exhausted, it will not be able to make any substantial investments into BAB even if it becomes clear these are required after the acquisition.

Source of BAB's current difficulties – It is not clear why BAB is in financial difficulties, for example whether the problems are due to a short term slow down in demand, or a more structural decline in demand for its products. If the financial difficulties are due to longer term problems then there may be little TKC can do to restore BAB's financial performance.

Employee integration – BAB seems to be quite a large company in relation to TKC. BAB currently employs 500, while TKC employs 900 across its three divisions. Acquiring 500 new employees will be a substantial management task for TKC, but if the integration of BAB and TKC's engineering businesses isn't successful this will reduce TKC's chances of gaining any synergies from the acquisition.

Part (c)

Top tips.

Although part (c) is divided into two parts, a number of the things that TKC needs to plan are very similar for both circumstances. And as with part (b), a number of clues about potential issues are given in the scenario, although they require a bit more lateral thinking here. For example, TKC is a listed company (meaning it has to plan what it is going to communicate to the stock market). Likewise, given the numbers of staff involved, what HR resources will be required to manage the process, and will TKC have sufficient resources to cope?

Although some issues were similar across both circumstances, there were also some specific issues, so you should have tried to identify some of these too. For example, how were the divisions going to be divested (eg sale as going concern vs liquidation), and what impact would the choice of divestment method have on any potential redundancy payments?

Notice, however, that the requirement asked you to 'recommend' the things TKC should plan. Your recommendations need to be justified and explained, so your answer should not have simply been a brief list of things TKC should consider, without any discussion of the points you have listed.

Note: The answers below are not exhaustive, and there are several additional relevant points you could have made which would have earned you marks. For example, both scenarios could involve substantial amounts of **senior management's time**, and are likely to involve specialist **legal advice**. These have to be planned and the costs budgeted for.

(i) Corporate reorganisation

Communication to investors and stock market - TKC is a publicly listed company, and so it needs to plan how it communicates it decision to divest the two divisions to the stock market. If investors see the divestment as a symptom that TKC is in financial difficulties, then its share price could be forced lower still. To try to prevent this, TKC needs to explain the commercial logic for the decision: that it is shedding loss-making activities in order to concentrate on its (profitable) engineering business, and improve the company's business focus for the future.

Nature of the divestment – It is not clear what form the divestment is going to take, or even whether TKC is planning to divest both divisions in the same way. The divisions could either be sold as going concerns to another company, sold through a management buy-out, or else their assets could be liquidated and the businesses closed.

TKC may wish to avoid liquidation if it can because if part of the group is closed it may further call into question the financial position of the company as a whole.

Financial implications – The nature of the divestment will also have financial implications for TKC. On the one hand, if the divisions are liquidated then the staff will have to be made redundant, requiring a potentially significant outflow of cash as redundancy payments. On the other hand, if TKC manages to the sell the division, then any cash raised from the sales could help fund potential acquisition of BAB if that goes ahead.

Dealing with employees and HR issues – In total TKC employs 900 people across its three divisions. Given that the three divisions have similar sized revenues, it is not unreasonable to assume they also have similar sized workforces, which means that TKC will be losing approximately 600 of its staff. This means the reorganisation will lead to a significant amount of work for TKC's human resources department – for example, arranging redundancy settlements or transfers of employment depending on the nature of the divestment. TKC will need to consider whether it has sufficient HR staff to deal with this, or whether it will need to hire additional temporary staff to help out.

Overcoming resistance from staff – Crucially though, TKC will also need to consider how it communicates the reorganisation to the staff. Again, the nature of this message will depend on the nature of the divestment, but regardless TKC should be prepared for resistance from the divisions' staff. Even if they are not being made redundant, the staff will still be concerned about how their jobs will change under new owners, and so TKC will need to plan how to deal with any resistance they encounter from the staff.

(ii) Proposed acquisition

Communication to stock market – In the same way that TKC needs to communicate its decision to divest the two divisions, so it would also need to communicate the logic behind its decision to acquire BAB. Some investors may be concerned that TKC's own falling share price and a lack of cash reserves mean this is not an appropriate time to be making a substantial acquisition. Again though, TKC needs to highlight the benefits of the acquisition: that the acquisition will make TKC the market leader in the UK, and will provide TKC with new opportunities to grow through exports.

Funding – Although the purchase price may be deflated due to BAB's financial difficulties, the acquisition is likely to involve a significant financial outlay. The dramatic fall in TKC's share price, coupled with its lack of cash reserves means that it is going to have to rely on debt financing to fund the acquisition. Therefore, a vital part of TKC's planning will be to secure the necessary credit it needs to make the acquisition.

Dealing with employees and HR issues – The acquisition would result in TKC acquiring up to 500 additional employees. Again, this could place a considerable burden on TKC's HR department as it tries to integrate the ex-BAB staff into its systems and policies; for example, including them in its pension scheme if it has one. As in the context of the divestment, TKC will need to consider whether it has sufficient staff to cope with this, or whether it will to hire additional temporary staff.

Overcoming resistance from staff – In the same way that TKC's own staff are likely to be resistant to the reorganisation, so BAB's staff may be anxious about the acquisition. It will be particularly important for TKC to identify who the key members of BAB's staff are and try to encourage them to remain with the company, otherwise TKC could be left with skills shortages in key aspects of the business (for example, the exports business which it has no prior experience of).

22 Telecommunications joint venture

Text reference. Joint ventures are discussed in Chapter 6 of your BPP Study Text.

Top tips. In **Part (a)**, you are only asked to 'explain the characteristics of a joint venture.' You are not asked to relate them specifically to the scenario.

In our answer we have made some passing references to the case study, as a couple of the points provide a useful link forward to parts (b) and (c). However, you do not need to do this. Also, remember that part (a) is only worth 5 marks, so don't go into detail on points which are more relevant to the later parts of the question.

For **Part (b)**, note you are asked to discuss the benefits to country C, not to either Y or one of the companies in C. Although a lot of the benefits of the joint venture might accrue initially to the venture partner in C, you need to think more widely about how they could then also benefit the country in general. For example, could new skills and new technology be transferred not only to the individual company, but also to other companies in C?

The political context of the scenario could also help you generate some ideas. Politically, a joint venture looks more acceptable than an acquisition by a foreign company, because more of the economic benefits (and the tax revenues) are likely to remain in C.

Part (c). Although there is only a single requirement – to evaluate the risks that Y should consider – there are still effectively two different sources of risk for you to consider here. On the one hand there are risks associated with the Y's potential partner: for example, will it have the necessary skills to be a valuable partner?

On the other hand, there are risks associated with Y itself. Y has previously always expanded via acquisitions, so what are the different issues it will face in a joint venture arrangement rather than controlling a fully owned subsidiary?

Note also, that part (c) asks you to evaluate the risks of entering a joint venture, rather than entering Country C. So, for example, discussions about political or economic risks in C were largely irrelevant, because they would have applied equally if Y had acquired a company there as opposed to entering into a joint venture.

Part (a)

Characteristics of a joint venture

Joint control – A joint venture is a contractual arrangement in which two or more companies undertake an economic activity which is subject to joint control.

New company – Joint ventures often result in the venture partners setting up a separate, new organisation in which they each hold an equity stake. In a number of joint ventures, the partners have equal stakes in the new company, but this is not necessarily the case. For example, if one partner provides the majority of capital for a venture, it is likely they will also control the majority share of the venture.

Exploit opportunities – Joint ventures are often used to enable the companies to exploit an opportunity which it would be difficult for any one of them to take advantage of individually.

Joint ventures are often used as a means of entering markets which are either closed to foreign companies or difficult for them to enter. Therefore Y might see a joint venture as a good way of entering C, given that the government there is under political pressure to ensure that the country benefits from any foreign investment.

Pooling skills and competencies – A joint venture can allow the partners to bring together different skills and competencies. For example, one partner might have extensive technical expertise, while another may have local market knowledge. This could well be the case with Y and a local partner in C.

Risks and rewards – Because the joint venture involves two or more partners, the risks and rewards involved are shared between the various partners. Joint ventures allow risks and capital commitment to be shared between the venture partners, so they can be a very useful way of undertaking expensive technology projects.

Part (b)

Benefits to Country C of the joint venture

Transfer of skills – As Y is a successful international company, its staff, and particularly its managers, are likely to have more commercial skills and experience than the staff at the company in C, a developing country. The joint venture would allow staff in C to work in conjunction with Y's staff to gain knowledge and skills. This would benefit C by increasing the skills in its labour market.

Technology transfer – It is also likely that Y will be using more modern technologies than the company in C. So again, the joint venture arrangement will allow the company to become familiar with new technologies, which it could then use in other aspects of its business in C, thereby potentially improving technology in C as a whole.

Investment – The national telecommunication company in C was using old equipment and needed considerable capital investment. The joint venture arrangement with Y will mean that the cost of this investment will be shared with Y, which may accelerate the investment programme.

Also, Y might be encouraged to make more investment through the joint venture than it would otherwise do if it simply acquired the company as a wholly owned subsidiary.

This investment in the telecommunications equipment should hopefully improve the quality of service that the customers in C get.

Competitive rivalry – If the joint venture company makes a major investment with one of the four local telecommunications companies, the other three might feel compelled to match this investment so that they do not lose market share. This investment should lead to benefits for all customers in C through improved telecommunications.

Benefits of improved telecommunications – If the telecommunications infrastructure in C is improved overall this may make C a more attractive location for foreign investment by companies in other industries.

Clustering – The joint venture company might be more likely to use local suppliers and components than would be the case if Y simply acquired the existing company as a subsidiary. The joint venture arrangement could benefit the supporting industries in C, and could bring new jobs to the local economy.

Future growth – If the joint venture model proves successful, then other international telecommunications companies, or other foreign companies, may be attracted to invest in C using a similar joint venture model. Any such additional investment will provide a further boost to C's economic development.

Tax revenues – C is likely to receive a greater proportion of tax revenue from the joint venture company than it would from a subsidiary of an international corporation. For example, if Y owned the company in full, it could use transfer pricing to reduce the level of taxable profits in C, and therefore the tax revenues which would accrue to C. Such a transfer pricing arrangement is less likely in a joint venture because it is a stand-alone legal entity.

Part (c)

Potential risks from potential partner

Skills of partner – The success of the joint venture will be strongly affected by how well the partner's skills support and complement Y's. Y is **entering the market at an early stage after deregulation**, and will rely on its partner's market knowledge and marketing skills to take advantage of opportunities in the market. If the partner doesn't deliver these skills, and Y has to do the majority of the marketing itself, in a market it doesn't really know, it will take longer for the joint venture to become established in C. Consequently its potential profits are likely to will be reduced.

Y also needs to be satisfied that its partner is going to contribute actively to the venture, rather than just using it as an opportunity to benefit from a skills and technology transfer from Y.

Partner's stability – Y should consider the financial stability of its partner, and the security of its customer base. Although the four companies in C each have approximately 25% of the local market at the moment, if there is a danger that large numbers of customers may leave a supplier soon then this may make an investment with that supplier worthwhile.

Reputation of venture partner – There is a risk to Y that its own reputation could be damaged by the actions of its partner if its partner acts unethically or illegally. Y's own professional judgment and integrity might be questioned if its partner is discredited.

Objectives from venture – The joint venture partner may have different objectives from Y. For example, they may have different opinions on the level of market growth they expect, and what this will mean for the joint venture's growth prospects. Equally, there may be differences of opinion as to how profits should be used. Should they be distributed to the shareholders, or should they be re-invested in the venture's growth?

If the two partners have different objectives, this is likely to lead to conflict, which could damage the performance of the venture.

Risks surrounding Y itself

No experience of joint ventures – Y has previously always expanded by acquiring subsidiaries, and so has no experience of joint venture arrangements. The skills required to manage the joint venture will be very different to managing a takeover. In particular, Y cannot impose its culture and working practices on the new operation, it will need to be sensitive to the local staff in C. If the integration of the two cultures is not managed properly, this will lead to conflict between the two partners.

Roles and responsibilities – Y and its partner will need to define clearly who is responsible for doing what; for example, Y might be responsible for IT and technology, and the local partner for marketing. These responsibilities need to be clearly defined at the outside to remove the chance for any disagreements and conflict. Equally, the way the joint venture is going to be managed, and who will hold the management roles, need to be clearly defined to prevent any conflicts.

Financial splits – Y and its partner will need to agree how the **costs of any investments are split**, and equally how the **profits are shared**. If Y is going to contribute the majority share of the capital investments, it could look to secure more than 50% share of the profit from the venture. Any such distribution of profits needs to be clarified with the venture partner at the outset – both to avoid conflicts later on, but also to avoid the risk of Y not getting the returns it believes it is due.

Lack of clear strategy – Y needs to have a clear idea of what it wants to achieve from the joint venture. One of the key issues it needs to consider is whether it views the joint venture as a permanent arrangement, or as a stepping stone to acquiring the local partner at a later date.

These longer term strategic plans might affect Y's objectives for growth and capturing an increasing share of the market. However, if Y does not have any strategic plans, there is a danger the venture could drift, and therefore it will not generate the returns Y might have expected.

Transfer of confidential information – One of the dangers of joint ventures is that partners can gain confidential information about each other which could be subsequently used competitively by one partner against the other. One of the main potential benefits of the venture to the partner in C is the transfer of technology and skills from Y. However, there is a risk that if the local company gains too much information then it might seek to leave the venture and compete directly with Y.

Political risk in C and security of assets – The government in C faced strong resistance to its privatisation plans. Therefore there is a risk that a future government might look to reverse the privatisation, and reduce foreign involvement in business in C. If this happens, Y's position in the joint venture might be under threat, and it might be difficult for Y to recover its assets and investment.

23 Electronic tracking equipment

Text reference: Strategic options and Lynch's expansion matrix are covered in Chapter 6 of the BPP Study text.

Part (a)

Top tip: This question requires a relatively straight forward application of Lynch's expansion matrix: looking at ways of expanding into new markets. Possible strategies include agency agreements, licensing / franchising agreements, joint ventures or acquisitions.

Note that the question verb is 'evaluate' so a sensible approach would be to consider the suitability, acceptability and feasibility of the strategies you suggest.

However, when evaluating the strategies, bear in mind that D's product is quite specialised and the volume of sales will be quite limited because the market only consists of police forces.

Also remember you are asked to evaluate **four** strategies, so make sure you do this. There are a total of 16 marks available, suggesting four per strategy, so you should try to divide your answer relatively evenly between the four strategies you choose.

Also, while you are evaluating the four strategies try to think which one seems to be the most appropriate for D to pursue. This will then provide a link to your answer for part (b).

However, make sure that your answer for part (b) makes a clear recommendation about which strategy D should pursue. In other words, which of the strategies you have evaluated in part (a) is likely to be most beneficial for D to follow?

Note: For tutorial purposes we have evaluated five possible strategies which D could have considered using. However, you should have only included four in your answer.

1. Agency agreements

D could continue to manufacture its products in its own factories in its home country, and then **export** the products to its targets countries. In such a scenario, D could also use local **sales and marketing agents** in the target countries to promote demand for its product.

Suitability – It is likely that the police forces in D's target countries will be funded by their governments. Therefore, if D selects agencies which already have established relationships with the relevant government departments in a country this could increase the chance of making sales in that country.

Acceptability – A potential risk with this approach comes from the level of control D will have over the agency, and accordingly how much effort the agency puts into setting D's product.

D will be totally reliant on the agency to generate sales for it, but if the agency doesn't devote much time and effort or resources to promoting D's product then this approach will not be able to generate the '**rapid growth**' the Managing Director wants. On this basis, an agency agreement may not be an acceptable strategy.

Feasibility – This is a relatively simple strategy, and also one which allows D to maintain control over the manufacturing standards and quality of its product.

Low capital requirement - There will be no need for D to acquire premises or employ staff in the target countries, which could be a particular benefit in the early stages of expansion before D establishes how lucrative the market in each country might be. If a market turns out not to be as lucrative as D had hoped, it can withdraw from that market relatively cheaply because it will not have invested any capital there.

Equally, D will not need to develop any in-depth knowledge of the business practices and customs in its target countries because agents will already have this local knowledge.

2. Licence agreement

Topic tip: The Examiner's answers indicated that a franchise agreement would not be appropriate here because D is dealing with a tangible product rather than a business concept. In his answer, the Examiner suggested that under a franchising agreement, the franchisor allows the franchisees to use a *process* or *business concept*, as well as the franchisor's name, in return for the payment of a franchise fee. However, in D's case, the agreement is to *manufacture specific products* rather than to use a *business concept*, so the Examiner held that a licence agreement is more appropriate than a franchise agreement.

Under a licensing agreement, a company in the target country could manufacture D's product using components supplied by D, and using D's manufacturing process.

Suitability – In order for licensing to be a successful strategy, D will need to find a suitable company in the target country that could manufacture the product to the appropriate standard, and then market and sell the product effectively. The scenario doesn't give any indication of how easily D would be able to find such a licence partner, but without one this strategy would not be viable.

However, if D can select a licensee which already has established relationships with the relevant government departments in a target country, D's sales opportunities should benefit from this.

Feasibility – Assuming that D can find a suitable company to act as its 'licensee' in a country, then strategy should be feasible. D would not need to build its own factory in the target country, nor employ any staff there, so the strategy doesn't impose any resource constraints on D, and could therefore be implemented relatively quickly.

Acceptability – The Board of Directors are keen to see both revenue and profits grow rapidly. A potential drawback of this strategy is that the licensee is likely to require a larger proportion of the profit than an agent would, because the licensee is adding value to the products by manufacturing it.

Another concern relates to preserving D's **intellectual property**. Not only is D's equipment protected by patents, but its manufacturing process also contains some sophisticated technology. Although D is likely to require any licensee to sign a confidentiality agreement before a license is granted, there is still a risk that the licensee may be able to use the knowledge it gains about D's product and processes to develop its own competitor products in time. The emergence of a potential competitor in this way could adversely affect D's ability to sustain revenue and profit growth.

On this basis, even if a suitable licensee company could be found, licensing doesn't appear to be an acceptable strategy.

3. Joint venture

D could establish a joint venture with an existing company in its target markets, and the joint venture would manufacture and market D's product in those markets.

Suitability – A joint venture (JV) arrangement will allow D to have a much **stronger influence** over the manufacturing and marketing process than a licensing arrangement because some of D's own employees will be involved with the JV.

D's greater involvement in the operation will also help it **develop its own knowledge** of the market in the target country, and in doing so may help D identify additional new product or market opportunities which may allow further revenue growth.

Similarly, D's active involvement in the JV will help D to **identify problems more quickly** than would be the case under an agency or licensing agreement.

Acceptability – Profit sharing – D will have to share the profits from the JV with its venture partner. The percentage split is likely to reflect the division of responsibilities between the venture partners, so if D's partner takes on the bulk of the responsibility for manufacturing and marketing that partner might also expect the majority share of the proceeds. This may prove contrary to the aim of maintaining D's profit growth.

Knowledge transfer – The directors may also be concerned about the degree of knowledge transfer about D's products and processes to the venture partner. As with a licencee, there is a risk that the venture partner could use the JV as a means of finding out about D's intellectual property and then set itself up as a competitor in future.

Feasibility – Capital costs - It is likely that any capital costs (for example, for new plant and equipment) will have to be jointly funded by D and its venture partner. Therefore a joint venture is likely to require greater capital investment by D than either a agency agreement or a licence. Also, if the venture proves unsuccessful, D would have greater financial exposure to losses than it would have under either of these two methods of expansion.

4. Acquisition

D may decide that, rather than working in partnership with another company, it would prefer to acquire an existing company in its target country outright and introduce its own manufacturing capability into that company to deal with local demand for its product.

Suitability – D is not working with a JV partner or a licensee so it would **retain full control** of its technology, thereby reducing the risk of knowledge being transferred out of the company to any potential future competitor.

Moreover, D would retail full control of the manufacturing, quality, marketing and sales processes in the organisation.

In this respect, establishing a wholly owned subsidiary in a country could be strategically important. If D subsequently wants to export in other surrounding countries, this operation would provide a useful base for doing so.

Acceptability – Moreover, D would not have to share any of the proceeds of the business with any other partners.

Feasibility – However, there are a number of issues with the feasibility of this strategy:

Target company – D would have to identify a suitable target company that was willing to be acquired, and it would then have to manage the acquisition and integration of that company into the 'D Group'. There is no evidence to suggest that D has made any acquisitions before, and this inexperience will add to the risk involved in this strategy.

Cost of acquisition – D needs to consider the costs involved. If it buys a relatively successful company, then the purchase price is likely to be high. If it buys a less successful firm, the purchase price may be lower but D is likely then to have to invest further in improving the firm's facilities and premises to bring them up to the standard required to host D's sophisticated technology.

Political issues – Some countries, and governments, look unfavourably on foreign owned companies and assets. Given that D's main customers are governments, it cannot afford to pursue an entry strategy which is not politically acceptable to the governments in its target countries.

Investment levels – Making an acquisition is likely to involve a far greater investment by D than any of the other strategies we have considered so far. However, the size of the potential market (for a specialist product with only a limited replacement market) may not justify the level of investment required.

Moreover, if D does enter a market via an acquisition but the acquisition does not prove successful, there will be significant **barriers to exit** which could make leaving the market expensive. (For example, if D closes down the company it had acquired, it could incur significant redundancy costs.)

Tutorial note. Although the question only asks for 4 options, this is a valid alternative strategy you could have evaluated.

Build its own plant in target country

Rather than entering some kind of partnership with, or acquiring, an existing company in its target countries, D could set up foreign divisions of its own in those countries.

This is likely to involve D acquiring the necessary land and then building its own manufacturing facility. It is also likely to require D to develop its own sales and marketing networks in the relevant countries.

Suitability – This approach would allow D to retain control over all aspects of manufacturing and marketing, and to retain all of the profits from the venture. Moreover, D would have modern, purpose-built factories for its manufacturing operations to use.

Acceptability / Feasibility – Building a factory is likely to involve **considerable capital investment** yet D will have no guarantee that the level of future sales it will generate will justify that investment.

If the operation provides unsuccessful and D wants to leave the market, it will then have the additional costs associated with closing the factory, selling the building and laying off the staff who work there.

D's **lack of previous experience or contacts** in its target countries will make it harder for D to enter the markets there. For example, D may be unfamiliar with local customs and business practices; it is unlikely to have any contacts among (buying) decision makers in the government; and it won't have any access to sales and distribution channels.

Slow growth – D's lack of existing contacts and networks, coupled with the time taken to build new premises, will mean that establishing its own operations in its target markets is likely to be a much slower means of growth than partnering with, or acquiring, an existing company.

This could be a particular issue here given the need to build a completely new factory, and therefore the risk of potential delays and problems associated with the construction project (in an unfamiliar country).

Part (b)

As the Directors of D have recognised, there can be a number of issues in establishing operations in foreign countries. Given that D has no experience of operating outside its country, and it is operating in a specialised business with limited scope for sales growth, D should not be too bullish with its expansion strategy.

Therefore, the level of investment and risk involved with an acquisition [or with establishing its own operations in a target market] cannot be justified. In the first instance, D is likely to be best served by entering an **agency agreement** while it gets a feel for the sales potential available. In time, if it becomes clear the sales potential in the target country (and neighbouring countries) justifies further investment, D could then consider moving to a licensing agreement, but initially D should look to establish agency agreements in its target countries.

Part (c)

Top tip: The question scenario identifies that D country only operates in a single country (its home country), but recognises that other countries will have different political, economic, cultural and legislative environments. How could these environmental differences affect performance between the different countries? For example, if the government in one country is looking to reduce spending while the government in another has no such restrictions?

Note that the question asks about performance *and control* issues. What difficulties could D face in controlling operations in foreign countries – especially as it no previous experience of doing so?

Different economic circumstances – At any time, different countries will be at different stages in their economic cycles. Therefore, some may be growing or generating a budget surplus while others may be in recession or suffering a budget deficit. These differences are likely to influence the amounts governments have available to spend on the equipment that D sells. This will affect D's performance in different countries.

Performance measurement could also be affected by the **relative wealth** of different countries. Sales (and sales prices) are likely to be relatively higher in more affluent countries compared to poorer countries, but costs (for example, labour costs) are also likely to be relatively higher in the more affluent countries. These differences could make it more difficult for the corporate centre to compare how well managers in different countries are managing performance.

Tax regimes – The different tax rates in different countries (either corporation tax rates or taxes on foreign investments) could also affect performance across different countries. Some governments may be more supportive of foreign investment than others.

Legal frameworks – Employment legislation, and health and safety legislation is likely to vary between countries. This may mean that D faces different costs in different countries, as a result of complying with the relevant legislation in each country.

Cultural and social differences – The culture and prevailing work in foreign countries could influence D's ability to control operations in those countries. For example, if D uses expatriate managers from its own country to manage its foreign operations, there could be problems if the foreign workers are used to working in a different way than D expects. **Language** could also be an issue if an expatriate manager has problems communicating effectively with the local workforce.

24 Plastics manufacturer

Text reference. Chapters 5 & 6 of the BPP Study text deal with Strategic options. Chapter 2 covers stakeholder management.

Marking scheme

				Marks
(a)	(i)	Each difficulty identified from scenario information and discussed to explain *why* it is a difficulty (not just repeated from the scenario)	1	
			Total up to	5
	(ii)	Strategies to deal with:		
		Price competition (price wars)	Up to 2	
		Problems in the home market	Up to 2	
		The need for overseas expansion	Up to 2	
		Problems with the labour force	Up to 2	
		Problems in the R&D department	Up to 2	
		Clear recommendations, based on evaluation of strategies	Up to 2	
			Total up to	12
(b)		Each point linked directly to the scenario material, and well discussed	Up to 2	
			Total up to	8
			Total	25

Part (a)

Top Tips. This question requires you to draw upon information presented in the scenario to inform your answer.

Requirement (a) (i) clearly directs you to the scenario – you should identify the difficulties facing F, and then discuss them. It is not sufficient to simply list the difficulties you read about in the scenario; a good answer should discuss the implications of them for F.

Likewise, (a) (ii) requires you to draw information from the scenario to shape your answer. Your need to identify a range of strategies that will help F specifically address the difficulties you have discussed in (a). Merely presenting a generic list of strategic options will not score well.

Notice also that (a) (ii) requires you to *evaluate* alternative strategies, so your answer should include a balanced appraisal of the suitability of the strategies you suggest; before *recommending* those that are most appropriate. Again, your are required to reach a conclusion based on your evaluation.

Easy marks. The scenario should generate a number of issues for you to talk about; and the examiner wanted you to relate your answers specifically to the scenario. If you did this (a) (i) should have offered some very easy marks, and should in turn have prompted you to identify relevant strategies for (a) (ii).

Examiner's comments. Part (a)(i) was poorly answered because candidates 'identified' difficulties rather than 'discussing' them. Part (a)(ii) was answered better, but while candidates identified a wide range of strategies they still failed to evaluate their appropriateness or make any final recommendations.

(i) The main difficulties facing F are:

- **Loss of market share**. F is suffering a reduction of turnover and profits as a result of foreign companies aggressively increasing their share of the beer crate market. If F does not react to this, it will find that the foreign companies overtake its market share leading F to lose further profits.

- **Reduced margins in beer crate market.** Because F is heavily dependent on two major products, it is vulnerable to any reduced margins earned on those products. One of those products is beer crates, and the recent consolidation in the brewing industry, coupled with increased availability of imported crates, has meant that consumers have an increased bargaining power to key the price of beer crates low. This has affected both turnover and margins.
- **Inflexible labour force**. The workforce appears very inflexible, and this inflexibility is leading to inefficiency in the production process and probably resistance to innovation. In turn, this inefficiency is also impacting on profitability, and may ultimately prevent F from reacting effectively to the increased competition form foreign competitors.
- **R&D department is not delivering commercial success**. The lack of commercial awareness within the R&D department means that F is not developing any new products which are commercially successful. This means that it is incurring significant overhead costs (on the R&D department) without realising any benefits to turnover and margins.
- **Poor communications with institutional shareholders**. F has failed to communicate its performance properly to its shareholders. Consequently there is a risk that they will not support future plans for the business, or provide additional capital if it is required to fund future initiatives.

(ii)

Top Tips. Your answer to this question should include strategies to address both the external market difficulties and the internal operational difficulties F is facing. The key difficulties the examiner highlights in his past exam review are: (i) problems of price wars; (ii) problems in the home market; (iii) the need to expand, possibly overseas; (iv) labour problems; and (v) research and development.

Up to 2 marks are available for each of these areas, with a further 2 for a clear recommendation as to which key strategies F should follow.

The answer below covers all these areas, but we have also included some supplementary points in text boxes. Although the points in the text boxes are relevant, you could still score well in this question without including them.

Loss of market share and reduced margins in beer crate market

F's most important priority must be to reverse the decline in the profitability of its beer crate business, caused by the loss of market share and reduction in profit margins.

There is unlikely to be any significant product differentiation for beer crates, and therefore price will play the key role in the product's success.

Pricing strategy

Competitive prices. In order to retain market share, F should aim to keep its price competitive against the foreign imports as their current aggressive growth strategy continues.

Reduce costs. Alongside this competitive pricing strategy, F needs to reduce costs wherever possible to restore profitability. Unfortunately, the inflexible and unionized working practices among F's workforce are likely to make it hard to reduce labour costs.

Although the institutional shareholders have suggested that F should **withdraw** from the beer crate market, this **is not a viable strategy**. F is still the dominant manufacturer in the home market, and if it withdrew from the market it would severely reduce its total sales. This would leave it carrying excessive fixed costs and so be faced with the costs of dismissing staff and closing capacity. Moreover, such a strategy is likely to be seen as a sign of weakness, and would merely encourage other competitors to target its remaining markets.

Market expansion

Market development. By contrast, if the longer term prospects for the home crate market do not look good, then F should look to supply to other overseas markets. In this way, they could increase production volumes and benefit from **economies of scale in production**. The market for beer crates is likely to be equally competitive overseas and so F should consider exporting other containers.

As a further benefit, once F has achieved cost reductions from economies of scale it would be able to compete more aggressively on price in the home market.

Overseas expansion

Foreign manufacturing plants. The fact that foreign competitors have been able to gain market share by competing aggressively on price, suggests that they have a lower cost base than F. F may be able to counteract this by setting up an overseas manufacturing plant of its own, to take advantage of lower operating costs and overheads.

Overseas acquisition. F may be able to combine the objectives of overseas market development and lower production costs by acquiring an existing overseas plastics manufacturer. However, F is likely **to need the support of its shareholders for this strategy**. Consequently, F's management will have to convince the shareholders of the benefits of this strategy, because the shareholders have proposed a withdrawal from the beer crate market.

Problems with the labour force and inflexible working practices

Inflexible working practices. If F is going to compete successfully with its foreign competitors, it will need to **streamline the working practices** within the company and make them more **flexible**.

Reduce bureaucracy. There is currently too much bureaucracy – with negotiating committees, precise job definitions and a complicated system of labour grades.

This bureaucracy is likely to mean that F has a **higher cost base** than leaner, more flexible competitors, and is therefore likely to be contributing to F's declining performance.

F needs to make its working practices more flexible, and simplify the employment structure. However, because the workforce is unionised, F will have to **negotiate with the unions** to get them to support any changes.

Staffing levels. One of the key issues to address will be whether F has more staff than it needs. It may be able to reduce operating costs by **making some staff redundant**. However, such a decision will have to be negotiated very carefully with the staff and the unions in order that it does not provoke strike action or other unrest.

If some staff are made redundant, F will incur a one-off charge for their redundancy payments, but in the longer term operating costs should be reduced. And if having a smaller, more efficient workforce means that F can compete more effectively in the longer term, then this one off cost is worth incurring – especially as the worst-case alternative may be that the company collapses.

Uncommercial R&D department

F is seeing its margins and market share in its core market (beer crates) come under increasing threat and so innovation and new product development could be critical in finding alternative areas for growth.

One such area could be electro-plastics, which is a much newer sector, and one in which F could potentially establish a competitive advantage if it is the first company to develop a successful product.

However, for F's new products to be a commercial success they have to **meet a market need**.

Marketing and market research. In order to identify which new products could be commercially successful, F needs to understand what sort of products it customers want.

The R&D department should then focus its time and resources on projects which are selected by the operational and marketing departments in the light of this market research information.

Links between R&D and marketing. The marketing department has an important role in indicating which products the R&D department should focus on, according to customer needs. But equally, once the R&D department has developed a new product, they need to work with the marketing department to generate consumer interest in the new product.

Given the current organisation structure, it is likely that there is not much communication between departments, so creating these links between departments will require a **change in the organisation's culture**.

Recommended strategies

F should focus on three key strategies to address the difficulties it is currently facing.

1 **Improve competitiveness to protect existing markets and market shares**. It should look to do this by reducing costs, in particular by reorganising current working practices.

2 **Look to develop new markets overseas** to reduce dependence on the home market.

3 **Look to develop new products**. It should do this by combining the new technological developments which the R&D department are working on, with an understanding of market needs provided by the marketing department.

Part (b)

Top tips. Although this part of the question is about stakeholder (shareholder) management rather than strategic options, you should still relate your answer directly to the scenario. The reasons why F needs the shareholder support stem from the difficulties and strategies which form the basis of (a).

A general answer about the importance of communicating with shareholders would have earned few marks here.

Depressed share price and unrest due to lack of information. Share prices are in part determined by expectations of future earnings. Because F has not kept its shareholders informed, they have very little knowledge about the company, its performance and its future plans. They do not know about the potentially exciting developments in electro-plastics for example. The only information they see is past performance, published in F's annual report and accounts.

As a result of this lack of knowledge, a group of institution shareholders has requested a strategic review and suggested that F should withdraw from its core market (beer crates). This is a potentially very damaging strategy, but it is one which may never have been suggested if the shareholders have been kept better informed.

Vulnerable to take-over bids. Perhaps most importantly of all, the poor results and reduced value of the company may make it vulnerable to a hostile take-over bid. If such a bid were received – even if it were under-valued – the shareholders may be tempted to accept it, because they have no information from the directors explaining why they shouldn't sell, and/or how business will improve in the future.

Alternatively, even if they were considering a sale, the directors should have been communicating any developments and issues with the shareholders so that they have an indication of what a fair value for the company would be based on the current projections.

Need for shareholder support. The Directors of F are potentially going to be faced with some major strategic decisions in the near future – foreign expansion, foreign acquisition, and workforce restructuring (which may lead to industrial unrest). The Directors will need the support of the shareholders to deliver these strategies, for example to provide additional finance in a rights issue, but if the shareholders feel alienated because of the lack of communication, they are unlikely to give their support.

No surprises. The company has reported uneven profits for the past five year, and this year it will have to report significantly reduce profits. If shareholders and financial analysts have not been informed of the reasons for this, and what F is doing to improve performance, the results are going to come as a nasty surprise. Investors and analysts do not like surprises, so the results are likely to lead to a fall in the company's value (share price).

25 Biotechnology company

Study Reference. Evaluation of strategic choices (suitability, acceptability, feasibility) is covered in Chapter 7 of the Study Text.

Alternative answer. This question provides a good illustration of the fact that there may often be more valid points that you could make in answer to an E3 question than you will have time for in the exam.

In particular, there are a large number of points you could make in relation to part (b).

The first answer below tries to show a wide range of these points for tutorial purposes. However, by doing so, the answer becomes quite long. Moreover, you would not need to make all the points we do to score a good pass to this question.

To illustrate this we have also presented a second answer (in a text box after the first answer) which would have scored a good mark for this question, and was written under strictly timed conditions.

This question illustrates that there is often no single right answer to business strategy questions. If you are asked to recommend an option (as in (d)) provided your recommendation is consistent with your previous answers and is sensible you will score marks for it. The two answers we have presented make different recommendations in part (d) but both are equally valid and would have both scored the marks available.

Marking scheme

			Marks
(a)	For a full description of suitability	Up to 2	
	For a full description of feasibility	Up to 2	
	For a full description of acceptability	Up to 2	
		Total up to	6
(b)	For evaluation of the cash flow guarantee from the venture capitalist	Up to 5	
	For evaluation of the purchase by the pharmaceutical company	Up to 5	
	For evaluation of the merger with another biotechnology company	Up to 5	
		Total up to	12
(c)	Identification of any reasonable alternative option	1	
	Evaluation of the alternative option	Up to 4	
		Total up to	5
(d)	Clear recommendation based on the evaluation	2	2
		Total	25

Part (a)

Top tips. A sensible way to approach requirement (a) would be to take each aspect of the SFA framework – suitability, feasibility, acceptability – in turn, and discuss how that aspect can be used to evaluate strategic options. Note your answer to (a) does not need to be specifically related to the options facing DDD.

Strategic choices are evaluated according to their **suitability** to the organisation and its current strategic logic; to how **feasible** it will be to implement them given the organisation's resources; and how **acceptable** they will be to the organisation's various stakeholders.

Suitability – A strategy must fit with an organisation's current operational circumstances and its strategic goals. In this context an organisation should consider the choices in relation to a corporate appraisal:

- How well does it exploit the organisation's **strengths** and distinctive **competences**?
- How well does it address any **weaknesses**?
- Does it help the organisation take advantages of **opportunities** available to it?
- Does it allow the organisation to deal with **threats** facing it?

Alongside these questions, an organisation should also consider whether a strategy will help it generate or maintain **competitive advantage** over its competitors.

The most suitable strategy for an organisation will be the one which allows it to do this most effectively.

Feasibility – For a strategy to be feasible, an organisation must have **sufficient resources** to carry it out successfully. In this context, resources include **money**, **technology**, **materials**, **staff** and **time**. If a strategy cannot be implemented using an organisation's existing competences, and therefore demands new competences to be acquired, it may not be feasible.

Acceptability – This aspect of the framework looks at the acceptability of a potential strategy to an organisation's various **stakeholder groups** – for example, customers, management, staff, shareholders and bankers. To assess a strategy's acceptability, an organisation should consider the values and interests of key stakeholders and then assess how well these fit with the strategy. Two key considerations when considering a strategy's acceptability will be the **financial return** it is expected to deliver, and the **level of risk** involved in adopting it.

Part (b)

> **Top tips.** Unlike for part (a), for requirement (b) you do need to apply the SFA framework specifically to the three options identified by the founders. Therefore a sensible approach here would be to apply the SFA framework to each option in turn; ie suitability of option 1, feasibility of option 1, acceptability of option 1, suitability of option 2 etc. It is also important to identify the different stakeholders involved here: the founders, the venture capitalists and the employees. What will the potential impact of the different options be for each of them?
>
> Note, however, that you are not asked to comment on the overall appropriateness of the options at this stage – that comes later in (d).
>
> **Easy marks**. If you approach (b) in a methodical way – working through the suitability, feasibility and acceptability of each option in turn – you should be able to score a good number of marks here.

1 Cash flow guarantee from venture capital company

Suitability

DDD's main weakness is a shortage of cash, and the guarantee from the venture capitalists will ensure there are sufficient funds to allow DDD to continue until the first drug is successfully launched in commercial quantities.

The injection of cash will not, in itself, add to DDD's strengths, but assuming the new drug proves commercially successful the funding could allow DDD a competitive advantage which it would have otherwise been denied.

The venture capitalists have only agreed to guarantee DDD's funding until the first drug is successfully launched, and so there may still be question marks about the **longer term funding requirements** between that launch and DDD's flotation, unless cash inflows from the launch of that drug are sufficient to support the business' cash needs.

However, to the extent that the venture capitalist **funding will meet cash needs** in the short to medium term and bring at least one new drug to market this option is suitable.

Acceptability

Venture capitalists – This plan will see a significant rise in the venture capitalist's shareholder in the company – from 15% to 60%. As the venture capitalists have proposed the plan, we can assume it is acceptable to them.

Founders – However, the increase in the venture capitalist's shareholding will mean that the **founders' stakes in the company are significantly reduced**. This may not be acceptable to the founders, particularly in the context of the profits they might make when the company is floated in five years time.

Employees – Similarly, the plan will not be acceptable to the employees because it will reduce the numbers of shares available to them through their share option scheme. Currently, the employees are prepared to accept relatively low salaries because they will receive shares in the company when it floats. However, if this option is removed they are likely to either **want higher salaries**, or will **leave the company** altogether. If too many employees leave, DDD's ability to develop its new drug may be jeopardized.

Feasibility

This option does not, in itself, affect the internal resources of the company so there are no problems about its feasibility.

2 Purchase by pharmaceutical company

Suitability

This option will allow at least some of the drugs which DDD is working on to be brought to market, but not by DDD as a company in its own right.

Given the foundations intention to float the company on the stock exchange, it seems likely that one of the strategic goals was to **run DDD as an independent company**. From that perspective, the outright purchase by another company is not a suitable option.

Acceptability

Venture capitalists

This option is **unlikely to be acceptable to the venture capitalists**, not least because they have proposed an alternative option. However, possibly more importantly, they are unlikely to be happy that whereas they invested in DDD expecting to see significant returns when it successfully launches its first new drug, they will no longer get the benefit of these returns. We do not know the terms of the deal under which the pharmaceutical company has offered to buy DDD (for cash, or for shares) but either way it is unlikely that the venture capitalists will receive the same returns as they would if DDD have successfully launched the new drug as an independent company.

Founders

This option **may not be acceptable to the founders** either, because while they currently have the independence and status of being their own bosses, under the new structure they will simply be employees (researchers) in a much larger company. If the large company offers the founders a favourable price to acquire DDD now, (rather than them having to wait 5 years to benefit from the flotation) the relative acceptability of this option may be increased. However, this will probably be unlikely – especially if the larger company is aware of DDD cash flow problems.

Employees

The employees will be concerned about the acquisition because the larger pharmaceutical company **only intends to retain 'a few of the staff'**. Therefore there is a risk that some of the current employees will be made redundant, which will not make this an acceptable option for them.

The other issue for all the employees to consider is that they will lose the potential benefits accruing from DDD's share option scheme in the event of it floating. However, if the larger company offered them higher base salaries than DDD did, they may be prepared to accept the security of a higher salary instead of the potential benefits of the share option scheme.

Feasibility

There are no problems with the feasibility of this option.

3 Merger with another biotechnology company

Suitability

Because the other biotechnology company's new drug will be launched in six months time this will provide **a short term cash injection** to support DDD until its first new drug is launched.

However, whereas DDD is then expecting to launch one new drug in most subsequent years, the other company is not expecting to have any other new drugs commercially available for another 5 years. Therefore, it is **debatable whether the other company has the same strength in developing new drugs** as DDD. If the merger effectively means that the other company provides a short-term cash injection in return for piggy-backing on DDD's competences in the longer term, then that is unlikely to be a suitable option for DDD.

Acceptability

Venture capitalists

Again, this option is **unlikely to be acceptable** to the venture capitalists, because it would mean DDD rejects the option they have proposed. Also the merger would **dilute the venture capitalist's share** in the new company which is unlikely to be acceptable.

Founders

As with the acquisition by a larger company, the merger would **reduce the founder's independence and autonomy**, because the directors of the other company would now be jointly responsible for business decisions and strategy. This change may not be acceptable to DDD's founders. Moreover, there is no indication of how long the founders would be expected to stay with the newly merged company. If they are expected to remain for a long time, they may find this restrictive.

Also, there is no indication whether the newly merger company would still **look to float in 5 years time**. If it would not, this again may be undesirable for DDD's founders.

<u>Employees</u>

The merger is very unlikely to be acceptable to the employees, because the rationalization of the workforce will mean that some **employees are made redundant**.

Also, if the newly merger company does not intend to float the employees who remain will **lose the potential benefits from the share option scheme**. It is possible, that they may be offered higher base salaries to compensate for this, but this appears unlikely since the other company has fewer new drugs in the pipeline that DDD and so **on-going cash flow could still be a problem** for the business.

<u>Feasibility</u>

The feasibility of this option will depend on how similar the research and development practices of the two companies are. The merger is the only option which will involve the integration **of the systems from two different companies**. This could mean that there are some significant changes to DDD's operating systems, and the **time taken** to complete the merger could also be an issue.

In addition, DDD's founders have **no experience of managing a merger** process which could increase the risk of the merger being unsuccessful.

Part (c)

Top tips. Requirement (c) asks you to evaluate one other option the founders might pursue. We have taken the view that DDD currently is spreading its resources too thinly over a large number of developments and so could rationalise the number of drugs in development. However, if you suggested a different alternative and evaluated its suitability, acceptability, and feasibility you would have got credit for this. For example, given the founders background as senior researchers in a university medical school might they consider whether there are any research grants which DDD could apply for to supplement its cash flow?

Examiner's comments. Parts (a) and (b) were generally well answered by most candidates. However (c) was generally not well answered. Very few candidates recognised the most obvious option to improve available cash flows by reducing the number of products in development from 12 to a more cost effective level.

At the moment, DDD has 12 drugs in development, a number of which may not be successfully launched. One option which DDD could pursue is to **reduce the number of drugs in development** and concentrate funds on those drugs which can be brought to market soonest.

<u>Suitability</u>

This option will not in itself generate an additional cash inflow for the business. It will only be suitable if by concentrating resources on a small number of drugs they can be **brought to market quickly enough** to cover the cash short-fall in nine months time.

There may also be issues around **which drugs to stop developing**. Those which can be developed most quickly may not be the ones which will be most commercially successful in the longer term.

Moreover, as with any development, there is no guarantee that the drugs which DDD chooses to continue with will be commercially successful.

<u>Acceptability</u>

Venture capitalists – This option may be acceptable to the venture capital company in that it doesn't involve any dilution of their share in the company. However, if reducing the number of drugs in development reduces DDD's future earnings this may be less acceptable to the venture capitalists. DDD's perceived earnings potential will affect its value when it floats on the stock exchange.

Founders – This option will be acceptable to the founders because it **maintains their independence and does not dilute their shareholding in the company**. As with the venture capitalists, however, the founders have a vested interest in not restricting DDD's future earnings too much however, because they will be the principal beneficiaries of a successful flotation. Because this option will reduce the number of new drugs DDD is working on at any time, it may decide to delay the flotation to allow the number of drugs launched to be increased before it floats.

Employees – This option is unlikely to be attractive to the researchers working on the drugs whose development is discontinued.

From the perspective that this option will not change the company structure or the employees' share options, it may be relatively more attractive, although not if the flotation is significantly delayed.

Feasibility

There should be no problems with the feasibility of this option.

Part (d)

Top tips. Requirement (d) is only worth two marks, so you should not spend too long on it. Do not repeat your answers from (b) or (c); but rather use them to reach a conclusion. You are asked to recommend one option only, so make sure you do just that!

DDD should select its preferred option by considering its impact on the three main stakeholder groups (venture capitalists, founders, employees).

Option 1 (Additional funding from venture capitalists) – This is relatively unattractive to the founders and the staff due to the reduction in shares available

Option 2 (Acquisition by large company) – This will not be acceptable to any of the stakeholder groups

Option 3 (Merger) – This is also unlikely to be acceptable to any of the stakeholder groups

Option 4 (Reduction in development portfolio) – This will be the most attractive for the founders and the staff, and should be acceptable to the venture capitalists.

Therefore, DDD should **reduce the number of drugs in development**.

Alternative answer to Question 25 (Biotechnology Company): see note above

Part (a)

Suitability

This means whether or not the proposed option makes strategic sense i.e. is it a logical fit with the company's activities. An example of this is an option that builds upon a critical success factor in which the company is proficient, or an environmental opportunity that the company is well placed to exploit.

Feasibility

Put simply, this is whether or not the company can successfully pursue the proposed option through to completion. Factors to be considered include, for example in DDD's case, regulatory approval or completion of successful clinical trials. Of more immediate concern to DDD is whether or not they have sufficient funds to bring their drugs to market.

Acceptability

This relates to whether or not the strategic option will be acceptable to the company's stakeholders. For example, in DDD the three options for funding must be assessed in the light of whether they provide an acceptable level of financial return and business control to the founder members, the 10 staff they employ and the venture capitalists.

Part (b)

Each option will be assessed using Johnson, Scholes and Whittington's framework: suitable, feasible, acceptable.

Option 1

Suitable

This option appears suitable. It would allow the company to pursue its mission to develop drugs for commercial use. Once this happens the stock market listing is much more likely to be obtained. The lack of cash is a major weakness for DDD and this option resolves this issue.

Acceptable

The founders will have mixed feelings with regards to this option.

Although it appears to guarantee the immediate future of DDD, releasing some of their equity via a subsequent floatation, the amount of equity they are having to trade appears very high.

The other employees will also have mixed feelings because although it may guarantee they get the opportunity to realise their share options they may also suffer a dilution of their value.

The venture capital firm will see this as a good deal. In exchange to underwriting DDD until it becomes commercially successful they get a massive increase in their financial returns. As an organisation that thrives on high risk and high reward investments this represents an excellent opportunity.

Feasible

This option appears feasible. There is no indication that the venture capitalists do not have the funds necessary to support the company until the first drug is successfully launched.

Option 2

Suitability

This option also appears suitable for bring the drugs to market. It would provide DDD with the resource required to see its drugs through to market, and a lack of resources is its key weakness at the moment.

However, it will mean that DDD no longer operates as an independent company, and so the founders may not think this is a suitable option if one of DDD's strategic goals is to operate as an independent company.

Acceptable

Acceptability will vary according to the parties. The venture capitalists will only view this as acceptable if it represents a better financial return based upon risk when compared to options 1 and 3.

The founders may prefer to retain a degree of independence and show some concern for the welfare of the other staff due to lose their jobs. This may depend upon the terms of the buy-out.

The other staff will be concerned as this option offers limited job security and they will be concerned as to the impact upon their share options.

Feasible

There should not be any problems with the feasibility of this option, although ultimately the success of this strategy may be subject to the takeover getting regulatory approval of the takeover and the ability of the two parties to agree to the sale, and to upon price and related conditions of the sale.

Option 3

Suitable

This option appears unsuitable. The combined entity would still be suffering a shortage of cash and there is no guarantee that enough funds would be available to see the first drug to market in 6 months. Equally important is that there is no assurance as to the commercial viability of the first drug the merger partner has developed.

Acceptable

This option does not seem acceptable to any of DDD's key stakeholders.

Other staff will fear for both their jobs and share options given the cash flow issues that are unresolved and the mention of staff rationalisation.

The founders may feel that they are tying themselves to a company with more problems than their own, given the 5 year wait to maturity of the merger partner's other drugs.

The venture capitalists may view this as a less attractive company than DDD. They are being asked to take on board a company that may extend the period of time in which a successful floatation may occur. This is unlikely to appeal to them as they are potentially able to realise their current investment in DDD within two years.

Feasible

This option appears to be unfeasible. Once again, regulatory approval would be required, which may delay the merger beyond the crucial 6 month deadline. Given the uncertainty over cash flow it is also highly unlikely that the key financial stakeholders such as DDD's venture capital partners and founders would agree to such a move, unless they were offered a significantly increased holding in the combined entity.

Part (c)

Alternative strategic option

It would seem that the biggest problem facing DDD is a gap between cash resources and investment strategy. The simplest way to solve this would be to focus on fewer drugs until such time that DDD starts to generate revenues.

In order to implement this strategy DDD should undertake an immediate review of its drugs portfolio and identify those drugs most likely to be commercially successful within the shortest time frames. Any drugs that fall outside of these parameters should be either mothballed, or alternatively sold to other biotechnology firms with an interest in purchasing them, which may even boost cash reserves. With the same number of staff focusing on fewer drugs the development cycle may be shortened.

This strategy would be suitable as it allows DDD to pursue its aim of developing drugs to bring to market. The feasibility appears high as it will allow the company to continue to trade whilst preserving its limited cash reserves. The founders, staff and venture capitalists should find this acceptable as it increases the likelihood of the company surviving to the point where it becomes an attractive floatation proposition thereby allowing them to realise their investments.

The main drawback of this strategy, however, is that it increases risk by focusing the company's resource on fewer drugs. Should the assessment of these drugs turn out to be wrong then DDD has a chance of pursuing unsuccessful drugs whilst spurning potentially lucrative ones.

Part (d)

It is recommended that Option 1 is pursued. This option is the only one that offers some sort of guarantee that the company will be financially supported until it can start to generate its own revenues.

Although this will lead to a significant dilution of the founders' investment, a successful floatation may well make them extremely wealthy anyway. By choosing the option that maintains the operational status quo there will be little or no disruption to the company giving it the stability to focus on developing drugs.

26 Educational publisher

Text reference: Evaluating strategic options is covered in Chapter 7 of the BPP Study Text.

Part (a)

Top tip: The scenario tells us the publishing market is highly competitive which suggests B will be keen to know what its competitors are doing and how they are performing. However, possibly more importantly, the Directors can also use the knowledge they build up about their own competitors to help develop their own strategies and improve B's own performance.

Strategy development – If B's directors gain an understanding of their competitors' strategies, they can use this to help develop their own strategies.

If the directors understand their **competitors' strengths and weaknesses,** this understanding could highlight areas for B to focus on. For example, B could target competitors' weaknesses in order to try to win business from them and increase its own market share.

Basis of competitive advantage – Equally, if B understands the basis on which its competitors are competing and their areas of competitive advantages, this can also help it determine the basis of its own strategy. For example, if one of the competitors is aiming to be the cost leader, B could look at that competitor's processes and see if there are any efficiencies of improvement B could introduce to reduce their own cost structure.

Increased profitability – B's directors believe that the three direct competitors are currently more profitable than B, although the directors have no evidence to support this. By improving their knowledge about the competitors, B's directors will be able to establish for certain how profitable they are.

The directors may also be able to establish why B's competitors are more profitable than it is. For example, if the competitors have outsourced any of their production and distribution processes, or relocated them to cheaper locations, this could suggest possible ways for B to increase its own profitability.

Responding to competitors' strategies – B could also benefit from trying to gain some knowledge about its competitors' future strategies as well as their current strategies. In this way, B should have a better chance of being able to respond to new products or innovations which the competitors are planning to introduce, thereby maintaining B's competitiveness in the market place. Although at the moment all the training companies seem to offer very similar training manuals, it is possible some of the competitors could be developing new products – for example, e-learning materials which students would find more appealing and more accessible that then traditional printed materials.

However, it is important that B does not simply imitate competitors' strategies but develops its own strategies to increase competitiveness, based on its own competences and resources.

Competitors' responses – Gaining competitor intelligence can also help B's directors gauge competitors' likely responses to any new strategies which B is planning to introduce.

Part (b)

Top Tips: The scenario talks about 'product development' and 'market development' opportunities, and the requirement then asks you to evaluate three strategies that would enable B to be more competitive.

A useful approach to this requirement would be to think of what 'product development' or 'market development' opportunities might exist for B, and then evaluate them: how suitable, acceptable or feasible are they?

Although the ideas of product and market development give a clear link to Ansoff's matrix, there is no requirement to discuss the matrix and you should not have wasted time doing so.

Note – The question asks you to evaluate **three** strategies only, so that is what you must do. However, for tutorial purposes we have included four possible strategies in our answer because these are all potential strategies you could have evaluated and which would have earned you marks in the exam.

Once you have evaluated the relative merits of the three strategies (in (b) (i)) you then need to recommend the most appropriates ones for B in the short term ((b) (ii)) and the long term ((b) (iii)). Think about these follow-up parts as you are evaluating the strategies in (b) (i). For example, a short term strategy needs to be relatively simple and quick to implement; whereas a longer term strategy can be more complex but should look to generate some kind of underlying competitive advantage?

Your recommendations in parts (ii) and (iii) should be guided by the points you have made in (b) (i), but make sure you give a clear recommendation for each part – don't simply re-evaluate the merits of each of the different strategies. To earn the marks here, you have to recommend a single strategy in each case.

(i) Currently, B only produces paper-based manuals, and it sells these through bookshops and online vendors, not directly to students. B could look to increase its competitiveness by reviewing its product range and the downstream supply chain through which it makes its products available to students.

1. <u>**Product format (product development)**</u> – Currently, B will incur significant printing and production costs associated with publishing their training manuals. However, an alternative strategy would be to offer the manuals in **electronic format**. For example, the manuals could be sold as e-books or in a downloadable online format.

Suitability – Reduced cost - By producing the manuals in electronic format, B's **costs would significantly reduced**: it wouldn't have to buy paper to print the manuals on, or incur packaging and freight costs for distributing the manuals to suppliers. As a result, B should also be able to sell its electronic books at a lower price than the hard copy manuals (and its competitors' manuals), thereby possibly enabling it to capture market share from its competitors.

Feasibility – Converting an existing hard copy manual to an e-book or a downloadable file is a relatively simple process, and so there shouldn't be any problems as to the feasibility of this strategy, although B may outsource the actual production of the e-products to a specialist producer.

Suitability – Usability – However, if the 'new' products are simply electronic versions of the existing manuals, this will not address the problem that the content is time-consuming to read, and students do not have time to read them. In this respect, B might consider allowing students to buy individual chapters of the downloadable manuals at any time, rather than having to buy the whole text in one bundle.

Acceptability – However, there is a danger that allowing students to buy single chapters may cannibalise sales if students choose to only buy a small number of chapters at any time (whereas they had previously bought a whole manual).

Acceptability – This strategy opens up the possibility that the manuals will be illegally reproduced, thereby damaging B's sales growth. There is a risk that a student could buy a single copy of the downloadable text, and then distribute it to friends and colleagues studying for the same courses meaning that those friends and colleagues won't buy the manuals themselves. The directors may consider that the extent of this risk may this strategy unacceptable.

2. **Product range (product development)** – At the moment, B seems only to produce a single type of manual which requires a lot of reading time to work through. However, as an alternative to this manual, B could develop some more interactive or user-friendly online material. For example, B could develop some online tutorials which only cover the key topics from each chapter of the manuals along with case studies and examples for students to work through to reinforce their understanding of subject areas.

   Suitability – The readers have said that B's existing manuals are very time-consuming to read, but time is often scarce for them. Therefore, an alternative product which is **less time-consuming** and more **user-friendly** should prove attractive to them. Users may find a product which focuses only on the key topics **more approachable** than one which covers everything in great detail.

   Also, because the new product is also online, it should be easier for users to work with than the bulky hard-copy manuals which were considered impractical. In time, the material could even be produced as a mobile phone application, making it even more convenient for students to access.

   Feasibility – This strategy will require B to create new materials for its online product because the text will not simply be copied from the existing hard copy manuals. Therefore, it is likely to take a significant amount of **time** to create the online materials in the first instance. This suggests this strategy is more appropriate in the longer term than in the short term.

   Acceptability – Moreover there is likely to be a significant cost involved, especially if B uses an external agency to design and develop interactive online materials. However, this product will be clearly differentiated from the products which B's competitors offer, and so could provide a useful tool for gaining market share. In addition, having a differentiated product may allow B to charge a higher price for it, in turn giving it a chance to improve profit margins which are currently low.

3. **Direct sales (Market development)** – Currently, B only sells its materials through bookshops or online vendors, rather than selling directly to students. This means that B has to pay some of the sales margin from the books to the 'agents' who have sold them.

   As an alternative, B could sell the books itself, allowing customers to purchase them directly from B's own website. In this way, B will retain all the profit from the sale, in turn increasing its profit margin, making this strategy **acceptable to B**. However, this option doesn't make the manuals any more user-friendly to the students so won't provide B with any means of differentiating itself from its competitors in that respect.

   Suitability – Ease of switching - A number of customers may already be buying materials online from online bookstores, in which case there should be very little switching cost in changing to buy the manuals directly from B. However, B will need to ensure that its products are still visible for students when they are looking to buy materials. If B's competitors continue to sell through the bookstores and online vendors, and if students look there to buy their books, then they may buy one of the competitor's books instead of B's. B may need to look at search engine optimisation, for example, so that students looking to buy a text online see that they can buy B's text directly from B.

   Feasibility – e-commerce capability - Although B currently has a website, it is unlikely that the company currently handles any e-commerce transactions. Therefore B will have to upgrade its website to provide the functionality required for customers to select manuals online, as well as providing a secure payment facility so that customers can pay for their books online.

   Feasibility – logistics – Under this strategy, B will also have to deliver (or oversee delivery of) individual manuals to private customers and the colleges whose students use its manuals. This will result in a much

greater number of deliveries than at present where B delivers bulk orders to a smaller number of bookshops.

Consequently B is likely to need to recruit additional logistics staff. Alternatively, B could outsource the packaging and distribution process to a specialist logistics firm – although it would need to consider the cost-benefit implications of this before choosing to do so. The fee paid to the logistics firm will reduce B's profit margin in a similar way that a commission paid to bookshops would.

Tutorial note. This fourth strategy is included here for tutorial purposes because it is a strategy you could have mentioned and would have earned marks for. Remember, though, that you should have only evaluated three strategies in your answer.

Cost reduction – Currently, B carries out the production process (typesetting and printing) in-house, and in Europe. However, it is possible that some of the production activities could be done more cheaply by using external contractors.

In particular, electronic versions of the manuals could be sent for printing by contractors based in countries outside mainland Europe, whose costs are cheaper.

Suitability – Cost reduction – This strategy should allow B to reduce its costs, and thereby improve margins.

Feasibility – Relationship management – However, although this strategy may reduce B's costs it will lead to a new problem of having to manage the relationship with the companies responsible for printing the materials. B will also need to ensure that the print quality of its manuals is not compromised by switching to new, cheaper printers.

Acceptability – Redundancies – This strategy is also likely to lead to redundancies amongst B's in-house production teams, and other one-off costs associated with shutting down the in-house production facilities.

Moreover, this strategy may effectively prove only to be an interim solution, with the longer term solution being the switch to using electronic media in preference to hard copy printed manuals.

(ii) **Short term option**: **Electronic formats** – In the short term, B should look to sell its materials in electronic formats (as e-books or as downloadable online files) rather than producing only hard copy versions of its manuals.

This strategy will reduce B's production and distribution costs, and will also allow B to sell directly to customers rather than using bookshops.

It should be relatively simply for B to introduce the facility for customers to buy the online materials through a secure payment facilities on B's own website, although there will be costs associated with increasing the functionality of the website.

In the short term, if B introduces electronic formats as an alternative medium, alongside printed materials, it will be able to gauge the relative popularity of each. If electronic formats prove more popular than the printed materials, then in time B can begin to reduce the number of printed manuals required.

(iii) **Long term option: Interactive manuals** – In the longer term, the most appropriate strategy will be to introduce a range of interactive online materials. Students do not find the current manuals very user-friendly because of their size and the length of time they take to read.

However, B and its three direct competitors only produce one style of text, in the format which students feel is difficult to work with. Although it will take time for B to develop a new style of learning material (hence it is a long term strategy) if B can do so it will provide a clear point of **differentiation** between B and its competitors.

In turn, this should provide B with a **competitive advantage** over its competitors, and thereby increase profitability – at least until competitors introduce similar products themselves.

27 Agriland

> **Text reference**: Stakeholders are covered in Chapter 2 of your BPP Study Text. Chapter 7 looks at evaluating strategic options.

Part (a)

> **Top tip:** Make sure you read this question properly before beginning your answer. You are not asked to describe stakeholder mapping, but rather to advise how it could be useful to ZZM in deciding the options to pursue. Do not waste time describing (or drawing!) Mendelow's matrix; instead, apply it to the scenario.

Establish interest and power – Stakeholder mapping could allow ZZM to identify the stakeholders who have an interest in its operations in Agriland, and then establish the degree of interest and power each stakeholder or groups of stakeholders has over its operations there.

Identify key players – In order for ZZM to be able to successfully pursue the options it chooses, those options must be acceptable to the stakeholders who have **high interest** in, and **high power** over, ZZM's operations in Agriland. Stakeholder mapping will allow ZZM to identify these key players; which would include, for example, the President of ZZM.

Manage stakeholders – By categorising the different groups of stakeholders according to their interest and power, ZZM can then work out how it should manage them.

In general terms, this should be as follows:

High interest and high power – make sure any options ZZM chooses to pursue are **acceptable** to them, and possibly even involve these stakeholders in deciding which options to pursue

Low interest but high power – keep them **satisfied**

High interest and low power – keep them **informed**

Low interest and low power – spend **minimal effort** on these groups.

Part (b)

> **Top tips:** The verb here is 'construct'. So you do not need to spend a lot of time explaining the reasons why you have a allocated a stakeholder to a specific category.
>
> Instead, you should identify all the stakeholders from the scenario, and then categorise them according to their level of interest and power. Don't forget that ZZM is a company, so you should not overlook its own shareholders as a stakeholder group.
>
> Note also that ZZM buys the agricultural products from the farmers' *co-operatives*: ZZM does not employ the farmers directly. (Make sure you read the scenario carefully!)
>
> Nonetheless, there is no single right answer to this question: provided you identify the relevant stakeholders and justify (briefly) the level of interest and power you have attributed to them, you will receive credit for this.

High interest and high power

President of Agriland and Government – ZZM's business plays an important part in Agriland's economy, and the President is keen to get ZZM to help him in the run-up to the election. The threat of nationalisation demonstrates the high level of power the President has.

Farmers' co-operatives – The co-operative has chosen to deal exclusively with ZZM, but the fact that it can trade with anyone is a threat to ZZM. If the co-operative stop selling to ZZM, ZZM will not have any inputs to use in its manufacturing process in Agriland.

Low interest but high power

ZZM's shareholders – Ultimately, ZZM needs to pursue strategies which deliver value to its shareholders. However, because ZZM is a multinational company, shareholders' interests in its business specifically in Agriland may be relatively low. However, the stakeholders' level of interest is likely to depend on the strategic importance of ZZM's business in Agriland to the performance of the company as a whole.

High interest and low power

Main opposition party – They have a strong interest because they want to nationalise foreign owned businesses, like ZZM. At the moment, as the opposition party, they have relatively low power. However, if they win the **forthcoming election**, then they will move to having **high interest** and **high power**.

Farm workers' union – The union is interested in getting a good deal for its members. The fact that workers' pay has not increased for two years suggests that the union's power is relatively low, but the fact that workers are starting to go on strike, suggests that its power may be increasing. If the workers go on strike, then there will not be any agricultural products for ZZM to buy.

Farm workers – The workers have benefitted from ZZM's efforts in improving production techniques and raising living conditions. However, because the workers are not employed by ZZM, individual workers are unlikely to be able to exert any significant power over ZZM.

Farm workers' families – Families will be interested in the continued improvement of their living conditions, and the development of the infrastructure in Agriland. However, they will not be able to exert any significant power over ZZM.

Low interest and low power

The scenario doesn't identify any stakeholder groups with low interest and low power.

Part (c)

Top tips: Make sure you read the requirement carefully: although it may look like a single requirement there are, in effect, two parts to it: (i) evaluate the three options suggested by the President, and then: (ii) identify and evaluate one further option of your own.

So, in total, you need to evaluate **four** options. There are eight marks available for this part of the question, suggesting there are two marks available for each option evaluated. So don't spend too long on any single option.

Nonetheless, you may still find it helpful to consider the suitability, acceptability and feasibility of each option: this **S,A,F framework** is very useful for evaluating options.

Giving a substantial donation to the President's party

ZZM and the President both have an interest in the current government winning the next election. If the opposition party wins the election, ZZM will be nationalised but will not receive any compensation.

However, if ZZM is seen to be supporting the current government financially, this will **antagonise the opposition party** still further, and could hasten the nationalisation process if the opposition party wins the election. In addition, such a situation would mean that ZZM has made a **'substantial donation' for no return**. This suggests this option will **not be acceptable** for ZZM.

Finally, given ZZM's desire to be good corporate citizen, it should be wary about making a donation to a Government which has allegations of corruption hanging over it. If the allegations are proved to be correct, being a donor to the political party could reflect badly on ZZM by association. This suggests the first option will **not be suitable** for ZZM.

Agreeing an extra tax

The introduction of an extra tax will reduce the profitability of ZZM's business in Agriland, and may mean that it becomes **uneconomic for ZZM to continue operating there**. However, we do not know how profitable ZZM's business in Agriland is, or what proportion of ZZM's overall business it represents to assess the impact of discontinuing operations.

However, if ZZM accepts the increased taxes, this could **create a dangerous precedent** in which other countries also increase the taxes ZZM has to pay. This suggests such an option will **not be acceptable** for ZZM.

The fact that ZZM's business is an important part of Agriland's economy should improve ZZM's bargaining power in any negotiations with the government. However, this option does not seem to have any benefits for ZZM, not least because ZZM does not actually employ the farm workers.

Opening a new agricultural processes factory

If the factory assists economic development in Agriland then this option could be seen as promoting ZZM's desire to be a **good corporate citizen**. So, in this respect this option **could be suitable** for ZZM.

However, we do not know how much the factory is likely to **cost,** and what the potential **economic benefits** of the factory are expected to be. ZZM needs to consider the financial aspects of the strategy in more detail before it can make a decision on this option. These financial aspects will determine whether or not this option is **acceptable** for ZZM.

Withdrawing from Agriland

Some analysts think that the government might lose the next election, which would mean that ZZM's business is nationalised with no compensation, regardless of whether it has followed any of the President's strategies.

Furthermore, the President has also suggested he is considering nationalising ZZM's operations if it does not support his strategies. The fact that he has stated the options are not mutually exclusive may suggest he is expected ZZM to support them all.

Given this context, ZZM should consider withdrawing its operations from Agriland, and **reinvesting in another country**. The disadvantage of such a strategy will be that it means ZZM loses the profits it is currently making from its operations, but there is a risk it could lose these anyway if it remains in Agriland.

Part (d)

Top tips: Make sure your answer for part (d) is consistent with your evaluations in part (c): which option did your evaluation suggest ZZM should try to pursue? However, do not simply repeat the points you made in part (c). The verb here is to 'recommend' so you need to choose one strategy which you think is the most appropriate for ZZM, and then explain why this is the case.

Make sure you select from all **four** options evaluated in part (c), not just the three originally presented in the question scenario.

Of the President's three options, the only one which may potentially be acceptable to ZZM is the third one: to open an agricultural processes factory in Agriland. However, the President's statement about the strategies **not being mutually exclusive** suggests that ZZM may need to adopt more than one of the three strategies.

ZZM also has to contend with the **uncertainty about the result of the next election**. If the opposition party wins, ZZM will be forced out of Agriland.

In addition, ZZM may have to content with social and economic changes in Agriland. Increased militancy and rising prices may have an adverse impact on its operations. Equally, ZZM should also consider whether there is a risk that its own name could become tarnished by any possible corruption scandals in the country.

Recommendation: Taking all these uncertainties and risks together, it is recommended that ZZM should **plan to withdraw** from its operations in Agriland. However, before making any final decisision, ZZM should consider the implications of such a withdrawal - in particular the impact it would have on the group's profit overall levels.

28 Relationship marketing

Study Reference. Data warehouses and data mining are covered in Chapter 8 of your BPP Study Text. Relationship marketing is also covered in Chapter 8.

Top tips. Requirement (a) is a test of factual knowledge, and does not require you to link your answer back to the scenario. You could have helped illustrate the difference between data mining and data warehousing by using an example, and there was a mark available for a relevant example. We have linked our example back to the scenario, but you did not need to do this.

In order to attempt requirement (b) you needed to know the 'Six Markets' model – a specific way of looking at the range of relationships involved in relationship marketing. If you did not know the model, you should not have attempted this question.

The way to approach (b) was to identify each of the 'Six markets' in turn and then provide an illustration of them in the context of B's business.

For requirement (c), there are a number of possible strategies B could use to develop relationship marketing and improve customer loyalty, but you only need to recommend three. The strategies could relate to any of the six markets. Note, however, that to score the marks available you need to explain why B should use the strategies.

Easy marks. If you knew the 'Six Markets' model, part (b) offered some easy marks because it is a simple application of this model. However, if you didn't know the model, this question was one to avoid.

Marking scheme

			Marks
(a)	Definition and explanation of data mining	Up to 3	
	Definition and explanation of data warehousing	Up to 3	
		Total up to	6
(b)	Description of relationship marketing	1	
	Contrast relationship marketing with transactional marketing	1	
	Application of each of the six markets (customer markets; referral markets; supplier markets; recruitment markets; influence markets; internal markets). For each market	Up to 2	
		Total up to	12
(c)	For each strategy recommended and supported with reasoned arguments	Up to 3	
		Total up to	7
		Total	25

Part (a)

Data warehouse – A data warehouse is a large-scale data collection and storage area, containing data from various operational systems, plus **reporting** and **query tools** which allow the data to be analysed. The key feature of a data warehouse is that it provides a single point for **storing a coherent set of information** which can then be used across an organisation for **management analysis** and decision making. The data warehouse is not an operational system, so the data in it remains static until it is next updated. For example, if B did introduce a customer credit card, the history of customers' transactions on their cards could be stored in a data warehouse, so that management could analyse spending patterns.

However, although the reporting and query tools within the warehouse should facilitate management reporting and analysis, data warehouses are primarily used for storing data rather than analysing data.

Data mining – By contrast, data mining is primarily concerned with **analysing data**. Data mining uses statistical analysis tools to look for **hidden patterns and relationships** (such as trends and correlations) in large pools of data. The value of data mining lies in its ability to highlight previously unknown relationships.

In this respect, data mining can give organisations a **better insight into customer behaviours**, and can lead to **increased sales through predicting future behaviour**. For example, if B were able to identify patterns in items which were purchased together, it could target its promotions to take advantage of this.

So, by identifying patterns and relationships, data mining can **guide decision making**.

Part (b)

The 'six markets' model' suggests that relationship marketing is applicable to six different markets, rather than just the market between producer and final consumer.

Customer markets – The customer market comprises the final consumers of a product or service, who remain the final goal for marketing activity. For B, this market comprises the **customers who visit its supermarkets and do their shopping there**. Issues such as customer satisfaction will be key here; in a competitive market, if customers are not satisfied with the service they receive they are likely to switch to a rival supermarket.

Referral markets – The referral market comprises people or organisations who, through their recommendation of a product or service, **persuade potential customers to join the customer market**. For example, customers who are impressed with the quality and price of the goods they buy at B might recommend B to their friends and

relatives. Equally, a lifestyle magazine or a newspaper might publish an article which reviews B more favourably than its competitors.

Influence markets – Influence markets are similar to referral markets in that they direct the choices of the customer market. However, whereas the referral market often includes personal recommendations, the influence market contains organisations and institutions which, by publishing their views, can **influence customer choices** en masse. For example, if a consumer association recommends that B has the most ethical relationships with its suppliers, this may encourage potential customers to shop at B.

Supplier markets – This aspect of the model highlights that organisations need to **establish and maintain good relationships with their suppliers**, in order to ensure that they can consistently meet the needs of the final consumers. This is a particularly relevant issue in the supermarket industry, because supermarkets are often criticised for trying to suppress the price they pay to their suppliers. However, as B tries to increase customer satisfaction its relationships with its suppliers will be important to ensure that it avoids any stock-outs, particularly among its most popular product lines.

Recruitment markets – This aspect of the model highlights the importance of **people in delivering service to an organisation's customers.** In order to provide good service to its customers a firm needs to recruit suitable staff, and its ability to do this can be enhanced by establishing good relationships with **recruitment agencies** (to source staff) or **local colleges** (to encourage students to consider working for it in due course). For example, a customer's experience of B could be affected by the quality of service they receive from the check-out operator when they pay for their shopping, so B will benefit by recruiting staff who are friendly and efficient.

Internal markets – In order to support the overall relationship between an organisation and its customers, the **internal departments** of the organisation need to **work efficiently and effectively together**. For example, if B's purchasing and internal logistics departments do not source sufficient produce to meet customer demand, customers are unlikely to be satisfied however good the level of face-to-face customer service they receive from shop staff. In this respect, if B does introduce data warehousing and data mining, the analysts looking at the data reports need to work closely with the purchasing departments to optimise the number and type of products being ordered.

Part (c)

Top tips. Note you are only required to recommend three strategies B could use to develop relationship marketing, and you should have only included three in your answer. For tutorial purposes we have included additional strategies which you could have included in your answer.

Targeted promotions – If B introduces the credit card and its data warehousing and data mining systems, it will be able to capture lots of information about customers' purchases. It could then use this to **send customers specifically targeted promotions and offers**. If customers receive offers which closely match their shopping patterns they are more likely to take advantage of those offers, thereby returning to B as repeat customers.

Offer discounts for repeat promotions – The market is fiercely competitive, and customers are price sensitive. Therefore if, when they pay for their shopping, B's customers receive a 'money off' discount for repeat purchases, B could in effect, **use price as an incentive to encourage loyalty**. To maximise the effectiveness of the offer, it should only remain open for a **limited time**.

Staff incentive programmes – B could introduce a **staff bonus scheme** which takes account of **customer satisfaction levels**. It appears that the high staff turnover is currently leading to poor levels of customer satisfaction, and in turn to poor customer retention rates. A bonus scheme operated throughout B would not only provide an **incentive for all internal markets** to contribute to improved customer satisfaction, it could also have the added benefit of **reducing staff turnover**.

Staff training – The current low levels of customer satisfaction may reflect poor customer service standards in B's stores, which would be consistent with having a high staff turnover rate and therefore lots of relatively inexperienced staff. One of the ways B could address this is to improve the quality of training it gives staff when they join. This will not only mean they can offer a better service to customers, but also if staff feel time is being invested in their training they may be more likely to remain at B for longer.

Mystery shopper – As the industry is very competitive it is important B compares the shopping experience (quality, value for money, customer service etc) it offers it customers with that of its rivals. One way it could do this is by introducing mystery shoppers who visit its stores and those of its competitors as if they were customers. These mystery shoppers could then identify areas where B needs to improve its customer offering.

Customer suggestions – One of the features of relationship marketing is emphasising the product benefits which are relevant to the customers. B could introduce customer comments or suggestions boxes in its stores to allow customers to suggest the improvements which would be most valuable to them. This has an added benefit of making customers feel valued, which could, in itself, improve customer loyalty.

Introduce new product ranges – If B introduces a data warehousing and data mining system, the resulting information it cold gather on customer tastes and spending habits may enable it to identify gaps in its product ranges. In which case, it could develop new products or introduce new ranges to fill those gaps, thereby improving its ability to meet customers' needs.

29 GHK Restaurants

Text reference: Porter's generic strategies are covered in Chapter 5 of the BPP Study Text. Information Systems are covered in Chapter 9.

Part (a)

Top tips: The scenario identifies that the restaurants in the GHK group seem to have a variety of different generic strategies: some are cost leaders, some are following differentiation strategies, some have focus strategies, but some are stuck in the middle. So make sure you link the ideas of Porter's model directly to the scenario. How can the generic strategies help GHK's owners maintain or improve profitability?

At an individual restaurant level, Porter's generic strategies could be used to help achieve a competitive advantage for the restaurants stuck in the middle. However, it is also worth considering whether this variety in strategies between the restaurants means that the group overall risks being stuck in the middle if it tries to use a single brand across the different restaurants.

Note that the question clearly tells you that you do not need to suggest individual strategies for each restaurant so you should not have wasted time doing this. Instead, you should have focused on the way GHK's owners can use Porter's model to help improve profitability overall.

Choosing a competitive strategy – Porter's logic behind his Three Generic Strategies Model is that a firm should follow only one of the generic strategies in order to achieve **competitive advantage**. According to Porter, if a firm tries to combine more than one of the strategies it risks becoming '**stuck in the middle**' and losing its competitive advantage.

Applying these ideas could help the owners of GHK assess whether their restaurants are following a coherent competitive strategy – either individually or as group - or whether they are becoming 'stuck in the middle.' If they are becoming 'stuck' in this way, the lack of a clear strategy might be contributing to the **decline in GHK's profits**.

Generic strategies – Porter suggests firms should choose a potential strategy based on one of three generic strategies: cost leadership, differentiation or focus.

Cost leadership - If GHK chooses to become a cost leader, it must ensure it has the lowest costs in the industry as a whole. By having a lower cost base than its competitors, GHK could achieve a greater profit than them, even if its sales prices were the same as theirs.

Although this aspect of Porter's strategy focuses primarily on cost rather than price, it appears that GHK's **restaurant near the railway** is pursuing this kind of strategy, since it claims to be 'the cheapest in town.' However, to maintain its profitability, the restaurant must ensure it can continue to keep its cost base lower than any of its competitors' cost bases.

Differentiation – If GHK chooses a strategy of differentiation, it must deliver a product or service which the industry as a whole believes to be unique. As a result of this uniqueness, GHK will be able charge its customers a **premium price**.

It appears that the extremely expensive **'fine dining' restaurant** in the historic country house is charging a premium price in this way. However, to maintain its profitability, the restaurant must ensure it maintains its distinguishing features – be they the quality of the menu; the service, or the ambience. These features are what differentiates the restaurant from others in the industry and they make attractive to customers, even though it is charging a premium price.

Focus – A focus strategy will involve segmenting the industry, such that GHK would then pursue a strategy of cost leadership or differentiation within a single segment of the restaurant industry.

Three of GHK's restaurants seem to following this type of strategy and tailoring their offering to a specific **market niche**: the barge restaurant specialising in **fish dishes**; the **steak house**; and the restaurant catering for **children's birthday parties**.

Stuck in the middle – GHK has eight restaurants in total. We have identified five of them as following one or other of Porter's generic strategies, but this means the other three - with conventional menus and average prices - are likely to be stuck in the middle.

In this respect, GHK needs to look urgently at finding a way of establishing a competitive advantage for these three restaurants. This should allow them to improve their profitability.

Strategy and marketing – We do not know whether all the restaurants in the chain are branded unilaterally as GHK restaurants, or whether they have retained their own names as well as their own styles and prices. If GHK is trying to run the restaurants as a single group, under a single brand name, then the analysis of the restaurants' current position, indicates that the **group as a whole is at risk of being 'stuck in the middle'** due to the diversity of its strategies.

In this respect, Porter's generic strategies model suggests that GHK would be best advised to run the restaurants as separate business units, and to develop marketing strategies which support each restaurant's individual characteristics.

However, even if GHK chooses to do this, it still needs to consider whether the restaurants' current strategies can deliver a **sustainable competitive advantage**. For example, the prices of foodstuffs and drinks are rising in GHK's country, which will increase its cost base. So, how sustainable is a cost leadership strategy, particularly as there is little evidence of specific technologies or processes which will allow GHK to sustain a lower cost base than any of its competitors?

Given the overall economic context in which GHK is operating, GHK's owners might decide that Porter's **focus strategies** (either cost-focus, or differentiation-focus) offer them the most practical way of maintaining or improving the profitability of their restaurants.

Part (b)

> **Top tips**: Although the question refers to 'a range of organisational information systems' you could usefully consider these systems at two different levels: systems which provide *strategic* information, and systems which provide *operational* information.
>
> Also, try to think of the sort of information which it would be useful for GHK's owners to find out about: the external competitive environment and market information; customer details and marketing information; and restaurant usage, costs and revenues.
>
> Moreover, note the focus of the question is on how GHK can use the systems to support its strategy: it is not about what information systems GHK could use. So don't spend your answer just talking about information systems: the value to GHK will be in the information which it can get out of the systems, rather than the systems themselves.

Market research – In order to decide look at the suitability of any potential strategies for its restaurants, GHK needs to have detailed **market** and **demographic information** to see whether the proposed strategies are suitable. For example, if GHK wants to pursue a strategy of differentiation, it will need to assess whether there are sufficient people who are willing to pay premium prices to eat in the restaurant in order for the restaurant to be profitable.

Market research could also identify **new opportunities**, especially if there is market demand which is currently not being met. This could allow GHK to adapt its strategy (particularly in the restaurants which are currently 'stuck in the middle') to cater for this latent demand. For example, market research might identify that customers want a restaurant which serves locally-sourced, organic food, and they would be prepared to pay a premium for this food. In this way, the findings from the market research could support a focus differentiation strategy.

Market share analysis – GHK should also try to get overall market revenue figures for the various market segments in which it operates, and compare its own performance against these overall market figures. This will

indicate whether its market share is increasing or decreasing, and therefore will give some indication of how successful GHK's strategies are proving.

Customer Information – We do not know whether customers need to book in advance to eat at GHK's restaurants, but it is likely they do for the 'fine dining' restaurant and for the birthday parties, at least.

Website – If GHK develops a website which customers can use for booking, this will allow GHK to build up a **database of contacts**. If customers give an e-mail address when they book, GHK can use these addresses for future e-marketing campaigns.

GHK could also introduce a **loyalty card programme** as a way of getting a database of customers, finding out which of its restaurants they use, and how frequently they use them.

Such information could have two different uses:

- **Customer relationship management** - On the one hand, it can be useful for customer relationship management. For example, GHK could send reminder emails to lapsed customers who have not been to one of its restaurants recently, or it could inform customers of any special offers they might be interested in at restaurants they have visited recently. Given that the local economy has shrunk recently, **maintaining customer numbers** is likely to be an important issue for GHK.
- **Trend analysis** - On the other hand, the database could be analysed to highlight patterns and trends in customer usage at the different restaurants. Understanding these trends could, in turn, be useful for marketing campaigns or operational decisions for example working out staffing levels.

Management Information Systems – GHK's owners are clearly concerned about the performance of their business. Therefore it will be important that they have timely and reliable management information which they can use to see how the restaurants are performing. For example, the owners might find it useful to have summary reports which provide them daily or weekly snapshots of restaurant revenues and customer numbers, and the gross profit margins at each of the restaurants.

Operational information systems – In order to provide this summary information, GHK will need a way of capturing detailed operational information. If the waiters and waitresses in all the restaurants recorded customer orders on **hand-held personal digital assistants** (PDAs) this information from these could be captured, and ultimately transmitted back to a **central data warehouse**. The PDAs could capture, for example, customer numbers, the days and times of orders, and the dishes being ordered. Analysing this information could highlight, for example, whether some items on the menu more popular than others, or whether some times of day busier than other.

This information could then be used to help the owners make decisions such as whether the **menus need changing**, or whether the opening hours need revising. For example, if there are some items on the menu which do not sell well, they should be removed or replaced. If they were removed, and the menus were shortened, this would mean that GHK needed to hold fewer ingredients in stock, which would be beneficial in a period of rising food prices. Equally, if there are times of day where customer numbers are low, the owners may decide not to open the restaurants all day, or they might decide to introduce some **special offers** to try to attract additional customers during those off-peak periods.

In addition to the hand-held PDA's, the **tills in the restaurants** should also be linked to the central data warehouse, so that the management information system can update figures for **sales receipts** and **cash takings** on a real time basis. Given that GHK is now in danger of making a loss for the first time, it will be important to be able to monitor sales figures closely, to see what impact any new strategies have on sales and cashflows.

Performance information – There is no indication that GHK has any key performance indicators (KPI's) for its restaurants. However, the information available from the operational information systems could be used in **KPI's**. The management accountant could report how well the restaurants are performing in certain key areas, for example, spend per customer head, or spend per waiter. These again can provide useful headline information to the owners to enable them to see how the business is performing in areas which are critical to its success.

30 JGS Antiques

Text reference: The Value Chain and SWOT analysis are discussed in Chapter 4 of your BPP Study Text. Information systems are covered in Chapter 9.

Marking scheme

			Marks
(a)	For each point made: if it relates to a factor from the scenario; if it is identified as a strength or weakness; and if its position in the value chain is identified: up to 2 marks available If only two out of three of these issues (factor from scenario; strength or weakness; position in value chain) are included, a maximum of 1 mark is available for each point made	Up to 2	
		Total up to	8
(b)	For each relevant suggestion or action identified, coupled with an explanation of why it is needed: up to 2 marks available If a suggestion or action is merely identified, then a maximum of 1 mark is available for each point made	Up to 2	
		Total up to	8
(c)	For an evaluation of the impact of e-commerce on each element of the value chain	Up to 3	
		Total up to	9
		Total	25

Part (a)

Top tip: The scenario contained a number of points which were either strengths and weaknesses, and these should have been relatively easy to identify. However, the requirement wasn't simply to analyse JGS's strengths and weaknesses.

You also had to classify these strengths and weaknesses according to the value chain activities to which they relate.

Look at the marking scheme again: there are up to 2 marks available for each point made. However, if you only produced a list of strengths and weaknesses (ie didn't use value chain categories) the maximum you could score for each point you made is 1 mark. Likewise, if you presented a list of value chain categories but didn't divide the points into strengths and weaknesses you would again be limited to 1 mark per point. Both value chain categories and classification as a strength or weakness had to be present to score 2 marks per point.

Examiner's comments: Most candidates were able to identify JGS' strengths and weaknesses; however, some then failed to apply these to JGS' value chain. Overall, those candidates who attempted to apply the strengths and weaknesses to the value chain scored well.

Some candidates took the approach of focusing on the strengths and weaknesses of the value chain model itself, rather than using the value chain to help understand JGS' strengths and weaknesses. This was an incorrect interpretation of the question and candidates who took this approach scored few marks.

Note: There are only 8 marks available, so you do not need to make all the points we have included below.

Strengths

Operations: The owners have developed a considerable income stream by charging for their respected consultancy advice about antiques.

Service: The owners have developed a national reputation in the antiques trade and their experience has allowed them to build up a loyal following of repeat customers.

Firm infrastructure: The business operates from a large modern shop in a fashionable area, which make its premises very valuable. If the owners sold the shop they could realise a substantial capital gain.

Human resource management: The business is run by the owners, and their experience in the antiques trade, and their reputation as experts, is a valuable asset for JGS.

Weaknesses

Inbound logistics:

The inconvenience of the shop's location may mean that people with antiques to sell may take them to another antiques dealer rather than bringing them to JGS.

Operations:

The location of the shop is not convenient for potential customers (antique traders and collectors) to visit, and the people who live nearby are not interested in buying antiques.

The owners are unable to attend antiques fairs because they need to be physically at the shop to keep it open.

Outbound logistics:

The inconvenience of the location may also be a weakness in relation to customers buying antiques; for example, a collector may choose not to buy an item due to the difficulty of transporting home, or JGS may have to bear the cost of transporting customers' purchases to their homes.

Security costs have also increased significantly in recent years, and these costs are presumably related to the cost of storing antiques at the shop. If these security costs continue to rise, storing antiques in the shop may become a weakness.

Marketing and sales:

The owners themselves believe that the location of the shop restricts the success of the business.

However, at the moment JGS's website is very basic, and although a number of people have visited it there is no scope for them to buy anything through the website.

Firm infrastructure:

The fixed costs relating to the shop premises have increased sharply over the last five years. This is likely to be contributing factor to the fact that the **business made a loss** for the first time in the last year.

Human resource management:

There appear to be no succession plans in place for when the owners retire. Given that they have been running the business since 1980 it is likely they will be approaching retirement age relatively soon.

Technology development

The business has only recently set up a website, and the website is very basic. As we have already noted, it does not have any e-commerce capabilities.

Part (b)

Top tip: The requirement asks you to 'Advise the owners...' what they need to do to facilitate e-commerce. Make sure you appreciate the context here: JGS is owned and run by two people, with who seemingly have limited IT skills. Therefore complex IT solutions are unlikely to be necessary or appropriate here. The most useful advice to the owners will be a series of practical steps or actions they can follow to implement an e-commerce facility for their business.

Notice also that the requirement asks you to advise the owners what they should do: (i) immediately, and (ii) on a continuing basis to carry out the e-commerce solution. Make sure you address both parts of the requirement.

Examiner's comments: Most candidates were able to identify a range of actions that would be required to facilitate e-commerce, including identification of additional hardware and software requirements, cataloguing and photographing antiques to display on the website, security features for the website, training and site maintenance. However, some candidates focused their answers on project planning and / or assessing the viability of an e-commerce solution. Neither of these approaches was required by the question and so scored very few marks.

The website currently only provides potential customers with some basic information about JGS; for example, its address and the opening times of the shop.

Although a number of people of people have visited the website, there has not been any increase in business as a result. Because the website has no e-commerce facility, people still have to come the shop in person in order to look at items, and thence to buy them.

One of the JGS's current weaknesses is that the location of its shop is very inconvenient for many antiques traders and collectors to visit. To remedy this weakness, JGS needs to develop the means for people to be able to view and purchase the antiques online, without physically having to come to the shop.

Immediate

Online catalogue – JGS will need to design and install (or get a web-designer to design and install) a new interactive website which allows customers to search for items to buy. The owners will also need to make a catalogue of all their antiques to enter onto the website, along with a photograph of each item and its price.

Although this may be less important initially, it would also be beneficial to tag each item with some general characteristics (eg clock, table) so that a customer can narrow their search by product characteristics rather than having to go through the catalogue item by item.

Secure payments mechanism – In order for customers to buy antiques online, JGS will need to provide a secure payments mechanism which will allow customers to make purchases using a debit or credit card.

Website security – More generally, JGS will need to ensure the website has good security to protect it against viruses or fraud.

The owners will also need to ensure that the **server** which hosts the website has **sufficient capacity** to support the increased level of traffic which they anticipate to use the upgraded website.

External consultants - It is unlikely that the owners will have the skills either to design the website themselves or to install the secure payments mechanism. In which case, they should employ a consultant to do it for them.

On-going basis

Catalogue updates - The owners will need to update the online catalogue when new inventory is acquired. Equally importantly, they will need to integrate the e-commerce system with the catalogue so that when an item is sold it is removed from the online catalogue to prevent it another customer attempting to buy it after it has already been sold.

Maintenance and support - It may also be beneficial for the owners to arrange some on-going maintenance and support for their website. For example, they may be able to arrange a maintenance agreement with the consultants who design the website, so that they support JGS with any routine maintenance or upgrades the owners may wish to make to the site in the future.

However, potentially the most important aspect of any maintenance agreement for the owners will be having someone they can call for help if the website crashes, or develops some other kind of operational problem.

Part (c)

Top tip: A useful way of approaching this question would be to consider how the introduction of e-commerce will help address some of the weaknesses of JGS's operations which were identified in part (a), or to build on some of its existing strengths.

However, note that, as in part (a) the question requires you to link your answer to the value chain, so it would be sensible to use value chain functions as headings for your answer.

Examiner's comments: In general, the candidates who applied the value chain successfully in part (a) of their answer did so again here. A good number of candidates correctly identified the beneficial impacts on marketing and sales, and on the inbound and outbound logistics of the business. However, far fewer identified the impact on other aspects of the value chain, for example, the impact of being able to sell the shop and generate an injection of cash from this sales.

Operations - The main impact of introducing e-commerce is that JGS is no longer reliant on its current shop as a physical site for their business. JGS will still need a site where it can store antiques, and it is likely to keep retain some kind of shop or showroom where the owners can make face-to-face sales. However, this can be moved to

new, cheaper premises, for example an out-of-town location which should also be easier for antique traders to get to.

Outbound logistics – The new location should provide a more convenient base from which to distribute the antiques, and it should also help to reduce the insurance and security costs relating to storing the antiques.

Marketing & Sales – e-commerce should increase the geographical reach of the business, and so should increase sales. Potential customers who previously couldn't visit JGS's shop (perhaps even international customers) can now search the website to look for items they may want to buy (and then also buy them online if they want to).

Firm infrastructure – The reduction in overheads and potential for increased sales should allow JGS return to profit. The owners will also receive an injection of cash from the proceeds of the sale of the shop, which should cover the costs of the website upgrade.

Human resource management – Once the website is running, the owners will be able to reduce the opening hours of their bricks and mortar shop, which will give them more opportunity to attend the Antiques Fairs which they have previously been unable to attend.

Technology – Once the website starts becoming a source of income for the business, then technology becomes a much more important aspect of its value chain. In effect, the website could become JGS's main 'shop'.

Procurement – As the website increases the geographical reach of JGS's customers it may also mean that the supply of antiques into the business also increases as more and more people become aware of it.

31 Futurist hotel

Text reference: PEST analysis and Porter's Five Forces model are assumed knowledge from E2, although they are revised briefly in the Introductory chapter at the start of the E3 Study text. Porter's generic strategies are covered in Chapter 5 of the E3 Study text.

Top Tips:

Part (a): Although PEST (PESTEL) analysis and Porter's Five Forces model are covered more extensively in the E2 syllabus than E3, they are deemed to be assumed knowledge at Strategic level, and you should have identified that they were the two models you were expected to use here.

The structure of the question should have helped you answer it. Part (i) asked you to explain the models, and then part (ii) asked they could help the team formulate their strategy. In other words, in part (i) you need to explain the models in general terms, and then in part (ii) you need to apply them specifically to the scenario. For example, how could an understanding of economic and social (demographic) factors affect the wedding business strategy?

Part (b) (i): From reading the scenario you should have identified that the 'De Luxe' hotel was following a differentiation strategy, while the 'Royal Albert' was the overall cost leader. Equally, understanding these strategic positions will be important for the Futurist's team as they come to design their own wedding package strategy, suggesting that it may be most appropriate for the Futurist to follow some kind of focus strategy.

Therefore, a sensible way to approach this part of the question would be to explain each of the generic strategies, and then apply them to the scenario.

The requirement for (b) (ii) refers to information systems strategies, so this might prompt you to look specifically at IS rather than IT or IM. Interestingly, however, the examiner's answers include not only Information Systems (IS) strategies, but also the supporting Information Technology (IT) strategies which would underpin them.

In our answer below we have tried to focus specifically on the IS strategies, rather than looking at any supporting IT strategies. However, as the marking guide indicates, you would also have earned marks if you had advised the team about how IT (as well as IS) strategies can help support the three generic strategies. Nonetheless, to score well, you should not simply describe IS or IT strategies in general terms, but you need to explain how they link to, and support, each of the generic strategies.

Examiner's comments: In part (a) (ii), many answers were particularly strong in their application of the PEST elements, but Porter's Five Forces model was generally less well applied. Many answers provided only a generic discussion of the forces which earned very few marks.

Marking scheme

			Marks
(a)	(i) PEST (PESTEL) model – identified and explained	Up to 2	
	Porter's Five Forces model – identified and explained	Up to 2	
		Total	4
	(ii) For explaining how PEST (PESTEL) model could be used to help formulate a wedding package strategy	Up to 4	
	For explaining how the Five Forces model could be used to help formulate a wedding package strategy	Up to 4	
	For explaining how both strategies could be used to help formulate a wedding package strategy	Up to 2	
		Total up to	6
(b)	(i) Explanation of how cost leadership strategy could help the team design a successful wedding package strategy	Up to 3	
	Explanation of how differentiation could help the team design a successful wedding package strategy	Up to 3	
	Explanation of how focus or niche strategy could help the team design a successful wedding package strategy	Up to 3	
		Total	9
	(ii) Application of IT/IS to overall cost leadership strategy (eg using IT/IS to track Futurist's costs, competitors' costs or supplier costs; using auction sites to purchase cheapest inputs)	Up to 2	
	Application of IT/IS to differentiation strategy (eg to give each wedding a unique identity; appropriately designed web/internet sites; access to wedding guest lists)	Up to 2	
	Application of IT/IS to focus strategy (eg for in depth market research for identifying valid demographic/market segments)	Up to 2	
		Total	6
		Total	25

(a) (i)

Two models that could be used to analyse the external environment are Porter's **Five Forces** and **PEST (or PESTEL) analysis**).

Porter's Five Forces looks at the competitive forces which determine the level of profits that can be sustained by an industry. The five competitive forces are:

(i) The threat of new entrants to the industry
(ii) The bargaining power of customers
(iii) The bargaining power of suppliers
(iv) The threat of substitute products
(v) The competitive rivalry between the existing firms in the industry.

PEST analysis helps to identify the external factors which constitute opportunities or threats to an organisation. The PEST acronym stands for:

Political factors – for example, any government regulation

Economic factors – for example, the rate of economic growth or recession

Social factors – for example, demographic trends among the population

Technological factors – for example, new inventions and new product development

Sometimes, these four factors are also supplemented by **E**nvironmental and **L**egal factors, such that PEST becomes PESTEL.

(a) (ii)

Five Forces model

Assessing profitability – The team could use the Five Forces model to assess the strength of the competition the Futurist is likely to face if it enters the market for wedding packages, and accordingly how profitable it is likely to be for the Futurist to enter the market. If the Five Forces are too strong, it may not be profitable for the Futurist to enter the market at all.

Choosing position in the market – The competitive rivalry between the firms in an industry is one of the forces which determine profitability. It will be important for the Futurist to assess the strength of this rivalry because there are already seven competitor hotels in the market. For example, if it seems that the competition is more intense is at the lower cost end of the market spectrum, then it may be more profitable for the Futurist to target the higher price end of the market.

PEST analysis

Understanding demand – The external environment will play an important role in determining the level of demand for any packages the Futurist might offer. For example, social trends, such as changes in the number of people getting married each year, will affect the demand for wedding packages overall.

Equally, economic and social factors could influence demand for particular types of wedding. For example, in a recession or in times of higher unemployment, the amount people are willing and able to spend on their wedding may be reduced, which may encourage the team to offer less expensive wedding packages. Equally, people may look to have smaller weddings, so the team may decide to offer a package for fewer than 100 guests.

Congruence between the two models

It is important that the team considers the consistency of any findings from the two models. For example, if the analysis of competitive rivalry (in the Five Forces model) suggests that the Futurist may be better advised to target the higher cost end of the market, but PEST analysis suggests that the economic environment means that lower cost packages may be more popular, the team will have to decide which of the two influences is likely to have more impact on the success of any potential strategy.

On-going review of the environment

While the models could assist the team in formulating their initial package strategy for the hotel, the team should also continue to monitor the environment to ensure that their strategy remains appropriate. For example, if additional hotels start offering wedding packages, will the Futurist need to make any changes to its packages in response to this new threat?

(b) (i)

Porter's three generic strategies suggest that, in order to compete successfully, the Futurist hotel should aim to pursue one of three strategies:

Cost leadership

Differentiation

Focus

Cost leadership

As a cost leader, the Futurist hotel should seek to have the lowest costs of any hotel in the market as a whole. To achieve this, the Futurist is likely to have to simplify and standardise it processes and its products (for example, its menu) so that is able to deliver a wedding package more cheaply than any of its competitors.

Sustainable competitive advantage - However, it is unlikely that this strategy is likely to give the Futurist a sustainable competitive advantage, because it does not appear to give the hotel any distinctive competences its competitors cannot replicate.

Consequently, the team should not look to adopt a cost leadership strategy for the design of their wedding packages.

Differentiation

If it follows a differentiation strategy, then the Futurist hotel needs to offer a level of service or quality that none of its competitors can match, so that customers perceive the Futurist's packages as being unique, and accordingly they are prepared to pay a premium price to host their wedding at the hotel.

Competition with 'De Luxe' hotel – The 'De Luxe' appears to be following a differentiation strategy, using its physical position (a castle in a beautiful, rural setting) and the high quality of its foods and facilities, to offer packages which customers perceive to be superior to any others on the market. This allows the 'De Luxe' to charge premium prices for its packages (starting at £500 per guest).

If the Futurist is going to pursue a differentiation strategy successfully, it will need to have some attributes or characteristics that distinguish it from all the other hotels (including the 'De Luxe') in the same way that the 'De Luxe' currently differentiates itself from the other six competitors. It is not clear from the scenario that the Futurist has any such differentiating characteristics, and if it doesn't, then a differentiation is unlikely to be appropriate for it.

Stuck in the middle

Nonetheless, an understanding of Porter's generic strategies should remind the team that the Futurist's packages are unlikely to be successful if they end up being 'stuck in the middle'. There are already five hotels which charge between £35-£50 per guest, and this is a danger that these hotels could become 'stuck in the middle' since they are neither the cost leader (the Royal Albert) or differentiators (like the 'De Luxe'). Similarly, unless the Futurist can replace the Royal Albert as the cost leader, or develop some underlying differentiating characteristics then there is also a danger that it could get 'stuck in the middle' which will restrict its profitability.

Focus Strategy

Given this context, it seems that the Futurist is most likely to be successful if it adopts a focus strategy.

Cost leadership focus - However, the difficulty that the Futurist faces is that the market for wedding packages is already a specific niche with the overall hotel market. Therefore, the Royal Albert's packages could be seen as following a cost leadership focus strategy, specifically targeting people who want to get married but who only have a very limited budget to spend on their weddings.

In this respect, it would appear that the Futurist should design a package using a differentiation focus strategy.

Differentiation focus - However, given the De Luxe's position in the market, the Futurist may not simply be able to use the quality of its wedding catering, or the standard of its rooms and facilities as its differentiating factors. Accordingly, the Futurist may need to highlight another aspect of its service which differentiates it from its competitors - for example, allowing customers to have flexibility in the number of guests they can invite (rather than standardising the package for 100 guests) or providing differentiation by hosting 'themed' wedding packages (for example, a Las Vegas-style package).

(b) (ii)

IS strategies and performance management – Whichever strategy the Futurist chooses to adopt, it will be very important that the hotel's management know how well the packages are performing.

On the one hand, there is an **internal, financial aspect** to such performance information. For example, how much revenue are the packages generating? How profitable are they? How is actual performance comparing to budgets or forecasts?

On the other hand, there could also be an **external aspect** to performance information. For example, what is the growth rate for the wedding package market overall, and what is the Futurists' share of that market?

It is very important that the Futurist's management team has sufficient information to be able to assess how successful the chosen strategy is proving.

Equally, if the strategy is not proving as successful as had been hoped, the Futurist's management team also need this information so that they can take any corrective action necessary to improve the hotel's performance.

Costs and margins – In relation to financial performance, it will be very important for the hotel's management to know how much the different elements of the packages costs; for example, the food. In turn, the relationship between this cost information and the prices the Futurist charges will determine the profitability of the packages. This focus on costs could be particularly important of the Futurist chooses a cost leadership strategy because of the related need to control and minimise costs wherever possible. In this respect, the Futurist could also use the internet to help identify and source goods (for example, fixtures and fittings for the hotel) at the cheapest price possible.

IS and operational processes – The hotel's information systems could contribute to the smooth running of the wedding packages themselves. For example, the hotel will need to ensure that all the guests are correctly allocated to their rooms, and if any guests have specific dietary requirements these are taken note of.

In this respect, although the Futurist's information systems on their own will not give the hotel a competitive advantage, if they do not operate effectively the systems could damages customers' perceptions of the hotel. This could be particularly important if the Futurist chooses a differentiation strategy.

Integration with other systems – It is not clear what proportion of the hotel's business the wedding packages will represent, but the Futurist will also take 'regular' room and restaurant bookings alongside the wedding packages. In this respect, it is important that any information systems used for the wedding packages are integrated with any other operating systems (eg, booking systems) the hotel uses. For example, the hotel will need to ensure that for any given night it has a sufficient number of rooms available to accommodate both wedding guests and any other non-wedding guests who had also booked to stay there. Equally, if a wedding party has booked the whole hotel, this needs to be recognised in any other operating systems the hotel uses, so that no other customers can book into the hotel or the restaurant at the same time.

32 LM recruitment agency

Text reference: IS and IT strategies are covered in Chapter 9 of the BPP Study Text for E3.

Top Tips:

You should have recognised from the scenario that a number of the current weaknesses in LM arise from it not having a common overall strategy for its IS and IT systems. Therefore, by implication, if it does have one this should help it overcome at least some of these problems.

In this respect, a sensible approach to part (a) (i) will be to address each of the current weaknesses in turn, and advise how a common overall strategy could help address them.

For part (a) (ii) it is important your answer focuses precisely on the question set: what the *contents* of the strategy should be (for example, the strategy should specify how IS and IT can be used to support the business.) However, you should not spend time discussing how the strategy should be formulated, or how it should be implemented. (This is the focus of part (b) of the question.)

Part (b) requires you to recommend a practical solution for how to implement the strategy. However, you shouldn't focus solely on the IS/IT aspects of the implementation; instead you should also consider a wider range of management issues. For example: who will be responsible for leading the strategy? Could a change agent be useful to help the implementation? What training and communication will be required for the staff? What is the timetable for implementation?

Examiner's comments: Part (a) (ii) of the question was not well answered. Many candidates based their answers on the *process* of strategy formulation, and not on the *contents* of the strategy. Discussions of the rational planning model were an incorrect approach to this question, and were neither required nor helpful here.

(a) (i)

Information Systems strategy (IS) decides the types of information available to members of the organisation.

Information Technology strategy (IT) determines the hardware, software, and communications used to deliver that information.

Increased strategic importance of IS / IT

As LM has grown rapidly, so have its information needs to enable communication, and to allow monitoring of activities. LM now needs an overall strategy for its information technology (IT) and information systems (IS) to ensure it can obtain the information it needs to sustain its growth.

Proper management attention

The managing partners do not currently appreciate IT's strategic significance for the business, which may suggest they are not monitoring how well it is adding value, or whether it is delivering any competitive advantage to the business.

Control levels of IT expenditure

The level of IT expenditure (£1 million) is the same as the forecast profits for the current year. However, as well as highlighting the importance of IT to the business, this size of this figure might also suggest that the current piecemeal approach to IS / IT is not efficient. For example, if each division buys its hardware and software separately, LM might be paying more for them than if it had central purchasing of IT. Therefore LM may be spending more on IT than it needs to.

To ensure integration and communication

LM's current strategy means that each division operates autonomously, but this is causing difficulties and inefficiencies in relation to IT - both internally, and in customer-facing transactions. For example, the lack of a common software means there are difficulties in transferring information between divisions.This could lead to inefficiency and mistakes.

Impact on customer service

The differences in style and quality between the divisions' web pages means that LM does not offer its clients a consistent level of service. and LM appears less professional to clients and customers that other agencies with better maintained sites. This could be very damaging because it may mean that LM loses revenue if clients transfer their business to its competitors.

Benefits of common overall strategy

LM's current problems reflect its current piecemeal approach to IS / IT, and the failure to recognise them as strategically important. Introducing a common overall strategy would address all these issues. In doing so, it should also lead to greater co-ordination and control, as well as improved performance within LM.

(a) (ii)

Note that this answer focuses specifically on IT and IS (and not IM) as the requirement asks about an 'overall strategy for IT and IS'.

Overall purpose of IS/IT strategy – The strategy needs to identify how information is going to be used in the business to support its operations and to achieve competitive advantage over its rivals, for example, through databases which allow it to match prospective candidates to vacancies more accurately than rival agencies can.

The strategy should also **highlight the benefits** (or deliverables) that IS/IT are expected to provide to LM so that expenditure and performance can be properly evaluated.

IS strategy

Support of the business

The strategy must formalise the ways in which information supports the business. Doing this will ensure LM addresses a number of the issues it is currently facing.

For example, although each division operates in specialist markets and so may need some bespoke features in its software. There still needs to be a way of sharing information between divisions.

The overall strategy could control these things by introducing a degree of standardisation to the software. Similarly the strategy could identify service standards for the website, to reduce the current levels of variation between the different divisions' pages.

IT strategy

Hardware and software

IT strategy could formalise the process for selecting and managing hardware and software. For example, it could identify the specification of computers to be used in the business, and could establish a consistent replacement policy across the divisions. Equally, the strategy could formalise purchasing procedures so that LM gets the best price for its purchases.

Performance measurement

The overall strategy also needs to indicate how performance is going to be controlled and measured. This could include setting parameters for the IT budget and performance measures; for example, in relation to IT expenditure (eg, as a proportion of client revenue) or in terms of service levels (eg, minimising the amount of time the website is 'Under construction').

(b)

Note: In the answer below we have suggested LM could use a change agent to help introduce the new strategy. Alternatively, you could alternatively have suggested using a project manager to do this. But remember, to score the marks available you need to explain how a project management could help implement LM's strategy, not the benefits of project management in general terms.

Board member responsibility

A member of the Executive Board should be given responsibility for the strategy as project owner. This would reinforce the importance of IS/IT to the organisation, and help ensure the strategy was implemented. Given his previous experience with IT, the Finance Director may be a sensible choice here. This should also avoid any conflicts which might arise from making one of the three divisional managing partners responsible for the strategy in preference to the other two.

Change agent

If the Finance Director does not have sufficient time to become directly involved in the change process a dedicated change agent must be appointed to implement the new strategy. The change agent's role could be crucial in selecting and implementing the new IT solution for the company, as well as selling the new strategy to key stakeholders within the business.

Plan with timetable and milestones

Because the strategy will necessitate changes to LM's current practice, target dates should be set for key changes to be implemented; for example, for the divisional web pages to all have a uniform style.

The timetable for change also needs to make provision for staff training, because LM's staff will need to know how to use any new IT systems which are introduced.

Stage model of change

Implementing the strategy will lead to a change in LM's current processes. Therefore change management will also be an important part of the implementation. The stage model approach: 'unfreeze – change – refreeze' could be useful here: to move LM away from its current processes, to learn a new approach, to establish new standards and to embed the new approach within the organisation.

Maintain communication

The 'unfreeze' stage of the change process also highlights the importance of consulting with staff, and dealing with issues and concerns they have about the change. In this respect, communication will be a key part of implementing the strategy: explaining why the strategy is needed, and how it will benefit the staff and the organisation.

Enable participation

Communication with the staff should help reduce resistance to the change, but nevertheless there may still be resistance to the new strategy. LM should be prepared for this, and have plans in place to deal with it; for example, by getting some of the staff to participate in designing some of the changes.

Consultation and stakeholder management

The three divisional managing partners also have a key role to play in implementing the strategy. The strategy will reduce the level of autonomy that each of the divisions has, but at the same time each of the divisions needs to retain the flexibility to serve its own niche market effectively. The managing partners will need to ensure that the specific IT requirements of their divisions can still be met within the overall context of the new strategy.

33 Y gardening services

Text reference: Information systems (IS), information technology (IT) and information management (IM) strategies are covered in Chapter 9 of your BPP study text.

Top tips:

For Part (a), note that the question requirement tells you that you should have assumed that Y secures the hotel contract. You should have realised that this will have such a fundamental change on Y's business that she will no longer be able to maintain her lifestyle strategy, and this should be the essence of your answer.

To score well in part (b) it is vital that demonstrate you know exactly what each of the strategies involve. For example, if you included an element IS strategy as part of IT strategy you would not score marks for this. You need to be very precise about the purpose and benefits of each of the different strategies. Equally, you need to look at the strategies specifically in the context of Y's business (which, for example, has previously had very little investment in IT).

The same points apply to part (c). You should deal with each of the three different strategies in turn and make sure your recommendations are specifically appropriate to each level of strategy. Equally, you must make sure that the actions you recommend are ones that Y may realistically be able to implement (given the size of her business and its previous lack of IT investment.)

(a)

Lifestyle business – To date, Y has deliberately kept her business small and has not been interested in its growth, such that she has only taken on a new client if an old one leaves, and she has not employed any staff. The focus of the business has been on Y's enjoyment and satisfaction rather than generating profit.

Change of circumstances – However, the changes in Y's family circumstances have meant that Y has had to change her approach to the business significantly. Winning the hotel contract means Y's income will increase, but in order to fulfil the contract alongside the existing customers Y will also have to employ at least four new staff.

Now, instead of providing enjoyment and satisfaction for Y, the focus of the business should be to provide a high quality of service for the hotel and to **generate sufficient profits** to pay the **staff** and any other **administrative costs** associated with the business now that it has grown (for example, IT costs).

This means that Y will no longer be able to maintain her lifestyle business strategy, but will have to adopt a more **commercial business strategy**.

(b)

Information systems (IS) strategy

<u>Purpose</u>

The IS strategy should identify the **systems** that will **enable Y to use information to support her new business strategy**. In this context, 'systems' will include the **activities, records** and **people** which Y will need to employ to meet the demands placed on the business, as well as the **technology** used.

<u>Benefits</u>

Business led – An IS strategy should be business-driven, so developing it will encourage Y to identify the ways in which information will support her new business strategy. Historically, Y's information systems have been very basic (based largely on her diary), but developing an IS strategy should encourage Y to appreciate that her IS strategy and the business strategy need to be inter-related.

Demands for information - For example, the IS strategy will focus on the demands the business may make for information (for example, knowing which staff members are allocated to which jobs at any time).

Creating new strategic options - However, by looking at the way information can be used strategically, Y may also be able to generate new ways of doing business which could allow her to secure a competitive advantage (for example, by working with a garden designer to create a library of possible landscaping features or plant borders that Y's customers might be interested in adding to their gardens.)

Commercial focus for information – Historically, the level of profit the business earned has not been of primary importance for Y, and she has been happy to rely on her diary as her source of business information. As the business takes on a more commercial focus, Y will need to look at information more critically: for example she should look at how much it costs her to undertake different jobs and to identify which clients are most profitable. Equally she will need to ensure the levels of service and quality provided to the hotel meets its expectations. The IS strategy should help Y define how she will generate the information she needs to manage the performance of the business.

Information technology (IT) strategy

<u>Purpose</u>

The IT strategy should define the technical solutions which Y needs to introduce in response to the demands identified by the IS strategy. In particular the IT strategy should identify the technology (hardware, software) which Y needs to acquire for the business.

<u>Benefits</u>

Support more complex business - Historically, Y has had very little IT to support her business, and she has relied on her mobile phone and her diary as her sources of control over the business. However, as the business expands this will no longer be appropriate. For example, now that Y employs staff she will need to record the jobs they are working on, and will also need to ensure they are paid correctly each month. Also, as the business grows, Y will need to ensure that all the customers are billed for the work done, and they settle their accounts. Having the appropriate IT systems in place will enable Y to achieve this.

Structured approach – Because Y has not used any computers or technological equipment in the past, introducing them will represent a significant change for her. The expenditure involved in buying computers for herself and her administrative assistant could also be relatively significant for a small business such as hers. Therefore it is important that the IT equipment Y buys is appropriate for the business, and also that she doesn't waste money buying equipment she doesn't need. An IT strategy (defining what computers, software and network links she needs) will help ensure this is the case.

Information management (IM) strategy

<u>Purpose</u>

The IM strategy will define the roles of Y's staff (and Y herself) in using the IT equipment, the relationships between them, and the design of any processes needed to exploit IT resources. The IM strategy should also define how data is stored and accessed.

<u>Benefits</u>

Define responsibilities – Historically Y has managed all the business' information herself, but now that the business has expanded, Y will be sharing some of the responsibilities with her administrative assistant. It is important that Y defines which tasks the assistant will do, and which she will continue to do herself. For example, Y should identify which files and records on the IT system the assistant is responsible for monitoring and updating, and which she will look after herself. These responsibilities should be defined in the IM strategy.

Information requirements – It is likely that Y will also require information about the business' performance on the hotel contract. The three gardeners, Y's assistant and Y herself may all be involved in collecting and collating this information. Again, the IM strategy will be important in defining who needs to provide what information (for example, at the end of each day, the gardeners may need to record the hours they have worked at the hotel (or at other clients), and the work they have done.)

(c)

IS strategy

Define business strategy – Before Y can define her IS strategy, she needs to define the business' strategy now that it has moved from being a lifestyle business to a more commercially oriented organisation.

Seek advice – However, the fact that Y would appear to have no experience of developing business or IS/IT strategies may also mean that she should not try to plan these all out herself. To this end, she should contact her accountant for help with this, and possibly also discuss the business' information requirements with an IT consultant.

Capture existing knowledge – Although Y has historically only used diaries to record this information, she has still built up some useful information about the business – for example in terms of seasonality of work, the time taken for different types of jobs, and customer feedback on the work done. It will be important for Y to analyse this information to identify and trends which can then be built into the future strategy of the business (for example, if there are specific aspects of Y's service which customers value, then it will important to try to ensure these are still provided in the future.)

IT strategy

Increased complexity – Y will have to manage the demands of the hotel contract alongside those of her existing clients, and, for the first time, she will also have to oversee the staff working for her. This means that Y's current IT systems – her diary and mobile phone – will no longer be sufficient for the business' requirements.

Expenditure requirements – As a result, Y will need to purchase the IT equipment which she needs for the business.

This is likely to include: computers for herself and her assistant; software packages (for recording written and numerical data); a printer; and a landline telephone point with broadband connection. Y may also want to provide mobile telephones for the gardeners so that she can contact them when they are at clients, and vice versa.

Depending on how successful the business becomes and how much Y wants it to grow, she may also consider creating a website for it.

Budget - However, before committing to any IT expenditure, Y should prepare a budget for that expenditure to ensure that it remains under control.

IM strategy

Identify information users – Whereas historically the only people who have needed information about Y's business have been her and her accountant, there will now be number of additional users. These will include: the administrative assistant, the gardeners, and the hotel.

Identify information requirements – Y will need to identify what information all the users require, and whether or not they need direct access to her information systems. For example, the administrative assistant will clearly need access to the records, but the gardeners are less likely to (although they are likely to want details of their pay and hours worked at the end of each month). Equally, it may be useful for Y to allow her accountant access to her records, to replace her current practice of handing over her diary at the end of each year.

Hotel information – The scenario has identified that the hotel is likely to be a very demanding client and will monitor performance very closely against contract specification. However, the scenario does not identify what information, if any, the hotel will want Y to provide about its performance. It will be important for Y to establish what information the hotel will want, and how it wants it provided, so that Y's IT systems can be configured to provide the relevant information (and also so that Y can monitor performance in these key areas).

Role of administrative assistant – We mentioned earlier that the IM strategy will identify the respective responsibilities of Y and her administrative assistant. However, Y will need to decide what aspects of the business she wants to keep looking after herself and which she wants to delegate to her assistant, so that these can be detailed in the strategy document.

34 IT outsourcing

Text reference. Outsourcing in the context of IT is dealt with in Chapter 9 of your BPP Study Text.

Marking scheme

			Marks
(a)	**Strategic level**		
	General identification of strategic level issues in relation to IT	1	
	Advantages related to the IT function of the merged organisation	Up to 2	
	Disadvantages related the IT function of the merged organisation	Up to 2	
	Managerial level		
	General identification of managerial level issues in relation to IT	1	
	Advantages related to the IT function of the merged organisation	Up to 2	
	Disadvantages related the IT function of the merged organisation	Up to 2	
	Tactical level		
	General identification of tactical level issues in relation to IT	1	
	Advantages related to the IT function of the merged organisation	Up to 2	
	Disadvantages related the IT function of the merged organisation	Up to 2	
		Total up to	15
(b)	1 mark for each relevant characteristic described and applied to BXA	1	
	(Relevant characteristics include: experience of similar work, capacity to do work, financial stability, cultural compatibility and fit with BXA's staff, track record of retaining transferred staff, openness during due diligence)		
	A maximum of 2 marks will be awarded for a generic list which is not applied specifically to BXA		
		Total up to	5
(c)	1 mark for each relevant factor to be included in the service level agreement	1	
	(Relevant factors may include: definition of the service and required performance, charges and procedures for charging, management information to be provided, right to audit figures, compliance with key obligations, benchmarking process to be used, termination arrangements)		
		Total up to	5
		Total	25

Part (a)

Top tips. The way to approach this question is to break down the requirement into its various parts. You are asked to discuss advantages and disadvantages, and you are asked to discuss them for each of three levels of the organisation.

However, note the requirement is to look at the advantages and disadvantages of outsourcing the IT function for the *merged organisation*.

Although the terminology of strategic, managerial and tactical levels (rather than strategic, tactical and operational) is unusual, the requirement to consider three levels of management should have given you a reasonable idea of how three levels should be differentiated.

It should also be reasonably clear that the marks available for this part of the question are easily divisible by three, emphasising the nature of the answer required: 5 marks for advantages and disadvantages at each level.

Notice how we have structured our answer: rather than working straight up or down the hierarchy, we have left the middle layer until last, since we think it is less clearly defined than the strategic and junior levels.

Easy marks. Some of the various advantages and disadvantages should be fairly easy to identify from your knowledge: such ideas as economies of scale, specialist skills, loss of control and improved cost forecasts are basic to any discussion of outsourcing. However, to maximise the credit you get for them make sure you apply them to the scenario.

Examiner's comments. The Examiner felt that answers to this question were generally poor: there was the usual problem of lack of application to the scenario and very few candidates were able to distinguish between the three levels of management.

The **strategic level of management** is concerned with decisions that set the overall, long-term direction the organisation is to take.

Potential advantages at this level include the following.

The supplier ought to be able to deploy **IT competences, skills and techniques of a higher order** than BXA can provide internally, thus equipping the company to handle the much greater complexity inherent in doubling in size by merger with CXA. This should also make future acquisitions easier to absorb.

Outsourcing ought to bring cost benefits through the **exploitation of the supplier's economies of scale**, though actually achieving these benefits would depend on satisfactory contract negotiations.

The merged company will have to do something about its IT strategy. Outsourcing should **reduce the risks involved** in what will be a major project.

Access to state of the art IT systems may spur a **complete strategic reappraisal** of internal methods and procedures, producing **transformational** rather than **incremental** improvement in the way the company does things. One obvious example of such change is **delayering and empowerment**. An insurance business runs on assessment of risk: much of the process can now be automated. Also, the role of middle managers as filters and processors of routine information can now be largely eliminated by the use of modern IT systems. Much flatter and more effective structures can result.

Potential disadvantages at the strategic level

There are two important strategic dangers involved in outsourcing such an important function. First, there is the **risk of losing internal IT capability**: this could stunt future developments.

Alongside this, and linked to it, is the **risk of losing control of the IT function** and the services it provides. This is a very serious problem, since IT may represent a **core competence** for a large insurance company: the growth of direct, telephone-based insurance services is a good example. A more immediate danger is, perhaps, the possibility that the chosen contractor will **exploit its position by raising charges unreasonably** at some future time.

The every day, **routine (tactical) level of management** will also be affected by outsourcing.

Potential advantages at the tactical level

Advantages should include the provision of **more capable, reliable and faster systems**, which should enhance customer service; better and faster response to operational IT problems; and a reduction in the training effort currently needed to keep the existing legacy systems in operation. Junior managers should find they have more time for non-IT related aspects of their jobs and will have more flexibility in the management of their staff, since work will be simplified and more standardised.

Potential disadvantages at the tactical level

Disadvantages will revolve around the **reliability and efficiency of the contractors and their staff**. It is at this level that there must be the greatest integration of work; contractor staff will be expected to understand and support operational rather than technical IT priorities.

The **intermediate level of management** between the strategic and the routine (the marginal level) will be affected by the levels both above and below it, since it will be responsible for implementing strategic decisions and for providing the first response to the operational problems that junior managers cannot solve.

Potential advantages at the managerial level

These will include improved **reliability and continuity** of systems, with a reduced risk of significant failure.

Access to **IT staff of a high quality for advice and assistance**: it may be possible to recruit some contractor staff for any remaining internal IT activities. **IT training resources** should also be improved.

Potential disadvantages at the managerial level

However, there will be the possibility of disadvantages too. These will be similar to those experienced by junior managers, though of greater significance.

Outsourcing would constitute a **significant change**, as would the merger with CX. The management of these changes and the stress associated with it would fall to this level of management. Staff would be unsettled and would require a clear lead. Also, staff at all levels must keep their eyes on the ball and not allow the changes taking place to distract them from their primary responsibilities to their customers. Middle managers such as department heads must make sure that this happens.

There is also a potential problem in the degree of retraining these managers would themselves require. They will tend to be older and **possibly less able to adjust** to the new methods and practices.

Part (b)

Top tips. You need to take note that there are only 5 marks available for here, and you should have scaled your answer accordingly.

The Examiner was quite mean with the marks for this requirement, a well-made point applied to the scenario being worth only one mark. However, this is possibly because there a quite a number of qualities that would be relevant and there are only five marks to play with.

Easy marks. There are no complexities here: you should be able to think of lots of qualities that would be desirable in any partner organisation... but make sure they are relevant to the scenario (see the examiner's comments below).

Examiner's comments. A comprehensive list without application to the scenario would not produce a pass mark.

Suppliers should be assessed for **general commercial suitability.** Factors to check would include creditworthiness, financial stability, length of service of key staff and cultural compatibility with BXA and CXA.

Technical characteristics should match the client's particular circumstances.

Perhaps the most important point is **track record** in similar circumstances. Suitable suppliers will have worked with other **financial services companies** and will understand the pressures and problems likely to arise during the proposed merger. As already mentioned, BXA has an opportunity to transform the way it works and the scale of its operations. Its chosen partner must have a record of **satisfactorily implemented innovation** if the company is to achieve the potential benefits of these changes.

It is likely that at least **some existing BXA IT staff will have their employment transferred** to the new contractor because of their experience and familiarity with the way the company does things. As a good employer, BXA should ensure that such staff are not disadvantaged by the move and should seek assurances from the contractor to that effect. Transferred staff should enjoy equivalent or better pay, conditions and training and career progression opportunities as they do at present.

BXA will wish to treat the contractor as a partner, since its efforts are likely to be so strategically important. The chosen contractor must therefore display **integrity, openness and commitment to BXA's plans and aspirations**. There must be no reason to doubt that a long-term relationship will be mutually advantageous.

Part (c)

Top tips. 'Identify' is a low-level instruction, corresponding to comprehension. A list of simply explained points such as ours provides an adequate answer. Again, there are only five marks available here.

Easy marks. As with the previous part of this question, there are some fairly obvious points to make, such as defining the service to be provided, reaction to faults and computation of charges.

Definition of strategic and operational roles to be discharged: this will include the call for innovation in the development of new systems.

Definition of standards of routine operational service, such as system uptime, installation of upgrades and operation of a help desk

Specification of the **basis of charging**, with a requirement that it should be transparent and subject to audit

Provision for arbitration or other alternative dispute resolution in the event of a dispute

Contract period and provision for early termination

Terms on which BXA staff are transferred

Method of **quality assurance** to be used, possibly including benchmarking and external audit

Ownership of any new **software** developed as a result of the changes planned for the organisation.

35 Supplying and outsourcing

Text reference. Chapter 4 deals with suppliers and the supply chain. Chapter 6 also contains material on outsourcing.

Marking scheme

			Marks
(a)	Each relevant advantage, related to C, and discussed (not simply stated)	Up to 2	
	Each relevant disadvantage, related to C, and discussed (not simply stated)	Up to 2	
		Total up to	10
(b)	Each relevant advantage, related to C, and discussed (not simply stated)	Up to 2	
	Each relevant advantage, related to C, and discussed (not simply stated)	Up to 2	
		Total up to	8
(c)	For each relevant stakeholder group identified	1	
	For each specific communication method relevant to the stakeholder identified	1	
		Total up to	7
		Total	25

Part (a)

Top tips. The way to approach this question is to use the information presented in the scenario to inform your answer. The key to doing well is to try to get as many ideas from the scenario as possible, and then *discuss* them. It is not sufficient to simply provide a list of advantages and disadvantages. A good answer should also present a balanced array of advantages and disadvantages.

Note, however, that the independent pharmacies are not the supermarkets, nor is there any suggestion in the scenario that the proposal to supply directly to the independent pharmacies means that C is not going to supply the supermarkets.

When this exam was sat, a number of students assumed one or other of these to be the case, and consequently answered a different question to the one the examiner intended. The question is actually asking what the advantages and disadvantages are of supplying directly to the independent pharmacies rather than supplying the pharmacies via the wholesalers.

There is an important message here: make sure you read the scenario carefully, and base your answer on the information given in the scenario.

Easy marks. The scenario should generate a number of issues for you to talk about; and the examiner wanted you to relate your answers specifically to the scenario.

Examiner's comments. Parts (a) and (b) were reasonably well answered. However, note that if the question asks for a 'discussion', a basic statement with no clarification is not sufficient to pass.

There are a number of advantages to C's proposal to supply directly to the pharmacies.

Advantages to C of supplying directly to the pharmacies

(i) **Increased profits** – Because the wholesalers are no longer taking part of the margin, C should earn increased profits from the new arrangement.

(ii) **Customer loyalty** – By offering a share of the increased margin to the pharmacies, C should be able to build a loyal customer base, and may be able to increase sales by capturing business which previously went to its competitors in the market.

(iii) **Customer relationships** – The removal of the wholesalers will **shorten the supply chain**, and will allow C to build closer relationships with the pharmacies. This could allow them to gain a better understanding of the market.

(iv) **Good public relations** – There may also be some public relations benefits to C from the new arrangement. If they are seen to be championing the cause of the small pharmacies, this would be a positive message to sell to the pharmaceutical industry.

In addition, there may be some **political capital** to be gained from the proposal, since government ministers have expressed concern about the power of the supermarkets.

However, there are also a number of disadvantages to the proposal.

Disadvantages to C of supplying directly to the pharmacies

Supplying directly to 4,000 independent pharmacies will require very different **logistical arrangements** to supplying to 10 wholesalers.

(i) **Higher inventory costs** – Under the new arrangements, C will have much higher inventory costs than it currently incurs, because it will have to hold all the inventories itself rather than having them held at wholesalers' premises.

(ii) **Increased distribution costs** – Equally, the new arrangements will increase C's distribution costs, as a result of servicing 4,000 destinations rather than 10. C may even have to increase their transport fleet to cope with the increased demand.

(iii) **Uncertainty of order levels** – It is also likely that the independent pharmacies ordering systems will not be as sophisticated as the wholesalers, which could make it harder for C to plan their deliveries and inventory levels in advance.

(iv) **Increased sales and marketing costs** – The new arrangements may also increase C's sales and marketing costs, because instead of dealing with 10 wholesalers it will now need to with 4,000 independent customers. It may need to take on additional sales staff to deal with this increased burden.

(v) **Threats to market share** – C could also **lose access to the main part of the market**. Supermarkets are taking a large share of the business and by refusing to supply them C will leave the market open to rivals to take increasing market share. This will particularly important if the independent pharmacy sector declines with the growth of supermarket pharmacies.

(vi) **Bad debt risks** – C's exposure to bad debt risks will increase. C will need to assess and monitor the credit worthiness of 4,000 clients rather than 10. This will be expensive and, it is assumed, some of the 4,000 may still end up as bad debts.

The additional costs arising from (i) – (vi) are likely to significantly reduce the benefits gained from not having to pay the wholesalers a share of the margin.

C may feel the increased number of customers is not desirable from a **supply chain management** perspective, and so it may decide not to supply all of the independent customers. Instead it may choose to concentrate resources on the pharmacists which buy relatively more drugs. However, restricting the market in this way will reduce sales below the level they would be if C continued to supply all the pharmacies.

It is also possible that the independent pharmacies may prefer dealing with a wholesaler rather than the manufacturing. Therefore, if C changes its practice some of the pharmacies may stop buying from it and choose to buy their drugs from one of C's six competitors who still use the wholesaler.

At a broader level, the **competition from the supermarkets** represents a potential threat to the long-term viability of the independent pharmacies. If the supermarkets can capture market share from the independents, possibly even forcing some of them out of business, then C's sales will decline unless it also moves to supply the supermarkets.

It is possible that the supermarkets may also use their buying power to depress the cost of the drugs supplied by the pharmaceutical companies. This again will present a threat to C's future income streams.

Part (b)

Top tips. Again, this requirement requires you to draw information from the scenario to shape your answer. This should have allowed you to relate the issues surrounding outsourcing specifically to the question, and this is what was required here. A general discussion of the advantages and disadvantages of outsourcing would not have scored well.

We have included a number of advantages and disadvantages all of which are relevant to the decision to outsource the transport function. However, this question is only worth 8 marks, and so you would not need to cover all these points to score well. The points in text boxes at the end of the 'advantages' and 'disadvantages' are relevant points which would have earned you marks if you included them, but you could have still passed the question without including them. Nonetheless, you would need a balance of advantages and disadvantages to pass the question, because the marks available were split between them.

There are a number of advantages to C's proposal to outsource the transport function if it decides to supply the independent pharmacies directly.

Advantages to C of outsourcing the transport function

(i) **Removes uncertainty over costs** – If C decides to supply the independent pharmacies directly, then its transport costs will increase significantly. However, by outsourcing the transport costs – and agreeing a contract for a fixed price with the transport company – then any uncertainty about the level of future costs is removed.

(ii) **Avoids capital expenditure** – The decision to outsource will mean that C does not have to increase the size of its transport fleet to cope with the extra number of deliveries required to service 4,000 independent pharmacies. This could result in a **considerable saving in capital expenditure** if C has a policy of buying assets rather than leasing them.

(iii) **Focus on core competences** – C will be **concentrating on its core business** of pharmaceutical manufacturing rather than diversifying into transport and distribution which it has less experience in.

(iv) **Benefit from economies of scale** – The transport company should benefit from economies of scale in transport and distribution costs which C cannot match. Therefore outsourcing should lead to cost savings at a cost per unit basis (although not all of these will be passed on to C because the transport company will look to make a profit on its operations).

(v) **Scalability of resources** – Outsourcing will allow **flexibility in transport services** which C could not provide in its own right. The transport company will be able to scale up or scale down resources depending on demand whereas C could not do this in its own right.

(vi) **Transfer of risk**. Providing the service agreement has penalty clauses built in, C can receive financial compensation for breakdowns in logistics which, if it operated its own logistics, it would not.

However, there are also a number of disadvantages to the proposal.

Disadvantages to C of outsourcing the transport function

(i) **Transport and distribution are crucial to the success of C's business model** – Although transport is not part of C's core business, under the new proposals the success of the transport and distribution network will be crucial to the relationship between C and the pharmacies. By outsourcing the transport function, C's control over the service delivery to its customers may be reduced, and if service levels slip then C's reputation with its customers will be affected. Management may decide that transport is too important a part of the business model to be outsourced.

(ii) **Loss of control** – The potential loss of control over the transport function is indicative of a general issue with outsourcing which C's management will need to be aware of. Outsourcing leads to a loss of managerial control, because it is more difficult to manage outside service providers than managing one's own employees.

(iii) **Redundancies and negative PR** – Because C already has a transport function, then the employees currently working in this area will be made redundant when it is outsourced, unless their contracts can be transferred to the external company. Such redeployment seems very unlikely though. The redundancies may generate negative publicity, which will reduce the PR benefits which we noted C could gain through being seen as a champion of the independent pharmacies.

(iv) **Tied in to contract** – If C signs a long-term deal with the transport company, it may find itself locked into an unsatisfactory contract, especially if it has no previous experience of arranging similar contracts.

(v) **Hidden costs** – There may also be hidden costs associated with the outsourcing contract. These could include the legal costs related to drawing up the contract for services between C and the transport company, and the time spent co-ordinating the contract.

Part (c)

Top tips. Although (c) was the shortest part of this question and there are only seven marks available, there are still essentially two stages to answering this question (identify the principal stakeholders; then recommend the most appropriate form of communication). You should have remembered the mnemonic 'ICE' to help identify types of shareholders: internal, connected, external.

However, because of the limited number of marks available you should have confined your answer to principal stakeholders only. Again, your answer must relate to the scenario. Any general discussions about types of stakeholders (or discussions about stakeholder mapping and Mendelow's matrix) would have earned no marks.

Remember that the main focus of the question is how C might best communicate the decision to the stakeholders.

Examiner's comments. Part (c) was poorly answered. Too many students gave a general discussion of Mendelow's matrix. This is not what the question asked for, and so any such answers earned no marks.

We recommend that the following stakeholders should be informed in the ways outlined below:

Internal stakeholders

Transport department staff – This group of stakeholders needs to be handled sensitively because this department is the one likely to be most affected by the changes. The message should be communicated by a member of the management team, accompanied by an HR representative, in a **face to face meeting** with the department.

Although we do not know whether the transport function is going to be outsourced, the staff are still likely to be concerned about the changes which the new proposals will have on their work. So the meeting should try to allay these concerns as far as possible, and show C to be a reasonable and considerate employer.

Connected stakeholders

Independent pharmacies – Initially, C should send a **letter to all the pharmacies** explaining the changes, with the letter including the date the changes will come into effect and the practical implications of them for the pharmacies' regular drugs orders. C should also consider setting up a **web-site** with some 'Frequently Asked Questions' which the pharmacies can consult to see how the changes will affect them.

Following the initial mail-out, should arrange some **area meetings**, in which the sales representative for an area invites the pharmacies in that area to come and discuss any issues with him or her. This face-to-face contact should help reinforce the relationship between C and the pharmacies.

C should also consider placing a general **announcement in the trade press** summarising the changes.

Wholesalers – The decision to stop using wholesalers should be communicated to each wholesaler individually in a meeting between a member of C's **management team** and a member of the wholesaler's management team. C should explain the reasons behind the decision, and also agree a timetable for implementing the new arrangements.

External shareholders

Doctors' surgeries – C should **write to all the doctors' surgeries** explaining why they are changing their distribution networks, and emphasising the benefits for the local pharmacies and the local communities.

Local communities – C should consider publicity in **local newspapers** to promote their public relations message that they are protecting the local community and the local traders against the encroachment of the supermarkets.

Both of these communications to external shareholders should be designed to encourage people to use the local pharmacies, because this will in turn support C's sales.

36 Contact Services

Text reference. Types of strategic change are discussed in chapter 12 of the BPP Study Text. Culture and the internal context of change are also discussed in Chapter 12.

Part (a)

Top tips. Part (a) asked you to analyse the type of change which the proposed strategy at Contact Services. Although you were not required to use any models in your answer, Balogun & Hope Hailey's matrix dealing with the nature and scope of change could have been a useful framework for your answer.

However, to score well you shouldn't spend a long time simply describing a theoretical model of change, but rather you should demonstrate your understanding of the model by applying it to analyse the specific type of change Contact Services is facing.

The answer below takes each of the four quadrants of the Balogun & Hope Hailey's matrix and then assesses the situation at Contact Services to see which quadrant it fits best. As with many E3 questions, there isn't a definitive right answer – is the change best viewed as adaptation or is it evolution? – but provided your argument is sensible, and you support it with evidence from the scenario, you will score marks.

Contact Services currently sells to a specialist **niche market** – the retail pharmacy market. Therefore the proposed strategic change – to sell to the **general retail market** – represents a **significant change to Contact Services' product and its market**. In this respect, it represents a **diversification strategy**.

We can analyse the type of change by applying Balogun & Hope Hailey's change matrix and looking at the nature and scope of the change.

Nature of change

The nature of a change looks at whether it is incremental or a one-off, 'Big Bang' change.

Incremental change builds on existing methods and approaches rather than challenging them. However, a **'Big Bang' change** involves a major change to existing methods, processes and cultures. Such an approach is usually required in times of crisis when rapid responses are required.

Scope of change

The scope of a change describes the extent of a change; the degree to which an organisation's business activities or its business model need changing. In this respect, a change can either be a **realignment** of a firm's existing strategy, or it can be a **transformational change** in which radical changes are made to the existing business model.

Types of change

Balogun & Hope Hailey's change matrix allows four different types of change to be identified: adaptation, reconstruction, evolution, revolution.

Adaptation is a change where the **existing business model is retained**, and the change only occurs incrementally. Because the proposed change at Contact Services represents a diversification of strategy, it is debatable whether the existing business model will remain valid.

The chief executive and the sales and marketing director may see the move to selling to the general retail industry as an adaptation of the existing model, but the reasons behind the software director's resistance to the change suggest that the change will involve a more significant transformation.

Reconstruction requires a significant, and rapid, change in the operations and process of an organisation often in **response to crisis** such as a long-term decline in performance. However, it does not involve any major change to the business model.

The proposed changes at Contact Services are borne out of a desire for growth, rather than being a rapid response to any critical problems facing the company. Therefore, they do not represent a reconstruction.

Revolution is rapid and wide ranging response to extreme pressures for change. It is likely to require a fundamental shift in the business model, and in the way a company operates. Although the proposed changes at Contact Services represent a diversification, the pace of change is unlikely to be rapid enough to represent a revolution.

Evolution is an incremental process that leads to a new business model. Evolutionary change often arises as a result of business analysis, leading to a **planned change**.

Evolution best describes the changes at Contact Services. The move into the generic retail market represents a **fundamental change in strategic direction** and it is likely that the company's processes and structure will have to change significantly to develop and sell the new packages successfully.

The change has come about due the chief executive's **desire to grow the business rather than in response to external financial pressures**. Therefore the changes are likely to be relatively incremental rather than requiring a sudden reconstruction of the business. In this respect, the proposed change at Contact Services may best be described as incremental.

Part (b)

Top tips. As with part (a), part (b) did not require you to use any specific models, however the reference to 'internal factors' should have alerted you that the Balogun & Hope Hailey's eight contextual features (the change kaleidoscope) might be a use framework here. The model identifies time, scope, preservation, diversity, capability, capacity, readiness and power as features which can affect the success of a change programme.

We have used this contextual features model in the answer below, but equally you could have used the Cultural web or the McKinsey 7S framework to help generate ideas instead.

The key point though is that you need to discuss enough different factors to earn a good proportion of the 15 marks available here. If you work on the basis of a maximum of 3 marks for each factor you discuss, you should be looking to identify 4 or 5 different factors here, and then apply them to the specific change scenario at Contact Services to score well.

Easy marks. If you were familiar with the contextual features model, you should have scored well in part (b) because the scenario gave plenty of clues about things that could affect the success of the proposed change: for example, the company wants to move to a bigger marketplace even though they are struggling to meet the demand from their existing marketplace; software is key to the project, but the software director is unenthusiastic about it, and appears to be alienated from his fellow directors etc.

Tutorial note. For tutorial purposes, the answer below includes all the headings from the contextual features model because all of them are relevant here. However, on the assumption that up to 3 marks would be available for each feature, you would not need to include all 8 features to pass this question.

The context of change

The context of change is provided by the organisational setting. It has many aspects and can therefore be very complex. However, we can organise the internal contextual features of change into eight main categories, to look at the way they could influence the success or failure of the chief executive's proposed change at Contact Services.

Time

No need to rush – Many companies are forced into changes in response to difficulties they are facing in their business. However, Contact Services does not appear to be facing any financial problems are so time is not pressing in that respect. This should allow them time to plan the changes carefully before implementing them.

Development time – Given that the software development team already appears to be under pressure to deliver and upgrade the current package, it also seems unlikely that they will be able to develop the software package for the general market quickly. Therefore a longer time scale may be more realistic anyway.

Chief executive's expectations – However, the chief executive wants to introduce the changes quickly to accelerate the growth of the company and make it an attractive acquisition target. So the timetable for change could become a **source of conflict** between the chief executive and the software director and his staff.

Scope of change

Evolution or adaptation – We have already suggested in part (a) that the proposed changes represent an evolutionary change, because the change from serving a niche market to serving a general retail market represents a substantial change of focus. This suggests the proposal might be more risky than if it were for an adaptive change only.

Changes to marketing mix – Moreover, Contact Services will need to develop new marketing skills for selling to a general market rather than to a specific niche market.

One possible threat to the success of the change is if the chief executive and the sales and marketing director underestimate the scope of the change.

Preservation

Software developers – The software development team are critical to the success of the proposed changes, and Contact Services' business more generally. Therefore it is vital that Contact Services **retains as many of its key software staff as possible**.

However, the software developers are already under constant pressure to meet the demands of existing customers, and so if their workload is increased still further a number may decide to leave.

If too many of the software developers leave Contact Services, the whole change project could be jeopardised.

Software development director – Persuading the software development director to support the changes will also be crucial to their success. Not only is a supportive director more likely to lead to support from the software developers themselves (and to stop them leaving), but the director will also need to play a key role in the design of the new product.

Diversity

Diversity of experience – Making changes is likely to be relatively easier in companies which have experience of different ways of doing things. However, it appears that Contact Services has very little diversity of experience and has been following a single, specialist, strategy for many years.

Therefore, it appears that the business' current experience does not support the chief executive's ambitious plans for expansion. It has never been a large business, nor has it had external investors.

Diversity of expectations – The goals of the sales team and those of the software developers seem to conflict. The sales team is making promises to customers that the developers are struggling to meet. As a result, quality standards are falling leading to customer dissatisfaction.

As the business expands, this scope for differences and conflict between the sales team and the developers will increase. If these differences adversely Contact Services' product they could hamper its efforts to enter the new markets successfully. The diversity of expectations between the Chief Executive and the software development director has already been highlighted.

Capability

Capability to manage change – Although the chief executive and the sales and marketing director are both keen on the proposed changes, the software development director and his team are far less so.

The chief executive will need to **convince the software team of the merits of the proposals** so that they support the changes. If the software team remain unconvinced and unenthusiastic, the changes are unlikely to be successful, because the developer's input is crucial to the project.

Past experience – We do not now anything about the **directors' past experiences of managing change**. We know that the chief executive is an entrepreneur and risk taker so it is possible he has led some change projects in previous roles. However, if he or the other two directors do not have any previous experience of leading change programmes this could hinder the proposals.

Equally, we do not know if any of the software team has experienced change processes before, such that their experience could be used to increase the changes of success here.

Capacity

People – The software development director already wants to acquire further resources to support the existing product, because he feels Contact Services software team is already working to capacity. Therefore, it is likely that Contact Services will need to **recruit a significant number of suitably skilled new developers** to support the planned expansion. This will not only increase costs, it will also take **time** – to recruit new staff, and to allow them to become familiar with the existing software.

This timetable may again be problematic for the chief executive if he wants to progress quickly, and the quality of Contact Services' packages could suffer still further if developers have to start work on a product before they fully understand it.

Funding – We do not have any details about Contact Services' financial position, but it seems likely that it will have to increase its borrowings to fund the expansion. Contact Services is a private company, and so cannot raise capital through an issue of shares on the stock market. It could look to the current shareholders for additional funding, but that means essentially looking to the directors.

The software development director is unlikely to fund changes he does not support, and the chief executive seems keener on getting money out of the company by selling it rather than investing in it further. Consequently, Contact Services' plans could be constrained by the amount of additional loan funding they can raise from their banks.

Readiness for change

The software developers would prefer to improve the existing software package they offer customers rather than moving to this new generic package. Therefore it is likely that they will **resist the chief executives proposed changes rather than supporting them**.

Moreover, since Contact Services has been **growing gradually** over the last three years, there is little no evidence to suggest it is ready for the significant changes proposed.

Power

The **chief executive appears to be the dominant power** at Contact Services, supported by the sales and marketing director. However, in practical terms, the success of the changes depends on the software team and the software development director.

The software development director appears justified in being cautious about the changes. However, there is a risk that the other directors will **force through the changes**, possibly even by buying out the software director's shares and replacing him with a new director. Such an aggressive strategy is unlikely to be successful, however, and could lead to Contact Services' revenues falling rather than the business growing if the reputation of its product falls further.

37 Heritage Trust

Study Reference. The role of change agents is discussed in chapter 12 of the BPP study text. Culture and change (including the ideas of the cultural web) are also discussed in Chapter 12.

Part (a)

Top tips. Part (a) is a purely knowledge based requirement. You are not asked to apply your knowledge to the scenario. However, note the requirement is only worth 5 marks, so you are not required to give an in-depth analysis of the role of a change agent in leading change. Note also that the verb is 'explain' which is only level 2 in the CIMA list of verbs, unlike 'discuss' (part b) which is a level 4 verb.

Easy marks. If you knew this subject area well, Part (a) should have offered some easy marks because it did not require any application. But there are only 5 marks available here.

A **change agent** is an individual or group that helps to bring about strategic change in an organisation. The agent has to manipulate and **exploit triggers for change** so that the drive for change gains momentum in an organisation.

The precise role of the change agent varies depending on the brief they have been given, but it is likely to include:

- Defining the change problem being faced
- Suggesting possible solutions to that problem
- Selecting and implementing a solution
- Gaining support from all involved

The change agent must possess the skills to **manage the transition process**, but must also have the determination to see the change through.

The change agent needs to **encourage** those who are going to be affected by change to participate and get involved in the management of the change. This helps stimulate interest and commitment to the change, and should help minimise fears and opposition to the change.

The change agent needs to **communicate** across a range of business units and functions, and across a network of different stakeholders, so that they all work together to enable the change to be implemented.

Part (b)

Top Tip. Unlike part (a), part (b) does require you to apply your knowledge specifically to the context and the scenario. Although you are not required to use any specific models, the reference to 'underlying organisational cultural issues' should have been a clue that the cultural web could be useful to you here.

A sensible approach would be to use the cultural web as a framework for your answer, and select five aspects of the web from which to identify the relevant cultural issues and explain their impact on the strategy. Note the question specifically requires you to select **five** underlying issues, so make sure you do: no more, no less!

The scenario gives a clear picture of a number of aspects of the Trust's existing culture, and suggests that the new Director General's strategy has been opposed because it challenges these.

The model answer below uses the cultural web as its framework, but if you explored the cultural perspectives using a different framework you would still score marks – provided you link the cultural issues directly to the resistance to the Director General's strategy.

To score well in this requirement you need to identify the relevant cultural issues at the Trust, and then explain why they have led to the Director General's strategy being resisted.

Easy marks. Part (b) requires detailed application to the scenario, but if you worked methodically through the scenario you should have been able to identify a number of issues which would have caused resistance to the Director General's plans.

Tutorial note: The answer below looks at all the aspects of the cultural web to illustrate the range of valid points you could have made here. However, we have shown the sixth aspect we cover ('stories') in a text box to reflect the fact that the question only asked for five. You would have scored marks for any five relevant issues, but for five only.

One of the main reasons why the Director General's strategy has been resisted by the Trust's managers is that she **failed to understand its culture** and therefore the way its staff behaved. The Trust's culture can be assessed by looking at its **cultural web**, and from this we can identify five underlying issues which have caused the Director General's plans to be resisted.

<u>Symbols</u>

Symbols are the **representations of an organisation's culture** – they can be visual (for example, large offices for managers) or verbal (for example, titles given to staff).

At the Trust, symbols such as the **accommodation** and **personal assistants** for the managers at the flagship properties indicate that these people are considered very important. Moreover, these symbols clearly demonstrate that importance to other people in the Trust.

Threats to status – The proposal to **remove the managers' personal assistants** would have involved removing a key status symbol, and would therefore have been very unpopular with the flagship managers. Furthermore, by making such a suggestion and challenging their status, the Director General would have immediately **made these managers hostile** to any other suggestions she might have had.

Power Structures

The power structures of an organisation reflect who has the real power in an organisation, and who has the greatest influence on decisions and the strategic direction of that organisation.

The **Trustees** are all well-known and respected figures in heritage and the arts and so this has promoted a culture in which **aesthetic importance** is valued above popularity with visitors.

The managers of the flagship properties have done little to challenge this, so we might suggest that they also have implicitly been preserving their own power.

Threat to power structures – However, the appointment of a Director General with a background in commerce rather than heritage and the arts, threatens to **challenging the whole purpose of the organisation**. Does it exist purely for heritage and artistic purposes or does it also seek to generate as much revenue as it can?

The Trustees appear to realise the need for change, but the flagship managers are likely to be more hostile, recognising that the need for a more commercial focus could jeopardise the privileges they earn, without seemingly having to do very much to justify them.

Organisational structures

The scenario does not tell us about the current organisational structure of the Trust, but it is likely that the organisational structure is likely to reflect the power structure.

However, the DG's proposals to recruit new business development managers illustrate that **commercial activities will no longer be secondary considerations** for the Trust.

The idea of introducing **commercially focused managers** represents a significant change in the Trust's priorities, but this again is likely to be unpopular with the existing property managers, particularly the flagship managers.

Control Systems

The control systems of an organisation concern the way it is controlled. They include financial systems, quality systems and rewards. Looking at the areas which are controlled most closely can indicate what is seen as most important to an organisation.

Allocation of budgets – The budgets at the Trust again reflect the **dominance and importance given to the flagship properties**, and art or antique collections of historical merit.

However, these controls suggest a **fairly inflexible environment**. The budget seems to be allocated according to a formula rather than to reflect the needs of the individual properties. For example, there does not seem to be any scope for the less high profile properties to get extra funding even if, for example, they need it for major repair works. In effect, the system seems designed to **reinforce the importance and prestige of the flagship properties**.

Inward-looking focus – The Trust's controls indicate an inward-looking focus (budgets to maintain the collections), rather than a focus on any external indicators, such as visitor numbers. This may indicate that the Trust is not used to having to measure performance, and, perhaps more importantly, it does not use performance as a means of allocating rewards.

Change of approach – In the context of control systems, the DG's proposal is likely to be unpopular for two different:

(i) it is using an **external measure** (visitor numbers) to allocate budgets, and it allocates the budget on **actual performance** rather than status

(ii) it could be seen to be **challenging the superiority and status of the 'flagship' properties**, by offering smaller properties the chance to increase their budgets if they can increase visitor numbers.

Rituals and Routines

The behaviour and actions of people in an organisation signal what is considered acceptable behaviour in that organisation.

The property managers seem to think it is acceptable to **lobby individual Trustees** to express their concerns with the DG's proposals.

Perhaps more importantly, the Directors seem to think it is **acceptable for them to write letters to the press and appear on television** to promote their views and gather support in opposition to the DG's plans.

Lobbying to resist changes – The DG was recruited by the Trustees specifically to help the Trust adjust to its new funding position, but the managers now seem to be trying to undermine her plans.

Ultimately, this is a short-sighted position, because if the Trust does not increase its funding, it will have a 15% reduction in income compared to its current position, suggesting that it will not be financially sustainable. However, this may **reflects the power structure** in the Trust, where financial and commercial interests are seen as less important than preserving the status of the flagship properties.

Stories

Stories are used by members of the organisation to illustrate the sorts of things it values.

In the Trust, the **stories reinforce the impression given by its power structures.** We have already seen that the power structures are directed towards heritage rather than promoting the popularity of the properties with the general public.

For example, by dismissing the **idea of linking budgets to visitor numbers** and accusing the DG of 'devaluing the historical significance of the properties in a search for popularity' the flagship property managers are suggesting that the **public are undiscerning**, and therefore cannot really be expected to appreciate the value of the properties they visit.

Self-interest vs. commercial management – Overall, the stories reinforce the idea that the managers **do not really value management and commerce**. The inference that the new DG cannot understand how the Trust operates because she has only run shops before can be seen as an attempt to denigrate her commercial background.

However, the reality behind the stories is probably that the managers feel threatened by someone actually reviewing whether they deserve their positions and privileges, but they are using their stories to try and disguise this concern.

Part (c)

Top tips. The scenario highlights that managers across the Trust have been particularly critical about the lack of consultation about the proposed changes. Resistance to change is often caused when the triggers for the change have not been communicated effectively.

Therefore, communication and consultation with the managers could be vital in overcoming resistance to the plans.

This is the approach we have taken in our answer below.

However, you could also have looked at this question in terms of a force field analysis, and looked at the issues which needed to be addressed to unfreeze the existing structure in order to facilitate change.

Note, however, that the question asks you to 'recommend the steps that could be taken' so you must make sure that your answer focuses on the possible steps to overcome the resistance rather than simply analysing the causes of the resistance itself.

Communication plays a vital role in the change management process, and the fact that the Trust's management have been very critical of the lack of consultation throughout the process suggests that the way the DG has communicated the changes and the need for change has not been very effective.

The manager's resistance could be overcome by a clear communication process, which should include the following steps.

Communication. As soon as possible, the DG should explain the need for the changes to the managers, in particular that the reduction in government grants means that the Trust needs to increase the income it generates from its own commercial activities.

One of the managers' concerns appears to be that they are concerned the DG is devaluing the history and culture of the Trust. However, by explaining the context of the changes, the DG might be able to reassure the managers that the changes are not designed to undermine their status within the organisation, but are driven by the economic pressures which the organisation will face going forward.

Education. In the communication process, the DG should also explain the aims of her strategy, and how it will address the issues caused by the reduction in government grants. She should also explain how she proposes to implement it.

Consultation. However, it is important that the managers are not simply told what the strategy is and how it will be implemented, but that they are consulted about it. Not only may the managers have valuable experience or suggestions which could help improve aspects of the strategy itself, but they are also more likely to support the strategy if they feel they have been involved in developing it.

Negotiation. Despite the communication and consultation process, there will inevitably still be some managers who still feel aggrieved by the changes, and by their loss of status. The will need to be a process of negotiation with these managers, and the Trust may need to make some concessions to encourage them to accept the changes.

Manipulation. The Trust may also need to manipulate some managers by appealing to their better nature and asking them to set aside their personal ambition for the good of the Trust as a whole.

38 Goldcorn

Text Reference. Types of change are discussed in chapter 12 of the BPP study text. Resistance to change is discussed in chapter 11; change and communication are discussed in chapter 12.

Part (a)

Top tips. Note that part (a) does not only require you analyse the current change programme, but also to compare it with the previous cost reduction efforts. In what way are the changes similar and in what ways are they different?

A good way to approach this question is to consider the characteristics of the two change programmes in turn, and highlight the differences between them. The scenario gives you a number of clues about the characteristics of the changes and you should use these as a framework around which to build your answer.

For example, you could consider: the level of change (strategic vs operational); the nature and scope of change (transformational vs adaptive; on-going vs one-off); whether the change is planned or forced; and whether the triggers for change are internal or external.

The finance director's proposal is much more extensive than previous change programmes, and in large part this reflects the changing environment in which Goldcorn is operating. We can highlight how the current programmes differs from the previous ones by looking at a number of key aspects of change.

Level of change

Change can take place at different levels within an organisation: from strategic changes which affect the whole outlook of the organisation, to process changes which affect individual business processes.

Current proposal – The current proposal for the **change to global production** is a **strategic change**. This is a change that affects the long-term direction of the entire organisation both in terms of its production capability and in terms of its market competitiveness.

Previous changes – Previous cost reduction exercises appear to have been at a lower level in the company, being restricted to individual factories. They have included changes at the **structural level**, for example with changes in the reporting structures.

However, the main focus of the previous changes seem to have been at a **process level**. For example, certain processes have been **outsourced** to try to improve efficiency, and similarly there have been selective redundancies.

These previous changes have been necessary to deliver the existing business strategy more efficiently and effectively. However, they have not tried to change the Goldcorn's overall strategy, whereas the FD's current proposal does.

Nonetheless, while the new proposal is primarily at the strategic level, implementing the changes will still include changes at the structural and process levels.

Nature and scope of change

The FD's proposal also differs from the previous cost reduction exercises in terms of the nature and scope of the change required.

Adaptive changes – The previous changes are have not tried to change the overall strategy or working practices. We could argue that outsourcing constitutes a **reconstruction** rather than simply an adaptation, but the nonetheless the changes have not fundamentally changed Goldcorn's existing structure.

Continuous change – Moreover, the previous cost reduction programmes seem to be an **on-going process** of trying to make Goldcorn most cost efficient. By contrast, the FD's globalisation proposal seems to be a **one-off change**.

Transformative changes – The FD's proposal will completely change Goldcorn's current structure and working practices. It could also require a major change in culture, as the manufacturing sites move from producing a range of products to mass-producing a single design.

The threat of the new entrant means that Goldcorn needs to take rapid and drastic action, with the FD recommending that his change programme be completed within six months. This wide-ranging and fast-paced change could be seen as a **revolution**.

Triggers for change

The trigger for the FD's proposal is **external**. The threat of the new external competitor has forced Goldcorn into making changes. Although it is now making plans for how to deal with the threat (so the change is planned to an extent) Goldcorn has essentially been **forced** to act by the external threat.

However, the triggers for the previous, smaller-scale changes have been **internal**. Goldcorn has **planned** the cost reduction programmes itself to improve its efficiency.

Predictability of outcome

The scale of the FD's proposals also means that it is much harder to predict their impact on Goldcorn compared to the smaller-scale changes. For example, these proposals will disrupt all the company's supply chains, both upstream and downstream, and they will fundamentally change the organisational structure – changing the manufacturing sites from profit centres to cost centres.

The FD has recognised the **extent of the uncertainty involved**, which is why he has suggested that the situation should be reviewed in two years time.

By contrast, the previous cost reduction exercises were much more small-scale and so their outcomes were more predictable.

Part (b)

Top tips. Make sure you read the question requirement very carefully before answering it. Before you can answer the requirement you need to identify who the key stakeholders are, and how the changes will affect them.

However, the requirement is not primarily about identifying the stakeholders, so you should not have spent time simply explaining why certain stakeholders are key. Instead you need to identify how the changes will affect these key stakeholders, and therefore what their concerns about the changes will be. Goldcorn's communications with the stakeholders will need to reassure them about their concerns. This is one of the main reasons why Goldcorn needs to communicate with its key stakeholders.

Shareholders

Shareholders will be concerned about the triggers which has prompted the FD's programme, in particular the apparent threat to Goldcorn's market share and profitability. They will want reassurance that the new strategy can be implemented successfully and the changes will enable Goldcorn to compete and add value despite the new competition.

It will be important for Goldcorn to communicate regularly with the shareholders to explain the nature and impact of the changes. However, because Goldcorn is listed on an international stock market it also needs to ensure it complies with the regulations about insider trading. Therefore it will be important to communicate information openly and equally.

Employees

The production employees in one factory are going to be made redundant – unless they are relocated internationally which seems very unlikely. The production employees at the other three factories will also be facing significant changes, due to the way production is being reorganised.

The extent of these changes are likely to be a major concern to the workers, and are likely to hit morale among the workforce. It will be very important for Goldcorn's management to communicate effectively with its workers to minimise any negative impact from the changes. To this extent, it will be important to communicate the reasons for the changes, and also to explain how the changes are going to be implemented and how they will affect the workers.

Local management

Local management may also be made redundant in the factory which closes but may be more likely to be relocated than production staff. Other management will need to work under a new cost centre structure with less autonomy than they previously had.

However, the local managers will also be key figures in implementing change and acting as change agents. Therefore their support will be vital for the successful implementation of the change programme.

Therefore they should not only be informed of the changes, but also consulted about the best ways of actually implementing them.

Customers

Customers will need to be reassured that they will still be able to get their Goldcorn vehicles, despite the changes in production structure.

Goldco

rn should run an advertising campaign in both the general press and the trade press to explain the changes, and also to highlight the benefits for the customer – for example, cheaper prices.

However, for this advertising message to be credible, Goldcorn needs to ensure that it can continue to supply all its customers during the change period. If dealers are unable to get the vehicles they want, this will render any advertising messages worthless. For this reason it may be necessary to stockpile some vehicles prior to the change.

Suppliers

Given the geographical shift in production there may need to be some changes in suppliers. These changes could be favourable to some suppliers where new production is located to their local factory, but for other suppliers the change may result in the termination of the relationship with Goldcorn.

It will be particularly important for Goldcorn to explain how the changes will affect the suppliers it continues to use, in order that those suppliers are able to guarantee the supply that Goldcorn needs from them.

Part (c)

Top tips. You may be tempted to think that the answer to this question lies in the reaction the workers who stand to lose their jobs will have to the changes.

However, while that is part of the answer, you shouldn't think only about individual people resisting change: aspects of the culture and structure of an organisation overall can also mean that the organisation tries to preserve its current ways of doing things rather than changing them.

Organisational culture and cultural barriers

The FD's proposal suggests fundamental changes that will affect the culture at Goldcorn. The new proposals will require the old culture based around **profit centres** and **geographical responsibility** will need to be unfrozen, and reset into a new global organisation.

However, the systems and procedures which Goldcorn has installed in the factories over the years to ensure they perform as well as they can may act as barriers to this change.

Power structures may be threatened by the redistribution of decision-making authority or resources, or the changing of lines of communication. For example, changing the factories from profit centres to cost centres indicates a reduction of decision-making authority in each factory.

This will affect the local managers in particular, and therefore they may be reluctant to implement changes which will be against their own interests.

Groups

Group inertia may block change where the changes are inconsistent with the preferred behaviour of teams and departments, or where they threaten their interests. The employees at the factory earmarked for closure are most likely to form a group to try to prevent the closure.

The marketing employees at all four factories may also form a group to resist change knowing that their jobs are most at risk from the centralisation of the marketing function.

If one or both of these groups are represented by a union they may also ask their union to support their cause as well.

However, their resistance may ultimately be futile, unless they can persuade Goldcorn that there is an alternative course of action it can follow and still fend off the threat of the new competitor.

Individual workers

Individual workers may also see the change as a threat. This may affect not only be workers in the factory that is destined to be closed, but also the employees in the other factories where there are likely to be substantial changes in work practices.

Workers will have got into **habits and routine** that they feel comfortable with, and the threat of having do things differently could make them feel uncomfortable.

For example, the globalisation and standardisation of production may mean they have to learn how to operate different machines on the production line.

Security. The workers are likely to see the change as threatening their security. For the site threatened with closure this will a loss of job security. But for workers at the other factories, the change will also lead to a loss of the security of familiarity.

The fear of the unknown could reduce worker's willingness and interest in **learning new skills**, not least because they may lack the confidence to take on a new challenge when their work practices change.

39 Chemico

Study Reference. Stakeholder analysis & CSR are discussed in Chapter 2 of the BPP Study Text; strategic alliances are discussed in Chapter 6, and change implementation is discussed in Chapter 12.

Part (a)

Top tips. The way to approach this question is to identify who the major stakeholders are, and then decide whether they will support or resist the proposal.

Note that there are effectively two aspects to the requirement:

– Identify the stakeholders' likely reactions to the proposal
– Consider the degree to which they will resist the proposal

If some stakeholder groups are likely to support the proposal rather than to resist it, you should say so.

Shareholders

Profitability – The shareholders will be keen that the **profitability** of the company is maintained because this will affect the return on their investments. Consequently, if developing the new product helps sustain profits they would be expected to support the proposal rather than resist it.

We do not know whether the shareholders are aware of the **alternative proposals** ChemiCo's directors have been considering (the alliance or the acquisition). If they are, and they think one of them would serve ChemiCo better commercially, then they may resist this first proposal in favour of one of these alternatives.

Risk of environmental pollution – As well as short term profitability, the shareholders are also likely to consider the longer term growth of their shares. In this respect, they may feel that the opportunities for enhancing the overall value of their investments would be jeopardised by the risk of toxic accidents.

Moreover, some of the larger institutional investors may decide they do not want to be associated with ChemiCo if its **corporate social responsibility** (CSR) policies are called into question.

The wider issue here is that ChemiCo must not been seen to **sacrificing safety in search for profits**.

Employees

Saving jobs – Given the lack of alternative employment opportunities in the region, keeping their jobs at the factory is crucial for the workers. So, from this perspective, the employees will support a change which seeks to preserve their jobs.

Health risks – However, avoiding health risks is also important to the workers. So the increased risk of toxic incidents attached to the new product will be a concern to them.

There is also a secondary issue here. We have assumed that the workers know about the health risks attached to the new product (because they have been highlighted by environmental campaigners). However, the directors may have convinced the workers that the risks are low, so that there are even less likely to resist the proposal.

Either way, the economic need to preserve their jobs is likely to mean that the workers are unlikely to resist the proposals.

Local residents

Conflicting interests – The local residents are likely to have the same dual interests as the staff. On the one hand, the community benefits from the **presence of a large employer** in the region (for example, people have more money to spend at local stores). If the proposal doesn't go ahead redundancies are likely, and this could have a knock-on effect throughout the rest of the regional economy (via the multiplier effect).

However, as with the employees the local residents will not welcome the introduction of a process which could potentially spill out **toxic waste**.

The residents are probably more likely to resist the proposal more than the workers, but it is debatable how much power residents alone could have to stop development.

Environmental campaigners

Environmental issues – The environmental campaigners will strongly oppose the proposals, because of the potential risk of toxic incident they present. The campaigners will be more concerned with the environmental costs of the proposal rather than the economic arguments for it.

Moreover, the campaigners have shown themselves to be **active in resisting the proposal**, and have already written to the local authorities. In terms of a force field analysis, the campaigners are likely to be the strongest resisting force acting against the proposal.

Regional government

Divided interests – Like the residents, the local authorities may also have split interests about the proposal.

On the one hand, they will want to **support ChemiCo as the largest employer** in the region, and they will want to keep income and jobs in the region. In this context, if they resist the proposal this could also discourage other potential investors who might have been looking to invest in the area.

However, on the other hand, the authorities will be aware of the **potential environmental risks** of the proposal, and will be concerned about any health risks the chemical processes might present.

Ultimately, the strength of their resistance is likely to depend on the level of toxic risk they think the new product presents.

Part (b)

Top tips. A good way to approach this question is to think what ChemiCo could gain from entering a strategic alliance, but also what the logistical issues and business risks might be from doing so.

The question asks you to 'evaluate the issues', so therefore you should present a balanced argument: you should look first at the potential advantages of the alliance, and then move on to look at its drawbacks. However, you must not just evaluate the advantages and disadvantages of strategic alliances in general – you must embed them in the context of the scenario and make them specifically relevant to ChemiCo.

Note: you are not asked conclude whether or not ChemiCo should enter the alliance, and so you should not do so.

Sharing competences – Alliances can be a valuable learning exercise for each partner. Entering into an alliance would allow ChemiCo and its partner to exploit complementary competences for their mutual advantage. Therefore before agreeing to form the alliance ChemiCo should consider what distinctive competences both it and the potential partner are bringing to the venture. Can they be used for mutual advantage?

Risk sharing – New product development presents many uncertainties as well as opportunities. So sharing the funding of expensive research via an alliance can spread the risk. However, it also means that future profits will have to be shared.

Goal congruence – One of the most important things for ChemiCo to do before entering an alliance will be to work out where there might be potential conflicts of interest between the two companies.

Disagreements many arise of profit shares, resources invested, management issues (including project management), overall control of the specification of the product to be developed, and marketing strategy.

These issues must be resolved in advance, and agreed on a contractual basis, so that each party is clear about its rights and responsibilities.

People and culture – The directors should also consider staff and cultural issues, and whether the companies can work together. For example, it may take a while for staff from both companies to trust each other, and to share ideas with each other. If the two companies cannot develop this trust between themselves, then the alliance is unlikely to be successful.

Partnership costs – The alliance will involve sharing tangible expenses such as capital contribution, but also sharing intangibles such as expertise. Having **joint ownership of patents for products** that are developed by an alliance could lead to disputes about a fair share of future returns from them, unless the agreement is carefully and thoroughly worded. There could also be similar issues surrounding the **ownership** and **use of any intellectual property** generated by the alliance. The alliance may therefore include significant legal costs to deal with any such issues.

Business risk – ChemiCo is a big company, and so is likely to be the larger partner in the alliance. There is a risk therefore that the alliance partner might use the alliance as a means of finding out about its ChemiCo's technology.

Alternatively, ChemiCo might decide is wants to use the alliance as a stepping stone to a future takeover of the smaller company.

Part (c)

Top tips. A sensible way to approach this question is to think about it in practical terms, rather than looking for theories and frameworks to base answer on.

For example, effective leadership and management will be required to bring the two companies together; good communication will be important so that staff in both companies know what is happening and how it will affect them.

Also, make sure you think about the specific context of the potential acquisition: a small, owner-managed business will be taken over by a much larger business. What will the implications of this be? (particularly in the smaller business).

Acquiring the plastics company would represent a **major organisational change** for ChemiCo. It will be necessary to integrate the target company's operations, techniques and people into the expanded company, while continuing to run the existing ChemiCo business.

Cultural issues – Mergers and acquisitions often fail to produce the expected benefits due to cultural incompatibilities between the two companies combining.

In this case, a small owner-managed business is being incorporated into a much bigger business. The policies and procedures which the staff from the small company are used to are likely to be very different to those in ChemiCo. If the acquisition is to be successful, the new staff will need to adapt to working within ChemiCo's structures. However, ChemiCo's management and staff can assist this process by making the new staff feel welcome into the business, and explaining how things are done.

Leadership – The success of the takeover will depend on effective leadership from ChemiCo's management.

The takeover is a **planned change**, and so the change process must be driven by the senior management. To be successful, the management must have a **clear vision** of their strategy for the merged business is going, and how to achieve it.

In turn this vision must be used to establish goals, and performance indicators, so that **performance across the whole business can be measured** against them.

Communication – Effective communication will be essential for both existing ChemiCo staff and staff from the newly acquired company to appreciate the reasons behind the deal, but perhaps more importantly to understand their roles and responsibilities in the new organisation going forward.

If staff from the local plastics company will be expected to use ChemiCo's policies and procedures then they will **need to be trained** so that they know what to do.

External communication – ChemiCo will need to decide how far the plastics business is rebranded (for example, will it be renamed ChemiCo Plastics?) and how the change of ownership is communicated to customers. It may be that the most practical solution is to allow the business to retain its current trading name, and reassure customers that business will continue as usual.

Management skills – The owner of the plastics business plans to retire, so ensuring a succession plan for running the plastics business will be essential. There may already be some managers in the business who can do this under this and effectively run it as an autonomous business unit within the ChemiCo 'group'.

It will be very important to establish what skills the staff within the business do have, because it is unlikely that ChemiCo's management know much about plastics manufacturing. Depending on the skills and commitment of the existing staff, it may be that ChemiCo have to recruit externally, to find a manager to run the new plastics division.

Redundancies – There are likely to be some redundancies after the acquisition, for example in the marketing and administration functions of the company being acquired. However, there may also be some redundancies in ChemiCo's production departments, because there is no guarantee the acquisition will completely reverse the decline in demand for ChemiCo's products.

The staff in both organisations will inevitably be apprehensive about the possibility of job losses. The best way to deal with such fears is to act as quickly as possible and determine whether any cuts are necessary. If they are, the cuts must be implemented fairly – for example, on basis of skills required going forward.

Given the lack of alternative employment opportunities in the region, losing their job will be a major problem for individual staff members. There is a chance that losing some of their colleagues will affect the morale of the staff who remain with the company.

To this end, ChemiCo could consider offering training and outplacement support to the staff being made redundant to help them try to find new jobs.

40 ProfTech

Text reference. Force field analysis and resistance to change are covered in Chapter 11 of the BPP Study Text. Styles of change management are discussed in Chapter 12.

Part (a)

Top tips. You should recognise that the scenario illustrates the forces driving change (competitive marketplace; student requirements; technology) and those resisting change (tutors).

Force field analysis will allow ProfTech's management to summarise these forces, but possibly more importantly it can provide a clear visual demonstration of the need to strengthen the driving forces and weaken the resisting forces.

Make sure you apply the force field model directly to the scenario: do not simply describe what force field analysis is. Remember, the question asks how the directors could *use* force field analysis. In this context, you should also consider whether there are any limitations on force field analysis' usefulness.

Remember though, there are only 6 marks available here and you are only asked for a brief discussion. So do not spend too long on any single aspect of the 'forces' identified in the force field analysis.

Lewin introduced the idea of force field analysis as a means of examining and evaluating the driving forces promoting change and the resisting forces acting against it.

If the e-learning facility is to be successfully introduced at ProfTech, then the **forces promoting** the change (particularly student feedback and the threat from competitors' products) need to be exploited and the **forces hindering** it (particularly staff resistance) need to be reduced.

Producing a force field analysis will require ProfTech's directors to **identify the various factors** that are promoting and hindering change.

Highlight key stakeholders

By listing the forces supporting and opposing the change, and identifying the relative strength and importance of each, forcefield analysis will identify the key stakeholders who will be affected by the change. This will include lecturers, students, students' employers, and internal functions at ProfTech such as the IT department and course material development teams.

This should prompt the directors to decide how to strengthen or weaken the more important forces as necessary.

However, although forcefield analysis can give these insights into how to manage change, it does not in itself explain how to overcome the resistance demonstrated by particular forces. So whilst the analysis will identify the tutors' attitudes as a major problem to ProfTech's e-learning facility, it will not actually show ProfTech how to deal with this resistance.

Appreciate different motives

Although forcefield diagrams show 'driving' and 'resisting' forces, they also highlight that people may resist change for different reasons. For example, some of ProfTech's tutors may resist the change because they fear it will reduce the amount of face-to-face contact they will have with their students, but others might resist it because they are afraid it will highlight their lack of IT skills.

By highlighting these different reasons, forcefield analysis will encourage the directors to realise that different solutions will be needed to manage the resistance to change.

Identify future state

The layout of a forcefield analysis diagram shows a current state and a desire future state. Having to think about the desired future state will prompt ProfTech's directors to establish more clearly the role they want e-learning to play in the future, and how the business' strategy will reflect this.

Again, though, forcefield analysis does not give a clear account of the resources needed to deliver this strategy, or a timetable for delivering it.

Part (b)

Top tips. As with part (a), the scenario provides some useful clues: the tutors would rather keep the method they are familiar with and like, rather than having to learn new skills. However, alongside this fear of uncertainty, do not forget there may also be issues of power and security. Might the online materials reduce the need for classroom teachers?

Also, to what extent is the resistance due to poor management and communication from ProfTech's management rather than being entirely due to the tutors? (Note this idea could also provide a link to part (c) of this question.)

The move to e-learning marks a major change in the way tutors deliver their material to students, and the potential size of the change may have prompted the tutors to resist it.

Fear of the unknown

Fear of the unknown is one of the main reasons people resist change, and it is likely to be a major reason behind the tutors resistance to the e-learning scheme. For example, if they are no longer going to be delivering lectures to students, what will they be required to do instead? Will they still have a job?

Dislike uncertainty

It appears that the e-learning project is not very clearly structured. Some tutors have introduced e-learning while others haven't. Consequently, there is likely to be a sense of uncertainty about how extensive the e-learning facility will be: for example, will e-learning modules be required for every subject area? Will students use e-learning modules alongside taught courses or will it replace them?

Any such uncertainty is likely to cause anxiety and resistance.

Potential loss of power

Some tutors may feel that the current situation of gives them a position of power and authority when teaching their students, so they may feel the change is a threat to this authority.

Potential reduction in quality

While some tutors might resist the change because of the impact they think it might have on them, others might resist it because of the impact they think it might have on the students. A number of ProfTech's tutors remain unconvinced about the benefits of e-learning and think that the best way for students to learn is through face-to-face tuition.

Cannot see the need for change

If the tutors believe that face-to-face learning is a better way for students to learn than e-learning then they will not see the need to change the current, face-to-face teaching style. For the change to be successful, ProfTech's directors will need to demonstrate the benefits of the new approach to the tutors.

In this respect, it may be that the tutors are interested purely in the quality of their teaching but have not considered the wider commercial issues at ProfTech. Students value the flexibility which e-learning offers, and Youtrain's e-learning facility is proving very popular. Whatever reservations the tutors may have about them, offering courses in a way which is convenient and popular with students will be crucial for ProfTech's success. The directors need to emphasise this point, but it would appear they have not yet done so.

Potential lack of skills

There is a wide range of attitudes among the tutors: some support the e-learning facility while others are resisting it. These differences in attitude may reflect differences in how happy the tutors are using technology. Some might be worried that the e-learning will expose that they are not very proficient with technology, and they will not be able to deliver their materials in the new format.

The tutors are used to delivering their materials face-to-face, and the new approach will present different challenges which they may be unprepared for, and so which they may not be able to carry out effectively.

Part (c)

Top tips. The scenario highlights that there is a lack of clarity and focus about the project: some tutors are developing e-learning materials, but others aren't. This lack of clarity suggests not only that the vision for change hasn't been communicated to all the tutors, but also that there is a lack of urgency in introducing the changes.

Establishing a sense of urgency, and communicating the vision for change are two of the eight steps in Kotter's eight set model for managing change.

So, although you are not required to use this model here, it could be a useful framework for answering this requirement. We have used it as a framework for our answer below.

(You might also wish to consider Kotter & Schlesinger's ideas about the different ways of dealing with change and managing resistance to change).

However, if you use either of these models, do not spend time explaining the models. Simply use them as a framework which you can then apply to help answer the question which has actually been set: advising ProfTech's directors of the approaches they may take to ensure ProfTech successfully implements its e-learning programme.

Develop a sense of urgency

ProfTech is currently the largest training college in its country but its market position is being threatened by Youtrain Co. Youtrain has introduced an e-learning system of its own, and there is a danger that if ProfTech does not respond then Youtrain will continue to erode its market share.

ProfTech's directors need to ensure that the tutors appreciate this commercial aspect, and recognise the threats to the business if they do not adopt e-learning.

Ensure key groups work together

ProfTech's tutors and IT department are both key stakeholders in delivering the project successfully. However, the relationship between the tutors and the IT department does not appear to be very supportive, with the tutors seeking to blame the IT department for anything which goes wrong.

For the e-learning facility to be success, ProfTech's directors need to ensure that the two groups of people work together rather than antagonising each other.

Develop vision for change

Although the directors are keen to have an e-learning product and want ProfTech's students to be able to take e-learning courses within two years, they do not appear to have identified a vision of how the change will be introduced.

To this end, the directors need to establish a project team to manage the implementation, and also to agree a detailed project plan – including a timetable for implementing the facility.

Leadership and top level support

The introduction of e-learning represents a significant change in ProfTech's business model. Therefore it is important that the directors demonstrate to the business that they support it, and will champion its introduction.

The Board clearly support the project – the directors have approved a budget for the e-learning product, and want all students to have the option of having online tuition within 2 years. However, it is important that this support is communicated to the business.

Communicate the vision

At the moment, a number of the tutors are not committed to the direction of the change, but in large part this might be because they do not know how the changes will affect them.

Accordingly, the directors need to communicate the reasons for the new strategy to the tutors, and need to make sure the directors understand what is involved in the change.

Tackle obstacles to change

At the moment, ProfTech's directors are worried about forcing staff to adopt e-learning where they know a number of them are resisting the change.

However, in order to implement the change successfully, ProfTech's senior management will have to tackle the obstacles to change. To this end, they will have to get the tutors to support the programme.

There are a number of ways in which the managers can try to overcome the resistance to change, for example:

- **Communicating the need for change**, and explaining to the tutors how it will affect them
- Providing them with any **support** they will need to develop the new material, and encouraging the tutors who support e-learning to demonstrate to their colleagues how it can be used
- Looking at a **bonus scheme**, whereby the tutors are rewarded for adopting the new programme

New staff

It is possible that, however much support they are offered, some staff will still resist the changes and so will leave ProfTech. When recruiting new tutors, ProfTech needs to hire people who are not only good tutors but also support the e-learning project, and so will help implement the new material.

Highlighting positive feedback

Being able to demonstrate successes early in the implementation will maintain the momentum required to introduce the e-learning facility as a whole. At the moment, ProfTech's students have commented critically about the variation in the quality of the materials. However, ProfTech should highlight any positive student feedback about the e-learning material to remind the tutors why the scheme is worth pursuing.

Consolidate improvements

Where e-learning will be an increasingly important revenue stream, ProfTech should measure the amount of online business it generates as a KPI. This will sustain the focus on driving online business, and will highlight the fact that developing ProfTech's e-learning capabilities is an on-going project. ProfTech will need to upgrade and improve its e-learning material regularly to ensure it retains its market leading position.

41 Callcom

Text reference. Triggers for changes and resistance to change are covered in Chapter 11 of the BPP Study Text.

Marking scheme

			Marks
(a)	For each external trigger identified and discussed, up to 2 marks	Up to 4	
	For each internal trigger identified and discussed, up to 2 marks	Up to 4	
		Total up to	7
(b)	For evaluation of each aspect of change management prior to wireless access project, up to 2 marks	Up to 6	
	For explaining how each stage in a stage model could help Callcom manage the project, up to 3 marks	Up to 8	
		Total up to	13
(c)	For each relevant reason discussed	Up to 2	
		Total up to	5
		Total	25

Part (a)

Top tips. A useful way to approach this question is to separate 'external triggers' and 'internal triggers' and use them as separate headings to structure your answer. Using the headings of PEST analysis would be a useful way of thinking about external triggers.

Note that the question also asks you to consider changes in Callcom's operations as well as its strategy. Some of the internal triggers (job cuts, training requirements) have prompted operational changes rather than strategic changes.

External triggers

Industry deregulation - The government's decision to privatise Callcom and deregulate the telecommunication industry, has forced Callcom to have to adopt a more competitive strategy rather than being able to sustain a monopoly position.

Technological developments – Developments in telecommunications technology have led to new products being available. Mobile phones, broadband, and wireless technology all offered opportunities for new product development, even though Callcom's venture into the mobile market was unsuccessful.

The development of **VOIP** may lead to changes at both the strategic and operational levels. At the strategic level, it may offer **growth opportunities** through additional wireless services. However, at an operational level, there are fears that VOIP technologies may lead to a change in the number and type of **network staff** which Callcom require.

Consumer trends – Public **demand for mobile phones and broadband access** has increased significantly across the market as a whole, and this has led a decline in fixed voice telephone revenues. However, Callcom has relied on these fixed voice revenues as its largest source of revenue so it will have to **develop its product portfolio** to ensure it has other revenue streams to replace the income from fixed line telephone networks if it continues to fall.

Internal triggers

Product decisions – Callcom's **senior managers** are responsible for directing its product and market strategies. So they will have developed Callcom's strategies for **entering the mobile phone and broadband markets**. Equally, the senior managers will have monitored the performance of Callcom's business units, and they will have identified that the **mobile phone business should be sold**.

Staffing levels – Callcom recently made some job cuts, which suggests that Callcom's managers have identified that staffing levels where higher than they needed to be, and so Callcom could make some efficiency savings by reducing its staff numbers. This is an operational change rather than a strategic change though.

Reaction to job cuts – When the job cuts were announced, the workers took strike action in attempt to prevent the cuts and to allow their colleagues to keep their jobs. The trade unions supported their members in this action. In effect, the unions and workers were trying to reverse the operational change proposed by the management.

Ownership and cultural change – As Callcom has developed from a state-owned monopoly to a listed company in a competitive industry, its organisation and culture needs to change to reflect its changed market position. However, Callcom is still more bureaucratic than many of its competitors, and slower to respond to market opportunities, so it would appear that this 'trigger' for change has only been partially activated.

Part (b)

Top tips. The requirement here is quite complex so you need to read it carefully to ensure you understand exactly what you need to do.

The question effectively has two parts: first you have to evaluate Callcom's success at managing change in the past; then second, you need to explain how a stage model could help it manage the current project.

Note also the verbs used. You are asked to evaluate the success at managing change in the past, so you need to consider where it has been successful and where it hasn't. What has it tried to change? Products? Staffing levels? How successful has it been in changing them?

You should have identified that a key problem Callcom has faced is resistance to the changes it has tried to implement.

This is the link between the two parts of the question. Historically, the changes Callcom has tried to introduce have been blighted by resistance, but if wireless project is to be a success this resistance needs to be overcome.

Can a stage model help it in this respect?

Note you are not asked to describe or explain stage models of change, and you should not have spent time doing so. Instead, you need to consider specifically how a stage model of change (Lewin's three stage model?) could be useful for Callcom. For example, could it get people to be more positive about change?

<u>Managing change to date</u>

Product diversification – Callcom has successfully managed to extend its product range so that it can offer broadband services and VOIP as well as its traditional fixed voice telephone services.

However, fixed voice telephone services remain Callcom's largest source of revenue. And given that fixed voice telephone market is now a **declining market**, it appears that Callcom still needs to make some more changes to its product portfolio to ensure its longer-term profitability.

Slow response – Although Callcom has managed to attract a significant number of broadband customers it was unable to achieve a profitable market share of the mobile phone market. Callcom's relatively bureaucratic culture means that it is slower to respond to opportunities than its rivals. If Callcom entered the mobile phone market after its rivals this is likely to have contributed to its failure to win market share.

Cultural change – Callcom's relatively bureaucratic culture and structure are a legacy of its history as a state-owned monopoly. Although Callcom has seen a number of young, dynamic companies successfully enter the telecommunications market, it **does not appear that Callcom has been able to change its style** (or has wanted to change its style) to become more dynamic and responsive. This is despite being a privatised company for over 25 years (since 1986).

Staff management – One of Callcom's biggest problems in managing change appears to be its **unionised workforce**. Even if a proposed change is in the best interests of Callcom as a whole, if it poses a threat to some of the workforce then they resist it – most notably through industrial action.

It would appear that when Callcom announced job cuts earlier this year (prompting a strike) it did not explain why the cuts were needed. Better **communication** and dialogue with the staff could have prevented the damaging industrial action.

Managing the wireless access project

Lewin suggested that organisations could use a three stage process for managing a change process, and the concepts behind the three stages could help Callcom in their wireless action project.

The project has already been met with some resistance by the engineers who are threatening industrial action if they do not receive a large pay increase.

Unfreeze – The unfreezing process involves reducing the forces that are resisting change. At Callcom this will involve management explaining to the staff (and the unions) why the changes are required, and in particular highlighting the dangers if Callcom does not take advantage of new opportunities as they arise.

If Callcom's competitors take advantage of the new technology and Callcom doesn't, it will not be able to compete effectively. This could ultimately jeopardise the survival of the company as a whole, and therefore the jobs everyone who works for it. Faced with this choice, the staff and unions are more likely to support the change.

Change – The change aspect will require Callcom's engineers adopting new behaviours and attitudes required to make the wireless project successful.

Communication will be critical here, because the staff will need to understand **what** needs to be done, and **why** it needs to be done.

The strong union representation at Callcom means that this communication should not be just with the staff but with their union representatives as well.

However, for the changes at Callcom to be successful, it is important that managers do not simply try to force them through regardless of any resistance from the staff. There may be good reasons why the staff might be objecting to the changes. For example, they may have identified practical issues and problems with the proposals which the managers have not foreseen.

Refreezing - Refreezing means introducing the necessary mechanisms, such as reward systems, to ensure that the new behaviours and attitudes are maintained.

For example, although Callcom's engineers have demanded a large pay rise for learning the new skills required to install wireless access points, this may not act as an incentive for ongoing improvement and productivity. Instead, Callcom could consider some kind of bonus scheme whereby engineers are rewarded for identifying improvements in the process for installing the wireless access points.

Ultimately, though, following the three stage model cannot guarantee the success of the wireless access project as a whole. The three stage model only focuses on the internal aspects of the change, but the overall success of the project will depend on external factors as well as internal factors. For example, Callcom will need to monitor technological developments to see if there are any changes to the technologies, and it will have to see how its competitors are responding to the opportunity. Callcom's pricing and marketing strategies could be crucial to the success of the project.

Part (c)

Top tips. A sensible approach to this question would be to take a practical approach. If you are facing change in your own life or work, what sorts of things might make you resist it?

You may be able to use your answer for the first part of (b) to help generate some ideas here. Callcom has had problems with its staff when introducing changes in the past, and in part these have been due to poor communication. If the reasons for change or the benefits it could bring are not clearly communicated, people are unlikely to support the change.

However, make sure that you answer to (c) does not duplicate points you have already made in (b).

Benefits not communicated – If Callcom's managers haven't explained the reasons for the change, and the benefits which will result from it, there is little motivation to change. In such circumstances the engineers might just view the change as 'change for change's sake', and reject it as unnecessary.

Fear of job losses – Callcom has already announced one round of job cuts earlier this year, and there is uncertainty about the impact VOIP will have on staff numbers. Therefore the engineers may associate change programmes with job losses, rather than as ways of improving the organisation's performance.

Fears about new technology – We do not know from the scenario how long the engineers have been working for Callcom, or experienced they are, but given the culture of the company it is likely that some have been working there for a long time. For them, changes which may also mean the introduction of new technologies, may be perceived as a threat. What if they do not understand the new technology or cannot cope with it? Again, do they risk losing their jobs?

Unwillingness to learn new skills – Alongside these concerns about being able to learn new skills, there may be some of the engineers who do not want to learn new skills. They may be quite content doing what they are doing, and so see no reason to change. To them, instead of being an opportunity to learn new skills, change might seen as forcing them to throw away existing skills.

Quality of new work – There may be concerns that new work will be more increasingly specialised and less interesting than their current work. For example, if the engineers currently carry out a wide variety of work, but then have to focus only on wireless installations, this may not be a very appealing change.

42 MMM University departments

Text reference. Objectives, including the characteristics of 'SMART' objectives, are discussed in Chapter 2 of the BPP Study Text for E3. The role of change agents in managing change is covered in Chapter 12.

Top tips.

Part (a) does not simply ask you to describe what 'SMART' objectives are (Specfic, Measurable, etc.) but rather to advise how MMM could use them to achieve the new control system's objectives. The key issue here is that, as they stand, the objectives for MMM's new control system do not demonstrate the 'SMART' characteristics. Therefore, the objectives will need to be modified in order for MMM to be able to assess whether they are being achieved or not.

A useful way to structure your answer would be to take the five aspects of the 'SMART' model as headings, describe the aspect briefly, and advise the Board how each aspect could be used to improve the objectives; for example, by making them measurable. This is the approach the Examiner's own answer took for this question.

Part (b). A key issue in part (b) (i) is to appreciate how the way in which MMM's 'culture' is likely to be embedded in the organisation. Therefore, the Board cannot simply impose a mechanical process to try to change the culture. Instead, MMM's culture will need to be changed more gradually; and the activities which you suggest in your answer need to contribute to this gradual change.

Part (b) (ii) – It seems likely that there will be some resistance to the new structure, not least from the Heads who will lose their jobs as a result of the change. Therefore, overcoming this resistance to change will be an important part of introducing the new structure. However, your answer shouldn't only address this issue; for example, don't simply discuss the various different ways of over-coming resistance to change (such as those suggested by Kotter & Schlesinger). Instead, try also to think of a range of practical issues that the Board need to consider – for example, what staffing levels will be required for the new structure? Will some staff have to be made redundant, and/or will others have to be recruited?

Part (c) – To score well here, you need to consider the specific role a change agent could play in the change process at MMM; not simply to discuss the role of a change agent in general terms.

Equally, you shouldn't spend time discussing the skills which a change agent needs to demonstrate. This was not asked for by the question, and so would have not earned you any marks.

Examiner's comments. In Part (a), many candidates were able to describe the SMART criteria, although surprisingly few candidates actually described all five aspects correctly. More importantly, very few candidates appeared able to apply the SMART criteria to MMM's objectives, and therefore to suggest how they could be made more specific, measurable, achievable etc.

Part (b) (i) was answered very badly. Many candidates treated the process of changing culture as a mechanistic one, rather than an abstract one, and focused on a structured approach such as 'Plan, Organise, Monitor, Implement.' Other answers merely re-wrote Kotter & Schlesinger's approaches to overcoming resistance to change, with little or no consideration of the specific difficulties of cultural change.

Marking scheme

			Marks
(a)	For describing each aspect of the 'SMART' model - up to 1 mark each	Up to 5	
	For relating each aspect of 'SMART' to MMM's objectives – up to 1 mark each	Up to 5	
		Total up to	10
(b) (i)	For each activity to be undertaken in relation to changing the University's culture, and the difficulties involved in changing culture – up to 2 marks each	Up to 5	
	(Valid points could include: Speed of change required, importance of communications, reward systems, symbols.)		
		Total up to	5
(b) (ii)	For each activity to be undertaken to introduce the new departmental structure – up to 2 marks each	Up to 5	
	(Valid points could include: reducing head count, planning/budgeting, training, overcoming resistance to change, project management.)	Total up to	5
(c)	For each activity that a change agent could undertake – 1 mark each	Up to 5	
	(Valid activities include: defining problems, examining the cause of the problem, identifying possible solutions, gaining support for solutions, disseminating advice/experience)		
		Total up to	5
		Total	25

(a)

The Board has introduced three new objectives, and the aim of the new control system will be to try to ensure that these objectives are achieved.

However, the objectives which have been introduced do not conform to the SMART criteria. As a result, it will be difficult to translate them into any specific targets for the Heads and their departments, and equally it will be harder for MMM to measure whether the objectives are being achieved or not.

If the Board used the SMART model, this would enable it to define its objectives more precisely, which in turn should help the Board measure whether the objectives are being achieved or not.

Specific – Objectives should be clearly defined so that everyone understands what they mean. However, MMM's objective 'To develop the Heads' motivation' doesn't appear to fulfil this function, because it seems unclear what it means to 'develop the Heads' motivation' or how this could be achieved.

Assuming that the Heads' motivation is related to the quality of education provided to students, a more specific objective could be something like 'To ensure that pass rates on all courses in the department exceed the national average.'

Measurable – The objectives need to be quantifiable so that performance can be measured against them, and consequently so that MMM can assess whether they are being achieved or not.

For example, the third objective would be improved if it quantified the level of income MMM wants to generate from external activities. For example, instead of seeking to 'encourage activities that generate income from external activities' the objective could be rewritten as 'To generate an additional £5 million income from external activities in the next year.'

Attainable (or achievable) – It must be feasible for the Heads and the departments to achieve any objectives which are set. If the objectives are felt to be unrealistic, the Heads will not even try to achieve them, which devalues the purpose of having objectives in the first place. Equally, setting unrealistic objectives will be demotivating for the Heads and their departments, because they know they will not be able to achieve their targets from the outset.

For example, if MMM currently generates £50 million income from external activities, the objective to generate an additional £5 million may seem to be achievable. However, if MMM currently only generates £10 million from external activities an increase of 50% may be felt to be unachievable in one year.

Relevant – The objectives set should be relevant to an organisation's mission statement, and should help the organisation achieve its mission.

MMM's mission 'to be the best' is very vague, and so it could be argued that almost any objectives could be relevant to it. In this respect, the aspect of relevance is likely to have little value in helping MMM to achieve the new control system's objectives. For example, although the objective 'To develop the Heads' motivation' is very vague, if the Heads of Departments become more motivated this should improve the performance of their departments, which in turn should contribute towards the overall aim of 'being the best'.

The aspect of relevance could also be used to highlight the importance of linking (strategic) objectives to the operational level and making them relevant to people's jobs on a day-to-day basis. For example, the objective to generate income from external activities could be linked to individuals' objectives to generate income from sponsorships or fund-raising.

Time-bound – The objectives need to define a date by which they should be achieved. If the objectives aren't time-bound, it will be difficult for an organisation to measure its progress towards achieving its objectives, because it doesn't know the time period which the objectives relate to.

For example, the objective 'to generate income from external activities' doesn't identify whether this income should be generated in the next year, or over the next five years, or even over a longer time period. By contrast, the alternative objective we have suggested – 'To generate an additional £5 million income from external activities in the next year' – clearly defines that the additional income needs to be generated in the next year.

Consequently, at the end of the next year, it will be easy for MMM to identify whether the objective as been achieved or not.

Currently, none of MMM's objectives are time-bound, so this is another area in which the SMART model could help MMM achieve the new control systems' objectives.

(b)

(i)

Gradual process - The university's culture will have evolved over time, and so the Board will not simply be able to change the culture as a one-off process. Therefore, the Board needs to accept that the process of changing MMM's culture will be a long and gradual one, and so it should not try to make any changes too quickly.

End point - Equally, however, before the Board seeks to make any changes it will need to identify what it wants the 'new' culture of the university to be, so that it can ensure that ensure any changes it introduces support the transition to this new culture.

These 'strategic' issues are likely to be the most challenging for the Board. However, there will also be more 'operational' issues which the Board will need to consider:

Communication – The Board will need to communicate with MMM's staff to explain the details of the new control system, and the potential impact it will have on them.

Reward system – Once MMM has defined its overall objectives and the objectives for the new departments, it will also need to define personal objectives for individual members of staff. It will be very important that these personal objectives are aligned to the departmental objectives; for example, so that any changes in behaviour which will be required to achieve a department's objectives are reinforced to the relevant staff.

Symbols – At a tangible level, the Board will need to approve a budget for the 'branding' of the new departments. For example, the new departments are likely to need new signage and stationery, and some offices may need to be relocated to fit with the revised structure.

(ii)

Departmental heads – The new departmental structure reduces the number of departments from six to three. Although each of the departments will be managed by one of the existing Heads of department, the restructure means that there will be three existing Heads who will no longer be in charge of a department.

The Board will have to decide which of the three existing Heads will be appointed as Heads of the new departments, but equally whether the other three Heads can be retained within the University or whether they will have to be made redundant.

Staffing requirements – The current staffing model will also have to be reviewed, to decide how staff from the existing six departments are apportioned to the three new departments. This is likely to be a major exercise, undertaken in consultation with the staff, and it will need to be overseen by MMM's human resources manager (if it has one). If MMM does not have a dedicated HR team, the Board should consider using HR consultants to manage the change.

Networks and internal communications – MMM will also have to consider how the restructure will affect internal communications. For example, if there are currently email groups set up by department, these will need to be redesigned for the new departments.

Equally MMM will need to consider whether any staff will need to move offices as a result of the restructure, and it will need to plan the logistics of any such moves.

Overcoming resistance to change – It is likely that there will be at least some resistance to the changes, for example from staff who cannot see the need for the changes or the benefits they can bring. The Board will need to identify ways of overcoming this resistance to change.

Once again, **communication** is likely to be very important here: communicating the 'vision' for change, and the potential benefits of the change may help overcome staff concerns about it.

The Board could also consider whether some of the staff could be involved in the change process. If staff feel they are involved in the change process, they may be less likely to resist the changes.

Wherever possible, however, MMM should avoid coercing staff into accepting the change, particularly as this is a change which the University has decided to make itself, rather than as a response to external environmental factors.

Training – In addition to the general communication issues identified above, the Board should also consider whether the staff need any more detailed training about how the changes will affect them and/or about how the university will operate under the new structure. Equally, if any staff are moving into new roles as a result of the restructuring, MMM will need to consider if they will need any training for their new roles.

In particular, this could apply to the Heads of the new departments. For example, a manager who has previously been the Head of an academic department may need some additional training before taking on the role as Head of the commercial department dealing with profit-making activities.

(c)

For the proposed changes at MMM to be effective, they need to be implemented effectively. MMM could use a change agent to manage the change process, and to be responsible for ensuring the changes are implemented successfully.

Importantly, however, MMM needs to recognise that the change agent's role is not actually to implement the changes themselves, but to manage and facilitate the process. MMM's Board and staff will still have to play a full part in implementing the changes though.

One of the change agent's key roles throughout the change process will be identifying problems and suggesting possible solutions for them. For example, one of the potential problems MMM faces is what to do with the three existing Heads who will no longer be Heads of Department under the new structure.

A change agent could assist in this aspect of the change problems as follows:

Defining the problem – what to do with the three Heads who will no longer have a Department to manage

Examining what causes the problem – the reduction in the number of departments

Considering how the problem can be overcome – redeploying the Heads elsewhere in the University

Suggesting possible alternative solutions – the Heads leave the University with a redundancy package

Gaining support from all involved – for example, discussing the options available with the Heads, HR and the Board.

Selecting and implementing a solution – for example, deciding when and where the Heads will be redeployed if a suitable alternative position can be found for them within MMM.

Crucially, if MMM uses an external change agent, the agent may already have experience (from previous projects) of the problems which MMM is facing. In this case, the change agent could use this experience to help MMM implement its change process as effectively as possible.

43 XYZ Chemical Co

Text reference. Corporate Social Responsibility (CSR) is discussed in Chapter 2 of the BPP Study Text for E3. Lewin's stage model of change is covered in Chapter 11.

Top tips. To score well in part (a), it is important that you don't simply consider the benefits of having a CSR policy in general terms, but rather you consider the benefits specifically for XYZ: for example, in relation its manufacturing process, and the health and safety of its workers.

Although part (b) is only worth 6 marks, the requirement sets out very clearly the different aspects of the CSR you need to consider: (i) manufacturing process (eg waste, noise and smell); (ii) procurement (eg Fair Trade); (iii) labour force (eg health & safety); and (iv) legal compliance. You should have treated each of the four aspects as the headings for your answer.

As with part (a), to score well in part (c) it is important that you don't simply describe the relevant theory (Lewin's stage model of change) in general terms, but instead you must apply it directly to the scenario. For example, part of the 'unfreeze' process involves explaining the reasons for the change to the staff. In XYZ's case, having a CSR policy could improve the working conditions for the staff (through reducing noise and smell, and making the manufacturing process safer), but there is also a more strategic benefit to having a CSR policy, since one is necessary in order for XYZ to become a listed company.

(a)

Enable listing – It seems that having a CSR policy is a fundamental pre-requisite for obtaining a stock market listing. So a major benefit of having a CSR policy will be that it makes XYZ eligible for listing in this respect. Obtaining a listing is important for XYZ because it should provide XYZ with access to the capital it needs to fund its expansion.

However, there could also be a number of benefits resulting from specific areas of the policy:

Waste reduction – Currently XYZ's manufacturing process produces large quantities of waste. A CSR policy is likely to focus on reducing the levels of waste overall, and also on making the manufacturing process less noisy and smelly.

At a basic level, improvements in these areas may reduce any public ill-feeling or opposition towards XYZ, or possible opposition to expansion plans which might involve building new or larger factories.

Equally, the drive to reduce levels of waste and reduce noise and smell may also make XYZ's processes more efficient, thereby potentially reducing costs and increasing profitability.

Diverse workforce – The fact that XYZ already has an ethnically diverse workforce suggests it offer equal opportunities to potential employees regardless of their ethnic origin.

A CSR policy is likely to reinforce the importance of equal opportunities in recruitment – regardless of ethnicity, age, etc.

Two specific benefits of this are:

(i) XYZ is giving itself as wide a pool of potential candidates to recruit new staff from (thereby hopefully allowing it to recruit the best staff possible). If XYZ is seen as a 'good employer' this will have the additional benefit that staff will want to stay working for it (thereby reducing staff turnover and associated costs (eg recruitment costs).

(ii) XYZ will hopefully avoid any costly litigation (for example on the grounds of age discrimination).

Accident prevention – A CSR policy is also likely to include provision for the health and safety of XYZ's workers. Again, it is important that XYZ tries to reduce the risk of accidents to being as low as possible, because accidents could have cost implications for the business:

- Every time there is an accident it is likely that the manufacturing process will have to be shut down until the accident is dealt with (meaning a loss of output)
- There is also a risk of litigation against XYZ if a member of staff is injured in an accident and it is proved that XYZ as the employer was negligent

More generally, the existence of some kind of risk management policies suggests that XYZ's senior management team is already aware of risks (both internal and external) and is trying to manage them. This is anther indicator of good management.

Sourcing fairly – As XYZ sources some of its raw materials from economically underdeveloped countries, it is important that XYZ pays (and is seen to pay) a fair price for these raw materials, and cannot be accused or exploiting the underdeveloped countries.

If XYZ is seen to be a good corporate citizen in this way, this could make it more attractive to potential investors, and in particular to **ethical investors**.

Attracting potential shareholders – As well as the specific benefits of the CSR policy, being seen as a socially responsible organisation could also be beneficial for XYZ when it comes to issue shares to the public.

Some people may be reluctant to invest in a company which is seen as socially irresponsible, because they will be worried about the longer term sustainability of the company and therefore also their investment in it.

Conversely, if XYZ is recognized as a good corporate citizen this is likely to make it more attractive to ethical investors. In time, if XYZ can get itself included on a CSR index – such as the 'FTSE4GOOD' index series – and if it performs well on the index, this could further increase its attractiveness to ethical investors.

(b)

XYZ's CSR policy needs to deal with the following matters:

<u>Manufacturing process</u>

Waste – The manufacturing process currently produces large quantities of waste, so XYZ should aim to recycle as much of its waste as possible.

However, XYZ should also try to reduce the levels of waste it produces; for example, by making sure its manufacturing processes are as efficient as possible, and by reducing resource usage as far as possible.

Noise – The manufacturing process is currently very noise, so the policy needs to identify how the noise levels may be reduced. In this respect, XYZ needs to consider both the level of noise pollution for the local neighbourhood around its manufacturing plant, and also the noise levels within the plant which the staff have to work in.

Smell – The manufacturing process is smelly as well as noisy, so the policy needs to address smell in a similar way to noise.

Procurement policy

Raw material procurement – As XYZ sources some of its materials from economically underdeveloped countries, its policy needs to define the basis on which it does business with companies in those countries. In particular, XYZ needs to highlight the importance of ensuring the price, and the terms and conditions it negotiates with supplies are fair.

<u>Labour force</u>

There are two issues in relation to the workforce which the CSR policy needs to address:

Equality – Ensuring that all **members** of the workforce are treated fairly and equally

Working conditions – Improving the conditions the staff have to work under. As well as the manufacturing process being noisy and smelly, there have also been a number of accidents. The CSR policy should therefore highlight XYZ's commitment to workplace safety.

Compliance

XYZ has always tried to comply with its country's laws, and it should continue to do this. However, CSR involves more than simply complying with basic legal requirements, so XYZ's policy should establish its basic principle of complying with the law before going on to highlight the other principles which will enable it to be a good corporate citizen.

(c)

Lewin suggested that there are three stages which need to be following in order for change to be implemented successfully – unfreeze, change, refreeze – and XYZ could use these three stages to implement its CSR policy.

Unfreeze

Explain need for change and benefits of change – The chances of XYZ's CSR policy being implemented successfully will be increased if it explains to the staff the reasons why such a policy is necessary before introducing it. The staff are more likely to accept any changes if they understand why they are necessary.

The need for change can be explained at two different levels:

Strategically, XYZ needs to have a CSR policy if it wants to become a listed company, and such a listing may be necessary to help the company grow.

At a more personal level, the CSR policy will deal, amongst other things, with the working conditions around the manufacturing process. In this respect, if the policy helps reduce the noise and smell the staff have to work with, and improves the safety of the process, this will be a direct benefit to the staff. Highlighting this to the staff may be the most persuasive way of getting them to support the change and 'unfreeze' their current behaviours in order to implement the change.

Change

Changing behaviours and processes – In order for the CSR policy to be effective, XYZ's staff will need to change their patterns of behavior to reflect the new guidelines set out in the policy.

The 'change' phase is mainly concerned with identifying the new, desirable behaviours, communicating them clearly to staff, and encouraging staff to 'buy into' them. For example, the CSR policy is likely to address issues of workplace safety, so it will be important that the staff know how they need to adapt their working practices to make them safer, and – perhaps more importantly – that the staff actually adopt the new, safer working practices.

Identification of change – One way XYZ could help ensure the policy is adopted successfully is by encouraging the staff to identify with role models from whom they can learn the new working practices. For example, the safety manager and team leaders must ensure they are following the new working practices, and then the staff will be encouraged to do likewise.

Manufacturing process – However, the success of the policy also depends on the manufacturing process being improved to reduce waste, noise and smell. In this respect, the 'change' stage of the model requires XYZ's engineering staff developing new production techniques which generate lower levels of pollution.

Refreeze

Embedding the change – In order for the CSR policy to be successful, XYZ will need to ensure the new patterns of behaviour (established during the 'change' phase) become embedded throughout the organisation, and that staff do not lapse back into old patterns of behaviour.

Habituation effects – To some extent, 'refreezing' may occur naturally over time. As staff become more familiar with the new working practices they will become more natural to them, so the temptation to revert to the old working practices is reduced.

Positive reinforcement – However, XYZ can also take measures to reinforce these habituation effects. For example, an element of the staff's appraisal (and, in turn, any bonuses they earn) could be linked to how well they perform in relation to the CSR policy. For example, an element of the engineers' bonuses could be linked to the amount they reduce waste from the manufacturing process each year, or the health and safety manager's bonus could be linked to the number of accidents each year.

44 WAL biscuit manufacturer

Text reference. Different types of changes are discussed in Chapter 12 of the BPP Study Text. The different ways which can be used to overcome resistance to change are discussed in Chapter 11.

Marking scheme

			Marks
(a)	For explaining circumstances where evolutionary change would be appropriate – 1 mark per valid point	Up to 2	
	For explaining circumstance where 'Big Bang' change would be appropriate – 1 mark per valid point	Up to 2	
		Total up to	4
(b) (i)	Modification: for each advantage or disadvantage of this approach evaluated – 1 mark each	Up to 3	
	Development: for each advantage or disadvantage of this approach evaluated – 1 mark each	Up to 3	
	Purchase: for each advantage or disadvantage of this approach evaluated – 1 mark each	Up to 3	
		Total up to	9
(b) (ii)	For overall recommendation	1	
	For justification for option recommended, and/or overall evaluation of issues determining the most appropriate option	Up to 2	
		Total up to	3
(c)	For identifying that R's resistance is a serious concern	1	
	For identifying appropriate techniques which could be used for overcoming resistance to change:		
	Education and communication	Up to 2	
	Participation and involvement	Up to 2	
	Facilitation and support	Up to 2	
	Negotiation and agreement	Up to 2	
	Maniputation and co-optation	Up to 2	
	Coercion	1	
		Total up to	9
		Total	25

(a)

Top tips.

Part (a). The requirement here is to explain *when* each type of change would be appropriate; not to explain what each type of change is. For example, although evolutionary change is likely to be slow and gradual, the relevant point here is that these characteristics mean it will only be appropriate in circumstances where an organisation has time to implement a change slowly and gradually.

However, note there are only 4 marks available for this requirement; 2 for each type of change. So don't spend too long on this part of the question; highlight the key circumstances when each type of change would be appropriate, and then move on.

Evolutionary change – Evolutionary change is an **incremental** process which is often undertaken in **anticipation** of the need for future change. This element of anticipation means that evolutionary change is likely to be appropriate in situations where management have **time to plan** the change, rather than being forced to change in response to external events. Similarly the incremental nature of the change means it is appropriate in situations where time is not critical, changes can be **introduced gradually**, and management will feel they are in control of the change process.

The fact that WAL is only changing its marketing software in response to the concern that it is being left behind by its competitors suggests that this change is reactive rather than proactive or planned in advance. Consequently, this suggests that evolutionary change may not be appropriate here.

'Big Bang' change – 'Big Bang' change is likely to be appropriate where an organisation has to make **wide-ranging** and **rapid change** due to changes in the competitive conditions it is facing. Unlike evolutionary change, which is essentially proactive, 'Big Bang' change tends to be reactive; **reacting to changes in competitive conditions** or the external environment.

Hence, the fact that WAL is looking to change its marketing software in response to the concern it is being left behind by its competitors and is losing customers suggests that 'Big Bang' change may be required to overhaul the current marketing information system.

(b)

Top tips.

Part (b) asks you to 'evaluate' the three solutions, so you need to consider the potential benefits of each, as well as what their limitations or disadvantages are.

The scenario highlights a number of potential benefits and limitations of each solution so finding relevant information for your answer should not have been a problem. However, it was important that you 'evaluate' the factors rather than simply re-writing information from the scenario.

For example, the scenario highlights quite clearly that the in-house IS/IT staff seemed unsure how long it would take to modify the software or develop new software in-house, and how much the in-house approaches would cost. The key point here is that this uncertainty is a disadvantage for both Solutions 1 and 2. You will earn the mark available for highlighting this disadvantage; not simply for describing the in-house staff's uncertainty about time and cost.

Note: There are 9 marks available for this part of the question, with 3 being allocated to each of the 3 solutions.

Our solution below identifies a range of valid arguments you could have included, but you would not have needed to make as many points as this to score the marks available.

Part (b) (ii). Your evaluations in (b) (i) should have helped you decide which of the solutions would be most appropriate for WAL to adopt. However, it is important that when making your recommendation you state your reasons clearly.

(i)

Modification

Evolutionary approach – This solution fits R's preference, and – if he has understood their opinions correctly – the preference of the IS/IT staff, for evolutionary change. The IS/IT staff are more likely to support a solution, and to be motivated to try to ensure that it is successful, if they feel their views about how it should be implemented have been listened to.

Limited experience – However, the fact that WAL's IS/IT staff have limited experience of the type of work required is a serious concern; not least because it may be accompanied by a lack of the skills needed to actually make the modifications required by the marketing staff.

Inherent limitations – However, perhaps more importantly, there may be inherent limitations and inadequacies in WAL's existing system, which cannot be addressed through a process of modification alone. As the existing system was a bought-in package, there may be elements of it which will be very difficult to modify to meet WAL's needs exactly. If the limitations of the existing package are too substantial, it is likely to be more cost effective for WAL to develop, or buy, an entirely new system rather than trying to modify the existing one.

Reliability of estimates – The IS/IT staff's lack of experience suggests it will be very difficult for them to estimate with any certainty how long the redesign will take. Although they have said they are confident it could be done within a year, their lack of experience may have led to them being over-optimistic and over-confident in their ability to deliver.

In the same way that the IS/IT staff have admitted they are unsure of the cost, it may be more realistic if they also admit they are unsure how long the modifications will take them to complete.

<u>Development</u>

Motivation for IS/IT staff – This solution, like Solution 1, fits the preference for evolutionary change. Moreover, as the IS/IT staff have expressed their enthusiasm for trying to develop the software, if they are given the opportunity to do so this should help motivate them.

Bespoke solution – Solution 2 is the only one which has the potential to provide the marketing staff with bespoke software, specifically tailored to meet their needs.

Lack of experience – However, the IS/IT staff's lack of software development experience could mean it takes them longer to develop the software than it would take more experienced developers. (Also, there could be a risk that the software developed may be inferior to that which could have been developed by more experienced developers).

Time and cost – However, the greatest concern about this solution comes from the uncertainty surrounding how long it will take and how much it could cost.

The IS/IT staff have already identified that it will cost 'considerably more' than Solution 1, but they have admitted that they can only make a rough estimate of the costs, because they don't know how long the project will take. The IS/IT staff's estimate that the project could take anywhere between six months and two years probably indicates their lack of experience in software development.

It seems unlikely that WAL can afford to wait two years for the new software given that it is already being left behind by competitors and losing customers as a result.

<u>Purchase</u>

Proven product – The software is already used by the majority of other biscuit manufacturers, and it is a proven product. Moreover, some of WAL's marketing staff – who have used the software before – appreciate its benefits, and have indicated that it would help them considerably in their jobs.

User acceptance - As the software will be used by the marketing staff, their views about which software to choose are important. It seems that choosing the industry standard software will be an acceptable choice them.

Speed of implementation – The external supplier has guaranteed that WAL's staff will be able to start using the software within three months of buying it. This is considerably sooner than either of the in-house solutions will be ready for use, and therefore fits better with the marketing department's requirement to move straightaway to a new system.

Competitive position – Currently WAL's marketing staff feel that WAL is being left behind by its competitors, but if WAL introduces the same software as the majority of its competitors this should enable it to catch up with them.

However, because this Solution will mean that WAL ends up using the same software as its competitors, it will not provide WAL with any competitive advantage over them, something which a bespoke package could potentially do.

Cost – WAL is already aware that purchasing the software would be an **expensive option.** However, at least with this solution WAL **knows, in advance, how much the software will cost**, because it will agree a purchase price with the supplier. This is likely to be seen as a benefit compared to the in-house options where the IS/IT staff are unsure of the cost, and so where costs could keep increasing if the projects take longer than expected.

Resistance to change – It is clear that R is opposed to this Solution, but he is responsible for procuring the replacement software. He is also concerned that 'Big Bang' changes have a history of failure at WAL. However, it is debatable how much implementing a new software package will require a change of culture at WAL; unlike previous 'Big Bang' changes.

Perhaps more importantly though, if the IS/IT staff are opposed to this solution, they may reluctant to provide IT support to the marketing department in the future, and any friction between the departments could be damaging for WAL going forward.

(ii)

Solution 1 should not be recommended because of the uncertainty about how long it will take and how much it will cost, given the IS/IT staff's lack of experience. Equally, the extent of the problems with the current system may mean that it is inherently unable to meet WAL's needs, and therefore moving to a completely new system is more appropriate than modifying the existing one.

Solution 2 should also not be recommended because of the IS/IT staff's lack of experience in software development, and the associated uncertainty about how long the project will take and how much it will cost. In addition, it seems that the marketing software is strategically important to WAL, so it would be taking a significant risk in giving the project to staff who have limited experience of software development.

Recommendation

Solution 3 should be recommended. The package being proposed is the market leading software, and WAL's marketing staff can testify that it will meet their needs and deliver considerable benefits, not least enabling WAL to catch up with its competitors. Although the package is expensive, WAL knows the cost involved at the start of the process, and the software can be installed much more quickly than would be case in either of the other two solutions.

(c)

Top tips.

The reference to 'overcoming resistance to change' in the requirement should have highlighted that Kotter & Schlesinger's framework is the relevant theory to use here. However, this does not mean that you should simply have described each of Kotter & Schlesinger's six methods for overcoming resistance to change in your answer.

The question asks how 'WAL could overcome the resistance to change' so it vital that you apply your knowledge of the model specifically to the scenario, and WAL's situation. For example, instead of simply identifying that 'Education and communication' is one possible way to overcome resistance to change, you should have advised how communicating with staff and educating them about why a purchased solution was required could help reduce their resistance to this solution.

The purchase solution is a 'Big Bang' approach, but R and the IS/IT staff appear resistant to change unless it is implemented slowly and gradually. R's resistance is likely to be a particularly serious obstacle for WAL, because his authority over the procurement process means he could potentially prevent WAL from buying the external package solution.

Education and communication – WAL needs to explain that the deficiencies in its current marketing system are so serious that they are making the company uncompetitive and causing it to lose customers. In the worst case, if WAL does not address these deficiencies quickly and successfully, its survival could be under threat. If WAL explains that the decision is being taken for the greater good of the company, then R and the IS/IT staff may more prepared to accept it.

Part of R's resistance also appears to come from the fact that previous 'Big Bang' projects have been unsuccessful. WAL needs to acknowledge this concern, but also to explain what actions it is taking to try to safeguard against past failings being repeated in this project.

Participation and involvement – R gives the impression that, although his department will have to do all the work to install the new software, they haven't been involved in choosing it. Therefore one way to help overcome their resistance to the purchased software would be to let key IS/IT staff see a demonstration of the software and ask any questions they may have of the vendor before a final decision is made to buy the package.

If the IS/IT staff feel they have been allowed to participate in the vendor selection they may be less resistant to the purchase solution – particularly if, by seeing the proposed package, they get a better idea of the benefits it can bring to WAL.

Facilitation and support – R appears to be concerned that WAL will encounter problems when it tries to implement the new package (as has been the case with previous 'Big Bang changes'). His concern is magnified because he feels his department will have to do all the work to integrate the new package into WAL's existing systems.

In this respect, it appears that at least some of R's resistance to the package comes from a fear of failure; for example, the fear that he and his department will take the blame and be held responsible if there are any problems with the new package. WAL should try to reassure R that this will not be case; for example, that his job security will not be under threat if the project is unsuccessful.

Moreover, the IS/IT staff should be provided with any training they need to help install and support the new software. WAL may also be able to get the software supplier to provide some of its own staff to help with the initial installation of the software.

Negotiation and agreement – R's comment about his department having to do all the work also suggests that they might be less resistant to the package solution if this were not the case. For example, the software supplier might offer a maintenance agreement which means WAL's marketing staff could address problems or queries about the software to the supplier (via a helpdesk) rather than to WAL's IS/IT staff. If WAL agreed to sign up for the maintenance agreement, this should reduce any resistance borne out of the level of work which the package would generate for the WAL's IS/IT staff.

In addition, while the majority of the WAL's IS/IT staff believe the change should be evolutionary, it appears that some support a 'Big Bang' approach. Therefore, WAL may be able to reduce resistance by assigning, as far as possible, those people who support the 'Big Bang' approach to work on the project, and leaving those staff who feel more comfortable with gradual change to work on 'business as usual' or more incremental projects in other parts of the business.

Coercion – Although this should only be used as a last resort, if WAL is unable to overcome resistance by any other means, it may have to force R and the IS/IT staff to accept the change. In the worst case, WAL may simply have to tell staff (including R) that it has made the decision to introduce the software package, and if they wish to continue working for the company, they will have to accept that decision.

45 JKL's growth

Text reference: Methods of strategic growth (organic growth; acquisitions) are discussed in Chapter 6 of your BPP Study text. Change agents are discussed in Chapter 12.

Top tips: You should have felt part (a) of this question was relatively approachable, because it was on a core area of the syllabus: a discussion of the relative advantages and disadvantages of organic growth vs acquisition as methods of growth. However, to score well it was important that discuss the advantages and disadvantages of each method specifically in relation to JKL, rather than just making general points. Also, whilst a lot of the advantages of organic growth are disadvantages of acquisition – and vice versa – to score well you need to try and make a number of diverse points. In other words, if you say one of the disadvantages of organic growth is that it is slow, you will not then also get a mark for saying that one of the advantages of acquisition is that it is fast. The two points are deemed to relate to the same issue, and will be marked as such.

Part (b) relates to the three reasons for failure which were clearly highlighted (as numbered points) in the scenario. Therefore a sensible approach would be to take each of the three issues in turn, consider how each might recur with the French acquisition, and then recommend how JKL could prevent this from happening.

You could have interpreted part (c) in two ways. Firstly, you could have discussed a step by step account of what the change agent could do to make the acquisition successful (and this is the general approach we have taken in the answer below). Alternatively, you could have discussed the impact the change agent could have on the acquisition process. Either approach would have been valid here. However, whichever approach you took, it is important that your answer focuses on what a change agent does: you will not earn marks for describing the skills required to be a successful change agent.

(a)

Organic growth

Advantages

Low risk – Organic growth is generally considered to involve less risk than making an acquisition, and JKL's past experience of its failed acquisition illustrates the risk involved in growing externally.

Expanding through organic growth means that JKL can exploit its own strengths whilst maintaining its existing **style of management** and **corporate culture.** Also, JKL will not face problems of having to integrate operating systems between different companies.

Growth in stages – JKL is a small company and so may only have limited resources. Organic growth is likely to be less onerous on its cash flow than making an acquisition. Organic growth can be managed gradually or in stages, whereas to make an acquisition JKL is likely to have to commit a large amount of funds in one go.

Disadvantages

Speed of growth – It is likely to take longer for a firm to grow organically, than if it acquires another firm. Organic growth is often achieved by a company reinvesting its profits into its growth. However, this means the speed of growth will be restricted by the level of profits available for reinvestment, and this could be a particular issue for JKL is it is still a small company.

Nature of growth – Organic growth is most suited to situations where a company is growing gradually, and using its existing markets. However, in this case, JKL is looking to break into a new market – in a foreign country (France) – and this represents a more significant change in JKL's strategy.

Access – As France is a new market for JKL, it is likely to lack the access to key suppliers and customers which established competitors will already have there. Moreover, none of JKL's staff speak fluent French, which could make it harder to establish contacts in the country.

Acquisition

In many ways, the advantages and disadvantages of making an acquisition can be seen as a mirror image of those for organic growth:

Advantages

Speed of growth – Making an acquisition would allow JKL to enter a new market (France) much more quickly than by growing organically. It may even allow JKL to gain access to a market which would otherwise be unattainable (given the absence of any customer contracts, and weak linguistic skills).

Acquiring skills – XYZ has a very good reputation in France, and acquisition will offer JKL the opportunity to widen its skill set. One of the criticisms of acquisitions is often that they benefit the company being acquired more than the company making the acquisition. However, in this case, XYZ's reputation and skill set look like it could be valuable for JKL to acquire.

Disadvantages

Risk – Acquisitions are likely to involve greater risk than organic growth, in particular with respect to the way the post-acquisition integration is managed.

Post-integration issues – JKL's experience has highlighted the potential problems involved in trying to integrate different cultures and systems, There could be clashes if the culture and management style of the acquired company is different to the acquisition one, and the likelihood of this happening could be increased by the fact that the company being acquired is in a foreign country. Post-integration problems could mean that the anticipated benefits of the acquisition are not actually realised.

(b)

Problems with accounting and control systems

Integration of accounting systems - We do not know the nature of JKL or XYZ's business and therefore how complex or specialised their accounting systems are. However, it is likely that the two companies will have different systems, and therefore JKL should aim to identify the differences between the two systems and integrate XYZ's accounting system (and possibly any related IT systems) with its own system as soon as possible after the acquisition.

This integration will be necessary to ensure that the group's results are prepared on a consistent basis; for example to ensure that inventories are valued on the same basis, and that depreciation policies are consistent.

If JKL employs a management accountant, that accountant should expect to play a key role in the integration process, possibly working in conjunction with the change agent.

Integration of control systems – In addition to the accounting systems, JKL needs to ensure that the control systems of the two companies are aligned. For example, if JKL offers performance-related bonus payments but XYZ doesn't, this disparity could lead to resentment among XYZ's staff and a lack of motivation. Therefore, it is important that the control systems of the two companies are aligned as soon as possible, and again the management accountant could play a key role in this process.

Corporate cultures

Cultural fit – It is likely that XYZ's corporate culture will be different to JKL's and if there is a lack of **cultural fit** between the two companies this could lead to the failure of the acquisition (as happened with the acquisition of LMN.)

Therefore, JKL should try to **understand XYZ's culture before it decides whether or not to make the acquisition**. If the cultures are too different (for example, if one workforce is heavily unionised and the other is not), JKL may decide not to make the acquisition.

Managing differences - If JKL decides that the differences are manageable, then it needs to identify which are the key differences that need to be reconciled in order for the acquisition to be successful. Perhaps more importantly though, JKL also needs to work out, in practical terms, what can be done to reconcile or work around the differences.

JKL's human resources manager (if it has one) and the change agent are likely to be very important to this aspect of the post-integration process.

Autocratic management style

Staff resentment – It would appear that JKL's senior management team didn't delegate any responsibility for the previous acquisition: they made decisions themselves and then told staff what to do, rather than encouraging any dialogue and discussion with the staff. Not surprisingly, the staff resented this approach, and so it is likely that their motivation dropped and they may have resisted some of the initiatives management tried to introduce.

Collaboration and participation - To avoid similar problems happening again, JKL's management need to be more flexible in their management style. There may still be occasions where they have to take a decision and impose it on the staff, but equally there may be times where it will be beneficial to get the staff more involved in the decision-making process. For example, the staff are more likely to understand the operational issues which may arise from the acquisition. Therefore, if management consult the staff, this may lead to better decisions being made, and it should also create a more positive attitude among the staff.

(c)

A change agent is an **individual or group that helps to bring about strategic change in an organisation.**

In part (b) we have already identified that a change agent could help integrate the accounting and control systems of JKL and XYZ as well as helping to reconcile the differences in corporate culture.

Also, provided that JKL's management adopt a less autocratic management style than they did for the acquisition of LMN, a change agent can also encourage staff to participate in the integration process and feel committed to it. This should help reduce any opposition to the integration.

However, perhaps the change agent's greatest value to JKL will come from identifying and defining potential problems in the acquisition and finding solutions to them.

Defining the problem – One obvious issue which will have to be addressed in the acquisition is that none of JKL's staff can speak fluently or correspond in French, while none of XYZ's staff can correspond in English. This is going to make communication between the two companies very difficult.

The change agent needs to highlight this problem to JKL's management and indicate the issues which could result from it. For example, how could the managers of the two companies discuss budgets or performance issues?

Suggesting possible solutions – At the simplest level, the solution is to increase the language skills in both companies. However, the change agent's value to JKL will come from suggesting ways in which this can be achieved.

In the **short term**, this could be achieved by each company hiring a translator as a temporary member of staff to facilitate any meetings or discussions between JKL and XYZ.

In the **longer term**, JKL could hire a language tutor to work with both companies to improve their skills in each other's language, or staff could be sent on external training courses to improve their language skills. As a more strategic point, the change agent could also suggest that, in future, advertisements for new staff in management roles specify a requirement for applicants to be bi-lingual in English and French.

Select and implement a solution – An important attribute of a change agent is the **ability to think creatively**, so this creativity should enable them to identify a range of possible solutions to a problem. However, the change agent then needs to discuss with the JKL's management to identify which solution to implement.

The change agent may be able to advise JKL's management which solution(s) may be most appropriate, but management should make the final decision about which one to adopt. However, the change agent can then be instrumental in implementing the solution. For example, if it is decided that all the managers should go on an external training course to improve their language skills, the agent could research the cost, quality and availability of possible courses which staff could then attend.

Gaining support from all involved – Even if the managers are sent on training courses, this will only benefit JKL and XYZ if the managers improve their language skills such that they can communicate more effectively. In this respect, the change agent needs to ensure that the managers understand the reasons why they need to go on the course, such that they co-operate in the learning process rather than resisting it.

At a more general level, the staff in both organisations are more likely to support the acquisition and subsequent integration processes if they can see the potential benefits of them. This is another area where the change agent could assist JKL: through communication with the staff, and encouraging them to be positive about the acquisition and trying to make it as successful as possible.

46 XZY Asia

Text reference: Ansoff's matrix is discussed in Chapter 6 of your BPP Study text. Stage models of change are covered in Chapter 11, and other issues to do with implementing change are covered in Chapter 12.

Marking scheme

			Marks
(a)	For explaining each quadrant of Ansoff's matrix, up to 1 mark each	Up to 4	
	For evaluating the appropriateness of strategies based on each quadrant of the matrix, up to 2 marks per quadrant	Up to 8	
	For additional evaluation of alternative strategies XZY could pursue to achieve continued growth	Up to 3	
		Total up to	12
(b)	For each difficulty the CEO may encounter as a result of the change in the organisational structure, up to 1 mark each	Up to 5	
	(Valid points could include: staff resistance, effect on morale, effect on XZY's profit or share price, cost of reorganisation, reorganisation may not be tackling the underlying problems, distracting management from other aspects of running the business)		
		Total up to	5

(c)	For selecting, explaining and applying an appropriate change management model, or a suitable process of change management	Up to 8	
		Total up to	8
		Total	25

Part (a)

Top tips: A sensible approach to this question would be to take each quadrant of Ansoff's matrix in turn, identify it by name and describe it briefly, and then evaluate how appropriate the strategies described by that quadrant would be for XZY.

A key issue is how well each strategy will allow XZY to maintain the growth rate of its profits and share price, but you should also consider the risks associated with each strategy.

There are 12 marks available for this requirement, and 4 quadrants in the matrix, so, as the marking scheme shows, there are 3 marks available for identifying, explaining and evaluating the appropriateness of each quadrant. Accordingly, don't spend too long evaluating any single quadrant.

Examiner's comments: This question should have been a relatively straightforward application of the Ansoff product/market matrix, and most candidates demonstrated a good understanding of the matrix. Many candidates were also able to apply the matrix correctly to XZY, although weaker answers tended to focus too much on describing the model rather than applying it to XZY.

Market penetration – XZY's current strategy of 'selling what we know to who we know' would seem to be a market penetration strategy, looking to achieve growth through exploiting the opportunities provided by existing products and existing markets.

Historically, this strategy has allowed XZY to generate high profits and a high share price.

However, it appears this strategy can't sustain profit growth any longer so XZY needs to find an alternative strategy in order to maintain the desired growth.

Product development – This strategy would involve XZY selling new products to its existing markets.

XZY has a broad range of well-regarded products. However, if the reason for the current downturn in growth rate is because these products are reaching the mature or decline phases of their lifecycle, then developing new products could be an appropriate strategy for XZY to pursue.

If, however, the reason growth is slowing down is due to a decline in economic growth in the Asian markets, then simply offering new products may not be appropriate. XZY may need to look to break into new markets instead.

Market development – This strategy would lead to XZY continuing to sell its existing products, but sell them to new markets.

So far, XZY has sold exclusively within Asia, but it could now look to expand to sell to a more global market. Such a strategy would be appropriate if the slow-down in growth rate is due to economic problems in the Asian markets which aren't replicated in other markets.

Alternatively, market development would be an appropriate strategy if XZY's products have reached maturity or decline in the Asian market, but would still be in a growth phase in other markets.

However, if the slow-down in growth is due to XZY's products reaching the maturity or decline phases of their lifecycle more universally, then market development would not be an appropriate strategy to pursue. Instead, XZY should be looking to develop some new products.

Diversification – This strategy would lead to XZY launching new products in new markets.

This strategy provides potentially the greatest opportunity to improve growth rates, because it combines the opportunities of product development (new products) and market development (new markets).

However, diversification is also the riskiest of the four possible strategies. Given that XYZ's current strategy of 'selling what we know to who we know' is essentially a low risk strategy, then the CEO may feel that changing strategy so dramatically represents too great a risk.

Part (b)

Top tips: It is important that you read the requirement carefully. The question asks about the range of 'difficulties which may be encountered in changing the organisational structure', but you shouldn't think these difficulties are confined to staff resisting change (although staff resistance may be one of the difficulties which may be encountered). For example, the CEO will also need to consider the potential costs of any restructuring, and also to assess whether restructuring the group actually help maintain profit growth.

Examiner's comments: Many candidates discussed the potential effect of the changes on employess and management, but some placed too much emphasis on the staff and their possible resistance to change. Candidates should also have recognised the potential costs associated with a change in organisational structure, and the impact this could have on profits. Very few candidates recognised that the reorganisation may not tackle XZY's underlying problems: for example, that its products are approaching the end of their life-cycles.

Staff resistance – Given the purpose of the reorganisation is to reduce employee numbers, staff will resist the changes if they fear their jobs are at risk. If staff morale and motivation falls, **productivity** or the **quality of output** may also fall. This in turn could undermine the objective of maintaining the profit growth rate.

Restructuring costs – Although the reorganisation is designed to save costs, there will be initial costs (for example, redundancy payments) associated with it. Therefore, in the first year, XZY's profits may be reduced further, rather than increased, which is likely to draw additional comment from the financial analysts and journalists.

Quality issues – The number of employees has grown by 20% since 20X8, but the HR director is now looking to restructure and reduce employee numbers. If staff numbers are reduced, but underlying production and workload remain basically the same, then the amount of work carried out per person will increase. If people's workload increases too much, then this could lead to a reduction in quality, which again could undermine revenues and share price.

Organisation structure – XZY currently has a functional structure, and it is likely to be relatively centralised and have quite a formal culture. We do not know what alternative organisational structure the HR director envisages in place of the existing functional structure, but if the proposed alternative involves a significant change in XYZ's culture this could further resentment and instability among the staff.

Weakness in underlying growth - The HR director's proposal doesn't tackle the underlying problem of low growth. Reducing staff numbers and cutting costs may increase profit in the short term, but they aren't long term solutions for increasing growth. For example, if a number of XZY's products are reaching the end of their product life cycles, this solution will not help in finding new products which can sustain growth in the future. However, by improving profits in the short term, this proposal may actually divert people's attention from these underlying problems.

Part (c)

Top tip: There are two ways of approaching this requirement (and the marking scheme indicates that either would be equally acceptable):

(i) Use a change management model (such as Lewin's stage model) and explain how this can guide the change process overall

(ii) Identify the strategies that the CEO could use to overcome resistance to change and thereby implement the change (for example, Kotter & Schlesinger's strategies.)

However, whichever approach you chose, to score well in this question you need to apply the model to the question and not simply describe the model.

Examiner's comments: Most candidates scored well here, and demonstrated good knowledge of change management models and the activities required to manage change successfully. Pleasingly, most candidates also applied their answers well to XZY.

Need for change: Given the likely resistance to the change, in order for the change programme to be implemented successfully, the CEO will need to make the staff aware of the need for change. A crucial part of the '**unfreezing**' stage of this change process will be to weaken the forces which are restraining change and increasing the readiness for change among the staff.

Effective communication will be vital here: taking time to explain to the need for change to the staff, and **consulting them** about the proposed changes may help the staff feel less insecure about the change process, and may therefore reduce their resistance to change.

Adapting to new structure - Once the CEO has prepared the organisation for change, the new structure will then have to be implemented. The **'change'** part of the process will involve the staff adjusting to their new roles and the new structure, and possibly learning new skills as part of the transition.

The success of this transition phase ultimately depends on staff buying into the new structure. However, the chances of this happening can be increased by making sure they have **role models** they can look to and who can show them how the new process works. So, for example, the CEO should make sure that managers and team leaders understand the new structure and are enthusiastic about the changes, because this enthusiasm should help the staff feel more positive about them.

Refreezing - Once the new structure has been introduced, it will be important to **embed the changes** into XZY; for example, making sure that the remaining staff understand their new roles and relationships and follow them, rather than reverting to what they did before the changes.

One of the ways in which XZY could encourage employees to embrace the changes is by having a **bonus scheme** which rewards staff who support the new structure and processes.

Leading change – For the change process to be successful it will need effective leadership. It seems that the CEO may be actively involved in the process, in which case he would be the most obvious leader. However, if the CEO is too busy with other strategic projects, he could appoint an alternative **change agent** to lead the process. However, in order for the change to be implemented successfully, it must be clear to the staff that XZY's senior management (for example, the Board of Directors) support the changes and support the change agent responsible for delivering them.

47 Operating theatre

Text reference. Both BPR and PI are dealt with in Chapter 10 of the BPP Study Text for E3.

Marking scheme

				Marks
(a)	(i)	Explanation of each technique (BPR and PI), highlighting differences between them	Up to 4	
		Role of IT in each technique	Up to 2	
			Total up to	6
	(ii)	Argument for and against OTIS being either BPR or PI	Up to 4	
			Total up to	4
(b)		For evaluation of three benefits to 4D, at up to 3 marks each	Up to 9	
		For evaluation of two benefits to society, at up to 3 marks each	Up to 6	
			Total up to	15
			Total	25

(a) (i)

> **Top tips**. This is a tricky question, because it not only requires you to know about BPR and PI but also to be able to distinguish between them.
>
> BPR is a fairly well-known idea and many candidates would have been able to give a reasonable account of its nature. However, the key to this question is identifying how PI is different from BPR. PI uses IT to streamline an existing process, whereas BPR seeks to achieve an enhanced outcome through a fundamental rethinking of the processes used to deliver that outcome.
>
> Notice also the emphasis on IT in the requirement. IT is likely to play a significant role in BPR in a contemporary business, and you must not overlook the IS / IT elements of your syllabus.
>
> **Examiner's comments.** Some candidates failed to mention the role of IT in the techniques. Most candidates could provide a definition of BPR, but fewer appeared to understand PI.

BPR may be seen as a late twentieth century aspect of **Scientific Management.** *Hammer and Champy* say that it is about 'fundamental rethinking and radical redesign of processes to achieve dramatic improvements in areas such as cost, quality and speed'.

The aim of BPR is **improvement** in the way things are done. It has its own philosophy, based on such ideas as focussing on **desired outcomes** rather than **existing tasks** and extending the **autonomy** of the people who perform the re-engineered tasks, and is most effective when there is a culture of **continuous improvement**.

By contrast, **PI** is not so much about the improvement of existing processes as the **development of completely new ones**. It is a more radical approach and less pervasive in that it tends to focus on a few key areas of the organisation.

Role of IT

In the BPR approach, IT is an **enabler**. Simple automation of processes is not BPR; the aim should be to **exploit the potential of IT** to enable the organisation to achieve its desired outcomes in ways that were previously impossible.

In **PI**, however, IT is often the **trigger for change**. Typically, its contribution will not be new ways of doing things so much as processes that achieve completely **new outcomes**.

A good example of the difference would be making airline reservations. Email would be an improvement to the basic technology of writing to a travel agent with details of the journeys required: it would enable faster communication. On-line booking would produce a completely new outcome in that the booking could be made, confirmed and paid for through direct access to the carrier's booking system.

(a) (ii)

> **Top tips**. Since the question asks for your opinion, the important thing to achieve here is an informed and sensible line of reasoning that reaches a conclusion. It does not really matter whether you think OTIS is BPR or PI, so long as you apply the differences of principle that distinguish these two ideas and relate them back to 4D's new technology. In fact, the nature of OTIS is such that it could be argued that it qualifies under either heading.

The effect of OTIS is one of **scale** only. It does not achieve any new **outcomes**, so it is arguably not PI.

The existing system depends on the physical presence of the students, surgeons and tutors in the operating theatre for interaction to take place. OTIS makes physical presence unnecessary but does **not change the nature** of what is achieved. It therefore does not qualify as PI, to the extent that a distinction can be made.

Even the ability to interact between locations anywhere in the world is **not a new outcome**, since basic satellite TV and telephone technology made this possible decades ago. All that OTIS does is speed the process up.

To this extent, because OTIS improves the way things are currently done, rather than creating a completely new process, it should be seen as an example of **BPR rather than PI**.

(b)

> **Top tips**. Note carefully the use of the question verb 'evaluate'; to evaluate means to 'appraise or assess the value of'. You must therefore make some value judgements to score well, and these should include limitations of the benefits as well as their upsides.
>
> Note also the specific requirements of the question: you need to evaluate *five benefits in total*: three for 4 D, and two for society.

Benefits of OTIS to 4D

(i) Increased student throughput and enhanced training

Lack of operating theatre gallery space means that only a limited number of students can watch any operation and take part in question/coaching sessions. OTIS will overcome this constraint, potentially increasing the throughput of students in this phase of their training, and enhancing the level of surgeon/student and learning group interaction, *without* a significant commensurate increase in cost per student (principally in terms of surgeons' and lecturers' time). This would **enhance the quality of the training**, while increasing the hospital's **surplus of revenue over cost** and **generating funds for investment** elsewhere.

This could be of significant long-term benefit, depending on the cost/revenue balance currently experienced by the hospital. It will be limited in the short term, due to the high development and set-up costs likely to be incurred by OTIS, the cost of promoting the service to remote medical/teaching institutions, and the cost of training in use of the system.

There may be additional issues to be resolved before OTIS becomes fully operational and accepted: for example, the privacy concerns of patients, technological risks (audio-visual failure in the middle of a remote student-conducted operation cannot be countenanced) and liability issues (will the hospital be liable for surgical errors committed under its supervision?)

(ii) Potential to develop new educational and medical services

4D might be able to develop new educational services using OTIS, perhaps in the field of post-graduate training in new surgical techniques: this would represent a **new revenue stream**, if it can be harnessed (eg in the form of subscription– or licence-only access to the system for this purpose). Another development with similar potential might be the provision of on-demand consultation for purposes of remote diagnosis, with 4D's staff observing and commenting on patients' symptoms in 'virtual' teams with remote colleagues.

While interesting, these may not constitute significant benefits, depending on the level of demand for each option, and whether and how much 4D is practically able to charge for the service. It may be argued that 4D should not seek to **over-exploit its medical/teaching staff**, whose work load is already likely to be heavy.

(iii) Enhanced reputation for excellence

The raised profile of 4D through its unique **world-wide exposure** may be valuable in various ways: in attracting additional government and medical/educational **grant funding**; in **attracting and retaining surgical 'talent'** as teaching surgeons; in attracting **quality students**; and in attracting links (and associated **knowledge-sharing**) with other prestigious hospitals. This is likely to be a significant benefit, as 4D is effectively in competition with other medical and educational institutions for all these core 'resources'.

Benefits of OTIS to society

(i) Raised standards of surgical training

OTIS makes the clinical expertise of 4D available on a regional, national and international basis. This should raise the standard of surgical training in under-resourced hospitals, both through observing the 4D surgical team *and* the 'reverse' procedure of supervision by them.

This is potentially a major benefit, particularly in developing countries, but the extent to which it will be of value in any given country or region will depend on the current standard of surgical training, and the availability of other teaching hospitals and clinical supervision. It may also be limited by lack of ICT infrastructure: countries most in need of the expertise may lack the

broadband internet service required for streaming of video footage and interactive guidance/support. They may also be unable to invest in the technology at their 'end' of the system.

(ii) Reduced costs of surgical services

The reduced cost of training surgeons (with less resources, space and personnel required) may enable hospitals to reduce the cost of surgery to patients and medical funds, and to have more resources left for other areas of their budgets.

Again, this is potentially a major benefit, particularly in developing countries, but the extent to which it will realistically be of value in any given country or region will depend on whether the demand for surgeons currently outstrips supply; whether surgeons, once trained, remain in the country or region; whether trained surgeons remain in the public sector – and whether cost savings are therefore available to fund-holders, and passed on to patients, or not. (Highly trained surgeons in areas where such skills are in short supply may choose to work in the private sector, or lucrative specialisms such as cosmetic surgery, in which the longer term benefit to society will be significantly reduced).

48 Insurance Company

Text reference: Business Process Re-engineering is covered in Chapter 10 of the BPP Study Text. Specifically, the principles of BPR are covered at Section 3.1 of Chapter 10.

Part (a)

Top tips: Hammer presented seven principles for BPR, and part (a) of the question is worth seven marks. Moreover, the requirement is to 'briefly explain' the principles. So, given the marks available, your explanation should indeed be 'brief', if you work on the basis of earning one mark for each principle you explain.

However, you should also note that the requirement only asks you to explain the principles. On this occasion, there is no requirement to link your answer back to the scenario; it is your technical knowledge (rather than your application skills) which is being tested here.

Business process re-engineering (BPR) is the fundamental redesign of business processes to achieve dramatic improvements in key measures of performance such as cost, quality, service and speed.

There are seven principles of BPR:

(i) **Focus on customer focused outcomes** – Processes should be designed to achieve a desired customer-focused outcome (for example, quality, service or speed) rather than being organised around existing tasks

(ii) **People who use the output from a process should perform that process** – If the staff who use the output of a process are involved in the operation of that process, the risk of errors should be reduced and so should time delays in the process

(iii) **Information processing should be included in the work which produces the information**. In other words, there shouldn't be a distinction between information **processing** and information **gathering**. The development of online databases can be crucial here, allowing users to have access to real time information, thus minimising delays in response to queries.

(iv) **Geographically-dispersed resources should be treated as if they are centralised** – For example, there should be a centralised database of suppliers which all departments use, so that they benefit from the economies of scale achieved by the central negotiation of supply contracts.

(v) **Parallel activities should be linked rather than integrated** – As far as possible, activities should be processed in parallel rather than sequentially. If tasks are performed sequentially, bottlenecks and delays might arise while waiting for the output of a previous process.

(vi) People should be **self-managing** and exercise greater **autonomy** over their work – The traditional distinction between workers and managers should be abolished. BPR aims to allow decisions to be made as quickly as possible and as near to the end customer as possible. This allows increased responsiveness, and also empowers the individuals who make the decisions.

(vii) Information should be captured once, and at source – If information is transferred from one data source to another there is a risk of human error. If information is only input into a system once, and is input as early as possible, the risk of error is reduced, and consistent replies can be obtained in response for any queries about the information.

Part (b)

> **Top tips**: Note that while part (a) was entirely a test of technical knowledge, part (b) is a test of both knowledge and application. You are asked to explain the stages in implementing a BPR exercise, but in the context of a BPR exercise that might be undertaken by C. So make sure you refer to C and its BPR exercise in your answer.
>
> The answer below is based on *Davenport and Short's* five-step approach to BPR.

Develop business vision and process objectives

The first stage in a BPR exercise is to develop the business vision and process objectives. In C's case, it seems that time reduction and quality improvement are key business objectives, and so the BPR exercise should aim to help C achieve these objectives.

C is aiming to use a BPR exercise to modernise the business and streamline its business model, thereby increasing the company's profitability. It is likely that the BPR exercise will look at ways of computerising the existing manual processes in order to **speed processes up**. In addition, C will want to find ways of **reducing the number of errors** in the paperwork customers received.

C should **set targets** at the beginning of the exercise which specify the speed with which enquiries will be answered and the acceptable level of errors in paperwork.

However, it is likely that the roles of the sales staff and the telephone operators will need to change for the introduction of a new improved operation, so the **impact of the changes on staff** should also be considered throughout the exercise so that it is not seen simply as a cost reduction exercise.

Identify the processes to be redesigned

C needs to improve the processes surrounding the communications between sales staff and customer, because these are crucial processes in the effective operation of C's business. Most of these processes are still paper-based. This makes them slow as well as increasing the risk of errors in the paperwork.

For example, when sales staff speak with customers they will record customers' details, and the nature of the risk to be covered, and then they will provide quotes for the policies which C provide for the customers. The scenario suggests that all this documentation is paper-based, but it could be more efficient to capture it all in an electronic database at source.

Given the fierce nature of competition in the industry, if customers feel that C's processes are slow and prone to error they will switch to using an alternative insurance company.

Understand and measure the existing processes

Before C changes any of its processes, it needs to map and understand its existing processes. It is important to understand all the different types of transactions that are currently undertaken, as well as understanding how the process works: what is undertaken when, why and by whom; where the key points of data capture are in the process; and where the bottlenecks and delays occur.

The BPR exercise may indicate that some of these processes need to be changed but it is important to understand them all before making any changes.

Identify change levers

The triggers for change have been declining margins, increased complaints about the slowness of C's processes, and the number of errors in customers' paperwork.

Given the fierce nature of competition, C needs to make its operations cost effective as soon as possible.

Although the majority of C's processes are still paper-based, some of them are computerised. Consequently, C should investigate the extent to which computerised data entry and the use of databases (data warehouses) could help solve the problem it is facing. It appears that there are a number of areas where IT / IS could be utilised to improve the efficiency of C's operations.

Design and build a prototype of the new process

Once a new system has been designed it should be developed and tested on a relatively small part of the business. The new system should not be viewed as the end of the BPR process – instead it should be viewed as a prototype which will then be refined based on feedback from the tests.

A selection of both telephone staff and the sales staff operating in customers' homes should be involved in testing any new system. Any feedback from customers should also be incorporated in subsequent versions of the prototype.

At C, because a number of staff have expressed concern about BPR and its implications for the business, some of the staff who are concerned about the BPR exercise should also be involved in testing the prototype. This will hopefully reassure them about the benefits of the new process for the business. However, before any new system is finally rolled out, all the staff who will be involved with it should be trained in how it works.

Part (c)

Top tips: In part (b) we identified that the first stage of a BPR exercise should be to develop the business' vision and its process objectives.

The link between the objectives and improvements is a useful one here: a BPR exercise will only be useful to an organisation if it delivers improvements to its business model. In turn, some of the improvements the Directors of C might expect to see should link to its objectives: reduced errors, quicker access to information, and improved customer satisfaction.

However, also think of the wider benefits of the BPR exercise: if it reduces the number of paper-based transactions the staff have to deal with, how is it likely to affect staff morale and motivation?

More rapid information processing and error reduction – It appears that the processes at C haven't been updated to take advantage of the IT / IS systems that are available today. In particular, relying on a predominantly paper-based system makes C's processes much slower than they need to be, but it also increases the opportunity for error as information is manually recorded and then transferred between systems. A new database-led system would prevent the need for re-keying and transferring information, and so should reduce the scope for errors in the system.

This system will also mean that C has reliable, **up-to-date information** about its customers. Any details the sales staff or telephone operators obtain about a customer can be entered into the central database on a real time basis, and the system can then be continually updated for other staff to use.

Moreover, no **paper-based transfers of information** from one part of the organisation to another will be necessary. Again, this reduces delays and reduces the risk of errors occurring.

Improved database system - If C develops an electronic database which stores all customer data, this should enable staff to respond to telephone enquiries more quickly. For example, if a phone operator receives a call, they can access the database and gather the relevant information to help them deal with the customer enquiry straight away. This faster response time should lead to improved customer satisfaction.

Better support for sales staff - Having an electronic (or online) database and improved technology should also help the sales staff when they visit potential customers. If the sales staff can access the database remotely (from laptops) they can get details of policies and premiums while they are with the customer, and so could potentially make a decision about a policy application straight away without having to return to the office to check details or process paperwork. Customers have complained about the slowness of C's current process, so speeding up the process should directly address these complaints.

Increased staff motivation – Not only have customers complained about the current sales process, but C's sales staff have also complained about them. Staff motivation and job satisfaction are likely to suffer if the staff feel they are having to work with out-dated processes and technology. Therefore, providing the sales staff with more up-to-date technology will not only allow them to do their job more effectively but it should also improve their motivation to do so.

Moreover, customers are likely to have a more favourable impression of the sales staff if the staff are able to provide quick and efficient service. If this, in turn, leads to the sales staff making more sales it is likely to increase their motivation still further.

Organisation structure - BPR's principle of working back from a desired 'customer-focused outcome' will help C to find the most efficient and effective way of delivering that outcome. This is likely to lead to a change in C's organisation structure or the tasks that individual people do, to reduce the level of internal communication required in response to telephone enquiries.

The degree of communication required internally to respond to telephone enquiries suggest that C's organisation structure is quite inflexible, and everyone has quite narrowly defined areas of responsibility. The increased focus on the customer may lead to a greater flexibility, as C's business will be organised around outcomes rather than tasks.

Greater process flexibility and speed – The paper-based nature of the C's current system means that tasks have to be done sequentially. However, one of the principles of BPR is that linked activities should be conducted in parallel rather than sequentially. In this case, if C improves its IT systems, and stores customer details electronically, staff may be able to deal with different aspects of a customer transaction in parallel, thereby speeding up the transaction process.

49 MNI University

Text reference. Levels of control measures are discussed at the beginning of Chapter 13 in your BPP Study Text, while control and performance measurement are covered in Chapter 14. Information systems are discussed in Chapter 9.

Marking scheme

			Marks
(a)	Classification of criticisms according to the three headings given	Up to 2	
	Advice on the role of control measures in implementing the new strategic plan	Up to 5	
		Total up to	7
(b)	Each relevant control identified, explained and justified in relation to the scenario – Up to 3 marks each. (Controls required, and therefore marked, for three areas only.)	Up to 9	9
(c)	For explaining how Information systems could support the new strategic plan at:		
	- Operational level	Up to 3	
	- Management level	Up to 3	
	- Strategic level	Up to 3	
		Total up to	9
		Total	25

Part (a)

Top tips. Make sure you read the question requirement carefully, because there are two distinct elements to it. First, you need to categorise the criticisms according to whether they are Operational; Management or Strategic. (It may be useful to think of Anthony's hierarchy here to get some ideas of what might be relevant to each level.)

Second, you need to advise the Vice-Chancellor how control measures can be important to the university and can help it implement its new strategic plan.

5 out of the 7 marks were available for the second of these two parts to the requirement. However, the examiner's comments are instructive here:

Examiner's comments: The main weakness of answers to this questions was that candidates failed to focus on the way control measures can help the University implement its strategic plan. Many candidates ignored this part of the question which meant that potential marks were missed.

Operational

- MNI could not accurately produce a head-count of the number of students enrolled
- Internal control of cash receipts was defective and in several areas there were discrepancies

Management

- MNI operated at a deficit: its expenditure exceeded its income
- Student drop-out and failure rates were greatly in excess of the national average
- The level of students complaints was very high and increasing
- MNI had a large number of debtors, mainly ex-students, but was not doing anything to collect outstanding amounts
- The level of staff turnover was abnormally high

Strategic

- The quality of education provided by MNI has been given the lowest possible rating: 'Poor'.

Usefulness of control measures in implementing the new strategic plan

The strategic plan needs to address the criticisms highlighted in the audits, and to improve MNI's performance in the eight areas identified.

Monitoring performance – Control measures will provide a framework for monitoring performance in these areas. The measures will force managers to assess MNI's actual performance compared to plan, and identify areas where further improvement is still needed.

Aligning goals and objectives - The control measures should be designed to ensure that day-to-day (operational) activities are aligned with MNI's strategic goals, and thereby help it to achieve its strategic goals. In this respect, the control measures could be presented as critical success factors (CSFs) supported by Key Performance Indicators (KPIs). If MNI monitors its performance against its KPIs – and takes corrective action if performance slips below the target level – this should help it achieve the goals set out in the strategic plan.

Part (b)

Tutorial note: The audit report identified eight criticisms; however, the question requirement specifically asks for you to concentrate on **three of the criticisms only**. Therefore you should have only looked at three of the criticisms in your answer.

For tutorial purposes, we have included all eight areas to show potential controls which you could have suggested to improve them. However, we must stress you should only have addressed three of them in your answer.

There are 9 marks available for recommending controls for three areas; meaning there are three marks per control. There is no instruction that you can only recommend one control to help improve each area of criticism. So, if you can think of, say, two controls for an area, you should include both of them. However, note you are asked to 'Recommend, with reasons...' so it is vital you discuss the reasons why you have recommended a particular control.

In the answer below we have started with the operational issues, and then worked through the management issues, and finally addressed the strategic issue.

Note that the operational issues lend themselves most easily to new controls, and so should be the quickest for MNI to resolve. Management issues are more complex than operational ones, and so are less likely to be solved by a quick solution. In turn, strategic issues are more complex again, and cannot be solved through any single actions or controls. They are likely to require a change in the overall approach and strategy of the organisation.

Examiner's comments: Many candidates provided a range of relevant control measures and described them reasonably well, but very few candidates discussed the reasons for the controls they had identified. If candidates do not answer all parts of the question ('Recommend, with reasons...') they will miss out on potential marks.

1 Inability to produce an accurate head count of students enrolled

If the university doesn't know how many students are enrolled, this will cause problems for resource planning (for example, allocating students to tutors) and also for obtaining government funding (because funding levels are likely to relate to student numbers).

Student database – All students should be registered on a central database which is continuously up-dated as new students join or existing students leave.

Identity cards – Based on the information in the database, each student should be given an identity card and a student number. MNI should ensure that students who do not have a valid identity card will not be able to use university facilities such as the library, student union or the sports centre (thereby also giving the students an incentive to make sure they are properly registered).

2 Defective internal control of cash receipts leading to discrepancies

There will be a number of cash transactions every day – for example, in the student union (canteen / bar) or the library. If cash controls are weak, there is a danger of theft and the shortfall of income against expenditure will be increased.

Pre-paid charge cards – MNI should try to minimise the number of cash transactions as far as possible. For example, students could all be given pre-pay (top up) cards which they use to pay for certain items (eg canteen lunches, library fees) by swiping through a card reader.

Cash handling procedures – MNI should also make sure that, as far as possible, there is a segregation of duties between staff who handle cash and those who account for cash. Cash should be banked frequently to ensure that large cash balances on not held on the university campus for any length of time.

3 Expenditure exceeds income

A situation in which expenditure exceeds income is clearly not sustainable in the long run because it would lead to MNI becoming insolvent.

The operational improvement suggested in points 1 and 2 could help this situation (for example, having accurate information on student numbers should allow MNI to claim the correct funding) but it is unlikely that operational improvement alone will make good the deficit.

Expenditure review – MNI's management should review all expenditure across the university as a whole and assess where savings can be made. For example, does it need 350 academic staff and 420 other staff for a student population of 8,000?

Income targets – As well as cutting costs, MNI should also consider ways it could increase its revenue. For example, could it increase student numbers above 8,000? Or could it increase its fees and prices for auxiliary services (such as meals) without seeing a disproportionate fall in demand?

Overall, MNI's management needs to control expenditure and income so that the university at least breaks even rather than operating at a deficit.

Possible improvements for the other areas of criticism in the report:

High student drop-out and failure rates

High drop-out rates indicate students are either unhappy with their courses or with life as MNI as a whole.

High failure rates may also indicate problems with the courses, or with the standard of tuition students receive.

Both of these issues are potentially damaging for MNI's reputation, and so could adversely affect student numbers (and therefore income).

Understanding reasons for leaving – MNI needs to understand the reasons why students drop out so that it deal with the causes of the problem. (For example, are drop-outs caused by poor tuition, poor facilities, or students finding they simply didn't like the subject they'd enrolled for?) If MNI conducted exit interviews, or had a questionnaire equivalent, for students who drop-out this should help gather the relevant information.

Analysis of failure rates – It is not clear if failure rates are universally poor across all departments or whether some departments and lecturers have worse rates than others. This should be analysed. If some departments are performing particularly poorly, the course programmes and the quality of the teaching should be subject to a detailed academic inspection.

High level of student complaints

As with the high drop-out rates, a high and increasing level of student complaints indicates that students are not satisfied, for example, either with the teaching or with their overall experience at MNI.

Analyse causes for complaint – It is not clear if there are any specific aspects of their courses or of the university in general which are prompting students to complain.

MNI needs to analyse the complaints they receive, and then address the issues which are leading to the most frequent complaints.

High numbers of debtors and lack of action to collect debts

The fact that a number of the debtors are ex-students may be linked to MNI's inability to produce a head count. If MNI never registered someone as a student, then it may well also have no record of them as a debtor. If MNI is letting debtors go uncollected, this will be damaging to its cashflow.

Link to student database – If a debtors ledger account is set up for every student when they enrol (through a link to the student database) then student debtors should no longer go unrecorded. If it doesn't already have it, MNI should also consider instigating a policy that students cannot graduate until all their debts to the university have been cleared.

Debt numbers – MNI should set some key performance indicators (KPIs) around the number and value of debtors outstanding, and the credit control department (or whoever is responsible for debtor management) should be monitored as to whether they achieve these KPIs.

High staff turnover

A high level of staff turnover (particularly among academic staff) may be contributing to the high failure rates and student dissatisfaction, especially if the better lecturers are leaving and being replaced with less good ones.

MNI will also incur costs in relation to advertising for, and recruiting, new staff.

Exit interviews – When staff leave, they should have an exit interview at which the reasons for their departure are discussed, along with any issues they have with working at MNI. This should highlight if there are any particular factors which are causing staff to leave; and, in turn, management should then focus on dealing with those issues.

Staff surveys – MNI should conduct surveys of all its staff (both academic and non-academic) to find out which aspects of their jobs they like and which they are less satisfied with. Management should then consider if there are any ways the main issues causing dissatisfaction can be addressed.

Poor quality of education

This criticism may be connected to a number of the others: high drop-out and failure rates; increasing student complaints; and high staff turnover. Moreover, if this rating is published externally it could damage MNI's reputation and may deter potential new students from applying. This will make it harder for MNI to increase income and to help reduce its operating deficit.

However, perhaps the most important implication of this criticism is that MNI's key aim for the next five years must be to improve the overall quality of its education. This improvement will need to be central to the new Strategic Plan.

Quality control - In order to assess whether the required quality improvements are being made, MNI should establish a quality control department, which carries out periodic quality audits on all departments and processes in the university.

The quality control department could also benchmark performance in key areas between departments. And if it identifies practices or processes one department is using which work particularly well, it could get these shared with other departments.

Performance targets – MNI can make quality integral to staff performance by including quality targets in the staff's performance management objectives. For example, academic staff could have a target of 'x% of students grading lectures as "Excellent".'

Part (c)

Top tips: Part (a) specifically asked you to break down the control hierarchy in MNI into three levels, in the way that the Anthony hierarchy looks at three different levels of control in an organisation. This approach – of looking at the three different levels – could also be useful here, because it could encourage you to look, in turn, at ways information systems can support the implementation of strategy at operational, managerial and overall strategic levels.

Also think of the ways information systems could help MNI implement the controls you have recommended in (b).

However, note that your answer should not have become a general discussion about information systems. To score well, you need to discuss the ways in which information systems would be specifically useful to MNI. You were not expected to describe the technology required to implement any of the systems though.

Examiner's comments: Many candidates provided technology based answers, outlining the information technology needs of the university. This was not the intended focus of the question, and meant that many candidates failed to address the ways information systems could support the new strategic plan (which was the question actually set).

Information systems (IS) can support the implementation of the strategic plan at each of the three levels of the control hierarchy: operational, management and strategic.

Operational

MNI's information systems need to provide up-to-date (real time) information about key **operational performance**. For example, the IS should be able to show how many students are enrolled at any time. MNI should also be able to use IS to review cash and debtors balances at any time.

In all of these cases, it is important that data is **'real time'** so that management can make decisions based on current figures. In this respect, the IS will need data capture mechanisms to ensure figures are continuously updated – for example, so that if a student joins or leaves this is picked up in the head count records.

Management

Performance measures and reporting – it is likely that one of the key steps in achieving the goals of the new strategic plan will be hitting revised performance targets for some of the areas criticised in the audit.

IS will used to provide reports showing performance against targets and KPIs which support the University's CSFs. For example, performance reports could indicate drop-out rates, complaint levels, and debtor numbers / values.

These reports will enable management to see if any further corrective action still needs to be taken (in the areas where actual performance continues to fall below the target level.)

Strategic

Performance reporting – In the same way that IS were used to support the analysis of performance against KPIs at management level, so they can allow MNI to assess performance against its CSFs at strategic level.

On-line classrooms – It is not clear to what extent, if any, MNI uses IS in its teaching. However, IS could play an important role here: for example if MNI introduced webcasts or online tutorials, students could use these to supplement their existing classroom lectures. In this way, IS could be a source of competitive advantage to MNI, as well as being a means of enabling performance measurement.

50 Management styles

Text reference. Chapter 13 includes Goold and Campbell's approaches to running divisionalised conglomerates. Chapters 11 & 12 discuss change management.

Marking scheme

			Marks
(a)	Definition of strategic control; definition of strategic planning; 1 mark each	2	
	Highlighting the differences between the two	2	
		Total	4
(b)	For each valid point made and embedded in the case (ie specifically about the impact the change in planning culture will have on the CEOs.)	Up to 2	
		Total up to	11
(c)	For each sensible stage / approach to change management, embedded in the case	Up to 2	
		Total up to	10
		Total	25

Part (a)

Top Tips. The scenario again provides you some useful information, and the explicit reference to Goold and Campbell's strategic management styles gives a clear indication of the issues you should be looking for.

Although (a) is only worth four marks it, the discussion of the different approaches to 'corporate parenting' it prompts should alert you to some of the issues that will be relevant in (b). Your answer to (a) should contain a brief definition of the two styles and then a comparison between the two.

Examiner's comments. Parts (a) and (b) were not well answered. This appeared to be due to a lack of syllabus knowledge, with candidates being unsure of the differences between the two styles.

The styles described by Goold and Campbell refer to the way a corporate parent seeks to influence the behaviour and returns from its business divisions. The **strategic planning** style involves a flexible strategic type of control influence and a fairly **high degree of central planning influence**. The corporate centre establishes extensive planning processes through which it works with business unit managers so that they make substantial contributions to strategic thinking. An emphasis is plan on longer-term strategic objectives, and performance targets are set in broad terms.

The **strategic control** style involves a fairly **low degree of planning influence from the centre**, but a tighter strategic control. The centre leaves the planning initiative to business unit managers, but it will then review plans

for acceptability. Firm targets are set for a range of financial an non-financial performance indicators and performance is judged against them.

The strategic planning style establishes the framework in which business unit managers can work, and then encourages them to contribute to strategic thinking within that framework, whereas the **strategic control style allows managers more freedom about how they work**, with the corporate centre being a resource they can use if they wish to, but they are not bound to do so.

The amount of **senior management time given to each business unit** is greater under a strategic planning style than a strategic control style. Under a strategic control style, senior management attention is focused on the core strategic issues.

Part (b)

Top tips. The key to doing well in (b) is to relate the impact of the changes directly to the CEOs of the former divisions. You should identify what the changes are, and then discuss the impact they will have on the CEOs. The question does not ask for a general discussion about changes in planning cultures, and you will score very few marks if your answer is not relevant to the scenario.

C used to operate a system of 'strategic control' so the CEOs of the former divisions in C will be used to operating under that system when dealing with their board of directors.

Business objectives. The CEOs were used to having a framework of objectives, both financial and non-financial, established for them by the corporate centre.

However, under the new structure, the overall framework will evolve from the planning process and each division, , will be expected to **develop its business plan in conjunction with the corporate centre** and through this contribute to the achievement of corporate goals This will represent a significant change for the divisional CEOs who are used to being given the framework, rather than having to go through a discursive process to set the framework itself. They may also find their proposals rejected.

Pursue own business strategies. The CEOs were used to planning and pursuing their own business strategies, within the overall business objectives guidelines set by the corporate centre.

However, under the new system, the CEOs will have to **develop strategies within a more closely defined framework** prescribed by the corporate centre. The strategies will be geared towards an overall corporate objective rather being driven by divisional objectives alone, as the old ones were.

The CEOs will find the new system **much more formal** than they are previously used to, with the centre having a far greater involvement in the decision making process.

Although the divisional CEOs will still have some degree of **autonomy**, it will be far less than they are used to and they may find this restrictive.

The need for formal planning and achieving central approval means management is likely to find the new process is **much more time-consuming** than the old process they were used to.

Group financial control. The divisional CEOs are also likely to find that the corporate centre now **controls expenditure and funding at a group level**, so they will now be competing with other divisions for scarce resources. They will not be used to doing this.

The centre will allocate resources according to which projects will deliver the best value for the group – rather than funds being allocating autonomously by division. The CEOs may find this frustrating, because it will mean they are not able to pursue projects they want to.

Discussions with the corporate centre. The CEOs will have been used to using the corporate centre as a sounding board to check that their plans and decisions are acceptable. In C the corporate centre would react to decisions and requests made by the divisional CEOs; it is unlikely to have imposed unilateral corporate decisions in its own right.

However, under the strategic planning system employed by B, the **centre will be much more proactive**, so the CEOs will now find themselves receiving directives initiated by the centre.

It is likely that the divisional CEOs may **resent the greater involvement of the centre**, perceiving it to be head office interference in their business. This will be particularly true if the involvement of the centre causes **delays in the decision-making process**.

Part (c)

Top tips. Part (c) requires you to show the process of change should be managed. There a number of models which are relevant to change management, and there is no single right way of managing change.

The model answer shown below is based on Kotter and Schlesinger's 'Six approaches' to dealing with change and resistance to change. However, provided you have described a logical model for implementing change, and applied it to the scenario, you will get credit for this. Once again, application to the scenario is important here to score well: remember the staff in question are senior staff, and B is keen to retain them after the acquisition.

Change can have a significant impact on people's circumstances, and the extent of the changes the CEOs are facing will mean that they are likely to be concerned about them. Some are likely to oppose them.

Therefore the changes will have to be **handled carefully so that B does not alienate the CEOs**, because it will want to retain them in the new business. The board of directors of C were removed but not the CEOs, suggesting that B sees them as valuable to the new business.

Nature and types of change

The scale of the re-organisation means that B is undertaking a **transformational change**, rather than an incremental change. Therefore it is likely that the board of directors will want to **implement the change programme quickly**, rather than introducing it gradually. However, they will still need to allow time for the CEOs to ask questions, provide comment and for them to be as reassured as possible about the changes ahead. Not doing so will delay change and may lead to a loss of divisional managers.

There is no single way to implement change successfully, but the manner in which a change is introduced is very important in it being implemented successfully. However, it will be useful to consider the following approaches to introducing the change.

Ways of implementing change

Communication and education. The structures and processes used at B need to be explained fully to the CEOs. This explanation should include a review of the benefits of the system which B operates, both for the CEOs as individuals, and for the company as a whole.

The **board of directors of B should be involved** in this communication process to demonstrate that the CEOs are important to the new business, but also that the changes themselves are important.

However, it would also be useful for some of the **CEOs from B's existing business to be involved**, so that they can explain the structure to their peer groups, and explain its benefits.

Throughout the communication process, it will be important to **encourage the new CEOs to ask any questions** they may have, so that the communication process is a two-way process. This should minimise the risk of any confusion.

Moving from a strategic control system to a strategic planning system will involve a large cultural change for the new CEOs. They will need clear guidance on how the **strategic planning process operates** at B; **what their involvement in it is;** and how their **behaviours will need to change** to fit into the new structure.

It will be useful for them to be given some **documentation about the strategic planning process**, and about their role in it.

Participation and involvement. It will be useful for some of the existing CEOs from B to discuss this with the new CEOs; and it would be useful to use the last strategic planning cycle as a case study to work through. This would demonstrate to the new joiners not only that the process actually works, but also what is required from them in the process. By working through the cycle, the new CEOs may even be able to identify areas where improvements can be made and included in the next planning cycle. If they feel that they are valued in the process, the new CEOs are less likely to resist the change.

In addition, allowing the two sets of CEOs to spend time together should help the new joiners feel more integrated into the business.

Facilitation and support. The new CEOs should have an **appraisal meeting** with the director they report to, to discuss the opportunities for them in the new company and to set their objectives going forward. The CEOs may initially feel that the changes will have a detrimental effect on them. However, the counselling managers can overcome the CEOs' negative perceptions by getting them to focus on the opportunities available going forward instead.

Negotiation. The appraisal system can be used to offer **rewards and incentives** for adapting to the new culture and performing successfully under it. The divisional CEOs will be relatively important employees in the new company, which may make B decide to offer them an initial incentive to stay with the company and embrace the new culture.

Co-optation. If there are some CEOs who continue to resist the changes, they could be co-opted into a change management team to **explain then changes to the other employees from C**. This will make it harder for them to resist the changes.

Coercion. Ultimately, if the CEOs remain unwilling to adapt, they should be removed from the business as quickly as possible. This will prevent any discontent from spreading amongst their staff.

51 JIK kitchen manufacturer

Text reference: Critical success factors are covered in Chapter 14 of the BPP Study Text for E3.

Marking scheme

				Marks
(a)		Aspects of current system which are appropriate; 1 mark each	Up to 3	
		Weaknesses in current control system; 1 mark each	Up to 7	
			Total up to	7
(b)		For each CSF recommended; 1 mark each	Up to 2	
		For justification of how the CSF could help JIK achieve future success; up to 2 marks each	Up to 4	
			Total up to	6
(c)	(i)	For each valid point made in relation to changes required to the current control system; 1 mark each	Up to 4	
			Total up to	4
	(ii)	For changes that will be required to the standard costing system; 1 mark per relevant point	Up to 3	
		For changes required to the reporting frequency; 1 mark per relevant point	Up to 3	
		For changes to information requirements; 1 mark per relevant point	Up to 4	
			Total up to	8
			Total	25

(a)

Top Tip:

The first paragraph of the scenario highlights that there are three core elements to JIK's business: manufacture, retail, and installation. However, the current control system focuses solely on the manufacturing process. This is important for requirement (a). How appropriate is it for JIK's control system only to report on one aspect of the business?

The clues in the scenario should have indicated that the majority of your answer for part (a) should be about the weaknesses in the current control system. However, because you are asked to 'evaluate' the system, you shouldn't have concentrated solely on the weaknesses, but should also have tried to have include some aspects of the current system which were appropriate.

Focus on manufacturing – JIK's current control system is focused exclusively on the efficiency of its manufacturing process. It is important that JIK's manufacturing process is efficient, so a degree of focus on the process is appropriate. However, it does not seem appropriate that the control system focuses solely on manufacturing given that JIK also **retails and installs kitchens**.

Reasons for customer complaints – There appears to be a high number of complaints in relation to the installation of 'Value' kitchens. However, it is not clear whether these complaints are due to problems in the manufacture of the doors, or due to problems with the installation. If JIK doesn't monitor the reasons for the complaints this is a weakness in its current control system, because correspondingly JIK will not have any information about areas where it can improve its performance.

Performance variables chosen – Reporting variances on three key aspects of the manufacturing process seems an appropriate way to monitor manufacturing efficiency. However, there is no indication why the three variances chosen (materials price; materials usage; and manufacturing labour efficiency) are the ones JIK has selected for its control system. For example, it may be that these are the easiest to measure, but they are not necessarily the one performance measures which JIK could choose to monitor.

Quality as well as efficiency - In particular, there doesn't seem to be any measure of the quality of the doors manufactured. Although JIK appears to be manufacturing its doors to a relatively low-cost model, it is still important that the quality of the doors meets customers' expectations, and the current control system doesn't seem to look at this aspect of performance.

Similarly, the focus for the Installation team seems to be on the number of kitchens they can install (with a bonus being paid if they exceed their annual target). However, the resulting focus on speed may also be contributing to the high level of complaints.

Luxury brand vs Value brand – It is likely that the current control system (with its focus on production efficiency) was established prior to two years ago when JIK introduced its new 'Lux-Style' kitchens. However, the success of the 'Lux-Style' range depends on their high quality rather than cost efficiency. Therefore, the current control system does not appear to be appropriate for the 'Lux-Style' range, because the **critical success factors** for this range are very different to those for the 'Value' range.

Poor understanding of performance – Another weakness in JIK's overall control system is that JIK does not seem to be aware of its profitability or the margins it is making, such that it was surprised to see that it only made 0.1% net profit in the last year. Using standard costing may be partly responsible for this, because it is not clear how often JIK updates the standard costs for each kitchen, or what variances there are between actual costs and standard costs. For example, if the actual cost of raw material inputs has increased but the standard costs attributed to each kitchen (and consequently the prices charged for each kitchen) have remained unchanged, JIK's margins will be lower than expected.

Timely reporting of information – JIK reports **weekly** on the variances it measures in its manufacturing process. While it is appropriate that variances are monitored and reported on a regular basis, weekly reporting may not necessarily always be the appropriate reporting period. If there is a major problem in the production process, leading to excessive waste of materials for example, then this needs to be identified and corrected as soon as possible rather than after the end of the reporting week. Therefore, it may be more appropriate for the performance of JIK's manufacturing process to be monitored on a **real-time basis.**

(b)

Top tips: The question specifically asked you for TWO CSFs which could help JIK achieve future success. Therefore, you should have only included two in your answer.

The two we have selected are **customer satisfaction**, and **quality of installations**. However, these are not the only CSFs which could be valid here. For example, **brand performance** and **manufacturing excellence** are two alternative CSFs you could have recommended.

(Brand management is likely to be increasingly important for JIK as it has two different brands ('Value' and 'Lux-Style') aimed at different market segments. The current control system already highlights that manufacturing is important to JIK. However, it only monitors some limited aspects of manufacturing. A CSF focusing on manufacturing excellence could also highlight the importance of flexibility, innovation and investments in technology, as well as the operational aspects of performance which are currently measured.)

You would have earned marks for any relevant CSF you recommended. However, to score well here, it is vital that the CSFs you recommend are specifically relevant to JIK, and you must justify why you have recommended them. Equally importantly, to score the marks here, it is vital that you recommended CSFs rather than KPIs (which would be the measures JIK could subsequently use to assess how well it was performing against its CSFs).

Examiner's comment: This question was poorly answered. A disappointingly small number of candidates were able to identify any relevant CSFs. In fact, most candidates who answered this question did not appear to understand what CSFs are, which demonstrates a clear lack of knowledge about an important part of the syllabus.

Quality of installations – JIK appears to receive a high number of complaints about the kitchens it has installed, for example major complaints are received about 10% of the 'Value' kitchens installed. This will direct cost implications for JIK because it will have to arrange for staff to return to the kitchens and fix the problem which customers are complaining about. Equally, the level of money back guarantees which have to be honoured also has a direct impact on JIK's financial performance and the low net profit.

Although it is important that the quality of the 'Value' kitchens installed meets customer expectations, the launch of the 'Lux-Style' kitchens reinforces the importance of JIK achieving a high quality of installations. If customers are paying, on average, £100,000 for each 'Lux-Style' kitchen they will expect their kitchens to be very high quality. If JIK doesn't have a good reputation for quality, it will be difficult for it to attract potential customers in future.

Interestingly, JIK has never received a complaint about a Lux-Style kitchen installation. However, it cannot afford any comments or complaints about the 'Value' kitchens to tarnish the reputation of the 'Lux-Style' brand.

Customer satisfaction – Repeat orders and recommendations are two of JIK's main sources of business. Therefore, it is vital that customers are satisfied with the kitchens they have installed, otherwise they will not use JIK again in future, or recommend JIK to other people.

Recommendations and customer feedback have become increasingly important with the development of social media, and if JIK's customers are giving negative feedback on the quality of its kitchens this could undermine the advertising JIK places in the local press.

Importantly, to achieve satisfaction, both the manufacturing and the installation processes have to work effectively. Not only do the kitchens have to be manufactured to the standard the customer expects, but also installed as the customer wants. In this respect, focusing on customer satisfaction addresses the problem with the current control system which focuses solely on the manufacturing process.

Moreover, customer satisfaction will reflect how durable the kitchens are over their whole life, and customers are unlikely to be happy if they have to replace their kitchens every couple of years because. So an element of this CSF also encourages JIK to look at the longer term performance of its kitchens rather than just the short term cost.

(c)

Top tips: Requirement (c) (i) is designed to test your ability to identify changes that are required to improve the performance of an inadequate/failing control system. However, the reference in the requirement to 'the CSFs recommended in part (b) of your answer' should have helped you answer (c) (i). What additional measures (eg qualitative; non-financial measures) will be required to enable JIK to assess how well it is performing against its CSFs? The idea of measuring performance against CSFs should also have suggested the importance of KPIs here.

To score well in (c) (ii) it is important that you answer all three parts of the question requirement, which covers: (i) changes to the standard costing system; (ii) changes to the reporting frequency; and (iii) changes to JIK's information requirements.

Note, however, that your answers to parts (b) and (c) (i) should have helped you identify possible changes to JIK's information requirements. The introduction of a new set of CSFs (and supporting KPIs) will mean that JIK needs to capture a greater range of performance information than it currently does. Does it currently have the appropriate hardware and software to enable it to capture all the information it needs in this respect?

(i)

Measuring quality – The CSFs recommended in part (b) both highlight the importance of quality, but JIK's current control system does not measure any aspects of quality because it only focuses production efficiency.

Quantitative and qualitative factors – The current control system looks at quantitative information (eg materials prices) as the basis for variance analysis. However, the CSFs will mean that JIK has to look at qualitative factors (eg customer satisfaction) as well as quantitative factors.

Internal and external focus – Highlighting customer satisfaction as a key factor in JIK's success also indicates that the control system will also have to look at information generated outside the organisation (eg customer satisfaction ratings) as well as internal information (eg materials usage). In this respect, the CSFs could encourage to take a more strategic approach management accounting, focusing on external, non-financial information as well as internally-generated and financial information.

KPIs – In order to measure how well it is performing in respect of its CSFs, JIK will need to introduce some related key performance indicators. For example, in relation to the quality of installations, JIK should introduce a KPI for the number of complaints received in relation to the Value kitchens (eg, major complaints received on less than 2% of installations).

(ii)

Standard costing system

Move away from standard costing – It seems likely that JIK will need to move away from its current standard costing system because the system is not aligned with the CSFs. In particular, the current system seems to focus on production efficiency rather than delivering quality and customer satisfaction.

Lux-Style vs Value range – Although JIK appears to use standard costing for all its manufacturing operations, the bespoke nature of the Lux-Style range suggests the cost of each Lux-Style kitchen should be determined on an individual basis depending on a customer's exact requirements.

Remuneration arrangements - Perhaps more importantly, though, JIK hasn't received any complaints about Lux-Style kitchen installations whereas it receives large numbers of complaints about the Value installations. This suggests that the differences in the time budgeted to install each kitchen, and the different remuneration arrangements may be contributing to the relatively high number of complaints in the 'Value' range. For example, the 'Value' teams may be trying to do too many jobs in order to try to increase their increase, but they are sacrificing quality for quantity. If this is the case, then the remuneration arrangements for the teams working on the 'Value' range may be need to be revised, for example by increasing the basic salary but restricting the amount of overtime teams can work.

Reporting frequency

Contingency approach - The frequency of reporting could vary for each KPI but it is unlikely that weekly reporting will be the most appropriate in all cases. For example, customer satisfaction scores will need to be measured over a longer reporting period. By contrast, operational performance measures (such as materials wastage) may be better reported on a real-time basis, so that any issues in the manufacturing process can be addressed as quickly as possible.

Information requirements

Increased requirements – The introduction of a range of CSFs and KPIs will mean that JIK has to gather information about a number of aspects of its performance, which it does not currently measure (eg, customer satisfaction, and the performance of the installation teams).

There are two issues for JIK to consider here:

- How it will **gather** the additional information (eg, using customer satisfaction surveys) and
- How it will **store** the information. Depending on the capability of its current management information system, JIK may have to upgrade its software to give it scope to record the additional information required.

In this respect, JIK may also consider also creating its customer satisfaction surveys on-line. Then, when customers complete the surveys the information can be integrated directly into JIK's systems.

Internal and external information – The increased focus on the customer means that JIK should also collect external information alongside internal performance information. For example, information about market growth and market share, will help JIK's management team to analyse the company's performance in the context of the industry as a whole.

Equally, external information (from a PEST analysis or Porter's Five Forces analysis) could also assist the management team in their strategic decision-making and strategy formation; for example, about whether JIK should continue to offer both the 'Value' and 'Lux-Style' ranges or whether it should just focus on one of the ranges.

52 NGV government department

Text reference: Control measures and performance measurement are covered in Chapter 13 of the BPP Study Text for E3. Knowledge management is covered in Chapter 9.

Top tips:

Part (a): When this question was set (in March 2011) the examiner's post exam guide acknowledged that this was a difficult question, requiring candidates to explain not only where NGV could benefit from financial ratio analysis, but also to establish (and explain) why financial ratio analysis is not currently occurring in NGV.

Identifying the weaknesses in NGV's current control system is essential to answer this question well. On the one hand, these weaknesses are contributing to the low return on investment. On the other hand, they also mean that financial ratio analysis will only be able to make a limited contribution unless the weaknesses are addressed first. For example, the lack of a management accounting function will make it difficult for the Director to get the financial information he needs to carry out his ratio analysis. Perhaps even more importantly, how can ROI be used as a performance measure all the time NGV is treated as cost centre rather than an investment centre?

Examiner's comments: This question was not well answered. Candidates answers to part (a) suggested they have a very limited understanding of financial ratio analysis, and most answers were based largely upon very brief (and unnecessary) descriptions of return on investment. Very few candidates identified the current weaknesses in NGV's financial information reporting structure, and how this has an impact upon the extent to which NGV could make sure of financial reporting analysis in producing an adequate ROI.

(a)

Financial ratio analysis – Depending on the ratios the Director chooses to use, financial ratio analysis could allow him to assess the profitability and returns NGV makes.

Currently, NGV does not have a management accounting function, and so the Director has to estimate how well the company is performing.

In this respect, introducing a more formal performance measurement system (ie formal ratio analysis) should allow the Director to exercise greater financial control.

Lack of control – The size of the department (320 staff with expenditure in the region of £20 – 25m) would suggest that it would benefit from a system of financial control, but it also seems rather surprising that a department of this size doesn't already have one in place. For example, it would be useful for the department to compare its actual expenditure against budgeted expenditure on a regular basis. And having an understanding of the amounts the department is actually spending would also be useful when agreeing the next year's budget with the government minister.

Moreover, the fact that NGV normally has a deficit at the end of the year suggests that it would benefit from tighter financial controls.

Lack of information – However, in practical terms, if NGV continues not to have a management accounting function, it may be debatable how the Director will be able to get the financial information he will require for his ratio analysis.

For example, we might expect the ratio analysis to take place in the context of periodic management accounts, comparing actual results to budget or forecast. But, in **the absence of a management accounting function**, or any regular management accounts, this information will not be available.

Organisation structure – Perhaps more importantly, NGV is not run as either a **profit centre** or an **investment centre**, and records neither the sales revenues accruing from its innovations in its own results, or its own assets on its balance sheet.

Given this, any ROI generated under the current accounting structure is likely to be rather misleading. In order for a meaningful ROI figures to be calculated, NGV would need to show the sales revenues accruing from its innovations in its own results, and would also need to show the value of the department's capital equipment on its own balances.

Change of policy – Consequently, under the current organisational structure, if the Director starts using financial ratio analysis it may have little impact on NGV's ROI.

However, if the introduction of financial ratio analysis were also accompanied by a reclassification of NGV as an **investment centre** (rather than a cost centre) the analysis should have more impact in helping NGV achieve an adequate ROI.

However, it is likely to be the **change in the classification of NGV** which is critical for helping NGV to produce an adequate ROI, not simply the introduction of financial ratio analysis into the current organisational structure.

(b)

Top tips:

For part (b), the scenario clearly identified that the current 'brain drain' is a problem for NGV, and this therefore means that improved knowledge management is important.

However, the question is asking *how* NGV should go about implementing a knowledge management strategy, rather than *why* it should implement one. Consequently, your answer should focus mainly on the process of implementing the strategy.

Whilst it is sensible to explain the context of the knowledge management strategy, and why it was required, you should have only included a short included to provide this context, and then focused the majority of your answer on the implementation process itself.

Also, while NGV will need some technological infrastructure in order to implement its knowledge management strategy, your answer should not been solely about technology requirements. It is equally important to consider the wider issues the implementation will raise: for example, can the staff be encouraged to use the system, and how can any resistance to it be overcome?

Knowledge management – The aim of NGV's knowledge management strategy will be to capture, organise and make widely available all the knowledge the department possesses, whether it is currently recorded (explicit) or in people's heads (tacit).

This is particularly important for NGV given the amount of '**tacit**' knowledge it currently possesses through its research experts, but which it is vulnerable to losing if these experts leave it to join a commercial organisation. Consequently, the knowledge management strategy should try to capture as much of NGV's 'tacit' knowledge as possible and convert it into '**explicit**' knowledge (by recording it and making it available to the organisation).

Senior management support – In order for the strategy to be successful, it will need to be supported by the Director and the other members of the senior management team within NGV. (The management structure of NGV is not identified in the scenario.) One important reason for this is that implementing the strategy will **cost money**, and will lead to **changes in operating procedures** for the staff. There may even need to be changes to the organizational structure; for example, NGV may need to **appoint knowledge managers** who are responsible for implementing the strategy. Knowledge managers could play a vital role in collecting and categorizing knowledge, and encouraging other people in NGV to use the available knowledge.

However, more generally, senior management support will be vital to approve the spending required to implement the strategy, and to help **overcome any resistance to change** when it is introduced.

It seems likely that the Director will support the strategy because he has already articulated his concern at the 'brain-drain' within NGV, and the lack of a system for capturing tacit knowledge.

Identify aims of the strategy – It is important that the aims of the strategy are identified early in the process so that the knowledge managers (or whoever else is responsible for implementing the strategy) know what they are trying to achieve. Identifying the aims will also be important for subsequently measuring how successful the strategy has been, and how well knowledge is used in the organisation.

Capturing and storing knowledge – NGV's size (320 staff) means that it will need some technological infrastructure in place to capture, store and distribute the knowledge. This is likely to take the form of an Organisational Management System (OMS), which could include databases, intranets and data mining tools.

It is important that the OMS doesn't only deal with explicit knowledge, but also helps NGV capture knowledge which is currently tacit so that in future it can be exploited by the department.

Structuring knowledge – In order for NGV to be able to maximise the value NGV can get from the knowledge it stores, the knowledge needs to be effectively **organised** and **accessible**. In this respect, NGV could look to build 'repositories of knowledge' in which a network of contents pages provide links to other databases where the actual knowledge is stored. This cataloguing of knowledge could be a complex and time-consuming process, so NGV may need to use an information specialist (such as a librarian) to help build the repository.

Pay review – However, as well as developing a system to capture to capture knowledge, NGV should also be looking to reduce the number of people leaving the department. In this respect, the Director could instigate a review of the current pay structures and pay rates, because it is likely that uncompetitive pay is exacerbating the current loss of tacit knowledge as NGV's staff are leaving to join other organisations who pay them more.

Cultural change - Importantly, however, as well as implementing the physical IT systems which will be necessary to capture and store knowledge, NGV will also have to address the 'softer' aspects of implementing the strategy.

Perhaps the most critical factor in the success of the strategy will be NGV's ability to create a culture of **knowledge sharing** within the department. If NGV's research staff continue to view knowledge as being their own personal possession, they will resist any demands to share this knowledge with the organisation. As a result, knowledge will continue to remain tacit rather than explicit.

In order to overcome the staff's resistance to change in this respect, NGV will need to convince them of the benefits of the new strategy – both for the department and for them as individuals – for example, by allowing NGV to undertake more complex and interesting research projects.

At a personal level, the **staff appraisal system** could also be amended so that staff are rewarded according to the amount they share knowledge and contribute knowledge to the knowledge management system.

Training and usage – Once the knowledge management technology is in place, the databases will need to be populated and NGV's staff trained and encouraged to use their contents. Again, the knowledge managers are likely to play a key role in encouraging the staff to use the OMS, but the staff are likely to need some formal training before they start using it.

53 ZZZ manufacturing company

Text reference: Performance measurement and performance management are covered in Chapters 13 & 14 of the BPP Study Text for E3.

(a)

Top tips:

Note that Part (a) doesn't ask you simply to evaluate the performance management system overall, but specifically in the context of assisting H to achieve the three objectives identified in the scenario: (i) maintaining the preferred supplier status; (ii) keeping expenditure within set limits; and (iii) developing the management skills of operational managers.

Although the question asks you to evaluate the performance management system, and therefore you should try to include some strengths as well as weaknesses, it should be clear from the scenario that the current system is essentially unsuitable for achieving the three objectives. For example, the PMS does not monitor any aspects of quality management, although guaranteeing the quality of its products is one of the key conditions of ZZZ retaining its preferred supplier status with MMM.

Maintaining ZZZ's preferred supplier status with MMM

The business from MMM currently constitutes 95% of ZZZ's revenue, which suggests that maintaining the preferred supplier position is the most important of H's objectives. ZZZ needs to achieve three main things in order to keep the contact:

Fulfil supply requirements – The business guarantee means that ZZZ has to supply MMM with at least £2 million worth of components each week, and this figure will be higher in some weeks depending on MMM's demand. Therefore H needs to ensure that ZZZ has the production capacity and flexibility to meet MMM's demands.

However, the PMS system does not address any aspects of production capacity or flexibility.

Maintain product quality – ZZZ will lose its preferred supplier status if there are two reports of failures relating to ZZZ's components. Therefore quality control and quality assurance should be very important to ZZZ. However, the PMS does not address any aspects of quality management.

Reduce prices – MMM insistence that ZZZ reduces its prices by 4% per year suggests that ZZZ needs to be actively monitoring its prices over time. However, the PMS system does not appear to compare actual prices with the previous year.

Faced with these price reductions, ZZZ should be looking to reduce its costs in order to preserve its margins despite the falling prices. However, the PMS does not appear to address any aspects of prospective cost or efficiency improvements.

Keep expenditure within budget limits

Budget control – The PMS is based exclusively on budget control, which suggests that it should be effective in allowing H to keep expenditure within budget limits.

Timeliness – However, the effectiveness of the PMS as a control system is dramatically reduced by the fact that it is based only on **quarterly reports**. H needs to be able to identify any potential areas of over-spending much more quickly than waiting for the next quarterly report.

Lack of detail – It is not clear what level of detail the PMS can produce, but H's discussions with operational managers only look at aggregate amounts.

Again, this dramatically reduces the system's effectiveness, because it will be difficult to identify (and then address) the causes of any expenditure variances simply by looking at aggregate figures.

Develop management skills

Exclusion from budgetary control – H's belief that operational managers should not be allowed to know the detail of any under or overspends in their cost centres, suggests that they are not involved in budgetary control in an effective way. This exclusion suggests that rather than developing their management skills, H is suppressing them.

Investment proposals – Similarly, excluding the operational managers from the preparation of the investment proposals also prevents them from being developing their management skills in this area either.

Summary

The PMS does not appear to help H achieve his objectives much at all, and therefore is ineffective in this respect.

(b)

Part (b): Your answer to part (a) - and the weaknesses in ZZZ's current performance management system you should have identified there – can then help you answer part (b). In effect, the FOUR improvements you recommend need to address some of the issues/weaknesses you have identified in part (a).

Although the requirement tells you that you must not recommend the introduction of the balanced scorecard as one of your four improvements, you could still recommend that ZZZ looks at non-financial performance indicators rather than concentrating solely on financial ones.

More timely reports – The PMS currently uses quarterly reports as the basis for comparing actual performance to budget. However, in order to improve H's ability to monitor and control actual performance, these performance reports need to be available on a more timely basis. As a minimum, H should be looking at variances on a monthly basis, but for some areas of performance he should consider whether daily or weekly reports can be produced. Some variance reporting for key aspects of the component manufacturing process could even be done on a 'real time' basis.

Review cost centre structure / cost centre reports – ZZZ currently has 2,000 cost centres and it produces expenditure reports for all of these cost centres. This is likely to be very time consuming for the budget accountant to produce, and H to review, (particularly if the frequency of reporting is increased), therefore ZZZ should consider whether it can reduce the number of different cost centres it has.

In addition, rather than simply producing reports which compare actual expenditure against budget, ZZZ should consider whether it could produce **exception reports** instead. In this way, rather than having to look a reports for all the cost centres in detail, H would be able to focus on those areas where actual performance is significantly different to expected (budgeted) level.

Corrective action – H's reluctance to discuss the detail of any expenditure with the operational managers appears to reduce his ability to understand the reasons for any variances, and perhaps more importantly, his ability to improve performance in the future. The operational managers are best placed to **identify ways of improving performance** going forward, and H should make better use of their knowledge in this respect. In this way, the PMS can be used to actively *manage* performance, rather than simply to report on historic performance.

Non-financial performance measures – The PMS appears to focus solely on financial performance. However, as the contract with MMM highlights, non-financial aspects of performance such as quality and reliability are also very important. Therefore, ZZZ should widen the range of performance measures it monitors, and should include non-financial measures alongside financial ones.

(c)

Part (c): Notice that the requirement here is specifically for performance measures that link directly towards ZZZ maintaining its preferred supplier status, not simply measures that would help improve ZZZ's performance in more general terms. The scenario identifies three main things ZZZ needs to achieve in order to keep its preferred supplier status: supply the level of business required; reduce prices by 4% per year, and ensure that its components do not fail.

The performance measures you recommend need to link directly to these aims.

Note: The requirement specifically asked you to recommend TWO performance measures. However, there are additional measures you could have recommended in addition to the two we have recommended below. For example, you could have recommended measures to do with production quantities and production reliability (based on the requirement to supply a minimum of £2million worth of components each week).

Equally, you could have recommended measures due to the timeliness or reliability of delivery to MMM (because MMM operates a JIT system and so will rely on ZZZ delivering its components as it needs them).

Provided you recommended relevant measures, and justified them, you would have earned marks for your recommendations even if they are different to ours.

% annual reduction in costs – As we mentioned in part (a), MMM's requirement that ZZZ reduces its prices by 4% year-on-year also means that it will have to reduce its costs each year.

Therefore, ZZZ should introduce a performance measure looking at cost reduction, because if ZZZ can improve the efficiency of its processes and reduce its costs, this should help it achieve MMM's price reduction target whilst still preserving its profit margins.

Component quality – In order to preserve its contract, ZZZ needs to ensure the quality and durability of its components. ZZZ will lose its preferred supplier status if there are two reports of its components failing either during production or ones MMM's cars are being driven by customers.

Therefore, ZZZ needs a performance measure which focuses on product quality and product reliability.

54 DLC telephone services

Text reference: Issues about strategic control and performance management are considered in Chapters 13 and 14 of your BPP Study text. Customer profitability analysis is covered in Chapter 8.

Top tips: For part (a), the scenario highlights that DLC's control system relies solely on budgetary control and ROCE as a measure of performance. You should have considered how useful budgets and ROCE are as control systems, but also what their limitations are. Make sure you do this specifically in the context of DLC, rather than in general terms. For example, is ROCE a suitable measure for a young, capital intensive company?

However, as well as considering budgets and ROCE individually you should also consider the limitations of DLC's control system focusing only on financial indicators. DLC's two key success factors are technological innovation and customer service. Shouldn't DLC have some indicators to show how well it is performing in these areas of the business? (Do not, however, let your answer become a long discussion of the Balanced Scorecard as an alternative performance management system. This was not required by the question.)

Part (b) builds on part (a) and specifically introduces the idea that DLC might benefit from having some non-financial performance measures. However, you need to think about this question carefully. You are asked how non-financial performance indicators (NFPIs) could help *evaluate* the two key success factors. This suggests you need to consider how NFPIs could help DLC monitor its performance against its key success factors, but also you need to consider the important of reviewing the success factors and any related KPIs. For example, if DLC consistently meets or exceeds a KPI it might be appropriate to introduce a new, more challenging target.

For part (c) you are again asked to evaluate: this time how customer profitability analysis (CPA) could assist the business in achieving its strategic aims. So you need to consider how CPA could be valuable to DLC, but also discuss its potential limitations. For example, could DLC actually implement CPA if sales are only reported in aggregate?

(a)

DLC's control system involves budgeting, preparing monthly management accounts and computing ROCE.

Usefulness

Budgets as a planning tool – The process of preparing a budget should encourage managers to think about the services planned for the budget period, and plan for any resource requirements needed to deliver the services which are planned. Preparing the budget should also provide a means of **co-ordinating activities** within the different areas of DLC's business.

Responsibility accounting – It is likely that the different areas of DLC's business (eg design, installation and maintenance) will have separate budgets. Therefore the budgets provide a framework for responsibility accounting for the managers of the different areas.

Performance evaluation – DLC prepares **monthly management accounts** preparing actual performance to budget. This should help X evaluate performance (for example which areas of the business area performing best against budget) and take corrective action where necessary – for example, if particular areas of the business are performing significantly worse than they were budgeted to.

Motivation – Provided that the budgets are deemed to be realistic and achievable by the managers and staff, then the budgeted figures could act to motivate staff – to try ensure actual results are favourable to budget.

Productivity – By measuring **ROCE,** DLC can see how effectively its capital is being employed. In this way, ROCE can provide a high level measure of the business' performance.

Limitations

Basis of budget preparation – The budgets appear to be produced simply by taking the previous year's actual figures and adding an adjustment for inflation. Therefore they don't allow for any expected variations in activity levels in the coming year compared to the previous year. For example, if DLC knows it is going to start work on a large contract in the coming year, but it didn't have any equivalent contracts in the previous year, then basing the budget on the prior year's actual figures is unrealistic.

There are two potential implications of this:

- The value of the budgets as a control measure is reduced, because managers could argue that many of the variances in actual performance against budget are due to the budgets not reflecting the actual level of activity
- If managers and staff think that the budgets are unrealistic and unachievable, then they may either ignore them or get de-motivated by the fact that their actual performance is so far away from budget

One way that DLC could improve its analysis of actual performance against a target is by **re-forecasting** its budget during the year, but again there is no evidence in the scenario to suggest it does this.

Level of detail – DLC's sales performance against budget is reported in total, but there is no sectional analysis. This means X, or any other senior managers, cannot tell whether revenue in some areas of the business is performing better than others. Again this is a weakness, because it means no corrective action can be taken to improve the performance of any areas which are doing less well.

Customer profitability analysis – Similarly, there appears to be no way of analysing the profitability of any individual customer or contract. X has acknowledged that the company is now too big for her to know the details and profitability of each contract, but DLC has no systems in place to allow this information to be recorded and analysed.

Inappropriateness of ROCE – X considers ROCE to be the best control measure available for her to use. However, ROCE may not actually be a suitable measure for DLC at the moment. ROCE is best suited to **mature organisations**, but DLC (founded three years ago) is still a relatively young company, and because it is successful it is likely to be growing quite fast.

Goal congruence – DLC's technological innovation also requires substantial, continued capital investment. However, using ROCE as a performance measure may discourage this investment. Making additional capital investment will depress ROCE (at least in the short term) and so managers may be unwilling to invest, whereas investment is likely to be necessary to maintain DLC's innovativeness and 'leading edge' skills.

Non-financial performance indicators – Although technological innovation and customer service are seen as **key success factors** for DLC, the company has no way of measuring how well it is performing in these aspects of its business. Although X considers that measuring ROCE can indicate how well DLC is performing in these areas, the company should have more detailed non-financial performance indicators which focus specifically on these two key areas of the business. Moreover, performance in these areas needs to be measured **more frequently than once a month** which is how often ROCE is computed.

(b)

Non-financial key success factors - DLC has identified Technological Innovation and Customer Service as its two key success factors, which suggests that it feels these are the areas in which it needs to outperform its competitors to remain successful.

These key success factors are non-financial, and so DLC should have some way of measuring performance in these non-financial areas as well the financial ones it currently measures. However, at the moment, DLC's control system focuses only on **financial performance**, and so doesn't provide any measures of non-financial performance.

CSFs and KPIs – Although DLC has not formally recognised them as such, Technological Innovation and Customer Service are, in effect, its critical success factors (CSFs).

Therefore, DLC would benefit from establishing some key performance indicators (KPIs) to show how well it is performing in these key areas. For example, measuring the number of customer complaints could provide an indicator of the level of customer service DLC is offering.

Timeliness of information – Currently, DLC's performance is only measured once per month, through the monthly management accounts and ROCE calculation. However, KPIs measuring the performance of the key operational processes could be reported much more frequently; for example, customer complaints could be reported on a daily basis. In this way, managers can take action to address any performance issues much more quickly than if they had to wait for the current monthly reports to become available.

Moreover, the current reports are unlikely to provide sufficient detail to allow the managers to identify any issues in the key operational processes.

Evaluating key success factors – To this end, monitoring its non-financial performance measures should provide X and the other managers with better information about how well DLC is **achieving** its key success factors. However, this doesn't, in itself, **assess the value** of (evaluate) the key success factors.

The value of the key success factors should be assessed in terms of how well achieving them allows DLC to **achieve it goals**. The business's goals are continued expansion, providing a rewarding lifestyle for X and secure well-paid jobs for the staff. Technological innovation and customer service are likely to be important for the continued expansion of the business, which in turn should provide secure, well-paid jobs for the staff.

Identifying additional success factors - However, some performance indicators to do with staff turnover may also provide a useful gauge of how secure and well-paid staff feel their jobs are. Similarly, performance indicators based on sales growth and new customers could help measure how well DLC is achieving its goal of continued expansion. Neither of these aspects of performance are addressed by the existing key success factors.

Therefore the process of developing a suite of non-financial performance measures could identify some additional key success factors alongside the two which DLC has currently identified.

(c)

Sales growth or profit growth - One of X's strategic aims for DLC is that the company should continue to expand in its current market segment. However, there is little value expanding if DLC does not increase its profitability by doing so; in other words, if the new customers it acquires when it expands are unprofitable to it.

Lack of profit information - However, X does not know the level of profitability generated by each customer or contract, and she has recognised this is a weakness for DLC. This weakness could be exacerbated as DLC expands, because there is a risk that the new customers it acquires may be unprofitable ones, and at the same time DLC may have to turn down potentially profitable contracts because it does not have the capacity to service them.

Customer profitability analysis (CPA) can help address these issues. CPA is the 'analysis of the revenue streams and service costs associated with specific customers or customer groups.' (*CIMA terminology*).

If DLC introduced CPA it could help identify which customers – or types of customers – are profitable and therefore DLC should look to retain. Equally, it could identify which customers do not generate any profit and therefore which DLC may benefit from no longer servicing.

New customers – If CPA allows DLC to identify which types of customer are profitable then this will help X decide which are likely to be the best new customers to accept as the company expands.

Equally, analysing trends in customer profitability may lead X to revise DLC's strategic aims, because it may suggest that customer groups in other market segments may provide better opportunities for profitable group in the future than DLC's current market/business segment.

Limitations with using CPA – Currently DLC's sales performance is only measured in aggregate. However, in order to use CPA, DLC will need to be able to analyse revenues and direct costs at an individual customer (or contract) level, as well as being able to assign indirect costs to an individual level. It is possible that DLC's management accounting systems may not currently be able to do this accurately, and there is a risk that if costs are wrongly apportioned customer profitability – and therefore X's decision making – will be distorted, and therefore DLC will turn down potentially profitable contracts and accept less lucrative ones.

DLC will also need understand how the **customer lifecycle** will affect profitability. Again, there may be customers which do not appear profitable initially, but may become increasingly profitable later on (for example, as their number of users increases.) Again, X's decision-making could be distorted if she only looks at customer profitability on a short term basis, rather than considering the potential longer term value that potential new clients offer.

55 Performance measurement

Text reference. Performance measurement and Neely's '4 CPs of measurement' are discussed in Chapter 14 of the Study Test.

Marking scheme

			Marks
(a)	For each appropriate *function* identified and described in general terms	1	
	For each function, if it is embedded in the case study material and described in terms of how it can help D, up to a further 1 ½ marks available	1 ½	
		Total up to	10
(b)	For each appropriate step or stage described in *developing* a performance measurement system in general terms	1	
	For each step or stage related to the case study to recommend how the performance measurement system should be developed at D, up to a further 1 mark available	1	
		Total up to	15
		Total	25

Part (a)

Top tips. The way to approach this question is to use specific issues highlighted in the scenario to guide your answer rather than answering too generally. Students who presented answers which were too general and did not relate to the specific issues highlighted in the scenario scored poorly.

The requirement did *not* ask you to describe a performance management system, or the benefits of a performance management system, but asked you specifically to apply them to D. Nonetheless, the examiner has still commented that many answers to this question were very general and did not address the problems D was facing.

Equally, you should not have spent time describing the current problems at D. You need to identify the problems from the scenario, because they can help indicate some of the areas where a performance measurement system could help D, but remember the question is asking about the performance measurement system, not the current problems at D.

A sensible way to approach this requirement was to select a suitable model of the functions of performance measurement systems, and then use that as a framework to explain how such a system could benefit D. In the model answer we have used Neely's 4 CPs, but you could have used PRIME equally well (Planning, Responsibility, Integration, Motivation, Evaluation).

However, students who tried to answer this requirement without using one of these frameworks scored poorly, because their answers lacked any clear structure.

The functions that an effective PMS will perform for D are shown below, and can be summarised as the 'Four CPs of Measurement'.

1 <u>Check position</u> – Effective performance measures will allow the partners to understand how well D is performing at present.

  The performance measures can be both financial (revenues, profitability) and non-financial (client satisfaction), and they should look to benchmark actual performance against target figures for each measure chosen.

  Performance can be measured for both the partnership as a whole and also for individual teams within the partnership.

Given the current problems with inter-term rivalry, the partners may wish to include a measure looking at the degree to which teams work together to secure business rather than the current practice of competing against one another.

The partners should also use PMS to benchmark D's overall performance in key measures against their competitors to gauge how well the partnership is performing.

2 Communicate position – Once the current performance levels have been measured, they should be communicated to the partnership's key stakeholders.

The key internal stakeholders here will be the partners (as both the owners of the business and the team leaders), and the consultants themselves. The consultants need to be aware of both the performance of their individual teams but also the partnership as a whole.

By communicating performance in the key measures chosen, D will be able to demonstrate how the current practices of teams competing against each other for business are damaging the firm. This in turn will help them justify the need for a new performance measurement system.

3 Confirm priorities – The performance measures chosen to be included in the PMS should be those which are important for the success of the business. By extension, their inclusion in the PMS communicates this importance to the stakeholders of the business.

Therefore the inclusion of measures around client satisfaction and knowledge sharing alongside the existing targets for new client acquisition will reinforce the importance of changing the organisational culture of the partnership.

Perhaps equally importantly, the new PMS will formalise this change, and communicate the new priorities to the consultants.

4 Compel progress – The consultants currently get paid large bonuses on the basis of their performance against a single performance measure – acquiring new clients.

We expect that the consultants will still be able to earn large bonuses, but in the future bonus payments will be linked to their performance across the range of multi-dimensional measures.

This should again help change the behavioural culture in the business, not least because the consultants' pay and career development prospects will now be linked directly to the new PMS. This will force the consultants to realise that it is no longer sufficient simply to bring new business to the practice at any cost, and that working together with colleagues and sharing knowledge with them instead of competing against them is equally important.

However, the new PMS will compel progress not only in individual consultants, but also across the partnership as a whole. If the partnership overall is failing to reach its performance targets this will be highlighted through the PMS, and so the partners will need to introduce remedial measures to improve performance.

Part (b)

Top tips. As with part (a), the way to approach this question is to think specifically about the context – the performance measurement system being developed is specifically for use in D.

However, note also that the question relates to the process that should be used in *developing* the performance measurement system, not in *operating* it.

Examiner's comments. This question was not well answered. In particular, in (b) candidates tended to focus on how a performance measurement system *operates* rather than how it should be *developed*.

D should go through the following stages when developing their performance measurement system:

1 Obtain senior management commitment and support for the project, and achieve buy in from the key stakeholders

It is important that the rationale for the new performance measurement system is communicated to all stakeholders in order to overcome potential barriers to its implementation. This will be particularly important in D, because although the partners are committed to the new multi-dimensional performance measurement system (PMS) the consultants who have earned high bonuses under the existing structure will need to be convinced of its merits.

The partners' support for the project could be demonstrated through a briefing to the consultants explaining the rational for the new PMS, and showing how it will benefit the partnership as a whole. They could also demonstrate that the new system is not designed to prevent the consultants from earning bonuses. By contrast, they will still be able to earn their bonuses, but in order to do so they must buy in to the new culture being promoted by the PMS.

2 Identify the key outputs required from the PMS

The key outputs should relate back to the stakeholders requirements. In D's case this will be providing cutting edge computer simulations for its clients (client requirement) in a manner which promotes the profit and reputation of the partnership (partner requirement).

3 Identify the key processes in providing the outputs

An effective control system needs to consider the inputs and processes in a system as well as the outputs from it. In D's case this should be done by documenting the business cycle from winning new business to delivering a finished model to a client. The documentation should involve a walkthrough of the current process, plus discussions with management and staff about the issues they face with the current process.

4 Identify the interfaces between the various parts of the firm and with other key service providers

D will need a number of people to all work together to provide a high quality service to their clients. For example, sharing knowledge between teams, and sharing best practice in customer relationship management will help teams improve the service they provide to their clients, alongside the current technical expertise they use in developing their models.

5 Develop performance indicators for the key processes

Performance indicators are critical for D to be able to measure how well it is managing the key areas of its business. Whilst there are obviously financial indicators around new business earned, chargeable hours billed and profits generated, the new multi-dimensional performance system should also look at non-financial indicators such as client satisfaction and levels of knowledge sharing between teams.

6 Identify data sources for performance indicators chosen

The data required will ultimately depend on the performance indicators which D chooses to measure (stage 5 above). As far as possible they should all be quantifiable, although it is likely that some measures may have to be qualitative.

The following are some possible measures D may consider using alongside the core financial indicators: chargeable time to non-chargeable time ratios; customer satisfaction surveys; percentage of key deadlines achieved; staff satisfaction surveys (particularly around aspects of training and development).

7 Develop reporting system

Again, the precise nature of how this is developed will depend on how D's management want to communicate information, but we suggest one suitable method will be through an electronic report circulated to the teams or posted on an intranet.

8 Implement the system

Note that the implementation of the new system should be accompanied by staff training to ensure that the consultants (and the partners) know how to interpret the data, and can identify which areas of performance need to be improved.

9 Review effectiveness of the system

There are three aspects to consider here:

- When the system is introduced initially it may have some bugs or faults in it. So the partners would be advised to pilot it on one team before rolling it out across the whole partnership.
- Once the system has been introduced it will be important to assess whether it does actually lead to any change in the culture and performance of the partnership.
- It will be important to regularly review the processes and indicators measured to ensure that they remain relevant if the nature and scope of D's work changes over time.

56 International acquisition

Text Reference. Performance measurement is covered in chapter 14 of the BPP Study Text.

Marking scheme

				Marks
(a)	For each element of information identified		½	
	For embedding the elements of information in the scenario and relating them to the target company, up to a further 1 ½ marks each		1½	
			Total up to	15
(b)	(i)	For each difficulty well explained in the context of the scenario	Up to 2	
			Total up to	6
	(ii)	For each disadvantage of ROI, well explained and related to the scenario	Up to 2	
			Total up to	4
			Total	25

Part (a)

Top tips. The way to approach (a) is to think about the context of the acquisition. EEE has historically produced high quality products. It is now looking to respond to competition by reducing the cost base of its production. So is it trying to move from a **differentiation** to a **cost leadership** strategy? What are the implications of this for its business model? What characteristics must an acquisition target have to help EEE achieve its aims?

Note the primary motivation for the acquisition is to reduce production costs, so the most important characteristics should relate to production capabilities, not the potential for market growth in the target's country.

However, note the wording of requirement (a) carefully – It does not ask you about the *characteristics* of a possible target, but rather the *information* EEE needs to assess the suitability of a potential target. A sensible approach would be to identify the factors EEE should consider in appraising the suitability of a target, and then the information it needs in order to assess those factors.

Marks available. The marking guide for this question indicates that up to two marks were available for each well-justified requirement relating to the target company, up to a total of 15 marks.

In the answer below we have identified eleven areas where EEE could seek information about the suitability of an acquisition target: production capabilities; production capacity; equipment; labour supply; supply chain; infrastructure; management and control; stakeholder interests; corporate image; market share; and financial analysis.

However, the marking guide suggests that you would not have needed to include all of them to score well in this question. 7 or 8 well justified, relevant areas should have been sufficient to secure a good mark.

Examiner's comments. This question was generally not well answered. Many candidates failed to read requirement (a) carefully enough and so failed to answer the question set. They were required to assess the suitability of the acquisition target (company) not the country which it is in. Detailed analysis of Porter's diamond was largely irrelevant here.

The reason for the decline in EEE's sales is that it has faced increasing competition from companies in neighbouring countries who have **lower production costs** than it. EEE is now looking to acquire one of these competitors to relocate its production to the acquisition in order to take advantage of its lower cost base.

However, before making the acquisition EEE needs to undertake some extensive intelligence to find out the strengths and weaknesses of potential targets.

<u>Production capabilities</u>

Quality standards – One of the key differences between EEE and its competitors is that EEE produces much higher quality goods than its competitors. By transferring production to the newly acquired division, EEE would have to accept a trade-off between lower costs and lower quality.

However, EEE will need to ensure that the products produced by the new manufacturer will still be sufficiently good quality to meet its **customers' requirements**.

Cost vs quality – In this context, EEE would be advised to undertake some market research to assess the relative importance of cost and quality in customers' purchasing decision. If low cost is the most important factor, then the suitability of potential targets will be affected by **how low (and possibly also how well controlled) their production costs are**. In effect, EEE would now be looking to adopt a cost leadership strategy instead of using quality as a differentiating factor compared to its competitors.

Product range and specification – Although the companies in the neighbouring countries are competitors to EEE, they may not be producing exactly the same products to EEE. Therefore EEE needs to be sure that the production lines can produce goods to the specifications and designs it requires.

<u>Production capacity</u>

EEE is looking to transfer its own production to the manufacturing division it acquires, alongside the division's existing production. Therefore, it should be looking for a company which has **sufficient capacity to take on EEE's production** while still maintaining its own existing production requirements. Alternatively, EEE should be looking to acquire a company which has **scope to expand its factory size** to meet the additional capacity requirements.

<u>Equipment</u>

EEE should look at the **age** and **condition** of target companies' production equipment. If a company has old equipment, there is a higher risk of failure or breakdown, potentially disrupting production. Equally, it may mean that EEE has to replace the equipment in the near future. (If this is the case, EEE should look for a reduction in the purchase price of the acquisition at allow for this. EEE may feel that if it can acquire the company cheaply, and then install new machinery to its own specification – or even use some of the machinery from the plant it is closing in F – this is an option which is worth considering).

<u>Labour supply</u>

In the same way that EEE needs to review the production equipment's capacity and its ability to deliver goods of sufficient quality, so it also needs to consider the **size and competencies of the labour pool** in potential target companies. For example, what are there skill levels if EEE needs them to take on additional tasks?

EEE should also look at the **external labour market** in the geographical area around the production plants, in case it needs to recruit additional staff to support additional demand. If any of the equipment production requires skilled labour, EEE should assess the availability of suitably skilled staff in the area.

<u>Supply chain</u>

The increased production levels post-acquisition are likely to increase the volume of materials bought in from suppliers. EEE will need to investigate that the target companies have secure contracts with their suppliers, and that the suppliers will be able to fulfil larger orders reliably.

<u>Infrastructure</u>

EEE should consider the geographic location of any potential acquisitions and the **infrastructure networks** around it. For example, if it hopes to use the new division to export products to a range of neighbouring countries, the location will need to be well served by road or rail links.

<u>Management and control</u>

EEE will also need to consider the **skills of the current management team** in the acquisition. Will the existing team be competent to manage the enlarged operation, or will EEE need to second some its own staff to manage the new division? Equally, EEE should assess the quality of **management and financial information** produced by the target companies, again with a view to assessing whether it will be able to provide sufficient information to allow it to **monitor the performance of the division** post-acquisition.

<u>Stakeholder analysis</u>

EEE needs to identify the key stakeholders in the target companies, and consider their response to a potential takeover.

Owners – As the companies are private companies, the owners' intentions are particularly important. Are they prepared to sell the company, or do they wish to retain control of an independent company, possibly growing it through acquisitions of their own? Would the current owners want to (or be prepared to) stay on and manage the division post-acquisition?

Employees – If EEE acquires the company will the current managers and staff be prepared to work for foreign owners? How well will the existing working culture fit with the organisational culture of EEE?

Suppliers – EEE will need to be confident that the target company's existing suppliers will be prepared to continue to supply the division once it has a parent in a foreign country.

Corporate image

Although EEE is looking to use the acquisition to reduce its production costs, it still needs to consider its corporate image. If the company it acquires has a **reputation** for producing very cheap, low quality goods, this could damage EEE's reputation for producing high quality products. Therefore, EEE should consider the reputation of potential target companies in their host countries, and in the industry more generally.

As part of its research into possible target companies, EEE should also assess what the competitor believes it **position in the industry** to be (in terms of cost and product quality).

Market share

One of the benefits of the acquisition for EEE will be to strengthen its (export) sales to neighbouring countries. Therefore the size of the potential company will be important; it needs to be sufficiently large so that by acquiring it, **EEE gains a significant share of the market** in its country.

EEE should also look at the size of the overall market in the target's country, to assess the **scope for future expansion**.

Market segments – As well as looking at overall sales, EEE should also assess the size and type of customers which the potential acquisitions serve. It will only be beneficial for EEE to acquire new customers if they can be **served profitably**.

Financial analysis

Finally EEE should examine the financial position of the targets very closely – including its financial statements for the last 3 –5 years, and its current budgets and forecasts. EEE should consider both the **profitability** and the liquidity of the operation.

Also , EEE should consider any **long-term contracts** from suppliers or leases which the target has already signed up to, and any **liabilities** which it may inherit as a result of the acquisition. In connection with this, EEE should also assess the pay and conditions for which the current employees work. (This could be important to make sure that there are no issues in respect of working time directives or minimum wage rates, for example, and also that EEE will not face any strike action if the workers are unhappy with their terms and conditions).

Conclusion

Ultimately, EEE's choice of which company to acquire should be decided by a combination of its potential to **revitalise EEE's sales**, the ease with which EEE can **incorporate and manage the division**, and the **price** which the vendors will be seeking for it.

As far as possible, in all of its investigations about the capabilities of potential acquisitions, EEE would be advised to substantiate its research through **direct observation** of the production line, rather than relying solely on discussions with management and looking at reports. In this way it can establish how the company *actually* operates rather than how its managers think/claim it operates.

Part (b)

Top tips. Although the scenario mentions ROI and RI as two possible approaches to performance measurement, you should not have limited your answer to (b) (i) too narrowly to the difficulties of applying these measures. You should also have considered the more general problems associated with performance measurement in a multinational organisation.

By contrast, requirement (b) (ii) focuses specifically on the disadvantages of EEE choosing ROI as its primary performance measure. So you should have kept your comments about ROI for (ii) and discussed the more general difficulties of performance measurement in a foreign subsidiary in part (i).

Examiner's comments. In (b), many candidates only focused on the difficulties of using ROI and RI as performance measures, rather than on the difficulties of measuring the performance of different divisions in different countries.

Marks available. The marking guide indicates that each difficulty well explained and relevant to the context of the scenario is worth up to 2 marks each, up to a maximum of 6 marks. Again, it would be possible to identify more difficulties than you need to score 6 marks. We have listed what we think are the most important difficulties in the answer below, but have included two additional ones in the box at the end of the answer. These are equally valid, and you would have earned marks for them if you included them in your answer.

(i) **Impact of becoming multinational** – Currently EEE is based entirely in F, and so the acquisition of the new division will mean it becomes a multinational company for the first time. Performance management in a multinational company brings different challenges to managing a company based in a single country.

When assessing the performance of the foreign division, EEE will need to allow for any differences in the economic conditions between F and the foreign country; for example, for example, **the potential impact of different inflation rates** on reported revenue and costs figures.

Impact of price differences on profits – Also, because F is more developed than its neighbouring countries, it is likely that products are likely to sell at a higher price in F than the neighbouring countries. Consequently, profitability could be affected by where products are sold to rather than the numbers of products sold.

Comparability of figures – The division may have different accounting policies than EEE, which would mean that its results are not necessarily comparable with other divisions. For example, if the foreign division **values assets differently**, this could lead to difficulties in comparing its performance to the other divisions using ROI or RI as the performance measures. Similarly if the age of the non-current assets is different across the various divisions, this could also distort comparisons.

Issues with **foreign currency translation** may also affect the comparability of divisions in different countries.

Furthermore, if EEE introduces a **transfer pricing** policy post-acquisition this could affect the profit the division reports. Therefore EEE must ensure the transfer prices applied are equitable and encourage the acquired decision to take decisions which are **in the best interests of the group** as a whole.

Division's expectations – We do not know what level of **performance measurement the division is used to**, or what level of management/financial information is available as a basis for performance measurement. If EEE wants to introduce more complex performance measurement processes, it will need to educate the division about them – explaining the benefits of them, and what information it needs for them.

Accordingly, EEE is likely to favour using some fairly simple performance measures initially.

Goal congruence – EEE needs to ensure that the performance measures it employs encourages the divisional managers to make decisions which are in the **best interests of the group as well as the division**. For example, the two approaches EEE is considering (ROI or RI) may **discourage the division from investing in new capital equipment**. This may mean the division may show a better performance in the short term than it would have done if it had made the investment, but its longer term performance (and therefore the longer term interests of the group) will be weakened by the lack of investment.

Other valid points

Selecting reference measures – One of the issues which EEE will face is deciding **what the most important performance factors of the division are**: for example, overall profitability, revenue growth, productivity levels, or returns on investment are all aspects of performance it could look to monitor, but they may require different behaviours from the division.

Financial and non-financial measures – There is a danger that EEE will concentrate primarily on financial performance. These measures are suitable for measuring the business's current and past performance, but are not necessarily helpful in shaping future strategies. EEE should also consider looking at **customer**-based measures, **business process**-based measures, and **innovation and learning** based measures as suggested by the **balanced scorecard**.

(ii) If EEE chooses ROI as its primary performance measure, it could face some problems surrounding the **application of non-current asset values** in the performance measurement calculation.

Encourages short-termism – One potential disadvantage of using ROI is that it may **cause EEE to reject some profitable opportunities**. If a return on investment is measured year by year, it may be below the target return in the first year, but then above it in subsequent years, as the net book value of the non-current assets decreases. However, it is possible EEE may reject the project because it needs to show a satisfactory profit and ROI to its shareholders in year one.

In this respect, **ROI encourages short-termist decision making**. By contrast, if EEE chooses RI as its primary performance measure it would not have this problem, because RI deducts an imputed interest charge for the use of assets, rather than using net book value in the calculation.

Discourages asset replacement – If profit remains constant year on year, **ROI increases as assets get older**. If ROI is calculated as a return on net assets, then net asset value reduces each year due to depreciation. If ROI is calculated as a return on gross assets, the costs of older assets is likely to be less than the cost of buying the equivalent asset now.

Consequently, using ROI **could discourage EEE from replacing older assets** with new assets. However, this could damage EEE's productivity and performance in the longer term. Again, ROI encourages short-termism.

Lack of flexibility – Another disadvantage of ROI is the **lack of flexibility applied to the discount factor.** EEE would need to apply the same discount factor to all projects or divisions, even if they have different levels of risk attached to them. Having identical target returns may be unsuitable for EEE now it is a multinational business.

Overall, RI is a more flexible performance measure than ROI. ROI may lead to EEE rejecting some investments which it would have accepted under RI. Therefore if it adopts ROI as its primary performance measure, its longer term performance may suffer.

57 SAH yachts

Text reference: The balanced scorecard is discussed in Chapter 14 of the BPP Study Text for E3.

Top tips:

Part (a): One of the main weaknesses of SAH's current control system is that it doesn't look at any non-financial measures of performance. The fact that N is considering the use of a Balanced Scorecard should have highlighted this point very clearly.

Although the question asked for strengths and weaknesses (and therefore you should have tried to give some of each) it should have been clear that the current control system didn't have many strengths, so the main focus of your answer should have been on its weaknesses.

Also, make sure your answer focuses on the strengths and weaknesses of SAH's control system, not the strengths and weaknesses of SAH as an organisation. This was not asked for in the question and you would not have earned any marks for evaluating SAH's strengths and weaknesses as an organisation.

Strengths

Cost control – SAH has an established system which allows it to control its manufacturing costs, which represent 60% of its total costs.

SAH has been using its standard costing system since 1985 which suggests N feels the system works well, and also that SAH's staff will be familiar with the system and interpreting the results it produces.

Weaknesses

Only focuses on financial performance – The current system only reports financial results, and the absence of any control over non-financial aspects of performance seems to be proving a problem for SAH. For example, its poor performance in relation to **non-financial indicators**, such as innovation ('old-fashioned' yachts) and product delivery (delivery times not being met), has led to SAH losing business.

Not aligned to customer requirements – The key features which customers are looking for in their yachts are quality, reliability and performance. Again though, SAH's current system does not report on any of these attributes.

Lack of integrated control – N has expressed his desire to have a control system that gives him 'integrated control' over all aspects of the business, but the current system does not give him this level of control.

Incomplete cost control – Moreover, the current system does not even control all of the costs within the business, because it only deals with manufacturing costs. Although manufacturing costs make up 60% of SAH's total costs, this still leaves 40% of uncontrolled, and many of these costs (such as marketing costs) may be unrelated to cost drivers in the manufacturing department.

Age of system – The current system was installed in 1985, meaning that it is now nearly 30 years old. Developments in technology during this time mean that the system is unlikely to be as effective as more contemporary systems, and therefore SAH could benefit from having a more up-to-date system.

Although the unacceptably low Return on Capital Employed (ROCE) is not entirely due to the control system, this coupled with the pressure on SAH's cash flow and the criticisms from customers may suggest that the current system is not allowing N to manage the business as effectively as he could do.

(b)

Top tips:

In (b) (i) there were a number of different measures you could have suggested, but note you were only asked for ONE for each perspective. The scenario should have given you some clues about possible scenarios. For example, SAH has lost business because the yachts look 'old-fashioned' and are 'too slow', so these are aspects which could be addressed by innovation. Equally, the customer perspective (or the internal business perspective) could address the failure to meet delivery times which currently happens for 30% of SAH's orders.

For tutorial purposes, we have included alternative measures in text boxes, but you could have earned marks for any relevant and appropriate measures - even if they were different to the ones we have suggested. However, to score well in (b) (i) it is vital that you justify the measures you have selected. Remember, the requirement asked you to '... select and justify...'.

Equally, in (b) (ii), notice that the requirement is very precise. You need to advise N of THREE potential problems. The context of the scenario could again have helped you here. It seems unlikely that N (or any of SAH's staff) have any experience of using the scorecard or of setting measures for it. So, for example, what problems could this generate in terms of knowing what the most appropriate measures to select are?

However, make sure your answers relate specifically to problems N might encounter from introducing the Scorecard, and you don't end up discussing general management issues such as resistance to change, or time constraints. To score well in this question, it is vital you focus on the specific difficulties of implementing the Scorecard (such as developing appropriate measures).

(i)

Applications of the Balanced Scorecard

Determine objectives and measures - The balanced scorecard seeks to translate mission and strategy into **objectives** and **measures**, looking at both financial and non-financial perspectives on performance.

Introducing the Balanced Scorecard should help make SAH more strategy-focused, and should help integrate the various features (financial and non-financial) which will help it to be successful. The scorecard can do this by translating the company's mission and strategy into specific objectives and targets for each of the departments, with these objectives being set against the different perspectives of the scorecard.

Link strategy to operations - In practical terms, SAH will need to identify what the key areas of performance it needs to improve in order to deliver its strategy successfully, and then it can use the Scorecard to measure how well it is performing against the targets its sets for each of those key areas of performance.

Balanced Scorecard measures

Financial perspective

Operating profit margins – Although SAH is profitable, its ROCE is currently unacceptably low. Improving its operating profit margins (profit before interest and tax) should help it improve its ROCE.

Net cash flow – The long lead times for each yacht mean that cash flow is very important for SAH, and it has been under pressure recently. If SAH could encourage customers to pay more quickly (or possibly even pay in instalments as the yachts are being built) this should help reduce the pressure on its cash flow and its overdraft.

Customer perspective

Achieving delivery times – In the last year, SAH failed to meet the promised delivery tem for 30% of its orders. This appears to be a major weakness for the company, so it needs to improve its performance in this respect in order to help retain existing customers and encourage them to recommend SAH to other potential customers.

Customer satisfaction – SAH's business comes from repeat orders and recommendations, which means that customer satisfaction is vital to maintain future orders. Given the competitive nature of the market, if customers are not happy with their quality and performance of their yacht, or the service they have received from SAH (eg, late delivery) they are less likely to make a repeat order in future or to recommend SAH to other potential customers.

Order book - As each yacht is built to order and there is a period of at least a year between an order being placed and a yacht being delivered, it is important for SAH to know it has continuity of demand. SAH can gauge the continued popularity of its yachts by the number of people who have placed an order for one.

Innovation and learning perspective

Number of design innovations – Recently, SAH has been losing business because potential customers have said that SAH's yachts look 'old-fashioned' and were 'too slow'. At the same time, SAH's costs have been rising due to the difficulties of obtaining the natural materials it needs. If SAH were to change its manufacturing process to use synthetic materials, this would allow it to reduce its costs and improve the performance of its yacht. Design innovations such as this can improve efficiency and reduce costs at the same time as meeting customers' requirements better.

Numbers of staff with relevant advanced qualifications – SAH employs school-leavers and trains them internally, unlike most of its competitors who employ university graduates who have studied yacht design and construction. This may be contributing to the criticism that SAH's yachts look old-fashioned, because SAH's staff are not familiar with new ideas and new techniques. In which case, it will be important that SAH either recruits some staff who are familiar with these new techniques, or sends its existing staff on external training courses so that they can learn them.

Similarly, the lack of staff with CAD/CAM experience appears to be slowing down the design process, which in turn could have a detrimental effect on SAH's cash flow.

Internal business perspective

Build time per yacht – If SAH was able to reduce the length of time it takes to build a yacht, it should be able to reduce the proportion of yachts it delivers late, sell more yachts (thereby increasing revenues and profits), and use its working capital more efficiently (in turn reducing the pressure on its cash flows).

Materials price variances – Whilst we could argue that using traditional skills and processes is a differentiating factor for SAH, in practice it appears that SAH's use of traditional processes and materials is actually reducing its competitiveness and profitability. For example, the prices of some of SAH's natural materials have risen by up to 40% in the last two years. Highlighting these price variances is important, and it may prompt SAH to change some aspects of its manufacturing process.

(b) (ii)

Conflicting measures

For a balanced scorecard to help improve the performance of an organisation, the measures chosen need to be congruent. However, this may not always be the case, and some measures may be seen as conflicting. For example, if SAH decides to send some of its designers on external training courses to learn how to use CAD/CAM techniques, this could be seen as conflicting with a measure to increase profits – in the short term, at least. It will be important for N to try to minimise any conflicts between the different measures in the scorecard.

Selecting measures

Given SAH's policy of recruiting school leavers, and the fact that the only control system currently in place is the standard costing system, it is debatable how many of the staff (if any) have experience of using a Balanced

Scorecard. Therefore, there are likely to be problems in selecting the most appropriate measures to use, and even **how many measures** to use.

It is important that SAH does not select too many measures, because this could lead to the impact of any results becoming lost in a sea of information. Equally, it is crucial that SAH selects measures that relate specifically to **value-adding processes**(*) and help it achieve its strategic aims, rather than simply selecting measures that are **easy to record**.

Again, though, the lack of experience may make it hard for SAH to formulate the performance measures it wants to use, particularly in relation to non-financial areas such as quality and innovation.

(*) : There could also be problems in agreeing what the key value-adding processes are. If these cannot be agreed, it will be impossible to determine what the most appropriate measures to use are.

Capturing information

Once the measures have been selected, and related performance targets set, SAH will need to capture the necessary information to see how well it is performing against those targets. It seems likely that the only performance information SAH currently records is manufacturing costs, meaning that N and the staff will need to devise ways of capturing the other information.

However, the ability to capture and record information may be limited by the scope of SAH's management information systems. The scenario doesn't mention whether SAH has any management information systems, but the company's traditional (almost archaic) culture and the age of its costing system, suggests that if it does have any systems they will be fairly basic.

Staff not understanding the need for the scorecard

SAH appears to be a very traditional company, which suggests that its staff may be reluctant to change. Given that SAH has reported a profit every year since its inception, and has been profitable using the current control system, the staff may not understand the reason why a more complex performance measurement system has to be introduced. In this case, they may resist the introduction of a new system, particularly, for example, if it means they now have to spend time recording different aspects of performance, rather than getting on with their jobs in the ways they are used to.

58 CCC car insurance

Text reference. The balanced scorecard is discussed in Chapter 14 of the BPP Study Text for E3.

Marking scheme

			Marks
(a)	For identifying that the Scorecard was developed to assist strategy implementation	1	
	Aligning each aspect of CCC's 'vision' to the perspectives of the Scorecard – 1 mark per aspect	Up to 4	
		Total	5

(b)	For appropriate recommendations for each perspective; correctly classified		
	Objectives – 1 mark each	Up to 4	
	Measures – 1 mark each	Up to 4	
	Targets – 1 mark each	Up to 4	
	Initiatives – 1 mark each	Up to 4	
		Total	16
(c)	For each drawback described – up to 2 marks each	Up to 4	
	Potential drawbacks include (but are not limited to): pursuit of one factor may hinder another; investment required; cultural change required/resistance to that change; may be complex to understand/ doesn't produce one single measure of performance.	Total	4
			25

(a)

Top tips. The requirement here does not ask you to advise what the Balanced Scorecard is, nor to describe what the four perspectives of it are. Instead, you are asked how using the Scorecard could help CCC deliver its value and strategy.

Did you notice that the four points in CCC's vision statement correspond very closely to the four perspectives of the scorecard?

Spotting this was crucial here, because it means that, if CCC introduces the Scorecard and then introduces performance measures for each perspective of the Scorecard, by doing so it should also address each aspect of the Vision statement.

Examiner's comments. Part (a) was not well answered. Most candidates chose to describe the four perspectives of the balanced scorecard, instead of discussing how the scorecard could assist in delivering the organisation's value and strategy. Although the scenario provided a vision statement which contained four statements which corresponded directly to the four balanced scorecard perspectives, very few candidates appeared to identify the link between CCC's vision statement and the balanced scorecard.

Strategic implementation – Although CCC has developed a vision statement and its overriding objective, it appears that it has been unable to implement its strategy successfully.

This highlights the importance of recognising strategic management as a process, involving strategic analysis, strategic choice and strategy implementation.

In order to develop its mission statement, vision statement and overriding objective, it seems likely that CCC has undertaken strategic analysis and made strategic choices. Therefore, the weakness in its strategic management process appears to be in its implementation.

Balanced Scorecard – Kaplan & Norton (who developed the Scorecard) suggested that one of its main uses is in enabling organisations to improve their strategic performance.

The scorecard seeks to translate mission and strategy into objectives and measures, in relation to the four perspectives in the scorecard; for example by setting measures and targets relating to each perspective. The Scorecard can also be used to communicate standards and targets to staff, and it can be used as a control mechanism. By providing the Directors with information on how CCC is performing against key measures, the Scorecard will enable them to assess how well CCC's strategy is being implemented, and what corrective action is required to improve its performance.

Scorecard perspectives – The four aspects of CCC's vision statement can be aligned to the four perspectives of the Scorecard:

Provide superior returns to our shareholders – This relates to the **financial perspective** of the scorecard: how CCC should create value for its shareholders to succeed financially.

Delight our customers – This reflects the **customer perspective** of the scorecard: how does CCC need to appear to its customers in order to achieve its vision.

Continually improve our business processes – This relates to the **internal business perspective** of the scorecard: what business processes CCC must excel at to achieve financial and customer objectives.

Learn from our mistakes and work smarter in the future – This illustrates the **innovation and learning perspective** of the scorecard: how can CCC continue to create value and maintain its competitive position through improvement and change?

If key performance measures were identified, and then monitored, for each of these perspectives, this should provide the Directors with more information with which to manage CCC's performance. In turn, this should help CCC implement its strategy more successfully.

(b)

Top Tips.

The key to this question is to define exactly what each of the aspects required is:

Objective – what CCC wants to achieve
Measure – a means of expressing the progress CCC is making towards an objective
Target – a specific value or deadline for achieving a measure
Initiative – the actions taken to achieve a target

Importantly, notice the distinction between measures and targets. Measures identify what is to be measured; targets are the specific values which CCC is aiming to achieve.

Note also that you are only asked to recommend suitable examples for each of the aspects; you do not have to give reasons to support your recommendation. Therefore your answers can be kept very brief.

The examples given in the answer below are not the only possible examples you could have given, and you would have earned marks if you recommended different examples, provided they were relevant and were attributed to the correct aspect (ie that what you recommended as a 'Measure' was indeed a measure and not a target.

The four perspectives which CCC should use, are the four perspectives identified in the Balanced Scorecard.

<u>Financial perspective</u>

Objective – To increase dividend yield on investors' shares

Measure – Dividend yield

Target – 8% dividend yield by the end of 20X3

Initiative – Improved customer retention to increase profits

Initiative – Cost cutting exercises or business process improvements designed to increase profits

<u>Customer perspective</u>

Objective – To increase customer satisfaction

Measure – Number of customer complaints

Target – Reduce the number of customer complaints to 1 per 100 transactions by the end of 20X3

Initiative – Increased staff training for sales executives

Measure – Number of customers renewing / not renewing their policies

Target – 95% of existing customers renew their policies in 20X2/20X3 (or Less than 5% of customers do not renew their policies)

Initiative – Properly promoted discount schemes linked to insurance renewals

Internal business perspective

Objective – Use up-to-date hardware and software

Measure – Age of PCs / Frequency with which PCs are replaced

Target – All PCs to be less than 2 years old by the end of 20X3

Initiative – Look to negotiate a deal with PC suppliers to provide new PCs at a competitive rate on an on-going basis.

Innovation and learning perspective

Objective – Raise the level of educational qualifications of CCC's staff

Measure – Number of staff with a higher education qualification (or Number of graduates employed)

Target – 50% of staff to have a higher education qualification by the end of 20X4

Initiative – Sponsor staff to attend part-time/evening higher education courses

(c)

Top Tips:

This question is essentially a test of knowledge, because there is no requirement to identify the drawbacks which CCC could face from using the Scorecard. Instead you are simply asked to discuss two drawbacks of the Balanced Scorecard itself.

However, it is important that the drawbacks you discuss relate specifically to the Balanced Scorecard, rather than being drawbacks of performance measurement in more general terms.

In our answer below we have suggested a number of potential drawbacks you could have discussed. However, you should only have discussed TWO, as instructed by the question requirement.

Difficulty in choosing measures – Some measures in the scorecard may conflict with each other. For example, the cost of training programmes (innovation and learning) may affect profits (financial). Sometimes it can be difficult to determine which combinations of measures will achieve the best results for a company overall.

Selecting measures – Companies may select measures because they are easy to measure, rather than selecting those which add value to the organisation. However, companies should measure those aspects of performance which are crucial in achieving their critical success factors, and in delivering value to their customers.

Appropriate measures – Measurement is only useful if it initiates appropriate action. Therefore measures should be developed by someone who understands the business processes concerned. If the measures are decided by senior managers or directors who do not understand the processes sufficiently, this could lead to inappropriate measures being chosen.

Time and cost taken to implement – It will take time for managers to decide what aspects of performance should be included in the scorecard. Time could also be required for training managers (and staff) how to use the Scorecard.

The Scorecard may also require investment in new software (for example, in order to measure additional aspects of performance). However, the benefits an organisation could gain from using the Scorecard may not justify the time and cost which will be incurred to introduce it.

Cultural change – For companies which have not used the Scorecard before, introducing it can require a significant cultural change. For example, if an organisation's current performance management system focuses solely on financial performance, the change to measuring (and managing) non-financial aspects of performance as well as financial ones could be difficult to achieve, particularly if it also affects reward schemes.

Given that introducing the Scorecard will be seen as a change, then there is also likely to be **resistance** to that change.

59 JALL independent retailer

Text reference. Issues around change management and overcoming resistance to change are discussed in Chapter 11 of your BPP Study Text. The Balanced Scorecard is covered in Chapter 14.

Marking scheme

		Marks
(a) (i) For each reason identified and explained	1	
	Total up to	6
(ii) For each way in which JALL could overcome resistance to change, discussed and applied to the scenario.	Up to 3	
(Candidates will be given credit if they apply either Lewin's 'Ice cube' model or Kotter & Schlesinger's methods of overcoming resistance to change.)		
	Total up to	7
(b) (i) For correctly identifying the four perspectives of the Scorecard	Up to 2	
For discussion of the way the Scorecard and its different perspectives can be used to manage performance	Up to 4	
	Total up to	6
(ii) For each relevant target identified, applied to a Scorecard perspective, and explained as to how it will incentivise performance	Up to 3	
	Total up to	6
	Total	25

Part (a) (i)

Top tips: The scenario provided a number of clues as to why JALL's staff, customers and suppliers may all resist the change in ownership. Remember that resistance to change won't only come from staff: customers and suppliers are also likely to be affected by the change, so they are likely to resist it too.

Examiner's comments: This question was well answered. Many candidates understood the reasons for possible resistance to change and applied their to the scenario.

Uncertainty about future – JALL is a long-established, family firm and its staff, customers and suppliers have all come to appreciate its values and culture. With the prospect of JALL being sold to LNR this could all change, but it is not clear what LNR's plans are for JALL.

This uncertainty about the future plans will prompt people to resist the change because they are unsure how it will affect them. The uncertainty will affect customers (will they still be able to buy stationery locally?), suppliers (will JALL continue to buy from them?) and staff.

Potential job losses – Perhaps the greatest uncertainty will be felt by JALL's staff who are not sure whether they will lose their jobs or not.

The fact that they could lose their jobs is, by itself, a reason for the staff to resist the change, but the fact that JALL has traditionally been a good place to work (with good morale, and bonuses every year) will intensify the resistance to change.

Lack of reasons – The uncertainty surrounding the change is made worse because it doesn't appear anyone has explained the reasons for the change. The staff in particular are likely to resist the change if they can't understand why it is necessary or why it is happening. JALL appears to have been a successful company, which makes the sudden change all the more unexpected.

The lack of any communication seems all the more surprising given that JALL's managers know their staff and major customers personally. This lack of communication could suggest that the sale has somehow been forced upon JALL which could again increase resistance to it.

Lack of skills – Another cause for concern, particularly among staff, is that even if they are not made redundant their jobs will change and they will need to learn new skills and working practices. For example, JALL appears to have been quite a traditional shop with no online sales, but the new owners might want to develop an online shop in which case staff may need to develop IT competences they do not currently have.

(ii)

Top tips: You could use two different frameworks for answering this requirement: one approach would be **Lewin's stage model of change** (unfreeze – change – refreeze), and possibly also **force field analysis** in the context of identifying ways of strengthening the driving forces for change and weakening the forces resisting change. The other approach would be to use Kotter & Schlesinger's different styles for overcoming resistance to change. The answer below is based on the **Kotter & Schlesinger** approach.

However, although Kotter & Schlesinger identify six approaches to overcoming resistance to change, we have only advised that five be used here, with "Manipulation and 'co-optation'" being the one omitted. Given the nature and context of the change, if staff feel they have been misled into supporting the changes, or given incomplete information about the changes, it is likely that they will continue to resist it in the longer term.

Importantly, however, whichever approach you took, you should not simply have provided a theoretical answer, but you should have applied the relevant model or process specifically to JALL and the scenario presented.

Examiner's comments: Candidates presented a good discussion of a range of methods for dealing with resistance to change. Many answers were based on Kotter & Schlesinger's methods of overcoming resistance, and, on the whole, candidates made some attempt to apply the methods to JALL.

Communication – One thing that appears completely absent so far is any communication about the **reasons for the change of ownership** and **how it will affect the main stakeholders (staff, suppliers and customers).** It is possible that if the stakeholders appreciate why the change is happening they might be more prepared to support, particularly if it won't affect them as much as they initially feared. For example, if customers are re-assured they will still be able to buy their stationery locally, in the same way they have previously done, then they are less likely to resist the change.

Participation and involvement – JALL's staff, in particular, are more likely to support the change if they are involved in it and helping to shape the company's future. For example, some of the staff could be invited to join **focus groups** to discuss aspects of JALL's integration into the LNR chain, and to try to minimise the need for compulsory redundancies.

Facilitation and support – Again, this is most relevant to the staff. Staff who are going to remain within the company but whose roles may change should be given **training** and support to help fulfil their new roles successfully. Alternatively, if any staff are made redundant, they should be given an **outplacement service** to help them find new jobs (for example, interview practice, or help with updating their CVs).

Negotiation and agreement – JALL's management should hold **discussions** with employees to resolve any areas of dispute about the change – for example, changes to terms and conditions, or salary changes.

The negotiations could also involve offering **incentives** to workers to encourage them to accept the changes – for example, if offering them additional payments to learn new skills and take on additional responsibilities.

Coercion – Although this should be seen as a last resort, management appear to have the power to force staff to accept the changes if they refuse to accept them voluntarily – for example, there do not appear to be any unions representing the staff. So, if staff continue to resist the changes, they could be told they will be made redundant if they are not prepared to work with the new regime.

This approach may be necessary if the other, more participatory approaches are unsuccessful. However, management need to beware that such any aggressive tactic may cause resentment among the remaining staff, even if the initial resistance to change has been overcome.

Part (b) (i)

> **Top tips**: As with so many E3 questions, it is important you read the requirement carefully here, and answer the question actually set. You are not asked to discuss the Balanced Scorecard model in general terms, but to discuss it specifically in the context of LNR managing its strategic performance.
>
> There were two marks (out of 6) available for identifying the four perspectives of the Balanced Scorecard, but the remaining four marks were earned for explaining how the LNR could use the scorecard to manage performance.
>
> Note, the requirement asks you to advise the management of LNR, not JALL. However, the requirement isn't entirely clear about whether you should be looking at ways the Balanced Scorecard could be used to manage JALL's strategic performance post-acquisition, or whether it is being used to manage LNR's overall strategic performance. The examiner's answer indicates that the first of these interpretations was the one he intended, however, the general gist of your answer should be the same whichever interpretation you had taken.
>
> **Examiner's comments**: Most candidates correctly identified the four perspectives of the Scorecard. However, few of them then adequately discussed how LRN could use the scorecard to manage its strategic performance.

Following the acquisition, LRN will want to ensure that JALL continues to perform successfully, and contributes to LRN achieving its strategic objectives.

Four perspectives - The balanced scorecard can be used to manage strategic performance by translating the organisation's vision and strategy into target measures in each of the four perspectives of the scorecard: **financial, customer, learning and growth (innovation)** and **internal business process** perspectives.

Target measures – The measures chosen should be those which are most integral to achieving LNR's strategy, and, as the scorecard emphasises, they are not confined to financial measures. For example, it is important to recognise the importance that customer focus and business processes can have on performance and the customer perspective and internal business process perspective respectively highlight this.

Performance management - Once the target measures have been established, LNR's management team should review actual performance against target as part of their periodic reporting process.

Provided the measures have been properly aligned to LNR's strategic objectives, this review process should help LNR manage strategic performance successfully. If a period end review indicates that performance in a certain measure is below target, then corrective action – in conjunction with the operational managers responsible for that business area - should be taken to improve it. In turn, if all the target measures are being achieved, then LNR should meet its strategic objectives.

(ii)

> **Top tips**: There are three key elements in the question requirement: (i) the use of targets; (ii) the Balanced Scorecard; (iii) incentivising staff performance.
>
> To score well you needed not only to explain how LNR could construct targets related to the Scorecard, but also to explain how these targets would help provide incentives to improve staff performance. As the examiner's comments indicate, few candidates actually did this.
>
> **Examiner's comments**. Many candidates failed to focus upon the need for targets within a staff incentive scheme, and instead just presented a range of Balanced Scorecard targets. In doing so, candidates failed to apply their targets to the question being asked. Once again, candidates must make sure they answer the question which has been set.

Alignment of objectives – It is important that the individual targets set for JALL's staff support LNR's overall strategic objectives.

Link to Scorecard measures – In the context of the Balanced Scorecard, individual performance management is a key component of strategic success. Linking staff targets to the scorecard measures can help achieve this success. Individual KPIs and action plans need to be linked to the Scorecard performance drivers. Therefore, the incentives (such as performance related pay) are designed to encourage individuals to achieve their targets, and in doing so, to enable the company to achieve its targets.

Hierarchy of scorecards (or objectives) – In this respect, there should be a hierarchy of scorecards within the group. So, for example, the JALL could have a company-wide scorecard; then the sales and marketing team could have a department scorecard based on the company-wide scorecard; and the sales managers and staff, in turn, have their own personal scorecards based on the department scorecard.

For example, JALL's overall vision and strategy might be: "To be the region's most popular retailer of office products and stationery."

In turn, extracts from the Scorecards could show:

Customer perspective: Extend product range

Marketing manager: Carry out market research to additional product lines capable of delivering additional revenue of € 250,000 per year.

Setting targets – The mechanism through which JALL's targets are set is likely to depend on the culture of the new organisation. If the culture is autocratic, the staff will be told what their targets are by their managers. If the culture is more participative, the staff are more likely to agree targets for the future with their managers. Either way, though, the targets will need to fit with the overall control measures identified in the Scorecard.

60 Computer company

Text reference. The balanced scorecard is discussed in Chapter 14 of the BPP Study Text for E3.

Marking scheme

			Marks
(a)	For identifying and correctly explaining each of the four components of the Balanced Scorecard	1 mark each	
		Total	4
(b)	For each appropriate and relevant measure, well justified and linked back to the question scenario.	Up to 2	
	Up to a maximum of 4 marks for each of the four perspectives		
		Total	16
(c)	For each relevant change management process discussed	Up to 2	
		Total	5
			25

Top tips.

Part (a) is a test of pure knowledge. However, be careful not to spend too long on this part. There are four marks available for an explanation of the four components of the Balanced Scorecard model – one mark per component. This means you only need to give a brief explanation for each component before moving on.

It is crucial that you read requirement for **part (b)** very carefully and notice that it asks for *measures*, not *targets*. So, for example; if you suggested that 'DD should ensure that all patents are registered' you would have scored no marks for this: it is a target, not a measure. However, you would have scored marks for including the measure 'Number of patented innovations.' This distinction may appear subtle, but once again it reinforces the importance of reading the question carefully, and answering the exact question that the examiner sets. A measure is a proposal for how performance should be measured in order to record and control it. A target is a statement of the level of performance which should be attained.

Note also that the question asks specifically for two measures for each of the components. If you gave more than two measures for any component you would only get marks for the first two you include.

Part (c) asks you to discuss the issues associated with introducing the balanced scorecard in the context of change management. Kaplan and Norton (who devised the balanced scorecard) produced a four stage approach for dealing with the practical problems of introducing the balanced scorecard for the first time. The answer below is based on their four stage approach. However, if you did not know this model, you could have still made some relevant points by applying more general principles of change management, such as the importance of keeping people informed about the changes, and the importance of explaining the need for the changes. Change management models such as Lewin's 'Unfreeze, move, refreeze' approach might also have been some help here.

Easy marks. Part (a) is a pure test of knowledge. If you had a good understanding of the Balanced Scorecard model, this should have given you some very easy marks.

Part (a)

The balanced scorecard aims to highlight the **financial and non-financial elements** of corporate performance, through measuring **four perspectives of performance**: financial, customer satisfaction, internal efficiency and innovation.

Financial perspective – This addresses the question, 'How can we succeed financially and create value for our shareholders?' and it covers measures such as growth, profitability, return on capital employed and shareholder value.

Customer perspective – This considers how an organisation must appear to its customers in order to achieve its vision. It asks the question 'What do new and existing customers expect of the organisation?' – aspects which could be measured in terms of quality, speed, reliability and value for money of the organisation's products.

Internal business perspective – This considers what business processes an organisation needs to excel at in order to achieve financial and customer objectives. For example, it could be measured in relation to the efficiency of the product development process.

Innovation and learning perspective – This considers how an organisation can continue to create value and maintain its competitive position through improvement and change. It could be measured, for example, in relation to the acquisition of new skills, or the development of new products.

Part (b)

Tutorial note. The question only asks you to provide **two** measures for each of the components of the balanced scorecard model. For tutorial purposes we have included a wider range of measures which would all have been relevant here in text boxes below, but you should only have included two measures for each component of the model. You would **not** have scored any additional marks if you included more than two measures for any of the components.

Some of the ideas may fit into more than one perspective; for example, the number of patents filed could be relevant to the internal business perspective or the innovation and learning perspective. However, you should not have simply repeated the same measure in more than one perspective, because you would not score any marks for the repeat.

Financial perspective

Cash flow – Currently, DD employs 30 scientists and engineers who are working on various research projects, but none of these projects have been made commercially available. Consequently, DD is not generating any sales revenue, and so has a negative cash flow. However, monitoring cash flow once it starts selling its products commercially will allow DD to measure how successful its sales are. DD cannot afford to continue with a negative cash flow if it is to become a successful commercial organisation.

Return on capital employed – DD does not have any shareholders, and is currently entirely dependent on the funding it receives from Mr X. However, as an entrepreneur Mr X will want to see a return on his investment. If DD does not start delivering an acceptable return on the capital Mr X has invested, he could withdraw his funding in favour of another investment opportunity.

NPV of R&D expenditure – Once DD's strategy changes to being a commercial organisation, it needs to focus more on projects whose financial benefits outweigh their costs. Measuring the NPV of projects will indicate how successfully they are achieving this.

Measuring NPV will also give an indication of how accurately DD forecasts the costs of developing a new product, and the level of sales it can generate from it. If DD's forecasts are over-optimistic, then it could be committing to project which will not generate value in the longer term.

Sales growth – Once DD starts marketing and selling its products commercially, looking at sales growth will provide a measure of how successful the products are in the marketplace.

Customer perspective

Customer feedback – DD has only been established for three years, and does not currently sell any of its processors. Therefore when DD starts selling commercially, it will be essential to develop a good reputation among customers and potential customers. Feedback from customers will provide a good measure of how well DD is delivering what its customers want.

Growth of market share – DD believes its innovative processor is significantly faster than any currently available. Therefore, once it introduces the processor commercially, DD should be able to gain market share from existing players in the market. Measuring the growth in their market share will enable DD to see how successfully it is doing this.

Percentage of sales from new products – A key factor in DD's growth over the longer term will be continuing to develop new products which meet customer needs better than any competitors' existing products can, so that DD builds up a balanced portfolio of products. One way DD can measure the success of new product development is by measuring sales from products developed in the last year as a percentage of total sales. Such a measure will indicate not only how successful DD is in its research and development of new products, but also how good it is at marketing them.

New customers acquired – As it is a new entrant into the market, a key factor in DD's commercial success will be its ability to attract new customers. Measuring the number of new customers acquired will enable DD to see how successfully it is doing this.

Internal business perspective

Actual introduction schedule compared to plan – One of the key changes which Mr X is looking to introduce at DD is moving the staff away from pure research projects onto the development of commercially viable products. One way he could introduce more discipline and structure over the development process is to develop a timetable for when new products become commercially available. Alongside this it would then be important to measure when the new products actually become commercially available compared to the original timetable.

Development vs research time – Another way of assessing how successfully the shift in focus from 'research' to 'research and development' is being adopted by the scientists will be to measure how much of their time is spent on pure research projects compared to how much is spent on their commercial development.

Time to develop new products – DD's cash flow will be affected by how quickly it can make new developments commercially available. One way of measuring the efficiency of the development process will be measuring the time between a new research idea being registered and it being developed into a commercially available product.

Level of defect rates – It is likely that DD will emphasise the speed of its processor when marketing it, as a source of differentiation from competitors' products. However, given that DD is aiming to supply superior products it needs to ensure that they all work as intended. A measure looking at the level of defects would help ensure that this desired level of quality is maintained.

Innovation and learning perspective

Number of patents filed – Although DD's engineers have published a number of academic papers, they have not filed any patents. However, patenting new ideas could help DD develop a competitive advantage over its rivals. Therefore, measuring the number of patents filed will indicate the scientist's success in developing commercially viable new products.

Number of modifications required in product development – Initially, it is likely that the pure research ideas will have to go through a number of modifications and prototypes as the scientists develop them into a commercially viable product. However, as the scientists become used to developing their ideas they should need less modifications to develop their initial idea into a product. Therefore measuring the number of modifications required will indicate how successfully the scientists are adapting to the new commercial process.

Cost per patent filed – Measuring the cost per patentable discovery would indicate the effectiveness of DD's researchers in developing new products.

Part (c)

As DD becomes more commercial it will need more **quantitative measures** of performance, and it can use the balanced scorecard to provide these. DD will also need to look at **external measures** alongside internal ones, and again it can use the balanced scorecard to introduce this balance.

However, the proposed change in strategy and culture will have a major impact on DD's staff and so it will have to be managed carefully because Mr X is keen to avoid losing any of the current research staff.

To this end, the balanced scorecard should be introduced via a four-stage approach.

Translating the vision – Mr X will need to explain what DD's new, more commercial, focus will mean to the research scientists in terms of their everyday work. Mr X will also need to explain the relevance of the four perspectives of the scorecard to the scientists' work, and in particular he will need to emphasise the impact of customer requirements compared to the previous scenario where the scientists work was governed purely by academic interest.

Communicating and linking – Once the overall approach has been explained, DD's strategy needs to be linked to departmental and individual objectives. Mr X should discuss and agree objectives with the researchers and the marketers based on the four perspectives of the balanced scorecard.

It is important to include the marketers as well as the researchers so that some of the new research going forward is market-led rather than being determined by academic interest.

Business planning – The scorecard can be used to help prioritise objectives and allocate resources in order to allow DD to make the best progress towards its strategic goals. At the moment, DD does not have a business plan and the scientists appear largely autonomous in their work. However, Mr X should develop a business plan and support that plan by ensuring that the scientists' efforts are concentrated on those projects which look like they will be the most successful commercially.

Feedback and learning – It will take time for the changes in culture and strategy to become embedded at DD. However, Mr X and all the staff will need to use feedback on performance issues constructively to promote progress against four perspectives of the balanced scorecard.

One area which may need to be revisited in the light of feedback is the balance of time the research staff spend on pure research projects compared to commercial development projects. Allowing the scientists sufficient time to pursue their own interests will help sustain their motivation, and should encourage them to remain with the company; but this needs to be balanced with the need for them to spend enough time on commercial developments to sustain the company's financial performance.

61 Global environmental charity

Text reference. The balanced scorecard is discussed in Chapter 14 of your BPP Study Text. Resistance to change, and overcoming resistance to change are discussed in Chapter 11.

Top tips. When answering **Part (a)**, it is very important that you recognise the context of the scenario. E is a charity, it is global, and it has 45 autonomous divisions – one for each country in which it operates. E has also been criticised for the lack of control and accountability within it, because each independent division does pretty much want it wants to.

So, the balanced scorecard can help E by establishing clearer goals for the organisation as a whole, and improving goal congruence. Importantly also, the scorecard doesn't just focus on profit measures, which could be useful since E is a charity rather than a company seeking to maximise profits.

However, given the apparent lack of control within E at the moment, will the Board and the CEOs have the skills to introduce the balanced scorecard successfully? How much will the culture of the organisation need to change? Will the CEOs resent it as a challenge to their autonomy / authority?

This last question provides a link between parts (a) and (b) of the question. If the divisional CEOs see the introduction of the balanced scorecard as a threat to their autonomy this is a reason why they might resist it.

Note that for **part (b)** you are specifically asked to discuss **four** reasons why the CEOs might resist the changes; so make sure your answer clearly discussed four separate reasons. Also, remember that you were asked to 'discuss' the reasons, so simply presenting a list of reasons would not have scored well. Similarly, make sure your answer focuses specifically on reasons why the CEOs in E would resist the change, rather than simply discussing general reasons why people might resist change.

Although you should still relate your answer for **part (c)** to the scenario, Kotter & Schlesinger's five ways of managing resistance to change should provide a good framework here. However, remember it is the CEOs who are resisting the change, so make sure your suggestions are appropriate to their position in the organisation.

Part (a)

Advantages

Help set goals – Currently the CEOs' meetings usually finish with no clear decisions about a unified direction of the charity to take. Using the scorecard will provide a framework to establish goals and objectives for the CEOs to work towards.

At the moment, the divisions all seem to act independently, largely because no clear decisions about strategy are agreed. Having the scorecard in place should help E focus on its key strategic goals, and should therefore make it harder for divisions to justify acting independently.

Goal congruence – The balanced scorecard will force the divisional CEOs to look at all aspects of the charity's objectives, and make them employ success measures for their particular division that support the corporate goals of the organisation as a whole.

Range of perspectives – The balanced scorecard looks at a range of perspectives rather than only financial, profit-driven ones. This is likely to be appropriate for E, since it is a charity and therefore its objectives are not primarily driven by shareholder value or profitability.

Value for money – Although E does not have shareholders, it still needs to show its donors that it is using the money they have donated effectively and efficiently and for the benefit of the causes it supports. If E adopts the balanced scorecard, it could set targets for how efficiently it uses its funds, and could then report to its donors about how well it has used the money that has been raised.

Internal and external factors – The balanced scorecard will encourage the CEOs to look at both internal and external factors. The environment is becomingly increasingly competitive, so E will need to find innovative ways of attracting funds, but it will also need to make sure its own internal processes are as efficient as possible so that as much of its money as possible can be allocated to its main goal – protecting endangered species and habitats.

Disadvantages

Too much information – The scorecard will lead to the CEOs having a wide range of performance measures to aim for, and being provided with a large amount of information about how their divisions have performed against those measures.

There is a danger that the CEOs (with no experience of any similar controls) will **not know how to interpret this information** or what to do with it. In which case, there is a danger they might simply ignore the information from the scorecard.

Equally, there is a danger that some of the measures could give **conflicting signals** to the CEOs, and so they may interpret the results incorrectly. The CEOs are likely to need quite a lot of training and guidance to use the scorecard.

Poorly constructed measures – E has not had a performance measurement system anything like the balanced scorecard before. There is a danger that if it introduces the scorecard, but the scorecard measures are poorly selected, they could generate responses which hadn't been foreseen and could actually damage performance rather than improving it. For example, although E needs to improve control and accountability, if the measures focus too much on these aspects of performance, then E could lose sight of the overall need to maintain its donations.

Applicability of measures – One of the four perspectives of the scorecard is 'Customers', but E doesn't have 'customers' in the sense, for example, that a retail organisation does. The Supervisory Board will have to clarify what each of the four perspectives means for E (for example, 'customers' could be 'beneficiaries') otherwise there is a danger that the divisional CEOs will view the scorecard as being irrelevant and will ignore it.

Concerns about poorly constructed measures or inapplicable measures mean that E will have to **validate the measures it proposes to use** very carefully before it actually begins to use the scorecard.

Culture change – Currently, the CEOs enjoy a lot of autonomy and have largely ignored any direction given to them by the Supervisory Board. For the balanced scorecard to be implemented, there will need to be a significant change in this corporate culture so that the CEOs follow the corporate plan rather than acting autonomously. The CEOs are likely to resist such a change.

Time to implement – The need to select appropriate measures to use and the potential cultural change involved, mean that the scorecard will not be a quick solution to E's problems. It seems that the Board view the introduction of a new performance measurement and control system as a matter of urgency. However, it is likely to take a considerable amount of time to develop, and implement, an appropriate scorecard.

Part (b)

Note: Make sure you clearly identify the **four** reasons you are discussing in turn.

1. **Fear of unknown** – Although the Supervisory Board have decided to introduce the new performance measurement system, there is no evidence that they have explained to the CEOs **what changes are going to be introduced** and **how the changes will affect them**. Even if the CEOs have been told a balanced scorecard system is going to be introduced, they may not know what this is. Consequently, the CEOs may be resisting the changes because they are an unknown quantity to them.

2. **Don't appreciate need for change** – The Supervisory Board have not explained to the CEOs why the changes are necessary. The CEOs may not be aware of the criticisms of E for its lack of direction. If they think E is performing better than it actually is, they may not appreciate the need for more formalised performance measurement and control. In which case, they might resist the changes as simply being bureaucracy being imposed on them, rather than appreciating that they are designed to help improve E's performance.

3. **Potential loss of power** – At the moment, the CEOs have a high degree of autonomy. However, they may be concerned that the introduction of a more rigorous performance measurement system will reduce this autonomy, and make them subject to more control.

   In particular, specific CEOs may resist the changes if they are worried about the performance of their divisions which might not be performing as well as others. By having a more effective performance measurement system, E will be able to identify those divisions which are not performing very well, but this is something it might not have been able to do previously.

4. **Lack of consultation** – It appears that the Supervisory Body have decided to implement the changes without any consultation with the CEOs. Given that the CEOs are relatively senior members of E, it is likely that some of them will be upset that they have not been consulted about the changes. Consequently, as a reaction to the lack of consultation, they will resist the changes.

Part (c)

Communication is crucial in overcoming resistance to change.

As a first step in overcoming the resistance to change, the Supervisory Board needs to communicate the reasons **why** the change is needed, and **how** the change will be introduced to the CEOs.

After this initial communication, the following steps could also be taken:

Education – The CEOs also need to be educated about the balanced scorecard: what it is intended to do, and how it should be used.

Participation – The CEOs should be consulted about the scorecard and encouraged to participate in designing the measures. If the CEOs feel they have contributed to the new performance measurement system they are less likely to resist it.

Negotiation – Some of the CEOs may still resist parts of the change, despite communication and education. The Supervisory Board may need to negotiate with the CEOs and may have to make some concessions to get the CEOs to agree the changes.

Manipulation – If some of the CEOs continue to resist the changes, the Board could try to make these CEOs feel guilty for doing so; for example, by explaining that the changes are proposed for the good of the organisation as a whole, and that their resistance threatens this greater good.

Coercion – If the CEOs continue to resist all 'voluntary' attempts to make them accept the changes, the Board could force them to do so. This might even involve threatening them with redundancy if they do not accept the changes and endorse the new performance measurement system.

62 RCH

Text reference. The 'strategic analysis, strategic choice, and strategic implementation' model of strategic management is discussed in Chapter 1 of your BPP Study Text. Critical success factors (CSFs) and key performance indicators (KPIs) are covered in Chapter 14.

Marking scheme

			Marks
(a)	For each valid point point:	1 mark each	
	Valid points could include: (i) a definition of strategic implementation; (ii) explanation that the three elements of the model are equally important; (iii) importance of interdependence between the elements; (iv) the model is not linear; (v) implementation is crucial if strategic plans are to be delivered.	Total	5
(b)	For each CSF identified:	1	
		Total	4
(c)	For each relevant KPI identified: 1 mark each	Up to 8	
	For recommendation why KPI is relevant / appropriate: 1 mark each	Up to 8	
	(No more than 2 KPIs accepted for any CSF)		
		Total, up to	16
			25

Part (a)

Top tip: The Examiner had intended that candidates would firstly define 'strategic implementation' and then discuss how it relates to strategic analysis and strategic choice (as shown in Johnson, Scholes and Whittington's model.)

However, it appears that many candidates didn't answer the question set, and did little more than define strategic implementation and describe what it involves. In doing so, they failed to explain that without implementation a strategic plan achieves nothing, and they failed to highlight the interdependence between the different elements of the model, which is a crucial aspect of it.

Examiner's comments: This question was generally not answered well, because most candidates failed to answer the question set. They defined 'strategic implementation' but failed to discuss why it was part of the model. Whilst a number of candidates adequately described the three elements of the model they failed to explain the interdependencies between them.

The focus of **strategic analysis** is on understanding the current strategic position of an organisation. **Strategic choice** involves choosing between the alternative strategies the organisation can pursue, while **strategic implementation** looks at how these strategies are actually put into practice.

Strategic implementation is the conversion of the strategy into detailed plans or objectives for operating units. Therefore it is a vital part of the strategic management process, because a strategy can only start delivering benefits to an organisation once it has been put into practice. In order to be beneficial to an organisation, a strategy must be able to be implemented. In this respect, the focus on strategic implementation highlights key issues such as resource availability, organisational structure and change management.

Johnson, Scholes and Whittington emphasise that the strategic management process should not be seen as a linear model, as for example, the traditional rational model portrays it. Rather, strategic implementation is **inter-**

linked with both strategic analysis and strategic choice. For example, in the process of implementing a strategy, an organisation might discover features of its resources and structure which will lead to it to re-evaluate its assessment of strategic position and strategic choices.

Part (b)

Top tips: Part (i) requires you to 'idenfify' four relevant CSFs, The verb is important here, as is the mark allocation: there are only 4 marks available. So you should not have spent time discussing, explaining or or justifying the CSFs you choice: simply 'identify' 4 suitable CSFs from the scenario and then move on. However, make sure you identify CSFs rather than KPIs. Also, note that the examiner insisted that financial performance was not a CSF, and so would gain no marks here or in part (ii). (see the Examiner's comments below.)

For Part (ii), you should have used the four CSFs you identified in part (i) and then identified two KPIs for each CSF – meaning you identified 8 KPIs in total. However, to score well in this question you also needed to provide clear reasons why the KPIs you chose were relevant and appropriate to each CSF identified.

Examiner's comments:

Part (i) was reasonably well answered with most candidates identifying suitable CSFs relating to customer satisfaction and product quality. However, some candidates tried to use the four headings from the balanced scorecard but this was not considered appropriate because financial performance is not a critical success factor. Also, some candidates did not appear to understand the difference between CSFs and KPIs, and identified a range of KPIs where CSFs were required.

Part (ii) was generally not answered well. Many of the KPIs provided were not measures, but were recommended activities or processes (for example, carrying out student surveys.) The key element of a KPI is that is has a measurable aim.

In addition to this weakness, very few candidates explained why the KPIs they recommended were suitable to the corresponding CSF, or to the context of TDM.

(i) Four critical success factors which be appropriate for TDM are:

- **Customer satisfaction** with courses and learning materials
- **Employee satisfaction**
- The **quality** of its teaching and materials
- **Reputation** and brand image

(ii) KPIs for each of the CSFs could be:

Customer satisfaction

Student satisfaction rating – at the end of a course, or at the end of a module within a course, students could be asked to complete a questionnaire rating their satisfaction with various aspects of the course (for example, the knowledge levels of the staff, the quality of the supporting materials, and the approachability / availability of staff to ask them questions).

If students are happy with the level of tuition they receive, they are more likely to book on subsequent courses with TDM than if they are dissatisfied with the courses. Similarly, they may share their experiences with their peers, in turn influencing their decision about where to book courses. Consequently, TDM needs to ensure that student satisfaction levels are maintained as high as possible, and it is important that TDM knows how its students (its customers) feel about the services it offers.

Client retention – A number of the students attending the courses aimed at professional qualifications are likely to have been funded by their employers. If employers continue to send their students to TDM rather than one of its rivals in the market, this suggests they are happy with the level of tuition and service their students are receiving. The pass rates that students achieve are likely to be a significant influence on client satisfaction in this respect.

Employee satisfaction

Staff turnover – The quality of TDM's teaching staff is crucial in maintaining customer satisfaction, so it is important for TDM to retain its best staff. TDM has been experiencing an increasing rate of employee turnover, and this could be indicative of dissatisfaction amongst the staff. The management at TDM should be keen to prevent this upward trend in staff turnover from increasing, making this an important measure to look at.

Staff absenteeism – High levels of absence are likely to also indicate dissatisfaction among the staff. If absenteeism is rising, in conjunction with employee turnover, then there is a danger that the quality of service provided to students will suffer. For example, if an experienced lecturer phones in 'sick' at short notice, their classes may have to be taken by an inexperienced lecturer who is not such an expert in a subject, meaning the students could receive lower quality tuition.

Quality of teaching and materials

Market share – TDM currently has the largest market share in its sector, despite carrying out relatively little marketing activity, and despite new entrants continually entering the market. It will important to monitor TDM's market share, because the share of the market TDM can capture will have a direct impact on its revenues and consequently on the wealth of RCH's shareholders. Customers will only continue to use TDM if they feel it is providing courses and materials which are high quality, and also which offer value for money. If market share starts to fall, it may be an indication TDM is not delvering this value for money to its customers.

Accreditations – TDM's courses will be accredited by academic and professional bodies. TDM has always concentrated on the quality of its courses and learning materials, so external accreditations will provide an independent corroboration of this quality. The quality of course tuition and learning materials, in turn, is likely to feed back into the level of customer satisfaction with TDM's courses.

Reputation and brand image

Brand reputation – TDM has never seen the need for market and customer research, and has always had a good reputation. However, given the continuing entrance of new competitors into the market, TDM needs to ensure that its brand reputation is maintained. This is important if TDM is to ensure potential customers will choose to come on its courses rather than going to one of its competitors.

Pass rates – TDM's students consistently achieve passes on a par with the national average. However, if some of TDM's rivals regularly achieve passes rates above the national average the competitors will be able to use this as a marketing message to try to win business away from TDM – particularly in respect of the professional qualifications business. If students, or their employers, think that selecting one tuition provider in preference to another can affect their chances of passing their exam, they are likely to select the tuition provider with the highest pass rate.

63 RTF

Text reference: The Balanced Scorecard is covered in Chapter 14 of the Study Text.

Part (a)

Top tip: This requirement is a test of knowledge only. You do not need to relate the balanced scorecard to the scenario: just explain briefly what the four perspectives are. And notice there are only 4 marks available here – in other words, 1 for each perspective.

The balanced scorecard is designed to provide information to help measure financial and non-financial performance.

Financial perspective – The financial aspect of the model encourages a business to consider how well it is creating value for its shareholders and whether it is succeeding financially? It looks at traditional financial measures such as growth, profitability and shareholder value.

Customer perspective – The customer aspect of the model focuses on how a business needs to appear to its customers in order to achieve its strategic vision. This perspective looks at what new and existing customers value from a business – for example, how important are cost, reliability, or quality to them? Is the business delivering what its customers want?

Innovation and Learning perspective – This aspect of the model looks at how well a business creates value and improves its competitive position through innovation and change. For example, how successful is it at acquiring new skills, or developing new products?

Internal business processes – This perspective considers the processes which a business needs to excel at in order to achieve its financial or customer-based objectives, and assesses how well those processes are performing..

Part (b)

Top tips: You are asked to recommend two appropriate measures for each of the four perspectives, so you need to recommend eight in total. However, do not recommend more than two for any individual perspective. You will only score marks for the first two recommendations you make.

We have shown two measures for each perspective, but there are a number of others you could have suggested and which would have been equally valid. For example, some alternative measures you could have suggested are:

– Financial perspective: net profit, return on capital employed
– Customer perspective: market share, number of customer complaints
– Innovation and learning perspective: number of new designs added to the library, professional qualifications or continuing professional development (CPD) undertaken by staff.
– Internal business processes: % of partner time spent on design work; number of contacts in database; number of contacts added to database.

Note that the requirement asks for *measures*, not *targets*, so you only have to indicate how performance should be measured (for example, by measuring gross profit), not the level of performance which should be attained (for example, to increase gross profit by x%).

Finally, note the mark allocation between parts (b) and (c) of the question. There are only 8 marks available for (for 8 recommendations!) in part (b), but there are 13 marks available for part (c). So although you may think part (b) looks easier, do not spend too long on it! You have only got time for a very brief discussion of each measure.

Financial perspective

Gross profit – There appear to be concerns about recording time spent on jobs and the resulting cost of jobs, so it will be important for RTF to measure and review the profitability of its jobs.

Profit per contract – There are concerns about the amount of time spent on designing 'one-off' houses. Measuring the profitability of these contracts would highlight whether this time is well spent or not.

Customer perspective

Number of repeat contracts – RTF has spent a lot of time and effort establishing a database of contacts, and building relationships with local government employees. However, RTF needs to be able assess whether these efforts are worthwhile, or whether it might be more profitable to look for new business elsewhere.

Number of new customers attracted – In order to increase revenues and grow the business, RTF will need to attract new customers. Measuring and analysing this area could also show the relative number of new customers each area of the business – government schemes or individual houses – is attracting.

Alternative measure:

New customers for 2020Design package - Selling the computerised design package marks a significant change in RTF's business strategy. It will be important to measure how successful the marketing manager is in licensing agents and selling the package.

Innovation and learning perspectives

Number of 'one-off' houses designed in the period – Designing one-off houses allows the partners the scope to express their creativity and produce innovative designs. It is important that RTF's partners continue to develop innovative ideas, because innovation could be a source of competitive advantage, especially for attracting wealthy individuals who are looking for 'designer' houses.

Technical qualifications earned by staff – RTF has invested in improving the education and technical background of its staff, so the success of this investment can be measured by looking at the technical qualifications its staff earn. Gaining relevant qualifications will also hopefully improve staff members' ability to do their jobs to a high standard.

Internal business perspectives

Number of projects completed on time and within budget – The focus in the local government housing scheme is on re-using library designs to produce homes on time and within budget. This measure will help show how efficiently RTF is doing this. The focus on achieving budget targets also links directly back to the financial perspectives of the scorecard dealing with profitability.

Design time per contact – The Management Accountant is concerned about the amount of time the partners are spending on the designs for 'one-off' houses. This measure will indicate how much longer the designs for the one-off houses take than designs based on library materials. This measure can also, more generally, provide an indication of staff efficiency, although RTF must be careful to ensure not encourage a culture in which staff sacrifice design quality in the quest for speed.

Part (c)

Top tips: Although this part of the requirement is probably the hardest, it is worth over half the marks for the whole question, so you cannot pass the question without picking up some marks here.

Kaplan and Norton (who devised the Balanced Scorecard) produced a four stage approach for organisations introducing the Scorecard for the first time. The answer below is based on this four stage approach.

However, if you did not know this approach you could still have earned some marks by applying more general principles of change management, such as the importance of communication and explaining the need for change.

However, you must not let your answer become a general discussion about change management. Remember, the question specifically asks how the Scorecard can be used to achieve the required changes.

Changes in strategy and culture

RTF is diversifying the scope of its activities, by starting to sell the 2020Design package in addition to its core architectural business.

Marketing and sales are likely to become a much more important part of the business, as illustrated by the recruitment of a dedicated Marketing Manager. As the business increases its **commercial focus** it will need more **quantitative performance measures**, and it can use the balanced scorecard to provide these.

However, RFT does not appear to have any **systematic way of measuring performance**, so introducing a Balanced Scorecard approach represents quite a significant change. Therefore, the introduction will need to be carefully managed.

To this end, the Balanced Scorecard should be introduced via a four-stage approach.

1. **Translating the vision** – Vision and strategy are at the centre of the Scorecard, and the four Scorecard perspectives are designed to help an organisation achieve its vision and strategy.

   RTF's current vision - focussing purely on design by RTF - may no longer be appropriate once it starts to sell the computerised design package.

   There are two implications of this:

   Developing a new vision – The partners need to consider how the development of the '2020 Design' package should be incorporated in the business' vision statement. If '2020 Design' is being sold to allow people to produce their own designs then the vision statement 'Your future designed by RTF: Today!' is no longer appropriate.

   Supporting the new vision – The partners need to communicate the change in vision to the staff in the business, so that the staff understand the logic for the change, and also how (if at all) the change will affect them.

2. **Communicating and linking** – For its new strategy to be successful, RTF needs to ensure that its operational objectives support its strategy and help it achieve its strategy.

   The Balanced Scorecard approach is designed to help organisations align their operational objectives with their strategies, but RTF has previously not had any systematic way of doing this.

   Structured objectives – The partners should discuss and agree objectives with the staff, so that the staff are working towards individual objectives which support RTF's overall strategy.

It will be particularly important that the Marketing Manager is also given objectives to work towards, since '2020Design' is a new project but also a potentially significant new income stream for the business.

If the business is split into divisions (eg local government housing, one-off housing) then divisional objectives should be set, linking the partnership's overall vision to individual staff objectives.

Reward management – We do not know whether RTF already has any performance-related pay (PRP) schemes for its staff, but it is possible that it could introduce a PRP scheme to reward staff for achieving their objectives.

3. **Business planning** – The scenario does not tell us anything about RTF's business plans, but given the lack of structured performance measurement, it is unlikely that RTF prepares any detailed business plans.

   However, the Scorecard could be used to help **prioritise objectives** and **allocate resources**, and in this respect it could help RTF develop a business plan for how best to achieve its strategic goals.

   Having a more structured approach to measuring performance could also encourage RTF to focus on the aspects of the business which look like they will be the most successful commercially.

   The **Marketing Manager** has a very important role in trying to identify the level of sales the '2020Design' package can achieve. Although RTF's market research has indicated that the package will be a viable commercial product, there is still a degree of uncertainty about the level of sales it can actually deliver.

4. **Feedback and learning** – The partners and staff at RTF will not only have to get used to using the balanced scorecard, but they will also have to adjust to the change in their strategy as a result of launching the '2020Design' package.

   They will realise that RTF is experiencing a significant period of change, but the partners need to make sure this change is viewed positively, and that they use the feedback on performance issues identified by the Scorecard in a constructive way.

   If the staff see that the changes allow them **new opportunities** they are more likely to support the changes than if they see the Scorecard as a way of imposing bureaucratic control, or the '2020Design' project as being a precursor to staff cuts.

   For example, measures in the 'Innovation and Learning' perspective might indicate there is an opportunity for staff training courses which allow staff to develop new skills, such that they could take on more of the 'one-off' design work which the partners currently do, allowing the partners to devote more time to promoting '2020 Design' at a strategic level.

64 B Supermarkets

Text references: Franchising as a method of growth is covered in Chapter 6 of the BPP Study Text. Sustainability is discussed in Chapter 2.

Marking scheme

				Marks
(a)	(i)	Calculating royalty fee (1 mark) and service and marketing contributions (1 mark)	Up to 2	
		Calculating number of franchises required	Up to 2	
			Total up to	4
	(ii)	Calculating initial outflow	1	
		Calculating annual inflows	1	
		Calculating PV factor (outflow/inflows) to break even [2.395]	1	
		Identifying when PV factor is achieved, using 12% discount rate	1	
		Identifying simply payback period	1	
			Total up to	4

(b)	Advising on marketing/branding factors which could affect the desirability of investing in the discount store franchise – up to 2 marks per relevant factor.		
	Relevant factors include: customer preferences; B's reputation; brand strength; competition; exclusivity; marketing support.	Up to 12	
	Advising on risk factors which could affect the desirability of investing in the discount store franchise – up to 2 marks per relevant factor.		
	Relevant factors include: length of franchise; opportunity cost; attitude to risk; reliability of estimates; investment in equipment.	Up to 10	
	Advising on implementation/operational factors which could affect the desirability of investing in the discount store franchise – up to 2 marks per relevant factor.		
	Relevant factors include: rules and guidelines; on-going royalty fees, and service fees; training provided; equipment provided.	Up to 10	
		Total up to	17
(c)	Evaluating how well the discount stores fit with each of B's environmental indicators:		
	Consumption of kilowatt hours – up to 2 marks	Up to 2	
	Number of free disposable plastic bags issued – up to 2 marks	Up to 2	
	Greenhouse gas emissions – up to 2 marks	Up to 2	
	Local amenity projects – up to 1 mark	1	
	Modes of distribution and transport – up to 3 marks	Up to 3	
		Total up to	10
(d)	For advising on the advantages of introducing the reformed planning and control system throughout B supermarkets – up to 2 marks per relevant advantage.	Up to 10	
	For advising on the disadvantages of introducing the reformed planning and control system throughout B supermarkets – up to 2 marks per relevant disadvantage.	Up to 10	
		Total up to	15
		Total	50

Top tips:

The calculations in **part (a)** should have been a very straight-forward break even calculation. You needed to calculate the royalty, service and marketing contribution fees B receives from each franchise *per year* (not per month), and then use this to calculate how many franchise it needs to grant in order to earn the €3 million income it requires per year.

(a)

	Per month (€)	Per Year (€)
Revenue per discount store	100,000	1,200,000
B's income per discount store		
Royalty fee (15% of revenue)	15,000	180,000
Service fee (5% of revenue)	5,000	60,000
Marketing contribution fee (5% of revenue)	5,000	60,000
	25,000	**300,000**

(Note: Fixed costs and variable operating costs are a cost to the stores, not to B)

B's minimum required income is €3 million per year. As each franchise store in Country P is expected to generate €300,000 income for B, it needs to grant at least **10 franchises** in order to generate the required income.

Part (b)

> **Top tip.**
>
> **Part (b) (i)** should have been another relatively straight-forward calculation; this time an NPV calculation. The franchisees incur an initial outflow, and then receive net cash inflows in subsequent periods. The key issue here is at what point the discounted value of the net cash inflows covers the initial cash outflow.

(i)

	Year 0 (€)	Year 1 (€)
Inflows		
Revenue (100,000 per month)		1,200,000
Outflows		
Franchise fees	60,000	
Training fee	20,400	
Equipment fee	150,000	
Royalty fee, service fee and marketing contribution fee payable (25% of revenue)		300,000
Fixed Costs (€2,000 per month)		24,000
Variable operating costs (65% of revenue)		780,000
Net inflow/(outflow)	(230,400)	96,000

Cumulative discount factor required for a franchisee to break even (230,000 / 96,000): 2.395.

The estimated cost of capital for entrepreneurs in Country P is 12%, which means a franchisee would need 3 years for a franchise to become financially worthwhile.

[*Tutorial Note*: The cumulative present value after 3 years is 2.402, using a discount factor of 12%. The franchisee needs a cumulative discount factor of 2.395 to break even.]

Using a simple payback method, with no discounting, a franchisee still needs 2 years and 5 months to pay back their initial investment.

(ii)

Top tips

Part (b) (ii) - The focus of this question is specifically on the desirability of investing in a franchise for a *discount store in Country P* (ie the situation described in the scenario), not about the desirability of investing in a franchise more generally.

Also, note the focus of your answer needs to be on the *entrepreneurs*. You have been asked about the factors which could influenced whether or not entrepreneurs decide to invest in the franchise – not, for example, the factors which could influence whether or not B decides to grant franchises in Country P.

Finally, note that the requirement only refers to 'factors' which are *likely to influence* the entrepreneurs, rather than whether these factors will make the entrepreneurs want to invest in the franchise or not. In other words, you need to give advice about the factors the entrepreneurs should consider when deciding whether or not to invest in a franchise, not what that decision itself should be.

The requirement provided you with three headings and you should have used these to structure your answer. Equally, you should have tried to come up with a range of points for each heading rather than, for example, concentrating on marketing/branding issues, and making very few points under the other headings.

For the second of the three headings (risk) you should also think about the relevance of the figures you calculated in part (b) (i). One factor which is likely influence the desirability of investing in a franchise will be the period for which the franchise is granted. If the franchise period is less than the period which makes it financially worthwhile for an franchisee to invest, how will this affect the desirability of having a franchise?

Marketing/Branding

Use of B's name – By investing in a franchise, the entrepreneur will be able to use B's name and its business model. B has been trading since 1963, and has established itself as a major, multi-national grocery business. It is one of the largest retailing companies in the world, and already has 5,168 discount stores within Europe.

In this respect, a potential entrepreneur might be attracted by the opportunity of becoming part of such a well-established and successful business model.

However, although the size of B's business means that its brand name should be known internationally, the fact that it does not currently conduct any business in P may mean that its brand is less strong there than in countries in which it does already operate.

Equally, because customer tastes and preferences differ from country to country, there is no guarantee that B's business model or brand will be attractive in P.

Competition – There aren't currently any discount stores in Country P.

On the one hand, this could be seen as an **opportunity** for the potential entrepreneurs. Because B's stores will be the first discount stores in P, this could give them a competitive advantage by virtue of being market leaders.

On the other hand this could be a **weakness**. The reason why there are currently no discount stores in P may be that the concept of discount stores is not attractive to the residents of P. B does not currently conduct any business in P, which may mean it does not understand the tastes and preferences of its customers properly. If the discount store model as a whole proves unsuccessful in P, then any decision to invest in one of the franchises is likely to be equally unsuccessful for the entrepreneurs.

Therefore, the entrepreneurs should undertake extensive market research and analysis before deciding whether to invest in a franchise. This research should assess customers' attitudes to discount stores, and whether they would use them. Equally the research should assess what value B's brand holds for customers in P, and whether this would encourage (or discourage) them from using the discount stores.

Alongside the customer-focused research, the entrepreneurs should also investigate the likely strength and speed of competitors' reaction if the discount store model proves successful. In this way, they can begin to assess whether, or for how long, B will be able to sustain any competitive advantage in Country P.

Exclusivity – We do not know how many franchises B is looking to grant in Country P, but before investing in one an entrepreneur will want re-assurance that they will not be competing directly with another franchise. In other words, the entrepreneur is likely to want the exclusive rights to operate within a certain geographical area. The larger this area is, the more attractive the franchise is likely to be to the entrepreneur.

Risk

Return on investment – When an entrepreneur purchases a franchise, their initial investment will be €230,400. Based on B's estimates of revenues and costs (see (b) (i)), the franchise will have to be offered for over three years in order to generate a positive net present value for the entrepreneur.

Reliability of estimates – However, there must also be an element of risk attached to the revenue and cost figures themselves. Not only have they been estimated by P rather than the entrepreneurs themselves, but there are also no existing discount stores in P to compare the estimates against. However, if, for example, the revenue figures turn out to be over-stated, then the franchises will be less attractive than B is initially suggesting.

Length of franchise – Nonetheless, the length of the franchise is likely to a crucial factor affecting an entrepreneur's decision about whether to invest in one or not. In basic terms, the longer the franchise the more attractive it is likely to be to the entrepreneur. However, some entrepreneurs may not want to be tied into a franchise contract for too long initially, in case it turns out not to be as beneficial as had been hoped. In this case, they may look to negotiate an initial franchise period of, say, 5 years, with the option to renew it for a longer period after that.

Legal position - The entrepreneur may also want to know their rights (or the compensation payable) if B decides to end the franchise or buy it back before the date which was originally agreed as the end of the franchise period.

Equipment – The expected useful life of the equipment could also affect any financial decision. The entrepreneur has to pay an initial €150,000 for equipment, but it is not clear whether, or how frequently, any subsequent outlays will be required for new equipment. Also, it is not clear who bears the responsibility and cost for servicing the equipment. However, these could be additional factors which could influence the desirability of investing in a franchise.

Opportunity cost – An entrepreneur also has to consider what alternative investment opportunities are available in P or might become available. By investing in B, the entrepreneur will reduce their scope for investing in any other opportunities which may arise, so they should only invest in B if they feel the potential returns it offers are greater than the returns they could get from any alternative ventures.

Franchise implementation and operation

Level of rules and restrictions – B, like any franchisor, will be concerned to ensure that the behaviour of its franchisees does not damage its brand or corporate identity. Therefore it is likely to have establish rules and guidelines which it will need to ensure the franchisees follow; for example there may be guidelines surrounding health and safety or corporate social responsibility.

The number and severity of the rules and restrictions which B seeks to impose on its franchisees is likely to influence the desirability of becoming a franchisee. If they are too severe, they could deter potential investors.

Level of fees payable – Another area of concern could be the level of on-going fees which are payable to B, and the amount of benefit which the franchisee will gain from them.

It is normal practice for a franchisee to have to pay a **royalty fee**, so this in itself may not be a concern to potential investors. However, if other franchisors require a lower fee, this may make B's proposed arrangement seem less attractive. Conversely, if other franchisors require a higher fee, investing in B's franchise could become relatively more attractive.

Equally, the entrepreneurs are likely to be interested to know what benefits they will get from the '**Service**' and '**Marketing contribution**' fees they have to pay, and how the rates B is charging (5% of revenue for each) compare to those of other franchisors.

Given B's position as a major multi-national retailer, the marketing support which it could provide the franchises could potentially be very helpful in helping them to acquire new customers and to become established in P. But the entrepreneurs are likely to want reassurance that the level of marketing support provided will be sufficient to help the new businesses achieve the level of sales which have been estimated. If it is not, this could significantly affect the desirability of investing in the franchise.

(c)

Top tips.

Part (c). The unseen part of the scenario reminds you that B has a number of environmental indicators it uses to measure its performance in relation to sustainability. These indicators are detailed in the pre-seen material, in the section about Corporate Social Responsibility.

The additional information provided in the unseen (about sustainability and the discount stores) relates directly to the indicators presented in the pre-seen material. Therefore, a sensible approach to this question (and the one the examiner intended candidates to take) was to use each of the indicators as a heading, and then think how the discount stores affect performance in relation to that indicator. To what extent will the discount stores business improve – or worsen – B's performance in relation to each of its sustainability indicators?

B has established a series of published indicators which it uses to measure its performance in respect of sustainability, and it will expect the discount stores in Country P to comply with the aspects of its corporate social responsibility policy which have given rise to these indicators.

Consumption of kilowatt hours

B's target is to reduce the amount of energy it consumes (kilowatt hours) per square metre of sales areas.

The discount stores in P will operate in new, purpose-built premises which are designed to be energy efficient. This energy efficiency should help B reduce its energy consumption per square metre of sales area, and therefore the stores contribute positively towards sustainability.

Number of free disposable plastic bags

Here, the target is to reduce the number of plastic bags provided to customers per square metre of sales area.

The discount stores will be able to operate without giving its customers free disposable plastic bags, which should contribute towards B achieving this target.

Greenhouse gas emissions

B's target here is to reduce the amount of carbon dioxide it emits per square metre of sales area.

B is hoping to operate the discount stores as 'carbon neutral' businesses, which should contribute positively to this aspect of sustainability.

Funding for local amenity projects.

B has committed to provide funding for the development of local amenity projects in all of the countries where B stores operate. As the discount stores will B's first stores in Country P, it is unlikely to have contributed to any local amenity projects in the country previously. Equally, however, there is no mention of B committing any funding once the discount stores are established.

So, in this respect, the discount stores have not yet led to any contribution to sustainability. Nevertheless, they could do if B commits funding to some amenity projects in P once the discount stores start trading.

Distribution and sourcing

Local sourcing – B currently sources approximately 20% of its product lines locally, with the majority of these being perishable items such as fruit and vegetables. However, the nature of the products the discount stores will sell means that only 10% of its product lines will be locally sourced. 90% will have to be imported.

Road and air transport – B currently transports much of its inventory by rail within Europe, and this has enabled B-Europe's stores to achieve higher reductions in carbon emissions per square metre of sales area than those in B-Asia and B-North America. The Asian and North American stores rarely receive inventory which has been transported by rail. This suggests that rail transport generates relatively less emissions than road or air transport.

B's imports into P will be split equally between road and air. This means that 45% of its products will be transported by road, and 45% by air. Since these are the modes of transport which generate relatively higher carbon emissions, the discount stores' transport requirements will hinder, rather than assist, B's attempts to increase sustainability through reduced greenhouse gas emisisons.

(d)

Top tips

Part (d). Here again, you need to use the pre-seen material as well as the unseen material. The section on 'Planning and management control' in the pre-seen material highlights a number of potential issues which B's current planning process. Therefore, ways in which the reformed process could help to address these issues could be advantages of the new process.

You also need to consider potential disadvantages of the reforms, because the question requirement clearly asks for both advantages and disadvantages which might arise from the reforms. However, you do not need to make any recommendations about how these disadvantages could be overcome, nor do you need to make any recommendations about possible alternative planning and control systems. The question requirement does not ask for these, and you would not have scored any marks for providing them.

Finally, note that to score well in this requirement, you need to address, specifically, the advantages and disadvantages of the proposed reforms to B's planning and management control system in Country P, and not simply to discuss the advantages and disadvantages of different styles of planning and management in general terms.

<u>Advantages</u>

B currently has a very bureaucratic and authoritarian management control system, in which the main board maintains very tight control over the regional boards. However, the reforms would give the regional directors greater authority to make their own decisions and control their own businesses.

Local knowledge – The regional directors should have a greater understanding about their own markets, and what strategies will work effectively in them, than the main board which has less local knowledge about the markets.

Responding to opportunities - The current control system often stifles planning initiatives in the regions, and creates tension between the centre and the regions. However, the new system will give the regional directors greater freedom to implement their own planning initiatives. This could be particularly beneficial if they are able to respond quickly to new opportunities which arise – for example, in relation to new products to sell – without first having to seek detailed approval from the main board.

Motivation – The greater authority and responsibility which the new system gives the regional directors should also help motivate the directors. The regional directors feel that the oppressive control from the corporate centre is preventing them doing their jobs effectively. But if they are given greater freedom to do their jobs, this should lead to them being more motivated.

If this increased motivation filters down through their teams it should hopefully lead to an improved performance in B's stores as well.

Staff development – By decentralising responsibilities, the reforms should help the personal development of the regional directors. Under the proposed new system, the regional directors will be responsible for agreeing profit targets with the CEO. Allowing the regional directors access to the CEO in this way will give them experience in dealing with more senior executives, and it could also help them think more strategically (by understanding the sorts of issues which the CEO is interested in).

Improved information systems – There are currently concerns about the accuracy and robustness of B's current inventory management systems, and problems with the inventory figures have sometimes led to stock-outs and corresponding losses of revenue.

The new system means that different business areas could use their own information systems, tailored specifically to their own needs. As a result, **better quality management information** should be available for control and decision-making, and, in turn, this will hopefully lead to performance improvements.

Disadvantages

Scalability – Although the reforms may work in relation to B Europe's Regional Director, there is no guarantee they could successfully be extended throughout B. For example, it is debatable whether the CEO will have time to agree profit targets with all the directors individually. But if he only agrees profits targets with some directors and not others, the ones who don't get to agree targets with him could feel excluded and resentful.

Increased responsibility – Whilst the increased responsibility which the reforms bring could serve to motivate some regional directors, there could equally be others who feel uneasy with the increased levels of responsibility. For example, some directors may feel uncomfortable having to decide what products to sell and where to source them from.

Moreover, if the directors make poor choices, those choices are likely to have a detrimental impact on B's performance.

Loss of control – Although the current system may stifle some initiatives, it does ensure that the main Board keeps control over the business. By increasing local authority and decision-making, the new system may make it harder for the Board to keep control. For example, the increased freedom that regional directors have may mean that the Board's strategic plans or initiatives may not actually be implemented.

Equally, if the initiatives which regional directors choose are all different from one another, the reforms could lead to a loss of uniformity within the Group, and potentially a weakening of B's brand identity.

Information systems – The reforms could lead to a number of different information systems being used within B. Although each has 'to be compatible' with the management control system, there could still be problems involved when comparing performance between different areas of the business. These problems would be avoided if B continued to use a standardised system.

Equally, if different areas of the business introduce their own information systems, there will be an additional **cost** involved in either buying or developing those systems, and then **training** staff to use them.

Cultural shift – As the Corporate Affairs Director has pointed out, introducing the reforms will require an element of cultural change at B. However, as B is a long-established company (founded in 1963) trying to change its culture prove difficult and time-consuming.

Moreover, there will inevitably be some resistance to the proposed reforms, and so B will also have to spend time and effort overcoming this resistance.

65 M plc

Text references: Corporate Social Responsibility is covered in Chapter 2 of the BPP Study Text. Porter's generic strategies are discussed in Chapter 5 and Lewin's three-step model of change is discussed in Chapter 11.

Top tips:

The calculations in (a) (i) should have been a relatively straight-forward break even calculation, although you need to work through the information provided in the scenario carefully to ensure you correctly identify how the proposals affect M's costs.

Also, it is important that you note the requirement is to calculate the number of *pages* of advertising required to break even, not the amount of advertising revenue required.

The calculations in part (a) (i) then provide a link into (a) (ii). How does the number of pages of advertising FREE needs to sell to break even compare to the number of pages of advertising The Daily Informer currently sells; and therefore what is the extent of the increase required? The amount of uplift required could be one factor which affects FREE's ability to achieve the level of sales required.

Part (a) (ii): The question requirement asks you to 'Discuss the factors which could *affect* FREE's ability to achieve the number of sales...'. As such, you should discuss the factors which could enhance FREE's ability to achieve the number of sales, as well as those which could hinder it. When this exam was sat, the examiner commented that most candidates only discussed the adverse factors which might prevent FREE from achieving the number of sales it needs to break even. However, there was no indication in the requirement that answers should be restricted in this way.

Part (a) (iii): To score well here, it was vital that you address each of the objectives in turn, and you address both the strategic and financial objectives. You should have used each objective as a heading for your answer, and then advised whether or not publishing a free newspaper fits with that objective.

The shift to publishing a free newspaper does not affect some of the objectives (either positively or negatively.) However, it was important that you made noted this against the appropriate objectives, rather than only discussing the objectives which were affected by the shift.

Part (a) (iv): This is another requirement, like (a) (ii) in which you need to avoid being too restrictive in your answer. It would be easy to focus solely on negative issues – such as redundancies, and the littering problem. However, there could also be some benefits from the proposal (such as potential increases in the number of staff required to deal with the additional advertising space). Equally, FREE will be printed on recycled newsprint which will reduce the environmental impact of its printing.

When answering this requirement, don't lose sight of what CSR is all about. It is not simply about minimising the negative effects of a firm's actions, but also about maximising the positive effects of them. Finally, note you need to consider three different elements of CSR principles: employment, the environment, and readership.

Part (b): The underlying task in this requirement is to 'evaluate' the likelihood that the proposed change will give the newspaper a sustainable competitive advantage. However, you are also told you should use Porter's generic strategies as a model to help you make this evaluation.

So a sensible approach would be to take each of the generic strategies in turn and then consider how likely they would be to generate a sustainable competitive advantage for the Newspaper Division. Note that the question doesn't simply ask about generating a 'competitive advantage' but a 'sustainable' one. So, for example, can strategies based on cost advantages ever provide a sustainable advantage, or can competitors always erode your cost advantage over time?

Part (c): This should have been a relatively straight forward requirement to end the question, although, as always in E3, it was important that you applied Lewin's model to the scenario rather than merely discussing the three stages in general terms.

Once again, a sensible way to do this would be to use each 'stage' as a heading for your answer and then think about the actions E could take within that stage to help manage the transition to the new working environment.

(a)

(i)

	Notes	**Daily Informer £000s**	**FREE £000s**
Revenue			
Circulation	*No sales revenue from FREE*	23,400	-
Advertising	*Balancing figure*	7,020	26,224
Total revenue		**30,420**	**26,224**
Costs			
Journalist salaries	*125 jobs lost @ £42k each*	8,400	3,150
Other staff costs	*£2.6 m savings*	4,810	2,210
Production costs - fixed	*Unchanged*	3,180	3,180
Production costs - variable	*1m copies per day @ 3p each; 312 days*	5,180	9,360
Advertising costs	*Additional costs of £0.5m*	1,000	1,500
Distribution costs	*45% saving*	4,680	2,574
IT	*50% saving*	4,000	2,000
Third party pictures/photos	*25% saving*	3,000	2,250
Total costs		**34,250**	**26,224**
Profit / (loss)		**(3,830)**	**-**

The projected costs for FREE are £26,224,000; therefore this is the amount of advertising revenue it needs to generate in order to break even.

The managing director, S, has stated that advertising space should be sold at £7,000 per page. Therefore, FREE needs to sell 3,746 pages per year (26,224/7), or 12 pages per day (3,746/312) in order to break even.

(ii)

Selling 12 pages of advertising per day marks a four-fold increase from The Daily Informer's current level of three pages. However, FREE's ability to attract this amount of advertising is likely to depend on potential advisers perceiving it as a successful newspaper.

Circulation – One of the key determinant's of FREE's success will be the level of circulation it can achieve. Again, the projected level (1,000,000) represents a major increase on the circulation levels which the Daily Informer currently achieves. Higher circulation figures should increase FREE's attractiveness to potential advertisers.

Price – FREE is offering its advertising at £7,000 per page which is cheaper than the Daily Informer's daily rate (of £7,500 per page). The lower price should make advertising space in FREE more attractive to advertisers. However, it is not clear how much the 'Opinion' charges for its advertising space. If the 'Opinion' charges less than FREE this might reduce the number of pages of advertising FREE can sell, because potential advertisers might opt to advertise in 'Opinion' instead.

Market segments – Advertisers will only want to advertise in FREE if they feel its readers will be potential customers for their products or services. FREE's proposed content (focusing on celebrity and lifestyle) and its distribution network (transport interchanges and leisure venues) suggests that its target readers should have a reasonably high spending power, making them attractive to advertisers. However, if FREE's readers don't match this profile, then advertisers will be reluctant to advertise in it.

(iii)

Strategic objectives

Meet the needs of readers for reliable and well informed news – The shift away from in-depth reporting towards celebrities and their activities might suggest that FREE will not fit with this objective.

However, although the different sections in the Daily Informer show it covered a very broad range of areas, they don't necessarily mean its coverage was reliable or well-informed. Similarly FREE's coverage, albeit on a more restricted range of topics, could still be reliable and well-informed, meaning it fits with the objective.

Also, the reduction in the Daily Informer's circulation figures over the last ten years suggests it is has not been meeting readers' needs effectively. If FREE can achieve (and sustain) the reader numbers it has predicted, this would actually suggest it will be meeting readers' needs more effectively, although it will be appealing to a different segment of readers than the Daily Informer did.

Expand the geographical spread of M plc's output to reach as many potential newspaper readers as possible – The reduced number of distribution points might suggest a contraction rather than an expansion in geographical spread. However, the dramatic increase in circulation (from 150,000 to 1,000,000 copies per day) fits suggests that FREE's business model fits well with the objective reach as many potential readers as possible.

Meeting the needs of native English speakers living in foreign countries – The current proposal for publishing a free newspaper does not address this objective.

Increase advertising income so that the group moves towards offering as many titles as possible free of charge – The fundamental logic behind FREE is to increase advertising so that it can be offered as a free title. And the forecasts suggest that annual advertising income will increase from £7.0m to £26.2m, which represents a very significant increase. Therefore the proposal fits very well with this objective.

Financial objectives

To ensure that revenue and operating profit grow by 4% on average per year – The Daily Informer is forecast to lose £3.8m in the year to 31 March 2013. So, if FREE achieves its intended level of advertising and breaks even it will contribute to the objective of growing profit, although total revenues will actually be lower (£26.2m vs. £30.4). However, the extent to which FREE contributes to the objective of increasing operating profits will depend on the amount of advertising revenue it can generate, and whether it can sustain or increase its advertising revenue in subsequent years.

To achieve steady growth in dividend per share – The proposed change to FREE does not directly address this objective.

To maintain gearing below 40% – The proposed change to FREE does not directly address this objective. However, if FREE contributes to a growth in operating profit this could in turn have a favourable impact on M plc's gearing ratio.

(iv)

The principles of corporate social responsibility suggest that M should try to maximise the positive impacts its actions have on stakeholders, whilst minimizing the negative effects of its actions.

Employment

The proposed change seems likely to lead to a number of people losing their jobs:

Journalists – The forecast indicates that 125 of the Daily Informer's 200 journalists will lose their jobs. Although some of these may be able to find alternative jobs, the experiences of the Opinion's journalists suggest it will difficult for them to do so.

Other staff – The forecast savings of £2.6 million suggest that 70 of the Daily Informer's 130 other staff will also lose their jobs (based on the average salary of £37,000). Again, the poor general economic situation means it is likely to be difficult for them to find alternative jobs.

Newsagents' staff – The new distribution arrangements will have knock on effects in job losses among retailers, particularly affecting staff in low paid jobs.

However, the proposed changes could also lead to some new jobs being created:

Distribution staff – The outsourced transport specialist is likely to need to recruit additional staff to distribute FREE at the 200 key points selected. These new jobs could, to some extent, offset the jobs lost in the newsagents.

Advertising – The extent of the increase in advertising pages sold per day (from 3 to 12) suggests that some additional jobs may be created, for example at advertising agencies, to prepare and produce these advertisements.

Nonetheless, on balance the proposed changes are likely to lead to net job losses. However, given that the Daily Informer was loss-making and its circulation had been declining rapidly, these job losses might be seen as preferable to the potential alternative that it closes altogether, meaning that all the staff working on the Daily Informer are made redundant.

The environment

Negative effect

Littering – The editor's experience from another free paper suggests that the proposed change could lead to a significant littering problem as people throw away their copies of FREE once they have read them.

Positive effect

Recycled newsprint – Recycled newsprint will be used in the production of FREE, instead of new newsprint.This should reduce the environmental impact of producing the paper. In addition, it is likely that FREE will contain significantly fewer pages than the Daily Informer and so less paper resources will be needed to produce each copy. (However, this saving will be counteracted by the increase in circulation.)

Fewer distribution points – The transport fleet currently delivers copies of the Daily Informer to 750 separate locations. However, FREE will only be distributed from 200 key points; meaning that there should be a reduction in carbon emissions associated with delivering the newspapers to their distribution points.

Readership

Changed readership – The Daily Informer positions itself as a family newspaper, and readers who value this perspective may view the proposed changes as undesirable. However, there remain other daily newspapers in the UK which these readers could buy if they want to.

The proposed change appears to be reflecting changes in society, and the wishes of customers as stakeholders. The number of people who are prepared to pay for a newspaper is declining, and M is responding to this. In this context, if 1 million people read FREE each day (compared to 150,000 reading the Daily Informer), it would appear that the change has had a positive effect for the 1 million readers as stakeholders.

In terms of the readers, it is almost inevitable that some readers will view the proposed change as a negative thing, while others will welcome it. However, this does not make the effects of the proposed change inconsistent with CSR principles.

(b)

Porter's generic competitive strategy model suggests that a firm needs to follow one of three strategies to generate a sustainable competitive advantage: cost leadership, differentiation, or focus.

Cost leadership

In order to pursue a cost leadership strategy successfully, M must be able to find a way of producing FREE at lower cost than its competitors could produce a similar paper.

However, it seems unlikely that M will be able to generate any sustainable competitive advantage in this way. The newspaper industry in the UK is mature and very competitive; and all the firms have similar production methods. Therefore, it is unlikely that FREE will be able to generate a sustainable cost advantage by modernizing its facilities. For example, although M's Newspaper Division modernized its printing press facilities three years ago, most of its competitors have now followed suit.

Nonetheless, a key aspect of the proposed change to FREE seems to be the £8m reduction in total costs, from £34.2m to £26.2m. This might suggest that M is trying to pursue some kind of cost leadership strategy; for example, by reducing the staff costs and the distribution costs associated with the paper.

However, it is still debatable whether any cost savings this generates will create a *sustainable* competitive advantage. Not only does FREE seem to be replicating a strategy already adopted by the 'Opinion', but also M has not made any changes which couldn't be imitated by other competitors.

In order to create a sustainable competitive advantage through cost leadership, FREE would need to be based on a low cost model that other newspaper producers could not replicate.

Differentiation

In order to pursue a differentiation strategy successfully, FREE must develop some unique characteristics which distinguish it from the rest of the newspaper industry, such that customers (in this case readers and advertisers) will value FREE more highly than all the other daily newspapers in the UK.

The Daily Informer appears to have been following a differentiation strategy, with its points of differentiation being 'the family' and its 'broad focus.' However, the proposed changes to convert the Daily Informer to FREE move away from these points of differentiation.

Defining the market

In effect, the national daily newspaper market in the UK seems to have been divided into two broad sub-groups: (i) free newspapers ('Opinion' & 'FREE'); and (ii) paid-for newspapers (the remaining nine others).

Therefore, in order to pursue a broad differentiation strategy, FREE would have to distinguish itself from both 'Opinion' *and* the nine paid-for newspapers.

Simply being free is not a source of sustainable competitive advantage, however. If the free business model proves successful, and allows FREE to gain market share from the paid-for newspapers, they could follow suit and become free newspapers.

Basis of differentiation

Instead, FREE could try to differentiate itself by providing content that its readers feel is superior to that offered by its competitors. For example, FREE could try to attract some of the 'star' journalists to write exclusive articles for it, and then use these to promote increased circulation.

Again, however, it is debatable whether such an approach is sustainable, because the other newspapers could respond by attracting other 'star' journalists to write articles for them. In order for FREE to develop a sustainable competitive advantage, it would need a strategy which its competitors will find difficult to replicate.

Focus strategies

In effect, the fact that S has stated that FREE must target the same market segment as 'Opinion' (rather than competing across the whole market) suggests that S is envisaging a focus strategy. In this respect, FREE would be targeting readers who do not want in-depth reporting, but who are interested in the activities of footballers and celebrities, along with lots of advertising.

However, it is difficult to see how this could be a source of competitive advantage for FREE, because it seems to be copying pretty much exactly the 'Opinion's' strategy, and targeting the same market segment. As a result, it is not clear how FREE is differentiating itself from 'Opinion.'

It is possible that the market segment may be large enough to sustain both newspapers. However, this is still no guarantee of sustainable competitive advantage, because there do not appear to be any significant barriers to entry to stop others of the daily newspapers also entering this segment in the future. In much the same way that FREE could enter the market to compete with Opinion, so other newspapers could also join the market and imitate both FREE and Opinion.

Moreover, another risk that FREE faces is that its target market segment appears to be quite different to the Daily Informer's target market. This could mean that FREE's journalists and editors don't have much experience at tailoring their stories to the demands of the new market segment. If FREE doesn't understand its customers' needs and desires properly it is unlikely to be successful. In this respect, there is a danger that the proposed change may lead to the Newspaper Division becoming 'stuck in the middle' to a degree; retaining some of the characteristics of the Daily Informer's style, and mixing them with a new style for FREE's new target market.

(c)

Unfreezing

Need for change – One of the key elements of the 'unfreezing' stage will be for E to make sure that the staff understand the reasons for the change. If the staff understand the reasons for the change they may be more likely to accept the changes.

In this respect, E should highlight the Daily Informer's significant (38%) drop in circulation during the last ten years, and the fact that it is forecast to make a loss for the year ended 31 March 2013, as it has also done for the last two years. Such figures mean that the Daily Informer cannot carry on as it is, and therefore some kind of change is necessary.

Competitive environment - E should also explain the context of the competitive environment in the UK, to highlight that changes in reading habits and the growth of alternative news media are going to further reduce the number of people who are prepared to pay for a newspaper. This again should highlight to the staff why the change is necessary.

Chief Executive's input – E could also point out to his staff that it was the Chief Executive who asked S and E to investigate the possibility of introducing a free newspaper. Therefore, E can explain that he has effectively been instructed to make the change, rather than doing it because he wants to cause disruption and uncertainty for his staff.

Change

Staff roles – The 'Opinion's' experience suggests that the transition to the new working environment will lead to changes in staff roles as well as to the number of staff employed. For example, the increased amount of advertising in the free paper suggests that staff will need to spend more time liaising with advertisers or advertising agencies, whereas less time will be devoted to editorial content or in-depth features within the newspaper.

Therefore E will need to identify for staff what their roles will be in FREE, and what will be expected of them. In this context, E will need to explain to staff how the culture and character of the paper will need to change – to reflect changes in its target audience – and how this will affect staff roles; for example, by requiring a greater focus on celebrities and sports stars rather than more 'serious' journalism.

Staff numbers – FREE will employ fewer journalists that the Daily Informer did, so a major element of the change process will be assessing whether the existing journalists can work on other titles within M plc, or whether they will have to be made redundant.

Reporting procedures – Not only will staff numbers be reduced in FREE, but the mix of staff and roles will be different than in the Daily Informer. This suggests that it is likely that new internal reporting procedures will be required. Equally, the details of these new procedures will need to be communicated to the staff; for example, so that if their department has been restructured they know who they will be reporting to under the new structure.

Reward and incentive schemes – E could also introduce new reward and incentive schemes which will help reinforce to staff the key areas of their roles and the patterns of behaviour which will be required if FREE is to be successful. For example, rather than being rewarded for the quality of their in-depth reporting, journalists could be rewarded for the number of exclusive celebrity interviews they are able to secure.

Management style – As the style and culture of FREE are likely to be significantly different to the Daily Informer, E may also need to modify the management style which will be used in FREE compared to that currently used in the Daily Informer. The combination of lower staff numbers and the shift in FREE's culture, suggests that a more informal style may now be appropriate. Any such change in management style will also help to reinforce to staff the contrast between the new and the old working environment.

Refreezing

After the changes have been introduced, it will be important that the staff adhere to the new patterns of behaviour and policies rather than reverting to the way things used to be done.

Bonuses and incentives – Bonuses and incentives can be a very useful for reinforcing the changes. For example, bonus targets should be set in relation to performance in key aspects of the new working environment.

Equally, staff members could be made aware that **future promotions** and **pay increases** will be linked to how well they accept the changes, and how well they perform in the new working environment.

Reinforcing success – E should also look to reinforce the benefits of the changes by highlighting success stories which have come about as a result of them; for example, by publicising increases in circulation figures if these show a significant growth.

66 M plc – Web division

Text reference: The BCG matrix is discussed in Chapter 4 of the BPP Study Text for E3, and Kotter & Schlesinger's approaches to overcoming resistance to change are covered in Chapter 11.

Top tips:

Part (a). The calculations in (a) (i) are not technically difficult. The key to scoring well here is to be methodical and work carefully through all the information provided in the scenario. Under the new pricing system, there will be three sources of revenue: daily subscriptions; weekly subscriptions; and advertising revenue. You need to make sure you pick up all of these in your calculations, and then compare the revenues from the new pricing systems to that from the existing system. The key issue here is whether the Web Division will increase its revenue by changing its pricing systems. So make sure you compare the revenues from the new pricing systems to the current advertising revenue.

Although two of the strategies appear to be beneficial (based on the figures provided) there must be a degree of uncertainty about the estimated figures used. How reliable are they? Have any of M's competitors adopted similar models which can be used for comparison? You should have considered practical issues like this in (a) (ii), but you should also have considered the decision from a strategic perspective. For example, how might the change affect M's competitive position, or how does it fit with its objectives?

Note, however, not to spend time discussing in (a) (ii) how well the strategy fits with M's objectives, because this forms the requirement for part (b).

Part (b). This question highlights the importance of using both the pre-seen and un-seen material to write your answers. The strategic and financial objectives are listed on pages 2 and 3 of the pre-seen material. Working through these in turn should highlight the potential conflicts arising from the new strategy.

To score well in this question you need to work through each of the objectives in turn and assess the extent to which the proposed change will conflict with them. The change will clearly conflict with some of the objectives more than others (eg, strategic objectives based around offering titles free of charge and trying to maximise reader numbers). However, even if there is no conflict with an objective you should still say so. So you should use each of the objectives as a heading for your answer, and then say whether there is a conflict or not.

(a)

(i)

Current **weekly** advertising revenue:

£6,000 per page × 5 pages ×7 days = £210,000

Possible pricing strategies

Forecast subscription revenues		*Strategy 1*	*Strategy 2*	*Strategy 3*
Daily subscriptions: price per page (£)		0.25	0.50	0.75
Daily subscriptions: forecast number of subscribers per day		4,000	3,500	1,500
Total weekly revenue from daily subscriptions (£)	1	**7,000**	**12,250**	**7,875**
Weekly subscriptions: price per week (£)		0.5	0.75	1.5
Weekly subscriptions: forecast number of subscribers per week		17,000	15,000	6,000
Total weekly revenue from weekly subscriptions (£)	2	**8,500**	**11,250**	**9,000**
Total weekly revenue from subscriptions	1+ 2	**15,500**	**23,500**	**16,875**
Forecast advertising revenues				
Advertising revenue per page sold (£)		4,000	3,750	2,500
Number of pages sold per day		7	9	10
Days advertising sold per week		7	7	7
Weekly advertising revenue (£)		**196,000**	**236,250**	**175,000**

Total weekly forecast revenues	*Strategy 1*	*Strategy 2*	*Strategy 3*
Subscriptions (£)	15,500	23,500	16,875
Advertising (£)	196,000	236,250	175,000
Total (£)	**211,500**	**259,750**	**191,875**
Uplift/shortfall vs current revenue			
Current revenue	210,000	210,000	210,000
Impact (£)	**1,500**	**49,750**	**-18,125**
Impact %	**1%**	**24%**	**-9%**

(ii)

Financial factors - The calculations in part (i) have indicated that Strategies 1 and 2 would help increase the Web Division's revenue, while Strategy 3 would lead to a reduction in revenue. From a purely financial basis, Strategy 2 is the most beneficial. If the figures are extrapolated to an annual basis, Strategy 2 leads to an increase in forecast revenues of £2,587,000 per year.

Financial and non-financial objectives – However, the decision may not be purely on financial factors, and X should also consider how well the different strategies fit with M plc's objectives (as discussed in part (b) below.)

Competitive position – M plc currently maintains all of its websites free of charge, so moving to a subscription-only service marks a change in strategy. It is not clear how many (if any) of M's competitors currently offer subscription-based or free sites, so X needs to consider how far the move could give M a competitive advantage over its competitors (by adopting a successful new business model before them) or whether the change is merely enabling M to catch up with its competitors (because they already use this business model, and it has proved successful for them). For example, in the UK, The Times has already successfully implemented The Times Online as a subscription-based site.

Sensitivities and uncertainty – The figures used in the calculations in (a) (i) are based on X's estimates. However, there are a number of uncertainties in these: subscription levels; the mix between daily and weekly subscriptions; the amount and price of advertising space sold.

Although X has used her experience of subscription-based websites and the feedback from market research in preparing her estimates, there is still a degree of uncertainty about how reliable the figures are. Therefore, X should look at how the impact on forecast revenues from modifying some of the variables used in the forecasts (eg, subscriber numbers or pages sold).

This is particularly important in relation to Strategy 1. Although, it looks marginally beneficial, if the number of pages of advertising sold were 6 rather than 7, the total weekly revenue it would generate would be £183,5000 rather than 211,500, a 13% shortfall on M's current weekly revenue.

Customer loyalty – Users who subscribe to the website are more likely to be loyal to it than users of the free website. This could be beneficial to M if it can sell additional products or services to these users. Therefore, the subscription model could generate additional revenues which are not currently included in the forecasts.

Customer profiling - Similarly, the subscription model could enable M to find out more details about its subscribers which could be useful in relation to selling advertising space. If M can highlight to potential advertisers that its readers fit particular market segments, this may encourage advertisers to buy advertising space in the paper.

External comparison - Again, we do not know if any other news websites have adopted a similar business model, but, if they have, it would be useful to compare the changes in their subscriber numbers (as a result of the change) to the assumptions and estimates X has used in the forecasts.

Scalability – It seems likely that, if the decision to move the 'Daily News' website to a subscription-based model proves successful, a number of M's other websites could also be changed to the subscription-based model. This should generate additional revenue increases for M plc. However, X needs to consider whether the subscription-based model is appropriate for some of the smaller websites. For example, would there be enough subscribers to make it worthwhile for advertisers still to advertise on them?

(b)

(i)

Strategic objectives

Expand the geographical spread of M plc's output to reach as many potential newspaper and website readers as possible – The 'Daily News' website currently receives 100,000 hits per day. If these hits are from different users, this suggests the website currently has at least 100,000 users. However, under the subscription-based model, the forecast maximum number of users is 21,000 (under Strategy 1). For Strategy 2 (which is forecast to generate the highest revenue) the number of users is expected to be 18,500.

Therefore moving to a subscription based model will lead to a significant reduction in the number of website readers, which **directly contradicts the objective**.

Increase advertising income so that the group moves towards offering as many news titles as possible free of charge to the public – Although the subscription-based model is likely to increase advertising income (in line with the first part of this objective) it **conflicts with the objective of offering news titles free of charge** to the public.

Meet the needs of readers for reliable and well informed news - The proposal does not appear to have any impact on M's ability to achieve this objective and so does not conflict with it.

Publish some newspapers which meet the needs of native English speakers in non-English speaking countries – The proposal does not appear to represent a conflict with this objective. Equally, however, moving to a subscription-only basis will not help M achieve the objective any better, so the proposal can be seen as neutral in respect of it.

Financial objectives

The proposal does not appear to conflict with any of M's financial objectives, and overall should help to achieve them.

To ensure that revenue and operating profit grow by an average of 4% per year – Assuming that the subscription-only website achieves the revenues forecast in X's estimates, the proposal (particularly Strategy 2) should help contribute towards this objective. However, by itself the proposal will only generate a very small increase in M plc's overall revenues.

To achieve steady growth in dividend per share – If the proposal helps to increase revenue and operating profit, then, in turn, this should enable to M plc to increase its dividend per share.

To maintain gearing below 40% – Again, if the proposal successfully increases revenues, it should help to reduce gearing slightly, because it should not require any additional capital expenditure.

Advice:

The proposal does contradict two of M plc's strategic objectives. However, at the same time it supports the strategic objective to increase advertising income, and it should contribute towards the achievement of all three financial objectives.

(ii)

X will have to persuade the Board that the benefits of the proposed change outweigh any disadvantages arising from the conflict with the strategic objectives.

Although the change will significantly reduce user numbers (conflicting with strategic objective 2), and mean that the website is no longer free (cf. strategic objective 4), it should increase the amount of advertising revenue. This is consistent with strategic objective 4 and all of the financial objectives. In this respect, X should highlight the potential financial benefits of the proposal.

This could be particularly important in encouraging the non-executive directors to support the proposal. They are currently dissatisfied with M's rate of growth and profitability and they want to see more positive action to secure the financial objectives; something which X could argue her proposal does.

In addition, X should explain that current practices in the industry have moved on since the objectives were established in 2005. In particular, she should highlight that strategic objective 4 is now outdated, and so basing strategic decisions in terms of their compliance with this objective may no longer be in M's best interest.

(c)

Top tips:

The important point to note in this question is how the BCG matrix can be used to develop product strategies for products in different quadrants of the matrix.

You will earn a small number of marks by describing the matrix and its axes, but in order to pass the requirement you then need to go on and apply the matrix to the scenario. The matrix's value to X will be in identifying those websites which should be built or held (stars, and cash cows) and those which should be divested or harvested (dogs, and some of the question marks).

However, there are also a number of practical issues you could consider. Is it actually feasible for X to put 200 websites onto one BCG matrix? And does M have good enough accounting systems to enable X to identify the 'sales' or net cash flows of each of its titles? Equally, how could X identify the total size of the each of the markets?

Remember, ultimately you need to be advising X in relation to which websites she should continue and which she should discontinue.

M plc's 200 websites are its portfolio of products, so the BCG matrix could be used to determine which of these products should be continued and which discontinued, on the basis of their **relative market shares** (the product's share of the market compared to its largest competitor's share) and their **market growth rates** (the market's annual rate of growth in sales volume).

The BCG matrix classifies products into four categories:

		Relative Market Share	
		High	*Low*
Market Growth Rate	*High*	Stars	Question marks
	Low	*Cash cows*	*Dogs*

The BCG matrix

An organisation can then use the matrix to analyse and plan its portfolio, and to try to create a balance between its products with the aim of maximising its competitive advantage.

In this respect, product strategies can be suggested for each of the four categories in the matrix:

Stars – build

Cash cow – hold, or harvest

Question marks – build, or harvest

Dogs – Divest

Consequently, looking at relative market share and market growth, alongside the profitability of each website, can help M decide which of its 200 sites it should look to grow and develop, and which it should discontinue. For example, if there are titles which have a high relative market share in fast growing markets (ie stars), M should look to invest in these titles and build them, even if they are not currently making a profit. Equally, M should ensure it holds a sufficient number of cash cows in order to fund the development of future stars.

Nonetheless, X needs to appreciate the potential difficulties she could face when using the BCG matrix. For example, in order to determine relative market share, she will need to establish the 'market' for each website – but is this a demographic segment, a subject interest, or a wider group of readers? Equally, she will need to obtain market data for each of the titles, possibly from external market analysts or research agencies.

In addition, the lack of detailed information about M's own websites could make it difficult for X to calculate M's share of the market for different websites.

These difficulties associated with using the BCG matrix suggest that X should not try to use it too prescriptively. Nonetheless, it could help give an indication of which websites (or even, which types of website) M plc should be looking to continue, and which it should consider discontinuing.

(d)

Top tips:

Note that in part (i) you are specifically asked for THREE improvements, so you need to identify your three improvements clearly. A sensible approach to this question would be to analyse the problems with the proposed programme (eg making the same number of people redundant from each department regardless of the size of the department), and then to recommend improvements to deal with those problems.

Part (ii): The reference in the requirement to 'overcoming resistance to change' should have indicated that Kotter & Schlesinger's ideas will be relevant here. Again, though, your answer should not be a theoretical discussion of Kotter & Schlesinger's different approaches for overcoming resistance to change, but you should have applied them specifically to the scenario. Remember, the question requirement has asked you to 'Advise Z...'

Remember also, the question refers specifically to the staff remaining in the division, so you would earn no marks for talking about ways of overcoming resistance from those staff who are being made redundant.

(i)

The aim of strategic headcount reduction programme is not simply to reduce costs but also to improve efficiency. As it stands, the current proposals (leading to the loss of 100 jobs) will lead to a reduction of costs in the short term, but they could end up causing inefficiencies and cost increases in the longer term.

Value and efficiency

Although one of the stated aims of the programme is to improve efficiency, the basis for selecting the employees to make redundant does not reflect this. Z's preference for choosing employees over 50 who are earning high salaries seems to be driven purely by short term cost savings. Not only is this approach likely to be illegal (on the grounds of age discrimination) but there is no reference to the value each employee contributes to M plc and the efficiency of their work.

By contrast, Z should review the business's needs, and how well each individual's skills match the business needs. Redundancies should then be made according to skills and competences rather than age and salaries. If necessary, Z should seek advice from an employment lawyer to ensure that any redundancies are not illegal on the grounds of discrimination.

Numbers of job losses from each department

The current proposals suggest that 10 people are made redundant from each of the 10 departments. However, this will have a disproportionate impact on some of the departments. In particular, the Web Security department currently only employs 11 people, so after the reduction there will only be one person working in the department, which means M's web security is likely to be seriously compromised.

Therefore, instead of making the same number of people redundant from each department, Z should take account of the current size and workloads of each department, and should look to make different numbers of people from each department redundant according to the department's ability to absorb the redundancies. Z should hold consultations with the departmental managers to gain a clear picture of the impact of the headcount reduction programme on each department.

Delegation of responsibility to managers

Although Z has imposed the programme and the numbers of people to be made redundant, the departmental managers then have to choose who to make redundant and notify those staff that they are being made redundant.

On the one hand the departmental managers could feel very uncomfortable having to make such decisions, which could adversely affect their motivation. Equally, the limited guidance they have been given means that managers could select people for redundancy according to their own personal preferences.

Instead of making the departmental managers solely responsible for the redundancy process, the HR department should retain responsibility for implementing the process. Equally, instead of arbitrarily selecting people to be made redundant, the HR department should work in conjunction with the divisional managers to select the people to be made redundant in relation to their skills and the business' requirements.

(ii)

Z could use a combination of the following approaches to help overcome resistance to the changes arising from the strategic headcount reduction programme. All these approaches involve dialogue and discussion with the staff, which is likely to be important given the scale and impact of the programme. To this extent, approaches such as coercion which try to force the staff to accept the changes are not likely to be appropriate here.

Participation and involvement: The staff are likely to resist the changes which they feel have been imposed on them without any consultation or communication. Therefore, one way Z could look to overcome the resistance is by inviting the staff to be more involved in the discussions about the structure of the Division after the headcount reduction programme.

Education and communication: The staff are also likely to resist the changes if they do not appreciate the need for them, and are not sure how the changes are going to affect them. Communication is vital in this respect. Z, or the Web Division's managing director, needs to explain to the staff why the changes were necessary, and how the headcount reduction programme will improve M's competitive position and efficiency. It could also help improve morale and staff motivation if the staff were reassured that the programme was designed to improve efficiency rather than because the division is failing.

Facilitation and support: The magnitude of the changes means that they are likely to have a significant effect on the working environment within the Web division. For example, staff's roles may have to change following the departure of certain colleagues. In this respect, it will be important that staff are given support and training as necessary to help them adjust to their new environment and any new aspects of the roles.

Negotiation: The scenario does not indicate how far working practices may have to change following the restructuring programme, but if changes are required negotiation may be necessary to encourage staff to accept them. For example, staff may have to be offered salary increases in return for taking on additional duties. However, Z may be reluctant to approve any salary increases, because this will reduce the cost-savings achieved from the redundancies. Z, in conjunction with M plc' management, may seek to transfer Web Division staff to other divisions, as an alternative to making them redundant.

67 F plc

Text reference: Mission statements and corporate social responsibility are covered in Chapter 2 of the BPP Study Text. Information systems and covered in Chapter 9.

Part (a)

Top tips:

Of the 25 marks available for part (a), 12 will be awarded for the calculations. This leaves 13 marks for your analysis of the figures and the final recommendation of which deal to offer. This breakdown of the marks should have highlighted that a simplistic analysis such as 'The Half-way house deal is the only one which meets both criteria (to pay back within one year, and to increase market share) and so is the deal which should be offered' is not sufficient here.

The reference in the scenario to the Divisional Accountant not supporting the General Manager's appraisal criteria should have also prompted you to question whether it was appropriate to base a strategic decision on one year's worth of figures. The Divisional Accountant has suggested looking at a three year period: what would the returns from the deals be over three years, and how would this differ to the figures in year 1?

Another potential issue here is the difference between cash flows and profitability. The General Manager's reference to paying back within year 1 suggests a focus on cash flows. However, it could be argued that this distorts the decision-making against the Exclusive deal. Although the cash outflows for purchasing the new freezers are incurred in Year 1 are greater, the retailers are subsequently obliged to sell the Desserts Division's products exclusively for a period of three years. So from an accounting perspective, the Division could look to spread the cost of the freezers over this three year period. This again suggests that evaluating the different deals over a three year period is preferable to looking at them over a single year (Year 1).

Examiner's comments:

Part (a) was not well answered. A common mistake was that many candidates only calculated either the year 1 profit for each deal or a three-year profit. It was necessary to undertake both in order to evaluate the difference in opinion resulting from the criteria set by the General Manager and the Accountant.

Many candidates recommended the 'Half-way House' deal, based largely on the calculation of payback within 1 year. In doing so, these candidates missed the point that one year was too short a time frame on which to make an important strategic decision, and this was considered to be a fundamental weakness in their discussions. The recommendation made by the management accountant in the unseen material should have given candidates guidance to consider the decision over a longer period.

Analysis of Freezer Deals: Year 1

Freezer deal		Exclusive	Half-way House	Free and Easy
Estimated take-up		5,000	2,700	135
		£	£	£
Net cost of freezers	(W1)	2,500,000	810,000	40,500
Marketing materials	(W2)	960,000	324,000	0
Cost		3,460,000	1,134,000	40,500
Additional contribution	(W3)	2,640,000	1,215,000	32,400
Cash Profit / (Loss)		(820,000)	81,000	(8,100)

W1:

	Exclusive	Half-way House	Free and Easy
Cost of each freezer (£)	500	500	500
Recharged to retailer	0	200	200
Net cost to Division	500	300	300
Take-up	5,000	2,700	135
Net cost of freezers	2,500,000	810,000	40,500

W2:

	Exclusive	Half-way House	Free and Easy
Marketing cost	= 16 x 12 x 5000	= 10 x 12 x 2700	0
	960,000	324,000	0

(Note: The costs of £16 and £10 given in scenario, are monthly costs not annual costs)

W3:

	Exclusive	Half-way House	Free and Easy
Additional monthly sales per retailer (£)	800	500	200
Retailers	5,000	2,700	135
Monthly sales (£)	4,000,000	1,350,000	27,000
Annual sales (£)	48,000,000	16,200,000	324,000
Contribution margin	5.5%	7.5%	10%
Contribution (£)	2,640,000	1,215,000	32,400

<u>Market share:</u>

Total monthly market sales: £ 50 million.

Impact of Freezer deals:

	Exclusive	Half-way House	Free and Easy
Additional monthly sales	£4,000,000	£1,350,000	£27,000
% increase in market share	8%	2.7%	0.05%

<u>Evaluation of deals</u>

The Divisional General Manager has insisted that any additional marketing spending must have a payback period of 1 year, and must increase market share.

However, these criteria also need to be judged alongside F plc's strategic aim to 'increase [the] profitability of each of its divisions through increased market share.

Payback period – The calculations show that the only deal under which the additional contribution from the deal exceeds the additional costs of the deal is the **Half-way house**. This deal is expected to generate an additional £81,000 in Year 1.

Market share – All three deals will increase F's share of the market for ice cream sold by independent retailers, although the Free and Easy deal only have a minimal increase, and so on this basis it can be ruled out as a realistic option. However, the Half-way house deal will increase F's share of the market from 7% to 9.7%, while the Exclusive deal will increase it even more; to 15%.

Marketing expenditure – The General Manager is willing to authorise £2 million expenditure. The Exclusive deal exceeds this, with expenditure of £3.3 million in Year 1 (largely due to the £2.5million spent to buy the new freezers). The expenditure required for the Half-way house deal looks as if it will be below the £2 million authorised, with the amount spent in the first year being £1.1million.

Therefore, on the basis that the Half-way House is the only one of the three deals which pays back within one year and increases market share, it may seem initially that this is the one which should be recommended.

However, there are a number of other factors which should be considered before a final recommendation is made.

Market research – One of the supplementary benefits of the deals is that they will enable the Desserts Division to conduct market research directly with consumers. In this respect, the Exclusive deal (which is expected to have the greatest take-up) could be the most beneficial, because it should give the Division the largest pool of customers to conduct market research on.

Advertising benefits – Equally, by having the greatest take-up, the Exclusive deal could allow the Division the best opportunities to increase its sales and profitability more generally through cross-selling. Each participating retailer will advertise the Desserts Division's products (not necessarily just ice creams) in its shops. In this respect, the Exclusive deal may be better able to contribute to the strategic aim of increasing profitability.

Short-termism – However, perhaps the most important consideration in the final recommendation is the time period being used to assess the financial performance of the deals. As the Divisional Accountant has suggested, looking at performance for one year only seems a very short time period, given the strategic nature of the investment (and the 'once and for all' expenditure of £2 million).

In this respect, it is important that the Division chooses the deal which will generate the greatest benefits in terms of profitability and market share in the **longer term**, thereby helping to achieve F plc's strategic aims.

3 year contributions - Given that the Exclusive deal means that the independent retailers will sell the Divisions products exclusively for three years, it may (as the Divisional Accountant believes) be more appropriate to look at the expected performance of the deals over a three year period rather than a one year period.

Looking at the respective returns from the deals over three years shows a very different picture from the one-year assessment, because the initial cash expenditure of supplying the freezers is not repeated in years two and three. (Although F is responsible for maintaining the freezers (under the terms of the Exclusive deal), there costs are expected to be minimal during the freezer's working life and so can be ignored from the calculations.)

Assuming that the marketing support continues at the same level in Years 2 and 3 as it was in Year 1, the revised results for the three deals are as follows:

Profitability in Years 2 and 3	Exclusive	Half-way House	Free and Easy
	£	£	£
Marketing costs	(960,000)	(324,000)	0
Additional contribution	2,640,000	1,215,000	32,400
Annual profit / loss	**1,680,000**	**891,000**	**32,400**
Cumulative profit/loss over 3 years			
Year 1	(820,000)	81,000	(8,100)
Year 2	1,680,000	891,000	32,400
Year 3	1,680,000	891,000	32,400
Cumulative	**2,540,000**	**1,863,000**	**64,800**

These revised figures suggest that the Exclusive deal generates significantly more profit than the Half-Way House deal over the three year period of the Exclusive deal.

Recommendation

Although the Half-Way House deal is the only one which meets the General Manager's original criteria, this may not be the best deal from a strategic perspective. The Exclusive Deal provides the Desserts Division with the greatest scope to increase market share, and also in the longer term also looks to be the most profitable.

Therefore, the deal which the Board should offer the independent retailers is the **Exclusive deal.**

The Exclusive deal would allow F to increase its market share to 15% (an increase of 8 percentage points), and can be expected to generate a profit of £2.5 million over three years (£677,000 more than the equivalent profit from the Half-Way House deal).

From a strategic perspective, this additional profit generated by the Exclusive Deal should be seen as more important than the fact that it does not pay back within one year, and that the expenditure required is greater than the £2 million originally proposed by the Divisional General Manager.

Part (b)

Top tips

Part (b) (i): The mission statement (given in the Pre-seen material) is important here. A number of points in the mission statement seem to refer to aspects of CSR. So does F need to have a specific aim to reinforce these points, or is their inclusion in the mission statement sufficient? To score well in this question you should have tried to give a balanced answer, including both advantages of having a strategic aim dealing with CSR and disadvantages of doing so.

Similarly, you could approach **part (b) (ii)** by considering the advantages and disadvantages of including the CSR report in the annual report. However, note that the requirement asks specifically about including the *internal* CSR report in the annual report, not simply including a CSR report in the annual report. So while you can earn some marks by highlighting the benefits of presenting an external CSR report, you also need to consider how appropriate it is likely to be to include an internal report in an external document.

Part (b) (iii): The last section of the unseen material should have highlighted some of the EEM is facing: a limited budget, no staff, very little contact with her boss, and resistance from the other managers. All of these issues are likely to reduce her effectiveness within F plc. So, in order to contribute more towards F plc meeting its CSR targets, the EEM will need to find ways of overcoming these problems. However, the examiner did not expect candidates to focus upon the day-to-day activities of the EEM, and to detail the reports she should produce and the targets she should monitor. The examiner pointed out this was an incorrect approach to answering this question because it ignored the information provided in the un-seen material which related directly to the current ineffectiveness of the EEM.

(b) (i)

Strategic aims and mission statement – F's strategic aims have been set in order to enable it to meet the obligations contained in its mission statement. F's mission statement does not currently mention Corporate Social Responsibility (CSR) directly, which could be seen as an indication that F does not need a strategic aim dealing with CSR.

However, although CSR is not explicitly mentioned in the mission statement, a number of references in it do suggest that F has recognised the importance of responsible business practice. For example, the statement refers to: sourcing high quality ingredients, using efficient processes, maintaining the highest standards of hygiene, and paying fair prices. All of these could be seen as ways of promoting responsible business practice, and the first three are echoed in F's existing strategic aims.

In this respect, introducing a strategic aim dealing with CSR could be seen as making the points implied by the mission statement more explicit, suggesting that F should one such strategic aim.

Reflecting current position - Finally, the Board should remember that the current mission statement was set in 2000, so some elements of it could now be outdated. CSR is becoming increasingly importance in the business environment, and F takes its CSR responsibility seriously, as it demonstrated by appointing an Environmental Effects Manager two year ago. If F introduced a strategic aim dealing with CSR, this would better demonstrate the Group's current attitude towards responsible business practices.

(b) (ii)

Demonstrate commitment to CSR – The Environmental Effects Manager's (EEM) annual report for the Board indicates how well F plc is progressing towards its CSR targets (in relation to fair trade, waste reduction and recycling, food labelling, transportation and energy usage) – all of which could be important information to include in the annual report. Given that this information is already available, F could use it to publicly demonstrate its commitment to CSR, whilst requiring little or no extra work to produce the report.

Disadvantages of reporting performance – However, if publishes the EEM's report externally in its current form, this will highlight areas where F has failed to achieve targets (for example, in relation to air kilometres travelled) as well as ones where it has performed well. In this respect, external readers of the report could end up being critical of F's failure to achieve certain targets rather than applauding the overall CSR initiatives that it has introduced, and those areas where targets have been exceeded (eg waste reduction).

Potential negative publicity – Equally, some elements of the EEM's report could lead to negative publicity if they are published externally. In particular, highlighting that two of the Meals Division's products are currently undergoing investigations by the Food Standard Authority in relation to inaccurate labelling could lead to customers choosing not to buy those products.

While it is important that the Board is aware of these issues, it may be less appropriate to report the detail to an external audience.

Modify internal report for inclusion in the annual report – Consequently, rather than simply including the existing internal report in its annual report, it may be preferable for F to edit the external version of the report. The internal CSR report should still form the basis of the external one, but any particularly sensitive or detailed information could be removed or reworded in the external report.

In this way, F will still be able to demonstrate that it takes CSR seriously (by producing a report) but with less risk of negative publicity arising from any particularly sensitive information being published.

(b) (iii)

Increased resource allocation – Currently, the Environmental Effects Manager (EEM) has no support staff to help her in her work, and the relatively small size of her budget (£100,000) means she has no scope to hire any.

Since the EEM is having to respond to an increased amount of external environmental legislation, advice and guidelines in additional to her regular work within F, she has more work than she can cope with. This overwork is likely to reduce the EEM's ability to help F achieve its CSR targets, so her effectiveness in this respect would be helped if she was able to **recruit some other staff** to help her.

In order for this to happen, the EEM's **budget** will need to be increased.

Improved communications – It appears that the EEM has very little communication with any of the senior management with F plc. The following actions can help rectify this:

Regular meetings - She has few opportunities to speak to the DoO (whom she reports to), so she may be unclear as to what aspects of her work she should be prioritising. To remedy this, the DoO should arrange regular meetings with the EEM so that they can discuss priorities and progress. For example, the EEM feels that her current activities do hot help F plc achieve its CSR targets; therefore it is important that she discusses her workload and activities to prioritise those which will help F achieve its CSR targets.

Feedback from Board - Although the EEM presents her CSR report to the Board, she never receives any formal feedback from them about it. One solution may be for the EEM to attend one of the Board meetings after the report has been produced. In this way, the Board could discuss any important issues with her, and they may even be able to make suggestions (which the EEM could then look to disseminate) as to how different areas of the business could improve their performance in relation to its CSR targets.

Overcoming resistance – Another issue which appears to be hindering the EEM's effectiveness is the lack of support she seems to receive from the managers within F plc. Some of them feel that CSR is better carried out locally rather than centrally, while others see CSR as a distraction from their work. Even though she has been working at F for two years, the EEM has not even met some of the managers yet.

The DoO should arrange meetings for the EEM with the managers so that she can explain her role within the group, address the concerns they may have, and possibly also consider ways in which she could help them in their work and vice versa.

Published CSR report - In addition, if the Board does decide to publish a CSR report in the Annual Report this will provide a clear indication that CSR is important to the group. In doing so, it should also highlight to the staff that the EEM and the work she is doing are also important. As a result, this could help to overcome some of the resistance to her, and improve the EEM's status and credibility within the organisation.

(c)

For part (c), note that the requirement asks you to look at three different ways in which information systems could be useful: implementing, monitoring and then reporting the CSR policy. Make sure you address all three areas in your answer.

Note also that the requirement refers specifically to F's CSR policy, and not performance or performance management in general terms, so make sure you include references specifically to CSR issues; for example levels of waste. The examiner stressed that generic discussions of IS/IT were awarded no marks, and answers needed to be applied directly to the implementation, monitoring and reporting of F's CSR policy.

Implementation

Setting targets – Although F plc has already set a range of targets associated with its CSR policy it is important that it regularly reviews them, to ensure they remain relevant and appropriate. Information systems (IS) could facilitate the collection of performance data and information which will assist in the formation of these targets. This data could either come from within F plc (subject to the capabilities of the information management system) or externally. For example, F could look at the performance of market-leading companies and then use its targets to help benchmark itself against those companies (eg in terms of waste reduction and process efficiency).

Communicating targets – F plc is a large and complex organisation, with about 10,000 full-time equivalent staff employed across three divisions in different parts of the United Kingdom. Information systems (IS) and the related information technology (IT) could play an important role in allowing the Board to communicate its CSR policy and the related targets across the group. For example, it is likely that F plc has some kind of intranet system, and the CSR targets could be published on the intranet so that all the staff know what they are.

Monitoring

Actual vs target – A key issue here will be monitoring how well F is actually performing against its CSR targets. Again, the standard information management system could be used to monitor CSR.

The advantage of a group-wide system is that it should enable consistency of comparison across the three divisions, for example to see which is being most effective in reducing the levels of wastage.

Real time analysis – The monitoring could be carried out on a real time basis, which would particularly benefit items such as waste reduction. For example, if the monitoring revealed that any of the production processes were wasting unexpected levels of ingredients, immediate action should be taken to stop the wastage, or at least reduce the levels of waste to a more acceptable level. It is possible the IS system could have some kind of automatic control so that if wastage exceeds a certain level the system automatically highlights the problem without requiring human intervention, for example producing exception reports showing products or processes which are suffering waste levels outside agreed parameters.

Reporting

Communication of performance – Once actual performance has been measured against the target, performance levels need to be reported. Although F plc have a standard information system, it is likely the focus of performance reports will vary from division to division.

The IS will enable the divisional accountants (or other people who prepare reports) to download the data they need for their division from the central system.

They could then make the reports available to authorised readers via the intranet, and could send the readers an e-mail alert to tell them the reports are ready to view.

Timeliness of reports - However, there may be limitations to the information which the standard information management system can provide. It has proved unreliable since its installation, and there may be limits to the amount and timeliness of the different reports it can produce.

If the current information management system cannot provide the information the Board need to monitor its CSR policy on a timely and reliable basis, then they may need to consider investing in a new management system which can do so. It is worth noting that the current system was installed ten years ago, and so may need upgrading (or replacing) soon anyway.

68 F plc – desserts division

Text reference: Approaches for overcoming resistance to change are given in Chapter 11 of the BPP Study Text for E3.

Part (a)

Top Tips:

The instruction in italics below the question requirement should have provided you with a clear framework for your answer. You need to do a calculation to work out whether the proposal is financially acceptable (ie whether it has a positive NPV and pays back within one year), then you need to work through the remaining conditions in turn and evaluate whether or not the proposal is consistent with them.

Of the twenty marks available, 10 are for calculations, and 10 are for the subsequent evaluation, so the qualitative analysis is equally important as the calculations. Also, note that you are asked to 'advise' the Board whether or not it should approve the relocation, so you need a short conclusion (based on your evaluation of the six conditions) giving the Board clear advice for its overall decision.

There are a number of potential points you could have made in your evaluation of the proposals, and, for tutorial purposes, the answer below tries to cover a range of these. However, because there are only 10 marks available for the evaluation and the final advice, we have included some of the points in text boxes as an indication that you wouldn't be expected to make them all in your answer.

Examiner's comments: The financial evaluation, including the NPV and payback calculation, was undertaken reasonably well by most candidates although some still made basic mistakes in the calculations. For example, many failed to calculate the redundancy payments correctly, because they omitted the 385 current vacancies. Also, some failed to use the correct discount factor, or did not use a 10 year time frame.

£'000	Yr 0	Yr 1 - 10 (per year)	Workings
Relocation costs	-1,820		
Local tax savings		75	
Incentives for factory jobs	5,040		5,600 x 90% @ £1,000 each
Incentives for office jobs	1,120		5,600 x 10% @ £2,000 each
Transport savings		300	
Redundancies	-4,229		[4,700-385] x 98% @ £1,000 each
Increased salary costs		-200	
	111	175	
Cumulative discount factor		5.019	Years 1 - 10 @ 15% = 5.019
Net Present value	111	878	
Total Net Present value		**989**	

Evaluation of six conditions of approval

1. **Positive Net Present Value** – The proposed relocation is expected to generate a positive net present value of £989,000 so this condition is met.

2. **Payback period** – The proposed relocation will generate a net cash inflow of £111,000 in Year 0, and is forecast to generate positive net cash inflows in all the subsequent years. Therefore, the proposal satisfies the condition to pay back within three years.

3. **Public image** – Redundancies – The proposed relocation will lead to 98% (4,229) of the Dessert Division's current employees in the North of England being made redundant. Given that unemployment in the region already seems to be quite high (as evidenced by there being a ready supply of manual labour for production work) the proposal is likely to be unpopular among the staff and local communities in the North of England. Consequently, it is likely to have an adverse impact on F's public image, particularly in the North of England.

   Relocation offer - Although F has offered its staff the possibility of relocating to the new site, relocating from the North of England to the West of England is unlikely to be feasible for many of the staff (hence the 98% redundancy rate. Therefore the offer of relocation will do little to help preserve F's public image in the local communities affected by the relocation.

   New job creation – However, as a counter balance to the closure of the division's site in the North of England, F has forecast that the new site in the West of England will employ 5,600 people. Therefore, in aggregate terms, the relocation will lead to the **creation of 900 new jobs**, which should generate positive publicity for F and hence help restore its public image.

   Public image in the West of England – Moreover, the move is likely to have a positive effect on F's public image in the West of England because of the number of new jobs it is creating there. Given the low number of employees who are expected to relocate from the existing site, F would need to employ about 5,500 new staff [5,600 – (4,315-4,229) = 5,514] in the West of England. This is likely to provide a significant boost to the local economy, especially since the fact that 'it should be easy to secure all the labour needed' suggests that unemployment rates there may currently be quite high.

4. **Contribution to Corporate Social Responsibility (CSR) targets** – F's CSR report for the year ended 31 December 2010 highlights that transportation is one of the five key CSR areas the company focuses on. Although the specific targets F has set appear to relate to the use of air travel rather than road travel, it is reasonable to expect that F will also want to reduce the number of road kilometres travelled. Therefore, given that road kilometres travelled increased by 5% in 2010, the opportunity to reduce road travel by 15% could be a significant positive contribution to the CSR targets.

5. **Consistency with mission statement** – F's mission statement highlights that the company is 'committed to continually seek ways to increase its return to investors'. The positive net present value of £989,000 over the first ten years indicates that the proposed relocation should contribute to an increased return for F plc's investors, compared to the return if the Dessert division stayed at its current site.

   The scenario does not indicate what impact the relocation will have on the Dessert division's production capacity (and hence its ability to expand market share, as also identified in the mission statement), but the increase in employee numbers suggests that the relocation has also been linked to the Division's expansion plans. In this respect, the proposed relocation is also consistent with F's mission statement.

   In addition, the mission statement highlights F's desire to use efficient processes, and, although the scenario does not give any detail about the operational facilities at the new site, the fact that the factory and distribution facilities are both modern will hopefully mean they are efficient to operate. Moreover, the reduction in operating costs (in Years 1-10 compared to the existing site) could also be seen as an indicator of increased efficiency, and therefore consistency with the mission statement.

6. **Contributing to F plc's strategic aims** – F's strategic aims refer to increased profitability through increased market share [aim (i)]; quality and product attractiveness [aim (ii)]; standards of food hygiene (aim (iii)]; and innovation and efficiency (aim (iv)].

   Although the proposed relocation does not appear to contradict any of these aims, it is nonetheless debatable how far it directly contributes to any of them.

The relocation will contribute to increased profitability, but this is primarily due to reduced operating costs rather than increased market share. As we have already suggested, the relocation may facilitate expansion and hence increased market share in future, but there is no guarantee of this at present.

Therefore it may be difficult to justify how far the proposal contributes to achieving F plc's strategic aims.

Advice:

The proposal generates a positive NPV, and seems to satisfy the conditions identified by the Board overall. Therefore, F plc's Board should approve the Dessert Division's proposed relocation to the West of England.

(b)

Top tip: The context of 'dealing with resistance to change' should have given you an indication that Kotter & Schlesinger's approaches for overcoming resistance to change could be a useful framework here. However, you shouldn't have simply worked through all six of the approaches in turn generically. To score well, you need to apply them critically to the scenario. For example, given that the Marketing staff distrust the Accountant (and feel he is spying on them), is manipulation and co-optation likely to be a suitable approach here?

Examiner's comment: Most candidates used either the Kotter & Schlesinger framework or Lewin's force field analysis to here, and either approach was acceptable provided it was applied directly to the problems identified in Goal 1.

The main weakness was that many candidates who identified 'manipulation' and 'coercion' failed to appreciate that they conflict with CIMA's ethical code and therefore should not be undertaken. At Strategic level, you are expected to think about the relevance or applicability of models, rather than simply applying them wholesale.

It appears that the Divisional marketing staff are suspicious of the Divisional Accountant and do not always understand or agree with the figures he produces. This has led to a difficult working relationship between the Accountant and the marketing staff, which may not be helped by the fact that the finance function is seen as the dominant force in the Division.

<u>Education and Communication</u>

Communicating Chief Executive's goals – At one level, it is important that the Accountant communicates the Chief Executive's message to all the marketing staff. If the marketing staff realise the Chief Executive has ordered that the meetings to change their character, and that a constructive working relationship be established this may help convince them of the need to change.

Education and communication about roles – However, a large part of the problem between the Accountant and the marketing staff appears to come from the fact that the Marketing staff do not understand the Accountant's figures, and do not understand his role in the department. In this respect, it will be vital for the Accountant to communicate his role in the department and educate the other staff about how (and why) he compiles his figures.

However, it is important that this communication is a **two-way process**. The Accountant must not simply tell the Marketing staff what his role is, he must also encourage the Marketing staff to explain why they feel he is spying on them, and what aspects of his figures they do not understand.

It is quite likely that many of the problems between the Marketing staff and the Accountant have arisen because neither fully understands the other's role and aims. Therefore, if both parties become more open with each other, and improve their communication, this should improve the working relationship, and in doing so, facilitate the change the Chief Executive wants to see.

<u>Participation and involvement</u>

Although the trigger for change has come from the Chief Executive, in general terms the working relationship can only improve if the various staff actually start working together rather than confronting each other.

In this respect, it is important that the Accountant tries to involve the marketing staff in changes wherever possible. For example, he could ask them for suggestions as to how the structure of their meetings could be improved to make them less confrontational. If the marketing staff feel they have been involved in shaping the change process they will have more of an interest in trying to ensure it is successful.

Facilitation and support

Shared responsibility – Although the Accountant has been delegated responsibility for overcoming the confrontations, it seems that both he and the Marketing staff are partly responsible for them. Therefore, ultimately the Marketing staff will also need to take some responsibility for overcoming them.

Working together - However, building on the ideas of education and greater involvement, the Accountant may be able to may be able to reduce the conflict and resistance from the Marketing staff by encouraging them to work more closely with him. For example, if the Accountant discussed his figures with the relevant members of the Marketing staff they would no longer be able to say they didn't understand them.

Equally, the Marketing staff may also be able to help the Accountant improve the quality of the figures, if they have more detailed knowledge about some of the operational issues behind the figures than he does.

It is quite likely that the Marketing staff's complaints have come when the Accountant has, unexpectedly, presented results which show the Marketing staff performing worse than forecast. By working more closely together, the Accountant and the Marketing staff can avoid these instances of 'unexpected bad news' which in turn should improve the working relationship between them.

Negotiation and agreement

Agree scope of meetings – We have already mentioned the possibility of the Accountant encouraging the Marketing staff to become involved with suggesting ways the meetings could be made more productive. However, this is a relatively informal involvement. The nature of the 'agreement' suggested here is a more formal arrangement. For example, **agreement** could be made about the frequency, timing and agendas for the meetings. There may also be an agreement the Accountant will circulate, in advance, any figures to be discussed in the meeting so that the Marketing staff have the chance to investigate any issues they highlight.

Negotiation - However, negotiation is important here as well. For example, the Accountant should discuss any proposals for the meetings (eg, frequency) with the Marketing staff, rather than just deciding them himself. Again, if the Marketing staff feel they have been consulted in the process they are likely to be less confrontational or resistant to it.

Coercion

Use of force – All the methods we have discussed so far are based in the context of the Accountant and the Marketing staff working constructively together to overcome their problems. However, the Accountant may find that some of the Marketing staff continue to resist any changes despite his efforts.

In the worst case, the Accountant may have to defer to the Finance Director or the Marketing Director and ask them to take the appropriate action against any staff members who are preventing a constructive working relationship being established.

However, the Accountant should be **very reluctant to resort to coercive tactics**. Given that the Marketing staff already distrust the Accountant (and think he is spying on them), such tactics may once damage the relationship between the Accountant and the Marketing staff even further, undoing whatever work has so far been done to improve the working relationship between the two parties.

(c)

Top Tip: The requirement here is specifically to 'recommend improvements', not, for example, to discuss the problems, or why they might have occurred.

However, it is important that you think about the context of the problems and what has caused them before you start to recommend your improvements. A number of the problems can be attributed (at least partially) to F plc's standard information management system. Therefore, there will be a degree of overlap in the possible recommendations to achieve different goals. However, you must avoid simply stating that the answer to each of the goals is to implement a new computerised system, or an ERP system. Instead, you should try to discuss the individual problems identified within each goal, and recommend a range of recommendation to address each specific problem.

Notice also that the scenario stated that any proposed changes must be self-financing. In addition to the comment below, the Examiner also noted that many candidates did not explore the financial implications of their recommendations.

Examiner's comments: Most candidates correctly reviewed each goal in turn and attempted to make a range of recommendations for each. Some candidates simply recommended a 'Just in Time' system to solve all of the problems identified in relation to Goal 2. This was a limited solution, and correspondingly was awarded limited credit.

Goal 2 - Reduce levels of wastage

Currently, 3.8% of ingredients are wasted at a cost of £7.5m. The target wastage figure is 2%, which equates to a waste cost of £3.9m; meaning that savings of £3.6m are required. These are major savings, so the measures required are likely to be quite extensive, but equally the potential benefits will justify significant spending to achieve them.

Inventory control system - The high levels of wastage appear to be directly linked to the problems in respect of inventory control. However, these are not confined to the Desserts Division, because all three divisions use F plc's standard information system. Therefore, in part, the Desserts Division will need F as a whole to improve its standard information system.

Requirement to be self-financing - The question of whether of not the new system will be self-financing could be an issue here, but if the system allows the Desserts Division to achieves it waste target then the 'benefits' of the system will be at least £3.6m per year. The cost of the new system is likely to be lower than this.

It seems likely that F needs an upgraded (or new) **software system which tracks receipts, storage and issues of materials**, and which will produce exception reports – for example, for raw materials where the quantities in stock fall outside agreed levels, or for raw material items for which large quantities have to be written off as unfit for use. In such cases, if an exception report is generated, the manager responsible should have to explain the reason for the exception.

Causes of wastage - However, it will still be necessary to identify the causes and locations of the wastage, and F plc could ask the internal audit department to carry out an investigation into this, and if necessary the Desserts Division may need to buy some new storage units if they are a factor in raw materials going bad.

More proactively, the division could also introduce a **staff incentive scheme** which asks operating staff to identify current areas of waste and propose ways of eliminating them. By encouraging staff participation in this way, and rewarding staff for good ideas, the Division may also be able to reduce turnover rate amongst staff.

Staffing and monitoring - The Desserts Division also needs to review its staffing procedures and controls. For example, it may be that warehouse staff are working without sufficient supervision or control, which allow them the opportunity to steal some raw materials. One way of increasing control would be to install CC TV cameras in the warehouse. This may cause resentment among some of the staff if they feel they are not trusted, but the Division could justify the need to install the cameras due to the levels of theft.

Goal 3- Physical inventory count

Reduce discrepancies – The current differences (5%) between the theoretical and the actual inventory counts should automatically be reduced if the measures recommended to achieve Goal 2 are introduced. For example, the current differences could be exacerbated by inaccuracies in the theoretical figures (resulting from the problems with F's information systems) and the levels of theft affecting the actual figures.

The context of inventory counts again highlights the importance of having reliable information systems. If the system-generated figures are not accurate, this reduces the value of undertaking inventory counts comparing these figures against the actual numbers in the warehouse.

Formalise process – However, given the value of materials which the Division appears to hold as inventory it is important the inventory counts are carried.

There is no indication how frequently these counts are currently carried out, or what processes are undertaken during them. Goal 3 has recommended that the counts should be carried out monthly basis, but it may even be preferable to count high value or high usage items more frequently than that (despite the increased cost of having additional counts). Also, the Division should establish more formal processes for the way all the counts are carried out, for example defining any involvement required from the warehouse staff. These should be introduced in conjunction with staff training.

Train staff – Currently, the process appears quite informal, with no regular group of people carrying out the counts. The reliability of the counts is likely to be increased if the people carrying out the counts are more regular, and have received training.

Goal 4 – Achieving 100% of potential revenue

The Divisional Accountant's estimate that 5% of the Division's potential revenue is lost due to poor inventory control suggests that in 2010 the Division lost approximately £29 million of sales revenue in this way. The scale of this figure again suggests inventory control issues are a major problem for the Division, but as we have already noted in relation to Goal 2 many of these are also group-wide issues (across F plc) rather than being specifically a problem for the Desserts Division.

Inventory control system - The remedial actions taken to achieve Goal 2 should also help to achieve Goal 4. However, the requirement to install a new information system is a Group-wide issue, and not one which the Desserts Division can achieve by itself.

Group approval required - Therefore in order for it to achieve Goal 4, the Divisional General Manager of the Desserts Division will have to stress to the Board of F plc the importance of upgrading the inventory control system across the group, such that they are prepared to sanction the necessary expenditure to develop (or buy in) a new system. However, given that the Chief Executive is the driving force behind the goals the Dessert Division is trying to achieve, this should make it easier for the Divisional General Manager to get the approval he needs, especially given the extent of the financial costs which appear to be arising from the misleading information from the current system.

Goal 5 – Timely management accounts

Resolving systems issues – Again, a proportion of the problem here is likely to come from the unreliability of F plc's standard information management system. Therefore, as with the solution to Goal 4, the achievement of Goal 5 will depend partly on the Board of F plc approving a new information system.

Resolving divisional issues – However, the lateness of the accounts is also likely to be partially due to the problems and issues specifically within the Division, and so the actions taken to achieve Goals 1 to 4 should help achieve this Goal (for example, having accurate inventory figures available for use immediately after the month end (or even on a real time basis).

However, if there are other additional issues which specifically slow down the production of the Desserts Division's management accountants compared to the other divisions then the management accountant will need to identify them and prepare a separate plan to resolve them.

Paper-based ordering – One such issue appears to arise in relation to the paper-based system for the ordering and receipt of goods. The management accountant should try to work with the relevant operational manager to see if the system can be modified into a standard form that is compatible with the F's standard information management system, such that an electronic system (which feeds directly into the information management system) can be used rather than a paper-based one.

69 DEF & WLS

Text reference. Stakeholder management is discussed in Chapter 2 of the BPP Study Text, as are mission statements. Evaluation of strategic options is covered in Chapter 7, while the BCG matrix is covered in Chapter 4.

Marking scheme

				Marks
(a)	(i)	Explanation of power/interest (using Mendelow) and recognition of appropriate approaches depending on level of power and interest	Up to 2	
		Each relevant approach explained – 1 mark each	Up to 5	
		(Relevant approaches could include prioritisation; weighting and scoring; satisficing; sequential attention; exercise of power)		
			Total up to	5
	(ii)	For discussing the current owners' logic behind the missions statement - 1 mark per relevant point	Up to 2	
		For discussing differences in IVB's aspirations and business approach compared to current owners – 1 mark per relevant point	Up to 3	
		Recognition that IVB will only hold 25% of the shares	1	
			Total up to	5
(b)	(i)	For each relevant measure of financial performance calculated: 1 mark each	Up to 7	
		(Measures include: Revenue growth per year, profit margin, profit growth per year, cash as % of profit, debtors as % of revenue, gearing, return on equity, P/E ratio)		
		For analysis of each measure of financial performance and its implications on the proposed acquisition – Up to 2 marks for each relevant point	Up to 12	
		Conclusion advising whether or not the acquisition is appropriate	Up to 2	
			Total up to	20
	(ii)	For advising of ways that acquiring WLS will help DEF achieve its objectives – 1 mark each	Up to 2	
		For advising of ways that WLS's activities conflict with DEF's mission statement – Up to 2 marks for each relevant point discussed	Up to 7	
		Conclusion advising whether or not the information in the report suggests acquisition is appropriate	Up to 4	
			Total up to	10
(c)		For each business area:		
		Identifying correct position in BCG matrix and explaining rationale – 1 mark each	Up to 5	
		Recommending appropriate strategy – 1 mark each	Up to 5	
			Total up to	10
			Total	50

Part (a)

Top tips. Although requirement (a) (i) is about stakeholder management, make sure you understand exactly what the requirement is asking before you answer it. It is not asking you to analyse DEF's stakeholders, and it is not asking you to explain Mendelow's matrix. However, the ideas behind Mendelow's matrix (identifying the key stakeholders according to their power and interest) are relevant here, because one way the Board of Directors could manage conflicting objectives is by prioritising the objectives of the stakeholders with the highest levels of power and interest.

Examiner's comments. In question (a) (i), nearly all the candidates presented a discussion of the Mendelow matrix, and then only referred to possible stakeholder management strategies used with that matrix. Candidates who gave a detailed stakeholder analysis for DEF using Mendelow's matrix wasted their time doing so, because this had not been asked for, and so would not earn any marks.

(a) (i)

Consistency with mission – The Board could evaluate how well each of the different stakeholder objectives allows DEF to achieve its mission. For example, the mission statement highlights DEF's intention to offer its customers a range of services of the highest quality. Consequently, the Board should assess the differing stakeholders' objectives in terms of how well they allow DEF to achieve this mission, and it should support those which are best aligned to its mission and its own strategic objectives.

Prioritisation of objectives – In this respect, the Board could specify that any option it considers makes must satisfy at least of its strategic objectives before it will be approved. In this way the Board could prioritise the stakeholders' competing objectives such that only ones which satisfy at least one strategic objective will be pursued.

Identify key stakeholders – The Board needs to identify which stakeholder groups it feels have high power and high interest in DEF's activities, because these are its key stakeholders. Any conflicts need to be resolved in such a way that they are acceptable to DEF's key stakeholders.

Weighing and scoring – In this respect, the Board could give weights to each stakeholder view, with the highest weightings being given to those stakeholders who views are most important to DEF. Different objectives could then be giving a weighting according to which stakeholders support it, or object to it, and the objective the highest score could be pursued.

Compromise – However, the Board may also need to highlight that there is a need to compromise in establishing and managing DEF's objectives. In this respect, the Board should explain to the different stakeholder groups that they may have to settle for less than it would ideally want to have. Again, however, the level of compromise the Board may ask different stakeholder groups to accept is likely to be linked to that group's importance to DEF.

(a) (ii)

Top tips: The key to answering this question well was to recognise the differences in approach taken by IVB and DEF. Doing so should then have highlighted the areas of the current mission statement which IVB is likely to challenge. For example, IVB is explicitly interested in profits and profitability but this isn't mentioned in the mission statement. Conversely, IVB is not interested in being a good corporate citizen or staff retention.

However, you should also have noticed that IVB currently only holds 25% of the shares. So, if the remaining shareholders object to IVB's proposed changes it is possible the mission statement may remain as it is for the time being.

Current mission statement – DEF's current mission statement focuses on the quality of service provided to customers and the quality of staff employed, maintaining high ethical standards, and being a good corporate citizen. However, these aims do not reflect IVB's focus on cost-cutting and short-term profitability.

This mission statement was formulated by the current Board of Directors, but once IVB has a representative on the Board, it is likely IVB will try to change the mission statement to reflect its own focus on business turnarounds and short term profitability.

Performance measures – The current mission statement emphasises customer service, quality, ethical standards and corporate citizenship as the bases on which DEF will seek to outperform its competitors. However, there is no reference to financial aspects of performance, such as profitability, return on investment or capital growth. It is likely that IVB will try to get some explicit commercial/financial measure of performance included in the mission statement.

Corporate citizenship – IVB's main focus seems to be on the short-term profitability it can generate for its shareholders. Shareholders appear to be the key stakeholder for IVB. Therefore issues such as ethical standards and being a good corporate citizen will be far less important.

People and staff – DEF currently aims to employ 'the best people' to help outperform its competitors. However, IVB's track record suggests a preference for cutting costs (including making large-scale redundancies) in the quest for short-term profit, rather than preserving the current workforce and continuing to employ the best people.

IVB's impact - If IVB only holds 25% of the shares it will not be able to force the other Board members to change the mission statement because it could still be out-voted by the other Board members. However, in future, the other LSGs may also wish to sell their shares, and if IVB also acquires these it could then secure a majority shareholding.

(b) (i)

Top tips. The note beneath the requirement clearly indicates that (b) (i) requires both calculations and then an evaluation of those calculations. In fact, of the 20 marks available, only 7 are for the calculations, so the commentary on the calculations is actually the more important part of the requirement.

To score well, it is important that you evaluate what the calculations indicate about WLS's performance and hence its suitability as a possible acquisition. In other words, you need to make some insightful comments about the calculations, rather than merely restating them. For example, rather than just saying that the debtors figure as a percentage of revenue has remained constant each year, you could say that this consistency suggests that WLS has a tight management of its working capital.

Your calculations in (b) (i) should have indicated that (from a financial perspective) WLS has been performing well. By contrast, the level of criticism identified in the audit report should have suggested that its performance in this area is much less good. Given DEF's own mission statement and its own position on CSR, the audit report suggests WLS's overall performance conflicts with DEF's position. What implications does this have for WLS's suitability as a potential acquisition target?

Importantly, however, although there are two distinct parts to the question – financial, then CSR – you then need to pull them together in order to advise the Board whether the proposed acquisition is an appropriate strategic option.

Examiner's comments. Question (b) (i) was not well answered by most candidates, with a number failing to undertake sensible financial analysis even though the calculations should have been fairly obvious (such as profit margin per year, growth in revenues, gearing levels.) However, many candidates could not identify even these most obvious calculations. The evaluation of the calculations was equally disappointing, with many candidates providing very superficial answers. A significant number of candidates failed to evaluate the calculations at all, and instead discussed general issues about the acquisition, such as cultural changes, impact on customers etc. The question specifically asked for an evaluation of financial performance, and general comments which were not relevant to the question set, earned no marks.

Question (b) (ii) was reasonably well answered, and most candidates correctly identified the differences between WLS's attitude and DEF's attitude to CSR, as found in the pre-seen material. However, most answers merely answered parts (i) and (ii) separately and failed to present an overall recommendation as to whether acquiring WLS is an appropriate strategic option for DEF.

WLS Financial performance

	2007	2008	2009	2010
Revenue	2,874	3,313	3,978	4,972
Annual growth (%)		15.3%	20.1%	25.0%
Cumulative growth (%)		15.3%	38.4%	73.0%
Retained Profit	632	795	1,074	1,492
Margin (%)	22.0%	24.0%	27.0%	30.0%
Net cash inflow	50	82	111	224
Cash inflow as % of revenue	1.7%	2.5%	2.8%	4.5%
Cash inflow as % of profit	7.9%	10.3%	10.3%	15.0%
Receivables	144	165	199	234
Receivables as % of revenue	5.0%	5.0%	5.0%	4.7%
Receivables as % of profit	22.8%	20.8%	18.5%	15.7%
Equity	308	1,103	2,177	3,669
Change in Equity		795	1,074	1,492
Debt	200	200	200	200
Debt + Equity	508	1,303	2,377	3,869
Gearing	39%	15%	8%	5%

Analysis of financial performance:

Revenue growth – WLS's revenue has grown each year (2007-2010) and the rate of growth appears to be increasing, both in absolute terms and in percentage terms.

Profit increases - WLS's profit has also increased year on year throughout the period. Interestingly, it is not just the absolute level of profit which has increased but also the margin. This suggests that WLS has not had to offer any significant discounts or price reductions in order to achieve its sales growth. It also suggests that WLS is beginning to benefit from some economies of scale as it has grown.

We are not given figures for any other cargo handling companies, but WLS's net profit margins (30% in 2010) look pretty high.

Cash flow – As well as being profitable throughout the period under review, WLS has also achieved a **positive cash flow** in each year.

Moreover, the net cash inflow has grown more rapidly over the period (in percentage terms) than retained profit has, such that cash inflow as a % of profit has increased from 8% (2007) to 15% (2010). This suggests that WLS has been effective in managing its liquidity and its cash flows.

Receivables – The ratio of receivables to revenue has remained constant over the period which suggests that WLS has maintained effective credit control despite its expansion. There is no indication of what credit terms WLS offers its customers, but the consistency in the % level of receivables may suggest it has one single set of terms which it applies for all its customers.

Equity – The equity figure has increased each year by exactly the same amount as the profit after interest and tax. This suggests that WLS has not paid any dividends in the period, and it may also suggest that the owners have been keen to use the retained profits from the business to finance its growth.

The lack of dividends may also indicate that the owners have been prepared to sacrifice their dividends in the short term to try to achieve a higher capital return when they come to sell the business in future. However, this seems slightly contradictory with the idea that the owners are looking for a quick sale; with the implication being that they may accept a lower price in order to secure a quick sale.

Debt and Gearing – WLS does not appear to have taken any new loans in the period, which suggests that the operating cashflow has been sufficient to fund the business in the short to medium term.

There is no indication as to when the current loan is due to be repaid, but WLS's positive cash flow suggests it should not have any problems repaying the loan when it becomes due.

Moreover, WLS's level of gearing is now very low, at 5% (down from 39% in 2007). This suggests WLS should not have too much difficulty obtaining additional loans in the future if it wanted to use debt financing to support its continued growth.

Sale price – The suggested sale price of $4 million represents a Price/Earnings (P/E) ratio of 2.7 (4,000/1,492).

There is no indication of how this compares to the P/E ratios of other companies in the cargo industry. However, it seems quite low given WLS's recent financial performance. This may therefore support the agent's claim that the owners are looking for a quick sale.

(b) (ii)

Although the analysis of WLS's financial performance suggests that acquiring the company may be an appropriate strategic option, the audit report prepared by QEG has highlighted some issues DEF needs to be aware of.

A number of QEG's findings suggest that WLS's operations are not aligned to DEF's mission statement and objectives:

High carbon footprint – WLS has a very high carbon footprint. However, one of DEF's specific strategic objectives is to minimise the pollution effects of the airport's operations. And, more generally, DEF seeks to be a good corporate citizen. Having a high carbon footprint contradicts these aims.

Unfair and discriminatory employment practices – WLS uses unfair and discriminatory employment practices in some countries. This again contradicts the aims expressed in DEF's mission statement to conform to the highest ethical standards and to be a good corporate citizen.

Poor customer service standards - WLS's customer service standards were found to be 'poor', with WLS seemingly having a 'couldn't care less attitude' to their customers. This appears to be completely at odds with DEF's strategic approach, which is based on achieving competitive advantage through the high quality of service it offers its customers.

Poor corporate citizen –The overall conclusion of QEG's report was that WLS 'is not a good corporate citizen', and consequently WLS was awarded the lowest possible rating in the audit report. Once again, this is at odds with the aim expressed in DEF's mission statement to be a good corporate citizen 'in everything that it does.'

In the light of QEG's findings about WLS, the Board will need to consider whether acquiring WLS is consistent with this aim of being a good corporate citizen, and therefore whether it is appropriate to acquire WLS.

Conclusion

The Board faces a dilemma here. WLS's financial performance suggests that it would be a suitable company to acquire, but the problems highlighted by the audit report suggest that the acquisition may not be appropriate in the context of DEF's mission statement. It is possible that the concerns over WLS's poor corporate citizenship may have led the current owners to sanction a lower sale price for the company. In this context, DEF also needs to consider the potential costs of rectifying the issues highlighted in QEG's report before deciding whether or not to proceed with the acquisition.

(c)

Top tips. The table in the unseen should have given you a useful framework for answering this question: look at each of the business segments in turn and consider its market prospects (growth) and DEF's likely position in the market (relative market share). This should enable to position each segment in one of the quadrants in the BCG matrix, and then you should have been able to recommend a suitable strategy for each segment position.

However, it is important that you explain why you have treated each segment as you have done - (see the Examiner's comments below).

Also, when recommending future strategies, it is important to think about their impact on DEF as a whole, and not simply quote the options in the model without thinking about them carefully. For example, aviation income is a cash cow, and the two possible strategies for a cash cow are 'hold' or 'harvest.' But, how appropriate would it be for DEF to 'harvest' aviation income?

Examiner's comments. There was some confusion in categorised the Car Parking segment, as many candidates considered this to be a 'dog' [rather than a 'question mark']. However, if candidates explain their categorisation clearly, then this was credited.

Aviation income

Cash cow - The scenario suggests that TUV airport is DEF's main competitor, but doesn't indicate the relative size of the two airports. However, it is likely that they are roughly the same size. Coupled with the combination of **strongly positive cash flow**, and some market growth in a **mature market**, this suggests that aviation income is a cash cow.

The two possible options for a cash cow are to **hold** or **harvest**. However, because aviation income currently contributes just below half of DEF's revenue [48% based on 2011 forecasts: D$ 11,232 / D$ 23,400] and because it generates a strong positive cashflow for the rest of the group, the appropriate choice here would seem to be **'hold'** and to continue to generate the cash flows needed to support DEF's desired growth from 2011-2015.

Retail concessions

DEF holds a monopoly over concessions at the airport, and has a strong regional market share. However, DEF is likely to only have a **relatively small share** of the overall retail concessions market.

Prior to 2009, the retail concessions market enjoyed **high growth**. Market growth has slowed in the last couple of years, but it is likely that this is due to the slowdown in the national retail market overall rather than a specific slowdown in the concessions market.

Question mark - Therefore it appears that the Board should treat the retail concessions business segment as a question mark (on the basis of it having a relatively low market share in a relatively fast growing market.)

On this basis, the BCG matrix would suggest that DEF should either **build** or **harvest** the retail concessions business segment. As the retail concessions are already forecast to generate a positive cash flow, it seems appropriate for DEF to look to **build** this segment.

If DEF were to shut down the retail concessions, their absence could adversely affect the airport's business as a whole, because passenger may choose to fly from other airports if DEF no longer had any shopping or catering facilities. Conversely, if DEF invests further in the retail side of its business, the extra shops and facilities will help support the projected increase in passenger numbers in the coming years.

Car parking

Question mark - DEF is likely to only be a **relatively small operator** in the car parking market as a whole and its market share also appears to be under threat from the increasing competition in the market. However, the projected growth in passenger numbers, and continued population growth more generally, suggest that the market still has **moderate to high growth prospects**. This again suggests that the car parking business segment is a question mark for DEF.

Importantly, although the car parking business currently produces a marginally positive cash flow, this could be under threat from competitors undercutting DEF's prices and offering additional services. The Board may be advised **wait and see** what impact these competitor actions have on the profitability and cash generating capacity of the car parking business before finalising a strategy for it. However, if cash flow looks like it is going to become negative DEF may be advised to **harvest** this segment, and stop operating its own car parks.

Other income

Although DEF's Other income comes from a mixture of revenue streams, it is likely that DEF only has a low relative market share for any of the them.

Property rental income seems to be a relatively important of DEF's Other income but DEF is not a major player in the property rental market.

Dog - The Commercial Director's feeling that the market position for Other income is 'declining both in growth and share' suggests that this business segment is a dog.

Accordingly, DEF would be advised to **divest** the business segments which make up its Other income.

However, before it sells any properties it currently rents out, DEF should consider whether it will need any additional properties for its own business in future. For example, if DEF introduces cargo handling services (as is proposed for 2014) it may need additional space for cargo storage.

Cargo handling / WLS

The cargo handling market is **growing rapidly**, although DEF currently has no presence in that market.

On the other hand, **WLS appears to be a significant player** in the cargo handing market, operating from numerous airports in America, Europe and Africa. It seems possible that if DEF acquires WLS, then cargo handling could become a **star** in its business portfolio. In this case, DEF would be advised to **build** this business segment.

However, if DEF decides not to acquire WLS it will need to **invest** to build its own business in this area.

70 DEF Airport

Text reference: Generic strategies are discussed in Chapter 5 of your BPP Study text. Strategic objectives and mission statements are covered in Chapter 2.

(a)

Top tips: Although the question requirement identified Porter's generic strategies as the framework for this question, you should not have spent a long time discussing the theory behind each of the strategies. You should have mentioned, briefly, how Porter suggests each strategy confers competitive advantage on an organisation, but then tailored your answer to the context of the scenario: how can the strategies help DEF achieve sustainable competitive advantage? (When this exam was sat, candidates who had done some background research about airports and their competitive strategies - following the release of the pre-seen material - could have used this research to inform their suggestions here.)

For (a) (i) it is vital you discuss low production *cost* and do not confuse this with low price. Porter's strategy is based on a company becoming the lowest cost provider in the industry, not necessarily charging the lowest prices. You also need to indicate how this cost leadership might translate into competitive advantage – for example, simply saying 'DEF will attract low cost airlines' is not good enough. Instead you should explain that being the cost leader would 'permit DEF to charge lower prices than its competitors for landing, servicing etc and yet still remain profitable, as a result of having lower costs than its competitors'.

The same logic applies to the other two parts of the question: to score well you must explain how Porter's strategy actually translates into a competitive advantage. When discussing differentiation, you should make reference to the ability to charge premium prices, and consider the implications of the passenger survey (mentioned in the unseen material) which suggests that high quality lounges and restaurants may provide a source of differentiation.

Note that in part (a) (iii) you should discuss **either** cost focus **or** differentiation focus. For tutorial purposes we have included both in our answer below, but you should have only included one or the other in your answers.

Sustainable competitive advantage – A firm can achieve sustainable competitive advantage if it can outperform its competitors and therefore continue to earn profits despite the effects of competition on it.

Porter argues that such competitive advantage can be achieved by using one of what he defines as the generic strategies: overall cost leadership, differentiation, or focus (cost focus or differentiation focus). So, according to Porter, if DEF wants to achieve sustainable competitive advantages it needs to adopt one of these generic strategies.

(i) Overall cost leadership

Cost control - If DEF chooses to pursue a cost leadership strategy it will need to control and reduce its costs so that they are lower than all the other airports it competes with. For example, DEF needs to ensure that its aviation-related costs (related to aircraft landings) are lower than all the other airports. In particular, DEF will need to have lower costs than TUV and the three other airports which are less than 80 kilometres away from it. If its cost base is lower than its competitors, DEF can then also charge lower prices than its competitors and yet still remain profitable.

Competitors' costs - At a practical level, in order to achieve cost leadership, DEF will need to have some information about its competitors' costs, so that it can benchmark its costs against theirs. This will enable DEF to identify any areas where cost-savings or efficiencies can be made, to allow its cost base to be lower than its competitors.

However, if DEF wants to follow a cost leadership approach, it may have to revise its mission statement: DEF is unlikely to be able to offer its customers 'a range of services that are of the highest quality' and at the same time have a lower cost base (and therefore offer lower prices) than its competitors. For example, DEF could lower its security costs by employing fewer security staff, but this could mean longer queues for passengers as they wait to pass through security. Equally, DEF might be able to renegotiate any contract services it has (for example, for cleaning the airport lounges) but if it pays less for these services, the service quality may suffer as a result (for example, the lounges may not be cleaned as thoroughly or as frequently).

Current costs - We already know that in some aspects of its business, DEF's costs are higher than its competitors, and therefore it is likely to be charging higher prices than its competitors. For example, DEF's car parking charges are higher than those charged by its competitors. This will need to be reversed if DEF is to pursue a cost leadership strategy.

Problems of identifying industry – The reference to car park charges highlights a potential complication in using Porter's generic strategies. We initially suggested that DEF's competitors were the other airports, but we have now identified that its competitors also include other car park operators, for example. In order to achieve overall cost leadership DEF would need to have a lower cost base than all its different competitors in the different markets in which it operates (aviation income, car parking, and other income).

Sustainability of competitive advantage - However, even if DEF manages to reduce costs and prices below its competitors in the short term, it is debatable whether this will allow it to achieve a sustainable competitive advantage. DEF does not appear to have any unique cost advantage over its competitors, so if it reduces it costs (and, in turn, prices) it is likely that its competitors will try to do the same. The only market in which DEF is likely to have a unique advantage is in retail concessions since it has a monopoly over granting licences. However, this advantage is not based on being a cost leader.

(ii) Differentiation

Premium prices - A differentiation strategy would entail DEF finding a way of differentiating itself from its competitors in such a way that its customers will pay a premium price to use DEF; for example, because of the quality and comfort of its airport lounges.

One area of business in which DEF can charge a premium price is for the provision of retail concessions because it has a monopoly over the granting of these. However, if DEF is going to pursue a differentiation strategy it needs to ensure that it has points of differentiation in all aspects of the business so that it can charge premium prices in all its different markets (aviation income, car parking etc.)

Distinctiveness - The Commercial Director's research into the survey of European air passengers could be instructive in this respect. The survey revealed that business and first class travellers value 'distinctiveness,' and it is likely they would therefore be prepared to pay a premium price for offering something which nobody else offers.

The survey results suggest that DEF would be able to achieve distinctiveness by: hosting only the major airlines and not the low-priced airlines; and having luxury passenger lounges, high class restaurants and large duty-free shops with an extensive range of exclusive brands.

Auxiliary services - DEF could look to enhance its distinctiveness by providing additional features which would appeal to business or first class travellers. For example, DEF could offer meeting rooms or conference facilities, or a chauffeur service in association with some of the major airlines.

Capital expenditure required – However, in order to achieve this distinctiveness, DEF is like to have to make some significant capital expenditure to upgrade its lounges and restaurants to a standard which is superior to that any of its competitors can offer.

Customer requirements - However, the Commercial Director's research also illustrates a potential problem in trying to use a differentiation strategy to achieve competitive advantage. While one type of passenger (airline passengers) may value distinctiveness, the other type of customer (the airlines) appear to be keen to negotiate the most cost effective deals they can with airports. Therefore, trying to charge premium prices to the airlines for using DEF airport is likely to be counter-productive, because it will encourage the airlines to use competitors' airports instead.

In this way, the range of different customers and markets DEF services, suggests that a focus strategy may be more appropriate for helping DEF achieve a competitive advantage than either one based on overall cost leadership or differentiation across the industry as a whole.

(iii)

Tutorial note: The requirement for part (iii) asks you discuss **either** Cost Focus **or** Differentiation Focus. Therefore in your answer you should only have discussed one or the other. However, for tutorial purposes, we have included both options here to indicate some of the possible ideas you could have included in your answers.

Cost focus

Whereas a cost leadership strategy would mean DEF aims to be the lower cost operator in the industry as a whole, a cost focus would mean it aims to be the lowest cost operator in a specific segment of the market, or **niche**.

Porter's logic here is that it should be easier for a firm to achieve competitive advantage in a particular niche than in the market as a whole.

Low cost airlines - One low cost airline, S already flies out of DEF and is looking to expand its operations at DEF. If DEF pursues a cost focus strategy, it could look to attract other low-cost airlines to use the airport, and it could tailor its strategies to providing a cost effective service for the low-cost airlines and their passengers.

Scope for growth - However, if DEF seeks to compete by lowering prices, it will need to be confident that it can secure, and accommodate, a sufficient increase in airline and passenger numbers to justify the lower fees it is charging the airlines.

However, as with the overall cost leadership approach, it is debatable how far a cost focus strategy would give DEF any unique competences compared to its rivals, and therefore how sustainable any competitive advantage would be.

Stuck in the middle – Moreover there is a danger that DEF's strategies could become confused. On the one hand, DEF could be trying to follow a cost focus strategy to attract low cost airlines; but, on the other, it could be trying to provide 'distinctiveness' and luxury which first class and business passengers want. Moreover, the European survey specifically identified that one aspect of distinctiveness was having an airport reserved for leading airlines, not low-cost carriers.

Consequently, DEF could find itself trying to serve two mutually exclusive markets: a situation which, in all likelihood, is doomed to failure. Porter referred to this position as being 'stuck in the middle', and he stressed that a business has to compete on the basis of either cost leadership or differentiation but it cannot try to do both.

Differentiation focus

As with a cost focus strategy, a differentiation focus strategy would mean that DEF seeks to achieve competitive advantage by concentrating on a specific market niche, and it then provides a quality of service to that niche than none of its competitors can match.

We have already identified that a differentiation strategy could be based on '**distinctiveness**', but a differentiation focus strategy would be based on offering distinctiveness to a more **narrowly defined market segment**. For

example, DEF could focus on the cargo handling service and if it could provide a better quality of service than any of its rivals (for example, not losing or damaging any cargo in transit) it could charge a premium price for this.

However, by definition, this kind of niche strategy is linked to a relatively restricted market . So although DEF may achieve a sustainable competitive advantage in a specific area of business, the **scale of the benefits** may not be great enough to generate significant profits and sustainable competitive advantage for the airport as a whole.

Focus based on location - In this respect, perhaps the best strategy for DEF to adopt is one where the focus relates to location. DEF's mission statement already points to differentiation on the basis of quality, but while this quality would not make DEF attractive to customers who live a long way from the airport, DEF could realistically seek to achieve competitive advantage by offering the highest standards of service to people who live within commuting distance of the airport.

(b)

Top tips: The unseen material identifies that IVB's strategic approach and objectives are very different to the LSG's who are the current shareholders in DEF. For example, IVB has a short-term focus, and does not appear to be interested in wider issues of social responsibility.

Notice that the requirement for (b) (i) refers to both 'approach to strategy formulation' and 'mission' so you need to address both in your answer. However, you need to make sure your answer focuses specifically on how IVB might challenge strategy formulation and mission: do not stray into discussing potential issues with DEF's objectives. You would get no marks for doing this, because that discussion is the requirement in (b) (ii).

Part (ii) deals specifically with the differences in objectives between DEF and IVB, and you should have been able to identify that IVB will object more strongly to some of DEF's objectives than others. For example, since IVB is interested in cost-cutting and short-term profits for its shareholders, it is likely to strongly oppose an objective to increase employment opportunities (for people living close to the airport.)

In your answer, you should have indicated whether IVB's challenge is likely to be strong or weak (in effect, what its level of interest in the objective is).

In relation to part (iii), the scenario does not indicate how many of the LSGs sell their shares to IVB. If IVB only buys 25% of the shares it will have a minority interest, and so its impact on DEF's operations will be less than if it acquires a controlling interest in the airport. However, you need to make clear in your answer what assumptions you have made about the level of interest IVB has acquired.

(i)

Long term vs short term focus - The Board seems to have adopted a **long term approach** to strategy formation, such that the development plan looks at passenger growth over the next two decades. In keeping with this, the Board seems to favour plans which are **phased and gradual** (for example, in respect of the development plans for the airport which are designed to avoid unexpected consequences for the local communities).

By contrast, IVB seems to favour an approach which looks at the short-term and short-term results, specifically profits. Consequently, IVB may challenge the Board's approach, if IVB feels DEF is not delivering sufficient **short-term profits for the shareholders**.

Social Responsibility – The Board's focus on 'Sustainable Aviation' highlights DEF's commitment to being a **good corporate citizen.** This idea of corporate citizenship, as well as the aim of maintaining the highest **ethical standards**, is clearly expressed in the DEF's mission statement. This again illustrates that DEF is concerned about its responsibilities to a wide range of **stakeholders** and not just in maximising short-term profits for its shareholders.

However, IVB does not appear to have any equivalent interest in social responsibility: its focus is exclusively on delivering **short-term profits for its shareholders**, rather than considering the interests of other stakeholders.

Owners' objectives – Currently, DEF is not listed on a stock exchange, but is owned by the four local state governments. In this respect, DEF's strategy may sometimes be influenced by **social objectives** (for example, promoting local jobs) as well as purely financial ones.

By contrast, IVB's focus will be on cost cutting, and this is likely to include cutting jobs in order to reduce the wage bill. Moreover, it is likely that IVB may want DEF to be a listed company in the future, thereby again increasing the importance of financial performance, and of ensuring that the results are in line with market, or analysts', expectations.

(ii)

Maintain/increase employment opportunities for people living close to the airport – This is the objective which IVB is likely to oppose most strongly. IVB will be looking to cut costs in order to increase short-term profitability, and one of the way of doing this will be through job cuts. Therefore IVB will be looking to reduce employment opportunities rather than increasing them.

Reduce visual and audible impact of the operation of the airport on the local environment – This objective reflects the current focus on corporate social responsibility and considering the social and environmental impacts of DEF's business. IVB appears solely interested in short-term financial returns. Therefore it is unlikely to be interested in the side-effects of the business.

If DEF incurs expenditure in order to reduce the visual and audible impact of its business, IVB will consider this to be unnecessary costs which could be cut in order to increase profits. Similarly, IVB may feel the desire to reduce visual and audible impact of the business may be restricting revenues, if, for example, DEF limits the number of "noisy aircraft" which it allows to use the airport.

IVB is likely to have a similar view on the objective to minimise the pollution effects of the operation of the airport. IVB is unlikely to be directly interested in the pollution effects of the airport, due to its focus on short-term profits. However, IVB may oppose this objective if it feels unnecessary costs are being spent trying to reduce pollution.

Create a passenger framework to meet the demands of forecast passenger numbers – Again, IVB is unlikely to have a strong interest be very interested in this objective, because it has a longer-term focus. However, IVB may oppose it if the objective means that DEF has to incur costs in the short-term in order to create the facilities or capacity to meet increased demand in the longer term. IVB is likely to have a similar stance on the objective to improve land-based access to the airport.

(iii)

Shareholding acquired - At this stage, we do not know how many of the LSGs are going to sell their shareholdings to IVB. However, this will be a crucial factor in determining what impact IVB can have on the future operations of the airport.

Minority holding – If only one LSG sells its shares to IVB, then IVB will only be a minority (25%) shareholder. Although IVB will have one representative on the Board, there will still be three of the existing LSG representatives on the Board.

In such a situation, although IVB is likely to challenge some of the airport's existing objectives, and try to encourage a greater focus on short-term cost-cutting and profitability, it will not be able to enforce any changes unless they are supported by the other shareholders, because the remaining LSGs will carry the majority (75%) in any vote.

However, having a fresh perspective on the Board could be beneficial in some respects, and IVB's commercial focus could bring a modernising influence on the Board. Moreover, because IVB is a bank, its involvement with the business may mean that additional sources of finance become available to DEF which were not available previously.

Majority holding - However, if IVB acquires the majority of the shares in DEF, then it will be able to bring about far greater changes at DEF. The whole culture of the business is likely to change, and instead of a focus on long-term, gradual development, there will be a shift to cost-cutting and short-term results, with a view to subsequently reselling the airport.

IVB's approach may indicate that they will prefer a **cost leadership** strategy (rather than one based on differentiation and quality), and so this may also see DEF seeking to increase the number of low-cost airlines which use the airport. Equally, IVB may look at way costs can be cut in what it sees to be 'non-core' areas of the business; for example, it might consider outsourcing the operation of the car park to a third party acting under a licence agreement with the airport.

Safety and security – Importantly though, however IVB looks to cut costs, it will be crucial that safety and security standards remain high at the airport. For example, IVB should not allow cost cutting to jeopardise maintenance works to the airport's runway, because if there is an accident and the subsequent investigation shows this was due to debris or potholes on the runway, this is likely to damage the airport's reputation and thereby could reduce the price at which IVB is able to sell it in the future.

(c)

Top tips: The scenario states that the assumption that "[revenue]... would have increased by 10% per year *until* the first year of actual operations in the year to 30 June 2014." Unfortunately, this is ambiguous. One interpretation is that the increases stop prior to the first year of operations (that is, in 2013) whereas the alternative interpretation is that the increases continue until the end of the first year of operations (that is, in 2014).

The interpretation you make will affect the results of your calculations, and so it is important that your subsequent reasons about whether DEF should (or shouldn't) undertake the project are consistent with the calculations you have made.

The examiner had actually intended that the question should be interpreted to mean 'until the end of the first year of operations', and this is the approach we have taken in the answer below. However, the examiner accepted that the alternative interpretation is also valid, and so candidates would receive credit for sensible reasoning based on that interpretation.

Revenue generated (D$):

2010	1,500,000
2011	1,650,000
2012	1,815,000
2013	1,996,500
2014	2,196,150

Expected profitability (D$)

	40%	30%	25%	*D $*
Revenue	2,196,150	2,196,150	2,196,150	
Contribution margin	878,460	658,845	549,038	
Probability	0.1	0.2	0.7	
Expected margin	87,846	131,769	384,326	**603,941**
Fixed costs				(400,000)
Expected profit				**203,941**

The calculations suggest that the cargo handling services project will generate additional profits of D$203,941 per year. This is marginally greater than the $200,000 threshold set by the Board of Directors.

Sensitivity - However, the figures assume that there is a constant 10% growth in income every year. Given that the expected values only exceed the target by less than D$4,000 (2%) this means any decision could be very sensitive to the actual growth in income being less than expected. Equally, the decision could be sensitive to any changes in fixed costs.

Uncertainty - In addition to this there is a lot of uncertainty in the forecast, as illustrated by the fact that DEF is uncertain what the contribution margin is likely to be. In practice, the target profit D$200,000 will only be reached if the actual contribution margin is 27.3% or above [(200,000 + 400,000)/2,196,150]. Based on the expected probabilities, we could suggest that this means there is only a 30% probability of the D$200,000 profit being generated, even if revenues increase at the expected rates.

However, we do not know how rigidly the target figure of D$ 200,000 will be enforced in any investment decision. The Finance Director's opinion seems to be that any project which would improve the airport's finances should be welcomed. Although there is a lot of uncertainty about the actual figures, it does seem likely that the project will improve the airport's finances.

Therefore, because the project looks likely to improve the airport's finances, and because its expected profitability meets the profitability target, it should be undertaken.

71 Aybe Asia

Text reference. Different approaches to strategic planning are discussed in Chapter 1 of your BPP study text, as is strategic management accounting. Scenario planning is discussed in Chapter 3. Ethics are covered in Chapter 2.

Marking scheme

				Marks
(a)	(i)	Explanation of traditional rational planning model	1	
		Justification for using traditional rational planning model	1	
		Assessment of nature of Asian market and differences to Aybe's existing markets	Up to 2	
		Conclusion about appropriateness of rational planning model	Up to 2	
			Total up to	6
	(ii)	For **each** alternative approach:		
		Appropriate alternative approach identified (1 mark); explanation of the strategy (1 mark); reasons why strategy is appropriate (1 mark)	Up to 3	
			Total up to	6
	(iii)	For each valid factor that Aybe should consider:	Up to 6	
			Total up to	6
(b)	(i)	Definition of strategic management accounting (including focus on external orientation)	Up to 2	
		Advice on relevance of strategic management accounting to current strategies	Up to 2	
		Advice on relevance of strategic management accounting for future strategies	Up to 2	
			Total up to	6
	(ii)	Description of scenario planning (including definition)	Up to 3	
		Advice on how companies can use scenario planning	Up to 2	
		Advice to Aybe about using scenario planning to help make its decision	Up to 4	
			Total	6
(c)		Calculation of total contribution margin	Up to 4	
		Calculation of correct total profit (accounting for fixed costs)	Up to 2	
		Evaluation of the Director's claim about achieving C$2m profit	Up to 4	
			Total up to	10
(d)		Identification of intimidation as the threat, and explanation of the director's threat (implied loss of job)	Up to 2	
		For each valid, relevant **internal** safeguard recommended: Up to 2 each	Up to 4	
		For each valid, relevant **external** safeguard recommended: Up to 2 each	Up to 4	
			Total up to	10
			Total	50

Part (a) (i)

> **Top tip**: The pre-seen material identified that Aybe has always used a rational model approach to strategic planning, meaning that this is the approach it is comfortable with. However, the Asian markets are much more dynamic and fast moving that Aybe's other markets. Is the rational model appropriate to such a fast paced environment, or is it more suited to a stable, more predictable environment?
>
> **Examiner's comment**:. Most candidates were able to apply their knowledge of the rational planning model to the scenario information, and avoided theoretical discussions. Consequently this question was reasonably well answered by most candidates.

Stability vs uncertainty – The traditional rational model provides a structure and order to strategic planning, but this is perhaps more appropriate to a stable and predictable environment than to a context of uncertainty.

Dynamic environment – However, Aybe's experience in Asia has suggested that the markets and environment there are uncertain. Also, as the Director of Operations has pointed out, the environment is very dynamic which makes it difficult to predict and forecast with any certainty. This dynamism and uncertainty are likely to make the rational model less appropriate to Aybe's Asian business than to other, more stable, parts of its business.

Lack of continuity - Moreover, Aybe's approach to the Asian business appears to be different to its approach to the rest of its business. The Board feel that continuity is important, and also appear to have established a strategic plan which looks to achieve growth through international expansion. But against this backdrop of continuity and growth, the Board are now considering closing the trading company in Asia. This is particularly surprising, since the separate trading company was only very recently established.

However, the possible closure again seems to reflect the dynamic changes in the environment: declining demand for IEC's products in Asia, increased protectionism and increasing labour costs. This dynamism and the corresponding need to revise strategic plans may not make the Asian markets a suitable environment in which to use the traditional rational planning model.

Review of strategic aims – Aybe has also decided to review its overall strategic aim of achieving growth through international expansion, and to assess whether it should concentrate on the domestic market instead. However, this overall strategic aim had only been published in the 2010 Annual Report, so it seems rather soon to be thinking about revising the aim. Nonetheless, the possible revision suggests Aybe is adopting a **more flexible approach** to strategic planning than the traditional rational model would provide.

(ii)

> **Top tip:** You are specifically asked to recommend **two** alternative approaches. The two we have recommended in our answer below are the **emergent** approach and **opportunism**.
>
> However, you could also have recommended incrementalism (or logical incrementalism), arguing that it would be appropriate for Aybe to respond to the changing conditions by making gradual changes to its strategy. This would be in-keeping with Aybe's seemingly conservative approach, and of preferring continuity over drastic change.
>
> You should have used your answer to (a) (i) and the problems you have identified with using the rational model to help you select two more appropriate approaches here.
>
> Whichever approaches you decide to use, in order to score well you need to (briefly) explain the strategy and then why it is appropriate for Aybe to use in the Asian markets. Linking your answer to the scenario is very important: answers which simply described different approaches to strategy in general terms scored poorly.
>
> **Examiner's comments**: Many candidates were able to identify and explain suitable alternative approaches to strategy, but unfortunately some failed to explain why the approaches they had identified were suitable to the Asian markets. This lack of application to the scenario was the main weakness in candidates' answers to this question.

Emergent approach – The traditional rational model views strategic planning as a **top-down** process, whereby a strategy is effectively imposed on an organisation. By contrast, the emergent approach sees strategy as something which emerges from an organisation. In effect, strategy is a **bottom up** process,

through which a strategy emerges from the way the organisation responds and adapts to changes in the environment.

Because Asia is an unfamiliar market for Aybe, and seeing it has a dynamic environment, an approach which allows Aybe to adapt its strategy to fit with that environment could be appropriate; in effect, following the notion of 'survival of the fittest'.

Opportunistic approach (or 'freewheeling opportunism') - Whereas the traditional rational model develops a prescriptive and structured approach to strategic planning, opportunism has the opposite approach. Opportunists would argue that rather than trying to plan ahead, organisations should simply take advantage of opportunities as they arise.

Such an approach could be appropriate for a dynamic and changeable environment (like Aybe's Asian markets) where it is difficult to predict ahead with any certainty. However, given that Aybe has traditionally valued continuity over change, the Board may be concerned that an opportunist strategy may lack coherence and control.

(iii)

Top tips: Although there are likely to be financial implications of withdrawing from Asia (eg the liability to the local entrepreneur) you should not have focused solely on this in your answer. There are also likely to be non-financial implications: for example, what will be the impact of Aybe's reputation? Moreover, if Aybe withdraws from Asia are there alternative markets it can move into to generate replacement sales and growth?

Examiner's comments: Most candidates identified a suitable range of factors that Aybe should consider, and this question was generally well answered. The main weakness in some candidates' scripts was a tendency to focus on short-term cost implications without considering the longer-term organisational issues for Aybe.

Sales potential – Although Aybe is considering withdrawing from the trading company this need not mean it withdraws from Asia completely. Although the trading company does not seem to have been as profitable as it had hoped, Aybe should consider whether it stops selling its products to Asia altogether or whether it needs to find an alternative channel. For example, if there is still a market for Aybe's products in Asia, it could consider using Asian sales agents to act on its behalf.

Exit barriers – Aybe and the local entrepreneur both have 50% shares in the trading company. If Aybe withdraws, the local entrepreneur will have to decide whether he wants to acquire Aybe's share and try to maintain the trading company himself, or whether the company should cease trading. If the company ceases trading, Aybe will be liable to pay the entrepreneur C$500,000. This exit payment could affect Aybe's decision of whether to withdraw or not.

Wider implications – The trading company seems to have been Aybe's first significant venture into Asia. If Aybe withdraws from the venture very quickly, this could be damaging for its reputation which could be problematic in two respects: (i) if Aybe wants to continue selling its products through sales agents, or (ii) if, in future, it wants to re-establish a joint venture company. (Although market conditions have worsened at the moment, they should improve again in future at which point Aybe might look to expand into Asia again. But if Aybe has a poor reputation in Asia, local businesses will be reluctant to become venture partners with it.)

Moreover, before withdrawing from the Asian company, Aybe should critically assess the growth prospects of its domestic market. If there are limited growth opportunities in the domestic market, the Board might be advised to persevere with looking at expansion into foreign markets.

Part (b) (i)

Top tip: Think about the features of strategic management accounting which disintinguish it from 'traditional' management accounting: a focus on external factors, and on non-financial information as well as on internally generated financial information. How could these features be useful to Aybe in developing and implementing strategies?

Examiner's comments: The focus of candidates' answers should have been upon the external orientation of strategic management accounting, and how this external focus could help Aybe develop its strategy. However, very few candidates made any reference to the external focus of strategic management accounting.

Strategic management accounting – Unlike 'traditional' management accounting which looks primarily at internally generated financial information, strategic management accounting looks at information which relates to **external factors**, and it looks at non-financial information and as well as financial information. For example, as well as looking at operating margins, strategic management accounting may also look at market growth, market share or customer profitability.

The external focus is important because Aybe needs to understand its environment as part of analysing its current strategic position and then developing its future strategic options.

Current strategies – Strategic management accounting can contribute to the success of Aybe's current strategies by **monitoring its performance** and **results** compared to competitors. For example, internally generated information shows Aybe's revenue increased from 2008-9. But if competitors' revenues grew more quickly, Aybe's relative market share would have fallen over the same period. Therefore it is important to understand Aybe's performance and results in the context of its competitors to gauge how successfully its current strategy seems to be working. (This argument applies equally to costs as well as revenues.)

Future strategies – It is very important for Aybe to consider the external environment when planning its future strategies. In this context, obtaining information about **markets** (eg size, growth), **customers** and **competitors** (eg number, size) should be a key part of strategic planning. For example, when Aybe was considering whether to launch the new trading company, it should have assessed this environmental information before deciding to proceed with the launch.

Forecasting – Strategic management accounting could also contribute to the success of future strategies in general by forecasting performance. These forecasts should not only look at Aybe's own performance but should also look at competitor's performance – so, for example, they could indicate what Aybe's relative market share might be, or how well it is managing its costs compared to its competitors.

(ii)

Top tip: This is another question where you need to apply your knowledge to the scenario. You shouldn't have simply defined or described scenario planning (or the various stages to it). Instead, you should have used this knowledge to consider how scenario planning could be useful to Aybe when thinking about whether or not to withdraw from the trading company in Asia.

Think about what scenario planning sets out to do: to identifying a range of plausible scenarios about how an organisation's environment may change in the future in a context of uncertainty. How would developing a range of scenarios about the future help Aybe in its decision whether or not to withdraw from the trading company? How might Aybe gain a better understanding of some of the uncertainties it is facing in the Asian markets?

Examiner's comments: This question was answered poorly. Most candidates were able to provide a basic definition of scenario planning, but few then went on to apply scenario planning to the potential decision to withdraw from the Asian market. Theoretical answers, lacking application to the scenario, will usually score poorly in the E3 exam.

Scenario planning involves developing a range of plausible views about how the business environment of an organisation might develop in the future, based on sets of key drivers for change about which there is a high level of uncertainty. (*Johnson, Scholes & Whittington*).

Recognise uncertainty – One of the key concepts behind scenario planning is that it does not aim to forecast what *will* happen; but rather it develops a *range* of futures. This recognises that there is a high level of uncertainty about the environment and the things that will actually happen to drive changes in the future. In this context, scenario planning could be useful for Aybe because of the dynamic and uncertain nature of the Asian markets. Aybe could use scenario planning to assess how a range of different scenarios could affect the performance of the trading company, and this could be useful in deciding whether or not to withdraw from the company.

Identify key causes of uncertainty – In order to prepare different scenarios, Aybe will have to identify what it considers to be the key factors which will affect the business environment and could lead to changes in that environment. For example, the factors could include: the length of the global recession, or the extent of protectionism in Asian countries. Again, identifying these factors could also be useful for Aybe in deciding whether or not to withdraw from the trading company.

Construct plausible scenarios and responses – In a scenario planning exercise, Aybe should construct a number of plausible scenarios of how its business environment might appear in the future. In doing so, Aybe can also begin to think how it would respond if any of these scenarios actually happened. In turn, this planning should help Aybe choose an appropriate strategic option as the future unfolds and some of the uncertainties get resolved.

For example, if some of the scenarios suggest that Aybe would benefit from remaining in the trading company while others suggest it would be better to withdraw, Aybe should wait and see if any of the scenarios start to happen and then take the necessary action based on the scenario outcomes it has constructed.

Part (c)

Top tips. This question should have been relatively straightforward, although it was important that you distinguished between contribution and profit.

The Director's claim is that the Asian business will achieve profit of at least C$2m in 2011, so this is after accounting for directly attributable fixed costs.

The requirement specified that 6 out of the 10 marks available here were for calculations; so, for the 4 remaining marks you should have evaluated the Director's claim in the light of the figures you have calculated.

Examiner's comments: A number of candidates labelled the Contribution margin ($2,240,00) as 'Gross profit' and then, having subtracted the fixed costs called the resulting $1,240,000 'Net profit'. Candidates at this level must appreciate the difference between contribution and profit, and those who failed to do so failed this requirement.

	A	B	C	Total
Average selling price per unit (C$)	350	6,200	85	
Average variable cost per unit (C$)	200	2,500	60	
Contribution per unit (C$)	150	3,700	25	
Sales volume per year	2,800	100	58,000	
Contribution per year (C$)	420,000	370,000	1,450,000	2,240,000
Directly attributable fixed costs per year (C$)				(1,000,000)
Profit per year (C$)				1,240,000

IEC's Asian business is forecast to make a contribution of C$ 2,240,000 but, once the C$ 1 million of fixed costs specifically associated with the Asian business are accounted for, the profit will only be C$ 1,240,000.

Moreover, the management accountant has established that revenue from the Asian business is declining and costs are rising, so the actual contribution may be lower than the forecast figures, if the forecast has not yet been updated to reflect these trends.

Either way, the Director of Operations' claim that IEC's Asian business will achieve a **profit** of at least C$ 2 million looks to be too optimistic; possibly because the Director has not taken account of the relevant fixed costs.

In addition, because Aybe only owns 50% of the trading company, it is likely that they will have to share the profits with the local entrepreneur. Therefore, the profit attributable to Aybe will be lower still, but the Director doesn't appear to have mentioned this.

Part (d)

Top tips: The Examiner has made it clear that he regards ethics and ethical issues as an integral part of business strategy. He has also indicated that a question could focus on either general ethical issues or specific points from CIMA's Code of Ethics. Therefore it is vital that you read the 'Code' thoroughly before your exam.

Although you could have attempted to answer this question without a detailed knowledge of the Code, it would have been made much easier if you know the range of safeguards which were recommended in the Code.

The requirement specifically asked you to recommend **two internal** safeguards and **two external** safeguards, so you should have recommended **four in total**. However, the Code includes a number more safeguards than this, so some alternatives ones you could have mentioned are included in text boxes in the answer.

Note that the question specifically asked you to 'explain the nature of the threat' and 'recommend ...safeguards.' You were not required to provide a general description of CIMA's Code of Ethics, but rather to apply the principles of the Code to the scenario.

Examiner's comments: Most candidates identified the threat of the management losing their job, but few correctly categorised this as 'Intimidation' according to the Code. A number of answers suggested sensible internal safeguards, but the discussion of external safeguards was less good. Resignation is not an external safeguard.

Threat:

Intimidation: CIMA's Code of Ethics defines intimidation threats as ones "which may occur when a professional accountant may be deterred from acting objectively by threats, actual or perceived" [*Para 100.10 (e)*]

In this case, the Director of Operations is threatening that if the Management Accountant does not support him, and they fall out, the Management Accountant could be asked to leave Aybe.

By saying 'I hope you won't fall into the same trap [as the previous Management Accountant]', the Director of Operations is trying to intimidate the Management Accountant into supporting his opinions about the Asian business, rather than looking objectively at the figures and forming his own opinion of them.

Safeguards:

Internal

1 **Policies and procedures to empower and encourage employees to communicate any ethical issues** that concern them to senior levels of management without fear of retribution.

In this case, the Management Accountant needs to be able to explain to a member of the management team that he is being threatened not to make an objective assessment of the facts and figures.

Moreover, the Management Accountant needs to know that whoever he talks to will listen to him impartially and will not automatically take the Director of Operations' side. The fact that the previous Management Accountant left Aybe shortly after a dispute with the Director might suggest that the Management Accountant felt ostracised or uncomfortable after the dispute.

2 **Policies and procedures to implement and monitor the quality of employee performance.**

Aspects of employee performance should include 'soft' skills such as relationship management, as well as more traditional measures such as meeting productivity targets or sales targets. In this respect, the monitoring process should pick up if there is a trend of one Director frequently falling out with staff and those staff leaving shortly afterwards. In this case it appears to be the Director's performance which is at fault, not the employee's.

Alternative internal safeguards [from *CIMA Code of Ethics, Para 200.16*]

- Leadership that stresses the importance of ethical behaviour and the expectation that employees will act in an ethical manner
- Appropriate disciplinary processes
- Timely communication of the employer's policies and procedures (including any changes to them) to all employees, and appropriate training and education on such policies and procedures
- Recruitment procedures in the employing organisation emphasising the importance of employing high calibre, competent staff
- Consultation with another appropriate professional accountant

External

1 **External review of the reports, returns and information produced by a professional accountant**

If the accountant knows that any reports he produces may be subject to an independent external review, he should want to ensure that they are properly prepared and accurate. In this case, the accountant should not be prepared to support a report saying that the Asian business will generate C$ 2 million profit because an external review could identify that a professional accountant could reasonably have been expected to know this was not realistic.

2 **Education, training and experience requirement for entry into the profession** – If the accountant is a member of a recognised professional body (such as CIMA) he will be aware of his duty to comply with a professional code of ethics, and to report any breaches of ethical requirements. Therefore the accountant will know he needs to report any threats which are designed to deter him from acting objectively.

Alternative external safeguards [from *CIMA Code of Ethics*, *Para 100.12*]

- Continuing professional development requirements
- Corporate governance regulations
- Professional or regulatory monitoring and disciplinary procedures

72 Aybe

Text reference: Different approaches to strategic planning are discussed in Chapter 1 of your BPP Study Text, Organisational structures are covered in Chapter 9. Methods of expansion and growth are discussed in Chapter 6, and Ethical issues are covered in Chapter 2.

(a) (i)	Explanation and characteristics of rational model	Up to 2	
	Discussion of relevance of rational planning model for use in the Asian markets	Up to 4	
		Total up to	5
(ii)	For each alternative strategy identified (1 mark) and explained (1 mark)	Up to 4	
	For explanation of why each alternative strategy may be appropriate for Aybe (1 mark each)	Up to 2	
		Total up to	6
(b)	For identifying and explaining functional structure	1	
	Evaluation of advantages of functional structure in relation to the Asian markets	2	
	Evaluation of disadvantages of functional structure in relation to the Asian markets	4	
	Discussion of the factors which affect the appropriateness of different structures in the Asian markets	4	
		Total	9
(c) (i)	For each control problem identified (1 mark) and explained (1 mark). Possible problems include: autonomy; controlling performance; reliability/integrity of agent; differences in culture; communication	Up to 4	
		Total up to	4
(ii)	For each control measure identified (1 mark) and explained (up to 2 marks)	Up to 6	
		Total up to	6
(d) (i)	Incremental profit forecast for 2010 - 2014	Up to 4	
		Total up to	4
(ii)	Calculation of incremental earnings per sharing for 2010 – 2014 (up to 2 marks) and incremental dividend per share (up to 2 marks)	Up to 4	
	Discussion of the implications of these revised figures for the shareholders	Up to 2	
		Total up to	6

(iii) For identifying that integrity and objectivity were the elements of CIMA's fundamental principles relevant to this scenario, and explaining how each was relevant (Up to 4 marks for each)	Up to 8	
For identifying that the request to destroy the original forecast is the issue which gives the Management Accountant an ethical dilemma	Up to 2	
	Total up to	10
	Total	50

(a)

> **Top tip.** The pre-seen material clearly identified that Aybe's current approach to strategy was based on the rational model, and the un-seen material then identified a number of characteristics of the Asian markets. Putting the two together would then allow you to discuss how relevant (or not) Aybe's rational planning approach is for its use in the fast moving Asian markets.
>
> **Examiner's comment.** This question was reasonably well answered, but beware of placing too much emphasis on a detailed discussion of the rational planning model. Make sure you spend sufficient time discussing its relevance to the Asian markets.

(i) Rational model – Aybe uses the rational model to carry out its strategic planning process. This suggests Aybe has a formal and structured approach to strategic planning, but also one which may be quite **slow** and **time-consuming**.

A formal, rational model approach to strategic planning would be relevant for environments which are **relatively stable**, and which Aybe knows well. However, it may be less relevant for Aybe as it tries to develop its Asian markets.

The Asian markets are **fast-moving** and highly **adaptive**, neither of which are characteristics which suit the rational model very well.

In addition, the market structures vary in the different Asian countries, so Aybe may need to have a degree of **flexibility** in its strategy to cope with the variation between countries. Again, however, the rational model may not be the most relevant strategic framework to provide this degree of flexibility.

(ii)

> **Top tip.** The question requirement asks for two alternative approaches to strategy. The two we have suggested are freewheeling opportunism and emergent strategy. However, you could also have suggested incrementalism (or logical incrementalism) and, provided you explained why you thought it might be appropriate for Aybe, you would have earned marks for this.
>
> You should have noted the link between this part of the question and the previous one. In (a) (i) you should have discussed the limitations of the rational planning model in respect of the Asian markets. The models you suggested here should be ones that allow Aybe to overcome those limitations.
>
> However, note the question is about 'approaches to strategy', not market entry strategies.
>
> **Examiner's comment.** The examiner noted that a few candidates took a completely incorrect approach to this question and discussed market entry strategies such as joint ventures or mergers. These were not considered relevant to the question set and so scored no marks.

Freewheeling opportunism – This approach to strategy suggests that organisations should not bother with strategic planning, but rather the organisations should respond to, and seize, opportunities as they arise.

The benefit of this approach is that it allows organisations to take advantage of opportunities quickly, rather than being slowed down by a formal strategic planning process. This appears to reflect the Director of Operations' view of strategy, and it may well be appropriate to the fast-moving and adaptive Asian markets where the pace of change may preclude a more formal strategic planning process.

Emergent strategy – An emergent strategy is one whose objective is unclear at the outset, but which develops during its lifetime as the strategy proceeds. An emergent strategy is appropriate for an organisation in an environment which is constantly changing.

The logic behind emergent strategies is that there is little point having a prescriptive strategy, and then having to change it regularly as the market changes. It is better for an organisation's strategy to change and develop as the market changes. Given that the Asian markets are highly adaptive and fast-moving nature, and that they are still reasonably unfamiliar to Aybe, an emergent strategy may well be more suitable that a prescriptive one which seeks to impose a strategy in advance.

(b)

Top tip. The question asks you to *evaluate* the suitability of Aybe's structure so you should have considered both the advantages and disadvantages of its current structure. Advantages you could have mentioned include: expertise, consistency and control; while disadvantages include: functional silos, inability to assess profitability and bureaucracy.

However, your answer shouldn't have just been a theoretical evaluation of the advantages and disadvantages of functional organisational structures: to score well you needed to evaluate their suitability in the specific context of Aybe's proposed expansion into the Asian markets.

Functional structure – Aybe's current organisational structure is organised along traditional functional lines. Consequently, it is likely that Aybe will have clearly defined departments for each of the functions performed within the business; for example, operations (production), marketing, and IT. Each of these departments is likely to have its own budget, and its performance will be monitored against budget, thereby allowing performance to be monitored and controlled.

Such a structure is quite logical because it reflects the work specialisation within the organisation, and it allows Aybe to recruit staff for each department with skills in that particular area.

However, Aybe's current structure could have a number of disadvantages in relation to the proposed expansion into the Asian markets:

Bureaucratic structure – Because they follow functional lines rather than business processes, functional structures can often be quite bureaucratic. This appears to be the case at Aybe, where the culture appears to be quite bureaucratic and **resistant to change**, as seen in the way the Board declined the consultant's review of the organisational structure in 2008. However, such a culture is unlikely to be appropriate to the Asian markets which are fast-moving and highly adaptive, and so where Aybe may need to respond quickly to changes in the business environment.

Co-ordination – Although people in each department will understand how their department works, they are less likely to understand how the business works as a whole. This may lead to problems in co-ordinating the work and output of different departments. This again could lead to problems in an environment which requires quick and flexible response to changes to the business environment.

Enterprise - The focus on individual departments may also lead staff to only think about their particular area of work rather than the efficiency and profitability of Aybe as a whole. It is likely that, rather than sharing knowledge and ideas between them, departments will be quite insular. This may place Aybe at a disadvantage in some Asian countries which are **highly entrepreneurial**, because Aybe's organisational structure is unlikely to encourage enterprise and innovation across the organisation as a whole.

Local involvement – In some Asian countries, there is a requirement for local involvement in any business enterprise. However, if this requirement extends to having a local representative on the Board of Aybe, it is difficult to see how this can be achieved within the current functional structure.

(c)

Top tip. Make sure you answer the question specifically set in (c) (i). The question wasn't about the problems Aybe might encounter if it chooses to operate abroad; nor was it about the generic problems involved in controlling an overseas business. It was specifically about the problems Aybe may face in controlling *agents* if it chose to use agency agreements as its method of expanding into Asia.

Your answer to (c) (ii) should then have followed on from (c) (i). Once you have identified the problems Aybe could face, you then need to advise ways which Aybe could use to deal with those problems.

Examiner's comment. Most candidates were able to identify a good range of relevant control measures in (c) (ii) relating to the problems identified in (c) (i); for example, suggesting having service level agreements, or locally-based Aybe managers to act as supervising agents. The main weakness in the answers, however, was the lack of explanation as to *why* the measures were relevant to the problems identified. Merely *listing* control measures would not have scored well, even if the measures were relevant.

(i) **Potential impact on reputation** – If Aybe conducts its business in Asia using agents, then the agents will be Aybe's primary point of contact with its customers. Therefore, if the agents behave unethically, or mis-sell Aybe's products, this will ultimately reflect badly on Aybe, by direct association with the agents. However, Aybe will not be able to directly control the way its agents act, because they remain separate entities.

Conflicting aims – Aybe will be dependent on the agent for the rate of sales growth in Asian. If Aybe wants to grow quickly, but the agent only wants to grow business more slowly, then Aybe won't be able to do anything about this directly. Again, the agents are independent businesses from Aybe, so Aybe has no direct control over them. This could be a particular problem if the agent acts on behalf of a number of different principals. If some of the others (potentially Aybe's competitors) are paying a more favourable commission than Aybe, then the agent will try to grow the competitors' business more quickly than Aybe's.

(ii) **Potential impact on reputation** – Before Aybe starts to use the agent, it should investigate the agent's background and trading record. Given the Director of Operations' experience in China, he may know some companies which already use agencies, and so could provide testimonials or background information on agents.

When Aybe signs an agency agreement with the agent, the agreement could cover aspects of behaviour and selling practices, as well as stipulating the basic commission payments which Aybe will pay the agent. This should help ensure the agent does not act in a way which could damage Aybe's reputation.

Feedback – Once the agent has started work, the most pertinent measure will be how potential clients view their meetings with the agent. It is possible Aybe could employ some kind of 'mystery shopper' tactic, in which it arranges for a known contact to act as a potential client. The contact could then report back on how the agent conducts the meeting.

Conflicting aims – A key control measure here will be the actual level of business the agent generates compared to Aybe's expectations. Aybe needs to receive regular reports from the agent detailing the level of business being generated.

Aybe also needs a way of verifying these reports, and so the initial agency agreement should entitle Aybe to have access to review the agent's management accounts or any other relevant books and records.

In terms of managing the level of performance, it may be possible to specify some kind of 'stepped' commission payment in the agency agreement, so that the agent's commission rate increases every time they reach an agreed level of business. This could provide the agent with an added incentive to sell Aybe's products in preference to a rival suppliers' products, and to sell as many of Aybe's products as possible.

(d)

Top tip. The calculations in (d) (i) were very simple and you should have found these easy marks. However, the calculations were only worth 4 marks.

More importantly, you should have realised that revising the profit forecast had implications for forecast earnings per share and forecast dividend per share, so in (d) (ii) you should have prepared additional calculations for these figures. 4 out of the 6 marks for (d) (ii) were available for these calculations.

But remember, these revised figures are only forecasts. They will not have any consequences for the shareholders unless they actually become reality, which must be debatable given the optimistic nature of the revised forecast.

The Examiner has indicated that he regards ethics and ethical issues as important aspects of enterprise strategy, and so you should always be prepared for a question on ethics and/or CIMA's Code of Ethics.

In this case, (d) (iii) did not require a general discussion about the Code of Ethics, though. Instead, you should have identified which elements of the code were relevant to the context, and then used them to evaluate how the Director's views represent an ethical dilemma for the Management Accountant. The ethical principles that were relevant here were: Integrity and Objectivity, and so these were the only ones you needed to mention in your answer.

Examiner's comment. (d) (iii) was poorly answered. A number of candidates showed a very poor knowledge of ethics altogether, while others demonstrated a detailed knowledge of CIMA's Code of Ethics but failed to apply it to the ethical dilemma presented in the scenario. Very few marks were awarded to candidates who merely described the Code or its principles, rather than applying them to the scenario.

(i)

	Actual 2009 C$m	Forecast 2010 C$m	Forecast 2011 C$m	Forecast 2012 C$m	Forecast 2013 C$m	Forecast 2014 C$m
Incremental revenue	5.00	6.25	7.81	9.77	12.21	15.26
Incremental cost	1.00	1.25	1.56	1.95	2.44	3.05
Incremental profit for the year	4.00	5.00	6.25	7.81	9.77	12.21

(ii) The incremental forecast based on the Director of Operations' assumptions shows significantly higher incremental profits than the Management Accountant's original forecast.

If the shareholders are presented with these figures, they are likely to expect higher future earnings – and in turn higher dividends – than if they expected incremental profits to be in line with the Management Accountant's original figures.

Impact on EPS and dividend per share

Based on the new incremental profit forecast, and assuming there are no new share issues, EPS and dividend per share would be as follows:

	Actual 2009 C$m	Forecast 2010 C$m	Forecast 2011 C$m	Forecast 2012 C$m	Forecast 2013 C$m	Forecast 2014 C$m
Incremental revenue	4.00	5.00	6.25	7.81	9.77	12.21
Earnings per share	0.022	0.028	0.035	0.043	0.054	0.068
Dividend per share	0.011	0.014	0.017	0.022	0.027	0.034

The extent of the uplift in the new figures is such that by 2014 dividend per share is now forecast to be C$0.034 as opposed to C$0.013 (an increase of 162%).

Reliability of figures – On the one hand, these new figures might please the shareholders who have been looking for increased growth and profitability. However, we do not know how reliable the Director of Operations' assumptions are. If his figures are not based on any realistic expectations and supported by opportunities in the market, then they may be mis-leading the shareholders into thinking Aybe's growth potential is greater than it actually is. It is important to remember that these are only forecast figures. Any earnings growth or dividends that the shareholders receive will be determined by Aybe's actual results rather than the Director's forecasts.

(iii) **Difference of opinion** – The management accountant prepared her figures in line with Aybe's normal procedures, but the Director of Operations believed the resulting forecast to be totally unrealistic. However, by itself, the fact that the Director felt the management accountant's forecast to be understated does not present an ethical dilemma.

The management accountant's position starts getting more difficult when the Director of Operations instructs her to **destroy the original forecast and present his alternative, higher figures**. On the one hand, part of the management accountant's role is to assist senior management in strategic decision-making, and the Director of Operations is asking for assistance in this way. On the other hand, the management accountant needs to be guided by the principles of **objectivity** and **integrity**.

Basis of figures – The management accountant's figures have been prepared after extensive consultation with Board members, operational managers and an external market research organisation. However, the Director of Operations' figures are based on his own instinct and personal experience.

Objectivity – Because the Director of Operations has insisted that the management use only his figures he is trying to exert undue influence to override the professional and business judgements of a number of other senior figures at Aybe, including the management accountant.

The principle of objectivity requires that professional accountants do not compromise their professional judgement due to the undue influence of others, and so in this respect the management accountant faces an ethical dilemma with respect to the objectivity of the figures.

Integrity – The management accountant should not be associated with a report which she believes to be misleading. The figures in the two forecasts are so different that they will lead to the Board having conflicting impressions of the profitability of the Asian expansion. If the management accountant simply presented the Director of Operations' figures without explaining that they were much higher than the original figures obtained by following Aybe's normal procedures, then her report would be misleading.

Ethical dilemma – It appears that the management accountant faces an ethical dilemma because the Director's behaviour is in conflict with the principles of objectivity and integrity.

If the management accountant had been allowed to present both her original figures and the Director's more bullish figures to the Board, with an explanation of the different perspectives, this dilemma would not have arisen. It is the Director's insistence that the original figures be destroyed such that the only figures presented to the Board are his revised figures that causes this ethical dilemma.

73 Power Utilities

Text reference: Different approaches to strategic planning are discussed in Chapter 1 of your BPP Study Text. Ethical issues are covered in Chapter 2, and CSFs in Chapter 14.

Marking scheme

				Marks
(a)	(i)	Description of rational planning model approach	Up to 4	
		Description of incremental approach	Up to 2	
			Total up to	6
	(ii)	Description of emergent approach	Up to 2	
		Suitability of emergent approach to PU	Max 2	
			Total up to	4
(b)	(i)	Calculating Capex cost of alternative methods	1	
		Calculating annual fees incurred under both methods	Up to 5	
		Applying discount factor	1	
		Calculating present value of future cash outflows for both methods	2	
		Calculating net present values	1	
			Total up to	10
	(ii)	Discussion of consequences of in-house solution	Up to 3	
		Discussion of consequences of outsourcing solution	Up to 3	
			Total up to	5
(c)	Outlining ethical issues and CIMA code of ethics		Up to 4	
	Relating Technical Director's views to elements of CIMA code – Up to 3 marks for each issue		Up to 6	
			Total up to	10

(d)	(i)	For each relevant CSF recommended, with reasons – Up to 2	Up to 8	8
	(ii)	Description of 'Information System'	Max 1	
		Discussion of the main attributes of an effective IS – 2 marks each	Up to 6	
			Total up to	7
			Total	50

(a)

> **Top tip.** Part (a) (i) asks you to compare and contrast two different approaches to strategic planning. A sensible way to do this would be to describe both approaches in turn, and then to highlight the differences between the characteristics of each.
>
> In part (ii) you are asked to advise the Directors of a third approach which will be suitable for PU's changed circumstances. Although there is not a single 'right way' of formulating strategy, an opportunistic approach (or freewheeling opportunism) is unlikely to be suitable for a company like PU, so the most appropriate strategy to suggest will be an emergent strategy.

(i) Rational Planning Approach

This approach is typically found in larger bureaucratic organisations such as PU, and is probably the model most commonly associated with the formation of strategic plans.

The rational planning model involves the formulation of a set of long-term strategic objectives leading to the generation and evaluation of strategic ideas and subsequently the selection of the strategies required to achieve the objectives. This rational planning approach is based upon a thorough analysis of the internal and external circumstances of an organisation. It is often favoured by larger organisations as it takes a holistic view of the whole company, leading to greater congruence and efficiency, as well as forcing the company to look externally and so take account of influential environmental factors.

Detractors of the rational planning approach point out that it is resource- and time-intensive. In dynamic environments it may be the case that the assumptions that the strategy is based upon may have changed substantially by the time implementation occurs, rendering it obsolete.

Incremental Approach

This approach views strategy as a series of small, logical steps allowing an organisation's strategy to evolve slowly and steadily. Whereas in the rational model, planning plays an important part in setting objectives and evaluation possible strategies, under the incremental approach strategy is not made by planning but by making gradual changes to an underlying logic.

The incremental approach has the advantage of allowing strategy to be tightly controlled. However, it is not likely to find favour with investors in publicly owned companies such as PU where investors will demand to know how the board intend to earn returns on their investment.

Moreover, whereas the rational model assumes that organisations try to select a strategy that will maximise profits or returns on investment, the incremental approach assumes that managers are more likely to pursue satisfactory goals. They are likely to support a strategy if it generates a satisfactory return, even though if the managers had explored other options, they may have been able to develop an alternative strategy which earned greater returns.

(ii) Alternative Approach

Mintzberg criticised the Rational approach to strategy and advocated a more flexible approach via Emergent strategies. These are strategies based upon 'crafting' patterns of behaviour found in the organisation. In order to capitalise on these an organisation must understand its own strengths and weaknesses as well as performing regular environmental analysis, to be aware of the opportunities and threats in the environment.

The advantage of this approach is that it encourages environmental openness and organisational flexibility to the needs of customers and markets. This will be especially useful to PU given it has faced enormous change in the form of privatisation. However an organisation should be wary of relying purely on emergent strategies as they may lead to reactive strategies and the lack of a long-term and coherent plan offered by the rational approach.

(b)

Top tip. All 10 marks for (b) (i) are given for the calculation, so it is important you spend enough time on this element of the question to score well. The calculations are not particularly difficult, so you should regard these as easy marks.

However, once you have done the calculations, you then need to discuss them in (b) (ii). Whilst it is obviously important to consider the financial aspect of the decision, it it also important to consider the customer service aspect of the different options and the potential implications for DP of a fatality or serious injury arising due to non-attendance within 60 minutes.

(i) Analysis of alternative methods

	In-house			**Outsource**		
	T0	T1 - T10		T0	T1 - T10	
Capex	(50,000)			(30,000)		
Annual fee		(8,000)			(1,800)	**W1**
10% DF/Annuity	1.000	6.145	**W2**	1.000	6.145	
PV	(50,000)	(49,160)		(30,000)	(11,061)	
NPV	**(99,160)**			**(41,061)**		
Engineers	75			38		
Urgent calls within 1 hr	100%			99%		
Non-urgent call	1 month			ASAP		

Workings

W1 6,000 urgent calls @ \$250 + 2,000 non-urgent calls @ \$150 = \$1.8m

W2 Assumed a 10 year appraisal period, annuity of 6.145 from tables

(ii) In house

Dealing with breakdowns in-house is undoubtedly the expensive option. Over a 10 year period the discounted cost is \$58m or 141% more expensive than outsourcing. This is reflection of both the greater set-up and ongoing costs. In exchange for greater cost however a slightly better level of service is offered to urgent calls as well as a higher degree of control over operations via the use of directly employed engineers.

Outsource

This option is commonly perceived to be the cheaper option and as discussed above this is certainly the case for PU. However the trade-off is loss of control over the activity, and potentially therefore you are putting your brand and corporate image in the hands of a third party. In this instance the level of service looks comparable but crucially there is a risk of death of serious injury in the 1% of urgent cases that may not be attended within 1 hour. Based on 6,000 calls a year this could result in 1 death annually (6,000 x 0.1%). The potential cost of litigation and loss of corporate reputation whilst unlikely to equate to \$58m over ten years is a significant disadvantage of the outsourcing approach here.

(c)

Top tip. You should always be prepared for a question on ethics or CIMA's Code of Ethics because the Examiner has indicated that he regards ethics and ethical issues as important aspects of business strategy.

In this case, the question did not ask for a general discussion about ethics, but you needed to specifically evaluate the extent to which the Technical Director's views presented an ethical dilemma for the Management Accountant.

Do they present the Management Accountant with an ethical dilemma, and if so, how/why? Which of the ethical principles are being challenged?

You should have identified that the principles of integrity and objectivity were relevant here, and then you could use them to evaluate how the Director's views represent an ethical dilemma for the Management Accountant.

Ethical dilemmas

The Technical Director (TD) is preparing to present financial information to the Board which is not complete in the sense that it does not take account of a serious and quantifiable risk in the form of death or serious injury. In addition to this it would appear that the TD is suppressing this information by telling the Management Accountant (MA) to mind his own business.

CIMA Code

CIMA has a published code informing its members as to the expected ethical standards that they are expected to meet. Foremost amongst these are:

Objectivity – the work of a MA should be true to the facts and free from bias and undue influence

Integrity – a MA should be honest and straightforward in all their professional and business relationships

Evaluation of the TD's views

'Not worth doing' the fatality analysis – this would fall under the **objectivity** criterion. Although the risk is small it may well be that the cost to PU in terms of compensating a victim's family and the negative publicity that follow may be materially high. To not present this to other board members may be knowingly hiding a significant potential cost to the business. Within the TD's analysis it would be likely that an expected outcome of the cost would be used giving quite a low figure, however expected values are not monetary values that actually occur and therefore the TD should be prudent and make the Board aware of both the expected value and potential worst case outcomes.

'Concentrate on your own job' – this would fall under the **integrity** criterion. The MA has rightly brought to the attention of the TD a potentially material omission. In telling the MA to mind his own business the TD is potentially knowingly presenting misleading information which is clearly not honest. However it may be that the FD has an honestly held believe that the information is not material and therefore not worth disclosing.

(d)

Top tip. This is another question which looks for you to apply your knowledge to the scenario.

In part (i) you do not need to describe what CSFs are, but rather recommend suitable CSFs for DP. Our answer below has suggested four possible CSFs, but there are others you could have suggested; for example: employee attitudes, because it will be important that staff morale is not adversely affected following DP's change from being a nationalised industry to a private sector company. Equally, it could be important for DP to develop a brand awareness to try to differentiate itself from its competitors and to secure a degree of customer loyalty to prevent its customers switching to rival suppliers.

Provided you suggested appropriate CSFs, and explained *why* they were relevant to DP as a company, you would have scored marks for your suggestions.

The point about applying your knowledge to the scenario also applies to part (ii). You are not asked to discuss the attributes of an effective Information System in general, but specifically what attributes of an Information System would help DP manage its attendance at breakdowns. Try to make your answer as practical as possible.

(i) CSFs for DP

Service reliability – DP must be able to provide a reliable and consistent flow of electricity to its customers. This could be measured by recording the incidents of power outages and average flow of current across its networks

Customer satisfaction – DP must be able to keep its existing client base happy. The acquisition of the company will have been valued in part on its future cashflows and these will only be fulfilled if DP is able to maintain and build upon its current customer base. Customer satisfaction could be tracked via periodic surveys.

Competitive prices – DP operates in a competitive industry that now has 9 players. As this represents a lot of free choice for customers for what appears to be a fairly undifferentiated product then the ability to compete on price is crucial. This could be measured by benchmarking its cost per kilowatt/hour against its rivals.

Safe processes – Heavy industry of any type carries a number of significant risks to employees and local communities. It is essential therefore for the safety of these stakeholders and the reputation of DP that is able to operate its power plants and electricity networks safely. This could be measured by the number of accidents that occur each quarter.

(ii) Information systems (IS) are any system either manual or computerised that is used by an organisation to capture raw data, process it into information allowing delivery of usable outputs and providing storage.

The attributes of an effective IS for DP in respect of breakdowns would include:

Central information store

All of the key information on customer addresses and breakdown history should be kept in one place for ease of access and updating. This would allow all engineers to retrieve the information they require in an efficient manner; for example, the database could include details of the layout plans of the electrical equipment at DP's bigger customers, which the engineers could use to help them, particularly if they are called to an urgent breakdown at one of these customers' premises. A central database would be used to achieve this information.

Report writing software

The senior management of DP will want to track performance of their engineers over time i.e. how many urgent calls are attended within 1 hour. This will require the ability to generate a range of reports. This will be especially crucial if the outsourcing option is chosen as DP will wish to monitor the performance of RSC against agreed KPI's in the outsourcing contract.

Remote access

The work carried out by DP's engineers will be almost exclusively carried out away from DP's premises. Therefore it is essential that they are able to access the IS in order to be able to download and upload information as and when required. This may involve equipping all engineers with hardware that can wirelessly dial into the IS via a secure VPN.

MOCK EXAMS

CIMA – Pillar E

Paper E3

Enterprise strategy

Mock Exam 1

You are allowed **three hours** to answer this question paper.
You are allowed **20 minutes** reading time **before the examination begins** during which you should read the question paper and, if you wish, highlight and/or make notes on the question paper. However, you are **not** allowed, **under any circumstances**, to open the answer book and start writing or use your calculator during this reading time.
You are strongly advised to carefully read ALL the question requirements before attempting the question concerned (that is all parts and/or sub-questions).
Answer the compulsory question in Section A.
Answer TWO of the three questions in Section B.

DO NOT OPEN THIS PAPER UNTIL YOU ARE READY TO START UNDER EXAMINATION CONDITIONS

BPP
LEARNING MEDIA

SECTION A

Strategic level pre-seen case material

Question 1

Clothing manufacturing in Europe

Since the 1960s there has been a decline in the number of UK and European clothing manufacturers due to competition from cheaper, and sometimes higher quality, imported clothes. The clothing industry generally has become much more fashion conscious and price sensitive. This has led to a reduced number of companies that are still in business in Europe. Some companies have moved all or part of their manufacturing processes to other countries to achieve a cheaper operating base, and up until recently this has allowed them to continue to compete on price.

Many companies have had contracts to supply High Street retailers for over four decades and are highly dependent on retaining these key customers who wield immense buying power over the small manufacturers. A number of family owned manufacturing companies, that had been highly profitable once, have ceased trading, or are operating at very low margins, as a direct result of the High Street retailers being able to dictate terms of business and prices.

An additional factor that has put the main High Street retailers under more price pressure has been the appearance and market growth of new High Street retailers and their new brands, who have procured their goods mainly from overseas sources.

The result is that the few companies that are based in the UK and Europe which are left in the business of clothing manufacturing are having to look very hard at their strategic plans in order for them to manage to maintain their business over the next few years.

History of Kadgee Fashions (Kadgee)

Kadgee was formed in post-World War Two in a European country, and has remained as an unlisted company, although its shares are now held by others outside of the founding family. Kadgee quickly established itself as a high quality manufacturer of both men's and ladies clothes. By the 1960s Kadgee had a turnover equivalent to €25 million, and had nine factories operating in two European countries.

During the late 1960s Kadgee suffered its first major fall in sales, and found that it had large stocks of men's clothes that had been manufactured without specific sales contracts. Kadgee managed to sell off some of the stocks, albeit at below cost price. However, the management decided that it should not manufacture clothes without a firm contract from a retailer in future.

In the early 1970s the range and design of its men's clothing was changed several times, but it continued to make little profit. In 1973, Kadgee sold its men's clothing range and designs and some of its manufacturing equipment to a large listed company. Kadgee decided to concentrate on expanding its ranges of ladies' clothing to meet the growing demands of its main customers (see below).

During the next few years, Kadgee consolidated its position and its profitability increased again. In the early 1980s its then Chief Designer persuaded the Managing Director to expand its clothing range to include a range of girls' clothes. This new limited range was launched in 1982 and was immediately sold out. Kadgee has positioned itself at the upper price range of clothing, and has never tried to mass produced low cost clothing.

During the 1980s Kadgee continued to expand its ranges of ladies and girls' clothes. A further change that occurred was that many of Kadgee's customers were starting to dictate the styles and types of clothing required and Kadgee's designers had to manufacture to customers' specifications.

However, during the 1990s Kadgee suffered a number of setbacks. It also saw many of its competitors suffer losses and cease trading. Kadgee had been able to stay profitable only because of its particular customer base and because it sold high quality clothes that commanded a premium price. However, Kadgee saw its margins on many product lines reduced greatly and also it started to lose many of its smaller customers, who choose to import, at much lower prices, clothing produced in Asia.

Kadgee's shareholders

Kadgee has remained an unlisted company. At the end of 20X5 29% of its shares were held by the company's founder who is no longer on the board, 60% by current directors, 11% by employees. The company has 200,000 shares of €0·10 each in issue and has a total of 400,000 authorised shares. The shares are not traded but the last time the shares were exchanged was eight years ago, when shares were purchased at €8·00 each.

Kadgee's customer base

Kadgee manufactures clothing for a number of European and international clothing retailers, including many well known High Street retailers. It manufactures clothing in the medium to higher price ranges and its customers require top quality designs and finishing to maintain their brand reputation.

The majority of Kadgee's clothing is manufactured for its customers under the customers' own label, for example, clothing manufactured for one of its customers called Portrait is labelled as 'Portrait'.

In 20X5, Kadgee's customer base, analysed by sales value, was as follows:

	20X5 revenue	*% of Kadgee's total sales*
	€m	%
Portrait	24.0	32.3
Forum	16.8	22.6
Diamond	13.5	18.1
Zeeb	5.1	6.9
JayJay	4.5	6.0
Other retailers of ladies' clothes	7.3	9.8
Haus (children's clothes only)	3.2	4.3
Total	74.4	100.0

Most of Kadgee's contracts are renewed at the start of each fashion season. Kadgee is currently negotiating for clothing sales for the summer season of 20X7.

Human Resources

In the clothing manufacturing business one of the most crucial aspects to achieve customer satisfaction is quality. Kadgee has been very fortunate in having a skilled, very dedicated workforce who have always adapted to new machinery and procedures and have been instrumental in suggesting ways in which quality could be improved. This has sometimes involved a very minor change in the design of a garment and the designers now work much more closely with the operational staff to ensure that the garments can be assembled as quickly and efficiently as possible.

Losses made by Kadgee

Kadgee has suffered from falling operating profit margins due to the pressure exerted by its customers over the last ten years. For the first time in Kadgee's history, it experienced losses for five years through to, and including, 20X2. During this time Kadgee increased its loans and its overdraft to finance operations.

In 20X0, Kadgee refinanced with a ten year loan, which was used to repay existing debt, and also to invest in the IT solutions discussed below, as well as to purchase some new machinery. Kadgee also invested in its design centre (see below), which was completed in 20X1.

During 20X1, the company invested in new IT solutions enabling its customers to be able to track all orders from the garment cutting process right through to completion of garments and through to the delivery to customers' premises.

The IT solutions also enabled Kadgee to monitor its production processes including machine usage, wastage at various stages of production and speed of production through the various stages. This has enabled Kadgee's management to reduce areas that did not add value to the finished garment. The use of TQM throughout the business has also increased Kadgee's efficiency and enabled it to eliminate some other areas which did not add value to the finished garments.

While margins are still low, Kadgee has been operating profitably again since 20X3, albeit at lower margins to those achieved in the past.

Changes in the supply chain

Many of Kadgee's customers have needed to speed up the process of supplying clothing to their shops, so as to meet the demands of the market and to remain competitive. Kadgee has worked closely with its customers in order to achieve shorter lead times from design to delivery of finished products.

In 20X1, Kadgee introduced a new design centre, centralised at its Head Office. The design centre uses computer aided design techniques, which has helped Kadgee's customers to appreciate the finished appearance of new designs. This seems to have helped Kadgee to win new business and to retain its current customers. It has also contributed to Kadgee's ability to speed up the process from design board to finished article. Kadgee has also benefited from working closer with its customers and this has resulted in additional orders, which Kadgee's customers' would otherwise have procured from overseas sources.

Growing competition from China

During the 1990s and into the 21st century China has had a massive impact on the textile industry. China's manufacturing base is forecast to grow further and this will have a negative impact on many companies operating at a higher cost base elsewhere.

Many European companies have spent millions of Euros establishing manufacturing bases outside their home countries in the last 15 years. Many have opened factories in countries which have much lower operating costs. These include countries such as Turkey, Sri Lanka and Pakistan, as well as Eastern European countries.

The companies which have set up operations in these low cost countries did so in an effort to cut costs by taking advantage of low overheads and lower labour rates, but still managed to maintain quality. However, even the companies that have moved some, or all, of their manufacturing bases and have taken steps to reduce their costs, now have to reconsider their cost base again. This is because of the very low cost of Chinese imports, which they are having difficulty competing against.

Following the relaxation of trade barriers, there has recently been a deluge of Chinese clothing imports into Europe, the UK and the USA.

The quality of Chinese manufactured clothing is improving rapidly and it is now globally recognised that the "Made in China" label represents clothing of a higher quality than many European manufactured garments. Furthermore, the Chinese manufactured garments are being produced at a substantially lower manufacturing cost.

Kadgee has so far been operating in a market that has not been significantly affected by imported goods, as it produces medium to higher priced clothing, rather than cheaper ranges of clothes. However, many of Kadgee's customers are now looking to reduce their costs by either buying more imported clothes or by negotiating substantial price cuts from their existing suppliers. The purchasing power of European retailers being exerted on its suppliers is immense and Kadgee is under much pressure to deliver high quality goods at reduced operating profit margins from all of its customers.

Date: It is now 1 November 20X6.

Appendix 1

Statement of financial position

	At 31 December			
	20X5		20X4	
	€'000	€'000	€'000	€'000
Non-current assets (net)		9,830		11,514
Current assets				
Inventory	8,220		6,334	
Trade receivables and rent prepayments	19,404		18,978	
Cash and short term investments	119		131	
		27,743		25,443
Total assets		37,573		36,957

Equity and liabilities

	At 31 December			
	20X5		20X4	
	€'000	€'000	€'000	€'000
Equity				
Paid in share capital	20		20	
Share premium reserve	450		450	
Retained profits	21,787		20,863	
		22,257		21,333
Non-current liabilities				
Loans: Bank loan at 8% interest per year (repayable in 2010)	4,500		4,500	
	21,787		20,863	
		22,257		21,333
Current liabilities				
Bank overdraft	1,520		940	
Trade payables and accruals	8,900		9,667	
Tax	396		517	
		10,816		11,124
Total equity and liabilities		37,573		36,957

Note. Paid in share capital represents 200,000 shares of €0·10 each at 31 December 20X5

Income Statement

	Year ended 31 December	
	20X5	20X4
	€'000	€'000
Revenue	74,420	75,553
Total operating costs	72,580	73,320
Operating profit	1,840	2,233
Finance costs	520	509
Tax expense (effective tax rate is 24%)	396	517
Profit for the period	924	1,207

Statement of changes in equity

	Share capital	*Share premium*	*Retained earnings*	*Total*
	€'000	€'000	€'000	€'000
Balance at 31 December 20X4	20	450	20,863	21,333
Profit for the period	–	–	924	924
Dividends paid	–	–	–	–
Balance at 31 December 20X5	20	450	21,787	22,257

Appendix 2

Kadgee's Cash Flow Statement

	At 31 December			
	20X5		20X4	
	€'000	€'000	€'000	€'000
Net cash inflow from operations				
Operating profit		1,840		2,233
Add back depreciation	1,965		1,949	
(Increase)/Decrease in inventory	(1,886)		(535)	
(Increase)/Decrease in trade receivables	(426)		(1,526)	
Increase/(Decrease) in trade payables and accruals	(767)		(604)	
		(1,114)		(716)
Net cash flow from operations		726		1,517
Finance costs paid		(520)		(509)
Taxation paid		(517)		(390)
Purchase of tangible fixed assets		(281)		(350)
Dividends paid		–		–
Cash Inflow/(Outflow) before financing		(592)		268
Increase/(Decrease) in bank overdraft		580		(194)
Increase/(Decrease) in cash and short term investments		(12)		74

Section A

Question 1

Unseen Case Material (Exam day material for Paper E3 only)

<u>Background</u>

Increasing competition in the clothing supply industry has seen clothing retailers looking to renegotiate their supply contracts with their existing suppliers. Kadgee is concerned that it may lose some of its major customers if it is unable to give them the price reductions they want.

<u>Possible relocation to China</u>

At the latest Board meeting, the Directors discussed the possibility of moving some of Kadgee's manufacturing to China. This could enable Kadgee to operate more profitably and would allow the company to be more confident in its ability to retain its existing customer base. Such a move would also allow Kadgee to compete more effectively in order to win new business.

The MD stated that Kadgee has also been approached by a Chinese clothes manufacturing company called LIN. LIN has proposed a joint venture with Kadgee, although the respective shares of the venture partners have not yet been decided.

LIN proposes that Kadgee should concentrate on doing what it does best, which is designing and distributing to the European market. Kadgee should continue to work with its current customers to agree designs, which could then be electronically transferred to a factory in China to manufacture. Kadgee would continue to supply its existing customers, but with clothes manufactured in China. This proposal would necessitate closure of all of Kadgee's European factories.

The proposed joint venture would require the construction of a large purpose built factory with manufacturing capacity of over 20 million garments per year. However, the Kadgee's Marketing Director and Operations Director are both concerned about whether the proposed joint venture will work well for the longer term.

<u>Investment in IT</u>

At the same Board meeting, the IT director also highlighted the importance of investing in IT in order to win new business. He presented a proposal to enhance Kadgee's existing IT systems to provide a secure extranet system which would be totally interactive, allowing existing, as well as new customers to browse through all of the available designs that Kadgee is offering to manufacture. The proposed system would allow customers to order online.

The system would also allow customers to personalise their orders, as they would be able to choose the colours, the materials and the designs they wanted. The IT director is confident that this additional functionality will allow Kadgee to secure a lot of new business as well as safeguarding existing customers. He is also confident that a price premium could be charged for clothes that are 'custom made' to customers' requirements, therefore enhancing the margins that could be achieved.

The proposal is forecast to cost €0.8 million for IT hardware and software, and will require additional IT maintenance and support costs of €0.2 million per year. The marketing budget would also need to be increased by €0.4 million per year for the first two years.

The IT director and the marketing director have almost secured their first new customer, BBZ, provided that the system is implemented. BBZ is a medium sized retailer in Europe and has not previously bought any clothing from Kadgee. It is forecast that the contribution to profit from BBZ's first order could be worth €0.2 million in the first year, and subsequent orders could generate, in total, a contribution of €0.4 million per year. However, BBZ have said they do not want to place any orders with Kadgee until the system is operational.

Two other medium sized customers who do not previously buy clothing from Kadgee have also expressed an interest in the 'custom made' production.

The marketing director has summarised the possible contributions to profit from these two other potential customers as follows:

	Probability	*Contribution to profit (€m)*				
		20X7	*20X8*	*20X9*	*20Y0*	*20Y1*
Both possible customers sign up	0.35	0.4	0.6	0.7	0.8	0.9
One of the two signs up	0.45	0.2	0.3	0.4	0.4	0.5
Neither of them signs up	0.2	–	–	–	–	–

The Operations Director is concerned about the whole logic behind the proposal, and argued that it is trying to shift Kadgee from having mass production systems into small scale batch production.

However, at the Board meeting, the Finance director said that he felt this proposal was well worth considering, but that he wanted to see an investment appraisal over five years before making any further decisions. He suggested that although the current bank loan has an interest rate of 8%, the risk-adjusted discount rate used for any new investments should be 10%.

Required

(a) **Discuss** the scope and nature of the changes which are likely to be required by Kadgee if it decides to adopt the proposal to:

(i) Relocate its own manufacturing operations to China
(ii) Enter into a joint venture with for manufacturing in China
(iii) Develop a new interactive ordering system **(15 marks)**

(b) **Produce** the investment appraisal the Finance director has asked for.

(Note: You should assume that all cash flows apart from the initial capital investment occur at the end of the year to which they relate). **(10 marks)**

(c) In the light of the investment appraisal, and of the circumstances in which Kadgee operates, **evaluate** the strategic benefits of IT director's proposal for Kadgee. **(10 marks)**

(d) **Analyse** the potential advantages and disadvantages to Kadgee of the proposal for the joint venture in China. **(15 marks)**

(Total = 50 marks)

SECTION B – 50 marks

Answer TWO of the THREE questions

Question 2

S4W is a publishing company whose customers include both large chains of booksellers and independent outlets.

The company owns three warehouses, strategically sited to ensure short delivery times to customers. The company's agents take orders using notebook computers, entering details while paying visits to customers. These are then downloaded into the head office order processing system and consolidated printouts of accepted orders are faxed to the relevant warehouse. Some orders are received at head office in writing and by telephone from booksellers. These orders received direct from customers are input immediately they are received and individual printouts of accepted orders are also faxed to the relevant warehouse.

At the end of each month the company sends an information pack to every bookseller. This includes marketing information, a listing of all orders booked during the previous month and a customer statement. The statement shows all unpaid invoices.

Each warehouse has its own local despatch system. When faxed orders are received, they are entered onto the system and, each Thursday, despatch documentation is produced. Orders are packed up and sent out on Thursdays and Fridays. The despatch system also produces the invoices. Where faxes are marked 'urgent', they are not entered onto the despatch system, but manual documentation is filled out and the order sent out straight away. Copy invoices are sent to the accounts department on a weekly basis for posting to customer accounts.

The company has called in a consultant to review its existing systems. Although the current systems are operating much as intended, the consultant has identified a number of shortcomings.

(1) The company does not have a long-term IS strategy.

(2) The sales and despatch process is extremely paper-intensive, with multiple keying in to systems at various points.

(3) Although the three warehouses use the same system as each other, the operating system installed is a proprietary one which is not compatible with the graphical interface-based OS at head office.

As a result of the consultant's preliminary review the company has decided to adopt a formal IS strategy to identify future development priorities.

Required

(a) **Explain** the benefits to S4W of an IS strategy and list the major stages in the development of such a strategy. **(15 marks)**

(b) **Compare** briefly the characteristics of information which S4W would use in strategic planning with those of information required for operational control. **(10 marks)**

(Total = 25 marks)

Question 3

S is a company which has traded very successfully within its domestic market for many years. It has achieved high levels of profitability in providing ground and soil sampling and testing services for a large range of clients in both the public and private sectors. This sampling is mainly undertaken to assess the suitability of former industrial land for building and public use.

In recent years, S has experienced strong competition and its Managing Director (L) has recognised that it is becoming more difficult to obtain new business from within its domestic market. Increasingly, it has been found necessary to offer more than the original basic ground and soil sampling and testing services in order to retain the loyalty of existing clients. This has necessitated a whole range of other services being offered such as testing for the presence of polluted substances in buildings, chemical analysis of water sources, geological surveys and providing for unfit land to be cleaned prior to becoming available for public use.

While these other services have been relatively successful, L is increasingly concerned about the prospects for sustaining the company's profitability because of increasing competition and saturation of the domestic market. With this in mind, L has asked you, as Management Accountant, to advise on the rationale for an overseas expansion strategy and the issues to be considered in its implementation.

Required

Produce a report to L which:

(a) **Explain**s the business case for expansion overseas. **(10 marks)**

(b) **Discuss**es the strategic and operational issues which the directors of S should consider before making a decision on whether to implement an overseas expansion strategy. **(15 marks)**

(Total = 25 marks)

Question 4

E is a multinational organisation and is one of the largest global producers of chocolate, coffee and other foodstuffs. E categorises the countries in which it operates as follows:

1 Less developed countries, from which E sources raw materials, but where there is no established local market for the finished products.

2 Fully developed countries, into which E imports raw materials, manufactures, and serves the local and export markets.

In every country in which E operates, it follows the OECD (Organisation for Economic Cooperation and Development) guidelines for multinationals.

In the particular case of country F, a less developed country, E has helped the local farmers to organise themselves into cooperatives to produce their crops. E has also funded schooling for the children of both the farmers and their workers, built and staffed a hospital and has provided other welfare benefits. E considers itself to be a good 'corporate citizen' and is used as an example of good practice on the OECD website.

Although the farmers' cooperatives are free to sell to E's two main competitors, they tend not to do so because of the close and friendly working relationship that they have with E. Both of E's main competitors are multinationals, but both are smaller than E.

E has recently been receiving some bad publicity in country F. The management of E feels that this is being organised by the government and the national labour union of country F. The government of F is reasonably supportive of business, but won the last election with a narrow majority. The government is now under pressure to raise the standard of living of the population. An election is due within the next fifteen months. The national labour union, which is increasingly being supported by the main opposition party in country F, is extremely anti-business. It would like to see all foreign companies removed from country F and all foreign-owned assets, and co-operatives nationalised.

The government of country F has stated that the prices paid for cocoa beans are too low, and that country F is not gaining sufficient tax revenue from the exports. The government of country F has threatened to impose an

export tariff on cocoa beans, unless prices are increased, and unless E opens a manufacturing facility in the country F. The management of E feels that it has been targeted by the government because it is the largest of the three multinationals operating in the country.

The national labour union of country F has argued that the farm workers are being victimised by the farmers, who have become too powerful because of the cooperatives. It states that the government of F should not allow the farmers to operate in this way.

The management of E does not want to build a factory because the transport costs from such a factory to the nearest market for finished products would force the company to operate the factory at a loss.

The Chief Executive of E is due to meet with government ministers from country F to discuss E's future operations and involvement in the country.

Required

(a) **Explain** the advantages to E of conducting a stakeholder analysis of its operations in country F. **(4 marks)**

(b) **Produce** a stakeholder analysis for E's operations in country F. **(14 marks)**

(c) **Evaluate** the options available to E in its approach to the government of country F and recommend the option that you consider to be the most appropriate. **(7 marks)**

(Total = 25 marks)

Answers

DO NOT TURN THIS PAGE UNTIL YOU HAVE COMPLETED THE MOCK EXAM

A plan of attack

We discussed the problem of which question to start with earlier, in 'Passing the E3' exam. (See page xi, in the front pages of this Kit.) Here we will merely reiterate our view that Question 1 is nearly always the best place to start but, if you do decide to start with a 25 mark Section B question, **make sure that you finish your answer in no more than 45 minutes**.

However, take a good look through the paper before diving in to answer questions.

<u>First things first</u>

In the first five minutes of reading time, look through the paper and work out which questions you are going to do, and the order in which you are going to attempt them.

We recommend you then spend the remaining fifteen minutes of reading time looking at the Section A scenario, identifying key information in the unseen material and highlighting the key requirements in the question.

The extra time spent on Section A will be helpful, regardless of the order in which you intend to answer the questions. If you decide to answer the Section A question first, the time spent will mean you are already immersed in the question when the writing time starts. If you intend to answer the question second or third, probably because you find it daunting, the question may look easier when you come back to it, because your initial analysis could generate further points whilst you're tackling the other questions.

If you are a bit **worried about the paper**, it is likely that you believe the Section A question will be daunting. In this case, you may prefer to do one or both of the optional questions before tackling it. Don't, however, fall into the trap of spending too long on the optional questions because they seem easier. You will still need to spend half of the three hours writing time available on the Section A Case Study, because it is worth 50% of the marks.

It's dangerous to be over-confident, but if you're **not too nervous** about the exam then you should turn straight to the compulsory Section A question, and tackle it first. You've got to answer it, so you might as well get it over and done with.

Make sure you answer every requirement and sub-requirement in the question, and also make sure you include plenty of examples from the scenario. Bear in mind that one thing you are being tested on is your ability to apply your knowledge to deal with the specific issues identified in the scenario.

<u>Analysing the questions</u>

Examiners are continually frustrated by candidates' apparent inability to dissect the requirements of a question correctly.

If you do not analyse the question requirements thoroughly, you are likely to produce answers which are largely irrelevant to the question. So, make sure you do the following:

- Dissect the question requirements: what are the issues the examiner want you to address?
- Identify all the requirements in the question: is there more than one requirement?
- Be aware of the verb used in the question: how much detail do you need to give in your answer?

<u>The questions themselves</u>

- **Question 1** looks at a clothing manufacturing which is facing increased competition from overseas competitors. The pre-seen and unseen material provide a large amount of information about the strategic context in which the company operates, and you should draw on this in your answer.

  The first part of the question looks at the type of change required by the company if it adopts a range of different strategies to improve competitiveness.

  The second part requires you to produce a relatively simple investment appraisal, based on figures provided in the unseen case study material, and then in part (c) you need to use these figures and your ability to evaluate strategic options to evaluate one of the specific strategies the company is considering.

  The final part of the question requires you to analyse the advantages and disadvantages of a joint venture as a means of overseas expansion.

- **Question 2** combines IT strategy and strategic planning, and you should have only attempted it if you felt comfortable with both parts of the question. The scenario is largely illustrative and the requirements are not as closely linked to its details as is often the case. Nevertheless, sometimes the Examiners set a question of this type and you must be prepared to answer it. The preparation of a solution does require a **sound knowledge of basic IT strategy** and this is a very popular topic with the Examiners. You would be well advised to ensure you are confident with your knowledge of IT strategy before you sit your exams.
- **Question 3** is only moderately difficult but many candidates would avoid it simply because it deals with **global strategy**. Nonetheless, you could face a question on this aspect of the syllabus in your exam, so make sure you can deal with it. Notice how the first requirement, for ten marks, asks about general principles, while the second part asks for a discussion specifically relevant to the subject company. In this situation it is imperative you tailor your answer to the company/scenario in question otherwise you will be losing easy marks.

  By contrast to the other optional questions, **Question 4**, has few purely knowledge-based requirements. Instead, the scenario provides the majority of the information you need to answer this question. However, although this question may seem easier than the other optional questions, do not fall into the trap of writing general answers about stakeholders. Make sure you read the scenario carefully to identify all the parties involved, and then consider the specific relationships they have (or could have) with company E.

No matter how many times we remind you…

Always, always **allocate your time** according to the marks for the question in total and for the parts of the questions. And always, always **follow the requirements exactly**.

You've got free time at the end of the exam…?

If you have allocated your time properly then you **shouldn't have time on your hands** at the end of the exam. If you find yourself with five or ten minutes spare, however, go back to **any parts of questions that you didn't finish** because you ran out of time.

Forget about it!

And don't worry if you found the paper difficult. It is more than likely other students did too. However, once you've finished the exam you cannot change your answers so don't spend time worrying about them. Instead, you should start thinking about your next exam and preparing for that.

SECTION A

Question 1

Marking scheme

			Marks
(a)	**Relocation of manufacturing operations** Up to 3 marks for discussion of scope of changes and up to 3 marks for nature of changes required	Up to 5	
	Joint venture Up to 3 marks for discussion of scope of changes and up to 3 marks for nature of changes required	Up to 5	
	New ordering system Up to 3 marks for discussion of scope of changes and up to 3 marks for nature of changes required	Up to 5	
		Total up to	15
(b)	Identify cash inflows from BBZ contract	1	
	Identify cash outflows: Hardware and software	½	
	IT maintenance and support	½	
	Marketing	½	
	Calculate probable cash inflows if: both customers sign up	2½	
	one customer signs up	2½	
	Calculate NPV of proposal	2½	
		Total	10
(c)	Each benefit evaluated and related specifically to the IT director's proposal	Up to 2	
		Total up to	10
(d)	Each potential advantage identified and related to Kadgee: up to 2 marks, up to a maximum of 8 marks for advantages	Up to 8	
	Each potential disadvantage identified and related to Kadgee: up to 2 marks, up to a maximum of 8 marks for disadvantages	Up to 8	
		Total up to	15
		Total	50

Part (a)

Text reference. Types of change are covered in Chapter 12 of the Study Text.

Top tips. The reference to scope and nature of the changes being required could have given you a clue that Balogun & Hope Hailey's change matrix might be useful as framework here.

However, if you used the matrix, you should not have spent time simply describing it. Instead you should have used it to help you analyse the types of change being described in the scenario.

Make sure your answer deals with all three of the proposals in turn because the speed and extent of change may not be the same for each of them.

There are 15 marks available, and there are three proposals to consider. So you should assume there are up to 5 marks available for discussing each requirement, and you should divide your time up between the three parts of the requirement accordingly.

> Also, when reading through the requirements for this question as a whole, you should have recognised that parts (c) and (d) look at the appropriateness of the two proposals, so you do not need to comment on that aspect of them here.
>
> Finally, note that the question is asking you about the type of change required by Kadgee (scope and nature of change), so you should have looked specifically at internal changes rather than changes in the external environment more generally. And for (a) (i) make sure you focus only on the changes, not the factors which might influence Kadgee's location decisions (eg Porter's diamond). You are not asked to discuss the factors which would affect where Kadgee decides to relocate, and so you would not score any marks for discussing them.

(i) Possible relocation of own manufacturing to China

Kadgee currently manufactures its own clothing from its European factories. However, the pressure to cut costs has prompted the Directors to look at the possibility of moving some or all of its manufacturing to China.

Scope of change

The proposal to move some or all of Kadgee's own manufacturing operations to China will represent a significant change to the detailed logistics of Kadgee's operations, and it will also result in a large number of Kadgee's existing manufacturing staff being made redundant.

However, it will not fundamentally change Kadgee's overall methods and approaches to clothes production. **Kadgee will still design and manufacture garments in-house**, and it will still be manufacturing for same customers. Although this is a major change geographically, it is not such a major change in the overall organisation of the company.

In this respect, the proposal should be seen as a **realignment rather than a transformation** of existing practices.

Nature of change

Moreover, the change is essentially **building on existing methods and approaches** rather than challenging them. So again, despite the major geographical change, the nature of the change could be seen as incremental rather than being a 'Big Bang' change.

However, the **trigger for the change** is the potential long-term decline in performance which Kadgee could suffer due to the threat of low-cost competition from China. This threat means that **significant and rapid change to Kadgee's operations is necessary**.

To this extent, the fact that the trigger for change is the response to the critical problems facing the company means the change is better seen as a **reconstruction rather than an adaptation**.

(ii) Joint venture

If Kadgee moves to a joint venture arrangement with LIN, not only do the manufacturing operations move geographically from Europe to China, but they move outside Kadgee's direct control.

Scope of change

In this option, **Kadgee will cease to be a manufacturing company**, and will become a design and distribution network. Again, it will result in a large number of manufacturing staff in the European factories losing their jobs.

However, the change in the focus of Kadgee's own competences represents a major **transformational change** to the existing business model. Kadgee will lose it manufacturing competences, and will rely on the joint venture partner to do its manufacturing.

Nature of change

The change from Kadgee being a manufacturing company to essentially being a design company represents a major change to its methods, processes and cultures.

If Kadgee pursues this option, it is likely to indicate that the external pressures of the changing competitive environment have forced it to take **decisive and rapid action** to retain its competitive advantage.

Moreover, once Kadgee has entered the joint venture, and once the new factory in China is built and ready to use, the changes to shift production to China are likely to take place quickly.

Therefore, the changes will be 'Big Bang' change, rather than an incremental change.

Looking at the scope and nature of this proposal together suggest that it is best seen as a revolution: a rapid and wide-ranging response to pressure for change, which leads to a fundamental shift in Kadgee's business model, and the way the company operates.

(iii) IT proposal

Scope of change

Building on existing capabilities – Whereas the relocation proposals will lead to the closure of Kadgee's European manufacturing operations, the IT proposal is more likely to lead to additional systems and processes being added to the existing operations.

So, in effect, the IT proposal is reinforcing Kadgee's current position.

Kadgee has historically designed quality designs in the medium to higher price range, and the IT proposal is designed to allow Kadgee to be able to charge a price premium.

Incremental change – In this respect, the change could be approached as an incremental change because it builds on existing methods. Although the new interactive online design and ordering process offers customers a lot more functionality, it is still building on existing processes rather than radically altering them.

In this respect, the change can be seen as a **realignment** of Kadgee's existing strategy.

However, the Operations Director's comment that the proposal is trying to shift Kadgee from a mass production environment to smaller scale batch production, suggests that there could be more far-reaching aspects of the change. If it changes the underlying culture of production, and the production processes, this is not an incremental change.

If the existing business model is being challenged – and changed – then the change is more of a **transformation** than a realignment.

Nature of change

Whereas the proposals to move manufacturing operations to China are extensive changes which will lead to the closure of Kadgee's European manufacturing operations, and will result in large numbers of redundancies, the IT-based proposal will have a smaller scale impact, certainly in the short term.

The IT director's proposal appears to **involve adding the new interactive functionality on top of Kadgee's existing production methods** and processes.

Therefore, it will involve a gradual change, rather than a sudden one-off change. In this respect, the change is best seen as **incremental**.

Part (b)

Top tips. Note that in this part of the question you only need to produce the investment appraisal. You do not need to comment on it here. However, you should have noted that you will need to use the figures you calculate to help advise your answer to part (c).

The mathematics in the calculations should not be difficult, and the figures are given in the scenario. So if you work logically through the figures, you should have been able to score some easy marks here.

	T_0 €m	Year 1 €m	Year 2 €m	Year 3 €m	Year 4 €m	Year 5 €m	Total
Cash inflows							
BBZ contract		0.20	0.40	0.40	0.40	0.40	1.8
Other potential customers (W)		0.23	0.35	0.43	0.46	0.54	2.0
	–	0.43	0.75	0.83	0.86	0.94	3.8
Cash outflows							
Hardware and software	(0.80)	–	–	–	–	–	
IT maintenance and support	–	(0.20)	(0.20)	(0.20)	(0.20)	(0.20)	
Marketing	–	(0.40)	(0.40)	–	–	–	
	(0.80)	(0.60)	(0.60)	(0.20)	(0.20)	(0.20)	(2.60)
Net cash flow	(0.80)	(0.17)	0.15	0.63	0.66	0.74	
Discount factor (10%)	1	0.909	0.826	0.751	0.683	0.621	
Net present value	(0.80)	(0.15)	0.12	0.47	0.45	0.46	**0.55**

Working

	Year 1 €m	Year 2 €m	Year 3 €m	Year 4 €m	Year 5 €m	
Weighted probabilities						
Both customers sign up	0.40	0.60	0.70	0.80	0.90	
× 0.35	0.14	0.21	0.25	0.28	0.32	(1)
One signs up	0.20	0.30	0.40	0.40	0.50	
× 0.45	0.09	0.14	0.18	0.18	0.22	(2)
(1) + (2)	0.23	0.35	0.43	0.46	0.54	

Part (c)

Top tips. The question asks you to *evaluate* the strategic benefits of the IT director's proposals, so you should first consider the advantages of the proposals and then move on to consider the limitations of them.

One of the key limitations seems to be that it is a niche strategy, and therefore whether it will provide sufficient income to be a valid alternative to Kadgee's existing customer base. The calculations from (b) should have helped you reach this conclusion, by highlighting not only the relatively low NPV of the project, but also the relative uncertainty about how many customers will actually sign up for the scheme.

Advantages

Increase margins – By offering customers flexibility, the IT director's proposal should allow Kadgee to charge a price premium. This will help increase margins. The reduction in margins through customers trying to force down prices is the key threat facing the business.

In effect, the IT director's proposal allows Kadgee to increase its margins through adopting a differentiation strategy.

Focus on quality manufacturing – Kadgee has traditionally been a high quality manufacturer. Adopting a differentiation type strategy continues this focus on quality.

Preserve jobs in Europe – This strategy will allow Kadgee to retain its manufacturing plants in Europe rather than having to relocate them in China. Therefore it will preserve jobs at the European factories.

Disadvantages

Price premium – The IT director's strategy is based on creating a situation in which Kadgee charges customers a premium price. However, the majority of customers are trying to reduce the price they pay, so the idea of wanting to charge a price premium seems rather contradictory in these market conditions.

This strategy does not make any reference to **reducing costs** which seems to be a critical issue for Kadgee.

Customer bargaining power – A key factor in the success of the strategy will be the relative bargaining power between Kadgee and its customers, and therefore Kadgee's ability to sustain its margins. However, as the trend for moving production to cheaper outlets in China illustrates, the larger customers have very strong bargaining power in the clothing manufacturing industry.

Niche market – The early indications are that ability to have 'custom made' clothing is attractive to smaller or medium sized customers, but there is no indication that Kadgee's large customers are interested in it.

These large customers are the ones wanting to reduce prices, so it seems unlikely that this proposal alone will safeguard Kadgee's existing customers.

Also, the value which the new proposal generates is likely to be quite small compared to the revenue Kadgee generates from its 'traditional' sales to its existing customers.

It appears that this proposal targets a niche segment of the market only, rather than being a strategy which Kadgee can use across its whole market. Even if the 'custom made' facility were to prove successful, there must be a **concern about how scalable it is**.

Uncertainty about demand – There is a 20% chance that only BBZ sign up for the new scheme. If this were the case, then the NPV of the project would be negative.

Even if all three potential customers sign up, the project only generates a net cash flow of €0.54 million over 5 years. Compared to the revenue that Kadgee currently gets from Portrait or Forum, these are still very small figures. As it stands, this proposal certainly cannot replace Kadgee's existing business.

Organisation structure – As the operations directors commented this proposal is likely to require Kadgee to change its production techniques from large scale manufacturing into small scale batch production. This will not only lead to it losing economies of scale, but there is also a question mark about whether Kadgee's production machinery is suitable for batch production.

Problems for marketing mix – An alternative to replacing large scale production with the customised range would be to offer the additional functionality alongside Kadgee's existing production range.

However, this would lead to confusion in Kadgee's marketing mix. On the one hand, it would be looking to reduce cost, but on the other it would be looking to create a niche market which charges a price premium.

Part (d)

Top tips. Do not let your answer to this question become a general discussion of the advantages of joint ventures as a means of entering a new overseas market. Make sure you relate it specifically to Kadgee's circumstances. For example, Kadgee could either relocate its own manufacturing operations to China or enter into this joint venture. So a useful approach to this question might be to consider the advantages and disadvantages of the joint venture compared to Kadgee relocating its own operations.

Also, if there is any relevant 'real world' knowledge you can include, make sure you do so. Although the pre-seen material did not identify the possibility of a joint venture, it clearly identified the issues Kadgee was facing and raised the importance of China as a location, so you could usefully have considered some of the ways clothing manufacturers have sought to respond to the threat of competition from lower cost countries in the real world.

Advantages

Gets into China – The joint venture will provide Kadgee with a means of getting its clothes produced in China, at the lower cost which its major customers want. However, the joint venture provides Kadgee with an alternative to having to build a wholly owned manufacturing operation in China.

Speed – Because LIN is already an established clothing manufacturer this should mean the joint venture will allow Kadgee to source clothes from China more quickly than if it had to establish its own manufacturing operations.

Supply chain networks – An important factor in this will be that LIN will already have pre-existing supply chain networks (for example, suppliers for raw materials such as cotton) whereas if Kadgee were to set up its own plant it would either have to arrange for its existing suppliers to transfer supply from its European plants to China, or it would have to set up contracts with new suppliers.

Benefit from local knowledge – The alliance with LIN will provide Kadgee with local knowledge about business cultures and business practices which it would not otherwise have. It will also overcome any potential language problems associated with moving into China. In this way, it could significantly ease Kadgee's entry route into operating in China.

Share of capital costs – There is likely to be a significant capital investment involved in building a new manufacturing plant in China. The joint venture will mean that these capital costs are shared between Kadgee and LIN, rather than Kadgee having to fund them all itself.

Offers scope for growth – The Chinese joint venture will build a large, purpose built factory to make Kadgee's clothes. Because the factory will be modern it should allow Kadgee to benefit from up-to-technology production technologies and efficiencies, thereby allowing it to obtain low costs.

Low costs on their own are a benefit to Kadgee, but if the factory increases Kadgee's **production capacity** it will provide a second benefit by allowing the scope for growth and potentially acquiring new customers – which Kadgee could acquire by offering to manufacture customers' clothes more cheaply than its rivals.

<u>Disadvantages</u>

Conflicts of interest – Conflicts of interest between Kadgee and LIN could potentially be a major disadvantage of the joint venture. Disagreements may arise over profit shares, and the relative shares of the partners have not yet been agreed. There could also be issues with the management of the joint venture – particularly around the quality of the garments produced. Kadgee will ultimately be responsible to its customers for the quality of the clothes, but they will produced by LIN.

Unequal interests – One of the main risks with joint venture arrangements is that venture partners can gain **confidential information** about each other which could subsequently be used competitively by one partner against the other.

This could be a risk for Kadgee here because LIN potentially stands to gain more from the venture. The venture will see Kadgee design and market the clothes and LIN make them. However, in time if **LIN develops its own design and marketing competences** (through working with Kadgee) it could eventually bypass Kadgee and deal directly with customers itself.

Ultimately the ability to actually make the clothes is crucial. Once Kadgee has lost its manufacturing capability, there is a risk that LIN can take over the supplier contracts for itself.

Profits shared – Kadgee will have to share the profits it earns from its clothing contracts with LIN so this will reduce its underlying profit.

Time taken to build new factory – LIN does not have any existing production facilities which can be used to make Kadgee clothing. The proposed new factory still has to be built. This means it might not be much quicker for Kadgee to partner with LIN than to build its own factory in China, and will be slower than if Kadgee decided to simply use existing Chinese clothing manufacturers to produce clothes for it as they were required.

SECTION B

Question 2

Marking scheme

			Marks
(a)	Each benefit to S4W of having an IS strategy: up to 2 marks each	Up to 10	
	Each stage of IS strategy development listed: 1 mark each	Up to 5	
		Total up to	15
(b)	Each relevant characteristic of strategic planning information identified and compared with operational information: up to 2 marks each	Up to 10	10
		Total	25

Part (a)

Text reference. Information strategy is covered in Chapter 9 of your BPP Study Text.

Top tips. This question is designed to cover the essential ideas relating information systems to strategy.

It is, perhaps, somewhat unrepresentative of the kind of question you are likely to get in the exam, which are more likely to deal with slightly more specialised topics, but it offers a very good workout on this general topic area.

Easy marks. The easiest marks are to be found in the basic theoretical models of principle relevant to part (a).

The value of information

Information is an organisational resource similar to human skills, fixed assets, goodwill and so forth. Planning in all these areas is desirable, so that the organisation can adapt to a changing environment.

An organisation's financial investment in information technology is substantial, especially with the proliferation of computing power around different departments. Moreover, information technology covers areas of management which previously would have been distinct: high volume data processing (a computer department); telecommunications (which may have been a general administrative function); office administration (PCs were bought to replace dedicated word processors, which were themselves purchased to replace typewriters). Many organisations report dissatisfaction with the outcomes of their investments. Some overall direction is therefore required. This is clearly the case at S4W where a variety of incompatible systems is in use.

What is an IS strategy?

A strategy is a long-term plan, concentrating on the overall performance of the system, stating long-term objectives and goals, and outlining the measures to achieve them. As information technology is so pervasive throughout the business, and can affect significantly the relationship an organisation has with its customers, the IS strategy should be developed with the overall corporate plan. This was not done at S4W.

Why should S4W have an IS strategy?

Not only does IS have to compete with other investments (eg other non-current assets) or expenditure programs for resources, but also implementing IS can be very disruptive. Moreover, with the growth of end-user computing, it is important that there is at least some central direction to ensure that the IS resources are used to the best advantage of the organisation. This will not be the case if the organisation is plagued with incompatible hardware and/or software.

Benefits to S4W of having an IS strategy

A strategy for information systems will therefore be part of the overall organisational strategy and will be geared to meeting organisational objectives. As significantly, it demonstrates the importance of IS to senior management and their commitment to it. Finally, it has the function of laying down the plan for managing IS in terms of technical standards and organisational responsibilities.

Developing an IS strategy

A strategy for information and information systems, therefore, need not be developed independently of other planning exercises. Arguably, each user department in specifying its commercial strategy should be able to state what information it is likely to need. Information will already be available about file sizes and so forth. If, however, an information strategy is a panic response to poorly controlled costs, and perceived poor value for money delivered by investments in information technology, the strategy exercise will be more tightly defined.

Stages in developing an IS strategy

Many strategy developments are likely to conform in some respects to the model outlined below.

(a) Personnel devising the strategy are given **terms of reference**. The brief may be very broad, or quite narrowly defined. The terms of reference may be developed from the overall organisational strategy.

(b) A **plan** is made for the strategy development exercise. This means defining in more detail what exactly is the subject of the study, from considerations of potential competitive advantage to purely technical decisions which need to be decided at strategic level. The plan would detail the timetable, required resources, and specify the outputs of the planning process.

(c) Strategy **definition**. Three types of document are written:

  (i) The information systems strategy details the long-term information plan to support business strategies or to create new strategic options.

  (ii) The information technology strategy seeks to provide a framework for the analysis and design of the organisation's technical infrastructure (eg communications, computing hardware open vs proprietary systems).

  (iii) The information management strategy details the management of information systems, in terms of necessary resources, authorisation procedures for systems development projects, cost control, and management of the technology (eg security policy).

(d) Strategy **implementation**. The strategy is then set to work. To be successful, the exercise should have a high profile within the organisation and there should be suitable commitment to it from senior management. This means that any demarcation problems should be sorted out.

(e) **Review**. The success of the strategy should be reviewed on a rolling basis.

Part (b)

Strategic planning, management control and operational control may be seen as **a hierarchy of planning and control** decisions. Management control is always in the middle of the range.

(a) Top level management make strategic plans, and low level managers make operational control decisions.

(b) Strategic planning tends to cover a longer time period than management control, whereas operational control is exercised day-to-day.

(c) The most important decisions are usually strategic, and the least important are operational.

Strategic planning is a process of deciding on objectives of the organisation, on changes in these objectives, on the resources used to attain these objectives and on the policies that are to govern the acquisition, use and disposition of these resources.

Operational control decisions ensure that specific tasks are carried out effectively and efficiently. It focuses on individual tasks, and is carried out within the strictly defined guidelines issued by strategic planning and management control systems.

Strategic information is used by the senior managers of S4W to plan the objectives of their organisation, and to assess whether the objectives are being met in practice. Such information includes overall profitability, the profitability of different segments of the business, future market prospects, the availability and cost of raising new funds, total cash needs, total manning levels and capital equipment needs.

Strategic information therefore:

- Is derived from both internal and external sources.
- Is summarised at high level.
- Is relevant to the long term.
- Deals with the whole organisation (although it might go into some detail).
- Is often prepared on an 'ad hoc' basis.
- Is both quantitative and qualitative
- Is incapable of providing complete certainty, given that the future cannot be predicted.

Operational information is used by 'front-line' managers such as S4W's warehouse foremen to ensure that specific tasks are planned and carried out properly. Operational information relates to the level of decision making referred to above as operational control. S4W's despatch procedures depend on detailed operational information: which quantities of books are to be despatched by which warehouse to which customers? The company's accounting function is also a heavy use of detailed operational information, not least for the preparation of invoices and statements.

Operational information

- Is derived almost entirely from internal sources.
- Is highly detailed, being the processing of raw data.
- Relates to the immediate term.
- Is task-specific.
- Is prepared constantly, or very frequently.
- Is largely quantitative.
- Has a high degree of accuracy.

Question 3

Text reference. Global business expansion is considered in Chapter 6 of your BPP Study Text.

Top tips. It is easy with this question to get bogged down in theoretical discussion about international expansion. As always, make it specific and relevant to the circumstances of the question. The examiner always points this out as an area of weakness in many answers. Remember, too, that this is a service business, because this has special consequences when expanding overseas. Required customer service levels in one country may not be expected in others, or vice versa, for example.

Easy marks. The business case for expansion revolves around the fact that the home market has become saturated. This does not automatically mean that the market overseas will be favourable, but it makes sense to at least consider it. As the company operates in a highly specialised and technical field, it is likely that the product (or service) life cycle is going to be at a different stage overseas, which could work to S's advantage. Full and thorough research of the market will be vital.

Note. Did you notice you were asked to produce a report? If you didn't you lost a very easy mark.

Marking scheme

			Marks
(a)	Each reason why S should expand overseas identified and explained: up to 2 each	Up to 10	10
(b)	Each strategic issue discussed and related to S: up to 2	Up to 8	
	Each operation issue discussed and related to S: up to 2	Up to 8	
	Overall mark for presenting answer as a report	1	
		Total up to	15
		Total	25

Part (a)

REPORT

To: Managing Director
From: Management Accountant
Date: November 20XX
Subject: International expansion plans

The company has been finding the domestic market for its services to be both highly competitive and increasingly saturated. This report sets out the **rationale** for overseas expansion and the **strategic and operational issues** that will be relevant when making the decision whether or not to market overseas.

The points made in this initial report are only an indication of the issues involved. Further **research** in the chosen overseas market will be essential.

1 Business case for expansion

1.1 A primary reason for overseas expansion that is encountered by many companies is that of **overcrowding of the domestic market**. S is finding it increasingly difficult to obtain new business at home, to the extent that we have had to offer an increasing range of services to retain customer loyalty. This new range of services has amounted to a **product development strategy** (per Ansoff's product-market matrix) that has been necessary in the domestic market. These additional services may or may not be attractive to the overseas market.

The **increased level of competition** has proved costly for the company as it has necessitated the development of additional services. There may be better returns available overseas if the level of local competition is less intense.

1.2 It is likely to be the case that S has **comparative advantage in service levels, skills and technology**, both through its traditional ground and soil sampling services and the development of its more highly specialist services. Lesser developed economies in particular may not have local companies with such highly developed skills, meaning that **entry barriers are low** and S should be able to establish a dominant position more quickly. The **economies of scale** likely to be enjoyed by S means that costs can be kept down and profitability higher.

1.3 A related point is that the **product life cycle** for the range of services that S provides may be at an earlier point in development overseas. This means that existing services will have a longer life, guaranteeing a longer period of profitability for services that have reached the mature stage in the domestic market.

1.4 Expansion overseas results in **geographic diversification** for the company, which means that it can focus on one service (ground and soil sampling) in a number of markets, not several different ones at home. This spreads the risk. In the long term, this may prove to be the most profitable strategy, and S may be able to scale down its additional services in the domestic market. It must be recognised however that the development of the overseas market could require significant investment before returns are achieved.

1.5 There may be **investment incentives** in overseas markets. The availability of venture capital or local government assistance in the form of grants can make overseas investment particularly attractive. S would need to investigate the possibilities here.

1.6 An overseas presence could help increase the **prestige** of S at home. This differentiating factor, in addition to a **reduced dependence** on the domestic market, could encourage S in the longer term to be even more innovative in the services it provides, as its risk is spread and it can afford to take some chances (that competitors cannot) and further enhance its competitive position.

Part (b)

2 Strategic and operational issues

Before getting involved overseas, S must consider both strategic and operational issues.

2.1 Strategic

(a) Most importantly, does overseas expansion 'fit' with the overall **mission and objectives** of the company? As a service business, S needs to make sure that its strengths and competences in soil sampling and testing will be well used overseas and will not deflect resources from the position that has been built up at home.

(b) The company needs to make sure that it has the internal **resources** to expand overseas. These will be chiefly financial, but it will also require a lot of time and staff effort. Marketing the services to an overseas country will be a significant project, and one which the company has not undertaken before.

(c) S needs to decide what overseas market to enter, and what its **level of involvement** will be. It is advisable to start off with only a few markets at the most, to limit not only the costs of entry and market communications, but also the likely number of competitors.

The choice of market is obviously very important. Not only must there be an **accessible demand** to make the market attractive, but S must assess its **comparative advantage** in that market. Prior experience in the provision of its range of services will be an advantage here. The **risk** associated with the market must also be assessed. This will include political stability, economic infrastructure and other external influences.

(d) The **longer term objectives** for the overseas venture need to be established. Is it merely a way of getting through what could be a temporary domestic slowdown, or is there going to be a full commitment to overseas expansion? This will necessitate some organisational changes for S, both in structure and management.

(e) The **form of involvement** needs to be considered. Will the services be provided by a dedicated overseas subsidiary, or will they be marketed via a licensing agreement with a local company? A joint venture with an existing company may provide quick, knowledgeable and less risky access to the chosen market. Unless the subsidiary route is chosen, S will have to relinquish some control, which it may not be prepared to do.

2.2 Operational

These are more short term needs than the strategic issues presented above. Sales levels, profitability, cash flows, market share and capital expenditure requirements need to be forecast and planned in detail. In order to be able to do this, the following issues need to be considered.

(a) The **needs and preferences** of the foreign target market need to be established. This can only be achieved via an extensive programme of **market research** to forecast likely demand and establish levels of competition. Dealing with likely foreign **competitor responses** to the presence of S (such as price cuts) must be planned in advance.

(b) The **cultural implications** of doing business in a foreign country must never be underestimated. S has no experience of conducting business overseas and this often requires sensitive handling and staffing. Market share will suffer if local preferences are not taken into account.

(c) This particular industry is heavily subject to, and driven by, **regulations**. S is familiar with the rules governing land quality, pollution and testing in its home market. The rules overseas are almost certain to be different in some respects, and it is imperative that local knowledge and expertise is employed to make sure that the rules are complied with.

(d) The **costs** of doing business overseas will be affected by factors such as foreign tax regimes, access to technology, and availability of physical resources.

(e) **Management skills** will be vital, both for staffing and the level of control over the operation. This will have implications for the organisation structure. For example, expatriate staff from the home country may need to be seconded to the overseas market to help local staff. As this is a service business, service levels are important and S will want to ensure that they are consistent wherever it is doing business.

As can be appreciated from the analysis above, any overseas expansion will need a significant amount of **research and analysis**, in order that what is a difficult decision can be made with some confidence. S needs to **plan** this proposed venture, **involve staff** at all levels, and examine all the factors involved.

Question 4

Study Reference. Stakeholder analysis is discussed in Chapter 2 of the BPP Study Text.

Marking scheme

			Marks
(a)	Helps to identify power and interest of each group	1	
	Identify need for support and agreement of most powerful stakeholders	1	
	Helps identify stakeholders who could cause most disruption	1	
	Helps identify how to deal with stakeholders	1	
		Total	4
(b)	Each relevant stakeholder identified, categorised (power/interest etc) and discussed	Up to 3	
		Total up to	14
(c)	Evaluation of each option given in the question scenario	Up to 2	
	For recommendation: well justified and consistent with evaluation	2	
		Total up to	7
		Total	25

Part (a)

Top tips. Requirement (a) is only worth 4 marks, so should be kept brief. Although Mendelow's matrix supplies the relevant theory here, you should not have spent time describing the matrix. Instead you need to explain specifically how it could be useful to E in the context of analysing its operations in F.

Stakeholder analysis will allow E to determine the level of **power** which stakeholders could have over their activities in F, and the likelihood that they will show an **interest** in E's activities there.

By establishing the power and interest of the various stakeholder groups, E can analyse the degree of influence they are likely to have on its operations, and therefore the **relationship E should seek to develop with its stakeholders**. This might mean working in conjunction with a key stakeholder to make sure a strategy is **acceptable** to them; or ensuring that other stakeholders are kept **satisfied by**, or kept **informed of**, E's proposed strategies.

Stakeholder analysis will be helpful to E as it considers its future operations in the F, and the possible opposition there might be to them.

For E to be able to implement its operations successfully in F, those operations will have to **be acceptable to the key stakeholders** who could otherwise disrupt E's plans. For example, if the political party in power after the election does not support multinational operations in F, it will be very difficult for E to continue its operations there at all.

Part (b)

Top tips. The scenario identifies a number of stakeholders, and you should have used these to produce your analysis in part (b). You should not have introduced additional generic stakeholders from outside the scenario, and you would not have scored any marks for doing so.

A useful way of structuring your answer to (b) would be to use the quadrants of Mendelow's matrix as the headings under which to group the different stakeholders. Another useful approach could be to identify groups whose support E needs, and to identify stakeholders who could cause disruption for E.

> **Easy marks.** Requirements (b) and (c) do not require any detailed technical knowledge; rather they require you to analyse the information given in the question scenario. If you worked through the scenario carefully, highlighting all the relevant stakeholders and issues, you should have been able to score well here. There are sufficient stake-holders identified in the scenario to provide an answer without you needing to include additional, generic ones.

<u>Key players – High power; high interest</u>

The government of F – The government of F has significant **power** to affect E's operating environment, for example through imposing duties or imposing wage legislation designed to **increase the standard of living in F**. The government has traditionally been reasonably supportive of business, but in the run up to the elections it is coming under increasing pressure to take a **tougher stance on multinational companies** in F. This will increase the level of **interest** it takes in E's activities, and will mean it views E in a less favourable light than it has traditionally done.

The opposition party in F – The government only has a narrow majority and therefore the **opposition party can exert considerable pressure** on the economic and social policies in F. Given that there will be an election in the next fifteen months, the opposition party could soon become the government, thereby increasing its power further.

The opposition party and the government appear to have different approaches to businesses and foreign investment, and so **business policy could be an important issue in the election**. This gives the opposition party a strong interest in E's activities.

The opposition party also has close links with the national labour union which is strongly anti-business and wants to see all foreign companies removed from F. This means that the opposition party's **interest is likely to be hostile** towards E.

The national labour union – While the national labour union has a degree of power in its own right, this **power is increased by its close links to the opposition party**, especially since the opposition party may soon become the government. The union's **interest in E is hostile**, because it would like to see all foreign companies removed from country F.

The other two multinationals operating in F – E is the largest of the three main producers operating in F. At the moment, the close working relationship between E and the farmers' cooperatives means that the cooperatives tend not to sell to E's competitors. However, if this relationship weakens the **competitors will try to gain business** from the cooperatives at E's expense.

However, while the other multinationals are E's rivals, their **interest is not entirely hostile**. Although the government is targeting E as the largest multinational, if E's negotiations fail, all the multinationals could suffer if harsher conditions are imposed on them. Moreover, the three multinationals might need to present a united front in trying to soften the stance of the national labour union and the opposition party towards foreign companies remaining in F.

<u>High power; low interest</u>

E's shareholders – E shareholders can be powerful in approving E's overall direction and policy, but they are more likely to be concerned with E's overall financial performance than the specific issues it faces in a single country. However, if E's operations in F make a significant contribution to its overall profit, then the shareholders are likely to be more interested in the outcome of E's discussions with the government.

Some shareholders may also be concerned at the suggestion that E is damaging the standard of living in F. Again, this issue in its own right is not so significant as the possibility that it may damage E's reputation as a good 'corporate citizen', which in turn could adversely affect revenues and profitability.

<u>Low power; high interest</u>

Farmers in F – The farmers have a good working relationship with E, but are ultimately **dependent on E** (or another foodstuff producer) to buy their crops. In this respect, the farmers have little power.

However, their **close relationship with E** suggests they will have a high degree of interest in E's future. For example, E has **helped the farmers form the cooperatives**, which improves their bargaining power when dealing with companies, and E has also helped with various other **welfare projects**. Consequently, the farmers are likely to want E to continue working in F.

The national labour union wants the government to break up the cooperatives, which would weaken the farmers' economic position. E's relationship with the farmers could well be discussed during E's meetings with the government, not least due to the union's claims that workers are being victimised by the farmers which E has supported.

Farm workers in F – Like the farmers, the farm workers have limited power over E. It is possible that they could withdraw their labour, but this presumes that there are alternative farmers they could go and work for, and this may not be the case.

However, like the farmers, the farm workers also have a strong interest in the situation. The farm workers are **dependent on the farmers for their jobs**, and the **farmers in turn depend on E** (or other producers) for their contracts to supply crops. If E were to leave and the demand for the farmers' produce was to fall as a result, this would affect the demand for farm labour, meaning the farmer workers would be likely to suffer a reduction in their incomes and their standards of living.

The OECD – The OECD has recognised E as an example of a **good corporate citizen**. Therefore the OECD will be keen for the farmers and farm workers in F to continue to receive a fair deal from E. Since E is a large company, the OECD will have a strong interest in E's position, but it is unlikely to be able to affect E's operations directly. If E is forced to agree any concessions which adversely affect the farmers, the OECD is likely to **express concern** at the changes, but it is unlikely to be able to reverse the decision.

Part (c)

> Note that for part (c) you need to make a recommendation at the end of your answer. This should also have alerted you to the fact that you need to evaluate at least two different options, giving you scope to then select your preferred one to recommend. Note the question only asks you to 'Evaluate' the options rather than to 'Identify and evaluate...' This is because the options you need to consider are identified in the scenario, so you should have limited yourself to these rather than inventing your own options.
>
> Although you might expect to have to evaluate options by looking at 'suitability, acceptability and feasibility' there are only 7 marks available here, so in this case you do not need to go into this much detail.

Although economically E might be best served by trying to **preserve its business as it currently is**, such an approach will **not be acceptable to the government** and therefore there seems little point in E considering this as an option.

Moreover, **it may be in E's interests to make some concessions to the current government**, because the government is more supportive to multinational companies than the opposition is. However, E needs to balance the cost of any concessions with the benefits from continuing to buy cocoa beans from F. Ultimately, E needs to try to maximise the returns it can earn for its shareholders.

Build manufacturing facility – The government wants E to open a manufacturing facility in F, but such a facility would operate at a loss. Therefore, this option is unlikely to be acceptable for E because it does not maximise the **returns it can earn for its shareholders**.

Increase prices paid to farmers – The government has stated that prices paid for cocoa beans are currently too low, and E could address this by increasing the prices it pays to farmers. Although this will mean E's profits are reduced, the bigger problem with this option is that is could be **politically damaging for the government**, because the labour union and the opposition party could illustrate it as another example of the farmers and the cooperatives being given favourable treatment.

Accept export tariff – The government has threatened to impose export tariffs if E does not built a manufacturing facility or increase prices. However, if the tariff is too high it might no longer make economic sense for E to source its cocoa beans from F. The government, however, is likely to view tariffs as a politically attractive option, because they are a way of earning additional income for F as a whole.

Provide additional infrastructure projects – One of the union's grievances is the disparity in living standards between the farmers and the farm workers. Currently, E can be seen as partly responsible for this due to the support it has given the farmers. One way E could address this is by funding some wider infrastructure projects which benefit the whole community. Such an approach would maintain E's image as a good corporate citizen, and would allow the government to demonstrate it has won concessions which benefit everyone.

<u>Recommendation</u>

E should try to negotiate an agreement with the government whereby the government introduces **a small export tariff** thereby providing some additional tax revenue, but alongside this E makes some **additional investments in infrastructure projects** which benefit the whole country, such as schools and hospitals for the general population rather than just the farmers' families.

This option will allow the government to demonstrate it has won concessions which **benefit the whole country**, but it should also mean it remains economically profitable for E to source its cocoa beans from F.

CIMA – Pillar E

Paper E3

Enterprise strategy

Mock Exam 2 (September 2012 exam)

You are allowed **three hours** to answer this question paper.
You are allowed **20 minutes** reading time **before the examination begins** during which you should read the question paper and, if you wish, highlight and/or make notes on the question paper. However, you are **not** allowed, **under any circumstances**, to open the answer book and start writing or use your calculator during this reading time.
You are strongly advised to carefully read ALL the question requirements before attempting the question concerned (that is all parts and/or sub-questions).
Answer the compulsory question in Section A.
Answer TWO of the three questions in Section B.

DO NOT OPEN THIS PAPER UNTIL YOU ARE READY TO START UNDER EXAMINATION CONDITIONS

PLEASE NOTE: THE PRE-SEEN MATERIAL FOR QUESTION 1 OF THIS EXAM IS THE SAME AS THE PRE-SEEN MATERIAL FOR QUESTION 1 OF THE MAY 2012 EXAM (B SUPERMARKETS – QUESTION 64 IN THIS KIT.)

SECTION A – 50 marks

Strategic level pre-seen case material

Question 1

Pre-seen case study

You should assume that the date 'now' is September 2012.

Introduction

B Supermarkets (B) was founded as a grocery retailer in a European country in 1963. Its sales consist mainly of food and household items including clothing. B now owns or franchises over 15,000 stores world-wide in 36 countries. The company has stores in Europe (in both eurozone and non-eurozone countries), Asia and North America. B's head office is located in a eurozone country. B has become one of the world's largest chains of stores.

B's Board thinks that there are opportunities to take advantage of the rapid economic growth of some Asian countries and the associated increases in demand for food and consumer goods.

Structure

The B Group is structured into a holding company, B, and three subsidiary companies which are located in each of the regions of the world in which it operates (Europe, Asia and North America). The subsidiary companies, referred to as "Regions" within B, are respectively B-Europe, B-Asia and B-North America.

Store operations, sales mix and staffing

B operates four types of store: supermarkets, hypermarkets, discount stores and convenience stores. For the purpose of this case study, the definition of each of these types of store is as follows:

A *supermarket* is a self-service store which sells a wide variety of food and household goods such as washing and cleaning materials, cooking utensils and other items which are easily carried by customers out of the store.

A *hypermarket* is a superstore or very large store which sells the same type of products as a supermarket but in addition it sells a wide range of other items such as consumer durable white goods, for example refrigerators, freezers, washing machines and furniture. Hypermarkets are often located on out-of-town sites.

A *discount store* is a retail store that sells a variety of goods such as electrical appliances and electronic equipment. Discount stores in general usually sell branded products and pursue a high-volume, low priced strategy and aim their marketing at customers who seek goods at prices which are usually less than can be found in a hypermarket.

A *convenience store* is a small shop or store in an urban area that sells goods which are purchased regularly by customers. These would typically include groceries, toiletries, alcoholic beverages, soft drinks and confectionery. They are convenient for shoppers as they are located in or near residential areas and are often open for long hours. Customers are willing to pay premium prices for the convenience of having the store close by.

B sells food products and clothing in its supermarkets and hypermarkets at a higher price than many of its competitors because the Board thinks that its customers are prepared to pay higher prices for better quality food products. B also sells good quality consumer durable products in its supermarkets and hypermarkets but it is forced to sell these at competitive prices as there is strong competition for the sale of such goods. B's discount stores sell good quality electrical products usually at lower prices than those charged in its supermarkets and hypermarkets, B only sells electronic equipment in its discount stores. Customers have a greater range from which to choose in the discount stores as compared with supermarkets and hypermarkets because the discount stores specialise in the goods which they sell. B's convenience stores do not have the availability of space to carry a wide range of products and they charge a higher price for the same brand and type of goods which it sells in its supermarkets.

Although B owns most of its stores, it has granted franchises for the operation of some stores which carry its name.

Nearly 0.5 million full-time equivalent staff are employed world-wide in the Group. B tries when possible to recruit local staff to fill job vacancies within its stores.

Value statement and mission

In recognition of the strong competitive and dynamic markets in which it operates, B's Board has established an overall value statement as follows: "We aim to satisfy our customers wherever we trade. We intend to employ different generic competitive strategies depending on the market segment in which our stores trade."

The Board has also produced the following mission statement:

"B practises sustainable investment within a healthy ethical and thoughtful culture and strives to achieve customer satisfaction by giving a courteous and efficient service, selling high quality goods at a reasonable price, sourcing goods from local suppliers where possible and causing the least damage possible to the natural environment. By this, we aim to satisfy the expectations of our shareholders by achieving consistent growth in our share price and also to enhance our reputation for being an environmentally responsible company."

Strategic objectives

The following objectives have been derived from the mission statement:

1. Build shareholder value through consistent growth in the company's share price.
2. Increase customer satisfaction ratings to 95% as measured by customer feedback surveys.
3. Increase commitment to local suppliers by working towards achieving 40% of our supplies from sources which are local to where B stores trade.
4. Reduce carbon emissions calculated by internationally agreed measures by at least 1% per year until B becomes totally carbon neutral.
5. Maximise returns to shareholders by employing different generic competitive strategies depending on the market segment in which B stores trade.

Financial objectives

The Board has set the following financial objectives:

1. Achieve consistent growth in earnings per share of 7% each year.
2. Maintain a dividend pay-out ratio of 50% each year.
3. Gearing levels as measured by long-term debt divided by long-term debt plus equity should not exceed 40% based on book value.

Governance

The main board comprises the Non-executive Chairman, the Chief Executive and nine Executive directors. These cover the functions of finance, human resources, corporate affairs (including legal and public relations), marketing, planning and procurement. There is also one executive director for each of the three regions, being the Regional Managing Directors of B-Europe, B-Asia and B-North America. There are also nine non-executive main board members in addition to the Chairman.

The main Board of Directors has separate committees responsible for audit, remuneration, appointments, corporate governance and risk assessment and control. The Risk Assessment and Control Committee's tasks were formerly included within the Audit Committee's role. It was agreed by the Board in 2009 that these tasks should be separated out in order not to overload the Audit Committee which has responsibilities to review the probity of the company. B's expansion has been very rapid in some countries. The expansion has been so rapid that B has not been able to carry out any internal audit activities in some of these countries to date. The regional boards do not have a committee structure.

Each of the Regional Managing Directors chairs his or her own Regional Board. All of the Regional Boards have their own directors for finance, human resources, corporate affairs, marketing, planning and procurement but their structure is different for the directors who have responsibility for the stores. In B-Asia, one regional director is responsible for the hypermarkets and supermarkets and another is responsible for discount stores and convenience stores. In B-North America, one regional director is responsible for the hypermarkets and supermarkets and another is responsible for discount stores (B does not have any convenience stores in North America). In B-Europe there is one regional director responsible for supermarkets and hypermarkets, one for discount stores and one for convenience stores. In all regions the regional directors have line accountability to their respective regional managing director and professional accountability to the relevant main board director. There are no non-executive directors on the regional boards. Appendix 1 shows the main board and regional board structures.

Treasury

Each of B's three regions has a regional treasury department managed by a regional treasurer who has direct accountability to the respective Regional Director of Finance and professional accountability to the Group Treasurer. The Group Treasurer manages the central corporate treasury department which is located in B's head office. The Group Treasurer, who is not a main board member, reports to the Director of Finance on the main board.

Shareholding, year-end share prices and dividends paid for the last five years

B is listed on a major European stock exchange within the eurozone and it wholly owns its subsidiaries. There are five major shareholders of B, including employees taken as a group, which between them hold 25% of the 1,350 million total shares in issue. The major shareholders comprise two long term investment trusts which each owns 4%, a hedge fund owns 5%, employees own 5% and the founding family trust owns 7% of the shares. The remaining 75% of shares are owned by the general public.

The year-end share prices and the dividends paid for the last five years were as follows:

	200	*2008*	*2009*	*2010*	*2011*
	€	€	€	€	€
Share price at 31 December	47.38	25.45	28.68	29.44	31.37
Net Dividend per share	1.54	1.54	1.54	1.62	1.65

Planning and management control

B has a very structured planning process. Each regional board produces a five year strategic plan for its region relating to specific objectives set for it by the main board and submits this to the main board for approval. The main board then produces a consolidated strategic plan for the whole company. This is reviewed on a three yearly cycle and results in a revised and updated group five year plan being produced every three years.

B's management control system, which operates throughout its regions and at head office, is well known in the industry to be bureaucratic and authoritarian. Strict financial authority levels for development purposes are imposed from the main Board. There is tension between the main Board and the regional boards. The regional board members feel that they are not able to manage effectively despite being located much closer to their own regional markets than the members of the main Board. The main Board members, on the other hand, think that they need to exercise tight control because they are remote from the markets. This often stifles planning initiatives within each region. This tension is also felt lower down the organisation as the regional board members exercise strict financial and management control over operational managers in their regions in order to ensure that the main Board directives are carried out.

Competitive overview

B operates in highly competitive markets for all the products it sells. The characteristics of each of the markets in which it operates are different. For example, there are different planning restrictions applying within each region. In some countries, B is required to operate each of its stores in a partnership arrangement with local enterprises, whereas no such restriction exists within other countries in which it trades. B needs to be aware of different customer tastes and preferences which differ from country to country. The following table provides a break-down of B's stores in each region.

	B Europe	*B Asia*	*B North America*
Supermarkets and hypermarkets	3,456	619	512
Discount stores	5,168	380	780
Convenience stores	4,586	35	

B is one of the largest retailing companies in the world and faces different levels of competition in each region. B's overall market share in terms of retail sales for all supermarkets, hypermarkets, discount stores and convenience stores in each of its regions is as follows:

	Market share
Europe	20%
Asia	1%
North America	1.5%

The following table shows the sales revenue and net operating profit earned by B in each of its regions for the year ended 31 December 2011:

	B Europe *€ million*	*B Asia* *€ million*	*B North America* *€ million*
Revenue	89,899	10,105	9,708
Net Operating Profit	4,795	743	673

B is constantly seeking other areas of the world into which it can expand, especially within Asia where it perceives many countries have an increasing population and strengthening economies.

Corporate Social Responsibility (CSR)

B is meeting its CSR obligations by establishing environmental targets for carbon emissions (greenhouse gas emissions), careful monitoring of its supply chain, undertaking sustainable investments and investing in its human capital.

Environmental targets for carbon emissions:

B's main board is keen to demonstrate the company's concern for the environment by pursuing continuous improvement in the reduction of its carbon emissions and by developing ways of increasing sustainability in its trading practices. A number of environmental indicators have been established to provide transparency in B's overall performance in respect of sustainability. These published measures were verified by B's statutory auditor and are calculated on a like-for-like basis for the stores in operation over the period measured.

In the year ended 31 December 2011, B reduced its consumption of kilowatt hours (kWh) per square metre of sales area as compared with the year ended 31 December 2008 by 9%. The target reduction for that period was 5%. In the same period it reduced the number of free disposable plastic bags provided to customers per square metre of sales area, by 51% against a target of 60%. Its overall greenhouse gas emissions (measured by kilogrammes of carbon dioxide per square metre of sales area) reduced by 1% in 2011 which was exactly on target.

B provides funding for the development of local amenity projects in all of the countries where B stores operate. (An amenity project is one which provides benefit to the local population, such as providing a park, community gardens or a swimming pool.)

Distribution and sourcing:

Distribution from suppliers across such a wide geographical area is an issue for B. While supplies are sourced from the country in which a store is located as much as possible, there is nevertheless still a requirement for transportation across long distances either by road or air. Approximately 20% of the physical quantity of goods sold across the group as a whole is sourced locally, that is within the country in which the goods are sold. These tend to be perishable items such as fruit and vegetables. The remaining 80% of goods are sourced from large international manufacturers and distributors. These tend to be large items such as electrical or electronic equipment which are bought under contracts which are set up by the regional procurement departments. B, due to its size and scope of operations, is able to place orders for goods made to its own specification and packaged as under its own brand label. Some contracts are agreed between manufacturers and the Group Procurement Director for the supply of goods to the whole of the B group world-wide.

B's inventory is rarely transported by rail except within Europe. This has resulted in lower average reductions in carbon emissions per square metre of sales area by stores operated by B-Asia and B-North America than for those stores operated by B-Europe. This is because the carbon emission statistics take into account the transportation of goods into B's stores.

Sustainable investments:

B aspires to become carbon neutral over the long term. The Board aims to reduce its carbon emissions by investing in state of the art technology in its new store developments and by carrying out modifications to existing stores.

Human Resources:

B prides itself on the training it provides to its staff. The training of store staff is carried out in store by specialist teams which operate in each country where B trades. In this way, B believes that training is consistent across all of its stores. In some countries, the training is considered to be at a sufficiently high level to be recognised by national training bodies. The average number of training hours per employee in the year ended 31 December 2011 was 17 compared with 13 hours in the year ended 31 December 2010. In 2011, B employed 45% more staff with declared disabilities compared with 2010.

Information systems and inventory management

In order to operate efficiently, B's Board has recognised that it must have up-to-date information systems including electronic point of sale (EPOS) systems. An EPOS system uses computers or specialised terminals that can be combined with other hardware such as bar-code readers to accurately capture the sale and adjust the inventory levels within the store. EPOS systems installation is on-going. B has installed EPOS systems in its stores in some countries but not in all its stores world-wide.

B's information systems are not perfect as stock-outs do occur from time-to-time, especially in the European stores. This can be damaging to sales revenue when stock-outs occur during peak sales periods such as the days leading up to a public holiday. In Asia and North America in particular, B's information technology systems sometimes provide misleading information. This has led to doubts in the minds of some head office staff about just how robust are B's inventory control systems.

As is normal in chain store groups, there is a certain degree of loss through theft by staff and customers. Another way that loss is suffered is through goods which have gone past their "sell-by" date and mainly relates to perishable food items which are wasted as they cannot be sold to the public. In most countries, such food items which cannot be sold to the public may be sold to local farmers for animal feed.

Regulatory issues

B's subsidiaries in Asia and North America have sometimes experienced governmental regulatory difficulties in some countries which have hindered the installation of improved information systems. To overcome some of these regulatory restrictions, B-Asia and B-North America have, on occasions, resorted to paying inducements to government officials in order for the regulations to be relaxed.

APPENDIX 1

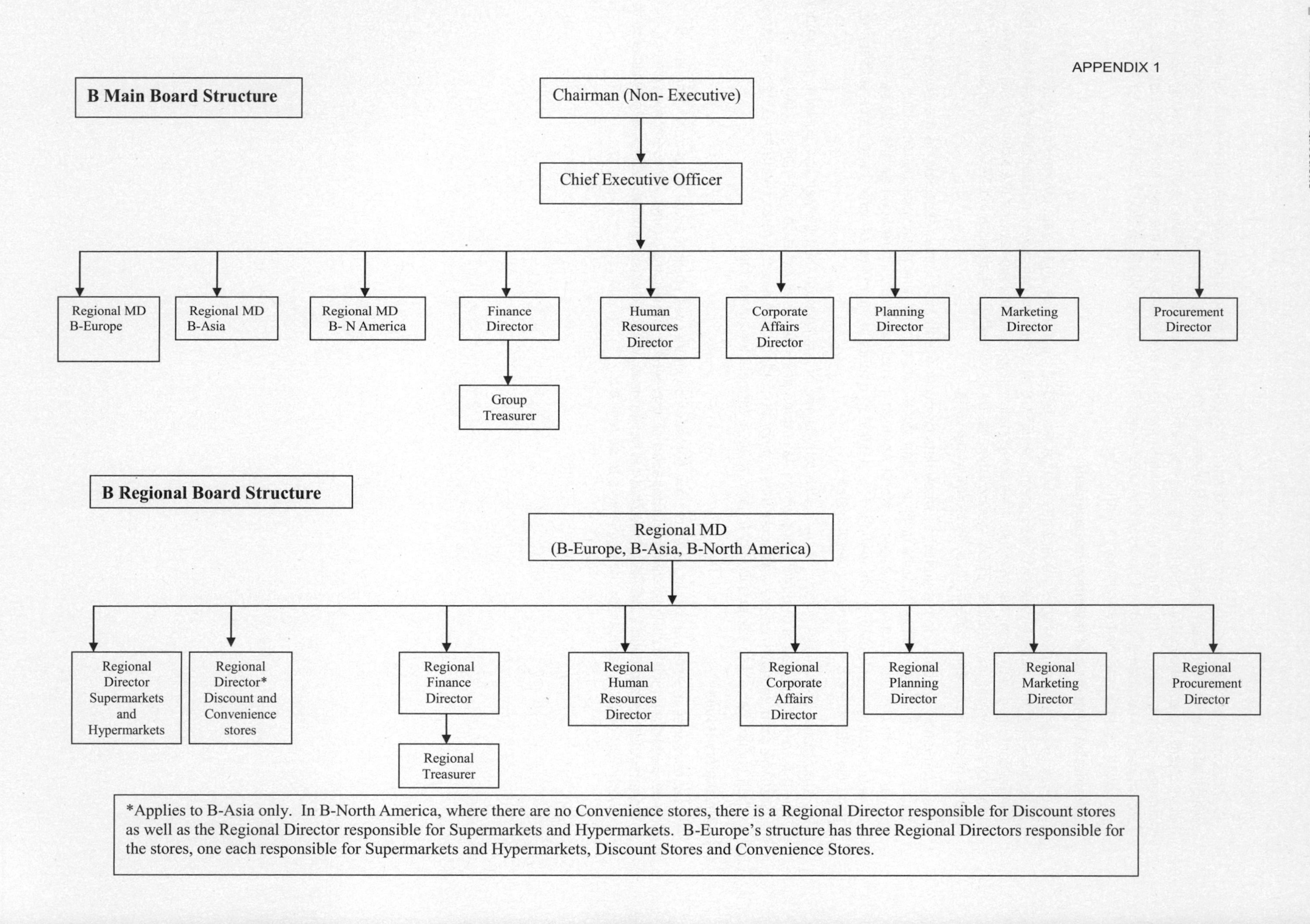
B Main Board Structure
Chairman (Non- Executive)
Chief Executive Officer
Regional MD B-Europe
Regional MD B-Asia
Regional MD B- N America
Finance Director
Group Treasurer
Human Resources Director
Corporate Affairs Director
Planning Director
Marketing Director
Procurement Director
B Regional Board Structure
Regional MD (B-Europe, B-Asia, B-North America)
Regional Director Supermarkets and Hypermarkets
Regional Director* Discount and Convenience stores
Regional Finance Director
Regional Treasurer
Regional Human Resources Director
Regional Corporate Affairs Director
Regional Planning Director
Regional Marketing Director
Regional Procurement Director
*Applies to B-Asia only. In B-North America, where there are no Convenience stores, there is a Regional Director responsible for Discount stores as well as the Regional Director responsible for Supermarkets and Hypermarkets. B-Europe's structure has three Regional Directors responsible for the stores, one each responsible for Supermarkets and Hypermarkets, Discount Stores and Convenience Stores.

B's income statement and statement of financial position.

Income statement for the year ended 31 December 2011

	Notes	€ million
Revenue		109,712
Operating costs		(103,501)
Net operating profit		6,211
Interest income		165
Finance costs		(852)
Corporate income tax		(1,933)
PROFIT FOR THE YEAR		3,591

Statement of financial position as at 31 December 2011

		€ million
ASSETS		
Non-current assets		57,502
Current assets		
Inventories		7,670
Trade and other receivables		1,521
Cash and cash equivalents		3,847
Total current assets		13,038
Total assets		70,540
EQUITY AND LIABILITIES		
Equity		
Share capital	1	2,025
Share premium		3,040
Retained earnings		18,954
Total equity		24,019
Non-current liabilities		
Long term borrowings		15,744
Current liabilities		
Trade and other payables		30,777
Total liabilities		46,521
Total equity and liabilities		70,540

Notes:

1 There are 1,350 million €1.50 shares currently in issue. The share price at 31 December 2011 was €31.37.

SECTION A

Question 1

Unseen Case Material (Exam day material for Paper E3 only)

Rationalisation in Country W

B's first venture to open stores outside Europe was in Country W in 1982. Initially, this was very successful but the current business environment is very competitive and the forecast results shown below have prompted questions about the continued viability of B's business operations in Country W.

B's business in Country W is organised into four sectors which cover the four different types of store which it operates there. Each sector has a sector manager who reports to the Regional Managing Director responsible for Country W. The individual store managers report to the sector managers who are senior to them.

Table 1: B's forecast sector profit/(loss) for Country W for year ended 31 December 2012

Sector	Supermarkets	Hypermarkets	Discount stores	Convenience stores	Total	%
	€ million	€ million	€ million	€ million	€ million	
Revenue	330	450	300	120	1,200	100
Costs						
Trading	198	243	225	72	738	62
Establishment	33	18	30	12	93	8
Regional Office	68	204	34	34	340	28
Profit/Loss	**31**	**(15)**	**11**	**2**	**29**	**2**

Notes:

The amounts in Table 1 have been converted from Country W's currency to euros.

Trading costs are all variable with revenue.

Establishment costs are all variable with revenue.

The regional office costs are all fixed. They comprise:

Insurances of €35 million

Property taxes of €100 million

B Supermarkets' management charge of €205 million. This is a central charge imposed by B Supermarkets: its basis is not disclosed to sector managers and it is a non-negotiable charge.

The regional office costs are apportioned on the basis of the floor areas of the sector's properties as shown below:

Supermarkets	Hypermarkets	Discount stores	Convenience stores
%	%	%	%
20	60	10	10

The Regional Managing Director responsible for Country W is very dissatisfied with the forecast sector trading results and considers that the forecast profit of €29 million is unacceptable. The Regional Managing Director responsible for Country W proposes to close the hypermarkets which he believes should improve the profit to €44 million.

However, the Sector Manager of Country W's Hypermarkets has argued that:

1. The current apportionment base of the regional office costs is unfair because these costs are not directly related to floor area but are more closely associated with the revenues generated by each of Country W's four trading sectors;
2. In terms of its trading performance, the Hypermarkets sector is Country W's best sector;

3. If any sector is to be closed, it should be the discount stores and the convenience stores because their combined forecast revenues in the year ended 31 December 2012 is only €420 million which is €30 million less than the Hypermarkets' revenue;

4. The regional office costs are too high and they contain a lot of wasteful expenditure: The sectors should not have to pay costs which they do not understand and did not authorise.

Competitive strategy

The Regional Managing Director responsible for Country W has attempted to manage B's business in Country W within the spirit of the company's mission statement, particularly 'selling high quality goods at a reasonable price'. However, he realises that this strategy has not been successful for all of the business sectors in Country W. The Sector Manager for Country W's Convenience Stores has commented that 'B's business in Country W is going nowhere: we are stuck in the middle. We should develop different competitive strategies to fit the characteristics of each of our four sectors'.

Country W's four sectors have the following characteristics:

Sector	B's Brand Characteristics	Customer Characteristics	Product Characteristics	Pricing	Competition	B's Market Share
Supermarkets	Many well sited supermarkets enable B to operate with a very economical cost structure.	Live locally. Value 24 hour opening. Middle income.	Wide variety of food and household goods.	Price sensitive.	Two well-established national chains each with 10% market share. Their supermarkets are often in inconvenient locations.	30%
Hypermarkets	Very highly regarded. High reputation for quality.	Willing to travel up to 50 miles. Affluent.	Consumer durables, high value items such as televisions, furniture, computers. Many up-market brands some of which are exclusive to B	Customers value quality and are willing to pay a premium for it.	Hypermarkets are a new concept in Country W. Only one recently founded competitor which is trading at a loss.	85%
Discount Stores	Highly regarded for its specialist range of products	Expect prices to be lower than in hypermarket. Mid and lower income groups.	Limited range of branded and 'own branded' goods.	Customers are extremely price sensitive.	Competition is mixed: some is very profitable, innovative and efficient: some is trading at a loss and very badly organized.	15%
Convenience Stores	No clear identity. Some stores are market leaders; others are market laggards.	Live locally. Mid and upper income groups.	Low value items.	Customers will pay a premium price if location convenient.	One national chain which has 65% of the market. Remaining 25% is fragmented.	10%

Required

(a) (i) **Calculate** the forecast sector contribution margins and the forecast total profit or loss for Country W for year ended 31 December 2012.

You should assume that:

- The Hypermarkets sector is closed on 30 September 2012.
- The Hypermarkets sector's costs and revenues accrue equally throughout 2012.

(3 marks)

(ii) **Calculate** the revised forecast sector profits and forecast total profit for Country W for year ended 31 December 2012.

You should assume that:

- The regional office costs are allocated on the basis of sector revenue.
- The Hypermarkets are not closed.

(3 marks)

(b) **Prepare** a report evaluating the strategic proposal, made by the Regional Managing Director responsible for Country W, to close the Hypermarkets sector.

In your report you should:

(i) **Discuss**, in turn, each of the four arguments put forward by the Sector Manager for Country W's Hypermarkets.

(12 marks)

(ii) **Advise** B of the strategic implications that closing the Hypermarkets might have on B's future operations within Country W.

(12 marks)

Your report should consider both the financial and non-financial effects of the proposal by the Regional Managing Director responsible for Country W to close the Hypermarkets sector.

(c) Assume all four sectors of B's business continue in Country W.

(i) **Recommend**, giving your reasons, which competitive strategy B should follow in future, in each of Country W's business sectors.

You should use Porter's model of generic competitive strategies in your answer. **(16 marks)**

(ii) **Advise** B of TWO limitations of Porter's model of generic competitive strategy. **(4 marks)**

(Total = 50 marks)

SECTION B – 50 marks

Answer Two of the Three questions - 25 marks each

Question 2

WWW is an international company based in Europe which trades principally in Asia and Europe. In its published Code of Ethics WWW has committed itself to 'being a company that will trade fairly and sustainably'. WWW has been following an expansion strategy which has led to the following three situations occurring:

Situation 1

At a recent presentation to investment analysts and financial journalists, WWW's Chief Executive Officer (CEO) gave a very optimistic forecast for the company's future, suggesting that revenue would double over the next three years and profits and dividends would increase by 50%.

However, the CEO had prepared his forecast in a hurry and had not had it confirmed by anybody else within WWW. He did not mention that WWW's home Government was considering taking legal action against WWW for underpayment of excise duties and had made a claim for large damages. If this claim was to be successful it would materially affect WWW's profit in the next year (20X3).

Situation 2

In connection with the legal case in 1, WWW's home Government had obtained a court order that all documents relating to WWW's export trade should be made available to the Government's lawyers.

However, many of the documents covered by the court order were the subject of confidentiality agreements between WWW and various entrepreneurs. These documents included details of patents and processes with a high commercial value and if knowledge of these became public it would destroy some of WWW's competitive advantage.

Situation 3

This situation, which is unconnected to situations 1 and 2, has also occurred. WWW has a joint venture agreement with a company, ZZZ. Under the terms of the joint venture agreement each company has to make regular returns of financial performance to the other. ZZZ is always late in making its returns, which are usually incomplete and contain many errors. ZZZ's accounting staff are very reluctant to co-operate with WWW's accounting staff and the working relationship between the two companies is poor.

WWW's financial controller has been involved in a review of the joint venture with ZZZ. Due to the many problems that ZZZ has caused him and his staff he has advised discontinuing the joint venture.

Required

(a) **Advise**, giving your reasons, whether each of the three situations is in conflict with CIMA's Code of Ethics

(i) Situation 1 **(4 marks)**

(ii) Situation 2 **(4 marks)**

(iii) Situation 3 **(4 marks)**

(b) **Advise** WWW of the stages of a procedure it could use to resolve ethical conflicts. **(7 marks)**

(c) **Recommend**, giving your reasons, TWO current ethical issues, other than those contained in CIMA's Code of Ethics, that could be included in WWW's Ethical Code. **(6 marks)**

(Total = 25 marks)

Question 3

HHH is a UK university. HHH's management board has identified student performance as a Critical Success Factor (CSF). HHH's management board has identified this CSF as it targets an area where it is currently underperforming compared to other UK universities.

HHH is aware of a nearby comparable university, SSS, which has had much success when several of its departments have worked together to improve their student performance. SSS has a culture of sharing knowledge and a knowledge management strategy. HHH does not have a culture of knowledge sharing. Within HHH, knowledge is regarded as the personal property of the individual and very few of its staff are prepared to share their knowledge with any of their colleagues. HHH has an abnormally high level of staff turnover compared to other universities. It is twice as high as that of SSS.

Student performance

Student performance is measured by HHH as the number of students successfully completing their courses. Those students who do not successfully complete their course are described as 'drop-outs'. The number of drop-outs is measured by the drop-out rate. HHH has access to data for all UK universities for student drop-out rates analysed by age and gender.

Drop-out rates vary greatly across HHH's academic departments. In some academic departments the drop-out rate is extremely high; in others it is very low, much better than the national average. Where the drop-out rate is much better than the national average, the departments have operated extensive schemes for student support. For example, students with personal problems can seek help from trained counsellors, students with financial problems have been helped to find part-time work and students with academic problems are given extra individual tuition from the academic staff.

In the departments where the drop-out rates are extremely high, none of these student support schemes is operating. The departments with the extremely high drop-out rates are not aware of how the departments with the very low drop-out rates support their students. The departments with the very low drop-out rates are unwilling to share their knowledge about how to reduce the drop-out rates as they have spent considerable time and effort developing their schemes and regard these as their own property.

HHH has not conducted any systematic analysis into its overall drop-out rate. Within its information systems, HHH has the following information about each of its students:

- Name
- Age
- Gender
- Address
- Educational record prior to joining HHH
- Educational record within HHH
- Academic department

HHH is aware that many universities have successfully used data mining to assist them in managing student performance.

Required

(a) Many organisations integrate their CSFs into their performance management systems by converting them to Key Performance Indicators (KPIs).

Explain, using examples, the advantages that HHH would gain by doing the same. **(3 marks)**

(b) **Advise** HHH's management board:

(i) of THREE benefits the university and its staff could expect to receive from the successful implementation of a knowledge management strategy. **(6 marks)**

(ii) of a total of FOUR social and technical problems HHH might encounter in operating a knowledge management system. **(8 marks)**

(c) **Explain** data mining and how the outputs of the analysis could be used by HHH to improve the student drop-out rates. **(8 marks)**

(Total = 25 marks)

Question 4

BBB is a fashion retailer with a chain of 20 shops, each with its own manager. BBB believes it can best compete by offering a wide selection of high quality products sold at a reasonable price. BBB has trained all its staff in customer care and prefers to employ staff who have worked for other fashion retailers.

As a large proportion of BBB's products are clothes which only remain fashionable for a short period, it is important that good inventory control is maintained. BBB has recently invested in a robotic system to improve materials handling in its warehouse.

As a service to its customers, BBB will deliver to their home, within 24 hours, any items bought from one of its shops. BBB's competitors do not offer such a service. BBB knows that it has demanding customers who appreciate the retail experience and after sales service which BBB offers. If a customer has any dissatisfaction with a purchase, BBB will make a refund without question. BBB frequently sends its regular customers special offers and invites them to fashion shows held in its shops.

BBB's head office is organised into departments which are responsible for the procurement of products, setting of personnel policies, investigating innovations in fashion retailing and general corporate administration.

BBB's management accountant has been investigating the acquisition of high-tech 'Smart Tills' which would provide the following information for each shop:

- Sales transactions and analysis
- Staff statistics (sales per staff member)
- Gross profit
- Inventory turnover and balances
- Audit information (a database recording all transactions)

If BBB replaces its existing tills with Smart Tills, it will be able to better manage cash and inventory and optimise its sales due to accurate real time information. This will have the benefits of identifying and controlling wastage and improve the accuracy of its forecasts.

The overall advantages offered by the Smart Tills are that BBB will be able to react more quickly to customer demand, ensure that it has sufficient stock in its shops, minimise wastage, reduce its investment in working capital and enable its head office to know, on a real-time basis, how well each of its shops is trading.

Required

(a) **Explain** how BBB could use Porter's Value Chain to achieve competitive advantage. Your answer should give examples from BBB of the NINE activities in the value chain and explain how each one of them could add value for BBB.

(13 marks)

(b) **Advise** BBB how it could improve its profits by use of Smart Tills.

(4 marks)

(c) **Recommend** FOUR key stages that BBB should include in a plan to introduce Smart Tills into all its shops.

(8 marks)

(Total = 25 marks)

Answers

DO NOT TURN THIS PAGE UNTIL YOU HAVE COMPLETED THE MOCK EXAM

BPP
LEARNING MEDIA

A plan of attack

As we mentioned in our 'plan of attack' for Mock Exam 1, the problem of which question to start with is discussed earlier in this Kit, in 'Passing the E3 exam; (page xi in the Front pages). Here we will once again reiterate our view that the compulsory Section A question (Question 1) is nearly always the best place to start but, if you do decide to start with a 25 mark Section B question, **make sure that you finish your answer in no more than 45 minutes**.

However, once again, take a good look at the paper before diving in to answer questions, and make sure you use your 20 minutes of reading time efficiently and effectively.

The next step

You may be thinking that this paper looks more straightforward than the first mock exam; alternatively, you may be thinking this paper actually looks more difficult.

Option 1 (this paper looks all right) – If you've read the requirements carefully, and you don't feel too daunted by this paper, then that's encouraging. You should feel even happier when you've got the compulsory question out of the way, so you should consider doing Question 1 first. However, remember the advice we have given you before: make sure your answer deals specifically with the question requirements, and relates directly to the organisation and issues described in the scenario.

Option 2 (don't like this paper) – If you think this paper looks challenging, you may want to get the optional questions done first before tackling the Section A case study. However, don't forget that you will need half of the three hours writing time to answer the case study, which is worth 50% of the total marks available.

The questions themselves

- **Question 1** begins with some short calculations focused around the financial impact of closing a division and of changing the way central costs are apportioned to divisions. These then link into part (b) of the requirement, where the basis of apportioning central costs and the potential decision to close the decision need to be discussed in more detail.

  Part (b) of this question requires you to write a report, which is worth 24 marks in total – almost half of the marks available in Question 1.

  The context for Part (c) is Porter's generic strategies, which is a core area of the syllabus. Therefore, you should have felt this part of the question was reasonably approachable, especially as the pre-seen material identified the characteristics of each of the divisions and the markets in which they operate. As such, this information should have helped you identify which of Porter's generic strategies would be most appropriate for each division to employ.

- **Question 2** tests your understanding of ethical issues and CIMA's Code of Ethics. The scenario identifies three situations which could present an ethical conflict, and you have to advise whether or not they do present a conflict. To score well in this question you need to have a good understanding of the Code, but equally you need to apply your knowledge specifically to the scenario rather than simply explaining the ethical principles in general terms.

  The question then looks at the steps an organisation could take to resolve an ethical conflict. This again draws on CIMA's Code of Ethics, which provides guidance on what these steps should be.

- **Question 3** starts with a very short requirement (3 marks) looking at the relationship between CSFs and KPIs, and their contribution to performance management systems.

  However, the main topics covered in this question are the benefits which knowledge management and data mining can bring to an organisation. Importantly, though, the question requires you to look at these benefits specifically in the context of the university described in the scenario, rather than looking at them in more general terms.

  Alongside these topics, part (b) (ii) looks at the social and technical problems which the university could face when introducing a knowledge management system, so issues around change management and resistance to change are also relevant here.

- The main topic area in **Question 4** is Porter's value chain, and how the value activities an organisation carries out can help it achieve competitive advantage. However, the question also looks at project management and project planning, so you should only have attempted this question is you feel confident about these topics as well as the value chain.

  Part (a) of this question should have been relatively straight forward, although it was important to apply the value chain directly to the scenario in the question rather than discussing the value chain and value activities in more general terms.

  Part (c) looks at project management and project planning. The scenario identifies that a retail chain is looking to introduce new tills into its shops, and the question requirement highlights the importance of project management and planning in this process.

Once again, let us remind you...

You must always **allocate your time** according to the marks for the question in total and for the parts of the questions within it. And you must always **follow the question requirements exactly**.

You've got free time at the end of the exam...?

If you have allocated your time properly then you **shouldn't have time on your hands** at the end of the exam. However, if you find yourself with five or ten minutes spare, go back to **any parts of questions that you didn't finish** because you ran out of time.

Forget about it!

As we've told you before, don't worry if you found the paper difficult. Once your three hours writing time is over, there is nothing more you can do with your answers, so forget about them. If this were your real exam, you'd need to forget about the exam once you'd finished and start thinking about the next one. Or, if it were your last exam, you could start celebrating!

Question 1

Text reference: Porter's generic strategies are covered in Chapter 5 of the BPP Study Text. Chapter 7 looks at evaluating strategic options.

Marking scheme

(a)	(i)	Calculating contributions from each sector	Up to 2	
		Calculating overall loss for Country W	1	
			Total up to	3
	(ii)	Calculating revised forecast profits for each sector	Up to 2	
		Recognition that total profit for Country W remains €29m	1	
			Total up to	3
(b)	(i)	For each relevant point discussed in relation to Argument 1: 1 mark each	Up to 3	
		(Relevant points include: insurance linked to floor area and revenue; property tax linked to floor area; no explanation of management charge)		
		Summary – some elements of argument are reasonable, but not all	1	
		For each relevant point discussed in relation to Argument 2: 1 mark each	Up to 3	
		(Relevant points include: lowest variable cost %; high contribution margin %, highest contributions)		
		Summary – hypermarket sector is best-performing sector	1	
		For each relevant point discussed in relation to Argument 3: 1 mark each	Up to 3	
		(Relevant points include: highest variable cost %'s; two lowest contribution margins; decision should be based on contribution, not revenue)		
		Summary – argument is not conclusive	1	
		For each relevant point discussed in relation to Argument 4: 1 mark each	Up to 2	
		(Relevant points include: no details of regional costs; sectors should bear a share of central costs)		
		Summary – difficult to justify this argument	1	
			Total up to	12
	(ii)	Analysis of financial impact (eg loss of contribution from hypermarkets; overall profits become a loss; regional office costs still incurred) – 1 mark per valid point	Up to 3	
		Possible loss of future contributions – hypermarkets are a new/growing concept	1	
		Effects on remaining sectors (eg future viability; possible closure of B's business in W) – 1 mark per valid point	Up to 3	
		Reputational damage	1	
		Impact on other stakeholders – up to 2 marks for impact on each stakeholder group (eg consumers; suppliers; government)	Up to 6	

	Conclusion – 1 mark per valid point	2	
	Report format	2	
		Total up to	12
(c)	For each sector (supermarkets; hypermarkets; discount stores; convenience stores): 1 mark per relevant point to justify the strategy being recommended; up to 3 marks per sector	Up to 12	
	For each sector: 1 mark for a clear recommendation of a valid strategy to follow, consistent with justification	Up to 4	
		Total up to	16
(d)	For each limitation explained – Up to 2 marks each	Up to 4	
		Total up to	4
		Total	50

Part (a)

Top tips:

Part (a) (i): A key point to note here is that, while you need to calculate B's forecast profit for Country W as a whole, you only need to calculate forecast *contribution* margins for the different sectors. Importantly, you are not asked to assess the forecast profit for the different sectors, and therefore you do not need to re-apportion the Regional Office costs (October-December) over the three remaining types of store. Instead you can simply deduct the total (€340 million) as a single figure from the total contribution generated by B's stores in Country W.

By contrast, the focus of **part (a) (ii)** was on the way the regional office costs were apportioned between the different sectors. However, the calculation here should still have been pretty straight-forward: re-allocating the regional office costs on the basis of sector revenue rather than floor area.

Part (a)

(i)

	Supermarkets (€ million)	Hypermarkets (€ million) *[to 30 Sept]*	Discount stores (€ million)	Convenience stores (€ million)	TOTAL (€ million)
Revenue	330.00	337.50	300.00	120.00	1,087.50
Variable costs					
Trading	198.00	182.25	225.00	72.00	677.25
Establishment	33.00	13.50	30.00	12.00	88.50
Contribution margin	99.00	141.75	45.00	36.00	321.75
Fixed costs - regional office costs					340.00
Profit/(loss)					**(18.25)**

(ii)

	Supermarkets (€ million)	Hypermarkets (€ million)	Discount stores (€ million)	Convenience stores (€ million)	TOTAL (€ million)
Revenue	330.00	450.00	300.00	120.00	1,200.00
Variable costs					
Trading	198.00	243.00	225.00	72.00	738.00
Establishment	33.00	18.00	30.00	12.00	93.00
Contribution margin	**99.00**	**189.00**	**45.00**	**36.00**	**369.00**
Fixed costs - regional office costs (W)	93.50	127.50	85.00	34.00	340.00
Profit/(loss)	**5.50**	**61.50**	**(40.00)**	**2.00**	**29.00**

(W)

Apportionment of fixed costs					
	330/1200 *340	450/1200 *340	300/1200 *340	120/1200 *340	
	93.50	127.50	85.00	34.00	340.00

(b)

Part (b): Firstly, did you notice that you have been asked to write a report, so have you presented your answer to this part of the question in an appropriate report format?

Part (b) (i): The Sector Manager has presented four arguments, and you need to address each of these in turn. Although the Manager clearly makes some debatable points, you shouldn't focus solely on these. Instead, you should try to give a balanced discussion – highlighting where the Manager's arguments are valid, as well as where they seem less justified.

Equally, it is important that you don't simply state whether you think the arguments are valid or not, but you discuss *why* you think this is the case. For example, in relation to argument 1, you should discuss why it is appropriate (or not appropriate) for the costs to be apportioned on the basis of floor area, and then why using revenues as the basis for apportionment is (or isn't) more appropriate. [see also 'Examiner's comment' below.]

Part (b) (ii): The requirement here asks for 'strategic implications' but then also gives you an extra clue as to the range of implications you should consider by noting that you should consider both the financial and non-financial implications of the decision to close the Hypermarkets sector. So make sure you do indeed consider both types of implications.

The calculation you carried out in part (a) (i) should have highlighted that closing the sector will have a significant negative financial impact, and suggests that B's operations in W could become loss-making overall. (B will still incur regional office costs, but it will have fewer sectors over which to re-apportion these costs.) What are the implications of this for B's future operations as a whole in W? Equally, what position does the Hypermarket sector play in B's product portfolio?

In terms of the non-financial implications of the decision: how might customers and suppliers react to the closure, for example, and how might their reactions affect B's other sectors?

Examiner's comments:

Part (b) (i) was not well answered by most candidates. Many candidates merely stated whether they felt the arguments were correct or incorrect, and gave little or no justification as to why they felt this.

In addition, many candidates made very naïve suggestions in relation to argument 3, stating that the Discount stores and Convenience stores should be closed as their combined revenue was lower than that of the Hypermarkets sector. However, such an approach completely ignores the fact that the most appropriate criterion to use in making such a decision is the sector's ability to generate contribution to profit, not simply the revenue it earns.

Part (b) (ii) was also not well answered. The main weakness was that many candidates only considered a very narrow range of implications, such as the impact on B's reputation and the effect on shareholders and employees. Very few candidates considered the impact of the closure on the remaining sectors and a similarly small number of candidates considered the financial impact and the loss of the contribution margin which the Hypermarkets sector would have earned if it had continued to trade.

REPORT

To: Regional Managing Director, Country W

From: Management Accountant

Date: [today]

Re: Proposed closure of the hypermarkets in Country W

This report discusses the Senior Manager's arguments against the proposal to close B's hypermarkets in Country W, and then considers the strategic implications which the proposed closure might have on B's future operations in W.

(i) Arguments made by the Senior Manager of the Hypermarkets

1. The current apportionment of the regional office costs is unfair

Management charge – The largest part of the regional office costs is the management charge. It is not clear what management services are included in this charge, and therefore what the fairest basis for apportioning them should be. For example, if a large part of the management charge relates to HR costs, then it may be more appropriate to apportion the charge on the basis of head count rather than floor area. But without further information it is not possible to say whether the basis of apportionment is fair or not. As the Senior Manager does not have this information either, it is equally not possible for him to judge whether the apportionment is fair or not.

Property taxes – Property taxes comprise the second largest element of the recharge. Floor area is likely to have some impact on the property taxes B pays for its stores, but is unlikely to be the only variable which affects them. For example, a store's location could also affect the level of property tax it has to pay. Therefore, the Senior Manager is partially justified in his argument, but there is no guarantee that property taxes are more closely correlated with store revenues than they are with floor area.

Insurance costs – Equally, it seems likely that insurance costs could be affected by both floor area and store revenues. Therefore, in the absence of any additional information, there is no clear reason why B should shift the basis of apportionment from floor area to store revenues. However, the Store Managers argument does suggest that B should at least investigate whether floor area is the most appropriate basis to use for apportioning insurance costs.

2. Trading performance

Contribution margin – The Senior Manager has argued that the Hypermarkets are B's best 'sector' in W, and Table 1 below supports this argument.

	Supermarkets (€ million)	%	Hypermarkets (€ million)	%	Discount stores (€ million)	%	Convenience stores (€ million)	%	Total (€ million)	%
Revenue	330		450		300		120		1,200	
Trading costs	198	60	243	54	225	75	72	60	738	61.5
Establishment costs	33	10	18	4	30	10	12	10	93	7.75
		70		58		85		70		69.25
Contribution	**99**	**30**	**189**	**42**	**45**	**15**	**36**	**30**	**369**	**30.75**

Table 1: Contributions to Profit, by Sector

Not only does the hypermarket sector generate the highest contribution to profit in monetary terms (€189 million) but it also earns the highest contribution to profit as a percentage of revenue (42%).

3. Discount and convenience stores should be closed because they generate least revenue

At the simplest level, the Manager's point is correct – the combined revenue which the Discount stores and the Convenience stores generate is €30 million lower than that generated by the hypermarkets.

However, it is not appropriate to decide whether or not to close a sector simply by looking at the revenue it currently generates.

On the one hand, although the revenue from these sectors is currently the lowest, there may be greater opportunities for growth in these sectors than in the hypermarkets sector, meaning their revenues could increase significantly in future years. In other words, B needs to consider the strategic future vale from retaining the divisions, not just the amount the currently contribute to the group.

But, more importantly, B should be looking at the **profitability** (contribution margin) of the different sectors, not simply the revenue they generate. In this respect, B should be concerned that the **contribution margin** generated by the discount stores (15%) is significantly lower than that generated by any of the other sectors. However, the contribution generated by the Convenience stores (30%) is the same as that generated by the Supermarkets, which would challenge the Manager's arguments that the Convenience Stores should be closed.

4. Regional office costs are too high and sectors should not have to pay for costs they do not understand and did not authorise

We do not know what costs the regional office is currently incurring, which means we cannot judge whether they are 'too high' or not.

The manager is justified in arguing that the sectors have not authorized these costs, but this does not mean that the sectors should not have to bear a share of these costs. For example, if insurance costs were not paid centrally, the Hypermarkets sector would need to arrange its own insurance, and so it is appropriate that the sector bears a share of the costs.

In this respect, although the Manager's arguments have a degree of validity in relation to the way the costs are recharged (without any explanation to, or authorisation from, the sectors), it is not valid to suggest that the sectors should not have to pay a share of the regional costs.

(ii) Strategic implications of closing the Hypermarkets sector.

Impact on profitability – Although B is currently forecasting a profit of €29 million for the year ended 31 December 2012, its revised forecast (if the hypermarkets sector is closed) shows a loss of €18.25 million (see (a) (i) above).

This decline in trading profit of €47.25 million reflects the three months contribution from the hypermarket sector which would be lost as a result of closing it.

Closure costs – In addition, if B closes the hypermarkets there will be costs associated with the closure; for example, redundancy costs payable to staff or costs associated with cancelling supplier contracts. Therefore, this will mean that B's final loss for the year ended 31 December 2012 is likely to be greater than the €18.25 million which has already been forecast.

Regional office costs – Importantly, although the decision to close the hypermarkets sector will reduce the contribution to profit the Group generates, it will not reduce the amount of regional office costs incurred (at least in the short term). But instead of being apportioned over four sectors, these costs will have to be apportioned over the three remaining sectors. Therefore the **contribution to profit which is lost** as a result of closing the hypermarket sector will translate directly into a reduction in B's overall profit.

Viability of Group – The forecast loss of €18.25 million suggests that unless the regional office costs can be significantly reduced, or the revenues from the three remaining sectors increased accordingly, it will no longer be viable for B to continue trading in W. In this way, the closure of the hypermarkets sector could precipitate the total closure of B's business in W.

Future growth – Hypermarkets are a new concept in W, yet B's hypermarkets are already very highly regarded and have established a high reputation for quality. Moreover, B has secured 85% of the market. This suggests that B is in a strong position to benefit from any future growth in the hypermarket sector in W. B's hypermarkets are forecast to generate €189 million contribution to profit in 2012, and this figure could increase significantly in the future if the sector grows.

If the hypermarket sector in W grows rapidly (as the concept becomes more established) then the hypermarkets would be a **star in B's portfolio** in W. This suggests that B should be looking to build the hypermarkets sector to increase the returns it can generate in future, rather than closing it.

Consumer perception – It is important to consider what impact closing the hypermarket sector could have on the performance of the other sectors more directly. In particular, the closure could have a negative impact on B's overall brand in W, and if consumers feel that the Group is in trouble they may be reluctant to purchase goods from B's other sectors.

Other stakeholders – Similarly, **suppliers** may be concerned about the closure; for example, if they feel that B is in financial trouble they may reduce the credit terms they offer B when supplying goods to its remaining business units.

Finally, the **government** or **local authorities** in B could also be concerned about the closures; for example, due to the loss of jobs which will result from them. If the relationship between B and the authorities becomes strained, this could mean that the authorities will look less favourably on any future proposals B submits for new developments in W.

Conclusion

The decision to close the hypermarkets division will have a significant negative impact on B's profits for the year ended 31 December 2012. However, perhaps more significantly, it could threaten the viability of B's remaining operations in B in the future.

(c)

Part (c) (i): The Table provided in the unseen material gives details about brand, customer and product characteristics, pricing and market share – all of which could be useful when deciding which of the generic strategies B should adopt for each sector.

Note that you are asked to recommend strategies for each of B's four sectors, so you should use each sector as a heading, and then consider how the characteristics of that sector make it suitable (or unsuitable) for the different generic strategies.

Remember that the two strategies are differentiation and *cost* leadership, not price leadership. So, in a sector in which B is pursuing a cost leadership strategy, the critical success factor is that B's *costs* are lower than its competitors' costs, not necessarily that its prices are lower than its competitors' prices.

Also, note that the verb here is 'recommend', so you need to give a clear recommendation as to which strategy B should follow – for each sector.

Part (c) (ii) should have been a relatively straight forward question, although it is important to note that you were asked to 'Advise B' of two limitations rather than simply to 'List' two limitations. In other words, you shouldn't simply have presented two bullet points, but should have given more detail about the limitations.

<u>**Supermarkets**</u>

Cost structure – B currently operates with a very economical cost structure, as a result of its well situated supermarkets. By contrast, many of the competitors' supermarkets are in inconvenient locations, which suggests they may have a less economical cost structure.

Market structure – B's market share (30%) is also significantly larger than that of its main competitors, the national chains with 10% market share each. This suggests that B should be able to benefit from economies of scale.

Costs and price – B's economical cost structure, possibly boosted by economies of scale, suggest that its costs should be lower than its competitors. This means that, even if B charges the same prices as its competitors, it would be able to earn a higher margin than them.

However, customers in the supermarket segment are **price sensitive**. Therefore, B could look to increase its market share by charging lower prices than its competitors, and thereby attract customers away from them. B's cost advantage over its competitors should mean that it can still make a satisfactory profit even if it charges a lower price than them.

Recommendation

Cost leadership strategy – B's cost advantages over its competitors suggest that its supermarkets should follow a cost leadership strategy. Because B already has a large market share and a number of supermarkets, it seems appropriate for it to compete across the market as a whole, rather than focusing more narrowly on specific niches within the market.

Hypermarkets

Quality – B's brand is very highly regarded, and it has a high reputation for quality. The hypermarkets stock a number of up-market brands, some of which are exclusive to B.

This approach seems to fit well with the characteristics of the customers in this sector. Hypermarket customers in W tend to be affluent, they appreciate quality, and are willing to pay a premium for it.

Current strategy – It seems that the hypermarket sector is already following a strategy of differentiation, based on the quality of its products.

Market leader – As hypermarkets are a new concept in W, B has been able to secure a position as the market leader, to the extent that it has 85% market share. If other companies identify the hypermarket sector as a profitable sector and look to enter it in the future, B will need a strategy which enables it to defend its position against these new entrants.

A differentiation strategy could enable it to do this. And, because this strategy fits well with the customer characteristics, B should continue to follow this strategy in the future.

Recommendation

Differentiation – B's current strategy of differentiation appears to have been successful so far, and B should continue to follow this strategy in the future; offering its customers high quality products and service, and wherever possible continuing to secure the exclusive rights to the up-market brands which are currently exclusive to it.

Discount stores

Narrow product range – B's discount stores are highly regarded for their specialist products, but they only offer a limited range of goods. This suggests that the discount stores should **focus** on particular niches within the market, rather than competing across the market as a whole.

Price sensitivity – Customers in the discount stores are extremely price sensitive and expect prices to be lower than in hypermarkets.

However, when thinking about whether to compete on price, B needs to beware that some of its competitors are very innovative and efficient, and profitable. This suggests that it is unlikely B will be able to achieve cost leadership in this sector.

Competitors – The competitors in this sector are mixed. While some appear successful (profitable, innovative and efficient) others appear much less so (trading at a loss, and being badly organised). It is not clear whether the successful competitors operate across all areas of the market or concentrate on specific niches.

If possible, B should try to select the niche which it is going to focus on as one in which the successful competitors have little presence.

Recommendation

Differentiation focus – B has developed a favourable brand reputation for its specialist range of products, and so its strategy should capitalise on this, and focus on the serving the needs of the customers who need these specialist products more effectively than any of the competitors.

<u>Convenience stores</u>

Lack of clear identity – The Sector Manager's comment that B's Convenience Stores are 'stuck in the middle' resonates with Porter's argument that companies which do not have a clearly identified generic strategy (either through cost leadership or differentiation) will not be successful.

This appears to be the case with B's convenience stores. The fact that some stores are market leaders and some are market laggards, means that customers are likely to be unsure about what the 'true' identity and strategy of B's convenience stores is.

Low market share – The market is currently dominated by a national chain which controls 65% of the market. As B only holds a market share of 10% it seems likely that it will be difficult for B to compete against the national chain, particularly on a cost leadership basis. However, the remaining 25% of the market is fragmented which suggests B could compete successfully in that aspect of the market.

Location – The convenience stores cater for mid- to upper-income groups, who are prepared to pay a premium price if the location of the stores is convenient. This suggests that B could be advised to focus on stores which are in good locations (convenient for mid and upper income groups), without any branches of the national chain nearby, and try to use location as a basis for differentiation.

Recommendation

Differentiation focus – B's convenience stores do not have any cost advantages and so will have to compete on the basis of differentiation rather than cost leadership. It seems unlikely that B will be able to compete successfully against the national chain across the market as a whole, and so it should focus on regions or locations where the market leader is relatively weak.

(c) (ii)

Stuck in the middle – In practice, many companies have pursued, quite successfully, strategies which Porter's model would categorise as stuck in the middle. For example, many supermarkets now offer 'value' ranges alongside 'premium' ranges to cater for different customer requirements.

In this way, Porter's model no longer reflects the full range of competitive strategies an organisation can choose from, and the development of models such as the **strategic clock** (which identifies a range of potential strategies) highlights this.

The importance of the customer – Porter's original model focused on cost (ie cost leadership) rather than price. In this respect, however, the model underplays the importance of the customer. Rational customers will seek value for money in their purchases, and this value for money is provided through a combination of **price** and **perceived product/service benefits**. For example, the customers in B's discount stores are extremely price sensitive, and so the price of the products they sell is likely to play an important part in determining the success of B's discount stores.

Defining the strategic unit – Porter's model suggests that if a firm has more than one competitive strategy, this will dilute its competitive advantage. But it seems impractical to suggest that a group of companies (such as B) should follow a single competitive strategy for all its business units if they have very different business models or operate in diverse markets. For example, it would seem impractical for B to try to follow the same strategy for its hypermarkets as for its discount stores.

In this respect it seems more appropriate to suggest that the model should only be applied at business unit level.

Defining the industry / market – Similar difficulties arise in relation to trying to determine which industry or market a firm is competing in, and therefore who its competitors are.

Question 2

Text reference: CIMA's Code of Ethics, and ethical issues more generally, are discussed in Chapter 2 of the BPP Study Text.

Marking scheme

			Marks
(a)	For each Situation:		
	For identifying the ethical principle relevant to the situation – 1 mark	Up to 3	
	For explaining the principle – 1 mark per situation	Up to 3	
	For reasons as to why the situation does (or doesn't) represent a conflict with the Code of Ethics – up to 2 marks per situation	Up to 6	
	For clear advice as to whether there is a conflict or not – 1 mark	Up to 3	
		Total up to	12
(b)	For each relevant and appropriate stage outlined – 1 mark each	Up to 7	
	For concluding comments, recognising that it may not be possible to resolve the conflicts entirely, due to multiple stakeholder interests	Up to 2	
		Total up to	7
(c)	For each appropriate issue identified – 1 mark each	Up to 2	
	For explaining the issue identified – 1 mark per issue	Up to 2	
	For explaining why the issue should be included in WWW's Code – 1 mark each issue	Up to 2	
		Total up to	6
		Total	25

Top tips

Part (a): It should have been relatively easy to identify which ethical principle is at risk in each of the 'situations' described in the scenario, and this would be a sensible place to start your answer in relation to each situation.

For each of the three situations, you should identify which of the five fundamental principles *could* be threatened by the issues identified, and then explain how the situation *could* lead to a conflict with the principle in question.

Then you should assess whether the situation *actually* represents a conflict with that principle. This assessment should form the basis of your advice..

Note that you have been asked to 'advise' whether (or not) each of the situations is in conflict with the Code of Ethics, so you need to give clear advice for each section of your answer, indicating whether there is a conflict or not.

(a)

Situation 1

Integrity – This situation could be in conflict with the fundamental principle of integrity.

CIMA's Code of Ethics highlights that the principle of integrity requires accountants to be 'honest, straightforward and truthful' in all business relationships. The principle of integrity also implies that accountants should not be

associated with any information which they believe contains a materially false or misleading statement, or which is misleading by omissions.

Contain a materially false or misleading statement – The CEO has presented a very optimistic forecast for WWW's profits, but this could be misleading if the government's claim for damages against the company is successful.

Omits information where such omission would be misleading – Although the government's claim for damages would 'materially affect' WWW's profit for 20X3 if it were successful, the CEO did not mention the claim in his presentation to the analysts and journalists. This omission is therefore misleading, because it prevents his audience from being aware that WWW's profit for 20X3 might be materially lower than the figure given in the forecast.

Tutorial Note:

The principle of integrity also requires professional accountants to disassociate themselves from statements or information which have been 'furnished recklessly'.

Contain statements or information furnished recklessly – The CEO prepared his forecast in a hurry, and did not check the figures with anyone else in WWW. Given that WWW is an international company, the CEO could be seen as reckless for presenting a forecast without asking anybody else in the company to confirm it. Such actions suggest the CEO has perfect knowledge of the company and its prospects, but that seems very unlikely.

Advice:

The CEO's forecast and presentation demonstrate the characteristics of communications which conflict with the principle of integrity. The CEO has not been honest in his dealings with the analysts and the journalists, and therefore Situation 1 represents a **conflict with the principle of integrity.**

Situation 2

Confidentiality – The principle which could be jeopardised here is confidentiality. The Code requires accountants and firms to refrain from disclosing, outside a firm, confidential information which has been acquired as a result of business relationships with that firm.

Many of the documents which the Government's lawyers have requested contain confidential information, which suggests there could be a conflict with the principle of confidentiality if they are handed over.

Exception: Legal proceedings – However, the Code makes an exception to the principle of confidentiality in the context of legal proceedings. In others words, the principle of confidentiality is not breached if confidential information is disclosed when it is required in the course of legal proceedings.

This is the case in Situation 2. WWW has been required to produce the documents as a result of the court order obtained by the Government.

Advice:

Although the documents contain confidential information, **Situation 2 does not represent a conflict with the Code.**

Situation 3

Objectivity – The principle which could be at stake in this situation is objectivity.

The principle of objectivity requires accountants not to allow bias, conflict of interest, or the undue influence of others to override their professional or business judgements.

Reasons for financial controller's decision - The financial controller's advice about discontinuing the joint venture appears to have been driven by the poor working relationship between the accounting staff in the two companies, and the problems which ZZZ has caused the financial controller and his staff.

By contrast, the financial controller does not appear to have considered the profitability of the joint venture, or the commercial benefits to WWW of continuing with it.

Conflict - In this respect, it appears that financial controller's decision has been biased as a result of the problems which he and his staff have encountered in working with ZZZ.

Advice:

This situation **represents a conflict with the Code**, and specifically with the principle of objectivity.

(b)

> **Part (b)**: The requirement looks at the stages which could be used to resolve ethical conflicts in general terms. For example, you should not have advised WWW of the stages it could take to resolve any of the specific situations given in the scenario. You were not asked to do this, and you would not have scored any marks for doing so.
>
> However, you should have noted that the question asked about the stages WWW could take to resolve the conflict, rather than the steps an individual could take to resolve a conflict. Therefore suggestions that it would be appropriate to 'resign' if the conflict could not be resolved were not suitable here, and would not have earned any marks.

WWW could use the following stages for resolving ethical conflicts:

Establish the all relevant facts and information

Identify the ethical issues which are involved, and **identify the fundamental ethical principles** related to the matter in question. These principles should be identified in WWW's published Code of Ethics, but alternatively WWW could refer to a Code published by a professional body such as CIMA (in its Code of Ethics).

Follow procedures – Where possible, WWW should follow its internal procedures when enquiring into the ethical conflict.

Identify potential courses of action – WWW should investigate possible courses of action which it could use to resolve the conflict, and should consider the potential consequences of each possible course of action.

The following questions could be relevant here:

- Can the conflict be resolved?
- What are the consequences if the conflict is not resolved?
- What stakeholders are affected by the conflict, or will be affected if it is not resolved?

Consultation – In order to help answer these questions, WWW needs to consult all the stakeholders who are affected by the conflict.

Resolution – Once WWW has established all the relevant facts, and considered the consequences of each possible course of action, it should then determine the appropriate course of action to resolve the conflict.

External advice – If WWW is not able to resolve the matter internally, it may need to seek external advice, either from its legal advisors, or from a relevant professional body (such as CIMA).

Compromise – However, it is important for WWW to recognise that, in some ethical conflicts, there may not be a way of resolving the conflict which is entirely wholly acceptable to all stakeholders. The resolution is likely to involving trading off the interests of one stakeholder group against those of another. Therefore, it is almost inevitable that there will need to be a degree of compromise in resolving the conflict.

(c)

> **Part (c)**: The first paragraph of the scenario identifies that WWW is committed to 'being a company that will trade fairly and sustainably.' This suggests that two ethical issues which could be added to WWW's Ethical Code are 'Fair Trade' and 'Sustainability'.
>
> However, these are not the only issues you could have suggested here, and issues to do with equal opportunities, for example, could have been equally appropriate. Note, however, that you need to give your reasons why WWW should include the issues you recommend in its Code of Ethics. So it is not sufficient simply to recommend the issue which should be included; you also need to explain why it should be included.
>
> Also, note that the requirement specifically asks you to recommend TWO issues which could be included in WWW's ethical code, so you should not have recommended any more than this.

WWW has committed itself to being a company which will trade fairly and sustainably, and therefore it could include the issues of 'Fair Trade' and 'Sustainability' in its Ethical Code.

Fair Trade – The key principle here will be that WWW pays it suppliers a fair price for the goods they produce and supply.

By including a commitment to fair trading in its Ethical Code, WWW will be recognising its **responsibility towards suppliers**, and its commitment not to use the bargaining power it could have over its suppliers to depress the price it pays them for the goods they supply.

In this way, WWW highlights that it is committed to stakeholder groups other than just its shareholders.

However, making a commitment to Fair Trade could also be beneficial to WWW in the context of ethical consumerism. WWW's consumers are likely to have a choice about whether or not to buy their products from it, and some consumers may choose to buy fair trade products in preference to ones which are sourced less ethically. Moreover, some customers may even be prepared to pay more for 'Fair Trade' products compared to one which come from less socially responsible sources.

Sustainability – The key issue here is that WWW appreciates the importance of long-term sustainability as well as short-term profitability.

Triple bottom line - Although the concept of sustainability is often used in relation to environmental sustainability, it should not be limited to environmental sustainability in WWW's ethical code. Instead, the issue of sustainability in the Code should cover aspects of **social justice** and **economic prosperity** as well as **environmental quality**.

In this way, the Code will highlight that if WWW does not behave in a way which is socially and environmentally responsible, its behaviour could damage its image and performance in the longer term; for example, through increased liability to environmental taxes, or through consumer boycotts.

By contrast, if WWW develops a reputation as a socially responsible company (through supporting the various aspects of sustainability) this could lead to increased business, because its actions will resonate with ethically conscious consumers.

In addition, WWW could link the idea of sustainability with that of creating a sustainable competitive advantage. This should highlight that if WWW does not conduct its activities in a sustainable way (either environmentally or socially) then the lifecycle of the company could ultimately be limited.

Question 3

Text reference: Knowledge management is discussed in Chapter 9 of the BPP Study Text for E3. Data mining is discussed in Chapter 8.

Marking scheme

		Marks	
(a)	For defining CSFs – 1 mark	1	
	For explaining the link between CSFs and KPIs – 1 mark	1	
	For explaining advantages to HHH of using CSFs and KPIs - 1 mark	1	
		Total up to	3
(b) (i)	Definition of knowledge management – 1 mark	1	
	For each relevant benefit of knowledge management identified – 1mark	Up to 3	
	For explaining how that benefit applies specifically to HHH – 1 mark per benefit	Up to 3	
		Total up to	6
(b) (ii)	For each relevant social and/or technical problem identified – 1 mark each	Up to 4	
	For explaining how each problem is a specific issue for HHH – 1 mark per problem	Up to 4	
		Total up to	8
(c)	Definition of data mining – up to 2 marks	Up to 2	
	For explaining how data mining could be used to understand factors which influence student drop-out rates – up to 2 marks per relevant point	Up to 4	
	For explaining how patterns identified through data mining could then be used to forecast student behaviour and to take action to prevent students from dropping-out – up to 2 marks per relevant point	Up to 6	
		Total up to	8
		Total	25

Top tips.

Part (a). There are only three marks available for this requirement, so keep your explanation brief! However, note that you are not merely asked to explain what CSFs and KPIs are, but to explain the advantages HHH would gain by using them in its performance management systems. The key point here is that HHH will need to have KPIs to measure how well it is performing against its CSFs. You can then give an example of a possible KPI which would be useful for HHH to monitor (eg drop out rates). Remember there are only three marks available for Part (a) though. It will be very easy to spend too long on this part of the question.

(a)

CSFs and performance management – HHH's CSFs should identify the areas which are central to its future success and therefore where it needs to perform well if it is to be successful overall.

CSFs and KPIs – Once HHH has identified which aspects of performance are crucial to future success it needs to be able to **measure** how well it is performing in relation to them. It can use KPIs to measure whether or not its CSFs are being achieved.

Examples – So, for example, measuring the number of students who do not complete each year of a course, or measuring the percentage of students who drop out each year, will allow HHH to monitor student performance.

(b)

Top tips.

Part (b) (i). To score well here it is important that you don't simply discuss the benefits of knowledge management systems, and the potential problems of using them, in general terms. Make sure your answers are linked specifically to HHH and the scenario provided. For example, the scenario has identified a number of problems arising from the way that HHH currently uses (or, more accurately, doesn't use) its knowledge. In turn, you should be able to identify the benefits from implementing a knowledge management strategy in relation to the way they could help overcome these current problems.

Part (b) (ii): Equally, although the implementation of the knowledge management strategy will lead to a change in the way the staff at HHH work, don't let your answer to part (b) (ii) become a general discussion about resistance to change.

Also note that the question requirement refers to social *and* technical problems. This should have highlighted that knowledge management systems do not only rely on the technology which supports them, but they also need a culture of knowledge sharing to be successful. How does this compare to the 'culture' which currently exists at HHH?

(i)

Improved student performance – One of the aims of HHH's knowledge management strategy should be to gather, organise and share knowledge and experience about areas of its business which will contribute to its future success.

In this respect, if the staff in the departments which currently have high student drop-out rates can learn more about how to improve student performance this should enable them to reduce the drop-out rates. In turn, this should allow the university to improve its performance in this area.

Reduce staff turnover – Currently HHH as an abnormally high level of staff turnover, and its staff turnover levels are double those of SSS, which has a culture of knowledge sharing.

Although there is no guarantee that introducing a knowledge management system will reduce staff turnover, if sharing knowledge helps improve performance this, in turn, should help improve the motivation and job satisfaction of HHH's staff. If staff value working for HHH because it is a successful organisation, this should help reduce staff turnover levels.

Increased collaboration between colleagues and departments – Currently very few of HHH's staff share knowledge with any of their colleagues. However, this lack of collaboration is likely to be stifling **innovation and creativity** within the University.

By contrast, if HHH implemented a knowledge management system, this should encourage staff to share ideas and experience with their colleagues, which in turn could lead to new opportunities for collaboration and innovation across the university. These should not only be restricted to new opportunities for how to improve student performance, but they could also extend into areas of academic research as well.

(ii)

Resistance from successful departments – Staff in the departments with low drop-outs rates have spent considerable time and effort developing their student support schemes, but the departments with high drop-out rates do not seem to have made much effort to introduce any student support schemes. Therefore, staff from the successful departments may oppose changes which they see as enabling the other departments to 'benefit' despite not having contributed anything to the schemes.

This resistance may be replicated in other areas, with staff not appreciating why they should share their any of their knowledge with other staff.

Demotivation – In a similar way, if staff feel that they have to share any knowledge and experience they gain, this may make them less motivated to build up their knowledge, preferring instead to let someone else do it and then making use of that knowledge.

Knowledge is power – Staff may be reluctant to share knowledge, because they may view knowledge as power. If a member of staff is the only person who has a particular piece of knowledge, that member of staff may feel that his or her knowledge increases their value to the university.

Therefore they will be reluctant to share their knowledge, particularly if they perceive that this will make them expendable to HHH, due to the fact they are no longer the only people who has the knowledge in question.

Cultural issues – The culture at HHH currently seems to dictate that staff and departments are very inward-looking and insular. However, the knowledge management scheme will require a much greater degree of collaboration and interaction between staff and departments.

In effect, the knowledge management system will need to be introduced and operated in the context of a wider cultural change, which emphasises the value of collaboration and knowledge sharing, and possibly also rewards it. For example, HHH may need to review staff objectives and reward schemes, so that staff are rewarded for sharing knowledge rather keeping it to themselves.

Limitations of knowledge systems – Although knowledge management systems are not solely reliant on information systems, HHH will need to consider how it is going to gather, capture and then share the necessary information. For example, given the apparent independence of the different departments, it seems likely that they will have different information systems. This could make it harder to share information and knowledge between different departments, if the various systems and incompatible.

Equally, it is likely that some of the knowledge may be **implicit,** or at least not currently recorded in **digital form.** Therefore, before it can be shared, the knowledge will need to be captured, and/or converted into a digital format.

(c)

Part (c). The structure of the requirement should help you answer it. Explaining what data mining is should help you appreciate how it could be used to improve the student drop-out rates (ie by uncovering relationships in data which can then be used to predict future behaviour).

However, note that the requirement doesn't simply ask how data mining could be used to help understand student drop-out rates; but rather how it could be used to help *improve* them. In effect, the question is asking how HHH could use the relationships it identifies through data mining to help prevent students from dropping out.

Data mining – Data mining is concerned with analysing large pools of data to highlight previously unknown patterns and relationships in that data.

Predicting future behaviour – One of the key benefits which accrue from data mining is the ability to use the patterns and relationships which have been identified to predict future behaviour. In HHH's case, the aspect of behaviour it wants to be able to predict is students dropping out of their courses.

Identify factors affecting drop-out rates - HHH could use data mining software to analyse data to try to identify what factors appear to be influencing student drop-out rates.

Because data mining software is designed to analyse large pools of data, HHH shouldn't be restricted to analysing only the performance of its own departments. It could also look at data for students in other UK universities to see what factors appear to be affecting their drop-out rates.

Importantly, if HHH can get a better understanding of the issues which are causing students to drop out of their causes, it can then develop plans to address those issues and thereby hopefully improve student retention rates.

Preventing drop-outs – If HHH can identify, in advance, the groups of students which are most at risk of dropping out it can then offer them additional support or guidance to try to prevent them dropping out of their courses.

For example, data mining might identify that foreign students who perform poorly in mock exams also fail their end of year exams and therefore cannot continue with their courses. In which case, action could be taken to offer extra tuition to students who fail their mock exams to help them improve their chances of passing their end of year exams and therefore being able to continue with their courses.

Question 4

Text references: Porter's value chain is discussed in Chapter 4 of the BPP Study Text.

Marking scheme

			Marks
(a)	For correctly applying each activity of the value chain to BBB – 1 mark per activity	Up to 9	
	For explaining the impact each activity has on BBB's competitive advantage – 1 mark per activity	Up to 9	
	(ie Up to 2 marks are available per activity; 1 for correct application of the activity; 1 for explaining its impact on BBB's competitive advantage)		
		Total up to	13
(b)	Benefits of having real-time information (eg reduced investment in working capital) – 1 mark per point	Up to 2	
	Benefits of improved analysis of sales transactions - 1 mark per point	Up to 2	
	Benefits from analysing staff sales (eg implications for customer service and training; staffing levels) – 1 mark per point	Up to 2	
		Total up to	4
(c)	For each relevant stage identified – 1 mark each	Up to 4	
	For explaining the benefit of including each stage in the plan – 1 mark per stage	Up to 4	
	(Relevant stages could include: consultation; appointing project leader/ team; training; designing output reports; after sales service)		
		Total up to	8
		Total	25

Top Tips.

Part (a).

The scenario provides a range of information about the different activities in BBB's value chain, and so you should have been able to use this to explain how the value chain could be applied by BBB.

However, note that the question requirement asks you to explain how BBB could use the value chain *to achieve competitive advantage*; not merely to explain what the value chain is, or to give examples of the different value activities at BBB.

The question requirement clearly asks you to give examples, from BBB, of all nine activities in the value chain so a sensible way to structure your answer would be to use each of the activities as headings and then explain how each of them could add value for BBB.

> But remember you need to explain how the activities add value and generate competitive advantage for BBB, not simply to explain what they are, or how they could add value to an organisation in general terms.

(a)

Competitive advantage – Porter argues that firms achieve competitive advantage through the way they organise and perform activities. Businesses are made up of value-creating activities, which create value for their customers.

The value chain helps firms identify how they are deploying their resources to satisfy customers, and how they are adding value for their customers. Therefore, by using the value chain, BBB should ensure that its activities are adding value for its customers, and this in turn could help it achieve competitive advantage.

Primary activities

Inbound logistics – BBB has invested in a **robotic system** to improve materials handling in its warehouse. This should improve the speed and efficiency with which items coming into the warehouse can be processed, and then, in turn, distributed on to BBB's shops. This should help BBB improve the service it provides to its customers by making new items available for them as quickly as possible. This is important because BBB's clothes only remain fashionable for a short period.

The improvements in materials handling in the warehouse should also reduce wastage, which will contribute to a greater margin.

Operations – BBB has trained all its staff in customer care, and tries to employ staff who already have experience of working in fashion retailers. By using staff who already have experience of working in other shops, BBB should ensure that the service it offers customers is at least as good as those other shops. And providing its staff with additional training in customer care may help BBB's performance exceed that of its competitors in this area of operations.

This is likely to be important given than BBB has demanding customers, but ones who appreciate the retail experience which BBB offers.

Outbound logistics – BBB will deliver any items bought in its shops to customers' home within 24 hours. BBB's competitors do not offer this service, and so this delivery activity is a feature which explicitly differentiates BBB from its competitors. Even if not all customers take advantage of this service, BBB knows that customers appreciate the after sales service which it offers.

Marketing and sales – BBB frequently sends its regular customers special offers and invites them to fashion shows held in its shops. By doing so, BBB keeps its customers informed about new products which have come into stock, and hopefully also encourages them to keep buying products from BBB.

In addition, by inviting its customers to fashion shows, BBB may help to make its customers feel valued, which should encourage them to continue buying products from it.

Service – If a customer is dissatisfied with any purchase, BBB will make a refund without any question. This is also likely to be one of the features which contributes to customers' appreciation of BBB's after sales service. By offering a refund without any question, BBB should be able to appease any dissatisfied customers, which, in turn, should help improve BBB's customer retention rates.

Support activities

Firm infrastructure – BBB's general corporate administration and infrastructure is unlikely to generate any competitive advantage in its own right. However, BBB needs a suitable departmental structure, management structure and management information to support its primary activities.

Moreover, planning, finance and quality control will all be important to BBB's strategic capability in its primary activities. So if BBB is able to organise these aspects of its infrastructure better than its competitors, this could provide a potential source of competitive advantage.

Human resource management – We have already identified that, when recruiting new staff, BBB prefers to employ people with previous experience at other fashion retailers. BBB also trains all of its staff in customer care.

This suggests that BBB's human resource management policies are geared towards providing customers with a good retail experience, which is something they appreciate. If BBB can provide its customers with a more favourable retail experience than its competitors, this should help it achieve competitive advantage over them.

Technology development – One of the head office departments investigates innovations in fashion retailing, and it seems likely that this has prompted BBB to investigate the introduction of 'Smart Tills' into its shops. By allowing BBB to manage inventory better and respond to customer demand more quickly, amongst other things, the 'Smart Tills' should help improve BBB's overall performance and competitiveness. Being able to respond quickly to changing customer demand is likely to be particularly important in fashion retailing because of the short periods of time for which clothes remain fashionable.

Procurement – BBB's competitive strategy is to offer a wide selection of high quality products at reasonable prices. Therefore its procurement function needs to be able to acquire an appropriate selection of products. Moreover, BBB needs to be able to procure its clothes quickly given the short period of time for which they will be in fashion. As a result, BBB's procurement activities play a vital part in underpinning its competitive advantage.

(b)

Top tips.

Part (b). Make sure you read the requirement carefully here. The question does not ask you how BBB could benefit from using the Smart Tills in general, but it asks specifically how using the Smart Tills could help BBB improve its profits.

Make sure you explain clearly how any benefits you identify will help BBB improve its profits.

Real time information – The Smart Tills will provide BBB with accurate, real time information about sales.

Inventory management – On the one hand this will allow BBB to manage its inventory more effectively. For example, it will have an up-to-date record of the inventory levels for any product, which will help managers know when to re-order. In this way, BBB should be able to reduce the risk of stock-outs (and therefore lost sales) but also over-ordering and having too much working capital tied up in inventory. Both of these aspects should improve profit.

Responsiveness to customer demand – Perhaps more importantly, the real time information should also increase BBB's responsiveness to customer demand. For example, the tills can provide an analysis of all the sales transactions, which should help BBB identify which products are selling well, and in which shops. This knowledge should be able to help BBB meet its customers' requirement better, for example, by increasing stocks of popular products, and possibly also by increasing stocks of similar, or complementary, products.

The more effectively BBB can meet its customers' requirements, the greater the revenue it should be able to generate. Increased revenues, in turn, should help improve profits.

Staff performance – The Tills will also provide BBB with information about the sales for each staff member, which could be used to help manage their performance. For example, staff could be given **incentive schemes** under which they qualify for a bonus if they achieve a sales target.

Equally, however, the Tills could identify if there are significant variations in the levels of income staff members generate. For example, some staff members may need additional training to improve their customer service skills and therefore make more sales. Alternatively, the level of sales staff members are generating in certain shops may be low because the shop is over-staffed. Either way, the sales statistics which the Tills provide should alert BBB to the potential issues, such that BBB can take action which could then lead to improved profitability.

(c)

Top tips.

Part (c). In general terms, you could approach this requirement as a question about project management. Although the question requirement refers to the key 'stages' it may be more helpful to think in terms of the activities which BBB needs to undertake in relation to implementing the new tills; for example, appointing a project leader; consulting with staff; and providing training.

Also, while the requirement asks you to 'Recommend...' rather than 'Recommend, with reasons...' it is nonetheless vital that you *explain* why you have recommended the stages that you have.

And finally, it is important that the stages you recommend are specifically relevant to the project to implement Smart Tills into BBB's shops, rather than merely being generic stages in the project management process.

Appoint project leader – The plan to introduce Smart Tills into all BBB's shops represents quite a major project for BBB. Therefore, BBB should appoint a project leader to oversee the project.

The project leader should understand the Smart Tills technology and the fashion retailing industry, and should have experience of managing change. If none of BBB's current managers have the necessary skills and/or experience to lead the project, BBB should employ an external consultant to lead the project.

Tutorial note: Appoint project team

You could also have suggested appointing a project team. As the project is likely to be a major undertaking for BBB, it could be beneficial to have dedicated staff working specifically on the project, rather than trying to combine working on the project alongside other routine aspects of their jobs.

Consultation with shop managers – The introduction of Smart Tills into the shops is likely to be a significant change for the shop managers, and therefore at least some of them may resist the change.

Therefore, before introducing the Tills, BBB should discuss the plan with the shop managers and explain why it wants to introduce the Tills. For example, BBB should highlight the benefits which the new Tills could bring, in terms of improved profitability.

However, it is important that the consultation is a two-way process, and so BBB should listen to any concerns the managers have about the plan. Not only is the managers' resistance likely to be reduced if they feel they have been listened to, but also some of the suggestions they make may smooth the implementation of the plan.

Training – Before the Tills are introduced into the shops, the managers and their staff will need to be trained how to use them.

It is likely that this training will need to be provided by the supplier of the Tills, but BBB will also need to consider when and how the training is given. For example, the staff from a shop cannot all receive training at the same time unless the shop is closed for the duration of the training.

Support Contract – Before the Tills are introduced, BBB also needs to ensure it has a contract in place with the supplier to provide on-going after-sales service and maintenance for the Tills.

Once BBB is using the Tills, they will be critical to its business. For example, if a Till breaks down, a shop may not be able to make any transactions for the period the Till is broken. Therefore, BBB should have a service level agreement in place with the supplier, which includes, amongst other things, response times for dealing with any breakdowns in the Tills.

Implementation – The Project Leader will have to plan how the Tills are to be introduced. For example, can the Tills be introduced to all 20 shops at the same time, or will the roll out of the new tills have to be phased? Equally, will there be a period in which the new Tills are run in parallel alongside the existing tills in the shops?

Post-implementation – Once the Tills have been introduced, the amount and quality of management information which is available should be significantly increased. Therefore the management accountant will need to determine what **additional management reports** should be produced to make use of the extra information which is now available.

CIMA – Pillar E

Paper E3

Enterprise strategy

Mock Exam 3 (November 2012 exam)

You are allowed **three hours** to answer this question paper.
You are allowed **20 minutes** reading time **before the examination begins** during which you should read the question paper and, if you wish, highlight and/or make notes on the question paper. However, you are **not** allowed, **under any circumstances**, to open the answer book and start writing or use your calculator during this reading time.
You are strongly advised to carefully read ALL the question requirements before attempting the question concerned (that is all parts and/or sub-questions).
Answer ALL compulsory questions in Section A.
Answer TWO of the three questions in Section B.

DO NOT OPEN THIS PAPER UNTIL YOU ARE READY TO START UNDER EXAMINATION CONDITIONS

BPP
LEARNING MEDIA

SECTION A – 50 marks

Strategic level pre-seen case material

Question 1

Pre-seen case study

V, a private limited company in a European country (SK), which is outside the Eurozone, was founded in 1972. The currency in SK is SK$. V is a travel business that offers three holiday (vacation) products. It has a network of 50 branches in a number of major cities throughout SK.

History of the company

V achieved steady growth until six years ago, when it found that its market share was eroding due to customers increasingly making online bookings with its competitors. Direct bookings for holidays through the internet have increased dramatically in recent years. Many holiday-makers find the speed and convenience of booking flights, accommodation or complete holidays online outweighs the benefits of discussing holiday alternatives with staff in a branch.

V's board had always taken the view that the friendly direct personal service that V offers through its branch network is a major differentiating factor between itself and other travel businesses and that this is highly valued by its customers. However, V found that in order to continue to compete it needed to establish its own online travel booking service, which it did five years ago. Until this point, V's board had never engaged in long-term planning. It had largely financed growth by reinvestment of funds generated by the business. The large investment in IT and IS five years ago required significant external funding and detailed investment appraisal.

Much of V's business is now transacted online through its website to the extent that 60% of its revenue in the year ended 30 June 2012 was earned through online bookings.

Current structure of V's business

V offers three types of holiday product. These are known within V as Package, Adventure and Prestige Travel. V only sells its own products and does not act as an agent for any other travel companies. It uses the services of other companies engaged in the travel industry such as chartered airlines and hotels which it pays for directly on behalf of its customers.

Package

"Package" provides holidays mainly for families with children aged up to their late teens. These typically are for accommodation in hotels (where meals are part of the package) or self-catering apartments (where no meals are provided within the package).

Adventure

"Adventure" caters for people aged mainly between 20 and 30, who want relatively cheap adventure based holidays such as trekking, sailing and cycling or who wish to go on inexpensive back-packing holidays mainly in Europe and Asia.

Prestige Travel

"Prestige Travel" provides expensive and bespoke holidays mainly sold to couples whose children have grown up and left home. The Prestige Travel product only provides accommodation in up-market international hotel chains in countries across the world.

All three of these products provide holidays which include flights to and from the holiday destinations and hotel or self-catering accommodation. V has its own customer representatives available at the holiday destinations to provide support to its customers. All-inclusive holidays (in which all food and drinks are provided within the holiday price) are offered within each of the three product offerings.

Support products

V supports its main products by offering travel insurance and foreign currency exchange. The travel insurance, which is provided by a major insurance company and for which V acts as an agent, is usually sold along with the holidays both by branch staff and by staff dealing with online bookings.

Currency exchange is available to anyone through V's branches irrespective of whether or not the customer has bought a holiday product from V. A new currency exchange product is provided by V through which a customer purchases an amount of currency, either in SK's home currency (SK$) or else in a foreign currency and this is credited on to a plastic card. The card is then capable of being read by automated teller machines (ATM's) in many countries across the world allowing the customer to withdraw cash in the local currency up to the amount that has been credited on to the card.

Marketing of products

V relies for the vast majority of its business on the literature, available in hard copy and online, which it provides on the holiday products it sells. Exceptionally, V is able to offer some of its existing holiday products at discount prices. These may be offered under any of the three main products offered but they are mostly cut-price holiday deals which are available under the Package holiday product label.

Sales structure

Staff in each of the 50 branches accept bookings from customers and all branches have direct IT access to head office. Online enquiries and bookings are received and processed centrally at head office, which is located in SK's capital city.

Branch managers have some discretion to offer discounts on holidays to customers. V offers a discount to customers who buy holidays through its online bookings. The branch managers have authority to reduce the price of a holiday booked at the branch up to the amount of the online discount if they feel it is necessary to do so in order to make the sale.

Financial information

V's revenue, split across the holiday and support products offered, for the financial year ended 30 June 2012 is summarised as follows:

	Revenue *SK$ million*
Package	90
Adventure	60
Prestige Travel	95
Support products	5

The overall net operating profit generated in the financial year to 30 June 2012 was SK$35 million and the profit for the year was SK$24 million, giving a profit to sales ratio of just under 10%. V's cash receipts fluctuate because of seasonal variations and also because V's customers pay for their holidays shortly before they depart.

Further details, including extracts from V's income statement for the year ended 30 June 2012 and statement of financial position as at 30 June 2012 are shown in Appendix 1.

Financial objectives

V's key financial objectives are as follows:

1. To grow earnings by, on average, 5% a year.
2. To pay out 80% of profits as dividends.

Foreign exchange risk

V has high exposure to foreign exchange risk as its revenues received and payments made are frequently in different currencies. It normally settles hotel bills and support costs, such as transfers between hotels and airports in the local currencies of the countries where the hotels are located. It normally pays charter airlines in the airline's home currency. Scheduled airline charges are settled in the currency required by the particular airline.

V is exposed to fluctuations in the cost of aircraft fuel incurred by airlines which are passed on to travel businesses. It has often been necessary for V to require its customers to make a supplementary payment to cover the cost of increases in aircraft fuel, sometimes after the customer had thought that the final payment for the holiday had been made.

Board composition and operational responsibilities

The Board of Directors comprises five people: an Executive Chairman (who also fulfils the role of Chief Executive), a Finance Director, an Operations Director, an IT Director and a Human Resources Director. The Executive Chairman founded the business in 1972. He has three grown-up children, two of whom successfully pursue different business interests and are not engaged in V's business at all. The third child, a son, is currently taking a "year out" from study and is going to university next year to study medicine.

The branch managers all report directly to the Operations Director. In addition, the Operations Director is responsible for liaising with airlines and hotels which provide the services offered by V's promotional literature. The IT Director is responsible for V's website and online enquiries and bookings. The Finance Director is responsible for V's financial and management accounting systems and has a small team of accountancy staff, including a part-qualified management accountant, reporting to her. The Human Resources Director has a small team of staff reporting to him.

Shareholding

There are 90 million SK$0.10 (10 cent) shares in issue and the shareholdings are as follows:

	% holding
Executive Chairman	52
Finance Director	12
Operations Director	12
IT Director	12
Human Resources Director	12

Employees

V employs 550 full-time equivalent staff. Turnover of staff is relatively low. High performance rewards in terms of bonuses are paid to staff in each branch if it meets or exceeds its quarterly sales targets. Similarly, staff who deal with online bookings receive a bonus if the online bookings meet or exceed quarterly sales targets. V's staff, both in the branches and those employed in dealing with online bookings, also receive an additional bonus if they are able to sell travel insurance along with a holiday product to customers.

Employee development for staff who are in direct contact with the public is provided through updates on products which V offers. Each member of branch and online booking staff undertakes a two day induction programme at the commencement of their employment with V. The emphasis of the induction programme is on customer service not on details relating to the products as it is expected that new staff will become familiar with such product details as they gain experience within V.

Safety

V publicly states that it takes great care to ensure that its customers are as safe as possible while on holiday. To date, V has found that accidents while on holiday are mainly suffered by very young children, Adventure customers and elderly customers. There has been an increase in instances over the last year where customers in resort hotels have suffered severe stomach complaints. This has particularly been the case in hotels located in resorts in warm climates.

Executive Chairman's statement to the press

V's Executive Chairman was quoted in the national press in SK in January 2012 as saying, "We are maintaining a comparatively high level of revenues and operating profit. This is in a period when our competitors are experiencing very difficult trading conditions. We feel we are achieving this due to our particular attention to customer service. He cited V's 40 years of experience in the travel industry and a previous 99% satisfaction rating from its customers as the reasons for its success. He went on to state that V intends to expand and diversify its holiday product range to provide more choice to customers.

Board meeting

At the next board meeting which took place after the Executive Chairman's statement to the press, the Operations Director expressed some concern. He cast doubt on whether V was able to provide sufficient funding, marketing and IT/IS resources to enable the product expansion to which the Executive Chairman referred. The Operations Director was of the opinion that V places insufficient emphasis on customer relationship marketing.

The Finance Director added at the same meeting that while V presently remained profitable overall, some products may be more profitable than others.

The Executive Chairman responded by saying that V's high level of customer service provides a sufficiently strong level of sales without the need to incur any other marketing costs. He added that since V achieved a high profit to sales ratio, which it has managed to maintain for a number of years, it really didn't matter about the profits generated by each customer group.

Retirement of the Executive Chairman

The Executive Chairman formally announced to the Board in July 2012 that he intends to retire on 30 June 2013 and wishes to sell part of his shareholding in the company. The Board members believe the time is now right for V, given its expansion plans, to enter a new stage in its financing arrangements, in the form of either debt or equity from new providers.

APPENDIX 1

Extracts from V's income statement and statement of financial position

Income statement for the year ended 30 June 2012

	Notes	*SK$ million*
Revenue		250
Operating costs		(215)
Net operating profit		35
Interest income		3
Finance costs		(4)
Corporate income tax	1	(10)
PROFIT FOR THE YEAR		24

Statement of financial position as at 30 June 2012

	Notes	*SK$ million*
ASSETS		
Non-current assets		123
Current assets		
Inventories		3
Trade and other receivables		70
Cash and cash equivalents		37
Total current assets		110
Total assets		233
EQUITY AND LIABILITIES		
Equity		
Share capital	2	9
Share premium		6
Retain earnings		60
Total equity		75
Non-current liabilities		
Long-term borrowings	3	50
Revenue received in advance		3
Current liabilities		
Trade and other payables		35
Revenue received in advance		70
Total liabilities		158
Total equity and liabilities		233

Notes:

1. The corporate income tax rate can be assumed to be 30%.
2. There are 90 million SK$0.10 (10 cent) shares currently in issue.
3. 30% of the long-term borrowings are due for repayment on 30 June 2014. The remainder is due for re-payment on 30 June 2020. There are debt covenants in operation currently which restrict V from having a gearing ratio measured by long-term debt divided by long-term debt plus equity of more than 50%.

SECTION A – 50 marks

[You are advise to spend no longer than 90 minutes on this question]

Answer this question

Question 1

Unseen Case Material

Customer profitability

At a recent Board meeting the Executive Chairman stated that he was not concerned with the level of profitability generated by each customer as, overall, V has achieved a high profit to sales ratio for a number of years. However, the Finance Director believes that a more detailed understanding of V's product profitability should be carried out by V before making any decision about future product expansion. Also at this Board meeting, the Executive Chairman stated that V should focus on the increasing demand for Prestige Travel holidays and that this is backed up by the fact that V's Prestige Travel products are the best performing for the business, based upon revenue earned.

Following the Board meeting, the Finance Director instructed the Management Accountant to undertake an analysis of the revenues, cost of sales and administration costs associated with each of V's holiday products. The following information was identified for the year ended 30 June 2012.

	Package	Adventure	Prestige Travel
Revenue from in-branch bookings	SK$9,000,000	SK$3,000,000	SK$85,500,000
Revenue from online bookings	SK$81,000,000	SK$57,000,000	SK$9,500,000
Total Revenue	SK$90,000,000	SK$60,000,000	SK$95,000,000
Cost of sales as a % of Total Revenue	60%	65%	75%

The Management Accountant has also analysed the sales revenues earned from each type of holiday product.

Average sales price of a holiday product booked in-branch	SK$3,000	SK$2,000	SK$5,000
Average sales price of a holiday product booked online	SK$2,700	SK$1,900	SK$5,000

Note: A 'holiday product booked' refers to a total holiday package and may vary in terms of the number of people booked onto each package. For example, a 'Package' holiday product may include 4 people (2 adults and 2 children). A 'Prestige Travel' holiday product may only include 2 people.

V's administration costs

In order to establish the net operating profit of each of V's holiday products, the Management Accountant has analysed the total administration costs of V. These administration costs are in addition to the cost of sales. He has identified that there are four administrative processes carried out by V's staff that make up the total administration costs, which are nearly all fixed. The Management Accountant has determined the average cost for each administrative process, which is shown below:

Administrative process	Average cost per process
1. In-branch holiday order processing	SK$600 per holiday product booked in-branch
2. Online holiday order processing	SK$200 per holiday product booked online
3. Late booking processing	SK$400 per late booking processed
4. After-sales queries/ complaints processing	SK$550 per after sales query/ complaint

Other information:	Package	Adventure	Prestige Travel
Late bookings processed as a % of total holiday products booked each year	35%	12%	6%
Number of after sales queries/ complaints as a % of total holiday products booked each year	27%	10%	75%

1. The administration costs of in-branch holiday order processing include the costs incurred in the time taken by branch staff discussing holiday options with customers and the subsequent completion of associated holiday ordering paperwork and administrative activities, including organising flights and hotel accommodation on behalf of the customer.
2. The administration costs of online holiday order processing are significantly less than in-branch costs due to less staff interface and the use of more automated order processing of hotel accommodation and flights.
3. Late booking administration costs are incurred if a customer books a holiday product within 2 weeks of departure. This requires administration time in processing accommodation, foreign currency and arranging flights at short notice. Late bookings, whether booked online or in-branch, are directed straight to a team at V's head office for processing. The costs are treated the same, whether booked online or in-branch. Late booking costs are in addition to the normal order processing costs.
4. After-sales queries administration costs result from customers changing their original bookings or making general enquiries after booking. This may include re-checking or making changes to flight or accommodation details. Sometimes errors occur during the booking process, for example due to staff in-branch processing orders incorrectly or due to customers using the website information incorrectly. Customers' complaints are dealt with by a specialist team at V's head office. Customer complaints are often due to customers being misled by customer sales representatives at the time of booking, largely due to the sales representatives not having sufficient product knowledge.

The Management Accountant has advised the Finance Director that the cost per administrative process identified in the table above are aggregate figures and give the average cost per holiday product booked.

Customer Relationship Marketing and E-business

V's Executive Chairman does not consider marketing to be a primary activity, as historically much of its business has come from word-of-mouth recommendations and repeat business. The Executive Chairman is confident that word-of-mouth recommendations have been successful in the past and will continue to be successful and that the high level of customer service offered by V is a key factor in this. However, the Operations Director, who is responsible for the marketing of V's products, considers that competitive forces have made customer retention more difficult. This is because customers are now more likely to shop around for the best holiday deals and are not necessarily loyal to one holiday tour operator. In particular, the main competitive threat to V appears to come from the proliferation of online holiday tour operators and travel agency services, many of which make use of sophisticated information systems.

The Operations Director believes that customer retention and loyalty could be improved by developing customer relationship marketing and by focusing more on 'e-business' and the use of V's information systems to transact more of its holiday product business.

Required

(a) **Discuss** the benefits to V of following an emergent approach to strategy development rather than undertaking a long-term planning approach. **(5 marks)**

(b) (i) **Analyse**, for each of in-branch and online bookings, the net operating profit and the net operating profit percentage for (i) Package, (ii) Adventure and (iii) Prestige Travel holiday products. **(15 marks)**

(ii) **Discuss** how V could improve the product profitability of each of its three holiday product types.

Your answer should take into account the results of your analysis in (b)(i) and also consider any other information that would be relevant in helping V's Board determine how it could improve its product profitability. **(10 marks)**

(c) (i) **Evaluate** the strategic and competitive impact a Customer Relationship Marketing approach could have on V's customer retention. **(8 marks)**

(ii) **Discuss** TWO strategic benefits and TWO strategic barriers to e-business for V. **(12 marks)**

(Total marks for Question One = 50 marks)

SECTION B – 50 marks

Answer TWO of the three questions in Section B – 25 marks each

Question 2

PPP, an electricity generating company based in a European country, Z, was a monopoly supplier until 1995. Z's Government de-regulated the electricity market in 1995 and since then PPP has faced increasing competition from eight other electricity generating companies competing in Z.

PPP currently generates its electricity using only fossil fuels. However, the electricity generating companies' customers (which supply electricity to the final users within Z) are increasingly concerned about environmental issues. Many of these customers are willing to change to a different electricity generating company which generates some of its electricity from renewable sources.

Since 2010, PPP has lost 5% of its customers to competitors who generate electricity from a range of sources, including renewables.

PPP's organisational structure is hierarchical, its decision making is often slow, and its management style is bureaucratic. Many of PPP's employees belong to trade unions and there is usually much resistance to any new initiatives or changes to working arrangements.

In 2010, Z's Government agreed to conform to an overall European Union target of generating 20% of electricity production from renewable sources such as hydro, nuclear and wind generated power by 2020. In 2011, Z's Government announced plans for incentive payments to be awarded to those electricity generating companies investing in projects to generate renewable energy. Through a government initiative called the 'Renewables Pledge', Z's electricity generators are all now required by law to provide a proportion of their electricity generation from renewable sources or pay a penalty fee to the Government.

In January 2012, the Chief Executive Officer (CEO) of PPP, who had been with the company since the 1970's, retired. He had always been sceptical of the Government's drive towards renewable energy and he had often blocked any initiatives for the company to move towards renewable electricity generation. The new CEO is a strong supporter of wind based electricity generation and he recently stated to the Board of Directors 'if PPP is to survive and thrive, it must develop a strategy for wind powered electricity generation. However, this cannot happen overnight as the old style of management must change so that we remain competitive in the industry. We simply must not continue to lose customers'.

The new CEO wishes to exploit Z's windy countryside in the north of the country for wind powered electricity generation. However, gaining planning permission for wind powered generators has proved to be difficult so far in Z. Many proposals have been delayed in the planning system, often due to local residents' opposition. On average, the planning application for a wind powered generator in Z takes 2 years for a decision to be made by local government. The national Government is introducing new laws to force local governments to make decisions more quickly.

The new technology needed to operate and manage wind powered electricity generation will require extensive investment and training in new techniques and skills and require changes to PPP's culture. PPP's engineers have threatened strike action in order to gain large pay increases to compensate for the new working arrangements. Large pay increases would make PPP uncompetitive in the industry.

Required

(a) **Explain** the internal and external triggers for change which have prompted the need for PPP to develop a strategy for wind powered electricity generation. **(6 marks)**

(b) **Evaluate**, using Lewin's Force Field Analysis model, the forces which are driving and restraining change in PPP. **(8 marks)**

(c) **Evaluate**:

(i) the **type** of change, in terms of speed and extent, which needs to occur in PPP in relation to both the move to wind powered electricity generation and its management culture. **(3 marks)**

(ii) the methods of managing resistance to change for PPP. **(8 marks)**

(Total for Question Two = 25 marks)

Question 3

GGG is a privately owned unlisted company which runs 20 residential care homes for the elderly. A residential care home for the elderly is a building where a number of older people live and receive care (that is, their physical needs are provided for), normally on a full-time basis. The elderly residents may pay the care home fees themselves or they may be paid by their relatives or by the local government authority.

The elderly residents of GGG's care homes are all capable of making decisions for themselves. All of GGG's care homes are located in and around two cities both located in the south of country X. GGG employs around 400 staff in the care homes, some of whom work part-time, and a small team of highly experienced administrators. GGG's care homes all have modern facilities and their staff are highly trained and dedicated. GGG has always been a profitable business, even though its care homes normally have a small amount of spare capacity. GGG has approximately 25% market share in the south of country X. The remainder of the market is shared by a small number of local government funded and operated care homes and some other small private businesses.

Due to the rising costs of operating care homes as a result of increased regulation and the general economic environment, a number of small privately owned care homes in the region have recently closed. The owners of some other privately owned care homes are considering closing or selling them. GGG is also aware that this trend is occurring nationally across country X.

A national shift in the demographics of the population in the last 30 years has resulted in a significant rise in the proportion of elderly members of society. Added to this, the increased social movement of families has resulted in an increasing demand for care home places for the elderly. GGG undertakes limited advertising, relying more on word-of-mouth recommendations and referrals from local hospitals and doctors to obtain its customers.

The prices charged to care home residents by the local government authority run care homes are lower than those charged by GGG, due to central government subsidies. However, the Managing Director of GGG is confident that the services and facilities provided by GGG are superior to those offered by the local government funded care homes.

Although GGG currently offers only full-time care for its elderly residents, there is a growing need for the market to offer 'relief care' packages. This is where elderly people, who do not normally live in residential care homes, could use any of the 20 care homes' facilities for short periods of time (normally 1 week), in order to enable their normal carers (usually family members) to take holidays or rest periods.

A number of GGG's elderly residents are often referred to local hospitals by their doctors for treatments and therapies. Many of GGG's staff are fully qualified nurses and these treatments and therapies could be undertaken by the staff of GGG in each of its care homes. These hospital visits for treatments and therapies can be disruptive and upsetting for residents who often prefer to remain in GGG's care homes and be cared for by staff with whom they are familiar. However, if GGG were to offer these additional facilities within its care homes it will need investment in training and new facilities.

Required

(a) **Analyse** the opportunities available to GGG, using Ansoff's strategic directional growth vector matrix. **(10 marks)**

(b) **Evaluate** the opportunities available to GGG in each of the four areas of the Ansoff strategic directional growth vector matrix using Johnson, Scholes and Whittington's Suitability, Acceptability and Feasibility framework. **(10 marks)**

(c) **Recommend**, with your justifications, which strategic directions, as set out in Ansoff's strategic directional growth vector matrix, would be most appropriate for GGG to follow. **(5 marks)**

(Total for Question Three = 25 marks)

Question 4

DDD Ltd is a medium sized engineering and manufacturing company. DDD designs, manufactures and installs combined heat and power (CHP) generators. These CHP generators provide an emergency back-up heat and electricity source if the normal national grid service is disrupted. DDD manufactures a range of small off-the-shelf CHP units for offices and shops and these are priced at approximately £20,000 each. DDD also manufactures large bespoke CHP units for customers and these units are priced between £250,000 and £500,000. DDD also provides contract service, repairs and maintenance operations for all of the units it sells. DDD currently has three large bespoke jobs in progress:

- a CHP unit for a large city hospital in its home country;
- two large CHP units for an overseas hotel chain; and
- a CHP unit in a large central government building in its home country.

DDD is very reliant on the expertise and industry knowledge of its staff and DDD often requires them to be able to work on several designs and installations at the same time. However, some of DDD's highly respected senior engineers often complain about difficulties of communication and coordination with senior managers. These senior engineers have also expressed their frustration at their lack of input to decisions. DDD has a high staff turnover compared to other similar organisations.

DDD currently has a functional organisational structure. However, some members of the Board think that the functional structure has sometimes resulted in a lack of integration of the key activities of the company, resulting in job disruption and delays. This can be a significant problem if the customer's contract includes penalties for late delivery of the product or service. Despite having a functional structure, DDD has a highly centralised decision making process, as some of the Directors believe that decentralisation would lead to a loss of control.

The Board of DDD is considering moving towards a divisionalised structure in order to provide more focus. However, having worked for a divisionalised organisation previously, the Finance Director has concerns that this type of structure may adversely affect DDD's performance. The Finance Director has recommended that a more flexible structure be considered. She also believes that a move towards a more decentralised approach to management and control would facilitate flexibility and innovation.

DDD has recently learnt that it has won a large contract for several large bespoke CHP units which will be used to support a major international sporting event which will take place in six years' time. This contract will require DDD's staff to work alongside many different organisations including government agencies, service suppliers, energy and management consultants and other large engineering companies. It will require DDD to design and install a range of CHP products in collaboration with other organisations, working to a fixed deadline date. This is the largest contract that DDD has ever undertaken, estimated to represent about 60% of its total sales revenue for each of the next six years. The Board of Directors is hopeful that if it is successful in delivering this contract, then it could lead to other similar prestigious contracts in the future.

Required

(a) **Evaluate** the benefits and drawbacks to DDD of having:

(i) A functional structure

(ii) A divisional structure **(6 marks)**

(b) **Evaluate** the benefits and drawbacks to DDD of having a centralised as compared to a decentralised decision making process. **(6 marks)**

(c) **Recommend**, with your justifications, an appropriate organisational structure for DDD to enable it to meet the needs of the large contract it has recently won. **(13 marks)**

(Total for Question Four = 25 marks)

Answers

DO NOT TURN THIS PAGE UNTIL YOU HAVE COMPLETED THE MOCK EXAM

A plan of attack

We discussed the problem of which question to start with earlier, in 'Passing the E3' exam. (See page xi, in the front pages of this Kit.) Here we will merely reiterate our view that Question 1 is often the best place to start but, you may decide you would prefer to select a question with no numbers or calculations in it, in which case you should start by doing your best Section B question first. However, if you do decide to start with a 25 mark Section B question, **make sure that you finish your answer in no more than 45 minutes**.

However, once again, make sure you take a good look through the paper before diving in to answer questions.

<u>First things first</u>

In the first five minutes of reading time, look through the paper and work out which questions you are going to do, and the order in which you are going to attempt them.

We recommend you then spend the remaining fifteen minutes of reading time looking at the Section A scenario, identifying key information in the unseen material and highlighting the key requirements in the question.

The extra time spent on Section A will be helpful, regardless of the order in which you intend to answer the questions. If you decide to answer the Section A question first, the time spent will mean you are already immersed in the question when the writing time starts. If you intend to answer the question second or third, probably because you find it daunting, the question may look easier when you come back to it, because your initial analysis could generate further points whilst you're tackling the other questions.

If you are a bit **worried about the paper**, it is likely that you believe the Section A question will be daunting. In this case, you may prefer to do one or both of the optional questions before tackling it. Don't, however, fall into the trap of spending too long on the optional questions because they seem easier. You will still need to spend half of the three hours writing time available on the Section A Case Study, because it is worth 50% of the marks.

It's dangerous to be over-confident, but if you're **not too nervous** about the exam then you should turn straight to the compulsory Section A question, and tackle it first. You've got to answer it, so you might as well get it over and done with.

Make sure you answer every requirement and sub-requirement in the question, and also make sure you include plenty of examples from the scenario. Bear in mind that one thing you are being tested on is your **ability to apply your knowledge** to deal with the specific issues identified in the scenario.

<u>Analysing the questions</u>

Examiners are continually frustrated by candidates' apparent inability to dissect the requirements of a question correctly.

If you do not analyse the question requirements thoroughly, you are likely to produce answers which are largely irrelevant to the question. So, make sure you do the following:

- Dissect the question requirements: what are the precise issues the examiner want you to address?
- Identify all the requirements in the question: is there more than one requirement?
- Be aware of the verb used in the question. What 'level' is the verb, based on CIMA's verb requirements, and therefore how far do you have to apply or use your knowledge to answer the question.

<u>The questions themselves</u>

- **Question 1** – Reading the pre-seen material (in advance of sitting the exam) should have alerted you to the increasing importance of online bookings for V travel business; and, perhaps not surprisingly, e-business is a key theme in Question 1.

  The question starts (part (a)) with a discussion of the benefits of emergent strategy (for 5 marks), but then the focus of part (b) is product profitability. Part (b) is worth 25 marks in total, and so forms the heart of this question.

  Part (b) (i) is, in effect, a product profitability analysis, and you need to work through it step by step to work out the profitability of the different products. However, you then need to use what you have found out about the differing profitability of different products and delivery channels in your answer to part (b) (ii): to discuss how the company's profitability could be increased. The contrast between the profitability of the online business and the (much lower) profitability of the in-branch business is a key issue here; picking up the theme from the pre-seen about the increasing importance of the online business.

However, whilst identifying the factors which cause the various types of holidays to have different profitabilities is important, the main focus of part (b) (ii) is actually how the company can improve the profitability of each of its products. In other words, how can it use the information from the profitability analysis to increase the products' profitability?

Part (c) tests your understanding of relationship marketing. However, to score well here you need to apply your understanding of relationship marketing specifically to the scenario. In particular you need to consider how much impact relationship marketing could have in helping the company retain customers – in the context of (the increasingly competitive) travel market.

Part (c) (ii) returns to the idea of e-business, and you should have found this a relatively easy requirement to end the question. However, to score well, you mustn't simply discuss benefits and barriers to e-business in general terms, but you need to apply them specifically to the scenario (including .

- **Question 2** tests your understanding of various aspects of change management: triggers for change; force field analysis; types of change; and methods for overcoming resistance to change. You shouldn't have found this question too daunting, given these are all core aspects of change management. However, it is important that you analyse all the requirements before you start planning your answer; in particular so that you avoid repeating yourself between parts (a) and (b). For part (a) you need only to *identify* what forces are driving change, but then in part (b) you need to go further and *evaluate* how strong they are; and how the strength of these driving forces compares to the strength of any forces resisting change.

- **Question 3** examines two key strategic frameworks: (i) Ansoff's matrix; and (ii) the Suitability, Acceptability, and Feasibility framework. So, hopefully, this is another question which should not have appeared too daunting. Moreover, the scenario identifies a number of opportunities which are available to the company in question, you should have been able to score a number of marks in part (a) purely by working through the scenario, identifying the opportunities, and then classifying them in the appropriate place in Ansoff's matrix.

  As with question 2, it is important here as well that your answers to part (b) don't simply repeat your answers from part (a). The logic between the two parts should be quite clear though. In part (a) you need to identify what the opportunities are; then in part (b) you need to evaluate whether these different opportunities are suitable, acceptable or feasible. On the basis of their suitability, acceptability and feasibility, you then need to recommend the most suitable opportunities (part (c)).

- **Question 4** looks at various issues to do with organisational structure. A lot of the theoretical ideas here should be familiar from E2. However, to score well in this question it is important that you evaluate the benefits and drawbacks of the different structures in relation to the scenario, rather than in generic terms.

  It is also important that you look at how the mark allocations were divided between the various parts of this question. The two 'evaluations' in parts (a) and (b) are only worth 6 marks each; while the 'recommendation' in part (c) is worth 13 marks. Therefore, it is important that you don't spend too long on parts (a) and (b) and don't leave yourself any time for part (c), which accounts for marginally over half the marks available for the question.

On which note, we repeat the points that we have stressed many times before. However, they can never be stressed enough:

Always make sure you **allocate your time** according to the marks for the question in total and for the parts of the questions.

And always, always **follow the verbs in the requirements exactly**.

You've got free time at the end of the exam...?

If you have allocated your time properly then you **shouldn't have time on your hands** at the end of the exam. If you find yourself with five or ten minutes spare, however, go back to **any parts of questions that you didn't finish** because you ran out of time.

Forget about it!

And don't worry if you found the paper difficult. It is more than likely that other students did too. However, once you've finished the exam you cannot change your answers so don't spend time worrying about them. Instead, you should start thinking about your next exam and preparing for that.

SECTION A

Question 1

Text reference: Approaches to strategic management are covered in Chapter 1 of the BPP Study Text. Relationship marketing, e-marketing and e-business are discussed in Chapter 8.

(a)

Top tips:

Although the context of this question is looking at the benefits of having an emergent approach to strategy rather than having a long-term planning approach, the focus of your answer needs to be specifically on the emergent approach, rather than being a comparison between the two.

A sensible place to start would be with a brief definition of emergent strategy, before moving on to look at its benefits.

It is important that you note the question asks you to *discuss* the *benefits* of an emergent approach. Note the verb is 'discuss', not, for example 'evaluate'. And not you are only asked to discuss the benefits, not the benefits and drawbacks, of such an approach. This means you must focus solely on the benefits; there are no marks available for discussing the drawbacks of using an emergent approach.

Equally, there are no marks available for discussing, or criticising a long-term planning approach.

Finally, make sure you relate the benefits of an emergent approach specifically to V, rather than just discussing them in general terms.

Emergent strategy – The key feature of emergent approaches to strategy is that they allow an organisation's strategy to develop, and evolve, over time; rather than being defined in advance as a result of a formal strategic planning process.

Responsiveness to change – A key benefit of having a strategy which evolves over time is that it will allow V to respond to **external triggers** (such as changing customer requirements) or changes in the external environment (such as new technologies) without having to keep changing a strategy which it has prescribed previously.

Product change – Also, by not being restricted to a long-term plan (for example, to sell packages to specific countries or regions only) V will be able to respond to **changing customer demands** and **market trends**. For example, if new types of holiday or new destinations become more popular, V will be able to change the packages it offers, or the price of its packages, in order to meet customer demand.

Process change – Equally, V also has to be able to respond effectively to changes in processes or technology. For example, five years ago it realised that in order to compete effectively, it had to adapt its business model and start selling holidays online as well as through its branch network. As competition in the industry intensifies, it will become increasingly important for V to be able to respond quickly and creatively to new trends, so that it doesn't get left behind by competitors.

Flexibility – The holiday market itself is likely to be an evolving one. Customers' preferences for the types of holidays they want, the destinations they want to visit, or the activities they want to include in their holidays are likely to change over time. This again highlights that V needs to be able to adapt to such changes, and an emergent approach an emergent strategy provides it with a strategic flexibility to do so which a more prescriptive, long-term approach might not.

Bottom up approach – In addition, there are likely to be occasions when V's shop staff and customer service representatives (who are dealing regularly with customers) get a better insight into customer requirements than V's senior management have. Staff can then adapt their behaviour or approach to fit with customer requirements, rather than having to follow an approach which has been dictated, top-down, by V's senior management.

Motivation – Moreover, the flexibility and ability to shape their own future (which emergent approaches give V's staff and managers) should help maintain their motivation levels. In addition, the emergent approach could also help V harness manager's creativity when shaping its future plans and strategies.

(b)

Top tips.

Part (b) (i): The subject area which this question covers is product profitability. However, although the verb requirement is 'analyse' what you actually need to do in part (i) is to calculate the profitability of V's different product types and distribution channels.

Make sure you understand exactly what calculations are required – and what a suitable layout will be – before starting your answer though. The requirement specifically identifies that you need to distinguish between the profitability of holidays booked in-branch and those booked online, so you need to calculate six different profitabilities: (i) Package in-branch; (ii) Package online; (iii) Adventure in-branch; (iv) Adventure online; (v) Prestige in-branch; (vi) Prestige online.

As the calculations for the costs of late bookings and after sales queries are based on figures for product totals, it seems sensible to structure the calculations by product, and this is the approach we have taken in the suggestion solution below.

The number of calculations required (for 15 marks) should have alerted you to the fact that there would be little (or no) time left for any analysis of the figures you have calculated. There are 15 marks available in total, so each 'profitability' calculated is worth 2.5 marks.

In effect, your opportunity to analyse the figures comes in part (ii). Before you can recommend ways to improve profitability (as required in part (ii)) you need to understand the relative costs and profitability of each of the products. You also need to identify what the largest cost items are: for example, after-service costs for Prestige travel.

However, your answer to part (b) (ii) must not simply be an analysis of the costs and profitabilities of the different products or sales channels. Although there are some marks available for this kind of an analysis (provided you add some insight, rather than simply repeating the figures or percentages) the main focus of your answer for **part (b) (ii)** should be how V can *improve* the profitability of the three different product types. In effect, the key word in the requirement is 'how.' What can V do differently in order to improve its profitability? For example; increasing the proportion of holidays booked online rather than in-branch.

Note also that the requirement refers to improving the profitability of 'each of [V's] holiday product types.' Therefore, you need to look at each of the three product types (Package; Adventure; and Prestige) individually, rather than suggesting more general improvements aimed at increasing the profitability of V's products as a whole.

(i)

Package holidays

	In-branch	*Online*	*Total*
Revenue	9,000,000	81,000,000	90,000,000
Gross margin	3,600,000	32,400,000	
Administrative costs			
Order processing (W1) (SK$600 each in branch; SK$200 online)	1,800,000	6,000,000	
Late booking (W2 × SK$400 each)	420,000	4,200,000	
After-sales (W3 × SK$550 each)	445,500	4,455,000	
Total administrative costs	2,665,500	14,655,000	
Net Operating Profit	**934,500**	**17,745,000**	**18,679,500**
Net Operating Profit %	**10.4%**	**21.9%**	**20.8%**

Workings

W1

Revenue	9,000,000	81,000,000
Average sales price	3,000	2,700
Number booked	3,000	30,000

	In-branch	Online
W2		
Late bookings; % of total number booked	35%	35%
Late bookings	1,050	10,500
W3		
After-sales queries %	27%	27%
After-sales queries	810	8,100

Adventure holidays

	In-branch	*Online*	*Total*
Revenue	3,000,000	57,000,000	60,000,000
Gross margin	1,050,000	19,950,000	
Administrative costs			
Order processing (W1) (SK$600 each in branch; SK$200 online)	900,000	6,000,000	
Late booking (W2 × SK$400 each)	72,000	1,440,000	
After-sales (W3 × SK$550 each)	82,500	1,650,000	
Total administrative costs	1,054,500	9,090,000	
Net Operating Profit	**(4,500)**	**10,860,000**	**10,855,500**
Net Operating Profit %	**-0.2%**	**19.1%**	**18.1%**

Workings		
W1		
Revenue	3,000,000	57,000,000
Average sales price	2,000	1,900
Number booked	1,500	30,000
W2		
Late bookings; % of total number booked	12%	12%
Late bookings	180	3,600
W3		
After-sales queries %	10%	10%
After-sales queries	150	3,000

Prestige travel

	In-branch	*Online*	*Total*
Revenue	85,500,000	9,500,000	95,000,000
Gross margin	21,375,000	2,375,000	
Administrative costs			
Order processing (W1) (SK$600 each in branch; SK$200 online)	10,260,000	380,000	
Late booking (W2 × SK$400 each)	410,400	45,600	
After-sales (W3 × SK$550 each)	7,053,750	783,750	
Total administrative costs	17,724,150	1,209,350	
Net Operating Profit	**3,650,850**	**1,165,650**	**4,816,500**
Net Operating Profit %	**4.3%**	**12.3%**	**5.1%**

Workings	*In-branch*	*Online*
W1		
Revenue	85,500,000	9,500,000
Average sales price	5,000	5,000
Number booked	17,100	1,900
W2		
Late bookings; % of total number booked	6%	6%
Late bookings	1,026	114
W3		
After-sales queries %	75%	75%
After-sales queries	12,825	1,425

(ii)

Tutorial Note: There are a number of valid points you could make here, and we have tried to include a range of them in the solution below. However, you would not need to make all of the points we have included to score well in this question.

Prestige Travel

Increase proportion of online sales – V's Prestige travel products currently generate a significantly lower net operating profit percentage (5.1%) than the other two product types (which generate 18.1% and 20.8% respectively).

At the same time, V sells a significantly higher proportion of Prestige holidays than other product types in-branch.

	Total	*In branch*	%	*Online*	%
Prestige	19,000	17,100	90.0%	1,900	10.0%
Package	33,000	3,000	9.1%	30,000	90.9%
Adventure	31,500	1,500	4.8%	30,000	95.2%

Administration costs – This mix between in-branch and online sales is a major reason why V's Prestige products generate the lowest profitability. As the table below illustrates, the administrative costs associated with in-branch orders are higher than for online sales, for all products. Consequently, the higher the proportion of sales made in-branch the lower the net operating margin is likely to be.

	Total admin costs (SK $)	*Products booked*	*Cost per booking (SK $)*
Package			
In-branch	2,665,500	3,000	888.50
Online	14,655,000	30,000	488.50
Total	17,320,500	33,000	524.86
Adventure			
In-branch	1,054,500	1,500	703.00
Online	9,090,000	30,000	303.00
Total	10,144,500	31,500	322.05
Prestige			
In-branch	17,724,150	17,100	1,036.50
Online	1,209,350	1,900	636.50
Total	18,933,500	19,000	996.50

Therefore, V could improve the product profitability of its Prestige products by increasing the proportion sold online.

Customer preferences – However, it would be useful for V to have more information about why its customers choose to buy Prestige products in-branch rather than online. If there are specific reasons which dissuade customers from buying Prestige products online, V could then address those issues, with a view to making online booking a more attractive proposition. For example, it may be that the customers feel that there isn't sufficient information available on V's online site to answer any questions they may have when compiling a bespoke travel package.

Discount levels – Alternatively, V could review its pricing policy and the level of discounts its offers to customers for booking online. In particular, V should consider what impact increasing the level of online discount might have on the mix of bookings between online and in-branch, and what the resulting impact of this might be on profitability.

Reduce level of after sales queries/complaints – The table of costs above shows that, even after allowing for the different mix in booking methods, the administrative costs incurred for Prestige products are still significantly higher than for other products. This is due to the number of after sales queries and/or complaints associated with Prestige products, which, at 75% of the number of products booked seems very high. Therefore, in order to improve profitability, V needs to reduce the number of these queries or complaints.

Understand reasons for after-sales queries - It is not clear what proportion of after-sales queries come from customers wishing to check or change their accommodation details, and what proportion come from customers complaining that they were misled when the sales representative made their booking. However, it will be important for V to collate this information, and then to analyse how the current booking process could be improved to reduce the level of after-sales queries (for example, by giving the sales representatives more training to improve their product knowledge.)

Equally, V should consider whether it could use IT systems to automate any aspects of after sales service, thereby reducing the cost of them. For example, it may be possible to allow customers to re-check bookings or make changes to their flights via an automated process, rather than having to contact the after-sales administration department directly.

Gross margin – V could also investigate why the gross margin it earns on prestige products (25%) is significantly lower than for the other products; for example, if it cannot benefit from any economies of scale (buying in bulk) when buying accommodation for 'bespoke' holidays.

If V could increase the underlying gross margin for Prestige travel this would improve its product profitability, regardless of how successful any cost reductions are. However, despite the Prestige holidays being 'expensive and bespoke' it is not clear how much scope there is for V to increase its prices; and what factors are causing this margin to be lower than that for other products.

<u>Adventure holidays</u>

Cost efficiency – The cost per booking for Adventure holidays is the lowest of the three product types, for both online and in-branch sales. In particular, the level of after sales queries and complaints for Adventure holidays (10% of total bookings) is significantly lower than for the other two products. This may reflect the fact that 95% of adventure holidays are booked online, so there is no risk of customers' requirements being misinterpreted by a sales representative during the booking process.

However, more generally, V should consider if there any aspects of the booking process for Adventure holidays which are different to those for the other products types, but which could be replicated for Package or Prestige travel in order to reduce the costs associated with them.

Consider offering online only – Adventure holidays have the lowest average sales price of the three types of product. This suggests that a 'low price, low cost' business model is the most appropriate for Adventure holidays. In particular, given the difference in administrative costs between bookings made in-branch and those made online, V could improve profitability by ensuring that the proportion of people booking on line is as high as possible.

Although 95% of Adventure holiday products are already bought online, this still leaves 5% being bought in-branch, and V makes a small loss on these products. Consequently, V could consider whether it stops offering Adventure holidays in-branch, and makes them only available online instead.

Package holidays

Late bookings – Although V's Package holidays generate the highest overall margin (20.8%) their average costs per booking are still significantly higher than those for Adventure holidays. One reason for this appears to be the proportion of late bookings which are made for Package holidays.

Given the choice of selling a holiday package at the last minute or not selling one at all, it is still more profitable for V to sell a package through a late booking. However, V should consider whether it can offer **discounts,** for example in the period three to four weeks before departure, to encourage customers to book earlier so it can avoid the costs associated with late bookings.

Alternatively, V could consider whether it only allows customers to **make late bookings online** so that it doesn't also incur the higher, in-branch costs associated with the booking.

After sales queries/complaints – The level of after sales queries and complaints is also relatively high for Package holidays (compared to Adventure holidays) so V should consider if this can be reduced in order to reduce costs and thereby improve profitability.

However, as we noted in relation to Prestige travel, it is not clear what proportion of the after-sales queries come from customers wishing to check or change their accommodation details, and what proportion come from customers complaining that they were misled when the sales representative made their booking. Here again, it will be important for V to analyse the reasons for the calls, and then assess whether the current booking process could be improved, and whether elements of the after sales service can be automated.

(c)

Top tips:

The verb here is to 'evaluate' the impact a CRM approach could have. So you need to think of the benefits such an approach could have for V; but then also whether there are any factors which could restrict how beneficial it will be. For example, given the proliferation of travel booking websites, how important will loyalty actually be to customers, compared to getting the best prices available?

Although the question refers to the 'strategic' and 'competitive' impact of a CRM approach, the focus of your answer should be on the 'impact' a CRM approach could have on V's business rather than trying to categorise impacts as to whether they are 'strategic' or 'competitive'.

Equally, note that the primary emphasis here is on the impact of relationship marketing, not relationship management; so, for example, you shouldn't spend time discussing the benefits to V of data mining, or customer profiling.

(i)

Customer relationship marketing – If V develops a customer relationship marketing approach this will mean it uses its marketing resources to retain its existing customers and make additional sales to them, rather than using its marketing resources solely to attract new customers. As such, a large proportion of V's marketing efforts will focus on developing long-term relationships with its existing customers, and securing their loyalty.

V should look to implement a relationship marketing approach through effective **customer relationship management**.

Strategic impact

Excellent customer service - In order for a CRM approach to be successful, V will need to develop and maintain **mutually valuable relationships** with its customers. In turn, this means that it will need to demonstrate a **clear commitment to its customers' needs**.

The level of customer complaints, particularly in relation to Prestige travel, suggests that V is not currently meeting its customer needs as well as it could do. However, adopting a CRM approach should encourage V to place greater emphasis on customer service; for example, customer sales representatives cannot afford to mislead customers at the time of booking if V hopes to develop a long-term relationship with those customers. Conversely, if V's customer sales representatives received more **training** – to improve their product knowledge and their customer service skills – this should result in improved customer loyalty and retention.

Proactive marketing – V's current approach appears to be rather passive; relying on word-of-mouth recommendations and repeat business. If V introduces a CRM approach, this will require it to take a more proactive approach to marketing; for example, contacting existing customers with details of holidays which may be of interest to them. This kind of reminder advertising could encourage customers to book their next holiday through V, in preference to using another travel agent.

Information systems – The success of this kind of advertising could also depend the quality of V's information systems. For example, V could look to capture data on customers' previous bookings, and then use data mining software to identify possible future bookings a customer may be interested in, based on their past bookings. However, it is not clear how much data V captures through its information systems, and therefore whether it has the IS/IT capability to implement such an initiative.

Value of relationship – Crucially, though, CRM will only have a beneficial impact on V's customer retention levels if customers feel that maintaining their relationship with V is valuable to them. Therefore, V will need to obtain feedback from any marketing activities to analyse whether customers perceived any value from the marketing, and from V, and whether this will encourage them to remain loyal to V.

<u>Competitive impact</u>

Competitive pressures – As the Operations Director has highlighted, the proliferation of online holiday tour operators and travel agency services has significantly increased the amount of choice customers have about where to book their holidays.

This increased choice is likely to make it harder for V to retain customers. In addition, the fact that customers are increasingly likely to shop around for the best holiday deals means they are less likely to remain loyal to a single travel agent.

These competitive pressures could limit the benefits which V may achieve by introducing a CRM approach, especially if customers are motivated by getting the best deal they can for a single transaction, rather than remaining loyal to a single provider.

Generic strategy – It seems that V is looking to differentiate itself from its competitors by the high levels of customer service it offers its customers. Again, though, if customers are motivated by getting the best holiday deal they can, it is debatable how important customer service will be for them when choosing which provider to use. In which case, a CRM approach will have relatively little benefit on V's customer retention rates.

Discounts – However, one way in which V could encourage loyalty, whilst recognising customers' desire to get good deals, would be to offer customers incentives or discounts on their next booking.

(ii)

Top tips:

Note the requirement refers to the benefits and barriers relating to e-*business*, rather than specifically e-*commerce*. Therefore you should consider aspects of e-procurement, and e-marketing, for example, and not just online sales.

Note also that the question asks specifically for TWO benefits and TWO barriers. As there are 12 marks available, this suggests there are three marks available for each benefit or barrier you discuss. You can only expect to score up to 1 mark for identifying a relevant barrier or benefit. The other 2 marks for each will come from discussing them; examining how (or why) the factors you have identified present a benefit or barrier to e-business at V.

<u>Strategic benefits</u>

1. New distribution channels

Online sales –The calculations in part (b) highlighted that packages sold online are more profitable for V than packages sold in-branch, due to the higher administrative costs incurred in-branch. Therefore if V can increase its level of online bookings this should improve the profitability of the company as a whole. Equally, if V can increase its online revenues, it could consider closing some, or all, of its branches, thereby reducing the costs associated with running them.

Increased coverage - In addition, increasing its online presence should allow V to reach a wider audience. Not only can customers throughout SK book holidays via V's online site (regardless of whether or not they live close to one of its branches), but V could also use links with other websites, or click-throughs, to increase the number of potential customers who visit its website and use its services.

Upstream supply chain – V may also be able to use e-business to improve the way it buys holiday accommodation and flights from hotels and airlines. It is possible that V could reduce its procurement costs and overheads through having improved linkages with its main suppliers. This in turn should also help V increase its profitability

2. Improved customer offering

Product information – A number of customer complaints arise as a result of customer sales representatives having insufficient product knowledge and misleading customers when they are making bookings. However, an e-business solution would mean customers would no longer have to deal with individual customer sales representatives, but could find details of possible accommodation, flights and packages on V's website. Whereas the level of service customers receive from different representatives could vary, the website will remove this variety, by providing a standardised message to all customers.

Equally, it will be easier for V to update the website for new products, and new deals, than it will be to share that information with all the customer sales representatives in its shops. Similarly, if V has e-mail addresses for customers or prospective customers (who have registered an interest in its products in the past) it can send them details of new products they may be interested in.

Possible other benefits:

Targeted marketing – E-business could also help V in relation to e-marketing and customer retention. If customers book their holidays online, this will allow V to develop a database of customer details and holidays booked. V could then use details about customers' interests and previous bookings as the basis for targeted marketing messages to those customers. If V is able to apply targeted marketing successfully, and suggest future holidays which appeal specifically to individual customers, this should increase the likelihood of those customers booking their holidays through V. (In this respect, e-business could play an important role if V decides to introduce a CRM approach).

Reduced publishing costs – It is likely that V currently incurs significant costs by producing large published brochures of holidays. These are unlikely to be a cost effective means of promotion, particularly if customers is only interested in one or two holidays within the brochure as a whole. In this way, if V reduces the amount and size of the published literature it produces, for example, by making this information available on line instead, such a change could help reduce its costs.

Decision making and control – It is not clear whether the management information and customer information collated from V's branches is as detailed as that which can be gathered from online sales. It is possible that V could receive better (or more detailed) information from online sales, which could then be used for control and decision-making. For example, looking at detailed analysis of the profitability of different types of holidays, or different types of customers, could provide some insight into ways to grow the business or increase profitability in future.

Strategic barriers

1. Customer preferences

Personalised service – It is likely that some customers, particularly those booking bespoke Prestige Travel holidays prefer to book their holidays in person, dealing with a customer sales representative, rather than online. There is a danger that if V no longer offers these customers an in-branch service they will switch to a different travel agent which does rather than using V's online service. This risk of losing these customers could therefore be a strategic barrier to e-business.

Although the number of customers who want this personal service may be relatively small, it is likely that they will be buying luxury, expensive holidays. Therefore, the revenue which V could lose if these customers took their business elsewhere is likely to be disproportional to the number of customers affected.

2. Costs

IT infrastructure – It is likely that V will have to upgrade its IT infrastructure to support its e-business operations. Any such upgrade could be expensive, and if V's management do not believe the benefits from e-business will justify the cost, they may oppose this expenditure.

Staff – Equally, e-business will require an extensive mix of staff - such as web designers, web technology support engineers, e-marketers; online security staff – and V may not currently employ the necessary staff. Again, there will be costs involved with recruiting the additional staff required.

Security – Finally, there could also be costs incurred to ensure the security of V's information systems. Data security needs to be paramount, since V will be holding confidential customer data. If there are concerns that V's current systems could be hacked into, or corrupted, then V will need to invest in additional systems security to reduce the risk of this happening. Equally, if customers are not confident that V's systems are secure, they are unlikely to be prepared to use them until any potential security weaknesses have been addressed.

Question 2

Text reference: Triggers for change, Force Field analysis, and Kotter & Schlesinger's methods of overcoming resistance to change are all discussed in Chapter 11 of the BPP Study Text. Types of change are covered in Chapter 12.

Importantly, however, there is relatively little 'text book knowledge' required to answer this question. By contrast, the information provided by the scenario is crucial, and you must make use of this in your answer.

Top tips:

Part (a): The scenario identifies a number of factors which have prompted PPP to develop wind powered electricity generation: for example, a new CEO who supports it; government regulations and initiatives designed to promote renewable energy; and changing customer attitudes.

Therefore, the 'triggers' you include in your answer should refer specifically to these factors identified in the scenario. You shouldn't introduce any additional triggers of your own.

Part (b): It is important that you recognise the way parts (a) and (b) of this question relate to each other, so that you don't end up simply repeating points from part (a) in part (b). The difference in verb requirements between the two parts is crucial.

In part (a) you are only asked to 'explain' what the triggers are. In part (b) you are asked to 'evaluate' the forces driving – and resisting – change. So your focus in part (b) shouldn't be on what the different forces are, but rather how strong they are. The key point about Force Field analysis is that it identifies that in order for change to be implemented successfully, the forces driving change have to be stronger than the forces resisting it.

Part (c) (i): Although the question refers to two potential changes (the move to wind powered electricity; and a change of management culture) you are asked to evaluate one *type* of change [singular] which would be needed to enable both changes.

Moreover, given that there are only *three marks* available for this part of the question, you cannot afford to spend too long on this part of the question. You should (briefly) identify the speed of change required; the extent of change required; and then decide which type of change would be most appropriate for that combination of speed and extent.

Part (c) (ii): Here again, note the verb requirement is 'evaluate'. This means it is not sufficient simply to list, or even discuss, different methods of managing change in generic terms. Instead you need to consider the different possible methods of managing change (or, more precisely, overcoming resistance to change) specifically in the context of PPP. In other words, would the different methods be appropriate and/or effective in this context?

For example, the scenario has identified that a large number of PPP's staff are union members, and the engineers have already threatened strike action. So this suggests that some kind of negotiation is likely to be essential in order to overcome the staff (and the unions') resistance to change.

(a)

Internal triggers

New CEO – The new CEO is a strong supporter of wind based electricity generation, whereas the previous CEO was sceptical about renewable electricity generation. The new CEO has argued that PPP must develop a strategy for wind powered electricity generation if it is to survive and thrive, therefore his appointment – and his position of authority in the company – represent a significant internal change trigger.

Loss of customers - The CEO's reference to 'surviving' and 'thriving' is likely to have been prompted by PPP's recent performance. In the last two years, PPP has lost 5% of its customers to competitors who generate electricity from renewable energy. In this respect, the recognition that PPP needs to start developing power from renewable sources in order to restore its competitiveness and improve customer retention can also be seen as an internal trigger for change.

<u>**External triggers**</u>

Customer concerns – As we have noted above, PPP has lost 5% of its customers in the last two years, to competitors who generate energy from renewable sources. This highlights not only that the PPP's customers are increasingly concerned about environmental issues, but also that they are prepared to switch generating companies to ones which they perceive are environmentally friendly. Therefore, customer pressure is an external trigger for change for PPP. If PPP doesn't start generating some of its electricity from renewable sources, it will becoming increasing unpopular with customers, and its market share will decline further in future.

Legal requirements and penalty fees – Z's government has agreed to conform to the overall European Union target of generating 20% of the country's electricity from renewable sources by 2020. Although this agreement by itself doesn't commit PPP to generating 20% of its electricity from renewable sources, it seems likely that the government's 'Renewable Pledge' initiative is connected to this national target, because the government needs a mechanism for ensuring that it can meet the overall target.

The fact that PPP is now required, by law, to generate a proportion of its electricity from renewable sources is likely to be a very strong external trigger for developing renewable energy (although not specifically wind power). If PPP doesn't comply with the legislation it will have to pay a penalty fee to the Government, which will reduce its profitability. Moreover, if it becomes known that PPP is failing to comply with the legislation (but other electricity generating companies *are* complying with it) this could prompt negative publicity for PPP, causing it to lose further customers.

Incentive schemes – The Government's incentives for electricity generating companies investing in renewable energy projects should make the investments more attractive to PPP. In effect, the government appears to be using 'carrot and stick' tactics; discouraging electricity generation from fossil fuels, whilst encouraging the use of renewable sources. This approach represents a very strong external trigger for change for PPP.

In conjunction with this, the government's legislation to speed up the planning process in relation to wind powered generators, could then make wind powered electricity generation an increasingly attractive source of renewable energy.

(b)

Lewin's Force Field analysis model indicates that, in order for change to be implemented successfully, the forces which are driving change need to be stronger than the forces which are resisting change.

<u>**Forces driving change**</u>

CEO – The new CEO appears to be a **powerful driving force for change**. He believes strongly that PPP needs to start generating wind powered electricity in order to survive and thrive. He also believes that PPP's style of management needs to change in order for PPP to remain competitive. And his position in the company, particularly in relation to his capacity for leading change, is likely to be a key element in driving that change forwards.

Governmental legislation and incentives – Legislation, both at national level and at European Union, also appears to be a strong driver for change. The fact that PPP is required by law to generate a proportion of its electricity from renewable sources suggests it has to change, because it currently generates all its electricity from fossil fuels. In this respect, the legal requirements to develop renewable energy are likely to be the **strongest driving force for change**. Ultimately, if PPP doesn't comply with them, its ability to continue trading successfully could be in jeopardy.

Customers – PPP's customers are becoming increasingly concerned about environmental issues, and they have demonstrated they are prepared to switch providers if their current provider doesn't generate at least some of its electricity from renewable sources. As the market in Z is strongly competitive, pressure from PPP's customers should provide a **strong driving force for change**. If PPP doesn't change it will continue to lose customers, which, again, could ultimately jeopardise its ability to continue trading.

Moreover, the strength of the PPP's customers as a driving force is likely to increase further as the other eight generating companies increase the amount of energy they produce from renewable sources increases. If PPP doesn't follow suit, the distinction between it and the other suppliers will increase, meaning increasing numbers of customers will stop buying their electricity from PPP.

Forces resisting change

Employees – Many of PPP's employees are resistant to change, and the fact that they belong to trade unions is likely to increase the strength of their resistance to change as a group. The unions are likely to be able to co-ordinate resistance to change (for example, through strike action) more effectively than employees acting individually could. PPP's engineers have already threatened to take strike action in response to the proposed new working arrangements.

Therefore, PPP's unionised work force should be seen as a strong force resisting change. However, PPP might be able to weaken this force by explaining why change is necessary, and possibly also negotiating some kind of compromise deals with the staff.

Skills - A secondary resisting force could be the employees' lack of skills required to generate wind powered electricity. However, this force should be seen as relatively weak. Although it will be costly and time-consuming to train staff in the new techniques, PPP should be able to arrange the training required.

Management style – It appears that PPP's current, bureaucratic management style is different from the management style the new CEO thinks PPP needs. However, there is likely to be an inherent resistance from PPP's management and staff towards efforts to change the style and culture of the organisation. Moreover, trying to change the culture of an organisation will be a slow and difficult process.

However, PPP (and, in particular, the CEO) may be able to weaken the resistance to change by explaining the importance of making the changes for the future success of the company. Therefore this force may only be a **relatively weak resisting force**.

Local residents – Objections from people living near proposed sites for wind powered generators appear to have delayed planning permission being granted for many of the sites. If PPP cannot get planning permission to build its generators, this will prevent it implementing its wind powered electricity generation strategy.

However, this force may be weakened by the new laws which the government has introduced aimed at speeding up the planning permission process. Equally, although local residents' groups could lobby the Government to prevent generators being built in their areas, the Government may overrule some of their objections because it knows that 20% of the electricity in Z has to be produced from renewable sources by 2020. Nonetheless, the residents' objections may present a **moderately strong resisting force**.

Evaluation

The two main external driving forces (legislation and customer requirements) both appear very strong. While some of the resisting forces (particularly staff and unions) also appear strong, if PPP communicates why change is crucial for PPP's future success it may be able to reduce the strength of the resistance to change.

(c) (i)

Change can be classified in relation to the **extent** of the change required and the **speed** with which that change has to be achieved.

Extent – The extent of change can range from the overall **transformation** of an organisation's central assumptions, culture and beliefs; to a **realignment** of its existing assumptions without any underlying change in the organisation's existing paradigm.

Speed – Change can range from an all-at-once, 'big bang' event to a series of step-by-step, incremental shifts.

With reference to the extent (scope) and speed(nature) of change required, Balogun and Hope Hailey identified four main types of change: adaptation, reconstruction, evolution and revolution.

Evolution – The move to wind powered generation, and the change in management culture, will both require a change in PPP's paradigm. Therefore PPP needs to implement a transformation process, rather than a realignment.

However, the complexity involved in changing the company's culture, as well as staff attitudes to change, mean that the change process will have to be managed slowly and carefully. Therefore, PPP needs to introduce evolutionary change, rather than revolutionary change.

(c) (ii)

Education and communication – Many of PPP's employees are likely to resist the changes, because they are concerned about the impact the changes will have on their working arrangements. The engineers may also be concerned they will need new skills to do their jobs.

It will be important for PPP to explain to the staff why the changes are required, and how the changes are likely to affect them. In particular, PPP should explain what the potential benefits will be; for example, the new skills which the engineers could learn through the training they will receive. Communicating the reasons for change, and the potential benefits of it, may help overcome the staff's negative perceptions of change.

However, it is important that any communications with the staff are open and honest, and that the staff are given the opportunity to raise any concerns they have about the changes.

Education and communication can often be a time-consuming method of managing change. However, given the evolutionary nature of the changes at PPP, the time taken to overcome change should not be a problem. Therefore, education and communication may be an appropriate method for PPP to use to help manage resistance to change.

Participation and involvement – PPP's staff, particularly the engineers, are likely to be vital to the success of the changes. Therefore, PPP should try to get the staff involved in the change process.

If staff feel they are being involved in the change process they may be less likely to resist it. However, perhaps more importantly, the engineers may be able to help PPP identify potential problems with proposed developments for wind generators, and suggest solutions to those problems.

Local residents are another important stakeholder group which PPP needs to manage. It may be difficult for PPP to get local residents to engage in the change process, rather than simply opposing it. However, PPP could try to get local residents to discuss their objections to the proposals so that it can work with them to revise the proposals in a way which overcomes those objections.

As with education and communication, this could be a time-consuming process; but again, the nature of the change facing PPP means that the speed with which it is implemented is not currently critical.

Facilitation and support – The engineers will need extensive training to develop the techniques and skills required to understand the technology used to generate wind powered electricity. However, although it appears that PPP is prepared to offer this training, PPP's engineers also want large pay increases as a result of the change. In this respect, training 'support' by itself doesn't appear sufficient to overcome their resistance to change. Nonetheless, training will still need to be offered as a key part of the change process, albeit alongside other methods of overcoming resistance.

PPP's staff may also need support in adapting to any changes in the company's culture more generally. For example, staff may need training to explain how the changes in culture and management styles will affect non-technical aspects of their jobs, such as performance management and staff development.

Negotiation and agreement – As many of PPP's staff belong to trade unions, it seems likely that there will need to be some negotiation in order to get them to accept the proposed changes.

The staff, backed by the unions, want large pay increases to compensate them for the new working arrangements, but PPP has argued that any such pay increases would make it uncompetitive in the industry. Equally, however, PPP cannot afford its engineers to take strike action as they have threatened to do.

Consequently, it seems that PPP will have to negotiate with the unions to try to agree a deal on pay and working conditions which will be acceptable to the staff, and yet also enables the company to remain competitive. In this context, PPP could consider using an external mediator to help resolve the disputes between itself and the unions.

Coercion – Although PPP may feel that the quickest way to overcome any resistance to change is to force people to accept it (for example, by making them redundant if they don't), such an approach would not be successful or acceptable.

On the one hand, even if staff accept the changes to protect their jobs, they will resent the changes and their motivation is likely to suffer as a result. On the other hand, perhaps more importantly, if the unions feel that staff are being forced to accept changes, this will increase the risk of strike action being taken.

Moreover, forcing staff to accept change is likely to be **unethical**, and therefore PPP should avoid using coercion as a means of overcoming resistance.

Coercion is only ever likely to be an acceptable method of overcoming resistance to change is rapid change is required. But, as PPP's change is evolutionary rather than revolutionary, that is not the case here.

Question 3

Text reference: Ansoff's matrix is discussed in Chapter 6 of the BPP Study Text. The 'suitability, acceptability and feasibility' framework for evaluating strategic options is discussed in Chapter 7.

Top tips:

Parts (a) and (b) of this question highlight why it is vital to analyse the question requirements before planning your answer. There is a natural progression between the two parts of the question, but if you don't identify this could you end up repeating yourself between (a) and (b).

Part (a) asks you to '*analyse*' the opportunities available; and Part (b) then asks your to '*evaluate*' these same opportunities.

The scenario highlights a number of potential opportunities which are available to GGG, so in part (a) you should identify what these opportunities are, and classify them into the appropriate quadrants of Ansoff's matrix, with reference to the ways in which they can enable GGG to expand (for example, by expanding into new market areas).

Then in **part (b)** you need to consider specifically how suitable, acceptable and feasible the opportunities are for GGG. Crucially, you shouldn't spend time restating what the opportunities are: you've already done this in part (a).

A sensible approach to part (b) would be to take each type of opportunity in turn (market penetration; market development; product development; and diversification) and then evaluate whether it is suitable, acceptable and feasible for GGG.

If you do this successfully, you should be able to generate up to 12 points for this part of the question (four types of opportunity; each analysed for the three aspects of Suitability, Acceptability and Feasibility). Given that there are only 10 marks available, this approach should enable you to score very highly on this part of the question – provided you apply the concepts of Suitability, Acceptability and Feasibility correctly.

Part (c): The linkages between the parts of the question follow through into part (c). Here you need to use your evaluation of the different opportunities (in part (b)) to identify which would be most appropriate for GGG.

However, there are three key points to note about this part of the requirement:

- The verb requirement is 'recommend'; so you must make it clear what you are recommending;
- You are asked to recommend 'strategic directions', not 'opportunities'. So, for example, you should recommend 'Market development'; rather than 'Buying additional care homes in the region'
- The requirement refers to strategic directions, not to a single strategic direction. So you have the opportunity to recommend more than one strategic direction. However, note that you have to justify why you have recommended the direction (or directions) you have; and your justification should be consistent with your evaluation (in part (b)) of the suitability, acceptability and feasibility of the different opportunities.

(a)

Ansoff's matrix suggests that will be four different types of opportunity available to GGG depending on the combination of new or existing products and markets it decides to pursue. These four types of opportunity are: market penetration, market development, product development and diversification.

Market penetration

A market penetration strategy would involve GGG increasing its share of its current market, using its current products.

Opportunities for growth - Currently, GGG only has a 25% share of the residential care home market in the south of X, so there should be scope to increase this share, in particular by attracting residents from other private care homes.

GGG's fees are likely to be significantly higher than the government-funded homes so residents may not be able to afford to move from government-funded homes into GGG's homes. However, a number of privately owned homes have closed recently, while others are considering closing. This should provide GGG with an opportunity to acquire some of their residents.

There seem to be two different opportunities for GGG in this respect. It could either wait until the homes have closed and then try to attract the residents to move into one of its homes. Alternatively, GGG could buy some of the homes which are being sold, as going concerns.

It is likely that GGG will have to increase the amount of advertising it undertakes if it wants to attract residents from other homes.

It may also have to consider reducing its fees, if they are significantly higher than those charged by the other homes. However, given that GGG prides itself on the quality of the services and facilities it offers, it seems unlikely it will want to reduce its fees too much.

Market development

A market development strategy could involve GGG increasing its revenue by offering its current product (residential care homes) in **new geographical areas** or to **different types of customer**. Given that GGG's care homes are run specifically for older people, there seems little scope to expand into different types of customer, without also changing the 'product' it offers. Therefore the opportunities for market development would appear more likely to come from geographical expansion.

Geographical expansion – Currently, GGG's care homes are located in and around two cities only. However, given the favourable demographic trends in X, it seems likely there will be opportunities for GGG to open additional homes. Given GGG's preference for word-of-mouth recommendations and referrals from local hospitals, it may prefer to focus its expansion on other cities in the south of X relatively close to its existing homes initially. If this expansion proves successful, GGG could then look to expand further so that it ultimately runs a national network of homes across X.

However, GGG will need to decide whether it looks to expand by opening new homes of its own, or whether it looks to acquire existing care homes which the current owners are looking to sell. Either way, though, this expansion is likely to require significant investment, but it is not clear how easily GGG (as a privately owned, unlisted company) could raise the necessary funds.

Product development

A product development strategy would involve GGG increasing its revenues by offering new products (services) in its existing markets.

'Relief care' packages – Currently, GGG's residents live in its care homes on a full-time basis. However, the growing need for 'relief care' packages, means that GGG could start accepting short-term residents (as 'relief care') in addition to its existing full-time residents.

The number of short-term residents GGG can accept at any time will be limited by the amount of spare capacity it has in its existing homes. However, GGG also needs to be aware of the potential opportunity cost of accepting residents on a short term basis; in other words, if it fills any spare capacity with short term residents it may then have to turn away residents who were hoping to move in on a full-time basis.

Treatments and therapies – A second product development opportunity would be for GGG to undertake, in-house, the treatments and therapies for which its residents are currently to local hospitals. It appears that many of GGG's staff (who are qualified nurses) already have the skills necessary to carry out the treatments. However, GGG would need additional investment in new facilities and training before it could offer these additional services in its care homes.

Diversification

A diversification strategy would involve GGG offering new service to new markets or groups of customers.

Treatments and therapies – GGG's current business model involves customers coming to its care homes as full-time residents, not specifically for treatment. However, an alternative model could be for GGG's nurses to provide a range of treatments and therapies for 'non-resident' patients who only stay in the homes for the duration of their treatment.

Although the majority of these people treated are likely still to be elderly, there is no need for this necessarily to be the case. For example, GGG's nurses and carers could provide therapies for people of all ages during their rehabilitation from injuries or accidents.

Because the idea of offering treatements in this way, is linked to GGG's current business, it represents a form of **related diversification**.

(b)

Tutorial note:

Although you do not need to describe Johnson, Scholes & Whittington's characteristics of suitability, acceptability and feasibility in your answer, it is important that appreciate what each represents, so that you evaluate appropriate points under each heading:

Suitability – The suitability of the opportunities depends on their strategic logic. Do they fit with GGG's current circumstances and the strategies it is already employing? Do they address any strategic issues which it is facing?

Acceptability – The acceptability of the opportunities will depend on how they fit with stakeholders' expectations. However, in order to assess the acceptability of the different opportunities, GGG will also need to identify who its key stakeholders are in relation to the opportunity, and what their expectations are.

Feasibility – The feasibility of the opportunities depends on whether GGG has sufficient resources and competences to implement them successfully.

Market penetration

Suitability – A market penetration strategy, particularly one based around filling the spare capacity in GGG's existing care homes, will not require any changes to its existing strategy. Therefore this strategy appears to be suitable for it.

There is no indication whether GGG opened all of its existing 20 care homes itself or whether it acquired some from other private businesses. If GGG has previously expanded through organic growth, market penetration based on buying additional homes may be less suitable.

Acceptability – Although GGG is profitable, there is no indication as to how far its **owners** want its profitability or market share to grow. A market penetration strategy (particularly one based around filling its existing spare capacity) is likely to present the **lowest risk** to GGG, but equally it seems to offer the lowest scope for future growth. However, if the owners are not looking for any significant growth then such a strategy could be acceptable to them.

Other key stakeholders to consider are GGG's **staff** and its **residents**. Market penetration is likely to be acceptable to the staff because it represents a continuation of their current activities. Similarly such an approach should be acceptable to the existing residents. The only issue which both staff and residents (or their families) may raise is that if the number of residents is consistently higher than at present (once any spare capacity has been filled) then staff numbers may also need to be increased to ensure that the standard of care is maintained at its existing high levels.

Feasibility – There do not appear to be any resource constraints with the strategy based on filling spare capacity. The only additional expenditure GGG is likely to have to make in the short term is on advertising to attract additional residents to fill the spare capacity.

If GGG takes on additional staff in the future, this will also increase its costs, but these costs should be covered by the additional revenue generated from having more residents.

If GGG looks to pursue a market penetration strategy by acquiring additional care homes, (or possibly by building extensions onto its existing 20 homes) it will need to consider whether it has enough sufficient financial resources to do this.

Market development

Suitability – The increase in the proportion of elderly members of society in X suggests that there should be increasing demand for care homes across the country. Therefore a strategy based on geographical expansion beyond the two city regions where GGG's homes are currently concentrated allows GGG to take advantage of the opportunity which is available to it. In this respect, the strategy is suitable.

It appears that GGG's current strategy is based on differentiation (offering superior services and facilities). Therefore, to maximise the suitability of this market development, GGG should look to expand into areas where the residents have sufficient wealth to pay for its services (in preference to the local authority care homes), but where there are not already too many existing privately-owned care homes.

However, the fact that GGG currently runs its homes in two specific areas may suggest that this geographical concentration fits with its current management style and structure. In turn, this may suggest that GGG's management style may be less well-suited to an organisation which is more spread out. For example, if senior managers take a keen role in the operation of the care homes, visiting the homes and holding meetings with their staff would be more difficult to do nationally, compared to a smaller geographical area.

Acceptability – Again, we do not know the owners' attitudes to risk and rewards so we cannot tell how acceptable this approach would be to them.

Opening new homes in new cities, is unlikely to affect the residents in GGG's existing homes, so there is no reason why this strategy should be unacceptable to them. Equally, provided GGG recruits new staff to work in the new homes, there is no reason why GGG's existing staff should find this strategy unacceptable. However, the strategy could be unacceptable to the staff if staff from GGG's existing homes are expected to transfer to the new homes.

Feasibility – A key issue here will be whether GGG can find suitable properties to use as care homes (or suitable land on which to build new care homes), whether it can find suitable existing care homes to acquire. Again, we do not know how much finance GGG has available to support its expansion, but that could also affect the feasibility of this strategy.

Equally, we do not know what timescale GGG is looking at for any expansion. It is likely to take longer for GGG to open new homes in new regions than to fill the spare capacity in its existing homes. If GGG is looking to achieve growth quickly, then a strategy based on establishing new care homes in new areas may not be feasible.

Product development

Tutorial note: This answer below assumes that the product development opportunity GGG chooses to pursue is that of 'relief care' packages. If you highlighted the provision of treatments and therapies as GGG's main product development opportunity, you should have evaluated that in this part of the question instead.

In our answers below, we have considered the provision of treatments as a diversification strategy, and evaluated it on that basis.

Suitability – If GGG decides to offer 'relief care' packages, it will be able to provide the same services and facilities to its short-term residents as its currently offer to its full-time residents. However, by opening up its homes to short-term residents, GGG will be taking advantage of a clear market opportunity, as there is a growing need for 'relief care' packages.

Equally, if residents come to GGG on a short-term basis, and are impressed by the service and facilities provided, they may subsequently return on a long-term basis as full-time residents.

Therefore this strategy appears to be suitable for GGG.

Acceptability – It is not clear how much extra work the relief care packages would entail for GGG's staff. Elderly people, finding themselves in unfamiliar circumstances, may need more care and attention than the full-time residents who already established and comfortable in their surroundings. In this respect, if the strategy creates significant extra work for the staff, and/or detracts from the level of care they can provide to the existing residents, it may be unacceptable to GGG's staff.

Equally, if the existing residents feel the change will detract from the service they receive, or from their quality of life in the care homes, it may also be unacceptable to them. For example, if the homes have communal sitting room areas, the full-time residents may be prefer to share these areas with other full-time residents they have got to know over time, rather than with short-term residents they don't know.

Feasibility – Caring for short-term residents should not require any additional skills or competences than caring for full-time residents, so the opportunity should be feasible in this respect.

However, one potential issue which could arise is this: If, as a result of taking on 'relief care' residents, GGG's care homes are full, they may have to turn away potential residents who are looking to move in on a permanent basis. Given that the core element of GGG's business is providing care for people on a full-time basis, if taking on relief care residents means it can no longer always do this, the feasibility of this opportunity could be questioned.

Equally, however, GGG may be able to overcome the problem by extending its care homes to include extra rooms; thereby increasing their capacity.

Diversification

Suitability – To the extent that GGG's nursing staff are experienced at caring for patients , and have the medical qualifications to provide the treatments required, this opportunity would appear to be suitable, although the nurses may need some additional training before they could start administering treatments.

However, GGG's current strategic purpose is providing residential care for the elderly. It is debatable how well a strategy focusing specifically on 'treatment' rather than 'care' fits with GGG's current position. Consequently, there should be concerns about the suitability of this opportunity.

Acceptability – Whilst the nurses may be develop their skills (through the additional training they would receive) and enhance their jobs, they may be less keen on the opportunity if it adds to their work-loads significantly.

This opportunity may also not prove acceptable to the existing full-time residents in GGG's homes, if there is a concern that staff will spend more time on the 'treatment' patients, detracting from the amount of time and care given to the existing full-time patients.

There could also be concerns from hospitals (and possibly the health authorities more generally) as to whether GGG's care homes are an acceptable place to be administering treatments, and whether standard of treatments will match that currently provided in hospitals.

Alternatively, however, some hospitals may be grateful for GGG's nurses carrying out some of the treatments if it reduces their own work loads. Equally, the standard of facilities and care patients would receive at GGG could be reviewed, and approved, by the relevant authorities before it starts carrying out any treatments.

Feasibility – GGG may have to recruit some additional nursing staff in order to implement this strategy. This will increase its costs, as will the cost of any additional training the staff require. However, the greater costs associated with this opportunity will be the investment needed in equipment and facilities in order to be able to provide the treatments. If these costs are too high, they could make this opportunity unfeasible.

Alternatively, if GGG needs to obtain a licence (or some similar regulatory approval in order to carry out the treatments it wants to); if it fails to get the necessary licences, this would automatically make the proposal unfeasible.

(c)

Market penetration – The combination of an increasing number of elderly people in X, combined with existing care homes closing or being put up for sale, provides an opportunity for GGG to grow whilst continuing to provide its existing services in its current market.

Growing through market penetration is likely to be the least risky option for GGG. Given the difficult economic environment, adopting a low-risk strategy appears sensible for GGG, particularly as it is already profitable, and – as a privately-owned unlisted company – isn't under any pressure from external investors to grow. Nonetheless, the market penetration strategy should still enable it to grow.

Therefore, market penetration would seem to be the most appropriate strategy for GGG to follow.

Product development – However, it could also be appropriate for GGG to pursue a product development strategy alongside its market penetration strategy. Therefore this option should also be recommended.

GGG already has the facilities and skills to cater for 'relief care' customers, and there is a growing market need for such packages. Therefore by pursuing this strategy, GGG could help satisfy the market, whilst also using 'relief care' customers to help fill any spare capacity it would otherwise have.

Question 4

Text reference: Chapter 10 of the BPP Study Text covers the advantages and disadvantages of different organisation structures.

Top tips:

Part (a): To score well here, it is important that you evaluate the benefits and drawbacks of the two structures specifically in relation to DDD. Don't just evaluate the benefits and drawbacks of the functional and divisional structures in general terms.

However, note that (for 6 marks) you have to evaluate four different things: (i) the benefits of a functional structure; (ii) the drawbacks of a functional structure; (iii) the benefits of a divisional structure; and (iv) the drawbacks of a divisional structure. This suggests that there are only around 2 marks available for each of the four elements, so you cannot afford to spend too long on any of them.

Part (b): It is important that you distinguish the wording of the requirement for part (b) from that for part (a). In part (a) you needed to look separately at the benefits and drawbacks of two different structures. However, although part (b) also refers to 'benefits and drawbacks' and to 'centralised and decentralised decision making processes', you shouldn't be looking to evaluate four different elements in the way that you did for part (a). The most obvious reason for this is that doing so would lead to a significant amount of duplication: in effect, the benefits of a centralised process will be the drawbacks of a decentralised process, and vice versa.

Instead, your main focus in part (b) should be on the centralised process; which is DDD's current process. So, in effect, you could approach this question as: Evaluate the benefits and drawbacks of DDD's current decision making process, in relation to the more decentralised process which has been proposed.

(a)

(i)

Benefits of a functional structure for DDD

Pooling of expertise – A functional structure means that staff carrying out similar, often specialist, tasks and activities are grouped together. By having such a structure, DDD's staff can pool their expertise, improving DDD's ability (despite only being a medium-sized firm) to compete effectively against larger firms.

Senior managers are close to the operation of their functions – A functional structure should lead to relatively simple lines of control, in which senior managers are close to the operation of their functions. Therefore, a functional structure should enable effective communications between DDD's engineers and their managers. However, it appears that this is not currently the case, as DDD's senior engineers have complained about the difficulties of communicating with their senior managers.

Drawbacks of a functional structure for DDD

Lack of communication and co-ordination between functions – The nature of functional structures means that staff tend to focus only on their own specific functions. Consequently, there is often a lack of communication and co-ordination between different functions. This appears to be the case at DDD, where the lack of integration between the company's key activities has resulted in job disruption and delays. Any such delays could be a particular problem in relation to the new contract which DDD has won for the major sporting event, and which has a fixed deadline date.

Value creation – Having a functional structure is also likely to mean that DDD's organisational structure doesn't reflect the business processes by which it creates value for its customers. This will make it difficult for DDD to identify where profits (or losses) are made for different products, and therefore to identify ways of increasing its profitability.

(ii)

If DDD introduced a divisional structure, the basis for its divisions could either be different product types (eg small unit; large units; repairs and maintenance) or different geographical regions.

Benefits of a divisional structure

Fits business structure – DDD offers a range of different products and services: small, off-the shelf CHP units; large bespoke units; and contract services, and repairs and maintenance. If DDD adopted a divisional structure according to these different product/service types, this would enable its staff to develop their expertise in relation to their specific products. This should help them improve the quality of the products and services they provide for DDD's customers.

Empowerment and motivation – DDD currently has a highly centralised decision-making process, and, for example, its senior engineers have expressed their frustration that they do not get any input into decisions. This may be contributing to DDD's high staff turnover. If DDD adopted a divisional structure, there should be a greater delegation of authority throughout the company. This should help motivate the divisional managers, and could also help motivate DDD's senior engineers if it provides them with more scope to contribute to the decision-making process.

Drawbacks of a divisional structure

Adverse impact on performance – Based on her previous experience of divisionalised structures, the Finance Director has expressed concern that moving to this kind of structure could adversely affect DDD's performance. Clearly, if moving to a divisional structure has an adverse affect on DDD's performance, it would not be advisable to adopt such a structure.

Duplication of activities – A divisional structure may lead to some duplication of activities, and therefore an increase in costs for DDD. For example, if each division has its own administration and IT activities, this could be less cost-effective than having single company-wide administration and IT departments. If DDD doesn't control its cost effectively, this could mean it has to increase its prices in order to maintain its profitability. In turn, this could lead to it becoming less competitive.

(b)

Centralised decision-making process

Benefits

Fits with current organisational structure – Functional organisational structures (such as DDD currently has) are well-suited to centralised decision-making processes. Therefore, DDD's current decision-making process fits well with its current organisational structure.

However, there are concerns that a functional organisational structure is not the most appropriate structure for DDD. If DDD changes its organisational structure in the future, this may also mean that it needs to change its decision-making process to fit with its new structure.

Control – As some of the Directors have indicated, having a centralised decision-making process allows them to retain control over the key decisions which are taken within DDD. In particular, a centralised process means that decisions can be co-ordinated more easily.

Costs - Related to this, a centralised process may also allow DDD to reduce costs associated with the decision-making process. A single decision can be taken centrally, rather than a number of localised decisions having to be taken, with the risk of duplication.

Goal congruence – Decisions taken centrally should be based on DDD's overall objectives. This should this lead to goal congruence throughout the company. However, if DDD adopted a decentralised decision-making process, decisions could be influenced by short-term or localised objectives of the people making them.

Drawbacks

Reduced moral and job satisfaction – Because all decisions are taken centrally, local managers and other staff will become frustrated at their lack of input to decisions. The senior engineers at DDD have already expressed their frustration at not being able to contribute to any decisions. This frustration is likely to lead to the engineers becoming less motivated, which could be a particular problem for DDD given the importance of the engineers to its business.

High staff turnover – It seems likely that staff frustration at not being involved in any decision-making has contributed to DDD's high staff turnover. This high staff turnover should be a concern for DDD, because when staff – particularly senior engineers – leave the company they not only take valuable knowledge and experience with them, but they could also join rival companies allowing those companies to benefit from that knowledge and experience at DDD's expense.

Imperfect information – The failure to involve engineers and other staff in any decision-making could also adversely affect the quality of decisions taken. It seems unlikely that DDD's Board have as much knowledge about all areas of the business as staff working in those areas. Consequently, the Board may end up taking decisions based on imperfect information, and those decisions could, in turn, adversely affect DDD's future performance.

Inflexibility – The Finance Director has suggested that DDD's current approach is making it inflexible. For example, the time taken to go through a formalised decision-making process, may prevent it from responding quickly to take advantage of new market opportunities.

Decentralised decision-making process

If DDD moves to a decentralised decision-making process, this would help it address the drawbacks of its current process.

Staff motivation and retention – In particular, if the senior engineers feel they have more input into decisions, this should increase their motivation, and should also help to reduce DDD's staff turnover rate.

Flexibility and innovation – The Finance Director has indicated she believes a decentralised approach could facilitate greater flexibility and innovation in DDD. Perhaps more importantly, decisions taken by staff who have a closer interaction with DDD's customers could also enable DDD to respond more effectively and quickly to customers' requirements.

Equally, if decisions need to be made about how to address slippage on products which are running late, it may be quicker to make these decisions locally rather than referring them through a centralised decision-making process.

In this respect, moving to a decentralised process may not only be able to reduce the level of penalties DDD has to pay, but it could also improve customer satisfaction because DDD has delivered its product on time.

(c)

Top tips:

Your answer to part (a) – in conjunction with the information provided in the scenario – should have alerted you to some of the problems with DDD's current structure; in particular, there seems to be a lack of flexibility and collaboration.

However, the nature of the new contract (requiring DDD to work alongside many different organisations) seems to suggest that flexibility and collaboration will be important attributes of the organisational structure you need to recommend here. In effect, demonstrating how well the structure you recommend can provide these attributes, should then act as your justification for your recommendation.

Note, however, that the verb requirement is 'Recommend...' Therefore the main focus of your answer should be highlighting the benefits of the structure you have recommended, and why it is appropriate for DDD to use here.

Remember that to score well in this question you need to apply your answer directly to DDD. So you shouldn't just explain the advantages of the organisational structure in general terms, but you need to explain specifically how they will be beneficial to DDD.

Collaboration – The new contract will require DDD's staff to work alongside many different organisations to design and install a range of products. There will need to be effective collaboration and communication, both within DDD and between DDD and its strategic partners, in order for this to work effectively.

One of the problems of DDD's current functional structure is likely to be that it encourages staff to focus solely on their own specialist areas, rather than collaborating with other departments. Therefore, DDD should be looking to introduce an organisational structure which promotes collaboration rather than discouraging it.

Flexibility – Similarly, the need to work with external partners within the constraints of a fixed deadline, is likely to mean that DDD will need a more flexible structure and approach than it currently has. For example, the fixed deadline means DDD cannot afford to have delays like it has sometimes had on jobs in the past; it will need to be flexible in order to overcome any slippage which occurs in the project.

The Finance Director has already recommended that DDD should be considering a more flexible structure; and winning the contract will reinforce the need for it to do this.

The nature of the contract (to design and install a range of *bespoke* generat0rs) is also likely to increase the need for innovation, alongside collaboration. The bespoke nature of the generators means DDD is likely to have to share ideas and skills with the other organisations involved in order to deliver the exact products required.

Matrix structure

The importance of collaboration and flexibility in meeting the needs of the new contract would suggest that some kind of matrix structure would be appropriate for DDD.

Two of the key characteristics of matrix structures are that they offer flexibility and they help improve communication. They also enable inter-disciplinary co-operation and a mixing of skills.

Dual authority – In a matrix structure, staff have two reporting lines: one to a functional manager, and a second to a product, or regional, (or in this case, project) manager. In this way, the dual authority in the organisation structure should help to ensure co-ordination between staff from different functional areas. Equally, the dual authority of a matrix structure should prevent functionalist specialists becoming focussed too narrowly on their own concerns, and consider the wider context of the project.

Project structure

The size and importance of the contract for DDD (representing about 60% of its total sales revenue) means that a project structure is likely to the most appropriate structure for DDD to apply for large bespoke projects, like the contract it has just won.

A project structure is an extension of a matrix structure, in which the dual authority sees staff reporting to a functional manager and a project manager.

Integrated approach - A project structure would enable DDD to create dedicated, **multi-disciplinary project teams** for each contract it is working on. Each team would work together on a project until it is completed, and then team members would return to their main functional areas until they are needed to join another project.

The introduction of team-based structure is also likely to be important for DDD. Such a structure should not only improve collaboration, but it should also allow staff (as members of the team) to have greater input into decision-making.

Moreover, bringing together staff with different specialist skills could also **facilitate innovation**, as they share ideas with one another.

In this respect, being part of a multi-disciplinary team could also benefit the individual staff members as well. For example, they can see new approaches or perspectives (which people from different functional backgrounds bring,) and they can possibly also develop new skills which have not previously been required in their 'functional' role.

Reporting lines

One of the potential criticisms of matrix structures is that they can lead to conflict and confusion. For example, there could be conflict between a functional manager and a product manager about the work a staff member should be doing. Equally, the dual authority could lead to confusion for the staff member; not knowing which manager's instructions take precedence if there is a conflict between them.

These potential drawbacks still apply for project structure, but the benefits to DDD from introducing the new structure in relation to the contract should outweigh the drawbacks.

Fit with management and control – One issue which DDD will need to address, however, is the 'fit' or potential lack of fit between a project structure and the centralised approach to management and control. The Finance Director has already suggested that DDD should move to a more decentralised approach to management and control, and such a change is likely to be necessary for DDD to maximise the benefits it can get from its new structure. If DDD retains a centralised approach to management and control, this will counteract the freedom and flexibility which the new structure is intended to provide.

Recommendation:

Matrix structure

Nonetheless, the importance of collaboration and flexibility in delivering the contract means that DDD needs to introduce some form of matrix structure. Given the self-contained nature of the contract, as well as its size and importance, a project structure would appear to be the most appropriate organisational structure for DDD to introduce to help it deliver the contract.

However, a project structure may be less appropriate for the routine repairs, maintenance and service areas of the business, where work is likely to be on-going rather than being attributable to specific projects.

Therefore, as an organisational structure for DDD as a whole, a matrix structure would be most appropriate. This could then be extended into a project structure specifically for one-off projects and contracts like the one DDD has just won.

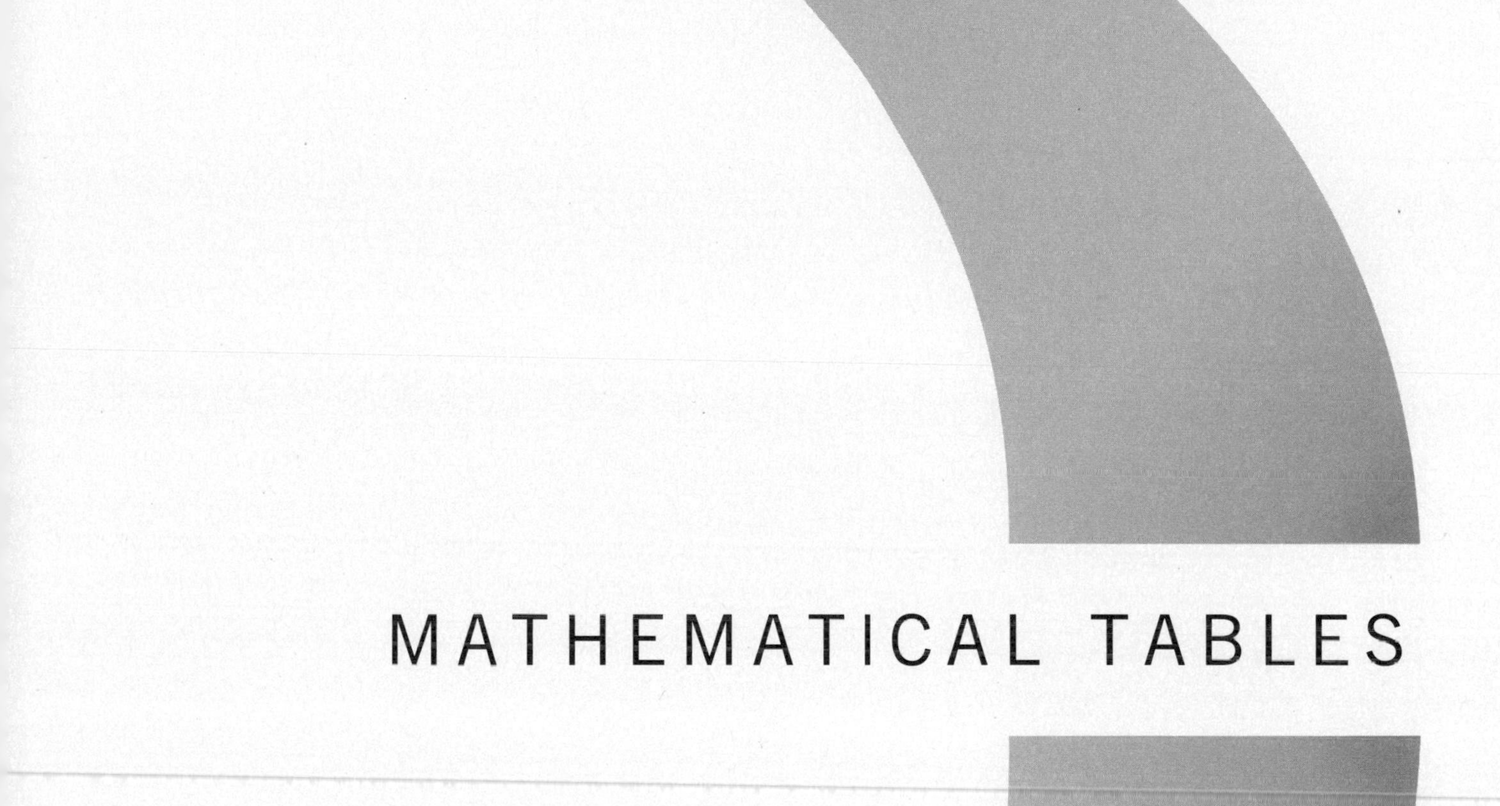

MATHEMATICAL TABLES

MATHEMATICAL TABLES

Present value table

Present value of 1.00 unit of currency, that is $(1+r)^{-n}$ where r = interest rate, n = number of periods until payment or receipt.

Periods (n)	Interest rates (r) 1%	2%	3%	4%	5%	6%	7%	8%	9%	10%
1	0.990	0.980	0.971	0.962	0.952	0.943	0.935	0.926	0.917	0.909
2	0.980	0.961	0.943	0.925	0.907	0.890	0.873	0.857	0.842	0.826
3	0.971	0.942	0.915	0.889	0.864	0.840	0.816	0.794	0.772	0.751
4	0.961	0.924	0.888	0.855	0.823	0.792	0.763	0.735	0.708	0.683
5	0.951	0.906	0.863	0.822	0.784	0.747	0.713	0.681	0.650	0.621
6	0.942	0.888	0.837	0.790	0.746	0.705	0.666	0.630	0.596	0.564
7	0.933	0.871	0.813	0.760	0.711	0.665	0.623	0.583	0.547	0.513
8	0.923	0.853	0.789	0.731	0.677	0.627	0.582	0.540	0.502	0.467
9	0.914	0.837	0.766	0.703	0.645	0.592	0.544	0.500	0.460	0.424
10	0.905	0.820	0.744	0.676	0.614	0.558	0.508	0.463	0.422	0.386
11	0.896	0.804	0.722	0.650	0.585	0.527	0.475	0.429	0.388	0.350
12	0.887	0.788	0.701	0.625	0.557	0.497	0.444	0.397	0.356	0.319
13	0.879	0.773	0.681	0.601	0.530	0.469	0.415	0.368	0.326	0.290
14	0.870	0.758	0.661	0.577	0.505	0.442	0.388	0.340	0.299	0.263
15	0.861	0.743	0.642	0.555	0.481	0.417	0.362	0.315	0.275	0.239
16	0.853	0.728	0.623	0.534	0.458	0.394	0.339	0.292	0.252	0.218
17	0.844	0.714	0.605	0.513	0.436	0.371	0.317	0.270	0.231	0.198
18	0.836	0.700	0.587	0.494	0.416	0.350	0.296	0.250	0.212	0.180
19	0.828	0.686	0.570	0.475	0.396	0.331	0.277	0.232	0.194	0.164
20	0.820	0.673	0.554	0.456	0.377	0.312	0.258	0.215	0.178	0.149

Periods (n)	Interest rates (r) 11%	12%	13%	14%	15%	16%	17%	18%	19%	20%
1	0.901	0.893	0.885	0.877	0.870	0.862	0.855	0.847	0.840	0.833
2	0.812	0.797	0.783	0.769	0.756	0.743	0.731	0.718	0.706	0.694
3	0.731	0.712	0.693	0.675	0.658	0.641	0.624	0.609	0.593	0.579
4	0.659	0.636	0.613	0.592	0.572	0.552	0.534	0.516	0.499	0.482
5	0.593	0.567	0.543	0.519	0.497	0.476	0.456	0.437	0.419	0.402
6	0.535	0.507	0.480	0.456	0.432	0.410	0.390	0.370	0.352	0.335
7	0.482	0.452	0.425	0.400	0.376	0.354	0.333	0.314	0.296	0.279
8	0.434	0.404	0.376	0.351	0.327	0.305	0.285	0.266	0.249	0.233
9	0.391	0.361	0.333	0.308	0.284	0.263	0.243	0.225	0.209	0.194
10	0.352	0.322	0.295	0.270	0.247	0.227	0.208	0.191	0.176	0.162
11	0.317	0.287	0.261	0.237	0.215	0.195	0.178	0.162	0.148	0.135
12	0.286	0.257	0.231	0.208	0.187	0.168	0.152	0.137	0.124	0.112
13	0.258	0.229	0.204	0.182	0.163	0.145	0.130	0.116	0.104	0.093
14	0.232	0.205	0.181	0.160	0.141	0.125	0.111	0.099	0.088	0.078
15	0.209	0.183	0.160	0.140	0.123	0.108	0.095	0.084	0.074	0.065
16	0.188	0.163	0.141	0.123	0.107	0.093	0.081	0.071	0.062	0.054
17	0.170	0.146	0.125	0.108	0.093	0.080	0.069	0.060	0.052	0.045
18	0.153	0.130	0.111	0.095	0.081	0.069	0.059	0.051	0.044	0.038
19	0.138	0.116	0.098	0.083	0.070	0.060	0.051	0.043	0.037	0.031
20	0.124	0.104	0.087	0.073	0.061	0.051	0.043	0.037	0.031	0.026

Cumulative present value table

This table shows the present value of 1.00 unit of currency per annum, receivable or payable at the end of each year for n years $\frac{1-(1+r)^{-n}}{r}$.

Periods (n)	Interest rates (r) 1%	2%	3%	4%	5%	6%	7%	8%	9%	10%
1	0.990	0.980	0.971	0.962	0.952	0.943	0.935	0.926	0.917	0.909
2	1.970	1.942	1.913	1.886	1.859	1.833	1.808	1.783	1.759	1.736
3	2.941	2.884	2.829	2.775	2.723	2.673	2.624	2.577	2.531	2.487
4	3.902	3.808	3.717	3.630	3.546	3.465	3.387	3.312	3.240	3.170
5	4.853	4.713	4.580	4.452	4.329	4.212	4.100	3.993	3.890	3.791
6	5.795	5.601	5.417	5.242	5.076	4.917	4.767	4.623	4.486	4.355
7	6.728	6.472	6.230	6.002	5.786	5.582	5.389	5.206	5.033	4.868
8	7.652	7.325	7.020	6.733	6.463	6.210	5.971	5.747	5.535	5.335
9	8.566	8.162	7.786	7.435	7.108	6.802	6.515	6.247	5.995	5.759
10	9.471	8.983	8.530	8.111	7.722	7.360	7.024	6.710	6.418	6.145
11	10.368	9.787	9.253	8.760	8.306	7.887	7.499	7.139	6.805	6.495
12	11.255	10.575	9.954	9.385	8.863	8.384	7.943	7.536	7.161	6.814
13	12.134	11.348	10.635	9.986	9.394	8.853	8.358	7.904	7.487	7.103
14	13.004	12.106	11.296	10.563	9.899	9.295	8.745	8.244	7.786	7.367
15	13.865	12.849	11.938	11.118	10.380	9.712	9.108	8.559	8.061	7.606
16	14.718	13.578	12.561	11.652	10.838	10.106	9.447	8.851	8.313	7.824
17	15.562	14.292	13.166	12.166	11.274	10.477	9.763	9.122	8.544	8.022
18	16.398	14.992	13.754	12.659	11.690	10.828	10.059	9.372	8.756	8.201
19	17.226	15.679	14.324	13.134	12.085	11.158	10.336	9.604	8.950	8.365
20	18.046	16.351	14.878	13.590	12.462	11.470	10.594	9.818	9.129	8.514

Periods (n)	Interest rates (r) 11%	12%	13%	14%	15%	16%	17%	18%	19%	20%
1	0.901	0.893	0.885	0.877	0.870	0.862	0.855	0.847	0.840	0.833
2	1.713	1.690	1.668	1.647	1.626	1.605	1.585	1.566	1.547	1.528
3	2.444	2.402	2.361	2.322	2.283	2.246	2.210	2.174	2.140	2.106
4	3.102	3.037	2.974	2.914	2.855	2.798	2.743	2.690	2.639	2.589
5	3.696	3.605	3.517	3.433	3.352	3.274	3.199	3.127	3.058	2.991
6	4.231	4.111	3.998	3.889	3.784	3.685	3.589	3.498	3.410	3.326
7	4.712	4.564	4.423	4.288	4.160	4.039	3.922	3.812	3.706	3.605
8	5.146	4.968	4.799	4.639	4.487	4.344	4.207	4.078	3.954	3.837
9	5.537	5.328	5.132	4.946	4.772	4.607	4.451	4.303	4.163	4.031
10	5.889	5.650	5.426	5.216	5.019	4.833	4.659	4.494	4.339	4.192
11	6.207	5.938	5.687	5.453	5.234	5.029	4.836	4.656	4.486	4.327
12	6.492	6.194	5.918	5.660	5.421	5.197	4.988	4.793	4.611	4.439
13	6.750	6.424	6.122	5.842	5.583	5.342	5.118	4.910	4.715	4.533
14	6.982	6.628	6.302	6.002	5.724	5.468	5.229	5.008	4.802	4.611
15	7.191	6.811	6.462	6.142	5.847	5.575	5.324	5.092	4.876	4.675
16	7.379	6.974	6.604	6.265	5.954	5.668	5.405	5.162	4.938	4.730
17	7.549	7.120	6.729	6.373	6.047	5.749	5.475	5.222	4.990	4.775
18	7.702	7.250	6.840	6.467	6.128	5.818	5.534	5.273	5.033	4.812
19	7.839	7.366	6.938	6.550	6.198	5.877	5.584	5.316	5.070	4.843
20	7.963	7.469	7.025	6.623	6.259	5.929	5.628	5.353	5.101	4.870

BPP
LEARNING MEDIA

Notes

Notes

Review Form – Paper E3 Enterprise Strategy (01/13)

Please help us to ensure that the CIMA learning materials we produce remain as accurate and user-friendly as possible. We cannot promise to answer every submission we receive, but we do promise that it will be read and taken into account when we up-date this Study Text.

Name: ______________________ **Address:** ______________________

____

____

How have you used this Study Text?
(Tick one box only)

☐ Home study (book only)

☐ On a course: college ______________

☐ With 'correspondence' package

☐ Other ______________

Why did you decide to purchase this Study Text? *(Tick one box only)*

☐ Have used BPP Texts in the past

☐ Recommendation by friend/colleague

☐ Recommendation by a lecturer at college

☐ Saw information on BPP website

☐ Saw advertising

☐ Other ______________

During the past six months do you recall seeing/receiving any of the following?
(Tick as many boxes as are relevant)

☐ Our advertisement in *Financial Management*

☐ Our advertisement in *Pass*

☐ Our advertisement in *PQ*

☐ Our brochure with a letter through the post

☐ Our website www.bpp.com

Which (if any) aspects of our advertising do you find useful?
(Tick as many boxes as are relevant)

☐ Prices and publication dates of new editions

☐ Information on Text content

☐ Facility to order books off-the-page

☐ None of the above

Which BPP products have you used?

Text	☐	*Success CD*	☐
Kit	☑	*i-Pass*	☐
Passcard	☐	*Interactive Passcard*	☐

Your ratings, comments and suggestions would be appreciated on the following areas.

	Very useful	*Useful*	*Not useful*
Introductory section	☐	☐	☐
Chapter introductions	☐	☐	☐
Key terms	☐	☐	☐
Quality of explanations	☐	☐	☐
Case studies and other examples	☐	☐	☐
Exam skills and alerts	☐	☐	☐
Questions and answers in each chapter	☐	☐	☐
Fast forwards and chapter roundups	☐	☐	☐
Quick quizzes	☐	☐	☐
Question Bank	☐	☐	☐
Answer Bank	☐	☐	☐
OT Bank	☐	☐	☐
Index	☐	☐	☐

Overall opinion of this Study Text *Excellent* ☐ *Good* ☐ *Adequate* ☐ *Poor* ☐

Do you intend to continue using BPP products? *Yes* ☐ *No* ☐

On the reverse of this page is space for you to write your comments about our Study Text We welcome your feedback.

The BPP Learning Media author of this edition can be e-mailed at: adrianthomas@bpp.com

Please return this form to: Stephen Osborne, CIMA Publishing Manager, BPP Learning Media Ltd, FREEPOST, London, W12 8BR

TELL US WHAT YOU THINK

Please note any further comments and suggestions/errors below. For example, was the text accurate, readable, concise, user-friendly and comprehensive?